Cover from First Edition

What reviewers are saying about *Modern Magick*

"If you follow this volume's clear lessons, in a year or two you you will not only have the knowledge and skills needed to understand other books on ceremonial magick, you will be a practicing ceremonial mage."
—eCauldron.net

"Kraig's *Modern Magick* remains one of the most lucid and practical texts available."
—Lon Milo DuQuette, author of *Enochian Vision Magick*; *Angels, Demons & Gods of the New Millennium*; and *Tarot of Ceremonial Magick*

"Superb! Every page clearly illustrates that here is an author who not only writes about magick, but has obviously practiced it successfully. This book is a must for the beginner as well as the advanced student who wants to effect 'change' and explore the 'worlds' beyond the physical plane."
—Cris Monnastre, former student of Israel Regardie

"I am sure that there are many, like myself, who consider it the missing key to the Golden Dawn system."
—Roger Williamson, author of *The Sun at Night*

"This is one of those rare books that is a seminal work of magick . . . [It] presents one of the most complete references on the Kabbalah that I have ever seen outside of the Jewish religion."
—DavensJournal.com

"This is a wonderful book!"
—David Godwin, author of *Godwin's Cabalistic Encyclopedia*

"This may well be the best book available for anyone who actually wants to begin doing magick, as opposed to merely reading about it."
—Donald Tyson, author of *The Fourth Book of Occult Philosophy* and *Enochian Magick for Beginners*

"*Modern Magick* is one of those 'must have' books . . . Everything is clear and concise. In other words: highly recommended."
—Lord Joshu, *P.A.N. Pipes*

"If you are looking for an effective key to unlocking the mysteries and experience of the Western magickal tradition, this is certainly an effective one."

—Kenneth Deigh, publisher and editor of *Mezlim Magazine*

"This is a book you will keep at the ready for research, advice, study, and a road map through the often confusing paths of the world of high magickal arts. Recommended!"

—Brother Shadow, *The Path*

"Gives the serious student all the tools needed to be a magician . . ."

—Pyramid Books

"This unusual book might well have been written by Aleister Crowley himself, from whom the author draws extensively yet always responsibly . . . Well written, informative, and extremely practical, this is essentially a work for the doer rather than the dreamy theorist."

—William Gray, author of *Temple Magick*

"At last a book that cuts through the mysteries of one of the most mysterious subjects. Mr. Kraig breaks down many doors that have deterred so many true seekers of light by giving detailed, understandable explanations of the secrets that others have covered up."

—Brook Martin, *Sunsight News*

What readers are saying about *Modern Magick*

"*Modern Magick* has had an incredible influence on my life. It has opened up gateways I never knew existed."

—C. R., Norman, OK

"I found it to be a very informative book covering just about every important aspect of the High Magickal arts."

—M. G., New York, NY

"Your own practical experience and your lucid commentary that pulls it all together make the book feel as if it were written specifically for me at just this time."

—R. A., London, England

"It is just the type of book I have been looking for over the past twenty years!"

—K. W., Saskatoon, Saskatchewan, Canada

"Your book amplifies and clarifies a lot of interesting things concerning the rituals and the ways of getting in touch with the powers."

—D. J., Stenhamra, Sweden

"Your book is wonderful. It is the reason why I am now practicing instead of just reading."

—R. J. C., Metarie, LA

"I am impressed with your practicality and logic."

—C. W. T., Medford, OR

"*Modern Magick* has been a great blessing for [a] beginner in the study of [the] esoteric arts like myself, and I deeply thank you for writing such a wonderful text."

—S. T. D., Santa Ana, CA

MODERN MAGICK

About the Author

Donald Michael Kraig received a B.A. in philosophy from the University of California, Los Angeles, and studied music there and at other colleges and universities. He received a fellowship to the University of Southern California where he received a certificate in multimedia, 3D graphics, animation, and web design, going on to help teach those classes there. As a musician, he performed before tens of thousands of people, including opening for acts ranging from Elton John to Great White. Don was a certified Tarot Grandmaster, was a member of numerous spiritual and magickal groups, and was initiated into several Tantric traditions. He was also certified as a clinical hypnotherapist by the National Guild of Hypnotists, the American Board of Hypnotherapy (ABH), and the Association for Integrative Psychology (AIP). He was certified to teach hypnotherapy by the ABH and was certified as a Master Practitioner of Neuro-Linguistic Programming by the AIP.

Don began teaching in the southern California area, and went on to give lectures and lead workshops throughout the United States and in Europe. He specialized in workshops covering the Kabalah, Tarot, magick, evocation, Tantra, hypnosis, past lives, the chakras, the Sri Yantra, and many other topics. Don passed from this world in 2014.

Revised and Expanded • *Over 150, 000 Sold*

MODERN MAGICK

TWELVE LESSONS IN THE HIGH MAGICKAL ARTS

DONALD MICHAEL KRAIG

Llewellyn Publications
Woodbury, Minnesota

Third Edition
Eighth Printing, 2018

Cover art © 2010 by John Blumen
Cover design by Ellen Dahl
Editing by Tom Bilstad
Interior illustrations on pages 33, 35, 41–43, 50, 54, 57–60, 78, 83, 133, 135, 139, 143, 155, 166, 194–198, 215–219, 225, 261, 315, 324, 343 and 349, © John Blumen. Art on pages 310–311, 327–328 provided by the author. All other art is by the Llewellyn art department.
Pentacle on page 113 © Chic Cicero and reprinted with permission.
Tarot cards on page 101 are from the *Golden Dawn Magical Tarot* and reprinted with permission.

Llewellyn is a registered trademark of Llewellyn Worldwide Ltd.

Library of Congress Cataloging-in-Publication Data (Pending)
ISBN: 978-0-7387-1578-0

Llewellyn Worldwide Ltd. does not participate in, endorse, or have any authority or responsibility concerning private business transactions between our authors and the public.
    All mail addressed to the author is forwarded, but the publisher cannot, unless specifically instructed by the author, give out an address or phone number.
    Any Internet references contained in this work are current at publication time, but the publisher cannot guarantee that a specific location will continue to be maintained. Please refer to the publisher's website for links to authors' websites and other sources.

Llewellyn Publications
A Division of Llewellyn Worldwide Ltd.
2143 Wooddale Drive
Woodbury, MN 55125-2989
www.llewellyn.com

Printed in the United States of America

Other Books by Donald Michael Kraig

The Magickal Diary

The Truth About Evocation of Spirits

The Truth About Psychic Powers

Modern Sex Magick

Tarot & Magic

The Resurrection Murders

Dedication to the Third Edition

There are so many people I would have to dedicate this book to that it would take an entire volume to list them all. I want to give my deepest thanks to Sandra and Carl Weschcke for their continued support and friendship; Michael Magee, Jonn Mumford, and Sunyata Saraswati, who started me in new spiritual directions; Tad James and Matt James, who helped me to further understand the power of the mind; and, most importantly, to all of those people who have read my books and attended my workshops, for you have taught me more than I would have believed possible. I hope you do not mind that I prefer not to think of you as readers or students or (heaven forbid!) fans—instead, I think of you as my friends.

Original Dedication

This book is dedicated to all of my teachers in the hope that what they shared with me I can now share with others. These teachers include: My parents, Frater A.M.A.G., Soror S.I.A.A., Frater D.D.C.F., Frater P., and others whose names I'll not use; Scott Cunningham and Raven [Grimassi], for their beautiful teachings; Rabbis Meriminsky and Haas; [Dr.] Michael Turk and Sifu Douglas Wong; and so many others. Further, this book is

Dedicated
with poignant memory
of what might have been
to AEGIS

Contents

And an Overview of the Subjects Covered in Each Lesson

SECTION ONE
THE OUTER ORDER

Getting Started; Dreams and the Dream Diary; The importance of delaying dream interpretation; The Ritual Diary and its use; Why you should also read other books on these subjects; Tarot Decks; The Relaxation Ritual; Definitions of Magick: White, Grey, and Black; The Story of Robin the Satanist; The Tarot Contemplation Ritual; Brief Divinatory Meanings of the Major Arcana Cards of the Tarot; Mythic and Factual Histories of the Tarot; Modern Tarot Evolution; My Theory for the Creation of the Tarot; Fortunetelling vs. Divination; The Split Hexagram Tarot Divination Spread; A Sample Tarot Reading; Learning the Tarot; Reasons for Regularly Performing the Lesser Banishing Ritual of the Pentagram (LBRP); Attitudes in Preparation for Ritual; Magickal Tools: Location, The Altar, Candles, The "Weapons," The Bell, The Robe; Drawing the Banishing Earth Pentagram in the Air; Appropriate Visualizations; Review; Bibliography.

Preparations for the LBRP including the Ritual Cleansing Bath; Physical Setup for the LBRP; The LBRP: The Kabalistic Cross (including the meaning of the words), The Formulation of the Pentagrams (including how the God names relate to one Deity), The Evocation of the Archangels, The Recapitulation of the Kabalistic Cross; How to Vibrate Words of Power (Vibratory Formulae); Psychic Attack and Psychic Self-Defense; The Four Solar Adorations; Advanced Work for the Four Adorations; Cultish Behavior of a Supposed Kabalah "Centre"; Hebrew; The Mythological History of the Kabalah; The Factual History of the Kabalah (including Merkabah Mysticism); The "Kosher Kabalah" and the "Wasp Kabalah"; The Dogmatic Kabalah; The Practical Kabalah; The Literal Kabalah (including Gematria, Notarikon, and Temurah); The Unwritten Kabalah; Introduction to The Tree of Life; The Flaming Sword; The Three Veils of Negative Existence; Formulation of the Universe; Freud; Reich; Kundalini, Libido, and Orgone; The Kabalistic Power Centers; The Ritual of the Middle Pillar; "Little Nasties"; Review; Bibliography.

tion Ritual for the Pentacle; Consecration Ritual for the Dagger; Consecration Ritual for the Chalice; The Value of Consecrations; Consecrations in a Group; Consecration Ritual for the Fire Wand; The Ritual of Magickal Obligation; Dealing With Non-Magickal People; SSOT-BME; Viewpoints and Biases; Review; Bibliography.

SECTION TWO
THE INNER ORDER

Our Direct Link to the Astral Plane; Positive Affirmations, Creative Visualization, and Why They May Not Work; Sphere of Availability; The Kabalistic System of Mental Magick including the Treasure Map; The Kabalistic Secret of Mental Magick; The Natures of High and Low (Art and Natural) Magick; A Timeline of Some Important Dates in the History of Witchcraft; A History of Fear, Hatred, and Persecution; Definition of a Talisman; The Difference Between Talismans and Amulets; The Stories of Three Students; Magickal vs. Natural Elements; Sympathetic Magick; Symbolism of the Magickal Elements; Designing Low Magick Talismans; Karma; The Best Times to Perform Low Magick Rituals; Skyclad; How to Describe the Purpose of Rituals; A Low Magick Ritual for Charging Talismans; Magickal Guardians; The Ideal Kabalistic Talisman; Types of Traditional Kabalistic Talismans; Correspondences for Talismans; Designing High Magick Talismans from Scratch, Including Pythagorean Numerology, Theosophical Reduction, A Talismanic Purpose Chart, Kabalistic Numerology, Austin Osman Spare and His Alphabet of Desire, and Using the Hermetic Rose Cross; The Final Design; An Important Secret Revealed; Supplement with Corrected Sigils of Olympian Spirits from the *Arbatel of Magick*, Planetary Symbols, Shapes for Talismans, Geomantic Figures, the Importance of Being Able to Design a Talisman from Scratch; Review, Bibliography.

On Doing One's Best; The Story of a Writer; Another Sample Talisman Design; Why You Shouldn't Incorporate Designs from Other Sources at this Time; Why a Kabalistic Talisman *May* Be More Powerful than a Low Magick Talisman; Plantary Associations with Days of the Week; Planetary (or Magickal) Hours and How to Calculate Them; Planetary or Magickal Hours Chart; The Simple Talisman Charging and Consecrating Ritual; Keys to Performing the Same Ritual with a Group; The Story of Mathers and the Peas; Ad-Libbing in Rituals; Language Styles; The Complete Ritual for Charging and Consecrating a Talisman; Texts for the Next Lesson; Three Reasons Some Magicians Don't Do Magick; Review; Bibliography.

Magick and Natural Laws; The Problem with Grimoires; How I Discovered the Three Secrets of Magickal Evocation: My Sources—The Whites, Dion Fortune; Six Revelations; Invocation or Channeling; Spiritism; Construction of the Triangle of the Art; The Magick Mirror; The Appropriate Location for the Triangle of the Art; A Drawing Attributed to Saint-Germain and How It Relates to Evocation; Methods of Altering Consciousness; Disclaimer; The Use of Goetic Seals; The Seal of Bael; A Ritual for Evocation; The Opening and Conjurations; The Questionings; Lies of Commission, Omission, and Obfuscation: The Welcome Unto the Spirit; The Purpose of the Ritual; The License to Depart; Other Seals of Spirits and Their Purposes; On Role-Playing Games; Books Needing Translation; The Yetziratic Sealing Rite; Pentacles from the Greater Key of Solomon; Elemental Entities: Gnomes, Sylphs, Undines, and Salamanders; Artificial Elemental; Ritual for the Creation of an Artificial Elemental; Notes to the Ritual; Spiritism and Channeling vs. Magickal Invocation; Guidelines for Invocation Rituals; The Bornless One; Review; Bibliography.

Sexuality; Cults and Preventing Sexual Manipulation; Sex Magick Techniques Including Thought Control, Inner Alchemy and Outer Alchemy; The Holy Letter; Wilhelm Reich; The Potent Orgasm, the Subconscious, and Symbols; A Sex Magick Ritual for a Couple; The Place of Comfort; Notes on the Ritual; Sex Magick Divinatory Techniques; The Yoni Mudra; Erotocomatose Lucidity; The Position Known as "the Crow"; Separating Love and Sex; Alchemy and Sex Magick; Karezza; Male Ejaculation Control and Multiple Orgasm; The Masters and Johnson "Squeeze" Technique; Conception Vessel One; The Magickal Elixir; The Powers of the Moon; The Mass of the Holy Ghost; Truths about Tantra and Kundalini Yoga; The Hahm-Sah Mantra; Shaktipat; Sex Magick Using Inner Alchemy; The Tantrik Ritual of Inner Alchemy; MahaTantra; God Eating; A Taoist Alchemical Ritual; KalaKakra: A Group Sex Magick Ritual; Personal Responsibility, STDs, and AIDS; Review; Bibliography.

Piscean and Aquarian Age Mentality; Three Things Needed to Work Any Magick; Where Magickal Secrets Come From; The False Notion of White, Black, and Grey Magick; Higher Spiritual Entities; Do what thou Wilt; Karma and Morality; Types of Non-Physical Entities on Other Planes: Etheric Body, Astral Body, Azoth, Artificial Elementals, The Empty Ones, Elementaries (Elementals), Larvae, Ghosts, Pseudo-Ghosts, Poltergeists; Thought Forms; *Forbidden Planet* and "Monsters from the Id"; The Shadow; Astral Projection; Astral LBRP; Concentration Cards Exercise; Mental Projection vs. Astral Projection; Methods to Develop Astral Projection; Bi-Locationality; Astral Travel; Astral Whiplash; The Ultimate Secret of Magick; Pathworking and Kabalistic Pathworking; Why Memorization of Correspondences is Important to Kabalistic Pathworking; An Example of Kabalistic Pathworking; Comments on the Example; The Ritual of the Paths; Hebrew for Gematria; Payment; Sandalphon; Discovering Your Guardian Angel; The Ceremony of the Paths; Directions for Future Study; Review; Bibliography.

Prefatory Comments on Three New Technologies of Magick: Neuro-Linguistic Programming, Chaos Magick, and Postmodern Magick; Discovering Your Timeline; In Time and Through Time; Working with Your Timeline; Changing Your Timeline; Jung's Judger and Perceiver; Other Keys for Successful Magickal Goals; Timeline Magick; Aggregation of Non-Essentials; An Incomplete History of Chaos Magick; Chaos and Chaos Magick; Other Chaos Magick Con-

cepts; Kia; Pandamonaeon; A Banishing Ritual; A Practical Chaos Magick Ritual; The Enlightenment, Modernism, and Postmodernism; Magick and Codes; The Practical Use of Symbols
for Magick from a Postmodern Perspective; Using Sigils to Change Codes; Three Methods to
Prevent Old Codes From Returning; Evoking Symbols; WWBD; The Abstract Sigil; Conclusion; Review; Bibliography.

A Ritual to Vastly Increase Personal Magickal Power.

Answers to the Self-Test Reviews from the Ends of Each Lesson.

New for the second edition. The *Modern Magick* FAQ: Answers to Frequently Asked Questions
I've Received about These Lessons and about Ceremonial Magick in General. On the Magickal
Elements and Associated Directions; On the Missing Archangel; On Determining if a Ritual
Worked; On Advice for Young Magicians; On What to Do if You Don't Have a Magickal Tool;
On the *Necronomicon*; On Joining Groups; On Ceremonial Magick and the Kabalah being Pa-
triarchal; On Chaos Magick; On Joining Several Magickal Groups and Covens; On Spirit Com-
munication; On Inertia of the Will; On Having Time; On Tarot Decks; On Satanism; On the
Ouija Board; On Talismans; On the Six-Rayed Star; Will You Do Magick For Me?

Course Glossary

Annotated Bibliography

Author's Note

The following series of progressive lessons in magick includes an easy-to-understand study of the Kabalah. In keeping with Kabalistic tradition I have chosen to refer to the Ultimate Divinity as "God." To both the Kabalists and myself, God is not seen as a male figure, even though God was described, in some instances, as anthropomorphically male. This was a symbolic convenience.

According to the Kabalah as I've learned it, the Ultimate Source of All is unitary, having united all dualities—up and down, left and right, positive and negative, magnetic and electric, male and female. It is believed that God cannot be limited to being either male or female. This idea is discussed further within these lessons.

I agree strongly with this point of view. When I use the word "God" as a representative of the Single Divine Source of All, I do not wish to imply the Deity is limited to masculine or feminine characteristics. The use of the word "God" to represent the Divine keeps with tradition and makes the use of English easier.

Some readers will also notice unusual spellings of the Hebrew when transliterated into English and when compared to some other books. Since there is no single, agreed-upon way of representing the sounds of Hebrew with English, I have chosen to represent the Hebrew by the way it sounds in modern (Ashkenazic) Hebrew, not by archaic spellings which can only be confusing. Thus, you will find "Sephiroht," the way it is pronounced by millions of people around the world today, instead of the old "Sephiroth."

It is hoped that this method of representing Hebrew will not offend anyone. Likewise, it is hoped that the usage of the term "God" for the Ultimate Divinity will not offend any who, like myself, values the importance of the feminine aspect of the Divine as is also described within the following pages.

Foreword

by Chic Cicero & Sandra Tabatha Cicero

What is magick? Ask a dozen people this question, and you may well get a dozen different answers. The subject of magick is one of those hot-button topics that triggers widely differing emotional reactions in people. Hollywood fantasy and horror films, while providing viewers with thrills and chills, have continued to disseminate half-truths and misinformation about what magick is, how it works, and why magicians practice it.

Magick is a process. In ancient times magick and religion were considered one and the same; they shared a fundamental origin and unity. Today, however, magick is often thought of as a distinct area of study, separate from religion. Modern magick is considered a refinement of medieval magick—the esoteric practices that were formulated in Europe during the era between antiquity and the Renaissance—practices that were created by a surplus of unemployed clergymen in medieval society. A Western magician practicing his craft in medieval times would have come from a Judeo-Christian background, and he would have thought of magick in simple terms, not in the psychological jargon that is used today. To the medieval magician, magick included the ancient arts of alchemy and astrology, but its most evident feature was working with spirits. Magickal texts of the period, known as *grimoires* ("grammars"), are primarily concerned with the interaction between the magician and the spirit world—an invisible world populated with hordes of spiritual entities: archangels, angels, planetary intelligences, elementals, and demons. Unlike medieval magicians, contemporary practitioners come from a wide variety of religious faiths—Christian, Jewish, Neo-Pagan, Wiccan, Buddhist, etc.—and yet all are able to use the techniques of modern magick to accomplish their goals.

Magick has its own set of attributes, mental processes, and natural or scientific laws, whereas religion depends more on faith, creed, and official doctrine. In short, religion is a specific belief or set of beliefs, values, and practices usually based on spiritual teachings. Magick is a method or mechanism for causing change in accordance with cosmic laws. This does not mean, however, that magick and faith are completely disconnected—very often they work together.

Is magick a form of miracle working, or merely an aspect of psychology? The most knowledgeable authorities on the subject have concluded that magick is a combination of both. It has been defined as "the method of science, the aim of religion." Famed nineteenth-century occultist Eliphas Levi posited that magick combined "in a single science that which is most certain in philosophy with that which is eternal and infallible in religion." In magick, faith and reason are not antithetical concepts; instead they are potent tools that, when used together, complement and empower the magician's ceremonial workings. If faith and reason can be likened to "two contending forces," then magick is the force that unites them. This seeming paradox is illustrated in the teachings of the Kabalah, wherein two opposing energies work together to power the engine we call the Universe, or as the Golden Dawn tells us, there are "Those forces betwixt which the equilibrium of the Universe dependeth."

Author Donald Michael Kraig has provided one of the clearest, most succinct definitions of magick ever written: "Magick is the science and art of causing change (in consciousness) to occur in conformity with will, using means not currently understood by traditional Western science . . ." In this case "will" is understood not in terms of the individual's petty wants and desires, but rather as an intention that is in harmony with the fundamental essence of the individual's Higher Self, and also in full accord with natural or cosmic law. More importantly, Kraig provides readers with a stunning revelation about the art of magick: magick is not supernatural—it is a completely natural phenomenon. With time, effort, and dedicated intent, anyone can perform acts of magick. To quote one of Kraig's most memorable lines: "Magick is not something you do, magick is something you are."

Modern Magick is not based upon a single set of teachings, although it draws upon systems as diverse as the Hermetic Order of the Golden Dawn, Solomonic magick, and sex magick. This book is therefore a complete and self-contained system of Western magick in its own right. The twelve lessons contained herein include a wealth of information on the Kabalah, creative visualization, the creation of talismans and ceremonial implements, magick mirrors, evocations, and much more.

When we first read *Modern Magick* in 1988, it was obvious to us that this book was destined to become a contemporary grimoire favored by ceremonial magicians from many different traditions. Clearly written in an instructional step-by-step lesson format, with plenty of practical exercises and review quizzes at the end of every chapter, *Modern Magick* has become an indispensible text for any magickal library. It has sold as many copies as has Israel Regardie's *The Golden Dawn*, but in a fraction of the time. Today books on ceremonial magick are plentiful, but very few of them can claim the title of "occult classic." *Modern Magick* is one that can. And with every new edition, it only gets better.

—Chic Cicero & Sandra Tabatha Cicero
Chief Adepts of the Hermetic Order
of the Golden Dawn

Foreword

by John Michael Greer

It can sometimes be difficult to remember just how hard it was, only a few decades ago, for an occult novice to find worthwhile instruction in magick. Nowadays nothing could be easier. Alongside the many magickal orders and schools available to newcomers, and the even greater abundance of Internet resources free for the downloading, any occult bookshop worth the name has plenty of good introductory handbooks for the magickal beginner, and publishers bring out more every year. Still, it wasn't always that way.

When I first began studying ceremonial magick, back in the middle years of the 1970s, books on magick were scarce, and books on magick that were worth reading were scarcer still. The handful of occult publishers that existed in those days kept some of the classics in print, and every year brought out a few new books—some of them good, others falling at various points below that mark. Those books did not appear on the shelves in ordinary bookstores. To get them, I used to take an hour-long bus ride from the down-at-heels Seattle suburb where I lived then to the university district north of downtown.

The attraction there was a store named Beltane, which closed many years ago but at that time was the one really good occult bookstore in the Seattle area. I would hand over money I'd saved from after-school jobs for some magickal tome I'd wanted for months or years, and leaf through books I couldn't afford in the hope of memorizing details I could scribble down in a notebook on the bus ride home. On the way, if I had enough money, I'd stop in at the handful of used book stores in town that carried occult books, and now and then find a treasure that became part of my slowly growing occult library. Most people who were learning magick in those days have similar memories.

What made the quest for occult books so pressing was that nearly everything available back then accepted the magickal ethos of an earlier era, and raised steep barriers in the face of the eager but uninstructed novice. Many volumes on ceremonial magick were little more than publicity for occult orders, not all of them still extant, and whetted the reader's appetite for magick while doing as little as possible to satisfy it. Many others focused entirely on magickal theory, and the handful of guides to magickal practice then available tended either to be cheap superficial paperbacks churned out by mass-market publishers, on the one hand, or daunting tomes that could have defined the opposite of "user-friendly," if that phrase had been invented yet.

Those of us who pursued magickal studies outside an occult order had to assemble our own curriculum from hints and scraps, and it's no exaggeration to say that many of us spent nearly as much time figuring out what we had to learn as we did learning it.

That changed over the course of the 1980s. Several books played crucial roles in that transformation in different parts of the occult community, but for ceremonial magicians, the most important was the original 1988 edition of the book you are holding in your hands.

Modern Magick effected a revolution in the way ceremonial magick was taught. In place of the vague hints, evasive language, and cryptic outlines that played so large a role in earlier magickal handbooks, it offered a clear and accessible guide to the basics of magick. An aspiring mage with no previous background at all could pick up a copy, study the teachings, practice the rituals and exercises, and come out the other side with a good working knowledge of the core of magickal theory and practice.

It's only fair to say that plenty of figures in the occult community criticized *Modern Magick* in harsh terms when it first saw print. Many of those criticisms were founded on honest disagreements about how magick should be taught, or what practices were suitable for novices; magicians have always been a fractious lot, and it's rare to find two of them who agree on much of anything. Some had murkier motives, rooted in the tangled ways that control over scarce information can be cashed in for prestige and power. The criticisms, though, did nothing to deter tens of thousands of readers from buying the original edition of *Modern Magick*, and turning it into one of the most successful magickal titles of its era.

Its impact was not limited to those it influenced directly, though. *Modern Magick* reset the bar for magickal textbooks, defining the approach to teaching magick that has become standard in the decades since its appearance. These days few occult authors can get away with portentous hints, skeletal outlines, and nothing more, as so many of their predecessors did; detailed, readable, user-friendly lessons that proceed step by step from basic principles to practical instructions have become essential. It's a measure of the triumph of *Modern Magick* that some of those occultists who criticized it most sharply on its publication went on to produce books of their own that borrowed its approach to teaching the magickal arts.

In effect, *Modern Magick* did exactly what its title implies, and made magick modern. In a field that had been all too full of evasions and unnecessary secrecy, it caught the first stirrings of the information age and presented the ancient art of ceremonial magick in up-to-date terms. This expanded and updated third edition is a worthy successor to the original volume. Today's occult newcomers will likely never know what it meant, back in the day, to find some crucial piece of occult lore in a dusty volume in the back of a used book shop; occult information is so abundant nowadays that it's easy to treat it as a given. Still, anyone who picks up this new edition of *Modern Magick* can at least know one familiar experience from those days: the delight of turning the pages of one of the classics of modern occult literature.

—John Michael Greer
Grand Archdruid
Ancient Order of
Druids in America

Foreword

by Lon Milo DuQuette

"Magick is not something you do, magick is something you are."
—DONALD MICHAEL KRAIG

I have been privileged in the sixty odd (very odd) years of this incarnation to count among my friends and colleagues some of the most talented, interesting, and influential individuals who have ever inhaled the rarified air of modern occultism. Some, like Israel Regardie, Robert Anton Wilson, Phyllis Seckler, Grady McMurtry, Helen Parsons Smith, Christopher S. Hyatt, and David Wilson (a.k.a. S. Jason Black), have (at least for the moment) *shuffled off this mortal coil*; many others, I'm delighted to say, are still here and continue to bless us with their work, wisdom, and experience. Occupying a prominent and respected chair among this august circle of adepts is my dear friend, Donald Michael Kraig.

I will no doubt embarrass him with my comments. If so, I must be resolute and remind him that it was *he* who invited *me* to pen a Foreword to this new edition of his classic tome, *Modern Magick*, and that he'll just have swallow (like the good boy he is) the undiluted medicine of my praise and admiration.

The measure of a magician is not to be weighed against the number of books he or she has written, or the amount of money amassed, or the number of fawning disciples held in tow (although Donald continues to earn a respectable trove of all these things). In the final analysis, the only meaningful credential a magician can present to the world is the *magician*. Has he or she evolved through the agency of magick? Is he or she a wiser, more balanced, more disciplined, more enlightened, more engaged, more self-aware individual? Is the individual a better friend, a better teacher, a better citizen, a better human being because of his or her involvement in this most personal of spiritual art forms? Most importantly, does the magician have the ability to laugh at *magician*?

The world of magickal literature is blessed with an abundance of scholars and historians. Magick is, after all, an extremely colorful and fascinating subject. Unfortunately the field is also cursed with individuals who appear to be exploiting their photographic memories and encyclopedic knowledge of esoterica not as a tool of self-mastery and self-discovery, but as a vehicle in which to flee themselves and a life of honest self-examination—individuals who make the art of magick their *lives*, rather than applying the art to make their lives *magick*.

If I were to give the novice magician one piece of advice at the beginning of his or her career, it would be, "Study and practice magick, but please, have a life!" When shopping for instruction, avoid like the plague the pompous, pretentious, paranoid poseur, with little or no sense of humor—steer clear of the "master" who has no interests or vocabulary outside the confines of his or her self-referential magickal universe. Most especially, shun those who spend an inordinate amount of time and ink attacking the character and work of rival magicians, authors, teachers, and/or anyone else who would dare write and teach on the same subjects.

Donald Michael Kraig is the antithesis of such creatures. It is evident everywhere in his writing. He is profoundly secure in the knowledge of who and what he is. He gives generously of the knowledge and wisdom he has gained from years of study and practice. More importantly he gives generously of himself. In the final analysis it is all the magician has to give.

For those who own, read, and use the first edition of *Modern Magick* I have some good news, some bad news, and some more good news:

The good news is—this new edition is not just a reprint of the old one upon which a fancy new cover has been wrapped. It is a renovation par excellence—a *Modern Magick* for a new generation of adepts-to-be—a new incarnation with a completely reorganized format, new chapters, and nearly 40 percent new material peppered liberally with fascinating anecdotes from Don's own magickal life experiences.

The bad news is—if you own, use, and enjoy the first edition of *Modern Magick* you are going to have to buy, use, and enjoy the new edition.

But the good news is—you will love it!

—Lon Milo DuQuette
Costa Mesa, California

My Life with the Spirits

*Low Magick—It's All in Your Head . . .
You Just Have No Idea How Big Your Head Is*

Foreword

by David F. Godwin

It's hard to say just when I became interested in ceremonial magick (the real thing, as opposed to magic tricks). Perhaps it had something to do with the statement of ads the Rosicrucians (AMORC) used to run in magazines such as *Mechanics Illustrated*: "What power did these men possess?" At some point I joined the now-defunct Mystic Arts Book Society, and one selection I received was Arthur Edward Waite's *Ceremonial Magic*. I was basically undeterred by Waite's Victorian tongue clucking over these medieval spells from resurrected grimoires, but the formulae were usually so involved and required so many exotic materials that any actual performance was totally impractical.

When Llewellyn published *The Golden Dawn* by Israel Regardie, I was further enthralled, especially by his descriptions of spiritual enlightenment, which he referred to as the *summum bonum*, or the Pearl of Great Price. I spent years studying the magickal systems of this *fin de siècle* secret magickal/occult society. I even tentatively practiced some of the simpler rituals. Unfortunately, Regardie's compilation consisted primarily of reproductions of late-nineteenth-century documents that were a bit flowery and obtuse, not composed with an eye to clarity but rather toward elaborate and quasi-poetic expression filled with much jargon not likely to be understood by non-initiates. Needless to say, fascinated or not, I never achieved much in the way of results.

Then came the first edition of Donald Michael Kraig's *Modern Magick*.

For the first time, the Golden Dawn system of magick began to make sense. Practical sense. For Donald does not just give you the mechanics, he tells you the part almost nobody had ever emphasized before. He tells you about the importance of *visualization*. You can't just say the words. That won't have much effect, if any, despite the instances in fiction where someone idly picks up a book, reads a few words, and inadvertently opens a portal to some eldritch entity. There has to be intent, and above all you have to *see* what is happening in your mind's eye. The cabalistic cross is not just schlag-schlag-schlag-schlag along with some mumbled Hebrew; it is a cross of light and power surging through your body. And so with all the exercises and practices and rituals.

After a daily practice of the "Lesser" Banishing Ritual of the Pentagram—or LBRP, as Donald conveniently calls it—for a couple of weeks, a light bulb exploded in the next room during the angelic invocation. *Something* was happening.

And this book is not just a comprehensible rehash of Regardie and the Golden Dawn documents. Donald has added voluminous tidbits, information, and techniques from his own illuminating experience. Here is material on dreams, Tarot, exercise, and many other topics that you simply won't find elsewhere. This is truly a step-by-step manual for the aspiring magician.

I learned a lot from this book. Perhaps most importantly, I learned the importance of the magickal attitude. After a certain amount of practice, things start to happen "in accordance with your will" even without ritual—so be careful what you will.

Now Mr. Kraig has given us a new edition of this seminal and all-important work, with added material and revisions for the sake of yet more clarity and accuracy. This book is a must-have for anyone with a serious interest in ceremonial magick or the Golden Dawn. It is the basic text of any magickal library.

—David F. Godwin
Godwin's Cabalistic Encyclopedia

Preface to the Third Edition

When I was asked to write a new edition of *Modern Magick*, I started to think back over the changes I had experienced since it was originally published. I tried to think back to the event that, after an amazing series of serendipitous coincidences, led to my writing these lessons. It wasn't directly due to my mother teaching me to read phonetically when I was three. It wasn't my fascination with reading that developed after devouring Robert A. Heinlein's *Have Spacesuit, Will Travel* when I was six or seven. Nor was it my writing a twelve-page story in third grade when the assignment only required one page. It wasn't my fascination with being a writer for the school paper that developed when I was in Daniel Webster Junior High School, either. In fact, I trace the direct beginning of this book to my time at UCLA.

I still remember an event during my second year. A friend and I were experimenting with hypnosis, and I went into a deep trance. "Why are you here?" she asked. I knew she wasn't asking why I was in that room.

From somewhere a message came to me. I blurted it out: "To learn; so I can teach."

Where the hell did that come from? At the time I was attending UCLA I had no desire to be any sort of teacher. I already knew what I wanted to do. I wanted to make TV programs. I was hoping to get into the motion picture–television department to further my studies. Being logical, I also had a fallback plan: if I didn't get into TV, I'd be a musician. I was a pretty good keyboardist, and had already performed all over Los Angeles, including some of the top clubs. Elliotz Mintz, who went on to be a publicist for John Lennon, Bob Dylan, and many others, had a TV show called *Head Shop*, and I had been on it with a band many times. And if not a filmmaker or musician, I was going to be . . . a magician! I was pretty good at that, too, having performed shows all over the city. I knew where I was going. *What happened?*

For some unknown reason, I didn't get into the UCLA film department. Musical groups I was in would have incredible success, and then get let down by managers or implode. And this was during a pre–Criss Angel, pre–David Blaine, pre–David Copperfield era when making a living by being a magician was difficult.

So I worked as a carney. I did telephone sales. And I continued studying the Kabalah and occultism in general. By this time I was living in Encinitas, California, north of San Diego. Through a series of curious events, I ended up sharing a home with an electrical engineer and his son. He also studied and gave treatments in Shiatzu—Oriental massage or acupressure—when few people knew what it was. He started teaching it to others from our house on a street named Vulcan. I asked if I could attend and he told me I could. By the third time through the classes, he asked me to assist.

One day he really surprised me. He said he had to be out of town for the following meeting of the class, and he wanted me to teach it. I felt very insecure, but he insisted that I knew enough to do it, so I agreed. He told his class, and some of the students talked with him privately, then came up to me. "We hear you know about the Kabalah," one of them said. "We'd like you to teach it to us."

I was shocked. This was totally unexpected. I held my thumb and first finger an inch apart. "I only know this much," I protested.

He held his thumb and forefinger a fraction of an inch apart. "But we only know this much," he said. So I agreed. The class was successful and people wanted to know more.

There was a nearby occult shop, and I went in and offered to teach classes on the Kabalah. At first it was once a week for four weeks. Over the next few years this expanded to six and then ten weeks. I taught it at other shops and expanded my offerings to other subjects while I continued my personal studies. I joined various metaphysical groups. A girlfriend dragged me to a class on Wicca. The teacher of that class turned out to be Raven Grimassi. I continued studying with him after that and I consider him both a mentor and a great friend. When my teacher of Shiatzu moved out, I had to find a new place to live. I ended up moving in with a person whose name I got from a card on the bulletin board of a tiny occult shop. As a result of that odd chance,

for the next six years I shared a two-bedroom apartment with Scott Cunningham.

I continued playing in bands. I worked in occult shops and in a shop for stage magicians. I gave workshops. I managed a costume shop. I became a courier for a bank. I put my basic course on the Kabalah and magick into fifty-two brief lessons. I was going to become a master of mail order. A man who already had a school with metaphysical mail-order classes got in touch with me and he had me rewrite the fifty-two lessons into fewer, but much larger, ones. He started to distribute them, but about four months later he vanished.

By this time, Scott was becoming quite a name and his success was inspiring. So I thought I'd give writing a book a try. I rewrote the lessons, again. That became the first edition of *Modern Magick*. I described what happened to me between the first two editions in the preface to the second edition. Since then, much has changed.

First, contrary to what I stated in my preface to the original edition, the number of practicing magicians has vastly increased. I like to think that this book had something to do with that change. Second, the antipathy and suspicion that once existed between Pagans and ceremonial magicians has all but vanished. This book was one of the first that respected both paths, and again, I like to think that this book had something to do with that change. Third, a new tradition in magick—Chaos Magick—has developed. Although as of this writing it's not very popular in the U.S.A., it has had incredible growth in Europe and the U.K. To keep the title of this book valid, I will be adding a new lesson that includes information on this and two other systems.

My life has changed over the years, too. One by one, all of my blood relatives, and almost all of my relatives by my mother and grandfather's remarriages, have left this incarnation. I have become honored with the title "Tarot Grandmaster" and have become deeply involved with hypnosis. I an now a certified hypnosis instructor and a master practitioner of Neuro-Linguistic Programming (NLP).

As I told one of my NLP instructors, "This is just like what I do . . . only different." That is, NLP is a form of magick that is focused on the use of the mind. Some of the first books on the subject were called *The Structure of Magic* (in two volumes). However, rather than focusing on NLP as an entirely original or unique form of magick, it is easy to incorporate many of its concepts to more completely and accurately explain traditional magickal concepts. In this way, incorporating some NLP concepts will make the magickal techniques in this book even more accessible to people today, helping to make the basic concepts more clear and resulting in greater success. It will make the magick more modern.

When I was revising, expanding, and writing this third edition I referred to it as "The Platinum Edition." Why? This is because platinum is generally worth about twice the value of gold. I don't mean to imply that the words on these pages are incredibly valuable in and of themselves. However, if you are willing to put in the study, the practice, and the work, you will discover that what you learn and experience is worth many times the value of gold. This is the Platinum Edition of *Modern Magick* because with it you can change your life to have a value many times that of mere gold. The true "edition of platinum," however, is not these lessons. If you're willing to put in the study and practice required by this path, the edition of platinum will be *you*.

Over the years I've communicated with thousands of people. Some of them are desperate for change and ask me to do a spell or ritual for them. Respectfully, I have to refuse. If I were to do a magickal rite to help you, the result might help you temporarily, but it would keep you weak and dependent on an outside source—me—for you to reach your goals. Having people dependent upon me is *not* the purpose of this work. Rather, it is to help you discover true self-empowerment, the ability for you to achieve your goals through your own work. So do not think that if you have a problem you can pick up these pages and mumble through a ritual without any understanding in order to get amazing results. That's what happens in the movies and comic books, not reality. You will discover that magick is not simply something you do, magick is something you are. It is a way of life. It is a way of approaching the world and the universe. It is a way to obtain what you want and need. And yes, it is a way to obtain power.

In fact, many people, especially when they're younger and feel disempowered, come to the study of magick in an attempt to gain power over others. If that's why you're here, I'm sorry, but such a goal is not in harmony with these lessons or reality. If you follow the practices revealed here you will discover rather quickly that the true power of magick is power over yourself. Those who hunger for power over others will quickly find failure and disappointment. But with perseverance, you will find that power over yourself and the ability to achieve whatever you desire really is the ultimate power. It is the true power of *Modern Magick*.

Preface to the Second Edition

A great many things have happened to me since *Modern Magick* was originally accepted for publication. I moved my home several times, including moves of thousands of miles. My mother died suddenly and one of my best friends died after a long illness. I have traveled all over the U.S. to give lectures. I have met thousands of people and answered thousands of letters. I went back to school with a Fellowship to USC where I received certificates in multimedia, 3D graphics, animation, and Web design for the Internet.

Modern Magick created major changes in my life. Directly and indirectly it has brought me new jobs and let me travel around the U.S. and visit Canada and England. Because of this book I have made many, many new friends.

Perhaps what pleases me most about the book are the many wonderful stories people have shared with me. I thought that *Modern Magick* would be just a book about how to do High Magick. Numerous people have written to me or talked to me in person to tell me that it changed their lives. Personally, I am more inclined to think that the people who went through major changes as a result of working with this book were ready to make the changes. *Modern Magick* was merely a kick in the direction they were already headed. But for whatever reason, I was very pleased that my writing has been able to help.

I had always hoped that *Modern Magick* would be used as a textbook for classes in magick. I have heard from many groups and individuals that they are using it for exactly that purpose. A bigger thrill is when I hear that groups are using it as a basis for study but are adding to it or changing things around. This means that people are thinking and growing. This means that magick is not simply the recapitulation of the actions of ancient, dead men and women, but a living and evolving science based upon those people's research, dedication, genius and originality. In many ways this book is simply a small testament to their wisdom. I do hope that even more groups will use *Modern Magick* as a guide for study, research and, most importantly, practice.

Although it was only a short time ago, when I wrote this book the number of volumes on High Magick that had been published was limited. Even many of the most valuable and most popular books on the subject had been written forty years earlier. Because of the small number of ceremonial magicians at the time (when compared with today), I had hoped this book would enjoy continuous but relatively small sales. I guessed that by this time, if it stayed in print, perhaps ten thousand copies would have been sold. To my surprise and delight I was off by a factor of ten.

I would like to think that the acceptance of the way I presented the information, combined with the fact that *Modern Magick* seems to have hit the market at exactly the right time, has helped make ceremonial magick more understandable and more usable for a greater number of people than ever before. There are far more practicing ceremonial magicians today than at any time in history, and I feel honored to have played a small part in that expansion.

When I first became highly active in the occult world, there was an attitude among ceremonial magicians and Pagans that they shouldn't mix. I am glad to say that has changed, opening the world of occultism to a pragmatic eclecticism: "If it works, I'll use it." *Modern Magick* was one of the first "Pagan-friendly" books on ceremonial magick. I hope that it has, in some small way, contributed to the acceptance of others' methods, bringing to Pagans and ceremonial magicians alike what I call "unity through diversity."

Many years ago I had a chance to go to a book signing by one of my favorite authors, Ursula K. Le Guin. She gave a reading from one of her novels, then started to sign books. When I got up to her I apologized. Everyone else had a bright, shiny, new edition of one or more of her books for her to sign. I presented an early edition of *A Wizard of Earthsea*, yellowing and obviously well read and well worn. Her entire face lit up. "I'm glad to see that somebody actually is reading my book," she told me.

This happened years before *Modern Magick* was even written. I have learned exactly how she feels. I find it amazing when I see a well-worn copy of my book that is filled with notes and comments. I wish I had the time to read all of those comments and see what people had highlighted or underlined. I've heard from many people that their first or second copy of this book was so used that they had to get another. Some have had copies hard bound. For all of this I am grateful.

I am also grateful to all of the people I met at Llewellyn, especially those who helped to make this project a success. I would like to thank Carl and Sandra Weschcke for taking a chance on me and Nancy Mostad for helping to get this through to publication.

And finally, I am most grateful to all of the people who have not only purchased this book, but have used it to help them on their individual paths to spirituality and magick. It is to them that I dedicate the new section of this book, the *Modern Magick* FAQ. I hope you find it as useful as the rest of the book.

Introduction

Looking back now, one particular event seems so very long ago. I was just turning thirteen. For me, it was a period of incredible excitement. Beside school, baseball, writing stories, playing music, doing magic tricks, skateboarding, and a paper route, I had spent the last four years preparing for what I thought was going to be the most important ritual of my life. In a matter of days I was to have my Bar Mitzvah and be initiated into Jewish manhood. Unexpectedly one of the rabbis on the staff of my temple called me into his office. This rabbi looked about ninety years old . . . and acted as if he were going on eighteen. He even wore tennis shoes under his rabbinical robes.

To me, Judaism had been very comfortable. No Hell or Hellfire. No "believe or be damned for eternity." Just love God and follow the "Negative Golden Rule":

Don't do unto others if you would not have them do the same unto you.

To a scientifically oriented person like myself—I loved everything scientific and of course did the odd experiment with my Gilbert chemistry set—this was a nice, safe, almost secular religion—until that old rabbi called me into his office.

He talked to me about my first responsibilities as a man within the Jewish community. I was overwhelmed with foreign information. Until now, this had been a virtually unknown part of my religion. In a few moments, that rabbi virtually blasted away my previously safe cocoon of Conservative Judaism.

Sure, we were supposed to wear a *Tallit* (prayer shawl) during certain ceremonies. It was a nice idea because, by wearing such a cloth, all were seen by God as being equal. (My young mind didn't think that God could see through the cloth to riches that might be worn beneath.) But now I was told the Tallit was supposed to have so many threads of such-and-such colors and be tied in a certain number of knots. What sort of craziness was this?

And then there was the *Tephillin* (phylactery). I was supposed to participate in certain prayer rituals called a *Minyan* that required a minimum of ten men. (Why ten and not eleven or nine?) During the Minyan we were supposed to each wear the Tephillin. The one for the arm was a box with prayers in it worn only on the left arm with the box near the heart. It was held on by a leather strap, which was then wound seven (why seven?) times around the arm. Then it was to be wound around the hand so as to form the Hebrew letter Shin, which combined with the knot on the head straps that forms the letter Dallet and a knot on the arm strap that forms the letter Yud spell out the word "Shadai," a name of God (I thought the name of God was that four-letter word which was never supposed to be pronounced). The other box was worn like a unicorn's horn between and just above the eyes. It had two straps that would come back over the head and then over the shoulders and down in front. The straps of both Tephillin were finished on one side and left unfinished on the other. They had to be worn with the finished side showing.

Suddenly, my safe, logical religion was illogical and no longer safe. I needed to find out the roots of my religion and discover the basis for what appeared foolish. Thus began a search and study which has so far taken decades, led to the Kabalah and ritual magick, and culminates in these lessons which you are now beginning to study.

In those years I have studied thousands of books and searched the United States and Western Europe. I have written for occult and New Age magazines and papers. I received a B.A. in Philosophy from U.C.L.A., am a Certified Tarot Grandmaster, a certified clinical hypnotherapist, a master practitioner of Neuro-Linguistic Programming, and have an honorary Doctorate in Metaphysics.

The lessons that you are beginning here are not something I have merely dreamed up. I have taught this course dozens of times in the Southern California area to hundreds of students. Each time it was taught I tried to improve and refine it. It was finally partially published for the first time as a mail-order course. Now those lessons are being published in book form to make them more widely available. You have the great advantage of having the entire course written out for you in far greater detail than any of the notes ever taken by any of my students. I am also able to present far more information than ever before.

I'd like to talk a bit on what this course covers. It is, naturally, on ritual, ceremonial, or art magick and the Kabalah: the philosophy behind magick (and, for that matter, all Abrahamic religion, too). It is primarily in the tradition of the Hermetic Order of the Golden Dawn, as within that group developed the union of numerous aspects of the Western Mystery Tradition. This book, however, is not the Golden Dawn and there are many differences between what is presented here and the Golden Dawn tradition. Further, this book has sections drawn from many other systems, including various Eastern, Pagan, Crowleyan (Thelemic), and more modern systems. Some of the topics to be covered include the Tarot, divination, the history of the Tarot, the Lesser Banishing Ritual of the Pentagram, the Banishing Ritual of the Hexagram, the Middle Pillar Ritual, the Circulation of the Body of Light, the Watchtower Ritual, meditation, the Tree of Life, the Three Pillars, the four Kabalistic Worlds, the history of the Kabalah, Gematria, Notarikon, Temurah, Bible interpretation, talismans, astral traveling, pathworking, healing, *The Keys of Solomon*, magickal rituals which you can design for any purpose, sex magick, and much more.

Obviously, this is more than can be covered in the following few hundred pages. After all, there are thousands of books available on these subjects, and it would be naïve to think I could capture all of that information in this one volume. There are, however, two things you should keep in mind:

1. *Sturgeon's Law.* This law states that 90 percent of everything is crap. It is named in honor of science-fiction author Theodore Sturgeon, who used it (originally calling it "Sturgeon's Revelation") because he was tired of defend-

ing science fiction to various literary critics in the 1950s. Supposedly, after being asked if he didn't agree that 90 percent of science fiction was crap, his response was that 90 percent of *everything* was crap. For the discussion here, I'm simply using this law to point out that of those thousands of books, much is repetitive and much more is useless guessing by people who haven't even tried the simplest ritual. That is, much of it really is crap. This course will leave you with the best of thousands of books, plus over twenty-five years of personal research and practice.

2. It is *not* the purpose of this book to completely explain all of these topics. The purpose of these pages is to introduce you to these ideas so that you can direct yourself in your life-long study of the occult (remember, "occult" means secret, as in "secret wisdom." It does not mean "evil"). This course will, however, give you more correct, immediately useful information on the Kabalah and ritual magick than any other single book or course presently in print. If you never read another book on magick, you will have everything you need to be a powerful, successful magician from the contents of these pages alone.

I'd like to talk now about the Golden Dawn. At the time when this magickal lodge formed in the late 1880s, there were few really good books available on either magick or the Kabalah. Most of the really good books on these subjects that exist today were written by members of the Golden Dawn, people who were associated with members, or people who knowingly or unknowingly were influenced by this group. These people include MacGregor Mathers, Aleister Crowley, Dr. F. I. Regardie, A. E. Waite, H. P. Blavatsky, Dion Fortune, P. F. Case, Chic and Sandra Tabatha Cicero, John Michael Geer, and many others. Much

of this course is derived from their writings, virtually millions of words presented here for the first time in an easy-to-follow, practical system of wisdom, spiritual development, and magick.

Many magickal rituals will be given in these lessons for you to practice. These should aid you in your psychic and magickal development. However, even though thousands of people throughout history have successfully shown their proficiency in magickal techniques, quite frankly I cannot guarantee your success. This is because the ability to perform magick successfully is dependent upon what you put into it. Your success is directly dependent upon the effort, practice, and consistency of your work. Many people, however, have told me of their great successes using the traditional techniques given in these pages.

The best way to use these pages is to first read through them quickly. Don't worry about not understanding something. During this first reading you are simply gaining an overview of what is here. Then the real work begins. Start going through these lessons, page by page, studying each of the ideas and practicing each of the techniques as they come up. Let me make clear at the outset that this course will not teach "Black Magick." You will *not* be required to do anything contrary to your moral or ethical values. You will not be "summoning up" any demons, devils, or evil entities.

Years ago, many Pagans, Wiccans, or Witches criticized those who claimed to be ceremonial magicians by saying that all they did was talk and read. They claimed that "magicians don't do magick." Unfortunately, I found myself in total agreement with them. In many cases that was true. In some cases today it remains true. But if you follow the instructions on the following pages, step by step, you will be that unique and powerful individual: a *practicing* ritual magician.

—Donald Michael Kraig

Section One
The Outer Order

*In magickal organizations such as orders and covens,
the Outer Order consists of a wider membership
wherein people are taught the basic theories and concepts of the group.
If people last through the trials and ordeals of this training—
proving their worthiness and dedication—
they move to the Inner Order.*

LESSON ONE

PART ONE

Getting Started

I want to start by telling you that all of the "fairy tales" and stories about the powers of wizards, witches, and magicians that you've heard or read all of your life are true. I don't mean that as some sort of metaphoric truth, but as a truth that is as real as the floor under your feet. Unfortunately, the truth of those stories is only partially true. The timing and methods described in those stories have been altered to make them more interesting as stories rather than as the reality that is hidden within them. Even so, I want to make this completely clear: *It is absolutely and without a doubt possible to create spells and rituals that will bring you money, love, wisdom, contentment, and more!*

The key difference between the "magic" in fairy tales and in movies and "magick" as practiced by tens of thousands of people around the world today and in the past is that most real magick does not occur instantaneously. As an example, if you worked a ritual to bring you money, it may take a week or two for the money to arrive. When it does arrive, it would come only by natural means. But, if you practice and properly perform your ritual, *come it must!*

No one can give you magickal powers.
You have to earn them.
There is only one way to do this:
Practice! Practice! Practice!

Magick—real magick—is an experimental science. One of the first things a scientist learns is to keep a record of his or her work. Therefore, as part of your work as a magician, it is important to keep a record of your practices, experiences, thoughts, and dreams. This should be done in two separate records, journals, or diaries.

The Dream Diary

Starting right now, today, you should start keeping a diary of your dreams. When you dream (and everybody does dream), one of four things may occur:

1. *Astral Work.* When doing astral work, you are learning lessons toward your spiritual, psychical, and magickal development as well as practicing these lessons. This occurs on what is called the "astral plane." You will learn more about the Kabalistic and magickal interpretation of the astral plane in later lessons.

2. *Psychological Messages.* Many times your unconscious mind needs to tell your conscious something, but your conscious refuses to or is unable to listen. In some dreams the unconscious sends a message, in symbols, to the conscious. This is a basis for one aspect of Freudian analysis.

3. *Play.* The mind, at rest, may wander aimlessly and meaninglessly, sending any sort of beautiful or bizarre pictures to your conscious.

4. *A combination of the above.*

If you have never kept a diary of your dreams, you will find that it is easy. Simply get a pad of paper and leave it with a pencil or pen by your bed at night. When you first wake up in the morning, write down what you remember. If you remember nothing, the entry in your diary may read, "I did not choose to remember my dreams," and that is okay. At first you may only remember a small amount, perhaps only one event or feeling. Within a month of steady practice, you will have trouble keeping your entries to less than a page.

Also, obtain a nice blank book or binder with blank paper, lined if you prefer, into which you should transfer your abbreviated notes from the bedside pad. Unless your handwriting is very legible, print your entry from the pad of paper by your bed into the new book. This will take a little longer, but in years to come it will be much easier to read. Be sure to date each entry.

As an alternative, you may wish to keep a computerized dream journal. You should still transfer the information from your pad to the computerized journal on a daily basis. You might consider this your "first ritual."

In a paragraph above I wrote about reading the diary in "years to come." This overview attitude is quite important. Do not, at this point, try to analyze each dream. Chances are at this time you will not be able to tell which of the four types of dreams mentioned earlier you are having. It is also unlikely that you will be able to interpret their individual meanings. Instead, look for repeated images or changes you find between recurring dreams or dreams with recurring themes. Please, please, *please* stay away from all of those ridiculous "meanings of your dreams" books!

Let me give you an example of how this diary can be important for you. One of my students had frequent dreams of being chased by soldiers and running and hiding. She had dreams such as these several times a month, and would wake up in a cold sweat, terrified. For her, the dream was a version of events that actually happened to her in her early life.

But after practicing some of the protection rituals from these lessons, her dreams, she told me, began to change. She no longer would hide and almost be discovered and raped. Instead, she would make her escape. For her, an old mental block that manifested in a fear of men and sex was broken down. As her feelings of security increased, her relationship with her boyfriend improved. This was represented by the change in her recurring dream. Similarly, you may be able to see positive changes occur in your life by being able to observe the changes in your dreams over time.

The Ritual or Magickal Diary

Starting later in this lesson you will be given rituals to perform at least once daily. They should never take more than half an hour while you are learning them, and much less time when they are memorized. In a second book, or in another file on your computer, you should keep a ritual diary. On page 10 is a suggested format for your diary. You may wish to make copies of this page and place them in a binder, then simply fill one out each day or for each ritual, or set of rituals, performed.

All of the data listed is important, and you should include information for each aspect every time you make an entry. In the future you will be able to see what conditions give you the greatest success when doing magick. Some people are most successful when they are happy and it is a warm night. Others have their greatest success when they are depressed and it is raining. Together, your ritual diary or magickal diary and dream diary become your own personal secret magickal text which is really only good for you.

By "Phase of Moon" I mean full, waning, or waxing. This information can be obtained from a local paper or an astrological calendar such as *Llewellyn's Moon Sign Book* or *Astrological Calendar*. There are also websites and computer applications that can provide you with this information. By "Weather Conditions" I mean rainy, cloudy, hot, muggy, warm, cold, etc. By "Emotions" I mean happy, sad, depressed, etc. By "Performance" I mean was it done well, fair, poorly, etc. By "Results" I mean how do you feel? What did you experience? Etc. You may also want to add comments to this section at a later date, in which case you should date the addition.

Oh, one last thing about rituals at this time. No, it is *not* acceptable to perform a ritual seven times in one day and forget doing them for the rest of the week. You may do them more often than once a day, but you should do them at least once every day. Regularity is important. Keep a record such as the one described for each ritual or set of rituals. If you do rituals in the morning, at noon, and in the evening of the same day, you'll have three pages like the ones on the next page in your ritual diary.

Tips for Remembering Dreams

You may not be aware of it, but research shows that you dream every night. In fact, you have several dreams each night. However, if you're like most people, you may not easily remember them. Ease at dream recall improves with practice over time. Be patient with yourself! Here are some tips or tricks that can help you to remember your dreams:

1. Every night, as you fall asleep, repeat silently to yourself: "I will remember my important dreams when I awake."

2. If you awake during the night and recall a dream but would rather go back to sleep, take a tissue or piece of paper, ball it up, and throw it into the middle of the floor. As you do so, tell yourself that it will remind you of the dream you just had. When you see the paper in such an unusual position after finally waking, it will trigger a memory of the dream.

3. When you do get up in the morning, record your dreams right away. Jot them down. Even if you are, uh, desperate to go to the bathroom, write something—*anything*—down on your pad of paper first. Transfer this—and expand on it as you remember more of the dream(s)—to your dream diary.

4. Record something in your dream diary daily. Make it a habit by doing this daily for a minimum of three weeks.

Ritual Diary Entry

DATE: **DAY:**   **TIME:**

Phase of Moon:

Weather Conditions:

Emotions:

Physical Condition:

Name of Rituals Performed:

Performance:

Results:

Using the Ritual Diary

While the importance of the ritual diary cannot be underestimated, its use is actually very simple. You can design a page such as on the previous page on your computer and fill it in after performing rituals, or you can make photocopies of that page and fill a binder with them. Here's an example:

Ritual Diary Entry

DATE: *March XX, 20XX*   **DAY:** *Tues.*   **TIME:** *8:45 p.m.*

Phase of Moon: *Waxing Moon in Leo*

Weather Conditions: *Cool evening. Windy. Clear sky.*

Emotions: *I feel excited about a new relationship, but I'm able to focus pretty well. I'm happy, but I also feel a bit insecure. Lots of "new relationship" energy.*

Physical Condition: *Awake and alert, feeling fine.*

Name of Rituals Performed: *RR; LBRP; BRH; MP; TCR; LBRP*

Performance: *The rituals were all performed with concentration and focus. I felt good about the way they turned out. Card drawn during TCR was the Hanged Man.*

Results: *The banishings cleared the area nicely, but I'm concerned about the Tarot card. It seems to indicate that I have to give up something in order to get something better. I wonder what that will be.*

Follow Up: April XX, 20XX. Well, the new relationships didn't work out. I left our dinner date in a huff, and put far too much money down on the restaurant table. We just did not have enough in common. I went to the _____ occult shop to cool off, and met an old friend, _____, there. We talked for a while, and I told her what had happened. She commiserated with me, and we went out for a drink to talk some more. We're going to see each other again this weekend. I'm thinking, perhaps these two relationships were indicated by the Hanged Man.

In the above example from my ritual diary, I used abbreviations for the rituals: RR is the Relaxation Ritual; LBRP is the Lesser Banishing Ritual of the Pentagram; BRH is the Banishing Ritual of the Hexagram; TCR is the Tarot Contemplation Ritual; LBRP is a repetition of the Lesser Banishing Ritual of the Pentagram. You'll learn to do all of these rituals as you study and practice from these lessons.

Most of the entries are pretty self-explanatory. The phase of the Moon was obtained from the *Llewellyn Astrological Calendar*.

In the "Results" section, I gave my initial impression of the information, message, or learnings I received from the Tarot card. The follow-up was entered about two weeks later. It seemed to indicate the validity of the original learnings.

This particular set of rituals and learnings showed me the accuracy of the Tarot, even with just one card. It also helped me to work with the idea of giving up something for something better.

Sometimes, follow-ups can be added to entries months or even years after the original entries. By studying such things as effectiveness and accuracy under different weather, emotional, and psychological conditions, you learn when you are more effective or less effective in your magick. In this way, your ritual diary can become your personal magickal grimoire or book of shadows. Be aware, however, that those results are personal and may or may not apply to others.

Getting the Most from This Course

As a result of giving these lessons many times, I realize that some of you may do no more than read this book. Many more people study occultism than practice it. Actually, if that's what you wish to do, it is fine. The structure of these lessons is such that if you only read them, they will actually give information to your unconscious mind, information that will positively influence the way you think about yourself and the world around you.

However, if you are really interested in learning how to *do* magick, I strongly suggest that before the seventh or eighth lesson you read at least one other book—preferably many more. Books are suggested in the bibliography that follows each lesson. You may select any of those books, or you may choose any book concerned with the Kabalah, the Tarot, or magick. The purpose of this is twofold:

1. So you get a slightly different view of the subject matter. I make no claim to being a guru or divine master. Studying the same subjects from different points of view is highly advisable.

2. So you can get a more in-depth study of a particular subject that interests you.

You do not need to buy a book. You can get it from the library, borrow it from a friend, or even pick one from your personal collection of books. In fact, it could be a book you have already read. It would be a good idea to keep a record of your readings, too. List the book's title and author, the date you completed it, and any comments you may have on the book.

Now, before giving you your first formal ritual, I want to tell you about the one thing which you should have in order to gain the most from this book: a Tarot deck. While this is not primarily a course in the Tarot, the Tarot does play a very important part in the study—a part not limited to "giving readings" or "fortunetelling."

The *best* decks for use in this course are:

• **The Golden Dawn Tarot.** There are two versions of this that I use. The first is the *Golden Dawn Magical Tarot* by Chic and Sandra Tabatha Cicero. I love the brilliant colors and the accuracy of the imagery. The other deck is *The Golden Dawn Tarot* by Robert Wang. Although there are a few minor symbolic errors in it, it was the first true deck based directly on the Golden Dawn's teachings. I am also not a big fan of his art. There are a couple of other decks that have been published claiming to be Golden Dawn decks, and you'll have to determine if they work for you.

• **The B.O.T.A. Tarot.** The Builders of the Adytum deck was designed by Paul Foster Case. It includes the Hebrew letters on the appropriate cards, a feature that so angered some of the leaders of the Golden Dawn that they booted Case from the order. Case vowed to never produce a colored version of the deck, but this desire was eventually ignored by his followers. However, if you can still get the black-and-white version and the book that goes with the deck so you can color in the cards yourself, you will find this a very valuable experience.

• **The Hermetic Tarot** by Godfrey Dawson is not well known, but it, too, is based on the Golden Dawn's teachings. Many years ago, before any Golden Dawn decks were published, this deck was available. When I taught the Golden Dawn system of Tarot, I encouraged people to use this deck. It is still a good choice.

Acceptable decks for this course include:

• *The Rider-Waite-Smith* Tarot. Even though Waite admitted in his original book on this deck that it didn't reveal all of the secrets, its popularity has made this deck part of many people's psyches. So if you're really familiar with it, you can certainly use it.

• Any Tarot decks based on the Rider-Waite-Smith, such as the *Universal Tarot, Aquarian Tarot, Morgan-Greer Tarot, Royal Fez Moroccan Tarot*, and many others. They seem to increase in number every month.

• Earlier Tarot decks (such as *the IJJ Swiss deck*) that are "standard," having twenty-two Major Arcana cards and fifty-six Minor Arcana cards in four suits for a total of seventy-eight cards.

Decks *not appropriate* for this course include:

• *The Crowley Thoth deck*, which is an excellent deck but so complex in symbolism it may be confusing for beginners. If you are not a beginner in working with the Tarot and you really like the Thoth deck, go ahead and use it. If you are not familiar with this deck, avoid it—for now.

Under no circumstances should you use a "non-standard" deck with this course. By non-standard I mean a deck with more or less than seventy-eight cards with a Major Arcana of twenty-two cards and a Minor Arcana with fifty-six cards divided into four suits. This would include decks such as the *Secret Dakini Oracle, I Ching cards, Gypsy Witch* fortunetelling cards, and many others. Although they are frequently called "Tarot" decks, they are more often considered "oracles" or "divinatory decks" so as not to confuse them with the seventy-eight cards of the Tarot. This is not to say that these decks are bad or wrong, only that they do not go with these lessons.

Tarot decks can be purchased at most major bookstores; however I suggest that you patronize metaphysical bookstores or occult supply shops. The people who work there are generally far more knowledgeable and helpful than those at a general bookstore who often have no interest or knowledge of occult topics. Also, when you buy from local shops you keep your tax money that pays for the fire department, police protection, and city services right in your community. If you don't have access to a local shop, many beautiful and unique decks that are suitable for this course are currently available through Llewellyn's website.

In the next column is your first ritual. Remember, it should be practiced at least once a day. You may have learned the ritual elsewhere. Many groups, organizations, and even doctors and psychological therapists teach forms of it. But although it is sim-ple, do not underestimate its importance. Walking seems simple now, but it was very difficult for you to learn—and you had to learn it before you could learn to run. This ritual will be used to prepare for every magickal ritual in this entire course.

The Relaxation Ritual

STEP ONE. Sit or lie in a place where you will not be disturbed for at least five minutes. Remember to unplug the telephone. Get comfortable. If you are sitting, your back should be straight. Whether sitting or lying down, your legs and arms should not be crossed. If sitting, rest your hands, palms down, in your lap. Remove glasses or contact lenses. Your eyes should be closed.

STEP TWO. Visualize a golden ball of beautiful, warm light surrounding your feet. If you cannot "see" the ball of light when you visualize it, that is okay. Just know that it is there. Truly know that if your powers of visualization were different, you would be able to see it. The ball of golden warm light always brings peace and total relaxation. Wherever the ball of light goes, tension flows away. Let it go, and as it goes, feel your feet filled with the warm, golden glow of peace and total relaxation.

STEP THREE. Now allow this ball of light to rise up your legs and up your torso. Then allow it to go down your arms to your fingers, and finally up your neck and into your head until you are completely covered with the warm, golden glow of total peace and relaxation, and all tension is gone. Allow the ball to move slowly. Take your time. Let go.

STEP FOUR. With your mind, spend a few moments exploring your body. If you notice tension anywhere, just send the ball of light there and the tension will vanish. With each breath allow yourself to become more and more relaxed.

STEP FIVE. Stay in this state of deep relaxation for a few moments. Know that you can return to this state whenever you like simply by doing the relaxation ritual. If you are having trouble sleeping, try this ritual when you lie down at night instead of suffering or taking dangerous pills. Be at one with yourself.

STEP SIX. When you are ready to come out of this state of deep relaxation, take three deep breaths and feel fresh life and energy coming into your body with each breath. Let that energy flow completely through you, from the ends of your hair to the tips of your fingers and toes. Become aware of the world around you and breathe in life.

STEP SEVEN. When you have returned to your regular awareness, record your experience in your ritual diary.

Now, before going further, spend a few days getting used to keeping your diaries, doing the ritual and obtaining a Tarot deck if you do not already have one that you wish to use with this course.

What is Magick?

In the first few pages we have already covered a surprising amount of material. We discussed dreams and ritual work, gave you a ritual to do daily, and told you how to keep a record of your work. This was to get you started on *practical work* as opposed to theoretical knowledge. The assumption was made, however, that you have a basic idea of exactly what magick is. But your definition may not be the same as mine, so let us now try to come to a workable definition of magick.

According to the famous occultist Aleister Crowley, magick is "the Science and Art of causing Change to occur in conformity with Will." Crowley was a member of the famous Hermetic Order of the Golden Dawn, which was mentioned earlier. Another member of the Golden Dawn was Dion Fortune. Her definition of magick was the same as Crowley's, except that she considered the "change" to be a change in consciousness. (Note: Fortune was a lay psychologist, someone who practiced psychology without being a medical doctor. She published several books on psychology under her real name, Violet Firth. Eventually, Freud felt there was no room for people to practice psychology without also being

a doctor. The field of "lay psychology" dried up for many years. Today, psychiatrists [medical doctors in the field of psychology] tend to specialize in the use of drugs for dealing with psychological problems and disorders, while psychologists deal with such issues without drugs and are usually not medical doctors.)

But what exactly do these definitions mean? Let's say that you do a magickal ritual to get fifty dollars. It, therefore, is your "Will" to get the money. You go out for a walk, and although when walking it is your habit to go right at a particular street corner, something makes you decide to turn to the left. A block down this street you meet an old friend who returns the fifty dollars you had loaned him several months ago.

What made you turn left? According to Crowley's definition, your magickal ritual would have caused some change in the physical world, which resulted in your turning in an unusual direction. Perhaps it was a smell, or a telepathic message from your friend, or from a higher entity telling you to "turn left!" If you ascribe to Dion Fortune's definition, then you would say that your ritual made a change in your consciousness, which gave you the information to turn to the left instead of the right.

In either case, three things are apparent:

1. No matter which definition you use, the actual result is the same.

2. The result functions *as if* there had been a change in the physical world, regardless of whether there had been a change in the physical world or just a change in your consciousness.

3. Magick works.

Unfortunately, either definition is still too broad. If you cause a change in conformity with Will and call it "magick," then almost anything you do is a magickal act. If it is your will to open a door, then you turn the knob and open the door, by the above definitions you have done a magickal act. In fact, Crowley (his name rhymes with "holy," not with "howdy") says that "every intentional act

Who Came Up with *That* Idea?

Somehow, a variety of myths have developed over time about getting supplies to use for your occult studies.

One of my favorite myths is:

You must never haggle over the price of supplies you are going to buy.

Who came up with that idea? If you can get some for a lower price, by all means do so. However, I do encourage you to support local stores, as it helps your community. Personally, I think this myth was developed by an "evil cartel of occult shop owners." Yeah, I know that no such cartel exists, but it would explain the source of the myth.

I learned about another myth from a few of my students. I hadn't seen it before they told me about it. According to them:

The only way to get a Tarot deck is to have someone give it to you.

Who came up with that idea? This is utter nonsense. What if someone gives you a deck that you can't stand? It could result in your disliking of the Tarot for years. I suggest that you look at many decks, find a deck you like and buy it (if you don't have one at present), and then use it.

Of course, it may be that you will find something by accident or be given a gift that is just perfect for you. You might even say that it was "intended" for you. When I was looking for a sword to use as a magickal tool, I searched all over for one with the right design. I had almost given up when I saw just what I needed hanging on the wall of a martial arts studio. I asked if it was for sale and the man there said I'd have to ask the owner who wouldn't be back for an hour.

I went away and considered the situation. Well, the truth was, I was pretty broke at the time. I came to the conclusion that I could only afford what I had in my pocket—thirty-four dollars.

An hour later I returned and met the owner and asked about the sword. He told me that he had brought it back from China himself. He had intended to use it for practice, but had never done so. (*Perfect*, I thought. *It was "virgin."*) Then he said, "I wasn't thinking of selling it, but I couldn't let it go for anything less than . . . thirty-four dollars."

Needless to say, that's still my magickal sword.

is a Magickal Act." If you follow his line of reasoning then, indeed, opening the door is a magickal act. While moving everything you do to the level of being part of your Will, and therefore magickal, has value, that idea is not what we are seeking at this time. For the purposes of this book, we need to make the definition of magick a bit longer:

***Magick** is the science and art of causing change (in consciousness) to occur in conformity with will,*

using means not currently understood
by traditional Western science.

We have added the idea that the magick is accomplished by some means not known by modern science. A ritual that causes something to occur does not make sense to current Western scientific thought. Therefore, "scientists" are inclined to think that real magick, since it doesn't fit into their worldview, is nothing more than supernatural hokum. But, *magick is not supernatural.*

Whether our entire universe came about either as the creation of an intelligent being or beings, or merely as the result of chance events, we still must come to the same conclusion: everything in the universe is natural! Some ancient cultures considered the apparent rise and fall of the Sun to be a supernatural event. As time passed, it was discovered that the seeming rise and fall of the Sun was, in fact, a natural event, caused by the rotation of the Earth.

Similarly, I am firmly convinced that one day magick will be understood in Western scientific terms. History proves this. Reading, writing, mathematics, astronomy, chemistry, medicine, physics, and more were all at one time deep occult secrets. Today, many of these things are taught to children before they begin school. The occultism of the past becomes the science of the future. Arthur C. Clarke, the famous science-fiction writer and author of *2001: A Space Odyssey*, wrote that "any sufficiently advanced technology is indistinguishable from magick." I totally concur.

In a sense, then, if you decide to do more than read these lessons and actually practice magick, you are a scientist of the future. That is why you should follow what is called "the scientific method." This method tries to control all variables in experiments and keeps accurate records of those experiments. This is why your ritual diary is so important. It will show how variables (weather, emotions, etc.) affect your experiments (rituals). I cannot overstress the importance of keeping your magickal and dream diaries.

We now have a definition of magick that is far more specific than either Crowley's or Fortune's. Since the results are the same, by the way, I will be dropping Fortune's "in consciousness" from the definition. But the definition we have so far is still not precise enough for our purposes. We have to add to our definition the goal or result of the magick.

I divide magick into three categories. It is important to note that these categories are used in this course. Other people differ as to their definition of the different types of magick. Some use fewer categories, others more. Here are the descriptions of each category.

White Magick. In Eastern cultures, White Magick is known as yoga. When most people speak of yoga, what they really mean is Hatha Yoga. Hatha (correct pronunciation: "hot-ha") Yoga involves the stretching of the body in order to prepare it for true yoga. The word "yoga" comes from the Sanskrit root *yug*, which means yoke or union. This "union" of true yoga is where you unite with, or yoke yourself to, your higher self or with God. White Magick, sometimes called mysticism, is the yoga of the West. Its goal has a variety of names including cosmic consciousness, enlightenment, the Knowledge and Conversation of your Holy Guardian Angel, realization of Self, and more. We will use the expression used by the Golden Dawn, which gives us the following definition of White Magick:

> **White Magick** *is the science and art of causing change to occur in conformity with will, using means not currently understood by traditional Western science, for the purpose of obtaining the Knowledge and Conversation of your Holy Guardian Angel.*

Black Magick. This category of magick has an easy definition, which needs little or no explanation:

> **Black Magick** *is the science and art of causing change to occur in conformity with will, using means not currently understood by traditional Western science, for the purpose of causing ei-*

ther physical or non-physical harm to yourself or others, and is done either consciously or unconsciously.

I will be discussing Black Magick only from the standpoint of how to avoid accidentally (or purposely) becoming a black magick practitioner.

Grey Magick. Grey is a mixture of white and black. Grey Magick can become either white or black (or remain grey), as we shall see. Here is the definition:

Grey Magick *is the science and art of causing change to occur in conformity with will, using means not currently understood by traditional Western science, for the purpose of causing either physical or non-physical good to yourself or others, and is done either consciously or unconsciously.*

Let us say that you do a spell to help a friend regain her health. By definition, this is Grey Magick because you are doing something for the physical good of another person. However, because you did the Grey Magick to help another, you end up feeling that you are closer to Divinity, closer to the Knowledge and Conversation of your Holy Guardian Angel. Thus, it is also White Magick.

On the other hand, let us say that you did a ritual to obtain a thousand dollars. Unlike some philosophies, the traditions of magick hold that *there is nothing wrong with using magickal abilities to advance yourself in this world.* Yes, it is perfectly fine to use your magickal abilities and knowledge to get ahead on this physical plane, to get money, friends, love, and fame. I frequently tell people that in the West it is difficult to be spiritual when you're wondering where your next meal will come from or how you will support your family. There's nothing wrong with using magick to help you attain your goals. In fact, you're encouraged to do so.

But . . . let's assume that after doing your ritual to obtain the thousand dollars your uncle dies in a car crash and leaves you a thousand dollars in his will. Yes, you have attained your goal, but you have done it using Black Magick; you have indirectly (or perhaps we could say directly) killed a person.

Some of you may even be thinking now, "Well, so what? I got the money I wanted." Yes, this is true. But there is always a price to pay. "As you sow, so shall ye reap." If you have caused evil, if you have been a source of spiritual darkness, it will surely return to you. In many Wiccan traditions it is believed that what you do will return to you threefold. Those doing Black Magick always have a price to pay, and sometimes that price is far heavier than expected.

I have a friend named Robin who freely admits that she used to be a Satanist and a black magician. She told me that she could always tell when a curse or black magick spell she had worked had come to fruition because something unfortunate would happen to her! This is not meant to be a lecture telling you that you should never do Black Magick. Rather, it is intended to show you what to expect if you try. Just as there is a law of gravity, so too is there an inviolable law of what is called in the East *karma*, and by Kabalists *Tikune* (pronounced "tee-koon"). Put out good and you will receive good. Put out evil, even unintentionally, and evil is what you will get. Such is the law.

So how can you avoid falling into the pit of the black magician? First, by practicing White Magick. This is why the first part of this course is only involved in teaching White Magick. Do not ignore this work, as this course is cumulative. Your development as a powerful (grey) magician and what happens in the future in this course is dependent upon what you are doing now. Second, before doing any Grey Magick you should always do a divination to determine the effect and the outcome of your magick. This is a reason why learning the Tarot or some other divinatory system is important.

On the pages following the next ritual you will discover meanings of the twenty-two Major Arcana cards of the Tarot. An "(R)" is followed by the meaning of the card if it appears to you during a reading in reversed (the picture is upside down) position.

The meanings here are based upon the teachings of the occultists and Kabalists A. E. Waite and S. L. MacGregor Mathers.

For the next few days you should become familiar with your deck and the definitions given here for the Major Arcana. For the time being, ignore any instruction books on the Tarot that you may have or which were included with the deck. Later, you can add to the system given here from information learned elsewhere. Using the cards for divination purposes will be explained in the next part of this lesson.

In the meantime, continue your diaries and the relaxation ritual, but after that ritual add the next ritual for daily practice, the Tarot Contemplation Ritual.

The Tarot Contemplation Ritual

STEP ONE. Remove the twenty-two cards of the Major Arcana. Take from the twenty-two cards (which should be numbered from 0 to 21) the cards numbered 6, 7, 10, 13, 15, and 18*. These will not be used at this time, so put them with the remainder of the deck. Keep the remaining cards of the Major Arcana with you while you perform the relaxation ritual.

STEP TWO. Immediately after completing the Relaxation Ritual, take the sixteen cards that remain from the Major Arcana and mix them up (shuffle them) in any manner you desire until you get a feeling it is time to stop. Note that this feeling may be very subtle. If you don't get such a feeling, stop mixing them after one minute.

STEP THREE. Select any one card and look at the picture on it for no more than three minutes.

STEP FOUR. Take three deep breaths and the Tarot contemplation ritual is complete.

STEP FIVE. Record the card name and number in your magickal diary. Also record any feelings, sensations, or ideas you received while looking at (contemplating) the card.

---

* There is nothing "wrong" with the cards that are removed at this time. However, without understanding them, the symbols on these cards may falsely appear as being negative, and contemplating them without understanding them could result in the imprinting of false or negative beliefs and ideas. As you learn more of the Tarot in the weeks to come, these cards will be returned and used in this ritual.

True Meanings of the Tarot?

When I first decided to learn the Tarot, I obtained a deck and three books on the Tarot by different authors. I figured I could take three different looks at the same thing and combine them into one whole. To my dismay, however, the meanings of the cards, as given by these authors, were radically different.

Over the years I've read scores of books on the Tarot. One book gave a listing of meanings by different authors, then gave the author's "summary" of the meanings. His summaries, however, were completely unrelated to what the others had written. Another author proposed placing huge sheets of paper on the walls (this was written pre-spreadsheet computer applications) and proposed that you write the names of the seventy-eight cards across the top, then, at the left, give the name of an author or a book, and under each card write the meanings given by the author for that card. In this way you could see similarities and correspondences between the various authors and come up with your own meaning.

The truth is this: *there are no "true meanings" for the Tarot cards.* Different Tarot readers and authors give different meanings for the cards based on the symbolism of the cards and their own backgrounds and training.

Some people simply look at the symbols on each card and come up with a meaning on the spot. Others have systems based on meanings given by Tarot interpreters or other "authorities." For example, I was taught a system for use with the Minor Arcana cards that is based on a type of numerology. Debunkers, however, consider it all junk and just broad psychological interpretations (I guess they never had a precise, in-depth reading).

The curious thing is that I have taught different systems of meanings for the cards, and they each result in valid readings. How is that possible? Consistency. As long as your system is internally consistent, with practice, the cards will produce viable readings. The cards pulled with the meanings you have for them result in a "meaningful coincidence," what the psychologist Jung called a "synchronicity."

What this means, then, is that as long as you work with a system of meanings for the cards that is internally consistent, they will eventually produce meaningful readings. So there are no ultimate "true" meanings for the Tarot cards. But if your system (or systems) is internally consistent, they will be true for you.

Brief Tarot Divinatory Meanings—The Major Arcana

0 FOOL: .... Folly, foolishness, extravagance. (R) Hesitation, carelessness, trouble from ignoring foolishness.

1 MAGICIAN: .... Skills, will power, self-confidence. (R) Wrong use of same, conceit, lack of skill.

2 HIGH PRIESTESS: .... Science, education, knowledge. (R) Ignorance, superficial knowledge.

3 EMPRESS: .... Fruitfulness, action, creativity. (R) Inaction due to vacillation, losing power.

4 EMPEROR: .... Power, effectiveness, reason. (R) Immature emotions, obstructions to plans.

5 HIEROPHANT: .... Mercy and goodness, a person who shows these qualities. (R) Overkindness, weakness.

6 LOVERS: .... A test which you will pass, a new love. (R) A failed test, lost love.

7 CHARIOT: .... Triumph, overcoming obstacles. (R) Defeat, obstacles overcome you.

8 STRENGTH: .... Spiritual power. (R) Physical power.

9 HERMIT: .... Caution or spiritual advancement. (R) Fear, overly cautious, unwise acts.

10 WHEEL OF FORTUNE: .... Good fortune, success, luck. (R) Bad luck, ill fortune.

11 JUSTICE: .... Balance, justice, equilibrium. (R) Imbalance, bigotry, bias.

12 HANGED MAN: .... Wisdom as a result of self-sacrifice. (R) Selfishness, trying to fit in with the crowd.

13 DEATH: .... An evolutionary change or transformation. (R) Stagnation.

14 TEMPERANCE: .... Combine or unite seemingly unlike things, moderation. (R) Clashing interests.

15 DEVIL: .... Something must happen, but in the long run it is for the good. (R) Something must happen, but for evil.

16 TOWER: .... Ruin, catastrophe, disruption. (R) The same, but to a lesser degree.

17 STAR: .... Hope and a bright future. (R) Expectations disappointed, barrenness.

18 MOON: .... Deception, hidden enemies. (R) Deceptions only slight.

19 SUN: .... Happiness and contentment. (R) The same, but to a lesser degree.

20 JUDGEMENT: .... Renewal, rebirths. (R) Setbacks and delays.

21 UNIVERSE: .... Assured success, completion. (R) Failure, inertia, evil reward.

PART TWO

The History of the Tarot—Mythical

In this part of the lesson I will be discussing the history of the Tarot and how to do a divination using the Tarot. Remember, becoming proficient in a divination system is necessary to prevent Grey Magick from becoming Black Magick. That is why this study is very important.

First, though, you might wonder why you should study the Tarot and not some other system. Perhaps you are already familiar with the Chinese *I Ching*, tea leaf reading, crystal gazing, astrological prediction, runic divination, or some other system. All of these systems, if studied in depth and mastered, are excellent. Aleister Crowley seems to have used the *I Ching* far more often than the Tarot. But as you have already seen with the Tarot Contemplation Ritual, and will see further on, in these lessons we will be using the Tarot for reasons other than just divinatory purposes. And it is my belief that the more you use the Tarot in any way, the more easily you will become proficient in its use in all ways.

You perhaps have heard the expression "worldview." It is a translation of the German term *Weltanschauung* (pronounced "velt-ahn-sha-oong," with the last two syllables run together and the final "g" almost silent) and is a concept found in German philosophy. The idea behind this expression is that you can have an underlying viewpoint that gives you a way to understand how people, our world, and the universe function and interrelate. It is a framework, lens, or filter through which a person sees the world. Some people have a worldview based upon politics, religion, or various psychological doctrines. Ritual magicians frequently have their worldview based upon the Kabalah and the Tarot. To "kick start" your understanding—and perhaps your adoption—of this worldview, the use of Tarot was already in one of the first rituals given here. As this course progresses, you will see how the Tarot plays even more important parts in traditional ritual magick.

There are actually two histories of the Tarot. One is factual; the other is made up of unproven and sometimes absurd theories. One of these unproven theories attributes an Egyptian heritage to the Tarot. A story of the Egyptian theory has it that Thoth, the god who functioned as the scribe to the other Egyptian gods, gave twenty-two pictures that illustrated great wisdom to the ancient temple mystery cult of Egypt. These pictures were hung on pillars in a temple underneath and between the legs of the famous Sphinx near the Great Pyramid of Cheops (pronounced "kee-ahps," this is the popular Greek name of the pharaoh who, in ancient Egyptian, is known as Khufu, pronounced "koo-foo." Khufu was the second pharaoh of the fourth dynasty who reigned from around 2589 B.C.E. to 2566 B.C.E.) on the Gizeh plateau, part of a necropolis that is situated on the outskirts of modern Cairo. An initiate into the mysteries would be led between the pillars and would have the symbolic meanings of the pictures explained to him by the initiator. From there the initiate would go via an underground passageway to the Great Pyramid itself, wherein he would receive full initiation. Unfortunately, there is no proof that this exact type of initiation ever took place.

Another story has it that a group of wise scholars, knowing that the famous library of Alexandria was going to be destroyed, met in the city of Fez, Morocco, to decide what to do. Some versions of this story say that the meeting was held after the destruction. One version of this story continues by saying that these scholars came from many lands and did not have a common language. Scholar-artists created a symbolic language with which they could communicate. The Tarot is a descendant of that artwork. Another version says that the wise men decided to make one great book containing all of the important wisdom of the world, which otherwise would be lost in the destruction of the library. In order that this great book would not also be destroyed, they decided to keep it hidden in the form of a gambling game, realizing that although humanity's search for wisdom might die, its thirst for quick gain and its lower nature would never disappear. Thus, according to these stories, was the Tarot born.

Again, there is no proof that any of these stories is in any way factual.

There are many other stories supposedly revealing the source of the Tarot. Some versions say that the Tarot was brought out of Egypt by the Gypsies. Note that the word "Gypsy" is derived from the word "Egyptian." This is because at one time it was believed that the Gypsies—or more accurately, the Romany people—came from Egypt. At that time, Egypt was thought of as being a source of all things mystical, magickal, and mysterious, and many Romany people did little to discourage the idea of their roots, adding to the mystery of their origin. Today, scholars are more inclined to think the Romany came from India.

Other stories, which do have a bit of possibility to them, have the Tarot developing out of gaming or fortunetelling systems from India or China. There is, however, no proof that any of these stories are true.

The History of the Tarot—Factual

We do have historical records of the following facts:

1. The first mention of the Tarot was made in 1332 by Alphonse XI, king of Leon and Castile. He banned them along with other gambling games.

2. In 1337, Johannes, a German monk, wrote that they "could be used to teach morality."

3. In 1392, Charles VI of France bought three sets of the Major Arcana from a man named Grigonneur.

4. By the 1400s, the Italian version, known as the Tarocchino, had over 100 cards including the Zodiac and the so-called Christian virtues.

Although the early fourteenth century is the earliest we can date the beginning of the Tarot, it is 100 years later before we can positively say that the Tarot first began to appear in Europe (in Italy, to be precise). Of course, nothing as complex as the Tarot appears overnight, so we may never know the exact origins and source of the Tarot, which has predecessors in India, Persia, China, and other locations.

Today, although there is a "standard" deck (in its framework, if not in its symbolism and style), there are a wide number of variations. Similarly, several hundred years ago there was also a great deal of non-standardization. At least one deck had over 140 cards. Tarot decks were used for gambling and instruction of the young (especially those who had not been taught how to read), but by the 1800s, the Tarot was used almost exclusively for fortunetelling. Most decks used at this time were based upon the deck of Charles VI, now known as the Grigonneur deck. One variation of this deck is the Visconti pack; another is the Marseilles Tarot. I mention them as versions of them are still available, and some modern decks are based on the formats of those early decks.

The Hermetic Order of the Golden Dawn made extensive use of the Tarot, and as already mentioned, we will be learning some of the more esoteric uses of the Tarot later in this course. A. E. Waite and Pamela Colman ("Pixie") Smith, both members of the Golden Dawn, designed what is today's most popular deck, the so-called Rider-Waite (or more accurately, the Rider-Waite-Smith) Tarot. When it was first released in 1909, it caught on very quickly for two reasons. First, it was the first time that all of the cards had symbolic pictures on them. Earlier decks did not have images on the Minor Arcana cards. Second, it marked the first time that a Tarot deck had been simultaneously published with a book explaining how to use the deck. In this instance, the book was Waite's *The Pictorial Key to the Tarot*. Of all of Waite's often ponderously written tomes, I find this one of the easiest of his books to read and understand.

The members of the Golden Dawn considered their "correct" version of the Tarot to be an important secret of the Order. Waite and Smith, who had taken solemn vows not to reveal the inner secrets of the Golden Dawn, kept their word. Many of the cards are designed with symbolism that varies considerably from the meanings given to the cards by the Golden Dawn, perhaps in order to fool the uninitiated.

Today, there are many decks based upon Waite and Smith's designs. More "original decks" (which

The Importance of Myth

Many people wonder why—even though we know that these myths of the origin of the Tarot are not historically accurate—"experts" keep repeating these myths as if they were true. Of course, we could simply acknowledge the obvious, that the "experts" aren't very expert and don't know what they're talking about. And maybe the true scholars of the Tarot should be making more of a fuss about historical accuracy. (In fact, a few are beginning to do so.)

However, I actually think it is *more* important to have the myths than to have only the historically accurate facts. I'm not denying that we should research and have accurate history. But once you know a date . . . so what? The Declaration of Independence was signed on July 4, 1776. You now know a date. So what? Far more important than simply knowing a date is knowing the meaning of what occurred on that day—what that date represents.

The story of a young George Washington admitting to his father that he cut down the cherry tree first appeared in a biography of Washington written by an ex-parson turned bookseller named Mason Locke Weems. It is generally conceded today that Weems simply made up the story.

But the story does several things for us, even today. It shows the value of honesty and integrity. In the case of the Weems' book, first published in 1800 (a year after Washington's death), it helped to establish a heroic figure as role model and part of the mythic history of a fledgling country. The story helped to make the myth of the man, and the mythic vision helped to make the nation, giving us the image of a country that stresses values including honesty and integrity. Having this as part of the nature of our country may have lead Alexis de Tocqueville to write in 1835—in contrast to what he had seen in his world travels through other countries—"America is great because she is good. If America ceases to be good, America will cease to be great."

Myths aren't just stories. They are stories that promote values that people choose to follow. We learn lessons through the actions of the people in the myths rather than from listening to lectures from parents or parental figures. Myths of bravery, integrity, honesty, and justice fill our early lives and world history. The ancient myths of Ulysses and Beowulf have been replaced by modern myths of Captain James T. Kirk and Luke Skywalker.

The mythic histories of the Tarot tell us more about the Tarot's true nature than do simple dates. They also tell us about our own natures and what we hold valuable. Therefore, the mythic histories of the Tarot are important not for objective historical fact, but for what the myths mean to me, to you, and to human civilization.

are actually based on Waite and Smith's work) are popping up almost every day. And all of these decks, according to the Golden Dawn tradition, are symbolically wrong. However, because of their massive use and popularity, they have developed a validity of their own, different though it may be from the Golden Dawn tradition.

Other members of the Golden Dawn who designed Tarot decks include Aleister Crowley (Thoth deck), who mixed the Golden Dawn ideas with his own system of Egyptian, Sumerian, and Tantric occultism (plus a good dose of perverse humor), and Paul Foster Case. Case's B.O.T.A. deck, which gives a version that seems halfway between the Golden Dawn deck and Waite's deck, was the first public revelation of the Golden Dawn attributions of the Hebrew alphabet with the Major Arcana cards.

I know some people who claim to be occultists and who collect Tarot decks. Their collection, in fact, is their only claim to knowing about the occult. But some decks which they collect are so distant from anything which could be called "metaphysical" that I wonder about their brand of occultism. One deck I saw has each card drawn by a different artist. Even though it is based on the Rider-Waite-Smith deck, it gets so silly that it even uses popular cartoon characters on them. Another deck, called the *Tarot of the Witches* (certainly an insult to most if not all Witches), was designed for a James Bond movie. The original printing of the pack even had the famous "007" in the form of a pistol design on the back of the deck.

In summary, there is no proof that the Tarot came from a single ancient source in Egypt, China, India, or anyplace else. That they were first introduced into Europe in the middle of the last millennium is known, but where they originally came from is one of the great unprovable (at this time) mysteries of the universe.

Now, I would like to give my unprovable guess as to how the cards developed. It is known that both India and China did have gaming systems that, to a minor extent, resembled a pack of cards. Although

unprovable, I maintain that it is likely that a traveler going from one of those countries to the Middle East, or perhaps a trader from the Middle East who went to India or China, somehow left one of these systems, or a version of it, in one of the Middle Eastern countries. Then, during one of the Crusades, a knight brought back one of these proto-decks and gave it to his lord or king, or described it and the ruler had one made.

Next, that lord or king, in a display of egotistical vanity ("I've got something you don't have") showed it to a peer, another lord or king. That second person decided to have it duplicated. Or, in a similar manner, the artist of one lord showed it to the artist of another lord, and the second artist either made a direct copy or made a version from memory. Moving from lord to lord, from king to king, the Tarot evolved.

There were, at that time, artist guilds that, like masons, may have included some form of mystical knowledge. Certainly many artists then, before then, and now were interested in the relationship between humanity and the divine. One of these artists could have added some mysticism in the Tarot art, and another could have added more. This progressed until we have the Tarot as it exists today.

But the most important question is "Does it matter where or how the Tarot developed?" To this there must be a loud "NO!" in answer, for the Tarot's use as a powerful mystical and magickal tool has been proven over the past several centuries.

Fortunetelling and Divination

It is important to understand the difference between fortunetelling and divination. Fortunetelling says that something *must* happen. Divination, such as with the Tarot cards, never says what must happen; it only indicates what will probably happen if you continue on the path you are currently traversing.

According to this view, you have the freedom to ensure something happens or prevent it from occurring. You have free will and the choice is always up to you. Fortunetelling would say that, as an exam-

Is the Rider-Waite-Smith Tarot the "Correct" Version?

I am often asked which version of the Tarot is the "real" one or the "most accurate" or the "correct" one. Due to its popularity, the Rider-Waite-Smith deck has become the *de facto* standard. But is the RWS the "most correct" deck?

Both Waite and Smith used the Golden Dawn deck. As part of their training, they would have had to create and use a copy of that deck. Some have even suggested that the RWS *is* the real Golden Dawn deck.

Of course, if you research Israel Regardie's book, *The Golden Dawn*, you'll immediately see that this is not the case. More importantly, even Waite admitted he was not revealing the full truth about the Tarot. In the introduction to his book, *The Pictorial Key to the Tarot*, Waite wrote:

The fact remains . . . that a Secret Tradition exists regarding the Tarot, and as there is always the possibility that some minor arcana of the Mysteries may be made public with a flourish of trumpets, it will be as well to go before the event and to warn those who are curious in such matters that any revelation will contain only a third part of the earth and sea and a third part of the stars of heaven in respect of the symbolism. This is for the simple reason that neither in root-matter nor in development has more been put into writing, so that much will remain to be said after any pretended unveiling. The guardians of certain temples of initiation who keep watch over mysteries of this order have therefore no cause for alarm.

He was making clear to his fellow Golden Dawners that he was not revealing the true secrets of the Tarot—or at least the Golden Dawn's secrets—to the profane.

So if this is the case, why look at the RWS Tarot at all?

The simple answer is that it works. The RWS is a great deck in and of itself. It needs no further justification than that. All of the numerous decks modeled on the RWS simply add to its success and validity.

So is there an ultimate and perfectly correct Tarot deck? The answer, unfortunately, is both "yes" and "no." There can never be a universal deck that is perfect for everyone because each person is a unique individual. The only deck that will be perfectly correct for you will be the one that, after years of practice, study, and meditation, you are inwardly urged to create.

Until that time, simply find a deck that follows the standard described earlier in this course and work with it. If you find something better later on, change and use it. If you come back later to the original one you liked, or change again, that's fine.

There is really only one important choice besides that the deck follow the standard number of cards and divisions: it should be a deck you will use regularly.

ple, you will have an accident on a boat on a specific date. Divination would tell you that a boat trip at that time could cause problems, and you are advised to stay away from boats. You can then either avoid the boat trip or be extra careful when on the boat. Fortunetelling says you have no choice—you will be on a boat at that time and you will have an accident. Divination says you have free will—you can move to the desert, or at least you can stay away from boats. In these lessons we strongly affirm free will, not pre-destination.

There is another reason, a very practical reason, for doing divination and not fortunetelling. In many states, counties, and cities, fortunetelling for money is not legal. If you decide to become involved with giving readings for people and intend to charge for them, I advise calling what you are doing psychologi-cal counseling, divination, or, if you obtain a minis-terial certificate, spiritual or religious counseling.

On the following pages I will give a method for doing a divination using just the Major Arcana cards. I will note here that a good reading can be given using only these twenty-two cards. They tend to rep-resent changing forces rather than the more static forces represented by the Minor Arcana. Using the Minor Arcana can give more detail, but using just the Major Arcana can give you more information on how things are changing or will change in your life.

In the diagram you can see two triangles (the "split hexagram") with an extra card between them. The upper triangle represents spiritual forces being brought down to the physical plane. The lower tri-angle shows conscious and unconscious desires and what is truly wanted or needed. The card in the cen-ter represents the final outcome of the matter under question. Here are step-by-step instructions on how to use this Tarot "spread" (layout) to determine the outcome of Grey Magick. This reading may be used for many purposes.

1. Set up the Major Arcana cards in a packet so that they are all facing one direction in nu-merical order. If they are facing down they

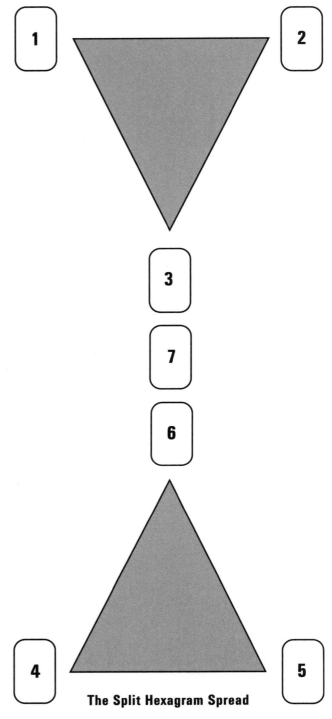

The Split Hexagram Spread

should have the card titled the Fool at the top of the pack. The 21 card, the Universe (or World), should be at the bottom.

2. Now, formulate your question. It should be in the style of "What will be the outcome if I use

magick to_____?"
Do *not* ask the cards "Should I do such-and-such?" as this puts the responsibility for your actions on the cards rather than on you. You should be seeking advice, not making the Tarot into a pseudo-mommy and asking for instructions.

3. While concentrating on your question, mix up the cards in any manner or fashion you desire. Continue to do so until you get a "feeling" it is time to stop. If you feel it is appropriate, mix the cards end for end so that in the reading, some may come up reversed.

4. Cut the cards into three piles to your left. Pick up the piles from right to left, reversing the order of the way you cut the cards.

5. Lay the cards, face down, on your table in the order shown in the diagram. The first three cards make up the upper, downward-pointing triangle. Cards 4, 5, and 6 make up the lower, upward-pointing triangle. The 7 card goes in the middle, between the two triangles.

6. When you turn over the cards, flip them in the same position so they don't change their upright or reversed orientation. Now, turn over cards in the positions 1 and 2. Both positions represent **unknown spiritual influences**. Card 2 will have a stronger effect on you than does card 1. Interpret these two cards.

7. Turn over the card in position 3. This represents **spiritual advice for the matter**. Interpret this card.

8. Turn over card 4. This card represents your **unconscious desires** in the matter. Don't be surprised if you discover that your real inner reason has little or no relation to your original or outer reason. Interpret this card.

9. Turn over card 5. This card represents your **conscious desires** in the matter. Interpret this card.

10. Now turn over card 6. This card will indicate **practical advice** in the matter. It may suggest changing your focus in order to achieve what you really want. It may advise you to go ahead or abandon the project. Of course, whether you continue with the project or not is up to you.

11. Turn over card 7. This is the **final outcome** if you go ahead and follow your current path at this time. Even if the reading so far has been positive, the outcome may be negative. This is because there may be other considerations which this short reading does not take into account. The Split Hexagram spread is a quick and easy method, but it is not intended to be totally and fully complete. It should be enough, however, to get you through this course of lessons.

Let's look now at a sample reading:

I mix up the cards while thinking, "What will be the outcome if I use magick to bring a new love into my life?" After cutting the cards and laying the spread, the cards are as follows: (see next page).

My interpretation is as follows:

Cards 1 and 2 indicate that this act would lead to great creativity (Empress) even though it could be seen as a wrongful use of magickal abilities (Magician [R]).

Card 3 indicates that it could lead to power and effectiveness (Emperor).

Card 4 indicates that inwardly I seek spiritual power more than just a sex partner (Strength).

Consciously, as card 5 indicates, I really do want a new love relationship (Lovers).

Card 6 gives me the practical advice that magick alone will not be enough to keep a good relationship, and that I must show mercy and goodness (Hierophant).

The Final Outcome, according to card 7, is that if I follow the advice given here, especially in card 6, my success in this matter is assured (Universe).

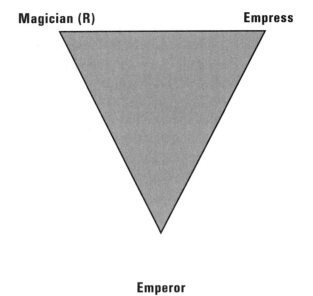

Magician (R)   Empress

Emperor

Universe

Hierophant

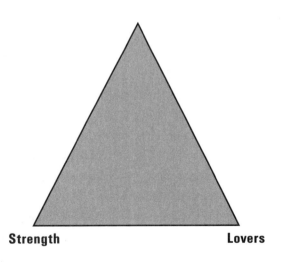

Strength   Lovers

Learning the Tarot

The only way to learn the Tarot is to use it constantly. Try memorizing the meanings of the cards, one card per day. Also try giving yourself small readings on a daily basis. However, don't count on the accurateness for at least a month. You were probably not too "accurate" when you first learned to ride a bicycle or drive a car, but as you practiced and became experienced, success in bike riding and driving not only was assured, it became a part of you and those skills became second nature for you. Today you just do them and don't even consciously think about them. Let me assure you that with just a few weeks or months of committed practice, you will be successful with your readings. They will surprise you with their accuracy. Be sure to continue with your daily practice of the Tarot Contemplation Ritual. Doing a reading or a ritual does not overcome the need for doing both.

This set of lessons is not about doing divinations, it's about learning the basics of practical magick. For this purpose the Major Arcana plays the most vital role. You will learn more of its importance later. For giving general readings to yourself and others, the Minor Arcana should be brought in, especially for in-depth readings. Unfortunately, there is only so much room in these lessons, and since the Minor Arcana does not play an intrinsic role in this course's study of magick, a thorough study of them will be left to other authors. Please do not think that the Minors are unimportant. Eventually you will want to learn more of their meanings. In dealing with the Tarot, however, this book's focus is limited to the Major Arcana.

After studying and practicing the system explained here for at least two months, feel free to study the Tarot on your own. I would repeat that there is no ultimate, correct meaning for each card. Different authors may give different meanings to the same card. Use their ideas to add to what you have learned here. Some suggested books on the Tarot are listed in this lesson's bibliography.

I would add to this interpretation that as card 6 indicates, I do not just need anybody; rather, I need someone who would enhance my spiritual practices.

PART THREE

The High Magick art is by nature different from certain aspects of other so-called "primitive" forms of magick as practiced by those involved in Witchcraft, Wicca, Voodoo, Brujeria, etc. The word "primitive" is not meant to insult followers of those or similar traditions any more than calling somebody such as Grandma Moses a "primitive artist" is insulting. Rather, it infers older styles and simpler ways. Many people I know who are involved in Wicca and Witchcraft are proud that their tradition is both old and simple.

But the very simplicity of these styles of magick has led to numerous books of spells and incantations, designed for the masses, which are, to a large extent, useless. The number of such books directly related to the Kabalistic ceremonial magickal art is small in quantity.

One of the big differences is that for many of the "primitive" techniques, all that seems to be necessary is the saying of a brief incantation and the ritual manipulation of a few objects: burning a candle, making a Voodoo symbol or *vévé*, and so forth. Sometimes the spells become mutilated over time so that the meanings of the original words become lost and the spell becomes nothing but sounds without any sense. Although this has also happened to some extent with ceremonial magick, a true magician always knows the exact meaning of every word and action of a ritual. This is why so much training, study, and practice goes into the making of a ceremonial magician.

The actual instructions for doing the next ritual that you will learn, the Lesser Banishing Ritual of the Pentagram, will be given in the following lesson. At this point there are probably some of you reading this who are groaning and thinking, "But I learned that ritual years ago! Besides, it's so simple." Well, if you think it is simple, you have never done it correctly and with full knowledge. It is a basic ritual, but it is not simple. It is short and easy to memorize, but not simple.

According to my dictionary, the word "basic" means "something that forms a base, like a basic in-gredient; something that is fundamental." I cannot overstress the fundamental nature of this ritual and how its practice will change your life and improve your psychic and magickal abilities. When *Modern Magick* was first published I had been doing it at least once daily for almost ten years and had no desire to stop. It is a basic, short ritual that forms the underpinnings to your training and will enhance your development as a true ceremonial magician.

Reasons for Performing the LBRP

There are three reasons for doing this ritual. The first and most important, yet most ethereal, is to *Know Yourself*. You will learn if you have the strength of will to stick to doing a ritual of this sort on a daily basis. As a result, you will discover more about your nature and who you are than ever before. You will develop a different feeling about yourself and your relationship to others and the world around you. It will affect you in many positive but subtle ways.

Second, it will expand your aura. This result is quite surprising. As your aura expands and brightens, you will also find yourself becoming stronger spiritually and psychologically than you have ever been before. This phenomenon is not imaginary. The expanded aura will enhance the feeling of *rapport* (pronounced "ra-pohr," with the "a" as in the word "rasp") others have for you. Rapport is a feeling of bonding between another person and you, based on their perception that you are trustworthy, have similar interests, are a good person, and are similar to them. Enhancing your rapport will result in others increasingly liking and respecting you, as well as coming to you more often for guidance and comfort. This won't happen overnight, but it will happen. You will realize that this is occurring when people start asking you questions like, "Is that a new dress? Did you lose some weight? Did you get your hair cut?" even though the dress was old, your hair is the same, and you haven't lost an ounce. Most people can unconsciously detect the aura and will be able to detect such a change in you. But they do not know that it is the aura which has changed, so they have to come up with something that they are familiar with, something on the physical plane such as your hair, clothes, or weight.

Third, this ritual (LBRP for short) will remove from your immediate area (banish) any unwanted influences. This banishing dispels negative and/or unwanted physical influences and non-physical ones including astral and elemental forces. This is one of the greatest defenses against psychic attack ever. The more you practice the LBRP, the more safe, the more at peace you will become.

The attitude you adopt when you perform this ritual is important. People working with computers have an expressive term: GIGO (pronounced "geegoh," with hard "g"s). It means "Garbage In, Garbage Out." If you put in garbage data, the result will be garbage, too. Put in accurate data and the result will be accurate. Similarly, you will get out of the ritual exactly what you put into it. Go into this ritual angry and you will come out of it feeling angrier. You should assume an attitude of beauty and joy. Doing the Relaxation Ritual immediately before the LBRP will aid you in achieving the desired state of consciousness.

You should be very positive, *sure* that when you call on the archangels they will be there, *sure* that the pentagrams are really there, *sure* that you are doing the very best you possibly can.

However, you should not "lust for results." Focus on the ritual, not what you expect the result of the ritual to be. If you perform the ritual with complete concentration, *you will be successful.* If you concentrate on something else, such as what you expect to experience or what you expect as a result of the ritual, you will divide your energies (between focusing on the performance of the ritual and focusing on supposed results) and the ritual will decrease in its effectiveness.

When you perform the ritual, you must understand that you are no longer in your house or apartment or building. Nor are you merely outdoors. Rather, you are in the *temple of the gods.* You are also in the *presence of divinity.* Wherever you are, when you do this ritual the area becomes a holy place. You should treat it as such.

Also remember that at this time you are a beginner, a student, a magician-in-training. You are not a high-ranking magus or wizard. Therefore, be modest, especially in the presence of the divine.

Physical Items for the LBRP

There are several physical things that you may want to use when you perform the LBRP. However, there is only one thing which you must have—a place where you can be alone and undisturbed. To do this ritual requires no more than ten minutes, and once it is memorized even less time is necessary. So the first thing you need to do is have a physical place where you can be sure you will be undisturbed for this brief length of time. For our purposes at this time, this ritual is not meant for the public's eyes.

Second, it is traditional to have an altar. This can be a small table covered with a black cloth, or the traditional "double cube." A good size for the traditional altar is 36 inches high by 18 inches square, giving an altar that is like two eighteen-inch cubes on top of one another (as above, so below). It also represents the earth plane because the number of sides of this altar that are external (top, bottom, the four sides of the upper cube, and the four sides of the lower) equal ten, the number of the Earth in the Kabalah (more on this later). Third, I have found that candles are much better than electric light for ritual work. I even prefer real candles to the wonderful, flickering LED lights that look like candles and are currently available very cheaply. However, those flickering, battery-powered lights are much safer, in that you won't be spilling candle wax or starting an undesired fire. There are also some older bulbs for lamps that plug into AC wall current that have the shape of a candle flame and actually flicker. Try any and all of them out, and see which one or ones work best for you.

For your work, you could have one candle for the altar, and maybe a few more for the room if you are doing the ritual inside. At this time use white candles. These can represent the purity (white) of spiritual energy (fire). Incense is also a nice touch and always adds to ritual work. Incense is said to represent prayers going up to God. At this point, the type of incense is not important. Merely find a scent that

Making an Altar

One of the things most ceremonial magicians learn to do is make things. From simple drawings to complex ritual items, taking the time to make them from scratch—or at least enhancing them with paint, colored glass "gems," and other features—gives you a feeling of accomplishment. Further, if you focus on the purpose of the item you are creating, it gives a magickal charge to the item.

You don't have to do everything. For example, you could go to a lumberyard and have them cut to size the pieces of wood you would use. In this case, you'd need four pieces that are 18 inches by 36 inches, two pieces that are 18 inches by 18 inches, and finally finishing nails and glue to put it together. Tell someone at the lumberyard that you are building a cabinet and they can help you with instructions. The sizes will have to be adjusted due to the thickness of the wood.

I made my altar in a very easy way. At an unfinished wood store they sell cubes of pressboard (also known as chipboard) that are 18 by 18 inches and have one side open. I simply nailed the two cubes together and added a piece of 18 by 36 inch plywood (1/2 inch thick) to cover the open sides of the cubes by using hinges and a magnetic latch. I have a pull in the shape of a majestic lion's head that allows me to open this door.

Before nailing the two cubes together, however, I used an electric saw to cut out a large U shape in the bottom side of the upper cube and the top side of the lower cube. When nailed together, this allowed for a "pass through" between both cubes, allowing me to store longer items, such as long wands and swords, within the altar. By having a hinged door, rather than a sealed box, the altar performs double duty as both a ritual altar and a place to store ritual items.

Upon adding several coats of paint (even with a sealer coat, this type of wood seems to drink up paint), and some wheels to make the altar moveable, I was finished. Traditionally, the altar is painted black to represent the fact that we are far from the true spiritual light which comes from above, even though it is from here that we must begin our starry climb. My first altar, however, was painted white and had on it a beautiful figure of the Tree of Life (more on this figure later) and also the protective Pentagram of Solomon from the book *The Goetia* on the top. These came from posters that I cut to size and glued to the side and top of the altar. I then painted over them with several coats of lacquer. If you do this, make sure that the coating will dry clear. Be aware that some lacquers that claim they dry clear actually dry to a dingy yellowish-brown. If you decide to make an altar that is not the traditional black double cube, carefully consider the meaning of any symbolism, including color, which you wish to use. You may wish to use a standard black altar for a time, or just put a black cloth over the altar, during this period of your training. You can always paint it with other colors and symbols later.

Finally, be sure to put several coats of protective finish on the *top* of your altar. The ideal choice would be the thick coating that tables in nightclubs and bars often have. This way, spilled wax from candles (and trust me, sooner or later you *will* spill wax) is easier to clean up. Alternatively, you can get a piece of glass to cover the top. A decorative trim that surrounds the top of the altar and extends above the top edges will assure you that the glass will not slip off. If you do use such a trim, take a look at your altar from a distance. Does it need matching trim at the bottom? How about around the center? The choice is up to you.

you like and use it. When I was starting, I preferred sandalwood or frankincense.

There are four traditional tools or "weapons" used by ceremonial magicians. Details of their construction will be given in later lessons. These tools are the wand, the cup, the dagger, and the pentacle. You could use a paper cup to represent elemental Water, salt (instead of a pentacle) to represent elemental Earth, a match (instead of a wand) to represent elemental Fire, and a feather or fan (instead of a dagger) to represent elemental Air.

Have a symbol for each of the elements on the altar, or have none of them. You should not have an imbalance in the energies the tools represent. If you do have the weapons, the Air symbol should be on the eastern part of the altar, the Fire symbol to the south, the Water symbol to the west, and the Earth symbol placed to the north. If you have the tools, they should be wrapped in a piece of silk or cotton when they are not being used: the wand in red, the chalice in blue, the dagger in yellow, and the pentacle in black. Sleight-of-hand magicians' supply shops usually have silk handkerchiefs available in these and other colors and shades at reasonable prices and in a variety of sizes.

You may also wish to use a bell. This can be used for marking the beginning and end of the ritual, as well as marking off various sections of more complex ceremonies. How big should it be? What should its shape be? That's up to you.

Another item to have is the proper clothes. Whereas some spiritual traditions use ritual nudity, ceremonial magick has always used special clothes. Traditionally, this is a black or white "Tau" robe, so called because when you hold your arms out to the side it looks like the Greek letter Tau. It is similar to the type of robes worn by people in choirs or angels in films. However, a robe is not necessary. The purpose of putting on a robe is to physically show both your conscious and your unconscious that you are no longer in your daily dress. It strongly shows that you are about to do something very special and spiritual. If you do not have access to the things needed to make or obtain a robe, simply go through your closet and find some clothes that you have not worn in a long time, or buy some new clothes. Wash them thoroughly. Now, only wear these clothes when you are going to do ritual work, and never for any other reason. Thus, even though they are "ordinary clothes," they become something magickal, and you will know that when you put them on you are going to do something special.

The Tau Robe

Robes are already available from a variety of sources, ranging from religious or metaphysical supply shops to school graduation suppliers. If you can sew, many sewing supply shops will have patterns for robes. An easy way to make such a robe is to get material that is as wide as your arms spread to the sides, from fingertip to fingertip. The length should be at least twice your height.

Lay the material out on the floor, folded over once. Then you should lay on top of the material with your neck at the fold and your feet toward the open end. Have a friend mark around your body in the shape of the Tau cross, with belled sleeves and a bottom that is much wider than the waist. The marks should be at least six to eight inches beyond your body where the arms meet your torso. Sew on the lines and trim off the excess material. Cut a hole for your head. Turn it inside out and try it on. You'll probably need to make a hem at the bottom, around the neck opening, and at the sleeves. Traditionally, the sleeves should reach to your first knuckle with your arms extended. You may actually have to add material to the sleeves to make them long enough.

I want to make something very clear to you:

You must not wait until you have all of your tools to start working on the LBRP.

You should start practicing and performing this ritual as soon as you begin studying its actual techniques in the next lesson. I am giving you some instructions on the tools you may wish to have so that you can start to gather or create them now. But, once

Tip for Tau Robe Design

Whether you make your own Tau Robe or purchase one, here's a tip that can make your magickal experience more pleasant.

Instead of simply letting the large, belled ends of the sleeves be open, sew them up about half way, from the bottom of the opening to the middle of the opening on both sides. This helps keep the bell of the sleeve in the proper, symbolic shape and position. More importantly for practical reasons, this small alteration results in something that most robes don't have: the equivalent of pockets! You can use this to store tissues, handkerchiefs, ritual instructions, small magickal tools, etc.

This small change to the basic design of a Tau Robe makes the life of the magician much easier.

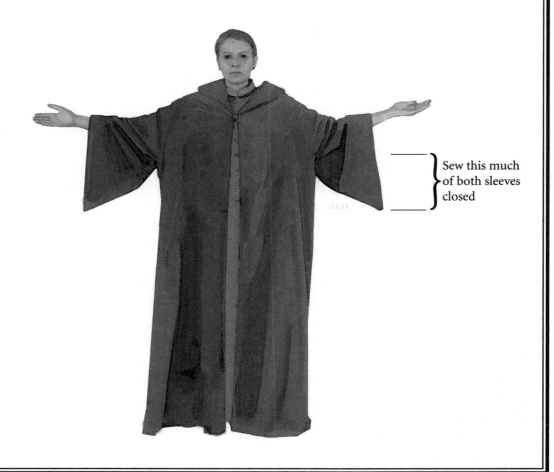

} Sew this much of both sleeves closed

you get into the instructions on how to do the ritual, begin practicing it immediately. The only thing you need to perform the ritual is space to be alone and undisturbed. This can be obtained by locking yourself into a bathroom if need be! And remember, the more you practice the ritual, the better at it you will become. The better you are at the LBRP, the better you will be—and the more successful you will be—in all of your rituals.

Drawing the Pentagram

In the LBRP you will be making large five-pointed stars (pentagrams) in the air in a specific way. Your left hand should remain relaxed and at your side. If you have a knife (*not* the Air knife; use another dagger for the LBRP), hold it in your right hand. If not, make a fist and point with either the extended index (first) finger, index and middle finger together, or even all of the extended fingers as if the entire hand were a blade. Point outside your left hip. Draw a line up above your head, then move the blade to the outside of your right hip. Next, move your blade so that it is outside your left shoulder, then horizontally across so that it is outside your right shoulder. Finally, move it back to the left hip, ending exactly where you began.

Your finger(s) or the tip of the knife should always be pointing forward, away from you. See the diagram on this page.

When you draw the pentagrams, you should visualize them as being a very bright and pure blue. It is the same color as you can see in an electric spark, the flame of a gas stove, or when a small dish of lighter fluid or alcohol is set ablaze. If you cannot visualize so well that you can actually "see" the pentagram in flame as you draw it, simply know beyond all doubt that if you had better-developed psychic vision you would be able to see it. *Know* that it is there. "See" the flame follow the tip of your blade or finger as you draw the pentagrams in the air, and know the flame is there.

How you use these lessons is up to you. Some of you will simply read through them and gain infor-

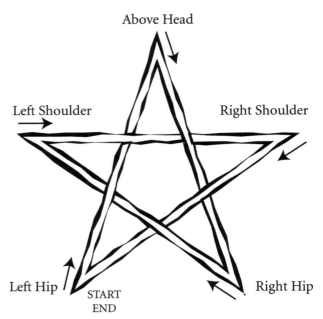

The Banishing (Earth) Pentagram

mation. Perhaps you'll compare them to what you already know. Perhaps you'll add what's here to the knowledge you already have. If this is the way you want to use these lessons, fantastic! I have a personal philosophy that you don't die when you stop breathing, you die when you stop learning. If you find that this information helps you, I think that's great.

Some of you will use this more like an encyclopedia. You'll study a bit here, refer to a section there, and maybe even practice a ritual or two. Perhaps you'll add some of the ideas and techniques to what you're already doing. Perhaps "digesting" small bits is exactly what you need at this time. If this is the way you want to use this, fantastic! My hope is that, in some way, you will get plenty out of your studies.

Some of you will use these lessons the way I hoped, as the best step-by-step introduction to magick available. That means you'll go through each lesson and take some time considering everything in it, practicing the techniques, learning and actually performing the rituals regularly, and checking that you have mastered the information in each lesson by answering the questions in the reviews. If this is the way you want to use this, fantastic! If you're using these lessons this way (and to repeat what I wrote earlier, I think you may find that reading through

2. Go above your head

3. Continue to your right hip

1. Start at your left hip

4. Move to outside your left shoulder

5. Draw across beyond your right shoulder

6. Finish exactly where you began

Position of pentagram shown for clarity. In practice, the pentagram is in *front* of the ritualist.

it once, perhaps fairly quickly at the beginning of your studies—doing an overview—is a good idea), when you get into actually doing the work, I suggest you study the material of each lesson for at least one month before going on to the next lesson.

There's no hurry. You have all the time in the world to succeed. It's when you think you don't have time that you will take shortcuts perhaps based on misunderstandings that can lead to failure. Success can be yours through regular study and practice.

Review

The following questions are designed to help you determine if you have mastered the information in Lesson One. Please try to answer them without looking at the text. The answers are in Appendix Two.

1. What is the "negative golden rule"?
2. What are the four things that can occur when you dream?
3. What is Sturgeon's Law?
4. What is your personal, secret, magickal text?
5. Why should you read other books on the Kabalah or magick?
6. Why, in your magickal diary, should you keep track of your emotional state?
7. How does Arthur C. Clarke compare magick and technology?
8. Define White Magick, Black Magick, and Grey Magick.
9. How can you avoid accidentally doing Black Magick?
10. What is the earliest mention of the Tarot in history?
11. What is the difference between divination and fortunetelling?
12. When doing a Tarot divination, why should you not ask "Should I do _____?" of the cards?
13. Give three reasons for doing the Lesser Banishing Ritual of the Pentagram.
14. When you draw a pentagram for the LBRP, what color should it be?
15. Why should the top of an altar have a heavy protective coating or be topped with a sheet of glass?

The following questions only you can answer.

1. This course presents the idea that God is neither male nor female. What do you think about that?
2. Are you keeping dream and ritual diaries?
3. What is the most important dream you've ever had?
4. Are you doing the Relaxation Ritual regularly?
5. Are you working with the Tarot?
6. Have you done any Tarot divinations? What is your most accurate result so far?
7. Which Tarot deck are you using with these lessons?
8. Why do you want to study magick?
9. Do you think you really understand this lesson?
10. What is your favorite myth? Why has it impacted you so strongly?
11. Have you ever tried to do magick, but it didn't work? Why do you think it failed?

Bibliography

For more information on these books, please see the annotated bibliography at the end of this book.

Ashcroft-Nowicki, Dolores. *The Ritual Magic Workbook.* Red Wheel/Weiser, 1998.

Bonewits, P. E. I. *Real Magic* (Revised Edition). Red Wheel/Weiser, 1989.

Cicero, Chic, and Sandra Tabatha Cicero. *The Essential Golden Dawn.* Llewellyn, 2003.

———. *Secrets of a Golden Dawn Temple.* Thoth Publications, 2004.

Crowley, Aleister. *Magick.* Weiser, 1998.

King, Francis, and Stephen Skinner. *Techniques of High Magic.* Destiny Books, 2000.

Kraig, Donald Michael. *Tarot & Magic.* Llewellyn, 2002.

Louis, Anthony. *Tarot Plain and Simple.* Llewellyn, 2002.

Regardie, Israel. *Foundations of Practical Magic.* Aeon Books, 2004.

———. *The Golden Dawn.* Llewellyn, 2002.

Wang, Robert. *The Qabalistic Tarot.* Marcus Aurelius Press, 2004.

———. *The Secret Temple.* Marcus Aurelius Press, 1993.

LESSON TWO

PART ONE

In this part of the lesson you will receive exact instructions for performing the Lesser Banishing Ritual of the Pentagram. Before going on in this lesson, go back and review part three of Lesson One. Be sure that you are totally familiar with all of the ideas in that section before proceeding to this section. By this time you should be familiar with keeping a dream diary and a ritual diary. It is possible that you may have discovered some insights into yourself and your magickal work as a result of your regular performance of the Tarot Contemplation Ritual.

Once you are sure you are familiar with the information and practices of Lesson One, you are ready to move on.

The Lesser Banishing Ritual of the Pentagram

Preliminaries

Initial preparation of the area: Start by determining where you will do this ritual. Give the area a good looking over. Go to the exact area where you will do the ritual. If you have an altar as described in the last lesson, put it in the center of your area. If you don't have an altar, use any small table, a chair, a stool, or even a piece of paper on the floor. Bring in a chair and place it at the west of the altar, so when you sit in the chair you will be looking over the altar toward the east. Make sure the area is clean. Dust, vacuum, and mop as necessary. If possible, make sure there is room to walk in a circle around the altar and chair without knocking anything over.

Initial preparation of yourself: Before starting the ritual you may wish to take a ritual cleansing bath. This type of bath is not intended to merely take the dirt off of your skin. Rather, it cleans negativity and the cares of the day from your spirit. First, take a shower to get the dirt off. Then run a warm bath. If you want, put some bath salts or Epsom salts with some nicely scented oil or perfume into the water. Then get in and just soak for a few minutes. Feel all of your cares, worries, and negativity going into the water. Now, pull the plug and let the water drain *while you stay in the water*. As the water slowly drains you will feel all of the negative things which were troubling you go down with the water. After all of the water has drained out of the tub, get out and dry yourself with a clean, fresh towel. Finally, put on your robe or special magickal clothes.

Final preparation of the space: If you have them, put the four tools that represent the magickal elements on top of your altar. Remember, have all of them present or use none of them. Put the Major Arcana cards for the Tarot Contemplation Ritual in a pile on top of the altar, too. According to the diagram below, you will start the ritual between the chair and the altar, facing east. If you have candles for use in this ritual, now is the time to light them and turn out any electric lights you have burning. Of course, if it is daylight, you will want to pull the drapes or close the curtains, etc. If, like me, you prefer candlelight, your goal should be to have the room lit only by candles. Also, light any incense you wish to burn at this time.

Final preparation of yourself: Take a few deep breaths. Inhale through the nose and exhale through the mouth. Do this slowly. Let any remaining cares, issues, or concerns leave with each exhalation. Be aware that you are about to enter a holy place.

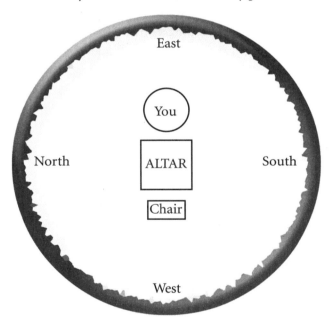

**Ritual Setup for the
Lesser Banishing Ritual of the Pentagram**

Sit in the chair, facing east, and do the Relaxation Ritual. Now stand, still facing east. Take the dagger (not the Air dagger) in your right hand, or point with your finger as described in the last lesson. Know that you are in the presence of God. The ritual has begun!

Part One: The Kabalistic Cross

STEP ONE. Rise from the chair and, walking clockwise, move around the altar to just east of it, remaining facing east (the position marked "You"). Visualize yourself getting larger and larger, taller and taller, until you tower above the room you are in. Continue this growing visualization until the city you live in is small beneath you. See the continent as tiny compared to your majestic body. Now even the planet Earth is small below you. However, no matter how small the planet Earth is, it is still firm and solid beneath your feet, anchoring you to the ground. You are completely safe and secure and will not float away.

Next visualize yourself growing so large that the planets of our solar system are like tiny toy rubber balls spinning near your feet. Soon they are too small to see as even the Milky Way galaxy becomes a small dot of light at your feet. Now visualize a dot of light coming from somewhere far above your head. Know that this is only a tiny bit of the light from this source, and if you saw the full brightness of this light you would immediately be blinded by its unearthly purity.

This tiny bit of the endless, limitless light forms a brilliant white sphere of pulsating light just above your head. It is nine inches in diameter, about the size of a dinner plate. It is brighter than ten thousand suns, but still only a tiny portion of the source of this divine, spiritual white light. Point to that sphere above your head with your dagger or finger(s) . . .

. . . and "bring it down" (by pointing) to your forehead, just above and between the eyes. Next, visualize this brilliance filling your head with divine light. While pointing to your forehead, vibrate: *Ah-TAH*. (The boldfaced syllable denotes emphasis. More on vibration later in this lesson.)

STEP TWO. Bring the point of the dagger (or your finger) firmly down your body until you are pointing toward the ground. Your hand with the blade finishes this straight line in a position that covers your groin. As you do this, visualize the light in your head coming down along with the blade (or finger), forming a beam of brilliant light that moves down through your body and beyond your feet down to the center of the planet Earth. Vibrate: *Mahl-**KOOT**.*

STEP THREE. Now bring the blade up to your right shoulder. As you do this, visualize the powerful stream of white light that runs down the center of your body begin to project a beam from the heart area out to your right, past the blade at your right shoulder. See this beam of light extend to the end of the universe, and beyond. Focus on this beam and vibrate: *Vih-G'Boo-**RAH**.*

STEP FIVE. Clasp your hands at your chest as if praying. If you are using a dagger, the point should be up, not pointing away from you, nor to the sides or down. Visualize within your chest, at the point covered by your folded hands, a brilliant golden glow. Vibrate the words: *Lih-Oh-**LAHM**, Ah-**MEN***.

STEP FOUR. Move the point of the blade horizontally to your left shoulder. As you do, visualize the beam of white light now extending through infinite space to your left. As you focus on this beam of light vibrate: *Vih-G'Doo-**LAH***.

The meaning of this first part of the LBRP is as follows: *Ah-**TAH*** means "you," or, more poetically, "Thine" in Hebrew. The visualization given above along with the proper pointing of the dagger (or finger) is for the purpose of indicating that you are linking your Higher Self with the Divine. *Mahl-**KOOT*** means "kingdom," and according to the Kabalah refers to our physical or "elemental" plane and the planet Earth. That is why you should be pointing down. *Vih-G'Boo-**RAH*** means "and the power" while *Vih-G'Doo-**LAH*** means "and the glory." *Lih-Oh-**LAHM*** means "forever," and *Ah-**MEN*** means, of course, "amen" (but you will learn the secret meaning of the word "amen" in a later lesson).

Thus, the first part of this ritual translates as "For Thine is the kingdom and the power and glory forever, amen." Does this sound familiar? It should. It is part of the Lord's Prayer. Curiously, this part of the Lord's Prayer does not occur in the first instance of the prayer in the Bible. It does appear in a later instance, giving the impression that it was added. Is this addition evidence that at least some of the early Christians knew the secrets of the Kabalah? We may never know. Several of the words used here refer directly to the symbol of primary import in the Kabalah, the Tree of Life. This will be discussed later.

Ritual Cleansing Bath Tips

Tip 1: If you add scented oil to the Epsom salts or directly to the water, be *very* careful. Some oils can be very irritating to tender and sensitive body tissues. Even a single drop of cinnamon can irritate and burn. If in doubt, don't use it. Either go without or use something professionally made and available from a metaphysical supply store or even a department store. If you have any allergies, be careful what you use, too. As an alternative, burn some incense or even a scented candle in the room.

Tip 2: Some people may not have a bathtub or simply don't like baths and prefer showers. You, too, can have the equivalent of a ritual cleansing bath. Begin by taking a shower to remove the dirt as described. Rinse off and, if you like, dry off. Get out of the shower. This is important as it physically indicates to your conscious and unconscious that you are no longer in a shower to get off the dirt.

Re-enter the shower. As the water pours over you, visualize or imagine that it is washing off all of your worries, cares, and negativity and carrying them down the drain. When the negativity is gone, dry off with a clean, fresh towel and put on your magickal robe or special clothes.

Variations of the Kabalistic Cross

Although the Kabalistic Cross seems to have been originally introduced as part of the LBRP, it has developed a life of its own. As a result, many variations of this part of the ritual have developed. Here are a few of them.

The Golden Dawn Variation: In Step Two, members of the Hermetic Order of the Golden Dawn folded their hands over the chest, at the point where the horizontal and vertical beams of light converge.

The Crowley Variation: Some followers of the teachings of Aleister Crowley also point to the chest, but they do so *between* Step One and Step Two. While at this point they add an additional name. Most resources give the word to be vibrated there as "Aiwass." Aiwass, Crowley believed, was the name of his (Crowley's) Holy Guardian Angel and was an extraterrestrial intelligence. Some followers simply use Aiwass at that point, however, it is likely that they should only use that until they contact their own Holy Guardian Angel, and then use the name of that entity.

The West Coast Thelemite Variation: Some Thelemites (followers of Crowley) on the West Coast of the U.S. believe that this ritual is related in some way to the famous grimoire, the *Goetia*. Crowley believed that the term "Goetia" meant "howling," so the people use a type of growling or howling of the words. Unfortunately, it's difficult to represent such vocalization using English. But to give you an idea, the first word, *Ah-TAH*, sounds something like "aaaaawwwwrrrrtaaaaaaaawwwwwrrrr."

The Alexandrian Variation: Alex Sanders (1926–1988) was the founder of the Alexandrian system of Wicca, one of the earliest forms of Neopaganism, developed slightly later than Gardnerian Wicca. Sanders, who claimed to have been initiated by his grandmother, blended Gardnerian concepts with even more ceremonial magick than was used by Gardner. In his variation, at Step One above, instead of *Ah-TAH*, he vibrates "Kether," and in Step Two points to the stomach.

Other variations: It seems like the variations developed for the Kabalistic Cross are unending. I have heard some people use AUM, AUMGN or even a combination such as AUM-EN instead of *Ah-MEN*. Those are obviously sound-alikes with some symbolic Eastern influences. One group, instead of *Ah-TAH*, uses Ah-Tor. I have no idea what that means or where it came from.

Which Is Right?

Throughout this course I will be giving variations of some rituals. That way you can see what other people are doing. The question is, which variation is "right"? Which way is the "correct" way?

In *Sane Occultism*, Dion Fortune wrote that there is no room for authority in occultism. I fully agree. I contend that magick is an experimental science. What I give works for many. Try it out. If it works, great. If it doesn't work, try something else. Your variation may not be the same as anyone else's, but if it works for you, that is the variation you should use. As it says in Crowley's *Book of the Law*, "Let success be your proof."

As a final note to this section, if you have not figured it out as yet, what you have done is to visualize yourself as the center of the universe with only the divine light coming through you. You may wish to remain in this position for a few minutes to feel its power.

Part Two: The Formulation of the Pentagrams

STEP ONE. Move forward to the easternmost edge of your circle. You should be at the point in first diagram labeled "East," and the second one on the next page labeled "Yud-Heh-Vahv-Heh." Face outward and away from the middle of the circle where your altar stands. In other words, you are at the east and facing east. Here, draw a pentagram as was described in the last lesson. Be sure to visualize the figure as a flaming, gas-jet blue pentagram as you draw.

STEP TWO. Inhale through the nose. As you do, feel energy flow from the ends of the universe through your nose and body, and down and out of the bottoms of your feet to the center of the Earth. As you inhale, both hands should be raised to the sides of your head by your ears. The dagger (or right-hand index finger) should be pointing forward. Your left hand (which should have remained at your side until now) is drawn into a similar position by your left ear, the index finger pointing forward, the rest of the fingers closed into a fist.

STEP THREE. Step forward with the left foot. At the same time thrust your hands forward so that they point to the exact middle of the glowing blue pentagram in front of you. (This position is known as a "God Form." This specific form is known as "the Enterer.") As you do this you should exhale and feel the energy come back up your body, out your arms and hands, through the center of the pentagram and to the ends of the universe. Visualize the energy as brilliant, fire-engine red. You should use the entire exhalation to vibrate the God name: *Yud-Heh-Vahv-Heh.*

STEP FOUR. Bring your hands back to your ears while bringing your left foot back to its original position. Put your left hand down by your side and point to the center of the pentagram with your right forefinger (or dagger). Now, following the arrow in the diagram above, trace a line in the air at the height of the center of the pentagram as you move in a clockwise direction around the edge of your circle's space. You should go 90 degrees so that you end up in the south, facing south. Again, see the diagram for the stopping location.

As you trace the line in the air between the pentagrams you should visualize a brilliant white light emanating from the tip of your finger or blade. At the south, repeat steps 1 and 2 of this part of the ritual, but vibrate *Ah-Doh-NYE.*

STEP FIVE. Repeat as above, but move to the west and vibrate: *Eh-Heh-YEH.*

STEP SIX. Repeat as above, but move to the north and vibrate: *AH-Glah.*

STEP SEVEN. Complete the circle by connecting a white line from the north to the east where you began. Then, moving in the same clockwise direction, return to the position at the east of your altar and face east (where it says "You"). *Note:* If you do not have room to walk in a circle, simply pivot where you stand.

STEP EIGHT. Now visualize the brilliant white circle expanding up and down to form a sphere above, below, and all around you. What you have done is create a sphere in brilliant white all around you with electric blue pentagrams at the quarters, which have been charged and sealed with names of God.

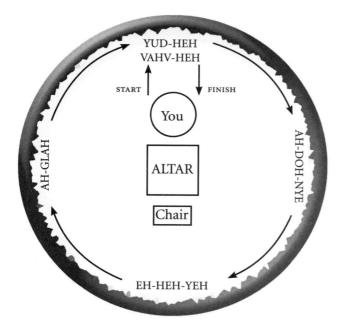

**Motions During the Formulation
of the Pentagrams**

One God—Many Names

In most major cities of the United States there are newspapers that are distributed free of charge (the ads pay all the costs), and they frequently have listings of events going on in the community. As a result of those listings early in my magickal career I twice went to see Jewish "scholars"—who were also rabbis—talk on the Kabalah. Perhaps things have changed since then—the Kabalah is becoming more popular—but I'll probably never do that again. Both times were wastes and showed that these men knew nothing of the Kabalah, or at least thought so little of their audiences that they chose to share none of their knowledge. One even went so far as to tell his primarily Jewish audience to forget about the Kabalah because Jews should only believe in one God and while "the Christians have given us three Gods [referring to the Christian Trinity of God the Father, God the Son, and God the Holy Spirit], the Kabalists have given us ten [referring to the ten names of God on the Tree of Life]." This shows a total lack of understanding, which must be cleared up now. Either that or these "scholars" must explain why the most famous and important historical rabbis, such as Isaac Luria and the Baal Shem Tov, were "polytheistic"

Kabalists. (The other rabbi, who came in forty-five minutes late and didn't apologize, talked about cats in a dark alley. To this day I have no idea what that had to do with the Kabalah!)

The Kabalah is a monotheistic tradition. In the Kabalah, the ultimate divine Source is beyond the comprehension of our mortal minds. But we can know and become in harmony with parts or aspects of the whole. These various aspects are *represented* by the different God names.

Let's compare this notion of the Divine to a very down-to-earth person whom we'll call John Smith. This "John Smith" goes by many different names:

1. His mother calls him "son."
2. His wife calls him "dear."
3. His daughter calls him "Daddy."
4. His son calls him "Dad."
5. His boss calls him "Smith."
6. His friends call him "Smitty."
7. His co-workers call him "John."
8. Old friends call him by his childhood nickname, "Binkey."
9. His mistress calls him "Honey-poo."
10. His business customers call him "Mr. Smith."

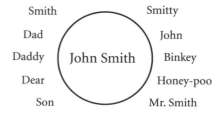

Thus we have one man with ten names. Further, the names represent the type of relationships people have with him. Imagine what he would think if his wife started to call him "Honey-poo"! Certainly he would take notice if his son, who had called him "Dad" for all of his life, said, "Father, there is something I want to talk to you about." In the same way, there are many names for God, but there is only one Source of All. We can learn more about that divine Source by learning about those aspects of God that are available to us, that is, by tuning in to what is represented by the names of God.

YUD-HEH-VAHV-HEH is known as the holy, ultimate, and unspeakable name of God. Its true pronunciation is unknown. In English we could say that it is formed of the letters Y-H-V-H. Jews never pronounce the word, instead saying Ah-doh-nye (or "Ha-Shem," Hebrew for "the Name"). By placing the Hebrew vowels of Ah-doh-nye (which means "my lord," not "lord" as some writers say) around the four letters that are known as the Tetragrammaton, the word "Yahovah" or "Jehovah" is formed. Therefore, to say God's true ultimate name is either of those, or a variation shows a total misunderstanding of this holy name. "Yahveh" or "Yahweh" is also a misnomer, an attempt to pronounce a word with no vowels. You see, YHVH may merely be an abbreviation for a longer word or a code for other letters. It is possible that some of the letters of this name are doubled. No one knows for sure. YUD-HEH-VAHV-HEH is the English transliteration for how the Hebrew letters, represented by the YHVH, are named.

The Y or YUD is said to represent archetypal masculinity (the Taoist Yang or Jungian Animus), and the first H, called the HEH Superior, represents archetypal femininity (the Taoist Yin or the Jungian Anima). The V, called VAHV in Hebrew, looks like an extended YUD (there is a deep, magickal mystery here) and represents physical masculinity, while the last H, the HEH inferior, represents physical femininity. Thus, this ultimate name of God, the Tetragrammaton (Greek for "four-lettered name"), the YHVH, says that God is the ultimate unity, a perfect blend of all dualities (as represented by the male-female symbolism), a unity of all opposites, on all planes. Certainly this is not a bad notion of the essence of Divinity.

EH-HEH-YEH is usually translated as "I am," but is more accurately translated in the infinitive form of "I shall be." It is the name God revealed to Moses at the burning bush. In the story, God tells Moses to go to Egypt and free the Hebrews, to which Moses asks, "Who shall I say sent me?" God's response is "Eh-heh-yeh ah-share Eh-heh-yeh." This is usually translated as "I am that I am," which never made sense to me and

always made me think that God was trying to be Popeye the Sailor. However, with the more accurate translation of "I shall be what I shall be" it makes perfect sense. God is saying to Moses, "I am beyond all names as I will be whatever I want to be." To me, that is a profound and sensible answer from God.

AH-GLAH is how the next God name is pronounced, but it is most commonly spelled AGLA. This is because it is an abbreviation for the words Ah-tah Gee-boor Lih-oh-lahm Ah-doh-nye. It means "Thou art great forever, my lord," and is from a Hebrew prayer.

There have been several different associations between the four quarters, the elements, and the God names and the archangels. These four God names are the ones currently most associated with the directions and magickal elements of the four quarters, as are associations for the following archangels.

Part Three: The Evocation of the Archangels

STEP ONE. Spread your arms straight out to the sides, so that your body forms a cross. If you have a dagger, the point should be up. Take a second or two once again to feel the energies flowing through you and making you a brilliant cross of light at the center of the universe. The cross also represents the four archetypal elements: Air, Earth, Fire, and Water (more on these later).

STEP TWO. Visualize a figure on a hill in front of you. The figure is dressed in yellow robes, which have some purplish highlights. The figure carries a caduceus wand. (This is a symbol used by doctors: a wand entwined by serpents. It was the wand carried by Mercury, the Roman god of medicine and the Greek Hermes. It also represents the life force.) The figure's robes wave in the wind. You should "feel" a breeze coming from behind the figure. Say: "Before me, **Rah-fay-EL**" (vibrate the name of this archangel).

STEP THREE. Without turning, visualize a figure standing behind you, dressed in blue with some orange highlights. The figure holds a cup in the form of a chalice encrusted with gems and is surrounded by waterfalls. Try to feel the moisture in the air. Say: "Behind me, **Gahb-ray-EL**" (vibrate the name).

The Magick Power of Three

It seems that since time began, people have found magick in numbers. A large part of the Kabalah, as you will find out soon, is related to numerology. The number three is important in the Kabalah, as it is in ancient Indian, Druidic, Christian, and other forms of mysticism.

Long after I wrote *Modern Magick* I had a realization about the God names used to charge the pentagrams. They all could be related to the number three. Specifically, if the pronunciation is slightly altered, they all have three syllables.

YHVH improperly becomes Je-hoh-vah.

Ah-do-nye has three syllables.

Eh-heh-yeh has three syllables, too.

Some people "improperly" make the fourth name Ah-gah-lah. I say "improperly" because most of our understanding of ancient Hebrew is based on re-creations, borrowings from related languages and guesswork. So although it does not fit modern Hebrew norms, it could be pronounced with three syllables. Besides, it's an acronym anyway and not a "real" word.

So should you alter the pronunciations for the advantage of having the symbolic three syllables for each of the God names? Try it out. If it works for you, use it. If it doesn't work, use the more accurate pronunciations given in these rituals.

STEP FOUR. To your right visualize a figure dressed in scarlet with green highlights. The figure holds a flaming sword and you should feel heat coming from this direction. Say: "On my right hand, **Mee-chai-EL**." (Vibrate the name. The "Ch" is a guttural sound as in the German "ach" or the Scottish "loch.")

STEP FIVE. To your left visualize a figure dressed in greens and browns on a fertile landscape. The figure holds some sheaves of wheat. Say: "And on my left hand, **Ohr-ree-EL**" (vibrate the name).

STEP SIX. Move your left foot out to your left and visualize another beautiful blue pentagram all around you, outlining your body. Say: "For about me flames the pentagram . . ."

STEP SEVEN. Visualize a golden hexagram, a six-pointed star sometimes called a Jewish star, within you, right where your heart is. Say: "And within me shines the six-rayed star."

Part Four: Repetition of the Kabalistic Cross
Repeat Part One of this ritual.

Again, other people have slightly different versions for the Evocation of the Archangels section. In one you would say, "Around me flames the pentagram, above me shines the six-rayed star." Another says, "Before me is the pentagram and behind me is the six-rayed star." They are minor differences, but you might like to try them and see how they affect you.

Some people do not perform the step out to the side with the left foot as in Step Six above. I continually stress the importance of using physical actions to stimulate the unconscious mind. Here, by stepping to the side separating your legs, and with your arms outstretched, the extremities of your body quite literally form a pentagram. You become the pentagram that is about you. However, try it without separating your legs and see which version works best for you.

After doing the LBRP, move clockwise around the altar and sit in the chair at the west of the altar, facing east toward the altar. Sit in your chair, take a breath and relax for a moment, and then do the Tarot Contemplation Ritual. Thus, the order for your practical daily work should now be as follows:

1. The Relaxation Ritual.
2. The Lesser Banishing Ritual of the Pentagram.
3. The Tarot Contemplation Ritual.

And of course, conclude by recording the ritual in your magickal or ritual diary.

Below you will find a summary that gives a schematic of the LBRP without any of the explanations. Refer to the instructions above while learning this ritual. Use the section below as a "cheat sheet" for as long as you need to do so, *but this ritual should be memorized!*

Vibratory Formulae

In the LBRP there are words that are meant to be said forcefully and with authority, such as "FOR ABOUT ME FLAMES THE PENTAGRAM." But there are also words in Hebrew that are meant to be "vibrated." You may have come across the expression before in your reading, and now the why and how will be explained in full.

It has long been an occult secret that all matter and all energy are made of vibration. Today many scientists depend on this being a fact in their research. If we follow the assumption that all matter is vibratory energy, then magick becomes a type of science that allows a person to affect vibrations. It becomes very valuable for us to develop an understanding of how to control vibratory energy.

The Lesser Banishing Ritual of the Pentagram

1. Touch your forehead, vibrate **Ah-Tah**.
2. Point down, covering the groin, vibrate **Mahl-Koot**.
3. Touch right shoulder, vibrate **Vih-G'boo-Rah**.
4. Touch left shoulder, vibrate **Vih-G'doo-Lah**.
5. Fold hands at chest, vibrate **Lih-Oh-Lahm, Ah-Men**.
6. Go to east, draw pentagram, point to center, vibrate **Yud-Heh-Vahv-Heh**
7. Carry line to south, draw pentagram, point to center, vibrate **Ah-Doh-Nye**.
8. Repeat, but carry line to west, vibrate **Eh-Heh-Yeh**.
9. Repeat, but carry line to north, vibrate **Ah-Glah**.
10. Carry line to east, completing circle, return to center.
11. Hands out, say:
    Before me, Rah-Fay-El,
    Behind me, Gahb-Ray-El,
    On my right hand, Mih-Chai-El,
    And on my left hand, Ohr-Ree-El.
    For about me flames the pentagram,
    And within me shines the six-rayed star.
12. Repeat Steps 1–5.

"For About Me Flames the Pentagram..."

There is a physical phenomenon known as *harmonic resonance*. This simply means that if one object vibrates powerfully enough, another object nearby will start to vibrate (or resonate) with the first if the second object has a natural vibratory rate in harmony with the first. As an example, if a violin note is played near a piano, the piano strings that have certain harmonic relationships to the violin note will sound without being touched; they will start to resonate. Thus, if you can control the vibration rate of one object, such as yourself, you will be able to cause certain reactions in other objects, such as those that exist on other planes of existence. Therefore, an understanding of how to vibrate words is essential for a magician.

There have been some incredibly complex ideas presented as the "secret" of vibrating words in the Kabalah. Some involve a convoluted system of bringing the sounds, through visualization, to different parts of the body. While nice, I have never found any practical use for this system, and it makes me think that it is one of the famous sets of ridiculous additions or "blinds" that have become attached to magick in order to keep the secrets away from those who either don't have a teacher or don't want to study and practice.

In my experience, and the experience of my many students, there are two really valuable methods of vibrating words, commonly known as the two vibratory formulae. The first is an internal (invocatory) formula. In this formula you cause a certain part of your body (actually part of your astral body) to vibrate. This is exemplified in the Kabalistic Cross part of the LBRP. Let's just look at the word "AH-TAH." What you should do here is fully inhale until there isn't room for one more drop of air. Then use the entire exhalation to vibrate the word. Thus, the word is elongated: AAAAHHHHHHH-TAAAAAAAHHHH. It should be vibrated loudly in an almost chant-like tone of voice. The pitch is usually higher than the normal pitch of your voice. It is almost shouted. Most importantly, you should feel it vibrate or resonate within your head. Likewise, MAHL-KOOT should be felt in the groin, VIH-G'BOO-RAH in the area of the right shoulder, etc.

The second vibratory method is the external (evocatory) formula. With this formula the intent is to excite the atmosphere (actually the so-called astral plane) around you. This is exemplified in the Formulation of the Pentagrams section of the LBRP. The method is quite similar to the invocatory formula. You inhale fully, and as you exhale you loudly vibrate the appropriate words, in this case God names. Here the God names are stretched out as: AAAAAAAH-HHH-GLAAAAAHHH. You should use the entire exhalation in sounding the God name or words when doing the evocatory vibratory formula. The big difference between the two formulae is that in the evocatory formula you should sense that the entire universe in front of you is resonating in harmony with your vibration. Your entire body and the entire universe should be experienced as vibrating to your call. The invocatory formula causes your body, mind, spirit, astral body, aura, etc., to vibrate in resonance with your voice.

There are some minor variations on these two basic formulae, such as seeing the words you wish to vibrate in flame before you and making the vibration charge and empower those flames.

The Great Voice

Some student-magicians do not have the luxury of a place where they can loudly, firmly, and authoritatively vibrate the God names and words of power. In fact, they need to keep their work a secret. This is difficult to do if you live in an apartment with paper-thin walls!

If you find yourself in such a position, you may use what is disguisedly called the "Great Voice." That is, you may do the vibratory formulae silently or very quietly, perhaps at the level of a whisper or quiet conversation. However, if you do so, you must still experience the vibratory phenomena. You must feel the various parts of your body vibrate when doing the invocatory vibratory formula. You must sense the entire universe resonating in harmony to your use of the evocatory formula. In other words, you must have the same results whether you vibrate loudly or in the Great Voice.

If you must use the Great Voice regularly, I suggest that you find a place to practice using your full, loud voice several times. Find a place where you can be alone to do this. When everything around you seems to "change" slightly, you will know you are vibrating the words correctly. These changes are not physical ones, but the area will "feel" different. If you practice by using the LBRP (a good idea), the area will feel cleaner and fresher. Some people notice an increase in the amount of natural, ambient light. You may also find that you will have to adjust the pitch of your voice either up or down in order to make everything vibrate correctly. When you hit the pitch which is correct for you, you will know it! Your voice will sound much louder and more commanding, and the air will seem to be alive with crackling energy. Then you will know what is meant when it is said that "the voice of a true magician is an awesome thing to hear."

To make a comparison, if you have ever been singing in a tile-covered shower stall, you will notice that your voice sounds normal, but at some pitches it suddenly booms out much louder and sounds fuller. That is the building literally resonating with your voice. That is the way you should feel when you vibrate a word.

As a final note to the LBRP, remember to record everything you are doing in your magickal diary. And, most importantly:

Do the LBRP with feeling!
Do it often!
"Enflame yourself with prayer!"

PART TWO

One of the biggest fears of many occultists is "psychic attack." However, the fact of the matter is that true psychic attacks are very rare. The reason they are so rare is that by the time a person has enough skills and talents to attack psychically, he or she also has enough mystical knowledge to know not to attack someone because of the negative repercussions that inevitably follow the attack. In the past twenty years I have had at least two hundred people ask for my help because they felt they were under psychic attack. I also know many metaphysical teachers and

psychics who have told me of their experiences with people who have come to them claiming to be under psychic attack. Of the hundreds of claims of psychic attack of which I have heard, perhaps five cases were real while the rest were imaginary.

Be that as it may, the *feeling* of being under psychic attack can be a very real feeling. The unconscious mind does not know the difference between reality or imagination, so the feeling that you are under psychic attack can actually result in the experience of every symptom of such attacks. This makes the attempt to determine whether a psychic attack is actually coming from an outside source difficult.

Further, our *psyches* are constantly under attack from society: salespeople order us to buy; TV ads order us to buy; friends, family and even strangers, knowingly or not, try to psychologically maneuver and influence us. Whenever we are in contact with other people, directly or indirectly, there are almost continuous attempts being made to manipulate us. Thus, we need to be aware of the day-to-day attempts at subtle sorts of brainwashing we are receiving along with having the knowledge of what to do if a real psychic attack does occur.

Although the common belief is that a real psychic attack involves a trained magick worker casting a spell, the reality is that this is rarely the case. Rather, it is caused by a person or persons who for some reason are angry with you. Their rage causes them to unknowingly direct a stream of energy filled with their anger toward you. They are probably not even aware that their thoughts and emotions are combining to have a negative effect on you (although they might relish the idea). What is even more likely, however, is that you simply *believe* that some negativity is coming toward you. In either case, you will still feel as if you are under attack, and both cases can be dealt with in the same way.

Signs of a Psychic Attack

Before determining that you should take action against a psychic attack—whether real or imagined—you will need to determine if you actually are under psychic attack. Several authorities give a wide

A Simple Tip if Your Room is Cockeyed

Masonic lodges are frequently designed to be aligned to the four directions. So are some synagogues, cathedrals, Indian temples, Asian buildings, and many others. In the past, and in many spiritual traditions, people understood the importance of aligning with the Earth's energies.

But in most of today's homes, such luxury is not thought about and may be rare. How, then, do you arrange a small room that is twelve degrees off of being truly aligned with the four directions? If you have some bookcases and furniture against the walls, trying to line things up according to the true directions leaves no room unless you remove all furniture. And even if you do, facing several degrees off of a corner to look at the east can feel odd and even downright weird. I've been there and done that with people, and after rituals people spend more time talking about how things felt "wrong" rather than spiritual effects of the ritual or other metaphysical topics.

So what can be done? Easy. Remember, ceremonial magick, with all of its décor and ritual items, is still practical. It has to be focused on obtaining results. So here is what you can do:

1. If the room has any windows, use curtains and drapes so when you are ready to do ritual during the day, you cannot tell where the Sun is.

2. Select one side of the room to be the "Spiritual East" and declare it as such. Perform the LBRP, and after the Evocation of the Archangels, and before the repetition of the Kabalistic Cross, say, "Before God and all the spiritual beings assembled here, I hereby declare that this side of the room is now, and in all future uses, the Spiritual East. So mote it be."

From this moment on, treat that side of the room as if it were the east in all situations, especially during rituals.

---

selection of symptoms that indicate a psychic attack. Dion Fortune, in her almost paranoid *Psychic Self-Defense*, lists such things as poltergeist activity or feelings of fear and paranoia. Unfortunately, poltergeist activity can have numerous causes other than psychic attack, and fears and paranoia can be caused by false beliefs and the inability to deal with them. Some of the books with lists of symptoms sound depressingly similar to the claims of some Christians that demons are responsible for all of your problems, from smoking and weight issues to gambling and money problems.

There is a simple rule to understand psychic attacks:

Psychic attacks always go after your weakest link.

Do you have problems sleeping? A psychic attack will go after your sleep patterns. Do you have serious asthma? A psychic attack will go after your breathing. Do you have problems with your stomach? A psychic attack will go after your digestion. Do you have certain fears? A psychic attack will make them stronger. Do you feel you're not as bright as others? A psychic attack will make you feel more insecure. Do you doubt the fidelity of your romantic partner? A psychic attack will increase your doubts and may harm the relationship.

However, any and all of these symptoms could have a completely natural cause and not be due to psychic attack at all. Therefore, as a common practice, think natural causes first, psychic attack last. Do everything you can to check out such symptoms via non-magickal means. Check with doctors, parapsychologists, psychologists, and anyone who might be able to help you resolve such issues. Remember, the chances are they are not from a real psychic attack. Only after you have eliminated all other potential causes should you consider that psychic attack may be behind the situation.

Technique to Overcome a Psychic Attack

This excellent method of repelling psychic attack is derived from Denning and Phillips' *Practical Guide to Psychic Self-Defense.*

STEP ONE. Close your eyes and pivot in a circle until you can sense the direction from which the real or imagined stream of negative energy is coming. Allow your senses to spread out as you slowly turn in a circle. The feeling of energy may be slight or strong. It may feel hot or cold. It may vibrate or seem to have a specific color or scent that shouldn't be there. As you spread out your astral senses, use them to look, feel, sense, hear, or taste something that doesn't belong there. That is the direction the stream of negative energy, real or imagined, is coming from.

STEP TWO. Once you find that direction, boldly face that way! The path of a magician is not one for cowards. Stand proudly and erect, and visualize on your forehead a bright, electric-blue pentagram with one point uppermost. Now bring your hands up to your forehead to surround the glowing star. The hands should be flat with the thumbs meeting at the brows and the fingers meeting above, palms out. Thus you have a triangle, the so-called "Triangle of Manifestation," surrounding the pentagram with the thumbs as the basal line of the triangle (see figure below).

STEP THREE. Now take a deep breath and, as you exhale, step forward with your left foot and thrust your hands forward while at the same time visualizing the pentagram on your forehead flying out in the direction you are facing. This will have the effect of sending away the negativity of the real or imagined psychic attack.

STEP FOUR. To keep it from returning set up a sphere of invulnerability by immediately performing the entire LBRP. (This is one of the reasons the LBRP should be memorized.)

Triangle of Manifestation to Project a Pentagram for Psychic Self-Defense

Psychic Attacks and the Lemon That Wasn't There

Some people question my comment that "the unconscious mind does not know the difference between reality and imagination." This is an important concept because, if it is true, it becomes easier to understand how simply believing or imagining that you are under psychic attack can have the same results as an actual attack.

Surprisingly, it's actually very easy to show how the imagination can control the physical body. Try this experiment:

Imagine yourself walking into your kitchen. See the countertops and hear the sound of your feet as you walk over to the refrigerator. Open the refrigerator and imagine you feel the sudden flow of cold air bursting out at you. See all of the foods in the refrigerator.

Now reach down and open the drawer where fruit is kept. Hear the sound of the drawer as you pull it out. Reach down into it and pull out a lemon. Feel its cool, firm, and bumpy surface in your hand. Bring it to your nose and imagine you can get that slightly sweet, slightly tart smell. Close the drawer and the refrigerator while holding on to the lemon.

In your mind's eye take the lemon to the counter. Imagine you open the drawer where you keep your knives and pull out a sharp one. Now, imagine that you carefully slice the lemon in half. It's a very juicy lemon and some of the juice spurts out. Take one of the halves and cut it in half.

With your imagination, pick up one of the quarters of the lemon and bring it to your face. Some of the juice runs onto your hand and you can feel it cold and astringent. The smell is pungent. And now, bring the slice of lemon up to your mouth and . . .

Take a big, juicy bite of the lemon!

Just chew it up. Taste that tart and sour juice.

Very good. Now, focus on your real, physical mouth. Do you notice how it has produced an increased amount of saliva? The production of saliva is controlled by your autonomic nervous system. You can't just say, "Mouth, give me more saliva!" and it happens. Something has to trigger it. Normally, that trigger is the taste of food or drink.

But there was no real lemon. It was just in your imagination. Yet, your unconscious (which controls the autonomic nervous system) reacted as if it were real. It produced more saliva.

Similarly, if you believe a psychic attack is taking place, your body and conscious mind will respond as if it were real.

Just like your mouth responded to the lemon that wasn't there.

Why Not Use a "Mirror Spell"?

I have often been asked, "Why not use a Mirror Spell to reverse a psychic attack?" A Mirror Spell is rather simple. You visualize a mirror to reflect any negative energy back to whoever sent it your way. There are two difficulties with this.

First, many psychic attacks are only our own belief that we are under attack. They can feel real, but the energy comes from within us. So if you reflect the energy back to the person who sent it—you'll be attacking yourself! Not a good idea.

It's better to get rid of the energy rather than create an endless loop that sends energy back to you as a result of your unknowing self-attack, which, in turn, is sent back to you. Or you may think that you know who is sending it and reflect the energy to that person, even though he or she was not involved at all. You'll be harming an innocent person.

The second reason is that most psychic attacks are not consciously directed. They are caused by a person's anger. That attacker didn't know what he or she was doing and they will face cosmic feedback (*karma* or the Kabbalistic "Ti-koon"). However, if you send back negative energy toward someone and are aware of what you are doing, you, too, will face the effects of karma. There are no "Lords of Karma" who will see that you are just returning the attack and you are not responsible. You are responsible for your actions, and if you act to harm someone—even if it is only reflecting what they sent to you—the karmic response will be the same as if you started the attack yourself.

Dealing with day-to-day attacks on your psyche from a multiplicity of sources is another matter. Doing the LBRP helps, but the problem is really one of awareness. The fact of the matter is that most of us are virtually unconscious—literally in a trance or asleep—for up to 95 percent of the time we are awake. "Awakening the sleepers" was a main focus of the work of Georges Gurdjieff. I also urge you to read as many books as you can on psychology and Neuro-Linguistic Programming (NLP), as this information will awaken you to how the mind works and how people manipulate one another.

Magickally, another way of becoming more awake to the world around us involves becoming more in tune with the universe. One way to do this is to record in your magickal diary the day, date, weather conditions, and phase of the Moon at the time of every ritual you perform. There are also four brief (less than thirty seconds each) rituals that will help attune you to the Sun as it daily traverses the sky.

The Four Solar Adorations

(Based on Aleister Crowley's *Liber Resh vel Helios*)

At Sunrise (or when you awaken). Face the east, make the sign of the Enterer [this was given in the LBRP], then stand upright with your arms up as if you were supporting a heavy pole above your head (see figure on next page). You will speak the following in a loud voice if possible. If not, use the "Great Voice" and speak silently.

Say:

"Hail unto Thee who art Ra in Thy rising, even unto Thee who art Ra in Thy strength. Who travelest over the heavens in Thy bark at the uprising of the Sun. Tahuti standeth in his splendor at the prow, and Ra-Hoor abideth at the helm. Hail unto Thee from the abodes of the night."

Resh at Sunrise

Finally, stamp the ground one time with your left foot and bring your left forefinger to your lips as if telling someone to be quiet. In fact, this it known as the Sign of Silence or the Sign of Horus.

Tahuti is the Egyptian for the god commonly known as Thoth. The rest of the symbolism can be easily understood by consulting a book on Egyptian gods.

Resh at Noon

At Noon. Face south, make the sign of the enterer. Form the Triangle of Manifestation, only hold it slightly above your head (here it represents the element of Fire as the previous position represents the element of Air). (See figure above.)

Say:

"Hail unto Thee who art Hathoor in Thy triumphing, even unto Thee who art Hathoor in Thy beauty, who travellest over the heavens in Thy bark at the mid-course of the Sun. Tahuti standeth in His splendor at the prow and Ra-Hoor abideth at the helm. Hail unto Thee from the abodes of the morning."

Make the Sign of Silence.

Resh at Sunset

At Sunset. Face west, make the sign of the enterer. Form the triangle with your hands, only do it over your stomach with the palms toward you, the thumbs at the top and the fingers pointed down. This position or God-form represents the element of Water (see diagram). Thus you have a downward pointing triangle in front of your stomach.

Say:

"Hail unto Thee who art Tum in Thy setting, even unto Thee who art Tum in Thy Joy. Who travellest over the heavens in Thy bark at the downgoing of the Sun. Tahuti standeth in His splendor at the prow and Ra-Hoor abideth at the helm. Hail unto Thee from the abodes of the day."

Make the Sign of Silence.

Resh at Midnight

At Midnight (or before you go to sleep). Face the north, make the sign of the enterer. Then step forward one pace with your left foot and raise your right hand above your head, palm forward, as if in greeting (see illustration):

You should be in the same position as seen in the 1950s cowboy films where an Indian warrior raises his right hand and says, "How!"

You now say:

"Hail unto Thee who art Khephera in Thy hiding, even unto Thee who art Khephera in Thy silence. Who travellest over the heavens in Thy bark at the midnight hour of the Sun. Tahuti standeth in his splendor at the prow and Ra-Hoor abideth at the helm. Hail unto Thee from the abodes of the evening."

Make the Sign of Silence. Of course, the God-form in the illustration above represents the element of Earth.

What's With the Funny Hand Signs?

Yes, magicians make funny signs with their hands. They also wave wands, swords, and daggers. Some people think this is all for show. Let me assure you it is not.

The mind and body are closely connected. By taking particular physical positions you can change the attitude of your mind. Let me give you two quick examples.

1. Sit in a chair with your legs slightly spread apart. Let your hands rest on your inner thighs, hanging loosely, fingers pointing down. Look at the ground between your feet. Frown. Take a deep breath and sigh as you exhale. Say out loud, "I really feel wonderful!" *This just feels wrong.* The physical position you are in is not in harmony with your audible expression. It feels wrong because your body is contradicting your statement.

2. Stand up straight. Throw your shoulders back. Look slightly up, above a horizontal view. Put a big smile on your face. Take a deep breath and say, "I feel terrible." Again, *it just feels wrong.* This new physical position is not in harmony with your new audible statement. The "wrong" feeling is because your body is contradicting your statement.

Over the years, as a result of logic and experimentation, it has been determined that the signs given in the Adorations above are physiological representations of the four elements. Remember and work with these poses.

In some of the original Golden Dawn documents, the position for midnight is given so that it looks as if you are giving the Nazi "Seig Heil!" salute. Some have claimed that it was a follower of Aleister Crowley who introduced the sign to Hitler and the Nazis.

It has been suggested by a few people that I changed the sign because I didn't like the Nazi associations. That is true. However, changes like that are not uncommon. Originally, when boys and girls performed the "Pledge of Allegiance" in U.S. schools, they also held their hand out as in the Nazi salute. This wasn't changed to the "hand over the heart" gesture until 1942. More importantly, some Golden Dawn temples make the sign with the flat of the hand vertical, like an archetypal karate chop. I have used all three methods and find the one described here to be the most effective. Try them all out and see which works best for you.

Advanced Work for the Four Adorations

If you find the Four Adorations very simple, you may wish to add the following visualizations. The overall purposes are:

1. To help you attune to the changes of the Sun,

2. To help you attune to the four magickal elements, and

3. To help you attune to the universe, and, hence, the Divine.

For this advanced work, when doing the adorations, simply add the following visualizations:

1. When you face east for the adoration at sunrise, visualize yourself imbued with the color yellow and filled with the qualities of air: heat and moisture.

2. When you face the south for the adoration at noon, visualize yourself imbued with the color red and filled with the qualities of fire: heat and dryness.

3. When you face the west for the adoration at sunset, visualize yourself imbued with the color blue and filled with qualities of water: cold and moisture.

4. When you face the north for the adoration at midnight, visualize yourself imbued with the colors of the fertile earth, especially greens and browns, and filled with the qualities of earth: cold and dryness.

To finish this part of the second lesson, let me reiterate that real psychic attack is very rare. One time I knew I was under psychic attack and decided to do nothing to see what would happen. The result was that I got six free books in the mail and a check for fifty dollars.

However, the sensation of being under psychic attack can be very real, so I urge you to learn the techniques of this lesson. Also, do not avoid the performance daily of the Four Adorations. Even if you are very ill, you can spend a few seconds doing them.

PART THREE

The Kabalah

Here is the section that many of you reading these lessons for the first time have been waiting for: the Kabalah. Since *Modern Magick* was first published, the Kabalah has become a pop sensation, thanks to the participation of some Hollywood personalities. I wish them well, but I regret to say that some of what they are practicing has little to do with any form of Kabalah I have studied—and there are numerous forms or "schools" that approach the Kabalah from different directions.

Just as an example, the so-called "red thread" popular among some Kabalists is more associated with Semitic folk magick. There is nothing wrong with that; it's just not the Kabalah. Similarly, selling blessed water is more along the line of what some Christian televangelists do. That is not a part of the Kabalah. Once, I went into one of the main locales of this supposed Kabalistic organization, at the "centre" of this popular revival. The first thing they tried to do was sell me a very expensive, multi-volume set of books. "Don't worry if you can't read the Hebrew or Aramaic these volumes are written in," I was told. "We'll tell you what page to look at every day and you'll get amazing changes in your health and well-being just by scanning the pages with your eyes."

I left, disgusted with what they were doing. And no, I didn't buy the books. So don't worry. The study and practice of the Kabalah—I would say the *real* Kabalah as I know it—is not going to make you a part of some materialistic pseudo-religious personality cult. In fact, I would say that the more you study the Kabalah, the more likely you are to see through attempted manipulation and the less likely you are to fall prey to any religious cult.

In the following pages I will be discussing a brief history and some of the basic theories of the Kabalah. One complaint I frequently hear from many people is that the Kabalah is confusing or boring. In fact, it is neither. But it may take several readings of the following material to get a feeling for the intricacies of Kabalistic thought. Just go through the following pages at your leisure while you practice the daily rituals which, to repeat, includes the Relaxation Ritual, LBRP and Tarot Contemplation Ritual. Also work with the Four Adorations and practice the technique for overcoming real or imagined psychic attack so you'll be ready if necessary. Although I have explained the Kabalah and its history hundreds of times in my classes, there are usually one or two people who do not immediately quite catch on to the ideas presented. So take a week or two practicing the rituals and perhaps making your robe and go over the following pages as many times as necessary.

It is said that there were three sacred "literatures" for the ancient Hebrews: the Torah (which is comprised of the first five books of the Jewish Bible, sometimes called the "Old Testament"), the Talmud (commentaries on the Torah), and the Kabalah (mystical interpretations of the Torah and speculations on the nature of God and the universe). The Torah was known as "the Body of the Tradition," and it was said that if ignorant people would read the Torah, they would profit from the experience. The Talmud was called the "Jew's Rational Soul," and those who were learned would profit in its study. The Kabalah was called the "Jew's Immortal Spirit," and the wise were advised to meditate upon it.

You may have noticed that different books and authors spell the word "Kabalah" in different ways. This is because the word "Kabalah" comes directly from the Hebrew and there is no precise transliteration between English and Hebrew. Some authorities claim that Jews spell it "Kabala," medieval Christian mystics spell it "Cabala," and occultists spell it "Qabala." If you include possible double letters (the "b" and the "l") plus either having a final "h" or not, there are something like twenty-four different potential spellings in English for the word. I agree with the learned Rabbi Lamed Ben Clifford (my friend Lon Milo DuQuette) who asks in *The Chicken Qabalah*, "Is there a correct way to spell the word Qabalah?" He answers, "Hell no!"

Thoughts on Hebrew

This gives me a chance to interject some thoughts concerning the Hebrew language. Many of the rituals in this course (such as the LBRP) will be using words from the Hebrew. But all languages, including Hebrew, change in their pronunciation over the centuries. As an example, the word "knight" that we today pronounce "nite" was originally pronounced "k-nigh-t" with a short "i" and the "gh" being a harsh guttural version of "ch," as in the Scottish word "loch." Thus, English has changed over the past few hundred years. Is it any wonder that Hebrew has changed over the past several thousand years?

Turning to look at Hebrew as it is spoken today in Israel and in synagogues around the world (and discounting local dialects) does not help our understanding of Hebrew pronunciation. Modern Hebrew is not the same as Biblical Hebrew. At the beginning of the last century a man named Eliezer ben Yehudah came to believe that Hebrew should once again become a living language. It had been relegated merely to religious documents and study rooms much in the way that Latin is today. Through his efforts, Hebrew, like a phoenix, rose from the dead and became a living language, and was adopted as the language of the state of Israel. This would compare with the idea of having all people in Italy learn Latin and use it as their everyday tongue.

But in the process of bringing Hebrew from death back to life, many changes in the language's very nature took place:

1. Certain letters that had two different sounds no longer do so (see the book *Sepher Yetzirah* for a list of all the original double-sounding letters).

2. The Hebrew letter called the "vah" or "vahv," usually having a "v" sound (although also sounding like "o" or "u"), may have originally sounded like our "w" and was called the "waw."

3. Even today certain Hebrew letters can have several sounds. The Aleph can sound like "ah,"

"eh," or "aw." The Yud can sound like "ee," "ay," or "eh." The Heh can indicate "ah" or "heh." The system of points and lines to indicate the vowels were added hundreds of years after Ezra compiled the Torah (circa 450–350 B.C.E.), so they may not be accurate.

4. Perhaps worst of all, mystically speaking, is that to make Hebrew a modern language, ben Yehudah had to take out much of Hebrew's wonderful lack of precision. As an example, the word in Hebrew "Oh-lahm" today generally means "world." Originally it seems to have meant "world," "universe," "aeons," and "forever." This showed that to the ancient Hebrew mind all of these things were related. Now, unfortunately, much of that knowledge is lost, as in modern Hebrew words are more meaning-specific.

5. Many Hebrew words were replaced by Aramaic words. As an example, in ancient Hebrew "Av" or "Ab" meant "father." In modern Hebrew the word for "father" is the Aramaic "Abba."

The next question is "Should we try to discover the ancient Hebrew pronunciation? After all, isn't the way the words are pronounced important?" The answer is yes, the way the words are pronounced is important. But no, it is not worth our time to seek out the ancient pronunciation of Hebrew. Most of the rituals used today were really created long after Biblical Hebrew was a mere memory.

In this course, the pronunciations used are those of modern Hebrew. In this way you will be tapping into the energies of millions of people who speak the tongue every day, rather than guessing at what ancient Hebrew may have sounded like.

After this digression, let us now return to this word of import, "Kabalah." Kabalah (or Kabbalah or Qabalah or Qabbalah or Kabala or Cabala or Q.B.L., etc.) comes from the Hebrew word that means "to receive," implying that the Kabalah is a "received" doctrine; that is, received from God. It also means that it is given by one person and received by another, usually in an oral manner. Thus, the true Kabalah was an oral, secret tradition, which for thousands of years was jealously guarded from the profane.

Like the Tarot, there are two types of histories of the Kabalah. The first given here is a mythological history, the second is the known, factual history.

The History of the Kabalah—Mythical

The Kabalah was a secret science known to the angels and to God before the creation of the universe. After Adam and Eve fell from grace in the Garden of Eden, an angel taught the wisdom to Adam so that grace and purity might be regained. (I notice similarities here between this story and that of Prometheus, who brought fire or "divine wisdom" to the human race. I wonder which story came first or if both are reinterpretations of earlier myths?) This knowledge Adam passed on to his sons, but was later forgotten or lost.

After the deluge, God not only gave the rainbow as a sign of his covenant with humanity, but also instructed Noah and his sons in the secret knowledge. But, as before, the knowledge was eventually forgotten or lost.

You may by now be seeing a trend developing for the reception and loss of this secret knowledge. Angels instructed Abraham in the wisdom. He, in turn, instructed Isaac and from there it went to Jacob. But during the captivity in Egypt it was again lost.

The knowledge was next recovered by Moses. Moses, so the story goes, spent forty days on the top of Mount Sinai, and traditionalists wish us to believe that all he obtained from God was two stone tablets with the Decalogue (Ten Commandments) on them. The mystical interpretation is that the first time Moses went up he received the secrets of the Kabalah from God, but destroyed them upon his return and seeing the people involved in idol worship. He returned to the top of the mountain, but now God would not allow Moses to share the secrets of the Kabalah with the common people. Instead, like little children (the name "Children of Israel" is very appropriate in this context) they were told what they could and could not

Possible Bragging Rights?

I think that this would be a good time to share a small tale of my personal history. Before I was born, my father decided to change the family name. You see, the family name had been "Katz." My father, Marvin Pershing Katz, had been a high school and college football hero. He was known as "Shovelhands Katz" because of his large hands and his ability to catch the ball. Even so, from his days as a child through his college years, he had been kidded by being called "Pussy Katz." After my older brother, Steven was born, my father decided to change the family name so his son would not be ridiculed. He changed it to "Kraig," keeping the "K" of "Katz" and giving the family a new name. May both my father and brother rest in peace.

So how is there bragging rights associated with that name? The name "Katz" is an abbreviation or acronym (in the Kabbalah it is called a *Notarikon*, of which more will be said later). It is short for "*K*ohain *Tz*eh-deck" (with the vowel "a" added between the initial letters of the two words). In Hebrew, those two words mean "righteous priest." This indicates that I *may* be a descendant of the ancient priestly caste. When in synagogue and called to the altar to say the blessings over the Torah, I am one of the tribe of the Kohanim. If this is accurate, then it would be my right to learn and share the Kabalah. But before you think this bit of knowledge has gone to my head, let me remind you that this "revelation" comes attached to these lessons as a sidebar to a section dealing with "mythological history."

do in the form of the Ten Commandments and the other 603 laws of the Torah. Moses, who already had received the Kabalah, was told that he could only give the secrets to his brother Aaron and through him to the future high priests of the Hebrews.

As a side note, in the late nineteenth and early twentieth centuries, the first real, great archaeological discoveries in Egypt took place. People around the world (especially occultists, who at times are not the most level-headed of people) were fascinated by the secrets of ancient Khem. Thus, when they read in the Bible that Moses was educated in Egypt, they assumed that the Kabalah had an Egyptian origin. While it is true that there were mystery schools in Egypt—in fact, Pythagoras studied at one—there is no proof that the Kabalah is taken directly from the wisdom of Egypt. However, it is likely that the Kabalah was influenced by the spiritual systems of ancient India, Egypt, Babylon, etc.

And so it was that the mystical secrets of the Kabalah were kept for hundreds of years by the He-

brew priesthood. But the common Hebrew man and woman did not learn the lessons of the Decalogue and the other laws which God had intended them to learn. Thus, God punished the people of Israel over and over until the destruction of the second Temple in the year 70 C.E. Rome had ordered the destruction, and had wanted rabble-rousers and freedom-loving troublemakers rounded up. One of these was a rabbi named Simeon ben (sometimes written "bar") Yochai. He managed to evade the Romans by hiding with his son in a cave for thirteen years (there is a special meaning in the number thirteen, which will be revealed later in this course). In the cave, these two learned men wrote down the secrets of the Kabalah for the first time in a large set of books titled *Sepher Ha-Zohar* or just the *Zohar* (Book of Splendor) and the small *Sepher Yetzirah* (Book of Formation). Later, when publishing became practical thanks to Gutenberg, these books became available to people all over the world. Thus it was that although the *Diaspora*— the exile of the Jews throughout the world after the destruction of the second temple—was decried by most Jews, mystical Jews have held that this diaspora was God's gift to all humankind, because in that way they were able to spread the divine wisdom of the Kabalah, rather than keep it hidden in a small section of the Middle East.

The History of the Kabalah–Factual

Little is known as to where the Kabalah actually originated. There do seem to be elements of ancient Chaldean, Egyptian, Babylonian, and even pre-Hindu Indian (what I refer to as "proto-Tantric") mysticism, as well as elements drawn from other, less well-known Semitic peoples hidden in its depths. More modern aspects of the Kabalah either were heavily influenced by Neoplatonic theories or, in fact, influenced the Neoplatonists.

The earliest known form of Hebrew mysticism (not counting earlier shamanistic forms that seem to exist in all primitive tribes and societies) was not even called Kabalah. The earliest form of Hebrew occultism was known as "Heh-cha-loht" (with the "ch" sounding like that in the Scottish word "loch"), which means "ascent." It is also known as Merkabah mysticism. The Merkabah was the name of the Throne of God in Hebrew, and it was the aim of the Merkabah mystics to be able to see God upon His Throne.

Unfortunately, most of the writings of the "Merkabah Riders" have been lost, so that full knowledge of their techniques is impossible. Although more and more is being uncovered, much is still debatable. From what little we know, the concepts of this tradition seem to be based upon mystical contemplation of the early chapters of Genesis and the vision of Ezekiel. These methods are known respectively as Mah-ah-seh B'ray-sheet and Mah-ah-seh Mer-kah-bah. From the fragments of Merkabah mysticism that still remain, it is assumed that the actual practices of these mystics involved "astral travel" through a series of seven "places" (planes?) by way of certain passwords, talismans, and secret signs while in a state of self-induced trance (possibly via self-hypnosis, physical duress, psychoactive drugs, or extended periods of sex). The names of each of the guards at each of the seven palaces had to be known so that they could be appeased in some way.

Unfortunately, the knowledge of those appeasement methods is also currently lost or unknown.

Although this has not been one of my interests, it is my hope that some intrepid individual or group does some spiritual and astral investigations and recovers the lost information. Perhaps it will be one of the people reading these lessons. To whet your appetite and to make this search easier, here, for the first time in any popular course or publication (to my knowledge) are the correct names of the guardians that are known (from the fragments of the book *Pirkei Heichaloht*):

First Palace: Dehaviel, Kashriel, Gahoriel, Botiel, Tofhiel, Dehariel, Matkiel, and Shuiel (though some say Sheviel).

Second Palace: Tagriel, Matpiel, Sarhiel, Arfiel, Sheharariel, Satriel, Regaiel, and Saheviel.

Third Palace: Shevooriel, Retzutziel, Shulmooiel, Savliel, Zehazahiel, Hadriel, and Bezariel. (*Note:* There are only seven guards listed in the fragments, not the usual eight, implying that one of the names has been lost.)

Fourth Palace: Pachdiel, Gevoortiel, Kazooiel, Shekhiniel, Shatkiel, Araviel, Kafiel, and Anaphiel.

Fifth Palace: Tachiel, Uziel, Gatiel, Getahiel, Safriel, Garafiel, Gariel, Dariel, and Falatriel. (*Note:* There are nine guards listed here, which is one too many.)

Sixth Palace: Katzmiel, Gehaghiel, Roomiel, Arsavrasbiel, Agroomiel, Faratziel, Mechakiel, and Tofariel.

Seventh Palace: For this palace there were two sets of names. They were described as one set for "ascending" and one for "descending," the meaning of which is unclear. My guess is that different names were used to enter and exit this palace.

The focus of this book is on the Kabalah, not on becoming a Merkabah Rider. Since other techniques (how to go into trance, how to astral travel) are needed and further information (the appropriate passwords and needed talismans) is unknown, I am not going to give a listing of the names of the rest of the guardians as this might lead to some unwise experimentation. My purpose in listing the names of the guards above (which in the tradition needed to be memorized) merely has been to show you the complexity of the system. Those who wish to go further into the topic have the name of one of the few sources in a preceding paragraph. If you experiment with this, I wish you good luck and hope you will share your results with the rest of us.

The final goal of the Merkabah Rider was to be able to gaze upon the Throne of God and upon God Himself. This was no easy task, as you can see from the small amount of material I have given above. Also, remember that even Moses was not allowed to view the face of God, for it was said that no mortal could gaze upon the face of God and survive.

There are obvious similarities to Egyptian lore as presented in the so-called *Egyptian Book of the Dead* (more accurately, the *Book of Coming Forth by Day*), especially the idea of going through various places, e.g., hells of the Egyptian afterlife (the Egyptian hells should not be confused with the Christian idea of Hell), and passing tests in order to pass safely through these nether realms. Did the Hebrews copy from the Egyptians, or vice versa? Or did both come from an older source? Or perhaps both cultures (along with others such as Tibetan and Amerind) just happened to tap into the same mystical current. Nobody knows.

The *Sepher Yetzirah*

Moving into the actual Kabalistic period of Hebrew mysticism, we come across the first well-known Kabalistic book, the *Sepher Yetzirah* or "Book of Formation." This book seems to be a combination of the earlier Merkabah mysticism and the more modern Kabalah. The *Sepher Yetzirah*, along with another work, the *Bahir*, have been traced back to the earliest centuries of the Common Era. Within them are discussions of such things as emanations from Divinity bringing about the universe. This idea is known today as Neoplatonism. However, if we assume that the Kabalah was either brought to the Egyptians by the Hebrews, or that the Egyptians had the knowl-

edge prior to the period of the enslavement of the Hebrews,* then it might be that Neoplatonism was a development of the Kabalah. As stated before, it is well documented that Pythagoras, who is still famous for the Pythagorean Theorem (the sum of the squares of two sides of a right triangle is equal to the square of the hypotenuse), studied mysticism and was initiated into Egyptian mystery schools. It is not unlikely that he learned some early form of Kabalah there and brought it back to his home in the Greek city-states. It is not impossible that Plato and his later followers adopted the idea of emanations as a result of studying in Pythagoras' mystery school, begun when Pythagoras returned to the Greek isles from the Middle East. Of course, this is speculation, but is based on probabilities.

That Kabalistic mysticism continued to develop during the centuries of the Common Era since the beginning of the diaspora cannot be disputed. It is one of the reasons that Jews were hated and feared. Part of the Kabalah is related to magickal abilities, and many people fear magick. In the fourteenth century, Moses de Leon made the first printing of the *Zohar*, the classic Kabalistic text. Some modern scholars, and some contemporaries of de Leon, have called it a fraud. They say that it was not the original *Zohar* of legend written by Simeon ben Yochai, and that de Leon forged the entire work. Although I do not claim to be a great archaeological scholar, I find this contention hard to accept. Parts of the whole long work in various forms have been discovered in other works dating before the fourteenth century. However, it does seem likely that de Leon did edit and add some of his own mystical philosophy to the *Zohar*. Even so, let us assume for a moment that Moses de Leon did create the *Zohar* as it is printed today (one current English translation fills five volumes). If so, it is a monumental work of mystical thought. Besides, whether it is ancient or relatively recent, it should be studied for what is in it, not for who wrote it.

---

* It is unlikely that the ancient Hebrews were ever actually enslaved by the Egyptians. There is no evidence that the Egyptians ever had such forms of slavery. It is more likely that they were simply an ethnic tribe within the control of Egypt. This is brought to light even in the story of the exodus where the Hebrews took their animals and possessions with them, and not long after melting their possessions of gold to form an idol. The concept of slavery is one where the slaves are possessions. They have nothing of their own. How could they have taken possessions, including lots of gold, when they would have had no possessions? It is clear that while the story of the Exodus may have some factual elements, much of it is mythologized.

God Has a Sense of Humor?

I have often been asked how you tell a good spiritual teacher from a bad one. Of course, he or she should have a thorough knowledge of a topic being shared, be willing to share it, be able to effectively communicate it, and not become egotistical about it. I'm sure there are lots of other things that would make up a good spiritual teacher, but I'm not trying to give a thorough answer to that question here. However, there are three things I would require of a spiritual teacher:

1. They have to sing.
2. They have to dance.
3. They have to laugh—especially at themselves.

If you find a spiritual or religious teacher who won't do these things, I would advise caution and even urge you to consider staying away. I hasten to add that I'm not saying the teacher has to be good at any of these things. I like to think I'm decent as a teacher and will sing and dance—but I'm no Josh Groban or Michael Flatley. And my singing and dancing gives me plenty of opportunities to laugh at myself.

That brings up another question. Does God fulfill these qualities? After all, who is a bigger spiritual teacher than God?

When it comes to singing, I would say "Absolutely." There is a famous Jewish prayer that includes the line, "Come, let us sing a new song. Let us joyfully proclaim the rock of our salvation." It's clear that God likes singing.

After the Hebrews escape across the divided Red Sea (actually that's a mistranslation; it should be the "Reed Sea," but that's another story), they begin to sing and dance. God tells them to stop because he wants no celebration over the deaths of so many Egyptians. The inference is that God would have enjoyed the singing and dancing at another time.

When it comes to laughter, God actually plays a practical joke on Moses. Moses asks to see God, but God tells him that no man can see his face and live. God tells Moses that this is what he'll do. "Stand upon a rock [...] and [I] will cover thee with my hand while I pass by. And I will take away mine hand, and thou shalt see my back parts . . ." (Exodus 33:21–23).

In other words, God "moons" Moses.

And let's not even talk about the time God punishes some men by giving them hemorrhoids (usually translated as "emerods" in 1 Samuel 5:6)!

Who said God doesn't have a sense of humor?

To sum up, the Kabalah is not a single book or simple mystical idea. Rather, it is a whole system of mystical thought and action. It is the mystical underpinnings for Judaism, Christianity, and (to a lesser extent) Islam. As the Middle Ages developed in Europe, many locations became Kabalistic centers, the most important ones being in Spain. But in 1492, the year Columbus sailed, the Jews were expelled from Spain. It is for this reason that some people believe that Columbus (actually Cristobal Colon was his name in Spanish, and "Colon" may have been a variation of "Cohen") may have been Jewish, and his trip, they believe, was to find a home for the expelled Jews. Be that as it may, many of the Jews returned to the Middle East, and a large, important Kabalistic center developed there in the city of Tzfat (usually transliterated as "Safed"), a town that still exists in modern Israel.

Two things happened that took the Kabalah away from being part of the mainstream of Judaism. One was a twelfth-century book by the respected Rabbi Moses Maimonides called A *Guide for the Perplexed*. In this book, supposedly "rational" (at least more rational than Kabalistic concepts in Western scientific terms) solutions to theoretical and philosophical problems in Judaism were given. Maimonides was trying to make Judaism compatible with the ideas of Aristotle.

A virtual war of words developed between the followers of Maimonides' "rational" approach (there is still much mysticism and magick even in his "rationality") and those who believed in the Kabalah. This "war" went on for years, the most famous proponent of the Kabalah being the Rabbi Nahmanides of the thirteenth century. Meanwhile, many schools of the Kabalah had developed, each with slightly different ideas of Kabalistic theory and practice, such as the schools of Isaac Luria (sixteenth century) and Isaac the Blind (late twelfth through early fourteenth centuries). The final blow to the Kabalah, along with the *Guide for the Perplexed*, came in the form of a man named Sabbatai Zvi (1626–1676).

A New Hope

Zvi (or Zebi, or Zwi) had an intense, charismatic personality. He was also very learned in both traditional and mystical (Kabalistic) Jewish knowledge. He became more and more popular in the Middle East until he was proclaimed by his followers as the Messiah, the savior of the Jews. He never denied that he was the Messiah. Word of his magickal powers, wisdom, and Godliness spread via Jewish traders to Jewish communities throughout the Middle East, Asia, and Europe. In the Middle East, where he spent most of his life, he developed many diehard zealots as followers. Finally,

the Islamic sultan could no longer ignore him. The resultant meeting between the two led to the discrediting of Zvi and his conversion to Islam, after which he was exiled to a prison in Albania, where he died as a false Messiah.

Deceived Jewry tried to forget and put out of their lives everything that reminded them of Zvi. In fact, many Jewish books wouldn't even give his name, only calling him "that one." Since Zvi was associated with the Kabalah and magick, this too was discarded and the position of Maimonides was accepted. Except for small groups of secretive believers, Judaism deserted the Kabalah.

The Kabalah was saved from being perhaps totally lost by those Christians whose goal was to study the inner teachings of Judaism in order to prove that Jesus was, in fact, the Christ, the Jewish Messiah, and thus turn all Jews into Christians. As you can see, there are still Jews in the world today, and the attempt failed. But it did cause the translations of many documents and books that had never before been translated out of the Hebrew or Aramaic. The possibility of real magickal secrets that were holy and not satanic in nature caught the fancy of many scholars and clerics, up to and including Eliphas Levi (born Alphonse Louis Constant). Levi's most famous work, translated poorly into English, is now in print under the title *Transcendental Magic*. His books and teachings helped start what has been called the "French Occult Revival" of the nineteenth century. At that time, many occult groups began to develop in France and spread to other countries, most notably Austria, Germany, and England. Some of these groups used their occultism to support questionable ethics, leading to "magickal wars" between occult groups in France, and the evil of Nazism in Germany.

Looking for a second back on the "lighter" side of occultism, we come in England to the Hermetic Order of the Golden Dawn, whose primary importance came in their taking the teachings of the Kabalah as a basis for their occultism and uniting it with other forms of occultism such as the magickal systems (or supposed magickal systems based on their sometimes incomplete knowledge) of Egypt, of Enochian magick, of the magick of Abramelin, and of mysticism from India, as well as other sources. We will deal with all of these as need be in this course.

The Kabalah that we study in this course is a modern Kabalah. The Kabalah is a philosophical system of life as well as a magickal system and, as such, has changed over the centuries to meet the needs of the people of the contemporary society. Besides differences in interpretations of the Kabalah based on different sects' attitudes, there are two major divisions in the Kabalah today.

Two Divisions of the Kabalah

First, there is what I call the "Kosher Kabalah." This has come about as a result of the need for a Jewish spiritual rebirth. Right now, in America at least, the number of Jews is rapidly decreasing. Oh, there may be more Jews numerically, but for many it is merely a group or cultural association and nothing more. Judaism is both a religion and a culture, and a person can be part of either or both. Thus, there can be religiously atheistic Jews who retain their cultural Judaism, and religious Jews who are alienated from archetypal Jewish culture.

I feel that part of the reason an increasing number of people who are culturally Jewish have abandoned the religious aspect of Judaism is at least in part due to the extreme lack of spirituality found in some of the major forms of Judaism. As I wrote in the introduction to the book, I initially experienced Judaism as very scientific combined with going to synagogue on the Sabbath and holidays and following the negative golden rule. Not too much spiritual there. This lack of spirituality may have resulted in a moving away from standard Judaism, and the fact that there is a disproportionately large percentage of Jews being attracted to various cults that disguise themselves as religions. But some Jews are looking toward their own spiritual roots and are rediscovering their Kabalistic heritage. The Kosher Kabalah,

then, has a particularly Jewish tone to it. It benefits all students of the mystical as we are obtaining more and more ancient Kabalistic works, which are finally being translated into modern languages. But, because it is so oriented toward one point of view, it is not our main concern.

The "WASP Kabalah" follows—or rather, leads—what has been called the Western mystery tradition as exemplified in the concepts of the Golden Dawn. This system of Kabalah *universalizes* the Kabalistic wisdom so that it may be accepted by all, no matter your particular faith or lack thereof. This "syncretistic" system of the Kabalah is the one that we will be studying. Because the Kabalah has been safeguarded for thousands of years by the Jewish culture it is obvious that it will have, in many instances, a Jewish flavor. That is partially why we will be using many words that are in Hebrew. However, since we will be studying the WASP Kabalah and not the Kosher Kabalah—since we are studying a universalized Kabalah—you do not have to be or become a Jew or Christian or Pagan or follow any particular religion or belief in order to study the philosophy and magickal techniques of the Kabalah and traditional Western ceremonial magick.

Four Branches of the Kabalah

There are four main branches to the Kabalah. Although the title of the divisions are clear, some of the aspects of each branch overlap.

1. *The Dogmatic Kabalah.* This concerns the study of the literatures of the Kabalah such as the *Torah*, the *Sepher Yetzirah*, the *Bahir*, the *Zohar*, and many others. Although their study is fascinating, it is not the focus of this course. The names of various books and appropriate sections from them or ideas from them will be given when they are needed, but the dogmatic Kabalah will not be a primary concern of these lessons.

2. *The Practical Kabalah.* This refers to the making of talismans and amulets via Kabalistic methods. It is the basis for Kabalistic magick

when mixed with the following two branches of Kabalistic study. The methods of the practical Kabalah are neither good nor bad, but can be used for what might be called "positive or negative" purposes. Therefore, it is necessary to first give you the work that will prepare you so that not only would you not have a desire to do magick for negative purposes, but so that you will understand the consequences that will result for yourself if you try to use magick for negative purposes. Thus, we will not be taking up the practical Kabalah for a few more lessons.

Please don't misinterpret the last paragraph to imply that if you follow the techniques as given in this course you will become a namby-pamby, fluffy-bunny magician who is all sweetness and light. No, by following the methods given here you can become a powerful magician, afraid of no other entity, physical or otherwise. But, rather than moving blindly with no understanding of the rules of the universe as explained by the Kabalah, by following these lessons and learning all the information, you can become a true wise man or woman, a wizard, a warrior of the light. You won't want to do negative magick because you'll have no need to do negative magick.

When we do get into the practical Kabalah and into Grey Magick, we will truly soar. Nor will we be limited to the kabalistic methods of magick. As an example, just in dealing with talismans we will be discussing Pagan, numerological, Rosicrucian, and other systems for making these devices.

3. *The Literal Kabalah.* This concerns the relationships between the numbers and letters of the Hebrew alphabet. The ancient Hebrews did not have separate figures to represent numbers, so they used the letters of their alphabet. It was believed that if two words had the same numerical total, they had a significant relationship to each other, and in some cases could be considered synonyms. As an example, *aheva* = 13 and *echod* = 13. Therefore, *aheva* is the same as *echod. Echod* is the Hebrew word meaning "one." Since in Judaism there is only one God, it also represents God. *Aheva* is Hebrew for "love." Therefore, according to this system, God is love. Further, the holiest name of God, the Tetragrammaton or YHVH, totals 26. Since 13 + 13 = 26, we can say that love (*aheva*) plus oneness (*echod*) equals the nature of God (YHVH). This process is known as *Gematria* ("geh-may-tree-yah"). As we go on in the lessons, you will see the vital import that Gematria plays in ceremonial magick. It will be explained more fully in another lesson. (By the way, do you remember that I said I would explain the meaning of the number 13 earlier in this lesson?)

Notarikon ("Noh-tayr-ih-kon") is another aspect of the literal Kabalah. It is a system of finding acronyms, where the first letters of a series of words gives a new word or words. English examples of this system would be Mothers Against Drunk Driving becoming MADD or North Atlantic Treaty Organization becoming NATO. (While I was in college I tried to form the Society to End Acronyms or SEA. Somehow it never caught on.) As you can see, they do not have to form familiar words, although they may do so. "Ah-tah Gee-boor Lih-oh-lahm Ah-doh-nye" is Hebrew for "Thou art great forever, my Lord." It is represented by the Notarikon (or acronym) AGLA, pronounced "Ah-glah," as given in the Lesser Banishing Ritual of the Pentagram. "Amen" in Hebrew is composed of three letters: aleph, mem, nun—AMN. They are a Notarikon for Al (pronounced "ehl" and meaning "God") Melech (meaning "king") Neh-eh-mahn (meaning "faithful"). Thus, Amen, the Notarikon for "Al Melech Neh-eh-mahn," means "God is our faithful king." The phrase is a repetitive refrain in a Hebrew call and response prayer, and is the inner meaning of the word "Amen."

Temurah ("teh-moo-rah") is a system of transposition of letters such as is used in cryptography and the making of codes. Its primary importance is in interpretation of the Torah (known as exegesis) and in making talismans. There are several different forms of Temurah, and theoretically, there's no reason why you could not make up your own. Here are some of the more popular methods of this system:

Avgad: A very simple kind of Temurah wherein any letter is replaced by the letter that follows it in the alphabet. Thus, in English, "a" is written as "b," "b" is written as "c," etc. The name of this method comes from the first four Hebrew letters, Alef (pronounced "a"), Bet (pronounced here as "v"), Gimmel ("g"), and Dallet ("d"), forming the word "avgad" and explaining that "a" becomes "b" and "g" becomes "d."

Aik Bekar: In this system, the twenty-two letters of the Hebrew alphabet plus the special "final" forms of five of the letters (they are only used at the end of words) are mixed according to a certain pattern. They are placed in nine boxes of three letters each. Thus is formed a figure three boxes high and three boxes across. In Aik Bekar you can have any letter in a box represent either of the other two letters in that box. In the first box—which has the letters aleph, yud, and koph (the "Aik" of Aik Bekar)—the yud could represent either the koph or the aleph. So, too, could the koph represent the aleph or the yud, and the aleph could represent either the yud or the koph. Although simple in design, this results in potentially complex codes.

A   Y   K
A = Y or K
Y = A or K
K = A or Y

The letters in the second box form the word "Bekar."

Achas B'tay-ah (the "ch" sounds like the Scottish word "loch"): This is similar to Aik Bekar. In this system there are seven boxes of three letters each, with one letter left over. Here again, a letter in one box is interchangeable with any of the other letters in that box.

There are several other systems of Temurah, including the simple expedient of transposing the first letter of the alphabet with the last, the second with the second to last, etc.

4. *The Unwritten Kabalah.* This fourth branch of the Kabalah refers to the correspondences on the sacred glyph known as the Tree of Life. It is one of the major keys to the entire Kabalistic system. Indeed, some people think it is the most important aspect of Kabalah. In the next part of this lesson we will begin the study of the Tree of Life.

But before going on to the next part, take a few days off and go over what you've studied so far. Take a break. This has been a lot of "stuff," and you've earned it. However, be sure to continue performing your rituals and keeping your diaries. If you intend to do so, you might also start building your altar and sewing your robe during this break. Maybe have a pizza. If you have it with pepperoni, it's not kosher—it might not even be good for you—but it sure tastes good.

PART FOUR

In this part of the lesson we begin the study of the mystical symbol known as the Tree of Life. In the garden of Eden as described in the book of Genesis of the Jewish Bible, there were two important trees growing with the other flora and fauna. One was the Tree of the Knowledge of Good and Evil. According to the exoteric interpretation of this passage, it was by eating from this tree that Adam and Eve fell from grace. God then drives Adam and Eve from the garden because the Tree of Life is there, and, as God says, "Behold, the man is become as one of us, to know good and evil; and now, lest he put forth his hand, and take also of the tree of life, and eat, and live forever." Although not having good syntax, this biblical quotation indicates clearly that the Tree of Life is considered to be highly important, capable of bringing eternal life. It is also capable of bringing much more, as we shall see.

Diagrams

Diagrams are frequently used to represent other things. A diagram of a miniature solar system can be used to represent the appearance of an atom. Its many valence levels filled with electrons are represented by the "orbiting planets," and the nucleus is represented by the stationary Sun. This works for most chemical considerations, but modern subatomic nuclear physics tends to ignore the solar system model of the atom, replacing it with tiny waves of energy that constantly move toward and away from the center of the atom. For most practical purposes, however, the solar system model of the atom works and is still taught in schools. It is only a map of the reality that gives us a way to understand the reality, but the map is not the territory; it is only a model.

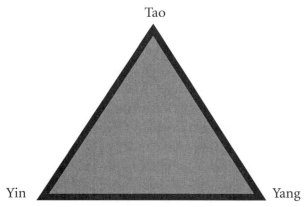

There are other models for other purposes. One such model, shown above, is a triangle with Yin and Yang at the lower angles and Tao at the top. Yin represents all things which are archetypically female: cold, wet, winter, receptivity, intuitiveness, etc. Yang represents all things which are archetypically male: warm, dry, summer, aggressiveness, logic, etc. Tao

represents the balance of these two ideas. Balance, according to Taoism, is the desired state. For a person to be balanced, he or she must have aspects of both Yin and Yang.

Other things can be reflected in this Yin-Yang-Tao triangle. Father, Son, Holy Spirit (the Holy Spirit in Gnosticism was seen as being female); liberal, conservative, centrist politics; body, mind, and spirit; and many other trinities. A most important one for modern philosophy was first written by the German philosopher Georg Wilhelm Friedrich Hegel (1770–1831) and is known as the Hegelian Dialectic, or the "Thesis-Antithesis-Synthesis Theory." This theory holds that if you have one condition or situation (thesis) but wish to change it to another, usually opposite condition or situation (antithesis), the result will not be either the new or old, but rather a mixture (synthesis) of the opposing positions. This is why revolutions rarely achieve their goals. Instead, they end as a mixture of what was and what was desired. The method of nature is evolution, not revolution.

The diagram that is important to the Kabalah above all others is the Tree of Life, as shown on the next page. As you can see, it is composed of ten circles forming three triangles: the highest one points up, then two triangles point down, and finally a single circle hangs pendant to the triangles at the bottom. Note that there are twenty-two paths numbered from 11 through 32 connecting the circles.

These circles are known as the *Sephiroht* (seh-fear-oht), the singular form being *Sephira* (seh-fear-ah). If you draw straight lines going from Sephira 1 to 2, 2 to 3, etc., up to 10, you will get the Lightning Bolt or Flaming Sword image also shown on the next page.

This is both the flaming sword which the Kerubim hold to keep people from getting back into the Garden of Eden and the path by which Divinity created the universe.

The Kabalistic Source of All

How can we know the ultimate Divinity? We only have mortal minds, which are limited. We see everything in

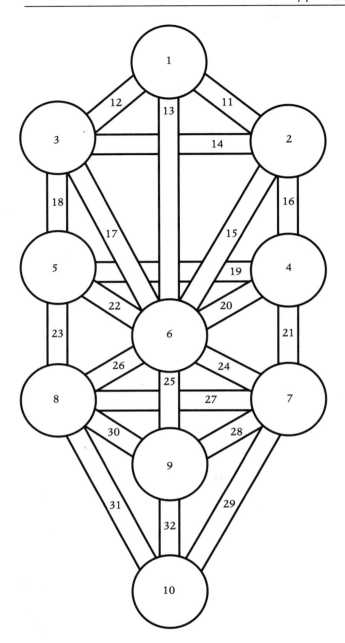

The Tree of Life

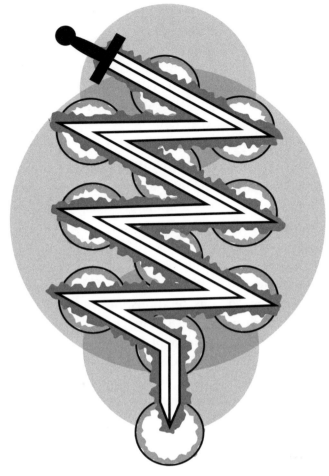

The Flaming Sword

dualities (me, not-me; up, down; stable, unstable; moving, stopped, etc.). Since the very nature of Divinity, by definition, must be beyond any sort of limitations, Divinity cannot have a dual nature. If Divinity is male, then Divinity is not female and thus is limited. Divinity is the ultimate unity, beyond duality. And since we have mortal, limited minds, the ultimate Divinity cannot be like anything we know. In fact, the ultimate speculation we can make about the nature of Divinity is that Divinity is *no-thing* which we can know. In Hebrew, the word for no-thing (nothing) is ***Ain***.

As soon as we put any qualities upon Divinity we limit the Source-of-All. As stated, a male God limits God to being not-female. A merciful Divinity does not have the righteous severity of being just. A Divinity that is limited cannot be the ultimate Divinity. It follows, therefore, that the only quality we can put upon Divinity is that Divinity is *without limit*. And the Hebrew expression for "without limit" is ***Ain Soph***.

As stated earlier, it was believed that anyone who beheld the face of God could not live. On this planet we can barely stand to look at the Sun on a bright day for more than a fraction of a second. It is too bright. Since we cannot behold a bright light, nor can we behold the "face of God," it follows that there is a relationship between the two, and that the first conceivable yet unknowable and unexperienceable aspect of Divinity is brightness beyond comprehension, brightness beyond any brightness of which we can conceive: *Limitless Light*. The Hebrew for "light without limit" is **Ain Soph Or**. These three conceptions are conceived to be above the Tree of Life with a "veil" beneath each, as shown in the following diagram:

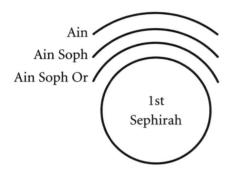

The Three Veils of Negative Existence

Because the word "Ain" means "nothing," these three conceptions above the first Sephirah have been called *the Three Veils of Negative Existence*. However, they have been called so wrongly, because in context Ain does not mean "nothing," but rather "no-thing" that our mortal minds can conceive, understand, or know.

The Formation of the Universe

The earliest known Kabalistic theory as to how the universe was formed comes from the *Sepher Yetzirah*. It holds that God moved the magickal Hebrew letters in such a way that the physical universe was formed. This is a basis of Grey Magick, which we will get into later in the course. Today, the most popular Kabalistic theory of the creation of the universe is the system described by the famous Rabbi Isaac Luria (1534–1572). According to Luria, before the creation Divinity filled the universe. Then, for some unknown reason, God decided to create. God allowed a tiny part of "Himself" to shrink out of the

universe, leaving a space. However, in some mysterious way God still filled this space much as a fragrant rose when removed from a room will still leave its essence or scent behind. This process Luria called "tzim-tzum."

God then sent a beam of energy from within "Himself" out into the newly abandoned space, apparently trying to create containers for this energy. But, for some reason unknown to us, God appears to have failed, with the result that the containers were shattered, forming the shells or what is known as the *Kellipoht*, the places where "demons" dwell. God attempted the process again, this time succeeding. The energy from the *Ain* went through the *Ain Soph*, through the *Ain Soph Or* and into the first Sephira. That Sephira filled with energy, then overflowed into Sephira number two. Sephira two filled and overflowed into Sephira three, and so forth down the Tree of Life into Sephira ten where an equilibrium, a balance, was established.

As the energy proceeds down the Tree, it goes from being very ethereal and spiritual in nature until in the tenth Sephira it manifests as the physical plane and our planet, Earth. Thus, this energy is seen as constantly creating our universe. This energy comes directly from Divinity, and without it all would instantly cease to be. With this simple way of looking at the Tree of Life we can see how truly God must love us to constantly be giving us existence.

Here is a type of mathematical way of looking at existence as represented by the Tree of Life: From no-thing comes Limitlessness (outer space). Filling this Limitlessness is Limitless Light (the big bang, or perhaps the space-time continuum). But this is all abstract. This is just energy. Now we need to develop solidity out of energy.

We start with the idea of position, what in plane geometry is called the point (first Sephira). By reflecting itself, the first point can create a second point (second Sephira). By joining the two points together we form a line. But there is nothing by which to judge length. So again, by reflection, we create a third point (third Sephira), which enables us to say that point

A Slightly Twisted Conversation on the Gender of God— From a Kabalistic Point of View

"So let me get this straight. According to the Kabalah, the ultimate nature of God is not male."

"Correct."

"So God is female."

"No, that would limit God."

"So God isn't male or female?"

"Not exactly. God is God. If God wants to be male, God can be male."

"That makes no sense. Either God is or is not male."

"That's your limited human thinking. God is beyond that."

"So God could be female, too?"

"God will be what God will be."

"So let me get this straight. Are you saying that God is male and female and not male and not female?"

"That's right. God is beyond dualities."

"Then is God androgynous?"

"As with the genders of male and female, God is beyond dualities. God can be seen as being androgynous and genderless."

"So when it comes to the Kabalistic concept of the gender of God, are you saying that God is androgynous and genderless, male and female, and neither male nor female?"

"Simultaneously."

"Well, that's as clear as mud! What about in the *Zohar* where things like the number of hairs in God's beard are discussed? Doesn't that mean God's male?"

"That was a metaphor used to help explain one part of the nature of God. You can look at a petal of a flower and examine that petal in depth, but you are not examining the entire flower."

A is closer to point B than B is to point C. Thus we have formed a triangle or plane. But this has all been what is called Euclidian: it exists on an imaginary two-dimensional surface with no thickness. To create a physical universe, we need substance, we need three dimensions. We need knowledge (Dah-at, the theoretical Sephira said to exist between the upper three and lower seven Sephiroht) in order to cross the void from two dimensions to three.

With the knowledge we create a fourth point (fourth Sephira), which with the previous three points gives us volume, and thus a third dimension. But these three-dimensional points are static, unmoving. We need another point to show motion (fifth Sephira) and still another to indicate time (sixth Sephira), for in the physical world time and space intermingle and cannot exist without one another.

So now we have something that has three dimensions and can move within the three dimensions. We still have nothing that can appreciate that existence. We add three more points (seventh, eighth, and ninth Sephiroht), which show:

a. The essence of life, called *Being* (*sat* in Sanskrit),

b. The ability to think, called *Consciousness* (*chit*), and

c. The ability to experience the sensation of something outside of one's self, called *Bliss* (*ananda*).

Therefore, the first idea of reality as can be appreciated by a mind is built up from the idea of a point through the idea of bliss, and summed up as all of reality in point ten, the tenth Sephira.

Now, I realize that what has been described here is very complex, and may, in fact, be confusing. But, like the Tarot, the only way to really learn about the Tree of Life is to study it, use it, confront it every day. As you learn more practical uses for the Tree of Life it will become quite easy to understand. In the meantime, spend a few days with this section before moving on to the next section. Remember, nobody said these lessons would be easy. But by the end of this course you will be able to understand the basic theories of the Tree of Life as presented here or in any book.

Understanding the Tree of Life, however, goes much deeper than some set of weird theories. The more you understand it, the more you will see how it can be used to understand and work with just about anything in life. It becomes a model, a paradigm for understanding how the spiritual planes, the physical planes, and your mind functions. Slowly, the Tree of Life will become part of your everyday life and thought. When that occurs you will have become a true mystic. And when you understand the universe as it is represented by the Tree of Life and can freely move about on the Tree as you wish, then you will be a true magician.

PART FIVE

By now it is hoped that you've been practicing the material for several weeks. That means before proceeding with this section you should really have the LBRP down pat. By this I mean you should not only have the words memorized, but you should also have all actions so well rehearsed you can do them without even thinking about them, and all of your visualizations should be clear. However, if you don't have everything memorized, at least transfer your notes to small cards or "cheat sheets" so you don't have to carry this book around.

The ritual I am about to describe is called the Middle Pillar Ritual. Its proper practice will result in greater vitality, aid in the task of self-mastery, help cultivate spiritual insight, and aid you in your white magickal quest, the search for union with the divine nature.

The Tree of Life exists everywhere, not just as circles on a piece of paper or as a philosophical construct. It also exists within the human being on a variety of levels. Picture yourself turning around and backing into the Tree of Life. This will give you a good idea of how the Tree exists on the body. The uppermost Sephira is just above the top of the head. The second Sephira is at the left side of the face, although it is on the right side of the Tree. The third Sephira is on the left side of the Tree and on the right side of the face. This continues down the entire body. We will be studying more of these relationships with the Tree of Life, part of the unwritten Kabalah, in the next lesson.

But for now we must turn our focus away from the Kabalah and toward India. Here, some of the most ancient of spiritual texts, the *Tantras*, speak of psychic centers known as *chakras*. (*Note:* The "ch" is pronounced very hard, as in the word "chalk," and *never* soft as if it were an "sh." That would require the word to start with a different Sanskrit letter, and people who pronounce it "shakras" may have never been trained in Sanskrit pronunciation. It may also be pronounced as "kahk-rahs.") The chakras exist in the energy fields around our bodies. There is also an energy stream known as *kundalini* (pronounced "koon-duh-lee-nee") which goes through these psychic centers. The oldest Tantras speak of only three major chakras: at the genitals, the heart, and at the top of the head. Later Tantras speak of four major

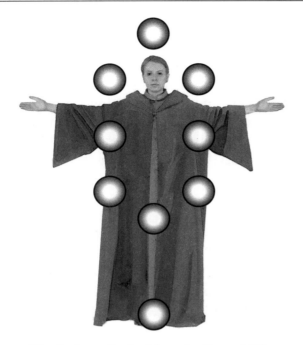

The Body as Backed into the Tree of Life

chakras: at the navel, the heart, the throat, and the top of the head. Even later books speak of six or seven major chakras, often disagreeing as to where the chakras are located. But most importantly, the books tell you that it is dangerous to attempt to raise the kundalini energy through the centers. To discover why this is so we must jump from ancient India to the late 1800s and Victorian Europe.

This was the era of Sigmund Freud (1856–1939). Although Freud outlived the Victorian era, much of his philosophy was heavily dependent upon his being raised in the Victorian period. It is also clear that Freud, a Jew, studied the Kabalah, in at least some cursory way. In his early writings on psychology Freud indicated that he believed that there was an actual, physical energy, a psycho-sexual energy, which he called "libido." Freud believed that this energy came from all parts of the body and would move to a single part of the body. He called this process "cathexis." He believed that all psychological problems could be traced to blockages of this psycho-sexual libido energy, and that was a problem.

Freud realized that if he was correct, the way to solve virtually all psychological problems would be

to unblock this sexual energy. This meant, of course, that he would have to encourage people to have sexual relations. Freud knew that in an age still rife with repressive Victorian morality, this would never be accepted. This was especially true since many of the people Freud worked with were unmarried.

Freud was a pragmatist. He knew he would have to change his theories so that he could still help people. I don't know if Freud was thinking in this direction, but it does seem to make sense that if getting energy moving would clear blockages, clearing blockages would also allow the energy to move freely. No matter how he came to this conclusion, Freud did change his notion of libido from an actual energy to a mere *desire*, which was capable of being focused in other directions. He called this process of focusing the energy in other directions "sublimation." Unfortunately, since there was no longer an actual energy that was stopped, Freud now needed to come up with a desire that was contrary to libido. This he called the "death wish." If it sounds confusing, it is. This is because Freud would not accept the reality of libido as an actual energy.

Meanwhile, one of Freud's most creative students, Wilhelm Reich (1897–1957), decided that Freud had been correct in the first place. He set out to discover and actually measure Freud's concept of psycho-sexual energy. Freud was quoted as saying that Reich was either a fraud or the future of the psychoanalytic movement. Later, Freud wrote the book *Civilization and Its Discontents* to denounce Reich's theories.

Reich's researches went far beyond the original theories of Freud. Reich called the psycho-sexual energy "orgone" and believed that he had seen it and measured it. Its color was a bright blue (such as in the LBRP). Reich invented group therapy, rebirthing, primal scream, bioenergetics, and certain educational systems; he also did sexological studies similar to Masters and Johnson decades before they began their research. Reich wrote several books on his theories and made devices (orgone accumulators) which he claimed could take orgone energy out of the environment to be used for healing purposes. For his efforts to enlighten the world, Reich was thrown in jail and his books were burned. (Here, in America, in the 1950s!)

My point in this is not to get you to read a particular book or author, nor is it to criticize the actions of our government in the middle of the McCarthy era. Rather, it is to show that Western science has studied and is well aware of the nature of the psycho-sexual energy. And this energy, originally called libido and later orgone in the West, is known as kundalini in India.

In India, however, the study of kundalini has gone on for thousands of years. As a result, they have a much deeper knowledge of it than does Western science. In a base and chaotic form it is said to lie "sleeping" in the area of the coccyx, the tip of the tailbone. On the surface of the body this appears at the perineum, the space between the sexual organs and the anus. Through imagination, special breathing and visualization methods, special sounds, or through sexual activity, this energy can be roused and sent up the spine, charging the psychic centers, the chakras, as it rises.

Here is where the danger supposedly lies. The energy does not rise smoothly. It stops and charges each chakra. If you are not ready to have a particular chakra charged with energy, if you have not reached the appropriate stage of psychic development, one of two things can happen:

1. The chakra will be charged and the sudden influx of energy will "blow you away," killing you, driving you insane, or, perhaps, enlightening you.

2. The raised energy will have no place to go. Then you are like a filled balloon that is in a state of tension, which cannot pop nor have the air in it released. Something eventually has to give. Remember, Freud said (originally) that

blockages were the cause of all psychological problems. If the kundalini becomes "stuck" at a lower chakra, it could result in a sexual obsession. Trying to raise the kundalini without proper instruction could also create severe physical problems. This is why in order to practice what is called kundalini yoga (which is a new name; its actual name is Laya Yoga), you should first get yourself a good teacher, known as a "guru."*

The ancient Kabalists were also aware of this energy. It is sometimes known in Hebrew as *Ruach* (pronounced "roo-ach," with the "ch" sounding like the German "ach"). It, too, cycles in the psychic centers. In the Kabalah there are five important psychic centers, each relating to a Sephira, and each also relating to a part of the psyche and the body of a human.

The *Yeh-chee-dah* (the "ch" as in the Scottish word "loch") is the psychic center just above the head. It is the deepest level of the subconscious. It is always in contact with the Divine and it is sometimes known as our Higher Self. It relates to that aspect of God represented by the God name *Eh-heh-yeh*.

Ruach, besides being the name of the energy we have been discussing, is also the name of the psychic center at the solar plexus. This is in the center of the torso above the stomach and just below the heart and breast. When this center is fully expanded it includes the heart. It represents our consciousness. Here we discover one of the basic differences between Eastern and Western mystical philosophy. In the East it is believed that our world is composed of nothing but vibrations. Our physical world is an illusion. This illusionary world called "Maya" is what is perceived by our consciousness by means of our senses. Therefore, our consciousness, by only seeing Maya, "slays" the true, inner reality. We are then told to "slay the slayer," eliminate our consciousness via meditation and other techniques. Western occultism, perhaps being more

---

* This is the "standard" story about the kundalini. Just recently I saw a post on an online forum from a person reading, "If this force awakens in an impure or out of balance form it can result in evil genius fanaticism delusions of grandeur, or mental illness (like manic depression and schizophrenia)." In recent years I've come to believe that this type of paranoia is far beyond a misinterpretation and may not be true at all. However, that discussion does not belong in this book and is more appropriate for a book on Tantra.

Regardie Agrees

One of the things about my life for which I feel very blessed is that I have had the good fortune to meet and spend time with some of the truly important people in occultism. One of these people was the late Dr. Francis Israel Regardie (1907–1985). Israel Regardie, who insisted I call him "Francis," was virtually alone in keeping the traditions of the Golden Dawn and Aleister Crowley alive between WWII and the 1960s, when his works were republished by Llewellyn and made available to a new generation.

At the time I met him, Francis lived in Studio City, California. While talking to him one day, I mentioned that I thought Reich's book, *The Function of the Orgasm*, was vitally important for understanding concepts of energy used in magick. Regardie strongly agreed.

It's nice when you're a young dabbler and one of the people you have respected and admired for years agrees with you!

pragmatic than its Eastern counterpart, says, "Let's not slay the slayer, but rather let us *perfect* the slayer so that it no longer only sees illusions." This is the process of developing the Will, which, by your ritual practice, you are now doing. The center relates to the God name *Yud-Heh-Vahv-Heh El-oh-ah V'dah-aht.*

The center known as *Nephesch* is located at the sexual organs. It represents the most superficial layer of our subconscious. It holds our lusts and urges and is capable of blocking the flow of energy between the Yeh-chee-dah and the Ruach. The God name here is *Sha-dai El Chai.*

We can compare these Kabalistic ideas with other types of psychology:

KABALAH	FREUD	TRANSACTIONAL ANALYSIS
Yeh-chee-dah	Superego	Adult
Ruach	Ego	Parent
Nephesch	Id	Child

In the Kabalistic system, there are two other psychic centers that need to be described.

The psychic center located at the feet is known as the *G'uph.* It represents the physical body. When standing, it actually goes above the feet and below

the feet, into the earth or surface below your feet. Its God name is *Ah-doh-nye Ha-ah-retz.*

The center at the base of the throat has no name in Hebrew, but is known as "the link." When activated, this center becomes the self-induced and self-devised link between the higher self (Yeh-chee-dah) and the conscious (Ruach). "The Link" is a good name, as it is a link between the centers above and below it. Its God name, borrowed from another Sephira, is *Yud-Heh-Vahv-Heh El-oh-heem.*

The energy we are going to work with is psychosexual in nature, and can be fully controlled by the mind (more on this in a later lesson). Problems can develop when you try to raise the energy from the sexual center because of the emphasis on the physical, earthy, and sexual nature of the energy. In our system we stress the psychological and spiritual nature of the energy; thus we can work in complete safety and without a guru. In this system we take the energy from our connection with the Divine, at the Yeh-chee-dah, and bring it down the "Middle Pillar" of our body. By the time the energy reaches the powerful sexual center it will have become so purified that, in effect, it spiritualizes the energies that otherwise might only be expressed in a sexual manner.

This does not mean that you will lose any desire for sex, only that when you do have sexual relations you will have a greater, even spiritual experience, and not simply a physical experience. This ritual will make you neither more nor less interested in sex.

The Ritual of the Middle Pillar

STEP ONE. Do the Relaxation Ritual.

STEP TWO. Do the LBRP. When finished, stand behind your altar (if you have one) with your hands at your sides, eyes closed, steady relaxed breathing, and, above all, try to get your mind into a still, quiet, and calm state.

STEP THREE. Focus your attention just above the top of your head. As a result of the LBRP there should be a sphere of white brilliance at this point. If not, visualize it. Take your time. Regard this white brilliance with a sort of awe: it is the spatial equivalent to the vital core of your being, your Higher Self, your link with the Divine. The result of this contemplation should be that the brilliance becomes even brighter. Now vibrate the God name **Eh-heh-yeh** three or four times. The sphere should get brighter still.

STEP FOUR. Now visualize a slender beam of light descending from the brilliance above your head through the center of your head, and stopping at the nape of your neck. Here the beam widens into a ball of light, although not as big as the one above. At this point you should be visualizing simultaneously the brilliant sphere above your head, the small ball of light at the base of your neck, and the beam of light connecting the two. Understand that this is the link between your conscious and your Higher Self, and the ball of light at your neck should grow in size and intensity. Vibrate the God name **Yud-Heh-Vahv-Heh El-oh-heem** three or four times.

STEP FIVE. Keeping the above in mind, cause a beam of light to descend from the ball of light at your neck, go down your torso, and light up the solar plexus in the form of a sphere. Understand that this represents your consciousness, and the ball should increase in brightness and intensity. You may feel as if you are being warmed by an internal sun. Vibrate the God name **Yud-Heh-Vahv-He El-oh-ah V'dah-aht** three or four times.

STEP SIX. In the same manner, see the light descend to the area of the genitals and form a sphere. Here, regard yourself as master of your "lower" self. The God name to be vibrated three or four times is **Shah-dai El Chai**.

STEP SEVEN. Again the light should descend, here to form a sphere which encompasses both feet and the ground; that is, the sphere should be half above the ground, covering the feet, and half below the ground, under the feet. The God name to be vibrated three or four times is **Ah-doh-nye Ha-ahr-etz**.

STEP EIGHT. At this point there should be large spheres of light above the head, at the throat, at the solar plexus, at the groin, and at the feet. Each sphere of light should be connected with the sphere above and below by a beam of light.

STEP NINE. Stay in this state for as long as you desire. Then, take a deep breath and, as you exhale, visualize the images fading and becoming invisible. They are still there, but they cannot now be seen. This completes the Middle Pillar Ritual.

Remember the instructions on vibrating words. Each vibrated word should be done so that you can feel the appropriate area of the body vibrating. If at any point you have trouble or difficulty in forming a sphere of light or a beam of light, do NOT struggle for minutes on end until you break out in a sweat. Rather, stop where you are and complete Step Nine with the progress you have made. Several things could have caused the problem. They are usually mental in nature, either from conscious or unconscious sources. By repeating this ritual daily you will eventually be able to overcome any problem in a very natural, gentle manner. You will be a better, stronger, happier person for it.

STEP TEN. Do the Tarot Contemplation Ritual. If you have been doing the ritual regularly for at least six weeks, you should begin using the all twenty-two cards of the Major Arcana.

STEP ELEVEN. Record results, feelings, experiences, etc., in your ritual diary.

Beware of the Little Nasties!

It is after about two or three months of regular work that some students start to report some unusual phenomena. They may think that they are seeing, hearing, or even feeling strange things! This is *perfectly normal*, and I'd like to explain exactly what's going on.

Without even knowing it, you have been working with what I call the "Astral Senses." The Astral Senses include the ability to see, hear, feel, taste, smell, etc. on the higher planes (the planes will be discussed in a few lessons). Anything that you experience now has always been there—only now, for the first time, you have opened your senses enough so that you can become aware of it.

I first became aware of these things while watching a boring program on T.V. Suddenly, out of nowhere, a large serpent seemed to come out of the floor and descend back into the floor about a foot away from its point of entry! A friend of mine calls these things "astral garbage." I call them "Little Nasties." *They cannot harm you in any way!*

Let me repeat that—the Little Nasties cannot hurt you. They can be bothersome, however. Sometimes I'll think that somebody is looking over my shoulder and I'll spin around to see who it is only to find empty air! One time, while talking to a person at a party—okay, it was a cute woman I was trying to impress—I thought I saw an old friend walk by. I turned away suddenly from the woman I was talking with in order to say hello to . . . a potted plant! When I turned back to the woman I was talking with she gave me a strange look and quickly made an excuse to leave. Oh well, I did say that they could be bothersome. I don't call them "Little Nasties" for nothing.

Other people have told me of seeing friends who weren't there, as I did, and others have heard voices calling them. Some people see bright, sparkly spots floating through the air. Perhaps even without training you have heard someone call your name, only no one did so. At that time, for a moment, your astral hearing was open enough to hear one of those Little Nasties.

Not everyone experiences these critters. You may never see, hear, or experience them in any way. While opening the astral senses is important, you may never be contacted by the Little Nasties and still become a very successful magician. If you have seen them, or do see them in the future, don't worry. It's not a psychic attack, and you are not going crazy. And they can't hurt you.

In fact, if you have the right attitude about Little Nasties, they can be sort of fun, especially at a boring party. In any event, don't be surprised if these guys bring a little silliness, fun, and, at times, exasperation into your life.

In all honesty, I am not really sure what they are. In some cases they seem to be what are called "elementals" (more on them in another lesson). In other cases, because you are working via visualization on the astral plane, you may, like a weird cosmic magnet, just be attracting meaningless astral junk. Little Nasties are not evil entities. Many children have "invisible playmates," and I believe that in many instances these are Little Nasties.

You will find a summary of the Middle Pillar Ritual on the next page. You may want to spend a month or longer mastering the information and ritual techniques of this lesson before moving to Lesson Three.

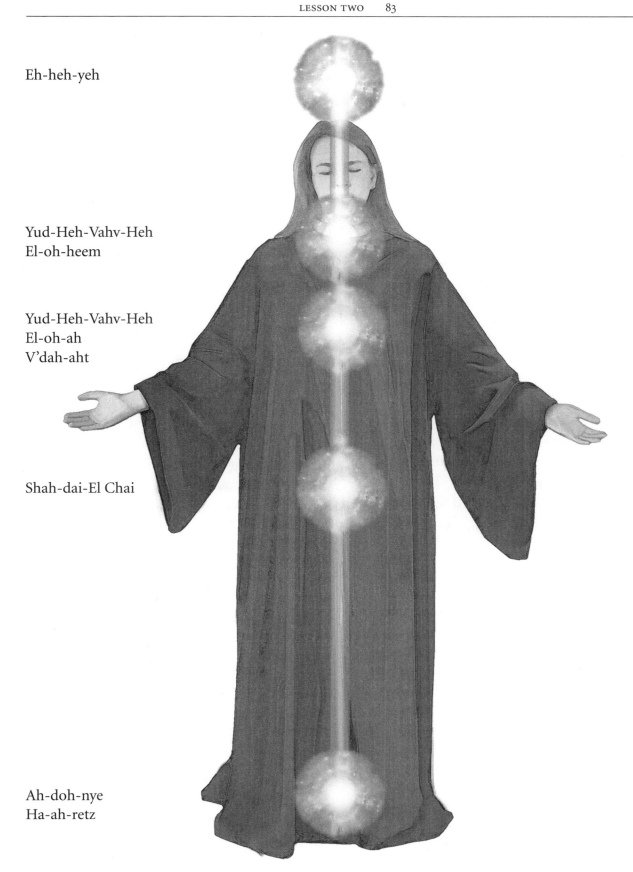

Eh-heh-yeh

Yud-Heh-Vahv-Heh
El-oh-heem

Yud-Heh-Vahv-Heh
El-oh-ah
V'dah-aht

Shah-dai-El Chai

Ah-doh-nye
Ha-ah-retz

The Middle Pillar Ritual

Review

The following questions are designed to help you determine if you have mastered the information in Lesson Two. Please try to answer them without looking at the text. The answers are in Appendix Two.

1. Name the four parts of the LBRP.

2. What do the Hebrew words of the Kabalistic Cross mean?

3. What is AGLA an abbreviation for?

4. Who is the Archangel of the north?

5. What is the "Great Voice"?

6. Why is it false to say that Kabalists have ten gods?

7. How do you make the sign of the element Water?

8. What are the three "literatures" of the ancient Hebrews?

9. What's wrong with using "Jehovah" as the name of God?

10. Name the man who made Hebrew into a modern, living language.

11. How do you "vibrate" words?

12. In what ways has the Hebrew letter Vahv been pronounced?

13. What was the earliest form of Hebrew mysticism?

14. Who started the French occult revival?

15. What are the four main branches of the Kabalah?

16. What are three signs that indicate a potentially good spiritual teacher?

17. How do you say "Without limit" in Hebrew?

18. What are the "Little Nasties"?

The following questions only you can answer.

1. Are you doing all of the rituals (Relaxation, LBRP, Middle Pillar, Tarot Contemplation) regularly?

2. Do you understand Kabalistic psychology?

3. Do you have a beginning understanding of the Kabalah and the Tree of Life?

4. Do you understand the idea of the Thesis-Antithesis-Synthesis Theory?

5. Have you ever been bothered by Little Nasties?

6. Do you understand the concept of "backing into" the Tree of Life?

7. Are you anxious to do some Practical and Grey Magick, or are you learning patiently?

8. What effects, if any, have you experienced from vibrating words?

9. Have you ever read something, not understood it, but when you came back to it, weeks or months later, discovered that it made perfect sense?

10. Have you been able to answer the questions of these first two lessons without going back through the text?

Bibliography

For more information on these books, please see the annotated bibliography at the end of these lessons.

Andrews, Ted. *Simplified Qabala Magic.* Llewellyn, 2003.

Crowley, Aleister. *Magick.* Weiser, 1998.

González-Wippler, Migene. *A Kabbalah for the Modern World.* Llewellyn, 2002.

Kaplan, Aryeh. *The Bahir.* Red Wheel/Weiser 1980.

———. *Sefer Yetzirah.* Weiser 1997.

King, Francis, and Stephen Skinner. *Techniques of High Magic.* Destiny Books, 2000.

Mathers, S. L. M. *The Kabbalah Unveiled.* Kessinger, 2007.

Regardie, Israel. *Ceremonial Magic.* Aeon, 2004.

———. *Foundations of Practical Magic.* Aeon, 2004.

———. *A Garden of Pomegranates.* Llewellyn, 1995.

———. *The Golden Dawn.* Llewellyn, 2002.

———. *The Middle Pillar.* Llewellyn, 2002.

———. *The One Year Manual.* Red Wheel/Weiser, 2007.

Sperling, Harry, Maurice Simon, and Paul Levertoff (translators). *The Zohar* (5 volumes). Soincino, 1984.

LESSON THREE

Prefatory Comments:

Reflection

We all read lots of things, from novels and magazines to advertisements, text messages, and "graphic novels" (what used to be called comic books). Most of these things are similar in that they're meant to impart information, and, in most cases, we forget the specifics about them. They're transient or short term at best. If you've been out of school for a few years, do you really remember everything from your textbooks? If you work for others, do you really remember everything from what was in that report you read last year?

Modern Magick was specifically designed to be different. That's why each section is called a "lesson" instead of a "chapter." Although you may choose to read it like other reading material, it's my hope that you will treat it as something special, a guide that can, quite literally, change the way you approach the rest of your life.

If you're willing to try it this way, I urge you to do two things before beginning a new lesson. First, reflect on what you've learned so far. Think about it: already you've learned a great deal about me, about keeping a dream diary, how to interpret dreams, how to keep a ritual diary, the history of the Tarot and how to choose a Tarot deck for use with this course, the Tarot Contemplation Ritual, the Relaxation Ritual, definitions of magick, divinatory meanings of the Major Arcana and how to do a Tarot reading, how to prepare for a ritual, the "weapons" or tools of a magician, how to draw an Earth Banishing Pentagram, how to take a Ritual Cleansing Bath, how to perform all the steps of the Lesser Banishing Ritual of the Pentagram, how to deal with psychic attack, how to perform the Four Solar Adorations, the mythological history of the Kabalah, a more factual history of the Kabalah, the four branches of Kabalah, the relation of Freud and Reich to magick, the Kabalistic power centers, the Middle Pillar Ritual, the effect of "Little Nasties," and much, much more. *You have done an incredible amount of learning and work and deserve recognition for this!* So reflect on all you've learned and practiced over the last eight weeks. You might even want to write down how your life has improved from this amount of work.

Once you've reflected on what you've learned and done, there is something else to do. This is very important for your future development and success: *Feel great about your accomplishments!* Over a mere eight weeks you have learned and practiced more real traditional Western ceremonial magick than 99 percent of the people in the world will ever do. You should feel good about what you've done. And you've done all this without parents or governments or employers forcing you to do this. You're what's called "self-actualized." You're amazing and should be proud.

I know, in the West we're trained not to feel pride. But I remember a statement from Aleister Crowley, who wrote, "An ounce of honest pride is better than a ton of false humility." Be proud of your true accomplishments. However, that doesn't mean you should become egotistical. I still remember my martial arts instructor, Sifu Douglas Wong, saying, "No matter how good you are, there is always someone better." So while you should be proud of your accomplishments, you can still be modest. Crowley continued his quotation by adding "an ounce of true humility is worth an ounce of honest pride." Eventually, when magick becomes a part of every moment of your life, you won't need feelings of pride to support you.

So revel in the feeling of your accomplishment, but don't stay there. Instead, use your reflections and feelings of pride in accomplishment as spurs to urge you to continue and to learn and practice more. Then forget about the pride and humility and move on. The third part of Crowley's quotation is "the man who works has no time to bother with either [pride or humility]."

PART ONE

Have you ever heard of a "Sunday Morning Christian"? A Sunday Morning Christian is a person who goes to church every Sunday (to be seen), sings very loudly (to be heard), and puts large bills in the collection plate. Then, in business, he does everything possible to steal and cheat. He lies about his friends

and enemies and he cheats on his wife. Yes, he puts on a big show of being a Christian for a few hours every Sunday, but when it comes to living every minute of the day after the manner of Jesus, what the Catholic Monk Thomas à Kempis (c.1380–1471) called "the Imitation of Christ," he fails miserably.

So what does this have to do with ceremonial magick? Like the Sunday Morning Christians who think that Christianity is something you do once a week, most people think that magick is something you do occasionally. This is totally wrong.

**Magick is *not* something you *do.*
Magick is something you are!**

I cannot stress this enough. To really be a magician means that your mindset is totally centered on magick. This means that no matter what you are doing, thinking, or saying, there is always in your mind the idea of how everything is related magickally. Thus, if you are talking politics, you might be thinking about how a politician is able to convince people to vote for him or her without ever mentioning a political platform. Certainly convincing people to do things for no apparent reason is a powerful form of magick. When you are cooking you might think about how the element of fire affects meats and their byproducts, as well as the changes fire makes to fruits, grains, and vegetables. When magick becomes your way of thinking, acting, and breathing, then, and only then, will you be a true magician.

This brings us back, for a moment, to the Hermetic Order of the Golden Dawn. There were really six degrees in the Golden Dawn, which, if you did well, would allow you to seek entrance into the inner order, commonly known as the R.R. *et* A.C. If you have studied a bit about the Golden Dawn, this may shock you: *The Golden Dawn was never a magickal order.* The inner order, with initials standing for the Latin phrase *Roseae Rubeae et Aureae Crucis* (Red Rose and Gold Cross) was where members did practice practical magick. The outer order, the Golden Dawn, did not.

The Golden Dawn did have several purposes in the order's overall scheme. It allowed people to meet and learn to have confidence in each other. It allowed people to learn the theories and philosophies that would later allow them to do practical magick. But for the purpose of this course, the most important aspects are that it initiated people and got them attuned to the four magickal elements.

Obviously, I cannot initiate you via a book. No one can (and I would highly question the notion of "astral initiation" offered by some organizations for Western traditions). But what is the need and purpose of initiation, anyway?

Initiation has two aspects: practical and mystical. On a practical level, initiation gives you nothing. Rather, it allows you to *begin* to follow a certain prescribed system of mystical and/or magickal work. As an example, a person initiated into the Neophyte degree of the Golden Dawn was to begin learning the Hebrew alphabet, the symbols of the planets and the zodiac, and he or she was also to begin doing the LBRP. The word "initiation" comes from a Latin root that means "to begin."

The mystical aspects of initiation are a different story. Imagine a private club that you want to enter. You knock on the door and the bouncer, who doesn't recognize you because you're not on the list of people allowed in, sends you away. Then, a person who knows both you and the bouncer comes up and introduces you to each other. From that time on you are a welcome guest in the private club. In this little story, the introduction to a higher, stronger force in the form of a bouncer, was your initiation. In reality, the mystical aspects of initiation not only introduce you to higher powers (or, if you prefer, your Higher Self), but also cause spiritual, emotional, and *physical* effects within you, which allow you to be easily recognized in the future by the higher powers.

There is another way to cause the inner changes that allow this recognition. You could go up to the bouncer day after day, week after week, and month after month if need be, talk to the bouncer and bring him presents and friendship until finally, without a third-party introduction, the bouncer allows you into the club. The way that this can be done is through faithfully performing the three keys to succeeding with the work of this course: practice, practice, practice.

In the Golden Dawn, an initiation into the Neophyte grade gave you membership, companionship with others of a like mind, and allowed both you and the other members of the order to see how well you could work together. Since by working your way through the lessons in this book you are not becoming a member of any order, that particular initiation is not vital to your advancement. The next four grades of the Golden Dawn attempted to get you in balance with the four magickal elements and, in fact, were sometimes referred to as the "elementary" or "elemental" grades. We will be learning about the magickal elements Earth, Air, Fire, and Water, one at a time and in their proper order.

The Neophyte grade of the Golden Dawn was not related to the elements. In fact, it was not considered to be the first degree of the order at all. It was called the 0=0 Grade. The next degree, known as the first degree or 1=10 (first degree equals the tenth Sephira) was associated with the element of Earth, so it is there we must now begin. We must become in total harmony with this element.

The Earth Element

Each of the four magickal elements are representative of alternate aspects of the qualities of temperature and moisture or humidity. Since in this lesson we are working with the element of Earth, let's examine its qualities. Obviously, Earth is not wet. Nor is it warm (except when infused with the element of Fire as seen in lava). Therefore, we can say that *the element Earth has the qualities of being dry and cool.*

The next step is to learn how to become aware of and in control of this element in our day-to-day life.

Exercise 1. Make a list of things that have the combined qualities of dryness and coolness. However, don't do this just out of your head. Rather, make a list of Earth things that you see each day.

Practice this for one week. Be sure to record the results each day in your magickal diary.

Exercise 2. Find a place filled with nature, such as a field or park. Wear as little clothing as you legally can (if possible, nudity is best, but do not break any laws), and sit or lie on the ground so that as much of your skin as possible is touching the ground. This is especially easy for someone wearing a flowing skirt (or kilt) with no underwear and then sitting on the ground with the fabric spread out. In this way there is nothing between the skin and the Earth. Spend some time contemplating, feeling the coolness and dryness of the Earth. You should do this at least three times within a week.

If you happen to find a grassy spot, or an area which has recently been watered, you may have a feeling that the magickal element of Earth has wetness in it. There are two responses to this. First, temperature and humidity are relative. It may be damp compared to desert sand, but it is dry compared to ocean water. Congratulations! This shows that you are thinking about the elements. However, the real answer to the idea that Earth has some wetness to it is that you are mistaking the physical soil for the magickal *archetypal* element Earth. A physical representation always lacks the purity of the archetype. Since we are physical and learn through our senses, we move in our minds from the physical imperfect object to the pure archetype. It is in this way we gain knowledge of the magickal elements.

Exercise 3. Spend a period of up to three minutes (no more), once a day, *imagining that you are the element Earth.* Feel the heaviness, the slowness, the coolness, and the dryness of pure elemental Earth. Feel the way you could absorb the pains and problems of the world (however, do *not* actually do so). Become Earth. Do this exercise daily for at least a week before moving to the next exercise.

Exercise 4. Once you have learned to "be Earth," the next step is to control elemental Earth. Take a moment and imagine yourself to be Earth. Bring the feeling from the previous exercise into your consciousness. Next, hold your hands nine to twelve inches apart, palms facing each other. Imagine a bottle or box between your hands. Now, as you exhale, visualize all of the Earth element that is in you going out with your breath and into the container between your hands. Three to five breaths should be enough to fill it. Then, with three breaths, inhale it back into you and go back to normal consciousness.

The Test. This will allow you to see whether or not you really have become in harmony with the magickal element Earth and also to see if you are able to control the element.

The next time that you feel lightheaded, giddy, unstable, not able to do your work, etc., form the container of Earth as described in Exercise 4. Then, once the container of Earth has been formed, with one big inhalation, draw the contents of the container back into you. Within five minutes you should feel stable and grounded.

The next time that you feel bloated, overweight, slowed down, etc., again form the container of Earth; only this time, visualize a large hole in the ground and drop the container into that hole. In your mind's eye, quickly see the hole close around the container. You should feel lighter in a few minutes, but it may be necessary to repeat this exercise up to five times to really feel light (but not like an "airhead") and energetic.

When you have succeeded at both parts of this test—increasing and decreasing the amount of elemental Earth within you—you will have mastered the element of Earth. However, if you do not succeed at it within a few days or weeks, don't worry about it. Just keep practicing. Remember, initiation is a *beginning*, not an end. Continue with your studies in this course. Do not stop and wait until you perfect your mastery of the element. If you continue your exercises, it *will* happen. Be sure to record the results of your experiments, whether they are good, bad, or indifferent, in your magick diary.

PART TWO

Before starting this part of this lesson, go back and reread the sections on the Kabalah in the previous lesson. As you are noticing by now, I am stressing

Boy, Was He Ticked Off!

There is a scene in the classic movie *A Christmas Story* where the main character, Ralphie, after weeks of anxious waiting, finally gets his precious Little Orphan Annie decoder ring in the mail. He dutifully records a secret message from the radio program and goes into the only place with privacy, the bathroom (much to the consternation of his desperate family), to decode what he thought must be a vitally important message using the ring. Slowly he translates the message, only to discover that the important secret communiqué from the radio was just an advertisement. Ralphie's combination of anger, disappointment, and frustration can be described in two words: he was "ticked off."

Back in the late nineteenth century, Aleister Crowley finally achieved his first initiation into what he thought was a true magickal group, the Hermetic Order of the Golden Dawn. As part of the initiation he was sworn to oaths that promised a horrible, dire fate if he ever gave away the order's secrets. And what were those secrets? The Hebrew alphabet and the astrological zodiac. *Whaaat?* Was that it? Crowley was ticked off.

In fact, from a superficial understanding of these things, he *should* have been ticked off. But, at least at that time, he missed the real secret: the Hebrew alphabet and astrology were interrelated and linked to magick. That information is commonplace among occultists today, but it was not known except in small magickal circles in the late 1800s. His initation also provided him with the opportunity to meet, communicate with, and practice ritual with some of the finest occultists of the Victorian age.

Perhaps he shouldn't have been ticked off at all.

going over previously presented material. One of the reasons for this is that the information and techniques presented in this course are *cumulative*. New information, techniques, and rituals are based on what appeared in earlier lessons. If you don't have the techniques down pat and don't have the previous information "under your belt" and understood, you may not be able to properly perform new rituals or understand new material. In order to help overcome this problem, you may notice that some important points and concepts are repeated. This is done on purpose to stress that information, not to make this course longer. For me, the most important part of this course is that you are able to use the lessons.

There is another interesting phenomenon I've noticed that is especially valuable if some material didn't quite make sense when you originally studied it. If you have not read that information for a while,

you may be surprised to discover that the material now makes more sense to you than it did during your earlier readings. I have a theory about this.

Have you ever noticed how, when typing on a computer, the cursor sometimes "hangs" for a few seconds? If you continue typing, the computer eventually catches up and the words you typed rapidly appear on the screen. This is because the computer has to do some processing in some way and puts the work of displaying what you've typed on hold. I think the mind may function in a similar way. The first time you study something it may not make sense, but after the mind has had time to "process" the information, it becomes clear. Your mind has had the time to digest the information subconsciously and intuitively come to an understanding of what was previously described. This is another reason to periodically review all of the lessons in this course.

The Map Is *Not* the Territory

One of the constant difficulties faced by aspiring magicians is mistaking a map for the territory. Obviously if you are traveling across the country, you are not going to mistake a map for the actual roads on which you are driving. Besides, it might actually be easier to fold up some roads than it is to fold up a map!

However, descriptions of the way the universe and various aspects of the universe function are also nothing more than maps. They guide us through the territory and may give us a way to understand it, but they are not the territory themselves. We frequently talk about multiple "planes" of existence, but these planes are not separate locations. The concept merely gives us an easier way to understand and work with the reality. Or, how about this: we each only have one mind. We may talk about the conscious and unconscious minds, the id, ego, and superconscious of Freud or the parent, child, and adult of transactional analysis, but they are only ways of understanding and working with the mind; they are not the mind itself.

Usually, if we think of roads, the map is something less physical—an easily destroyable piece of paper. In the case of Exercise 2, however, the physical world is a map, just a representation of the real essence of elemental Earth. Physical soil or earth is a map of archetypal elemental Earth. They are not the same. The map—the physical earth—is a limited representation of the territory—archetypal elemental Earth. It may give you a limited idea of the territory, but it is not the territory and should not be confused with the actual territory.

We are going to be looking again at that central glyph of the Kabalah, the Tree of Life. There are many ways to study the Tree, and in this part of the lesson we are going to look at a few of the ways to analyze the symbol.

The Three Pillars

Look at the image of Tree of Life on the next page. The figure has been divided into three large pillars. The pillar on the left is composed of the 3rd, 5th, and 8th Sephiroht, and is known as the "Pillar of Severity." On the right, the pillar is composed of the 2nd, 4th, and 7th Sephiroht. Being opposite of the pillar on the left, the one on the right is known as the "Pillar of Mercy." Balancing the two outer pillars is the Middle Pillar. It is composed of the 1st, 6th, 9th, and 10th Sephiroht, and is also known as the "Pillar of Mildness."

It is interesting to note that the Pillar of Severity, on the left, is considered to be female while the Pillar of Mercy is considered to be masculine; a reversal of what might be considered an archetypal norm. However, if you study Jungian theories of archetypes, you will find that just as there is the kind, helping, beneficial "Great Mother," so, too, is there the feminine element that works against you, known as the "Terrible Mother." See, for example, myths of evil older women (the Witch in "Hansel and Gretel"), and deceptive and powerful younger ones (Circe in *The Odyssey*). As mentioned earlier, there appear to be some links between the Kabalah and the source of Indian Tantra, what I refer to as proto-Tantra. One of the most powerful Tantric images is that of the goddess Kali. She is viewed as strong and powerful, even violent and terrifying. But she is also kindly and loving—Kali Ma (mother Kali). Further, in Tantra, there is the view that archetypal female power is outgoing, electric, and stimulating while archetypal male power is receptive, magnetic, and calming. Female is force, male is form. The Kabalah seems to agree with

Pillar of
Mildness

Pillar of
Severity

Pillar of
Mercy

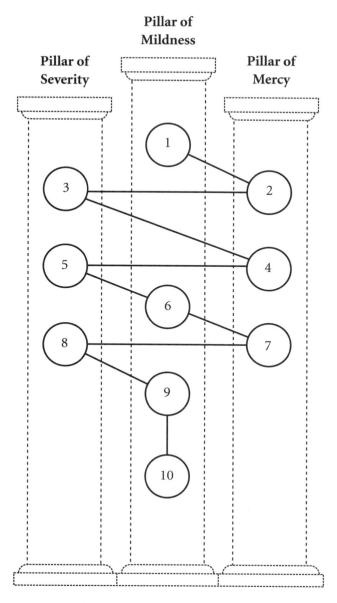

Tree of Life: The Three Pillars

actions and realize that Victory (7th Sephira) can come about through Wisdom and the ability to endure. We can show Mercy (4th Sephira) instead of a short temper, and achieve a desired Victory not through strength alone.

Think about this in terms of wars. No war was ever decided on the battlefield unless the enemy was completely obliterated. Battles bring people to the bargaining table and then the politicians determine the way to victory. If the peace agreements are wise, future wars can be eliminated and in time foes can become allies. See, for example, the peace agreements between Japan and the U.S. after World War II. If the peace agreements are not wise, future wars are inevitable. This happened to Germany after World War I when the victorious "Triple Entente" powers demanded enormous reparations from the losing Germany, partially causing the destruction of Germany's economy and allowing the country to be taken over by Hitler and the Nazi party.

The Pillar of Severity. To be severe, we must have an Understanding (3rd Sephira) of the laws of the universe and the Strength (5th Sephira) to empower them justly, but never yielding to giving mercy, only justice. This will result in an outward display of power and Splendor (8th Sephira) that hides the lack of humanity and mercy residing beneath the surface.

A person on this pillar is filled with what is called, in German, *Schadenfreude*, which is the taking of delight in the suffering of another. It's not enough to be victorious, but you have to gloat at the failure or suffering of others. There's no equivalent word in English. The closest concept I know of is the idea of being a "bad winner." Unfortunately, many people live with this philosophy: it's not enough for me to win, but I also have to see you in a state of misery. The problem with this attitude, of course, is that eventually, someone who is bigger and meaner than you will come around, and you will be that person's victim.

The Pillar of Mildness. To be mild, we must realize that we live in the Kingdom (10th Sephira) of Earth and we are not gods. Therefore, in whatever

this concept in some ways, such as in relation to the Three Pillars, but not in all situations. Be aware that both potentials are there.

The next image is another version of the Tree of Life. On it, each Sephira has its name both in transliterated Hebrew and the English translation of the Hebrew. Compare the two versions of the Tree of Life and follow along as the meanings of the Pillars are described.

The Pillar of Mercy. To be merciful, we must have the Wisdom (2nd Sephira) to see the results of our

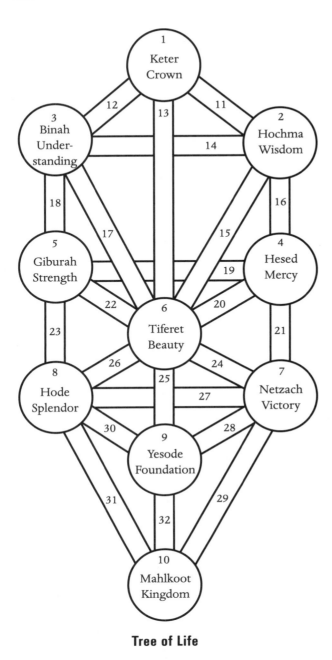

Tree of Life

sary. Sometimes we need to be severe, for it would be foolish to be weak in the face of evil. At other times it may just be foolish to get upset over minor issues, and it is wiser to let them go. At the end of the day, however, finding oneself approaching the world from the vantage point of the Middle Pillar brings the greatest and longest-lasting rewards to our world, our personal kingdom.

So this, then, is one way to understand the Tree of Life, the system of the Three Pillars. If we are not successful in our efforts toward achieving any particular goal, we can see where we are unbalanced, i.e., focused toward one side of the Tree. We can then seek to add some of the balancing characteristics from the opposite side of the Tree. The result moves us to the center, toward the Pillar of Mildness, which could also be called the Pillar of True Manifestation.

The Three Triangles

The next system of looking at the Tree is known as the Three Triangles. As can be seen from the diagram on the next page, the Tree of Life can be divided into three triangles, the top one pointing upward and the other two pointing downward.

The Celestial Triangle. The uppermost triangle, composed of the first three Sephiroht, is known as the Celestial Triangle. It starts at a single point, which means that it comes from the unity of God and divides into two sides. This shows that although Divinity is a unity, everything which manifests can be seen in the form of a duality: male and female, up and down, in and out, hot and cold, magnetic and electric, force and form, etc. It is one of the duties of a magician to learn to overcome everything that seems to be in opposition in order to achieve unity with Divinity. (This is an ancient secret of the Kabalah and is understood by Tantrics. It will be discussed in a later lesson.) As an example, the magician must learn that day is not opposite to night, but rather both day and night are a natural part of the Earth's spinning on its axis. Also, it is in this uppermost triangle that we can see those qualities of beings who are truly celestial in nature. They have Wisdom and Understanding. Thus, they are capable of wearing the Crown of cre-

we strive for we must seek a Foundation (9th Sephirah) of Beauty (6th Sephira) by trying to avoid the extremes of overseverity and too much mercy. In this way we can seek to Crown (1st Sephira) our efforts with success.

Some people mistakenly think that we need to always be on the Middle Pillar. Unfortunately, this is not always possible. The entire Tree of Life, as a model for approaching the world, shows that we need to be able to tap into any of the pillars when neces-

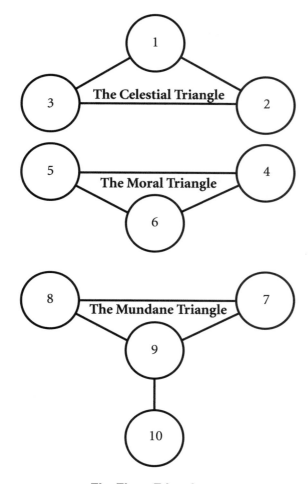

The Three Triangles

hand, if we show only strength and are totally unmerciful, we might be able to achieve our goals (although never without difficulty), but we will have no friends, have no real love, and our "success" becomes meaningless. By developing Strength *and* Mercy we exhibit a Beauty that aids us in achieving all of our goals, and gives us happiness in what we do achieve. Thus, the sides of this triangle should guide us and form what is called the "moral compass."

The Mundane Triangle. The lowest triangle is called the Mundane Triangle. It is an apt name. It concerns physical plane successes only, not mental and spiritual ones as are found in the Moral and Celestial triangles. Here, a Victory followed by too much Mercy leads to defeat, while the Splendor of a Victory, if not tempered with Mercy, leads to revolution and ruin. When balanced, a Foun-

ation and rule both the visible, physical world, and the higher planes of existence.

It should also be noted that from the single point of the Divine, there is an even division to the two sides of this triangle, male and female. It is evenly balanced. Some have claimed that the Kabalah is sexist. I would deny this completely. The Kabalah is definitely not sexist, although some Kabalists and Kabalistic writers, often reflecting their time and environment more than the Kabalah, definitely present sexist ideas. That should be seen as a reflection on them, not on the Kabalah.

The Moral Triangle. The central triangle which points down is called the Moral Triangle. A combination of Strength and Mercy results in the development of Beauty. If we have too much mercy, we become weak and unable to complete our goals. People take advantage of us, and we die young. On the other

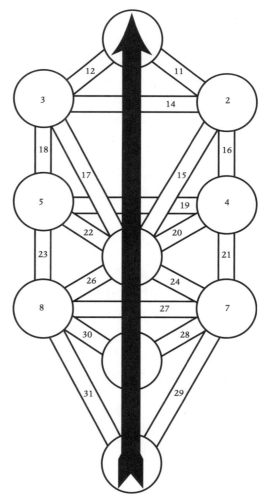

The Path of the Arrow

dation for success in this world exists and a Kingdom, as represented by the one Sephira hanging pendant to the Three Triangles, may be founded.

As you can see, each system of understanding the Tree of Life helps to explain the other systems. Go back for a second and look at the diagram of the Three Pillars. We can say that the path of a mystic or Yogi, whose intent it is to rejoin with the Divine (at Keter, the 1st Sephira), follows the Middle Pillar. This path, sometimes known as the "Path of the Arrow," as shown on the previous page, is like the path an arrow flies if pointed straight up from Mahlkoot to Keter. The yogi sits in meditation until he or she can simply "hop" from the lowest to the highest.

From reading the previous sections, you should be able to understand how a magician needs full access to all of the Sephiroht of the Tree, not just the middle pillar. A magician follows a path that can take him or her from Sephira to Sephira, going through and learning about each one while also covering each of the connecting twenty-two paths, winding about like a snake. In fact, the path of the magician is sometimes known as the *Path of the Serpent*. At each Sephira, on each of the connecting paths, the magician learns new things and has new and exciting experiences, which the mystic or yogi will never know. The yogi merely sits in meditation until ready to make the jump to the top of the Tree. The magician takes a more circuitous route. Each can achieve the goal of unity with Divinity—White Magick—in the same amount of time. It is their own determination and abilities that speed or delay the coming of unity, of Nirvana, of the ultimate mystical ecstasy ceremonial magicians refer to as obtaining "the Knowledge and Conversation of Your Holy Guardian Angel."

I like to use an understanding of the Three Triangles as a basis for psychology. By understanding which Sephira a person is "at," I can recommend what the person needs to do for improvement. If, for example, a person always finds himself or herself being taken advantage of, I believe that person to be "in" the Sephira Hesed, number 4, Mercy. That person needs to develop more inner strength, strength enough to say "No!" to someone who is trying to take advantage of him or her. Then, instead of being the person everyone thinks of as being a sucker, people will be able to learn for the first time what he or she thinks about, cares about, and wants to do. They will see this person for the beautiful entity that person is.

Beware, again, of mistaking the map for the territory. What I described here is only a representation. Nobody is ever psychologically "in" a Sephira. This just provides a model that can help in obtaining one of the most powerful forms of magick in the world: personal change.

The Four Worlds

Another method of looking at the Tree is called the method of the Four Worlds. Look at the diagram on the next page showing one of the systems of understanding the Four Worlds. Dividing lines have been drawn between the triangles, as previously described. Thus, each triangle and the single tenth Sephira represents a "World."

The topmost triangle, composed of the 1st, 2nd, and 3rd Sephiroht, is known as Ha-oh-lam Atziloot, which means the World of Archetypes, or Emanations. It is the Divine world wherein exist the thoughts of God. It is in this world that the aspects of the powers of God, as represented by the Names of God, are said to exist.

The middle triangle, composed of the 4th, 5th, and 6th Sephiroht, is known as Ha-oh-lahm B'riyah, which means the World of Creation. It is not yet real in a physical sense; it is far more of the conscious mind. It is in this world that the archangels are said to exist.

The bottommost triangle is formed of the 7th, 8th, and 9th Sephiroht and is known as Ha-oh-lahm Yetzirah, or the World of Formation. It is considered by some to be equal to the astral plane, which is the basis for everything that exists in the physical universe. It is in this world that the various "orders" of angels are said to exist.

The 10th Sephira in this system all by itself forms Ha-oh-lahm Ahssiah, the World of Action. It is the

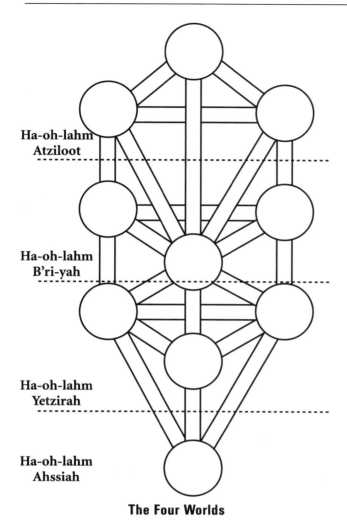

Ha-oh-lahm
Atziloot

Ha-oh-lahm
B'ri-yah

Ha-oh-lahm
Yetzirah

Ha-oh-lahm
Ahssiah

The Four Worlds

world wherein the four elements, and hence the physical universe, exist and wherein physical action can occur.

But what good does this Four Worlds system do? Let us assume that God wishes to create a universe. The first thing God would need to do is perceive the need for something. Here God is operating in the world of Atziloot. Next, God would see that a universe composed of Air, Earth, Fire, Water, and living things was necessary. Here God would be operating in the world of B'ri-yah. Next God would begin doing whatever was necessary to create the universe. Here God would be operating in the world of Yetzirah. Finally, God would put life and action into the formed parts of the universe, and would be operating in the world of Ahssiah.

But this course is about practical magick. How does this information apply to us and how can we use it on a practical level? Let us say that you need something to hold your papers and notes when doing a ritual. You see a need, and therefore are in the world of Atziloot. Next, you begin to visualize it. It is made of wood, higher in the back than in the front so that the papers are at a nice angle, and there is a ledge at the bottom of the front so that the papers do not slide off. A battery-powered light illuminates the papers. Here you are in the world of B'ri-yah as you "create" the stand in your mind. Now you go out and buy the wood, cut it to size, assemble the stand, and finish it with an attractive and appropriate paint job. Here you are in the world of Formation, Ha-oh-lahm Yetzirah. Finally, you put it to use, and you are then operating in the world of Ahssiah. *If you have ever desired anything but have not been able to bring it into your own world, then it is most likely that you have overlooked the importance of one of the Four Worlds.* We will learn more about the process of bringing things into our lives (Grey Magick) in later lessons.

As stated earlier, the Kabalah has changed over time and has not been a static, unchanging system. There are other versions of the Four Worlds. One system holds that the divisions of the Four Worlds should show only the topmost Sephira, Keter, as being in the first World. The next two Sephiroht are in the second World. Sephiroht four through nine make up the third World of Yetzirah, and the fourth World is made up only of the final Sephira, Mahl-koot.

Another system holds that there is a full Tree of Life within each Sephira on the Tree of Life! Thus, there would be 100 Sephiroht to deal with. You could have Keter in Keter, Hochma in Keter, and up to ten different Sephiroht in each Sephira. With this system the Worlds get quite complicated.

Yet another system puts four Trees of Life on top of each other, with each Tree representing a world (see the diagram on the next page). In this system there are forty Sephiroht. Finally, another system says that there is a full Tree of Life within

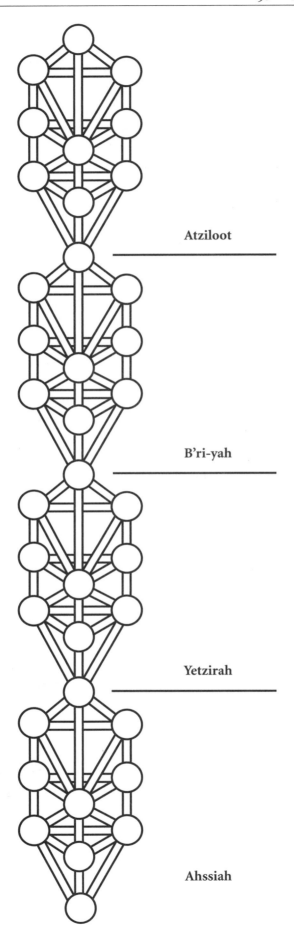

Atziloot

B'ri-yah

Yetzirah

Ahssiah

each of the 40 Sephiroht for a total of 400 Sephiroht! Although going into detail on the meaning of this last system is far too advanced and complicated for this course, you might wish to spend some time contemplating the different Worlds and the various ideas of Trees of Life within the Sephiroht.

PART THREE

The Secrets of True Meditation

This section is a very special part of this course. What this part of the lesson consists of is simple, safe, and practical information on what meditation is and on how to meditate. Although you are encouraged to meditate on a daily basis as a necessary part of your own spiritual development, you are free to practice the technique given here as you will. It is not part of your suggested daily ritual practice. I do strongly suggest, however, that you either make time to practice it daily for at least several months, or just include it as part of your daily ritual.

In recent years there has been quite a furor concerning how to meditate and the benefits you can obtain from the practice of meditation. Recently, I saw a show on TV where two sleight-of-hand magicians tried to debunk the value of meditation. That's sort of like hiring a garbage collector to prove that brain surgery is useless! That show was a sad embarrassment.

There have been many books that have seen print over the last twenty-five years or so with titles such as *How to Meditate* or *One Hundred and One Ways to Meditate* or *Meditation for Idiots* or something similar. They wouldn't have been published if there was no interest in meditation. Most of these books have good points and bad points, beginning with trying to define exactly what meditation is. Without a definition of what meditation is, you can hardly be taught how to do it!

One group of authors tried to equate meditation with contemplation or concentration. This is probably because (a) their teachers didn't know any better, (b) they don't know any better, or (c) they simply looked up the meaning of the word "meditation" in a dictionary.

Most English dictionaries will define meditation as some form of contemplation. The two words are seemingly almost synonyms. Thus, those teachers who equate meditation with contemplation would have you simply look at an object, listen to a sound, or contemplate a thought and call it meditation. It is not.

Meditation as it really exists is derived from an Eastern idea based not on contemplation, but silence—the silence of the mind. In his book *Meditation and the Bible*, Aryeh Kaplan clearly shows that techniques used by the ancient Hebrew mystics and prophets were similar to those of the ancient Indian mystics. Unfortunately, most of the ancient Hebrew techniques have been lost along with the writings of the Merkabah mystics. But here is the basic theory behind meditation:

> *Try for a second to rid your mind of all thought, to make it perfectly quiet. Unless you know what real meditation is and have practiced it, it is inevitable that you will fail at this seemingly simple request. A voice will run through your head saying such things as "There, I'm quiet now," or "Am I doing this right?" or "How long do I have to keep this up?"*

**In true meditation
the goal is to silence the inner voice.**

In another lesson we will learn that our unconscious (in this course the term "unconscious" is synonymous with "subconscious") is our direct link to Divinity, to God. Since, by definition, God must be all knowledgeable (otherwise something else could be greater than God; if there is something greater than God, then that greater Thing must be the true God and what we have been calling God is only a false God or subordinate deity), our unconscious must have a link to all knowledge, to the secret wisdom of the universe, to enlightenment.

But that little voice which constantly is speaking in our head usually shuts out the even smaller voice of our unconscious mind. One of the things that can occur in our dreams is that our unconscious speaks to us through symbols which are sometimes difficult to understand. In true meditation our unconscious can speak to our conscious directly, sharing its wisdom.

What follows is a method for true meditation. There are other well-publicized schools of meditation that charge over a hundred dollars to teach you a technique for meditation. According to their website, the current cost to learn basic Transcendental Meditation is $2,000.00 US, and they have more advanced courses that cost more. There is nothing wrong with these courses and some of them are very good. Unfortunately, some of these schools brag about how their techniques result in lowered blood pressure and increased IQs. This bragging is absurd. Any form of relaxation (such as the Relaxation Ritual) will result in lowered blood pressure. Also, the same social scientists who used to say a person's IQ did not change over a lifetime are now teaching classes in how to raise your IQ through study and concentration.

Although true meditation will have the effect of increasing one's IQ and lowering blood pressure, these are merely additional side benefits. The true benefit of real meditation is the experience of oneness with Divinity; that form of White Magick known as enlightenment or cosmic consciousness.

True meditation has three steps:

1. Relaxation. The purpose of this step is to get rid of any physical tension or pain so that the physical body will not get in the way of the next steps.

2. Contemplation. The purpose of this step is to completely unite your consciousness with a sound, object, idea, drawing, etc. Notice that relaxation and contemplation are both *parts* of true meditation, but do not constitute the whole.

3. Negation. In this step (the step which is usually left out of lessons on how to meditate), you eliminate from your mind all consciousness of what you have been contemplating. Since your consciousness has become united with what you have been contemplating, it (your consciousness) also leaves when you get rid of the object of your contemplation. The result is a state wherein your consciousness is not blocking the already existent link between you and the Divine. This is White Magick, the state of true bliss, and is the ultimate and only goal of true meditation. Unless one tries it and achieves the true meditative state, no words can fully explain it. It is beyond conscious communication of thought.

In the following form of meditation, you will be focusing on a familiar object. Some traditional books would have you meditate on the ancient Indian Tantric Tattva or Tattwa symbols. These are specially colored geometric figures including triangles, squares, and ovoid shapes, which represent the elements. A traditional pre-Kabalistic system is to focus on the first letter of the Hebrew alphabet. While this may have been fine for cultures where visual stimulation was not as complex as in Western film and television-loving cultures, or in modern cultures used to working with those symbols, I have found through personal work and research done during my classes that Westerners often need something different, something more visually complex. That is what is offered here.

A Technique of True Meditation

STEP ONE. Perform the Relaxation Ritual.

STEP TWO. Perform the LBRP. Always be sure to do a protection ritual of some kind before meditating.

STEP THREE. Shuffle the Major Arcana cards (practice this for several weeks with cards 6, 7, 10, 13, 15, and 18 left out) and randomly select one to use. This will be the object that you will use for the contemplation part of this technique.

STEP FOUR. If you feel the need, do the Relaxation Ritual again.

STEP FIVE. Scanning: This step works in a way similar in nature to the method by which an old television with a big picture tube produces an image. In a picture tube is a device called an "electron gun," which shoots electrons in a small single beam toward

the screen, forming a "scan line" across the front of the tube. The beam from the electron gun then jumps back to just below the first line and repeats the process. If you look closely at the front of such a TV set when it is on, you can see the lines. You cannot see the lines as they are made because the process is done so fast that your eye cannot follow it. This speed, combined with the way your mind holds on to a picture, is what gives the appearance that you have a solid and moving picture on your TV.

In this meditation technique, scanning is done this way:

1. Start by looking at the upper right-hand corner of your chosen card.

2. Look at a horizontal strip of the card about a half inch in height, from the top of the strip to the bottom. Move your vision from right to left across the width of the card. Thus you should have a strip of the card in your mind composed of the uppermost half-inch of the card.

3. Now return to the right-hand side of the card and scan again across the card, from right to left, covering another half-inch strip immediately below your previous scan.

4. Repeat this process until you have totally covered the card.

What you are doing is observing the card, from top to bottom, a half inch at a time. Try to remember as much of each strip or "scan" as you can, but don't worry about perfection. You will get better with practice. See the image at the top of the following page.

STEP SIX. Contemplation: In this step you will become fully involved with the object. Put simply, the technique is to reproduce the previous step of scanning, but within your mind's eye.

1. Put down the card so that you can no longer see its face.

2. By memory, go through and visualize the entire scanning process.

Scanning

De-Scanning

"The Magician" Card from the *Golden Dawn Magical Tarot*

Go one strip at a time until you have reproduced—in your imagination and to the best of your ability—the entire card. The first time you do this, and for many times to follow, you will probably miss many symbols, images, and colors, and perhaps you will only be able to recall and mentally create the outline of larger shapes that were on the card. It is not important that you are completely accurate with your visualization, but your visualization abilities will improve with this practice. This does not mean that it is permissible to be lazy or overly brief in this process. You must do the very best that you can. This step should take between three and four minutes, but if you wish it may take longer.

STEP SEVEN. Negation:

1. Starting again in the upper right-hand corner of the card that you have now visualized through the scanning procedure, take the topmost strip that you scanned and, moving from right to left, erase the image. That is, you "descan" it; you make that first and topmost strip disappear. In your mind's eye you should still see a card, but with its top half-inch being removed.

2. Return to the top right-hand corner of what is left of your visualized card and repeat the process, taking off another strip.

3. Continue this de-scanning, erasing process until the entire card is gone from your mind. Duration for this step: about one and one-half to three minutes, maximum. See the image at the bottom of the previous column.

STEP EIGHT. The State of True Meditation: At this point, a very interesting phenomenon will occur. Your consciousness, which has been caught up in the act of scanning and de-scanning the visualized card, will also be "gone" (actually it will only be silent) by the time the card is gone. Your consciousness will be silent and the monologue in your head will be stopped. This will give your unconscious a chance to speak to you and give you possibly important messages and information.

When you first try this process, it is common for the true meditative state to last for only a brief instant. The inner voice returns and asks something like, "Am I silent? Did I do this right?" As soon as the voice comes back, the meditation is over.

As you practice this technique you will be able to make that instant of true meditation last a minute, five minutes, or more. As this state stretches out in length you will have a new feeling come over you, a feeling of being in total harmony with the universe, of having all knowledge and knowing that although things must evolve to a better state, all things are exactly as they should be at this instant in time. This is known as cosmic consciousness or enlightenment. It is, as I have said, really impossible to speak of this state of feeling, this state of existence. You must experience it and discover its beauty for yourself.

As stated at the beginning of this section, it is not required that you practice meditation. Nor is it required that you practice this particular method of meditation. However, sooner or later you will come to realize that meditation should become a part of your daily life. When you do decide to meditate on a regular basis, if you choose to use another system of meditation than is described here, do not deceive yourself into thinking that you are really meditating if all you are doing is concentrating or relaxing. Those are aspects of true meditation, but they are not meditation in and of themselves.

Also, you will find that all of your rituals and exercises will be greatly improved by practicing true meditation.

PART FOUR

In this portion we will be focusing on what is known as the "unwritten Kabalah." On the next two pages you will find a list of correspondences; that is, a list of how various things and ideas correspond with the Sephiroht on the Tree of Life. In this section you will learn the information necessary to understand the list.

As you can see, by the left of each row are the numbers 1 through 10. These, as you probably guessed, represent the numbers associated with each of the Sephiroht. The first column gives the name of each Sephira as they would be pronounced in Hebrew. The next column gives the translation of those names into English. I would like to mention here that some texts, especially those written for a primarily Jewish readership, sometimes give alternate names and/or spellings for the Sephiroht. For example, Giburah is frequently called "Pachad," which means "fear." It may also be spelled "Givurah." However, this type of study falls more appropriately under the subject of the dogmatic Kabalah that, for the most part, is beyond the scope and purpose of the present course.

The third column is labeled "Color (Q.S.)." Kabalistically, there are four sets of colors (one for each of the four Kabalistic Worlds) that are related to the Sephiroht. They are named after the court cards of the Minor Arcana of the Tarot. In the Golden Dawn, initiates were expected to know all of the color scales. However, for our purposes, the most important version of the colors for the ten Sephiroht is called the Queen Scale (hence the "Q.S."), which are the colors given here.

The Queen Scale colors are associated with the world known as B'ri-yah. Traditionally it is believed that it is more important to become familiar with the Queen Scale sephirotic colors than with the other scales of color. Note that there are four colors associated with the 10th Sephira. This is because the 10th Sephira relates to the Earth, the world of the four archetypal elements: Air, Earth, Fire, and Water. By now you should be beginning to become familiar with the element Earth as a result of the exercises given earlier in this lesson. You will become familiar with the other elements later in this course.

Kabalistic Correspondences

	Sephira	Translation	Color (Q.S.)
1	Keter	Crown	White Brilliance
2	Hochma	Wisdom	Gray
3	Binah	Understanding	Black
4	Hesed	Mercy	Blue
5	Giburah	Strength	Scarlet
6	Tiferet	Beauty	Gold
7	Netzach	Victory	Emerald
8	Hode	Splendor	Orange
9	Yesode	Foundation	Violet
10	Mahlkoot	Kingdom	Citrine, Brown Olive, Black

	Scents	Chakras	God Name
1	Ambergris	Crown	Eh-Heh-Yeh
2	Musk	3rd Eye	Yah
3	Myrrh; Civet	Throat	YHVH El-oh-heem
4	Cedar	—	El
5	Tobacco	Heart	El-oh-heem Gi-boor
6	Olibanum	—	YHVH El-oh-ah V'dah-aht
7	Rose; Red Sandal	Solar Plexus	YHVH Tz'vah-oht
8	Storax	Genitals	El-oh-heem Tz'vah-oht
9	Jasmine	Root	Sha-dai El Chai
10	Dittany of Crete	—	Ah-doh-nai Mel-ech

[YHVH = Yud Heh Vahv Heh]

	Body	Planets	Metal	Stone
1	Cranium	1st Swirlings	—	Diamond
2	Left Face	Zodiac	—	Star Ruby; Turquoise
3	Right Face	Saturn	Lead	Pearl; Star Sapphire
4	Left Arm	Jupiter	Tin	Sapphire; Amethyst
5	Right Arm	Mars	Iron	Ruby
6	Breast	Sol	Gold	Topaz
7	Loins; Hips	Venus	Copper	Emerald
8	Loins; Legs	Mercury	Mercury	Quartz
9	Genitals	Luna	Silver	Quartz
10	Feet	4 Elements	—	Rock Crystal

	Archangel	Translation	"Soul"	Translation
1	Metatron	Angel of the Presence	Yechidah	Higher Self
2	Ratziel	Herald of Deity	Hai-yah	Life Force
3	Tzaphkiel	Contemplation of God	Neshamah	Intuition
4	Tzadkiel	Justice of God	—	—
5	Khamael	Severity of God	—	—
6	Raphael	Divine Physician	Ruach	Intellect
7	Haniel	Grace of God	—	—
8	Michael	Protector of God	—	—
9	Gabriel	Man-God	Nephesch	Lower Self
10	Sandalphon	Messiah	G'uph	Physical Self

	Angelic Order	Translation
1	Chai-oht Ha Kah-desh	Holy Living Ones
2	Auphaneem	Wheels
3	Araleem	Thrones
4	Chasmaleem	Brilliant Ones
5	Serapheem	Fiery Serpents
6	Malacheem	Messengers
7	Eloheem	Gods and Goddesses
8	Beney Eloheem	Children of the Gods and Goddesses
9	Kerubeem	Strong Ones
10	Asheem	Souls of Fire

	YHVH	Creature	Tool	Plant
1	Tip of Yud	God	Crown	Almond (aflower)
2	Heh (superior)	Man	Inner Robe	Amaranth
3	—	Woman	Outer Robe	Cypress
4	—	Unicorn	Wand	Rush; Olive
5	—	Basilisk	Sword	Cactus
6	Vahv	Phoenix	Lamen	Sunflower
7	—	Lynx	Lamp	Rose
8	—	Hermaphrodite	Names	Orchid
9	—	Elephant	Scent	Comfrey
10	Heh (inferior)	Sphinx	Circle	Lily; Ivy; Willow

It would be a good idea for you to make up a separate Tree of Life for each of the columns of correspondences. This can give you a visual image that cannot be duplicated by cerebral, left-brain, mental processes. For the colors, color in each Sephira with the appropriate color. The 10th Sephira has an "X" drawn through it and should be colored in like this:

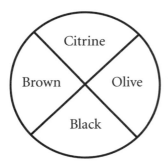

Violet and green make olive; orange and green make citrine; orange and violet make the peculiar shade of brown used here, technically known as russet.

The next column associates various scents, odors, and incenses with the Sephiroht. Note that the association for the 5th Sephira, Giburah, is listed as tobacco. Today there are so many adulterants allowed to be added to tobacco that its purity, and therefore its value, is questionable. It was originally chosen, according to Aleister Crowley, because tobacco is said to be the favorite "scent" of men who work hard, and Giburah does mean "strength." For a long time I questioned the value of tobacco as a magickal incense, as I would usually just open up a cigarette and drop the generally awful-smelling stuff on a block of hot charcoal. Then one day I went into a shop that sells wide varieties of tobacco for pipe smokers. Here I found several relatively untainted tobaccos, which have worked excellently for me. Try finding some you like, some of which give you a feeling of strength and power, the essence of Giburah. *You will NEVER become a magician if all you can do is blindly follow obsolete patterns.* Tradition can only be a guide.

In fact, it would be appropriate to use any scent that gives you that feeling of strength and power,

whether or not it contains tobacco. In a similar manner you can "correct" any of the listings on the chart of Kabalistic correspondences so that it is correct for you.

It should be apparent to you at this point that I tend to be eclectic in my beliefs and I welcome change and newness. However, some of the correspondences date back thousands of years. They have lasted this long for only one reason: the thousands of people who have used them have discovered that they are accurate and that they work. Thus, although I do hope that you will closely examine and work with all of the correspondences, you should have a good, thoughtful, and valid reason for changing what has worked for so many for so long.

The next column relates the Sephiroht to the chakras. Because many people are familiar with the chakras, I have included them here as another way of becoming familiar with the Sephiroht. Unfortunately, deep study of the chakras is not really part of the curricula of this course. If the chakras interest you and you would like to do more study on them, consult the bibliography for books that go into detail on the subject.

The next column gives the God name associated with each Sephira. Remember, although there are many God names, these refer to aspects of a monotheistic deity, not to a polytheistic pantheon. In other words, they represent the faces or potencies of a singular deity. Note here, as shown in the parenthetical note on the page of Kabalistic correspondences, that when you see the letters "YHVH" as a God name they should be pronounced "Yud-Heh-Vahv-Heh." Otherwise, the column is self-explanatory.

We have already shown how the Sephiroht can be related to the physical body. That is, a person is seen as backing into the Tree of Life. The next column gives the traditional associations. This is followed by a column listing the planets. Note that the first Sephira is associated with "1st Swirlings." This may refer to the original big bang which formed our physical universe, or it may refer to the galactic gas clouds that, due to gravity, condensed and began to spin. They eventually formed the galaxies and individual star systems. Or, it may refer to something altogether different. It will not be a vital part of our magickal system, so it is not an essential bit of knowledge. The second Sephira is related to the entire zodiacal belt, not to a planet as such. The tenth Sephira, which is related to the planet Earth, is also the sphere of the four archetypal elements.

The next column gives the metals associated with the Sephiroht. Notice here that the first, second, and tenth Sephiroht have no metallic associations. This is followed by a column associating the Sephiroht with stones.

The Kabalistic view of the higher planes shows a very ordered universe. Each entity or power essence has others in its command to do its bidding. A simple diagram of this would be as follows:

The Unknowable Divinity
Aspects of God   (**The God Names**)
The Archangels
The Angels   (**The Orders of Angels**)

The aspects of Divinity are represented by the God names. The angels are frequently dealt with in groups known as "orders." The angels do the bidding of the archangels; the archangels obey God; God assigns the archangels tasks appropriate to their nature. The relationship an archangel has with Divinity is via the aspect of the Ultimate Source, which is represented by the God names. The whole, rather militaristic structure is controlled by the unknowable divinity, the Ain. You will find a column with the correspondences that gives the Hebrew names of the archangels followed by a column with the translations of the Hebrew names.

The next column relates to the personality or "soul," and has already been discussed. It is presented here in brief, and much more detail will be added at a later time. This is followed by the transliteration of the Hebrew, giving the Hebrew sounds in English. This is followed by a listing of the Angelic Orders, and then by the translations of those Hebrew terms.

It is interesting to note that several of the names of the orders of angels are terms used by Ezekiel in his revelation. If you understand traditional Hebrew mysticism, the mystical book of Ezekiel becomes easier to comprehend. If you do not, you can come up with absurd theories as one NASA scientist did, claiming that Ezekiel saw an alien space vehicle. He claimed that the descriptions Ezekiel used were merely a way of reporting the action of the space ship! He failed to see that his interpretation of Ezekiel was his way of trying to understand mystical terms without including mysticism. That would be like trying to describe the recipe of a cake while claiming that flour was really "flower" and you should grind up petals from a rose in order to make devil's food cake!

Coming back to Earth, most scholars believe that this angelic train-of-command was copied from various Semitic peoples who had long lists of djinns and the like.

Next come the magickally important Hebrew letters Yud-Heh-Vahv-Heh, YHVH for short, the Tetragrammaton. I have already discussed it, but let's add some more information. The Yud looks like this: י. The upper tip of the Yud is associated with the first Sephira. The rest of the Yud, along with the Heh (which looks like this: ה), is associated with the second through fourth Sephiroht. The Vahv is an elongated Yud and looks like this: ו. It is related to the fourth through ninth Sephiroht. Notice the overlap between the Vahv and Heh. The second or last Heh is related to the tenth Sephira. The first Heh is known as the Heh Superior (Sup.) and the second Heh is known as the Heh Inferior (Inf.).

Hebrew is read from right to left, and the Tetragrammaton looks like this:

Vertically, it looks like this:

The creatures in the next column are both real and unreal, while the tools of the following column are magickal tools. The lamen is a medallion hung around the neck to represent a certain power or quality. The names are the various God, archangelic, and angelic names, along with other words of power. The traditional magician of the Middle Ages wore two robes: an outer robe, representing the silence necessary to being a magician, which concealed a hidden, inner robe of truth. Today, most magicians wear only one robe, the two robes being more symbolic than actual.

Finally, the last column is self-explanatory with the sole added note that the plant associated with the first Sephira is an almond "aflower." That is, it should be blooming.

This list of Kabalistic correspondences is by no means complete. But it is a good start. I suggest that you make up a series of Trees of Life, each one filled out with one of the columns. You may wish also to make up a very large Tree of Life putting many of the correspondences associated with a Sephira in the drawing of that Sephira. I urge a deep study of the correspondences now. Their importance will become clearer to you as we move into the study of Grey Magick. For a far more complete version of these correspondences, get *777* by Aleister Crowley, *Godwin's Cabalistic Encyclopedia* by David Godwin, or *The Complete Magician's Tables* by Stephen Skinner. These books are vital encyclopedias necessary for research performed by a modern practicing ceremonial magician.

PART FIVE

If you feel you have been successful with the Middle Pillar Ritual, you may go on to an advanced version of the ritual. Visualize each Sephira, each power center, in the colors given on the correspondence list. Dah-aht is lavender, and for Mahl-koot use black. The Sephiroht should be connected with a beam of white light. You may also vibrate the name of the archangel after vibrating the God name. Dah-aht at the throat does not have a Kabalistic archangelic name, so we borrow from another language called Enochian or Angelic. Use: El-ex-ar-peh Co-mah-nah-nu Tahb-ih-toh-ehm.

The Circulation of the Body of Light

While the advanced Middle Pillar Ritual is a valuable addition to your practices, its success will depend in part upon your visualization abilities. Visualization, in this sense, does not necessarily mean that you must "see" the colors. Rather, it could mean that you "know" or "feel" that the colors are there. This does not mean "hope" they are there—you must know that if your astral vision were open you would easily be able to see the colors in your mind's eye. You must *know* that the colors *are* there whether you see them or not.

Even if you have not mastered the advanced version of the Middle Pillar Ritual as given above, you should now add a new ritual to your daily practice. It should add no more than two or three minutes to the total time of your daily work. There are three parts to it.

Start by doing the same daily practices you have done up to now: the Relaxation Ritual, the LBRP, and the Middle Pillar Ritual. However—and this is important—do *not* visualize the Middle Pillar vanishing. Keep the pillar in your mind's eye as strong as possible.

FIRST PART. While keeping the visualization of the Middle Pillar, refocus your attention on Keter, the white brilliance just above your head. Visualize this brilliance in a state of extreme strength, needing to radiate out even more energy. Visualize it sending a current of energy down into the head and to the *left* shoulder. Let this energy pass down the left side of your body to your left foot. Feel it move to your right foot, up the right side of your body, to your head, and back up to Keter.

This motion should be synchronized with your breath. When you exhale, feel the energy go down your left side. When you inhale, feel the energy go up your right side. You should have the sensation of a circle of energy swirling around you. Move the energy, with your breath, in six to ten cycles—more if you like.

Feel free to expand the energy further out to the sides, to the ends of the universe, if you wish. Most commonly, it is seen as going out about three feet from the body. You might also wish to experiment with what happens if you contract the energy so that it goes down the left side of the spine and up the right side of the spine.

SECOND PART. This immediately follows the first part of this ritual. It is similar to that part, but instead of directing the energy down one side and up the other, here you should direct the energy down the *front* of your body and up the back. Be sure to synchronize your breath so that as you exhale the energy goes down the front of your body and, as you inhale, it goes up your back, to your head and up to Keter. Repeat six to ten times.

THIRD PART: "THE MUMMY." This immediately follows the second part of this ritual. Revisualize the entire Middle Pillar. This time, focus your attention on Mahl-koot, at the feet. From the upper right side of this spherical power center, *visualize the energy curling up in a tight spiral to the front of the left leg.* From here it continues around the back and moves upward in a counter-clockwise spiral around your body. It is as if you are being wrapped like an Egyptian mummy, from the feet to the head. Instead of cloth, however, you are being wrapped in spiraling energy.

You should feel a whirling of spiritual power as the pure spiritual light and energy rises up in spirals from your feet to above your head, from Mahl-koot to Keter. At Keter you should visualize the energy exploding out like a water fountain in all directions. This energy lands at your feet and begins to rise in the spiral again. As you inhale, feel the energy rise toward Keter. As you exhale, feel it explode outward toward Mahl-koot at your feet. As in the first and second parts, do it for six to ten cycles or more if you wish. Then, take a very deep breath, and as you exhale, see the energy disappear visually, but know that it is still there, invisibly.

Finish by doing the Tarot Contemplation Ritual and filling out your ritual diary.

Warning: Although it sounds simple and rather benign, the Circulation of the Body of Light is a very powerful ritual. You may rock back and forth, feel dizzy, or even fall over as a result of your direction of spiritual energy. The first time I tried this I literally fell to the ground, overcome with the energy. I know that if people are just reading this or have jumped to this section without practicing the previous material for two or more months, this may sound absurd. And to you, it will be absurd. But if you have actually performed all the work and all the practices described previously, you will discover that I am not understating what can happen. If anything, I'm understating just how *wang-boom!* powerful this ritual can be. If you do experience any of these phenomena, don't get terrified or petrified. With a few days of practice you will be in control of that amazing energy.

In the Chinese yoga manual titled *The Secret of the Golden Flower* it says that "when the light circulates, the powers of the whole body arrange themselves before its throne, just as a holy king takes possession of a capital and lays down rules of order, and all approach with tribute. Therefore, you have only to make the Light circulate; that is the deepest and most wonderful secret. The light is easy to move, and if allowed to go long enough in a circle it crystallizes itself; it is this condition of which it is said 'silently in the morning thou fliest upward.'"

The energy used in the Circulation of the Body of Light ritual is so powerful that it can be used for healing purposes. Simply use visualization to direct the energy that you have learned to control down your arms and out through your hands. This healing technique is especially good for people who are drained and low on energy. It is good as an aid for people who are *recovering* from almost any physical ailment. It can be used without fear on people who have serious, chronic diseases. However, you should follow these rules:

1. *Never* attempt to heal a person without first getting that person's permission to do so.

2. If a person has a *minor* cold or flu, do not attempt to heal that person. They need the "disease" to get rid of the toxins that are in the body. If the disease has run its course and the person is still weak but recovering, then it is okay to help him or her recover faster. Place one hand on the forehead and the other on the lower stomach and send the energy that you have learned to control.

3. If a person has a serious, life-threatening disease, focus your attention and hands near the area where the disease is most obvious. Visualize the disease leaving his or her body and fading into nothingness while you fill their body with new, life-giving energy. As soon as you sense that the person you are working on is filled with energy, do the LBRP to make sure that absolutely nothing unwanted comes back.

4. Do not use this technique for a person who has a high fever. Instead, hold their hands and visualize the illness leaving their body (and staying away from your body!). Visualize the illness fading to nothing. Do the LBRP. Finally, if you wish, you may send *small* amounts of energy, which your mind colors a cooling, healing blue.

5. Always finish with the LBRP, the Middle Pillar Ritual, and the Circulation of the Body of Light Ritual for yourself. Then run your hands under cool, fresh water for at least a minute. This cleanses you and helps to protect you from accidentally allowing any illness back into you.

6. Always work in cooperation with medical doctors. *Under no circumstances should you ever advise a person to not follow a doctor's advice or not seek the aid of a professional therapist!* If you honestly feel that a particular medical treatment is not helping someone, you can advise that person to get a second opinion from another licensed physician.

On the next page is a diagram of the Tarot as it exists on the Tree of Life. I am not going to make any comments on it at this time. Rather, I want you to spend some time looking at it and trying to discover the relationships between the Tarot and the Kabalistic correspondences given earlier in the lesson. I am presenting it now, seemingly unrelated to the material in the preceding and following paragraphs, to draw attention to it. It may be the most important diagram for the magickal techniques that will be given later in this course. It will be explained later, at the proper time, but I want you to get some familiarity with it now so that it will not be something startlingly new when its importance becomes evident. Study it with your Tarot cards in hand and compare with what has already been given.

Before moving on to the next part of this lesson, there is another thing I wish to clarify for you. You may be thinking that I will be adding on to the basic daily rituals until you have no time to do anything else! This is not the case. There is only one more basic ritual that you must learn. Do not give up. Do not omit any part of the rituals. Do not skip a day unless it is *impossible* not to. Everything that you are now doing is White Magick, moving you toward unity with Divinity. It is also your preparation for doing Grey Magick. If you memorize the rituals they should not take longer than fifteen minutes. And, in a short time, this course will give you a method for doing the rituals anytime, anywhere, via a special mental process. It will take even less time to perform

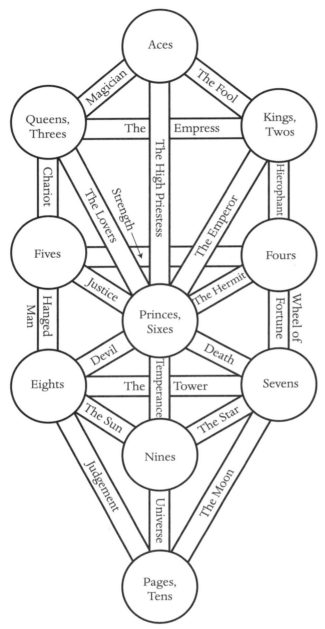

The Tarot on the Tree of Life

the rituals, and it will simultaneously give you more personal power. Don't give up! You can do it and amazing things await.

Sometimes in my classes I have had students tell me that although they carry out the rituals with extreme care, they feel nothing within themselves (or without) as a result of their ritual practice and work.

They want to know why they are failing and what they are doing wrong.

The answer is that there is nothing wrong and that they are not failing. The energies involved in the rituals are continually at work throughout the physical and spiritual universe. The energy goes around and through all things, both physical and non-physical. It is everywhere. If you did not feel the motion of the energy before, there is no guarantee that you will sense it after you have begun practicing the rituals. Magick permits us to *utilize* these forces in ways non-magicians cannot comprehend. This does not depend upon whether you feel these energies.

It is not necessary that you have any weird experiences or unusual sensations as a result of the practice of the rituals in this course. If the rituals are done properly, the desired results must inevitably occur. If you throw a ball in the air, it must come down. This is the law of gravity, and the ball will come down even if you're not consciously aware of any sensation due to gravity. If you do the rituals properly, you must get the desired results. This is the cosmic law of magick.

Sometimes, unusual experiences or sensations can actually get in the way of psychic development. Some people get sidetracked into trying to produce psychic phenomena. They end up spending time trying to do relatively useless things such as levitation or being able to see what symbol is on the back of a card. While spending time bending spoons (and what good is a bent spoon, anyway?) they ignore their magickal work and retard their magickal and spiritual progress.

So, some of you may feel or sense the energies that have been described in this and in previous lessons. Some of you, for a while, may not. But, as Bill Murray chanted in the movie *Meatballs,* "It just doesn't matter!" If you do the rituals properly, the magick will work.

Know that you can do the rituals successfully. *Dare* to do them. Then just *Do* them! Finally, *Be Silent* about your achievements.

PART SIX

In this section I am going to be discussing primarily the use of the magickal tool known as the pentacle and its construction. First, however, I need to discuss the system of the magickal elements.

As you may know, and as I have already briefly discussed, in the West we have a system of "four magickal elements." Well, this is not true now, nor to my knowledge has it ever been true. As far as I can tell, calling our system a "four element" system is a blind to fool those outside the temples of wisdom.

The fact is that there have always been five magickal elements. According to the *Sepher Yetzirah*, one of the oldest Kabalistic documents extant, their order is as follows:

The *SPIRIT* of God
AIR emanated from Spirit
WATER emanated from Air
Part of the water became *EARTH*
FIRE emanated from Water

Note that some people call the system as listed in the *Sepher Yetzirah* a "three element" system. This is because the element of Spirit is ignored and the element of Earth is not even considered a separately emanated element, but rather a mere part of elemental Water. Some later Kabalistic systems contend that elemental Earth is only a combination of Air and Water or a mixture of Air, Water, and Fire. In any event, even though elemental Earth may be considered a secondary element in the traditional Kabalah, it is still an element. Include Spirit and Earth with the Three Element Kabalistic system and we have our five elements of magick.

In the West the magickal four elements are frequently pictured around a pentagram. Isn't it obvious that there must be a fifth element so that each point of the pentagram can have a magickal element associated with it? The missing element, of course, is the source of the other four elements, Spirit. Spirit is the source of all that exists and is the divine light from beyond Keter. These are the symbols of the five elements:

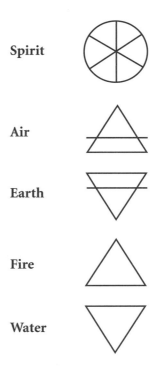

Spirit

Air

Earth

Fire

Water

Below, the symbols of the elements show which element is associated with each point of the pentagram.

But to get a really good idea as to how the elements interrelate, we must travel briefly to China. In Chinese mysticism there has never been a doubt or mislabeling of the number of elements of magick. They do have slightly different names, however, and here is how the Chinese and Western systems correspond:

CHINESE	WESTERN
Fire	Fire
Earth	Earth
Metal	Air
Water	Water
Wood	Spirit

In the diagram below, you can see that the distribution of the Chinese elements around the pentagram are in a slightly different order than in the Western system shown above. But the Chinese system is well thought out. If you go clockwise around the pentagram of the five Oriental elements, you are following what is called "the Cycle of Creation or Generation." Here is a symbolic explanation of this cycle:

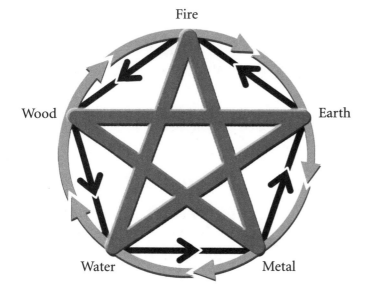

Fire burns down things and they eventually become Earth.
Metals are mined from Earth.
Water comes through Metal pipes.
Wood is created from the vital nutrients in Water.
Fire comes from burning wood.

Obviously, this is a modern interpretation; however, it aids in remembering this cycle. If you follow the paths of the arms of the pentagram, you are fol-

lowing what is called "the Cycle of Control or Destruction." Here is a modern explanation of this cycle:

Fire purifies or destroys Metal.
Metal, in the form of an axe blade, forms or destroys Wood.
Wood tools can be used to control Earth.
Dams of Earth control Water.
Water extinguishes (destroys) Fire.

Thus we can see in the Oriental system that a particular magickal element can be used to do one of three things:

1. Enhance itself (Fire + Fire = 2 Fire).
2. Enhance another element (adding Fire to Wood increases Earth).
3. Counter another element (Water counters the effect of Fire).

Now that you've had a chance to see a thought-provoking system of working with the magickal elements, let me tell you that the Western system, in my opinion, is much easier, especially when discussing the elemental tools. The pentacle really has only two important purposes: it collects and directs the energies of elemental Earth. What you use the energy for, and how you use it, is up to you. If you feel light-headed, it can ground you. If you feel that you are under psychic attack via the elements of Spirit, Air, Fire, or Water, it can reflect those energies back upon their source. If you are attacked using the element of Earth, it can either reflect the elemental energy or, even better, store it for your future positive use. Thus, for the operative magician, the pentacle is primarily a defensive weapon, meant never to be used as a weapon except in case of being attacked. It can also, as mentioned, be used to direct and store Earth energy for whatever purpose you desire.

The next problem for us—now that we know the purpose of the pentacle—is an appropriate construction. Most tradition-based books recommend using a disk of wood or metal up to nine inches in diameter. Now, as I have already said, this tool is also a defensive weapon. Grabbing a nine-inch circle of wood or metal and trying to direct it in the proper direction to dispel an attack on you would be like having someone jump you with a knife while you struggle to find a huge old shotgun that doesn't even fire accurately!

The answer to this problem is twofold. Firstly, an object six inches in diameter is far easier to use if you have average-sized hands. Secondly, if the object, instead of being flat, is *concave*, it will return any energy from any direction, back toward the direction from which it came. This creates a situation of "instant karma" for your attacker.

What you can do is carve out (or buy) a shallow wooden bowl. The interior must be as perfectly concave as possible, although the back may be flat so that it can be balanced on a table or altar. A small ring of wood or metal placed on a table will allow you to balance a bowl with a round bottom on that table or altar. Metal can be used for your pentacle, but it is slightly harder to paint a metallic surface than a wooden one.

Lightly sand the surface and put on a white undercoat or primer. With a fine line brush draw an "X" from edge to edge on both sides of your pentacle. This should divide both surfaces into four large triangles. Paint these citrine, olive, black, and brown, as listed earlier in this lesson. Paint both sides. The black section on both sides should be directly opposite or back-to-back of each other. In this way when you hold the pentacle from the bottom you will be holding black on both sides of the pentacle. If the undercoat shows through, use a second coat.

Using a compass, draw a circle three-eighths of an inch from the outer edge of the pentacle. Paint the ring white from the line to the edge. Either freehand or with the aid of a compass, draw out a pentagram (or hexagram) so the points of the arms just touch the white ring that you have drawn on the front and back of the pentacle. The lines of the pentagram should be about three-eighths of an inch in width. If any of the background colors show through these white lines, keep adding coats of white paint until the white is opaque.

Next, fill in the circle with the Hebrew letters of the God name, angelic name, etc., and the appropriate sigils as given on the next page. These should

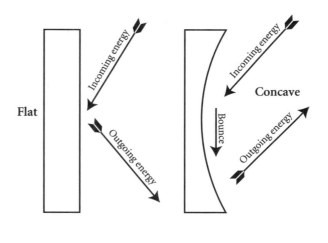

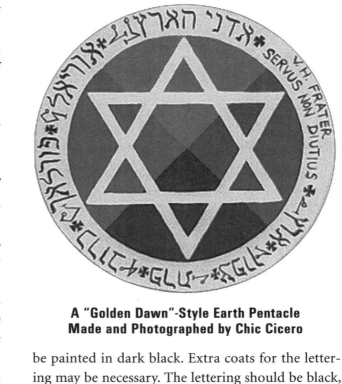

**A "Golden Dawn"-Style Earth Pentacle
Made and Photographed by Chic Cicero**

be painted in dark black. Extra coats for the lettering may be necessary. The lettering should be black, not grey. Finally, cover the entire pentacle with a protective clear coat of lacquer. I suggest the use of Varathane liquid plastic gloss.

If you want more information on how to work with the paints and colors, I suggest the book *The Secret Temple* by Robert Wang or *Secrets of a Golden Dawn Temple* by Chic and Sandra Tabatha Cicero.

Both provide methods for building the Golden Dawn tools. If you get either book, you will see that the Golden Dawn used not a pentacle with a pentagram on it, but more of "hexacle" with a hexagram on it (see photograph above).

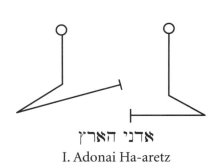

אדני הארץ

I. Adonai Ha-aretz

אוריא

II. Auriel

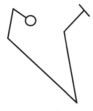

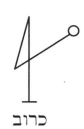

פורלאך

III. Phorlakh

כרוב

IV. Kerub

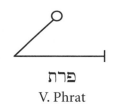

פרת

V. Phrat

צפון

VI. Tzaphon

ארץ

VII. Aretz

VIII. The Motto

Symbols and Hebrew for the Pentacle

What's a Pentacle, Anyway?

So why did the Golden Dawn call this a pentacle, anyway, if it has hexagram on it? Doesn't the prefix "pent" mean "five"?

Yes, it's true that the prefix "pent" means "five," and perhaps it might be best just to say that a pentagram is a five-pointed star and a pentacle is an object with a pentagram on it. The problem, as usual, is with language. You see, although we pronounced the words and spell them "pent-," they may have a different source.

It is quite possible that pentacles were originally meant to be worn like some form of protective jewelry. In that case, the beginning of the word is derived from the prefix *pend-*, meaning something that hangs like a pendant.

Alternatively, the word "pentacle" may be derived from the Latin *pentaculum*, which may mean a "small painting," such as is drawn on a talisman or, in this case, a pentacle. In that case almost anything could be on it.

Whatever the true source of the word, if you want to create a pentacle in the style of the Golden Dawn, paint a hexagram on it. If you are not making a Golden Dawn pentacle, there is no reason you cannot put a pentagram on your pentacle. Experiment and see what works best for you.

The Magickal Motto

Finally, if you notice, there is a space listed on the page for a "motto." This is the Golden Dawn equivalent of a magickal name. Just as putting on your magickal robes tells your subconscious that something special is happening, so too does referring to yourself by your magickal name or motto add to this intuitive understanding. Today, magicians tend to take the choice of a magickal name or motto very seriously, often spending hours agonizing over just the right choice to represent their goal as a magician. Some magicians take the magickal names of someone they admire for their magickal ability, real or imagined, such as "Merlyn" or other historical or mythical characters. Some people, instead of a name per se, use a phrase representing something they stand for or believe. The Golden Dawn mottoes were usually in Latin, but any language will do. Here is a list of samples:

Anima Pura Sit. Let the soul be pure.
Demon Est Deus Inversus. The Devil is the
    inverse of God.
Deo Duce Comite Ferro. With God as my leader
    and the sword as my companion.
Finem Respice. Have regard to the end.
Perdurabo. I will last through.
Sacrementum Regis. The sacrament of a king.
Sapere Aude. Dare to be wise.
Iehi Aour. Let there be light.

Members of the Golden Dawn, as well as in other magickal orders, will often refer to each other by the initials of their magickal mottoes in correspondence and within rituals. Thus, you would have Frater or Soror (brother or sister) D.D.C.F., D.E.D.I., S.A., etc. As you rise through the degrees of an order, some people change their motto. Often you will be entitled to use honorifics such as "Greatly Honored Frater," too.

English, Latin, Hebrew, Greek, Enochian, or any other language would be fine to use for your magickal name or motto. You should spend some time considering what name you will use. True, you can always change, but you will find that its choice will be important and more and more meaningful to you as you evolve magickally.

One last thing in this part of the lesson. Although people today may look back in wonder at the members of the original Golden Dawn, it should be remembered that beside being great occultists, they were also just men and women doing the best they could to excel, just like you and me. You see, they had in their possession a large book of family mottoes. Most of the members simply took their long-standing family motto as their magickal motto. Others just looked through the book and selected a motto they liked. Oh my!

PART SEVEN

Perhaps you have wondered what the difference is between "ceremonial" magick and "ritual" magick. Many people use them interchangeably as synonyms and, in fact, their dictionary definitions are quite similar. However, in magickal philosophy there is an important difference. Anyone can do a ritual. It can be a magickal ritual or a ritual of another kind, such as a shaving ritual wherein you shave yourself according to a certain pattern. After a period of practice, some rituals, such as a shaving ritual, become habits. To break the ritual, that is, to follow an unusual pattern, can cause problems. It can make you feel uncomfortable, and can possibly be harmful. If you don't believe me, try shaving yourself in a different manner than usual. Start in a different location or shave in a different direction. But don't be surprised—and don't blame me!—if you end up cutting and nicking yourself in many places. This, then, gives you three important caveats:

Never let your magickal rituals become habits. Always perform them with full awareness. Be present in any ritual even if you have been doing it daily for years.

My definition of a ceremony is a "group ritual." That is, it only takes one person to do a ritual while it takes several people to perform a ceremony. Thus, in order to do ceremonial magick you must have a group of some sort.

Although all of the magickal techniques in this course will be presented so that they can be performed by the individual ritualist, in the future there will be notes given on how to do some rituals with a group. This leads to the question of the values and drawbacks of groups.

Merits and Challenges of Working with a Group

The benefits of magickal groups are threefold:

1. *Camaraderie.* Sometimes, being a magician can be a lonely prospect, and it is nice to have friends who have similar interests. They can give you feedback on what you're doing and give guidance. Even if you choose not to be part of a group, I urge you to consider attending an occasional festival or convention. Camaraderie and socialization, even for a short period of time, are very beneficial.

2. *Specialization.* Everyone in a magickal group, to some degree, must have similar knowledge. That's one of the things that holds groups together. No one, however, can be an expert in all fields of occultism. In a group, one person may be a specialist with the Tarot (although everyone in the group may be familiar with the Tarot), another a specialist in astrology, another in occult history, and another in ceremony and ritual. Thus, the more people you have, the greater the chance that a subject your group needs information on will be known by one of the members.

3. *Power.* In spite of the fact that some people will deny it, the truth is that the more people you have, the higher the levels of psychic/magickal energy may be generated. Perhaps you have experienced the flows of energy at a rock concert or football game. This is nothing more than poorly controlled psychic or magickal energy. With magick we learn how to control this energy via the techniques you have been learning and further techniques to come. Obviously, the intensity is increased in proportion to the number of people present. Further, the amount of energy increases *exponentially* rather than via simple addition. This means that if one person generates "E" amount of psychic energy,

2 people (may) generate 2E

3 people (may) generate 4E

4 people (may) generate 8E

5 people (may) generate 16E

6 people (may) generate 32E

7 people (may) generate 64E, etc.

As you can see, even a few people together can have a much stronger effect than a large number working individually. This, by the way, is not a theory I made up. It is based on Einstein's field theories and is accepted by most occultists with whom I am familiar.

This does not mean, however, that having a group of people will automatically make you successful in your magickal work. A competent and experienced individual magician may be far more in control of the psycho-magickal energy than a group. Sometimes an individual may be more successful than a group for just this reason. This is also why I wrote above that a group of people *may* be able to generate more than an individual. Certainly a group of incompetents would not be able to outdo one well-trained magician.

This brings us to the challenges associated with groups. I had a close friend, a well-respected author of several books on magickal topics, who died several years ago. He believed that although you could have group rituals, the idea of working with a single group on a regular basis was obsolete and impractical. This opinion was due to his personal experience with some groups. I, too, have experienced much the same. Always, and I do mean *always*, the problems associated with groups are based on one problem and one problem only: personal psychology. Cliques form and people locked out of the cliques feel hurt and left out. Person A won't work with person B because person B is too (a) smart, (b) dumb, (c) ugly, (d) beautiful, or (e) other. Somebody institutes plots against the leader. Somebody wants to change the group so that it fits his or her personal image of what the group should be rather than changing himself or herself so as to fit in with the group. It's all so very stupid.

This sort of nonsense has gone on for years between groups too. Various groups calling themselves Rosicrucian all insist that only they are the real Rosicrucians and all of the other groups are frauds. Various Witchcraft and Wiccan groups involve themselves in this same sort of foolishness. One famous magickal group currently has about five or six people claiming to be the true leader of the organization, each leading their own group, and each claiming that the others are frauds and fakes. This disagreement has led to outrageous name-calling and expensive court cases. What can a person who wants to work with a group of others with similar interests do?

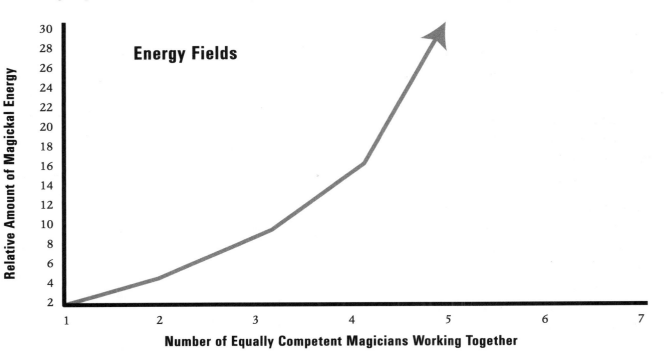

Gotcha!

It never fails that people will look through a large volume, such as *Modern Magick*, looking for typos, minor contradictions. and tiny inconsistencies. Well, if you want to look, go ahead.

So earlier, in the section on dealing with psychic attack I wrote that you shouldn't do mirror spells because you'd consciously be doing a form of Black Magick, sending negative energy to someone, and that would eventually have repercussions on you. Yet in the section on making a pentacle I advise making the pentacle concave so it would direct negative energy back to where it originated. Essentially, it would be a type of mirroring spell.

Now, I could just say that yes, this is an inconsistency, and quote some famous people with what they thought about consistency:

"Consistency is contrary to nature, contrary to life. The only completely consistent people are dead."

—Aldous Huxley

"Consistency requires you to be as ignorant today as you were a year ago."

—Bernard Berenson

"Consistency is the last refuge of the unimaginative."

—Oscar Wilde

"A foolish consistency is the hobgoblin of little minds, adored by little statesmen and philosophers and divines.

—Ralph Waldo Emerson

"Consistency is the quality of a stagnant mind."

—John Sloan

"Consistency is a virtue for trains . . ."

—Stephen Vizinczey

However, this would be a "cop-out" and not represent the truth. In reality, there is no inconsistency and both of the original concepts are correct when taken *in context*. Even though *Modern Magick* covers a wide ground, it is still meant to take people from introductory level and intermediate level up to the point of preparing people to be advanced magicians. That means because I want to introduce you to all of this material, it is impossible to cover everything in depth and you should think about everything that is written.

The reason I advise against performing mirroring spells to oppose psychic attack is that the vast majority of such attacks may be unintended, accidental, self-created, or imagined. Turning negative energy on to someone who is simply angry with you and didn't mean to hurt you is cruel and uncalled for. Turning it on yourself is just plain foolish.

In a situation where you would use the qualities of the Earth pentacle, you would be fully aware of who and where the negative energy is coming from. For the purposes as will be described later in this book, it would primarily be used with specific non-physical entities *after* you have tried other remedies. For a fictionalized version of its use, see my novel *The Resurrection Murders*.

So, there is no contradiction here. Sorry. If you're really into finding that sort of thing, you'll have to keep looking.

First, he or she can forget about the whole thing. But if that doesn't work, he or she can start a group from scratch. Then, as more and more people become involved, each person, in the tradition of the Freemasons, must be accepted by all of the current members of the group before the person is allowed to join. Thus, the people must first meet on a social level before becoming involved on a magickal level. The group must be a small circle of friends. Some Witches claim the size of a magickal group should be no more than thirteen. Hence, thirteen is the maximum size of many covens.

Also, the goal of all the people in the magickal group must be unified. There must be no ulterior motives for any of the people being in the group. Israel Regardie strongly suggested that all people involved with occultism should go through psychotherapy. For a long time I felt that this was because he was a Reichian therapist. But because of my experience with many groups and with the experiences told to me by others, I am at a point now where I am inclined to agree with the good doctor.

Unfortunately, most of us have neither the time nor desire to go to some sort of therapist or counselor, and many people can't afford it. Also, there is a wide degree of quality among therapists. Sometimes I think that many people became professional therapists in the hopes of solving their own deep mental problems, and, failing that, try to help others without recognizing that everything they do goes through the "filter" of their personal psychological issues. Don't get me wrong, there are numerous wonderful, skilled, and dedicated counselors and therapists, but how will you know if you have a good one, a person who won't begin by having you locked up for studying the occult?

Luckily, there is an answer. It is a powerful therapeutic and magickal technique that can be used which I call the I.O.B.

I.O.B.

The I.O.B. technique is not new, but it is a new interpretation of traditional Golden Dawn magickal techniques and medieval counseling techniques. The

Golden Dawn aspect includes a simple version of the formulation of "telesmatic images" and certain banishing techniques. The medieval counseling technique is commonly called "exorcism."

Of course, ever since the movie *The Exorcist*, people have become familiar with the idea of exorcism, or at least an exaggerated and fictionalized idea of the process. It is commonly thought of as a way to get rid of demons or devils (if they exist) that may be "possessing" a person. If you haven't noticed, possessing demons are fairly rare these days (although some fundamentalist Christian sects blame everything from smoking and gambling to poverty and cancer on demons). Yet, in medieval literature they seemed to be fairly common. We must ask ourselves, "What happened to them?" The conclusion must be that either they have almost totally ceased to bother people, they never existed, or the modern interpretation of these "demons" is different. Well, there is no reason to believe that the demons said to possess people in the Middle Ages have changed, and with all the reports of exorcisms during that period, there is little reason to assume that all those reports were faulty. Therefore, we may assume that the "demons" are being handled in a different manner. If you look at the actual reports of the exorcisms from that time you must be struck by the similarity between the descriptions of the "possessed" and people who today would be described as having certain physical or mental problems. So, even if we are to assume that some exorcisms did deal with demon possession, it seems that many functioned as a sort of early psychotherapy in the tradition of what is today known as "psychodrama."

These techniques are not associated only with medieval Christian philosophy. Similar techniques were used in some initiatic systems. But for our purposes here, the most important thing to know is that in many cases the exorcisms worked.

The Golden Dawn system of telesmatic images is based on a complex technique of visualizations according to a pre-established code of image construction. The members of the order would find an entity and build up its appearance for visualization using a complex set of rules. It is too involved to discuss in its full form here. The idea, however, is to create an image of something which in itself is devoid of form. Thus, "justice" could be made to have a specific image. So could "freedom" become a particular angel or archangel. "Intolerance" could be visualized as a demon with a set of features determined by the telesmatic system. Then, once this image was created, it could be given a "life" of its own (to a limited extent). Finally, it could be dealt with as if it were a living, breathing entity like you or me.

Notice that I said that something like "intolerance" could be given form. Likewise, any quality, good or bad, can be given form. It is this idea, along with the idea that exorcism was an early technology for dealing with unwanted psychological issues, that is the basis of the I.O.B. technique.

A word of warning: It may be that going to a positive, growth-oriented psychotherapist who is not against occult studies may be better for you than attempting the I.O.B. technique to deal with your "inner demons." This is because the I.O.B. technique is the only thing in this entire course that could be considered dangerous. By this I do not mean that demons might attack you or you might get ill. What I mean is that through this technique you will learn more about your true nature than you may be able to accept. It is said that over the doors of the ancient mystery schools was seen the phrase "Know Thyself." Really knowing yourself can be the most awe-inspiring and frightening experience imaginable. So, if you opt to attempt this technique and find yourself scared, physically ill or feeling lost, *stop immediately!* The mind has certain blocks and safeguards, which prevent us from learning the innermost truths about ourselves until we are ready to accept them. Go slow, be gentle, and if you try this system be kind to yourself. It is very powerful.

The "I" in I.O.B. stands for "Identify." Your first and perhaps most challenging task in this technique is to identify aspects of yourself that you no longer wish to possess. Are you hard-headed? Egotistical? Self-centered? Insecure? Indecisive? Whatever it is, your first task is to identify it. Now, at the beginning this is quite safe, although it might not be too easy to admit to those things which you consider to be your own faults. Later, it will become easier to admit your faults on a conscious level, but your unconscious may resist your conscious. This will be the time to go easy. Never force something if it will not come easily. Work on one thing at a time. This process may be time-consuming, but it is far shorter and cheaper than Freudian analysis (Freud actually wrote that he wanted his system to take a long time and cost patients a lot of money). And it does work.

The "O" in I.O.B. stands for "Objectify." This second step is the easiest and most fun. The idea here is to build up an image that represents what you have identified. This can be any form, although it should preferably be capable of life. Thus, a rock would not be as good for this technique as would an elf, or a dog, or the image of a demon.

Let's assume that you have determined that one of the things which you wish to rid yourself of is hardheadedness, the inability to change. In this step we want to objectify this hardheadedness, make it into a thing. We can make up any image, but for our purpose here let us give it a somewhat human appearance. Its face must have firmly chiseled features, and he (let's make it male) has an army helmet on. His eyes are steel grey. He is tall and strong, but the joints of his legs and hips do not work, so his strength is useless. He is wearing a metallic jumpsuit, and beneath it are seen hard muscles, which never relax. In fact, in some places the muscles look like nuts and bolts. Although it is hidden, it is possible to sense that he feels great pain because he can never relax: he must always be hard, there is a fear of not being right, etc. In this way an image of hardheadedness is built up. All of the things I mentioned are objectifications of the archetype of hardheadedness. If this happens to be an aspect of yourself that you wish to work on, you can start with what I have given and continue. What color is his skin and hair? (Don't be limited by standard or "normal" colors.) Is he holding anything? Doing anything?

Lastly, name this creation. You can use any name as long as it is not the name of someone you know or know of. Again, it does not have to be standard. "I-gis" (hard "g") is short and applicable. "Grelflexor" is an interesting and perfectly acceptable appellation.

Spend some time making this image as concrete as possible in your mind. You may wish to draw it if you have some artistic abilities. Also, it does not have to be in human form. It can be shaped like a bizarre animal. In fact, that might even be better.

Once you have "created" this image, the next step is to give it life. Visualize the figure and do the LBRP around both you and the figure. If you have made a painting or sculpture or decoupage of the image, use that as a focus of the LBRP. Use your mind and visualization abilities to make the physical art creation and the mental image unite.

Next, do the Middle Pillar technique. When you sense the energy in the Middle Pillar is at a peak, take a deep breath and, with a full exhalation, send the life-giving (literally) energy down your arms and out your hands toward the figure that you have mentally created. If you have a physical representation of the image, send it toward that figure.

The "B" in I.O.B. stands for "Banish." This is the magickal equivalent of exorcism. However, this process of banishment—though based on the Lesser Banishing Ritual of the Pentagram—is a little tricky because we are banishing an unwanted part of ourselves. Now, let's go through this step by step.

STEP ONE. Purify the outside of yourself with a ritual bath as already described.

STEP TWO. Do the Relaxation Ritual.

STEP THREE. If you have a picture or sculpture of your objectification, look at it for a few minutes. Then put the physical image away and work it up in your imagination. If you have no physical image, simply build it up in your imagination. Make it as real as you possibly can.

STEP FOUR. As part of your visualization you should see a wispy cord or rope-like construction connecting you and the figure. It should be connected to both your body and the body of your objectification at the solar plexus. If it does not have a

solar plexus, then it should be attached to its heart area or head.

(Remember, your visualization needs to be only as good as you can make it. It does not have to be perfect. In fact, if you are not good at visualizing things, simply know—not think or believe, but *know*—that it is there and that if your psychic vision were better you would be able to see it.)

STEP FIVE. Now, take your dagger and make a physical motion that cuts the connecting cord close to your body. If you do not have a dagger, use two fingers of your right hand as if they were a pair of scissors. The important thing to remember about this step is that it should be both physical (you should do an action) and mental (you should visualize the cutting of the cord).

STEP SIX. Immediately, and without so much as a nanosecond's pause after Step Five, make the sign of the enterer (take a step forward with your left foot as you thrust your arms forward, dagger or right forefinger along with the left forefinger pointing straight ahead) directly at the newly separated figure. At the same time, project a bright blue pentagram at the figure from your fingers and shout, "[Name of the object], be gone!" This should cause the visualization to move a short distance away and stay there long enough for you to perform . . .

STEP SEVEN. The LBRP. Perform the complete Lesser Banishing Ritual of the Pentagram. When this is completed, make sure the figure you created is *outside* of your protective circle. Make sure that there is no trace of the severed cord that existed between you and the figure. If a small, vestigial piece of it remains, that's okay, but anything attached to you should be completely within your circle, while anything attached to the figure outside of your circle must not enter the circle at all.

STEP EIGHT. Determine which magickal tool would be the appropriate weapon to destroy the figure. Here are some possible examples:

For hardheadedness (unwillingness to change): The chalice.

For fickleness: The pentacle.

For sloth: The wand.

For lack of clear thinking: The dagger.

As you can see, the appropriate tool represents the opposite qualities of what you wish to rid yourself. Water is always changing, so the chalice is a good weapon against unwillingness to change. The solidity of Earth, as represented by the pentacle, is a good weapon against constantly changing the mind. The energy represented by the Fire wand is a good weapon against laziness, and since Air represents our higher faculties, Air's tool, the dagger, is a good weapon against lack of clear thinking. If you do not have a set of the traditional tools, use whatever you have that represents the appropriate element.

STEP NINE. Point the appropriate magickal weapon at the figure (be sure to drink the contents of the chalice if it is filled *before* doing this!). The instructions for how to point the pentacle are to simply hold it by the black sections and face the concave side in the direction you wish to point. Pointing the wand and dagger are obvious. Hold the chalice by its stem or base with the section for holding fluid facing out, away from you. If you do not have the tools as yet, just use the outward-facing palms of your hands. Say:

By the power and in the name of Sha-dai El Chai [vibrate the God name] I command you, _____ (name of your created image), to dissolve, vanish, depart, disappear. You are banished forever and may not return. So mote it be!

This must be said with authority, as if you were a mighty king or queen talking to your lowliest subject. Remember, though, that it is not you that will destroy what you don't want, but the power of the Divine going through you. ("Mote" is an Old English word meaning "must.")

STEP TEN. Do the Middle Pillar Ritual very briefly. Then, as in the Circulation of the Body of Light, feel the energy come down from above, but this time direct it down your arms and out your hands, through the appropriate magickal tool (if you have it), through the center of the pentagram in front of you from the LBRP (it must not go anywhere else), and into your creation. Visualize the energy getting stronger and the figure getting weaker and increasingly transparent. With each exhalation, the energy leaving you should be stronger and stronger until the created figure is totally overpowered and vanishes into nothingness. Continue this sending of energy, in the name of Divinity, for at least a minute after the figure is totally destroyed.

STEP ELEVEN. Now hold your arms up in the air at about a sixty-degree angle so they form a large letter "V" above your head. If you used a magickal tool, it should be in the right hand, pointing up. Look upward and say:

Hail unto Thee, Lord of the Universe. Hail unto Thee, whom nature hath not formed. Not unto me, but unto Thee be the power and the glory for ever and ever, AMEN.

STEP TWELVE. Once again, do the LBRP. Then, visualize your magickal circle fading from your attention, but know that it is still there. Write down the results in your diary.

The I.O.B. technique can help you solve many of your problems. But remember, at this time you are just a magician in training. A chef learning to cook does not always have his or her food come out perfectly, and your I.O.B. technique may not be perfect at first either. You may need to repeat this technique several times in order to rid yourself of some aspect of your being or behavior you do not want. If you have created (or purchased) an artistic version of your visualization, it should be totally destroyed after doing the I.O.B. And if the problem is not succumbing to your work, go on to another aspect of your personality you wish to change or eliminate and come back to the previous problem later.

If you, and the other members of your group, practice the I.O.B. technique regularly, it is possible that your group will work harmoniously together. And if you want to work alone, your own work on the I.O.B. technique will make you a better person.

Nature Abhors a Vacuum of the Mind, Too

While I have received numerous letters of success from people using the I.O.B. technique, I've also received messages from people who have only had temporary success. I had used the technique for making personal change and other forms of magickal work with great success, and frankly I didn't understand why some people were having problems.

Although I had occasionally studied hypnosis on my own for a long time, there had been no structure to my studies. It was only in late 1999 that I took my first professional class in hypnosis and hypnotherapy. It was there that I found the solution to the problem.

There is an old saying, originated as a scientific concept by Aristotle, and known as *horror vacui*, that "nature abhors a vacuum." By this he meant that an empty space would always try to suck in a liquid or gas.

In that basic hypnosis class, the instructor pointed out that helping people stop smoking was the "bread and butter" for many hypnotists. Often, however, people who try and use hypnosis to stop smoking make an error that leads to failure. The process of smoking includes activities and takes time. You have to get your cigarettes, take one out of the pack, put it in your mouth, find a lighter or match to start it, take the time to smoke it, find a place to put it out, find a place for the butt, and put the cigarettes and lighter or match away. If you simply use hypnosis to help a person stop smoking, he or she is left with a blank spot, an emptiness, and a bunch of unused time. Something will fill up that time and replace the activity. If you don't give a person something to do during that time, the person will do so by themselves. And the easiest thing to do is fall back into old patterns and start smoking again.

So in professional hypnotherapy to stop smoking, the hypnotist works with a client before the hypnosis begins to figure out something to fill up that time with one or more activities.

This led me to a great "aha!" moment. If you get rid of something in the I.O.B. and don't replace it with something, the demon you banished could return and fill up the vacuum you created.

The solution, then, is to come up with replacement activities. If, for example, you're working on hardheadedness, come up with simple activities—perhaps just reading about other people's beliefs with an open mind—to replace what you banished.

Yes, nature does abhor a vacuum, even if that vacuum is in your mind. It will fill it with something. Choose for yourself what you want to fill the vacuum with before nature (or your unconscious, that little devil!) does it for you, and establish it as a habit through repetition.

Review

The following questions are designed to help you determine if you have mastered the information in Lesson Three. Please try to answer them without looking at the text. The answers are in Appendix Two.

1. What are the qualities of the element Earth?
2. Name the Three Pillars of the Tree of Life.
3. Name the Three Triangles of the Tree of Life.
4. Name the Four Worlds of the Kabalah.
5. What is the goal of true meditation?
6. What are the three steps of true meditation?
7. What is "scanning" as related to meditation?
8. What four colors are associated with elemental Earth in the Queen Scale?
9. How can you be assured of never becoming a real magician?
10. In the Kabalah, what is the heavenly order of things?
11. When is it okay to heal a person who has not given you permission to do so?
12. Are rituals a failure if you sense no immediate change within yourself or outside yourself?
13. Why is the expression "four magickal elements" incorrect?
14. How do the Chinese elements correspond to the Western magickal elements?
15. Why is it a good idea to make a concave pentacle?
16. List three benefits of being involved in a magickal group.
17. What language should you use for your magickal motto?
18. What does I.O.B. mean?

The following questions only you can answer.

1. Are you regularly performing all of the rituals?
2. Do you meditate?
3. Are you mastering the Earth element?
4. Are you memorizing the correspondences?
5. Do you look up the meanings of any words in this course that you are unfamiliar with? For example, did you know that a basilisk has the head, wings, and feet of a rooster with a barbed serpent's tail? It was said to be hatched from a chicken's egg that a toad or serpent sat on. Its breath and gaze were said to be fatal. It was also known as a cockatrice.
6. What will you use the I.O.B. for? How can you use it in a way not mentioned in the book?
7. Have you ever failed at achieving a goal? Which of the Four Worlds did you leave out?
8. What is your favorite color? When you wear it, how does it make you feel? If you put on a different color, based on the Queen Scale colors, do you feel changed?
9. Have you "felt anything" from the rituals? If not, are you okay without any unusual sensation? Why or why not? What does that say about your feelings on magick?
10. When you started the lessons in this course, what was your goal? Did you seek to learn magick to have power over one or more people? What is your goal now?

Bibliography

For more information on these books, please see the annotated bibliography at the end of this course.

Crowley, Aleister. *Magick.* Weiser, 1998.

———. *777 and other Qabalistic Writings of Aleister Crowley.* Weiser Books, 1986.

Fortune, Dion. *The Mystical Qabalah.* Lulu.com, 2008.

Godwin, David. *Godwin's Cabalistic Encyclopedia.* Llewellyn, 2002.

Gray, William G. *The Ladder of Lights.* Red Wheel/Weiser, 1981.

Judith, Anodea. *Wheels of Life.* Llewellyn, 1999.

Knight, Gareth. *A Practical Guide to Qabalistic Symbolism.* Red Wheel/Weiser, 2008.

Leadbeater, Charles. *The Chakras.* Quest, 1973.

Mumford, Jonn. *A Chakra & Kundalini Workbook.* Llewellyn, 2002.

Regardie, Israel. *A Garden of Pomegranates.* Llewellyn, 1995.

———. *The Golden Dawn.* Llewellyn, 2002.

———. *The Middle Pillar.* Llewellyn, 2002.

——— *The Tree of Life.* Llewellyn, 2000.

Skinner, Stephen. *The Complete Magician's Tables.* Llewellyn, 2007.

LESSON FOUR

PART ONE

Occult groups usually have various levels known as degrees or grades. They follow a certain logical pattern, such as going up the Tree of Life or simply making sure that you understand the increasing information needed to achieve the group's highest level. The Hermetic Order of the Golden Dawn did an interesting thing. After you finished the basic introductory grade of Neophyte, identified as the 0=0 degree, you would go through a combination pattern. The next four degrees were linked to the first through fourth Sephiroht of the Tree of Life and to the magickal elements.

The Air Element

In this book we will be focusing on linking ourselves to understanding and working with the elements. In the previous lesson, we worked with Earth. In this lesson, aligned with the initiatic pattern of the Golden Dawn and other Western groups, we move on to the study of the magickal element of Air. As a reminder, go back and make sure that you've mastered the techniques in the previous lesson. In fact, look over all of the things you have learned since you started working with this book. When finished, you should start with the exercises below as soon as possible. If, after working the exercises for Earth in the previous lesson you are not satisfied with your understanding of and feelings of unity with the element Earth, continue with those exercises for up to two more weeks. Then do them sporadically as you will. However, you should begin the exercises below immediately.

The element of Air has the qualities of being warm and moist. The following exercises will help you to become more aware of this element in your daily life.

Exercise 1. Observe those things around you that have the combined qualities of warmth and moistness. Remember, all of these elemental qualities are relative. Steam is a form of the element Air, and it has much more moisture and warmth than does the vapor from dry ice. However, the cold vapor from the dry ice also has the element of Air within it. See if you can determine the relative Airy qualities as you experience them. Make a list of all these things and record it in your magickal diary. Do this exercise daily for one week.

Exercise 2. Find a spot where you can be out-of-doors and alone. Take with you an outdoor reclining lounger, the type that has nylon webbing spaced around an aluminum frame. If you don't have one of these, a folding chair will suffice. The idea here is to be elevated above the ground and have as much of the physical air surrounding your body as possible.

Remove all of your clothing and lie on the lounger or sit in the chair. If you cannot find a place where this is possible, wear as little clothing as you can. For men, a brief men's swimming suit is fine, and for women a tiny bikini will do. The object here is not nudity, but rather to allow as much air to touch your body as possible.

What you will be doing is known as "elemental pore breathing." To do this, start off by doing the Relaxation Ritual. Next, become very aware of your breath. Become aware of the slow in-and-out motion of the physical air. Notice the way the air feels as it comes in through the nose, goes down the air pipe, and into the lungs. Sense, visualize, or just imagine the interchange of oxygen and carbon dioxide within the lungs, and feel the CO_2-laden air as it goes out of the lungs, through the air pipe, and out the nose and mouth.

Now imagine that your entire body is nothing but a large breathing apparatus. Imagine that every part of your body only has the function of breathing. Further, visualize or imagine that your skin is part of this system. As you physically breathe, imagine that *every pore* of your skin is also breathing. However, just as your lungs breathe in physical air, your pores

should be breathing in elemental Air. Feel it going in and out of you, cleansing, purifying, and vitalizing your entire body.

Try this exercise at different times of the day and, if possible, at different locations. Air is the second most changeable of the elements and you can experience it in many different ways. Do this exercise daily for at least a week. If you wish, you may do it for a longer period of time—it's a really fun exercise and you're going to enjoy it—but after a week go on to the next exercise.

Exercise 3. Spend a period of up to three minutes (no more), once a day, imagining that *you are the element Air*. Feel the lightness, the floating giddiness, the warmth and moistness of Air. Feel how physical things don't seem to matter and learn the true meaning of the term "airhead" while understanding that it is merely a description and not a negative comment. This is not said in jest, but in all seriousness. Become Air.

Do this exercise for a week only, no more. Do not repeat it (if repeating it is your desire) for at least a month. Do not repeat it more often than one week out of a month. That is, no more than twelve weeks per year, one week at a time. If you notice that you are having trouble finishing your normal work, *halt this exercise immediately.* In a day or two you will be back to normal. Also, doing Exercise 3 from the section on the element of Earth from the previous lesson will help overcome the problem of absorbing too much Air, which is the cause of becoming an "airhead" in the negative sense.

Exercise 4. Once you have learned how to "be Air" (without allowing it to take over your life), the next step is to take greater conscious control of the element. Take a moment and imagine yourself to be Air. Bring the feeling from the last exercise into your consciousness. Next, hold your hands nine to twelve inches apart, palms facing each other. Visualize or just imagine a bottle or box between your hands. Now, as you exhale, visualize all of the Air element that is in you going out with your breath and being trapped in the container between your hands. Three

Why Do I Gotta . . . ?

"A month? You expect me to study just one lesson a month? Why? I could be waaay beyond that by now. Why can't I just go as fast as possible? Why do I gotta . . . ?"

Hold on a minute there, Speed Racer! *Modern Magick* is not just a bunch of lessons to read. Well, I suppose you could do that if you wanted to, but unlike other books that have the aim to teach you *about* magick, the purpose of this course is to help you *become a powerful magician.*

Many of the techniques given here need to be memorized so that you can forget about the technique and throw yourself into the practice. In other words, the practice needs to become a habit.

In 1960, Dr. Maxwell Maltz published *Psycho-Cybernetics: A New Way to Get More Living Out of Life.* Maltz was a plastic surgeon who observed an interesting phenomenon. He saw that it took about twenty-one days after an amputation for a patient to develop the "phantom limb" sensation, a feeling that there was still a limb where the amputation had been and that it was hurting, aching, itching, etc. He derived from this that it took three weeks (twenty-one days) to install a new habit.

The thinking behind this is that to install a habit we have to bombard our brains for this length of time—without an interruption—to produce the new connections and energy/information flows within the brain that will break an old habit and/or establish a new habit. If there is an interruption, you have to begin the twenty-one-day period of repetition again.

I do not know if this is exactly what happens for one main reason. Although I believe that the brain (the grey stuff between the ears) is linked to the mind, I'm not sure they are the same. If they are not, then changing the brain may or may not change the mind. For evidence to support this, scientists have mapped out the brain, and although a section of the brain attributed to a certain behavior may be damaged, the person can still either perform or redevelop that behavior.

If we assume that the brain is not the mind, is there any evidence that it takes twenty-one days for the mind to develop a habit? Maltz discovered that if he worked with patients wanting plastic surgery, giving them positive visualizations to focus upon for three weeks, it would alter the patients' mindset and many would go so far as to cancel the surgery.

This may have been achieved simply because Maltz wanted it to happen so his patients complied (one aspect that leads to success with hypnotherapy). Whatever the cause, this three-week rule has become a standard theory in behavior-changing work.

I figured I could give you a week to get the basics of any lesson going, and three weeks to practice, turning rituals and techniques into habits. During that time, I hope you will also further your study of the materials in the lesson. So yes, you "gotta."

By the way, Maltz's books are based on visualization techniques, and I'll be covering some secret methods for that in these lessons. In the meantime, you may want to look at Dr. Maltz's books.

to five breaths should be enough to fill it. Then, with three breaths, inhale it back into yourself and go back to normal consciousness.

The Test. This test will allow you to see whether or not you really have become in harmony with the magickal element of Air. It will also allow you to objectively judge whether you are actually able to control the element.

The next time you feel heavy, bloated, slow, or lazy, form the container of Air as described in the previous exercise. Once the container of Air has been formed, with one big inhalation draw the contents of the container back into you. Within five minutes you should feel relaxed and refreshed, lighter, and anxious to do those tasks you wish to do.

The next time that you feel lightheaded, giddy, overly silly, unstable, etc., again form the container of Air. Next, visualize a large "black hole" in the physical air in front of you. When your container is filled to overflowing with your excess elemental Air, "throw" the container into the black hole. That is, visualize yourself tossing the container of elemental Air into the black hole, and then see the hole sealing itself up after your container has entered it. You should feel more grounded and balanced in a few minutes. It may be necessary to repeat this "black hole" experiment two or three times to feel totally normal.

When you have passed both parts of this test to your satisfaction, you will have mastered the element of Air. As I said about elemental Earth, if you do not succeed at such mastery within a few days or weeks, *don't worry about it.* Just keep practicing. With one or more of the magickal elements it may take only a few hours or days to master. Other elements may take considerably longer. But remember, there is no race to succeed. Do not give up! Just keep practicing without worrying about the results. Eventually *you will succeed,* as have all who have diligently practiced. Don't forget to record the results of your experiments—good, bad, or indifferent—in your magickal diary every day.

PART TWO

As I said before, anyone can do a ritual, but a ceremony really takes a group to perform properly. Let's assume that you have gathered a group of people together, and all of you are studying via this course. Here, then, is a practical and valuable group ritual you can perform together.

A Healing Ceremony

This is a ceremony to help someone who needs to be healed. There should be a minimum of three people, plus the person to be healed. This particular ceremony should not be used on someone who has a fever. Nor should it be used on someone who has a minor cold or flu, as those "dis-eases" are needed to cleanse the body of toxins due to the poor living habits that made the person susceptible to the germs that are always around us. However, when most of the cold or flu is over and the ill person is just very tired from the effects of this illness, this ceremony is effective. It is also good for chronic diseases. The only exception to the above rules is if the cold or flu is life threatening.

This ceremony will not replace the treatment of a regular physician, an M.D., nor should you reverse a doctor's instructions. But after this ceremony a doctor may need to change a treatment when a patient is found to be better or totally healed.

STEP ONE. Have the person in your group who is most adept at doing a divination (such as with the Tarot) perform one to see if it is appropriate to do the healing. If not, follow that advice. Trust the divination.

STEP TWO. If the answer from the divination is positive, ask the ill person if he or she freely gives permission for the group to do this healing ceremony. If the answer is no, do not go further. Even if the person has previously begged for a healing, the question should still be asked. If the answer is positive, prepare the area as follows:

a. Form a ring of chairs with enough room allowed to easily walk around outside the circle of chairs. There may be more chairs than people.

b. In the center should be the altar with the usual paraphernalia upon it. Another chair, for the person being healed, should be stationed in front of the altar, facing east. The ill person should sit in the chair, facing east, throughout the ceremony, especially if that person is not part of your practicing group. Others should sit in the circle of chairs where they will See diagram on the next page.

STEP THREE. A person should be chosen to lead the relaxation ritual. Let that person use a low, deep, relaxing voice, almost as if trying to coax a small child to fall asleep.

STEP FOUR. Let one person do the LBRP. The Kabalistic Cross should be done from behind the altar, facing east. The formulation of the pentagrams should be done by walking *outside* the circle of chairs so that all are enclosed. The Evocation of the Archangels and the repetition of the Kabalistic Cross should be done facing east, from "behind" the altar. That is, you should be west of the altar facing toward the east. If you do not have an altar, perform this from behind the person who is to be healed.

It is also possible to have one person do the Kabalistic Cross, another do the formulation of the pentagrams, another do the Evocation of the Archangels, and the first person repeat the Kabalistic Cross. Personally, I have not found this to be as effective as having one person do the entire LBRP, but try both ways and see which you prefer. The person being healed should not be actively involved in the performance of the LBRP.

All of the members of the circle who are sitting in their chairs should be focusing intensely on the ritual being performed. They should add their own visualizations to those of the person(s) doing the ritual. No one, save the person to be healed, should ever be doing nothing within the circle once the ceremony starts.

STEP FIVE. Let all the ritualists, save one predetermined ritualist, come forward and form a tight circle, holding hands, around the person to be healed. In this position, let all do the Middle Pillar Ritual. The one remaining ritualist should stand in the east, facing west (toward the people), also doing the Middle Pillar Ritual, but should imagine himself or herself as being a hundred feet tall, and both watching and partaking of this ritual.

STEP SIX. The person in the east should hold in his or her right hand either a dagger (for chronic or mild problems) or the wand (for more severe problems). When the Middle Pillar Ritual is complete, this person should hold up his or her arms as if in blessing, and walk directly toward the circle of participants, saying:

I come in the power of light,
I come in the power of wisdom,
I come in the mercy of the light,
The light hath healing in its wings.

STEP SEVEN. By this time he or she should be next to the circle of people centered around the person to be healed. With the tool he or she has carried, this person should point either toward the top of the ill person's head or toward the particular part of the body wherein lies the problem to be healed.

At this instant, all in the circle should imagine a giant, bright light above the center of the circle. This is a group Keter rather than an individual Keter. Each ritualist should see a beam of light shoot out from the group Keter toward the person with the tool, sending vast amounts of pure, healing energy. When the lone ritualist feels this has been accomplished, he or she should direct this huge amount of combined group and spiritual energy down to the tool and into the body of the person being healed.

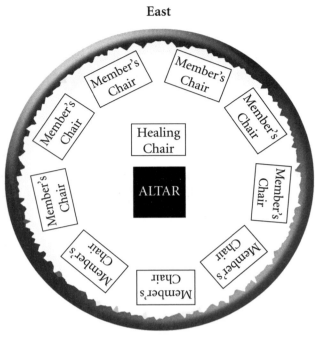

East

Circle for a Healing Ceremony

STEP EIGHT. When the ritualist senses that the ill person under the magickal tool has the energy running clearly through him or her, the ritualist should start vibrating (at a very low pitch) the vowel sound "AH." All, save the person being healed, should join in with the intonation of the vowel, letting it rise in pitch and volume. When the ritualist feels it can get no higher, he or she should say "now" as a cue for all the ritualists to shout "GLAH" (thus making AH-GLAH or AGLA as in the LBRP) and clap their hands loudly, thus breaking the circle of energy. This keeps the energy within the person being healed and prevents it from flowing back into the ceremonialists. Immediately, the main ritualist turns east, raises both hands (still holding the tool in the right hand), and says,

Not unto me but unto Thee be the power and the glory forever.

All ritualists vibrate **AH-MEN** and return to their seats.

STEP NINE. The LBRP is repeated as before.

Here Ends the Healing Ceremony.

As stated within the text of the ritual, the sudden breaking of the circle with claps and a shout is to prevent any of the energy from going back into the ritualists. Although it would not hurt them, since it is positive, it would lower the power and intensity of the healing. It also prevents a "negative backlash," which is frequently suffered by healers who are naturally talented but have no magickal experience, knowledge, or training. Sometimes this type of healer ends up temporarily suffering from the same symptoms as the person being healed. This negative backlash is totally avoided by the techniques of the above ceremony.

Some of you may be wondering about my associations for wand and dagger. I will have more to say on this subject later in this very lesson.

PART THREE

In this section I will be sharing some ideas on symbolism with you, starting with one of the oldest and best-known symbols, the cross. The cross is far older than Christianity. It has always been revered as a spiritual and religious symbol. This is why early Christians usurped the cross as "their" symbol. Various non-Christian traditions had used forms of the cross far back into antiquity. By using the cross as their new symbol it was thought that it would be easier to convince the Pagans that they should worship a similar God, one who had the same symbol. In a similar fashion, Pagan holy places were usurped by Christians and changed into churches. Thus, if a Pagan wished to worship at a sacred site, he or she would have to go into the church and worship there.

The earliest Christians used the symbol of a fish drawn with one continuous line (see figure below) to represent their faith. Some Christians say that this is because Jesus was said to be a fisherman, although nowhere in the New Testament does it mention him fishing.

Also, it is said to represent Christianity because the Greek word for fish, *icthys*, is an acronym (or Notarikon!) for the Greek words meaning "Jesus Christ, the son of God, the Savior." On an astrologi-

That "Old Time Religion" is Fishy!

Some readers may question my claims about the mythic aspects of Christianity. That's good! Dion Fortune said there is no room for authority in occultism. I say, "Don't take my word for it. Check it out yourself."

The concept of Christianity is firmly based on the astrological concepts of the Piscean age. As such, *in its creation*, it is "old age" as opposed to the coming new age, the age of Aquarius. The symbol of Pisces shows two fish going in opposite directions. Thus, we have people preaching peace while planning and practicing warfare. We have societies split in two. We have people extolling competition rather than cooperation. When we finally fully enter the next age this will change, but as the song says, we are only at the "dawning" of the age of Aquarius.

In the previous paragraph I didn't mean to imply that the church fathers sat around in a circle planning a religion to fit the characteristics of the Piscean age. Rather, they were so heavily influenced by the energies of the new Piscean age that they couldn't help but create a Piscean-oriented religion with a focus on fish and fishing. To survive in the coming age Christianity (and all other religions) will have to evolve. But that will be up to the members of each religion.

As shown in the main body of the text of this lesson, the earliest symbol for Christianity was that of a fish drawn with a single line. One of Jesus' famous miracles is that of the loaves and fishes. He uses metaphors related to fishing. About the only thing they don't do is worship Dagon, the ancient Semitic god who, according to Jewish tradition (which the early Christians knew), was in the form of a fish.

According to Austen Layard, who excavated Babylon in the nineteenth century, the high priest of Dagon would put on a garment made of a giant fish with the head of the fish forming a miter at the head of the priest. According to Alexander Hislop in his 1858 book *The Two Babylons*, "The two-horned mitre, which the Pope wears, when he sits on the high altar at Rome and receives the adoration of the Cardinals, is the very mitre worn by the priests of Dagon, the fish-god of the Philistines and Babylonians."

That sure looks like a fish with an open mouth to me. The decorations even look like a fish's eyes. But then, that's just my opinion . . .

cal basis, Jesus wasn't a fisherman, but a *fish man*; that is, an archetype of the Piscean Age. There are many dates given for the beginning of the Age of Pisces (the astrological sign is represented by two fish), but they all center around the start of the common era, within a few hundred years of the year 1 C.E.

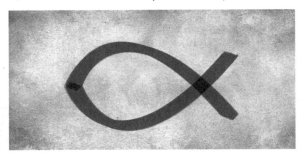

Early Christian Fish Symbol

Great charismatic leaders with large followings of sometimes mindless devotees are typical of the Piscean Age. Thus, from the dawning of this age we have had Alexander the Great, Jesus, Cromwell, some of the popes, Arthur of England, Mussolini, Hitler, Roosevelt, Kennedy, Marx, Stalin, Mao, Falwell, Rev. Moon, Jim Jones, Prabhupada, Gandhi, and many others. I am not trying to equate the qualities of goodness or badness between these men, only to indicate their charisma and ability to attract an utterly devoted, sometimes mindless following. Nor should I have left out the women, such as Joan of Arc, Blavatsky, Besant, McPherson, Anthony, Sanger, Peron, and others. These women, too, attracted and still attract many followers. Jesus, as a Piscean Age archetype, is perfectly represented by the symbol of the fish.

One of the earliest forms of the cross was known in ancient Egypt. It had a loop at the top and was (and still is) known as the Crux Ansata, the looped cross, Isis' sandal strap, and most commonly as the ankh. Many people following a spiritual path try to ignore the inherent sexuality of the ankh. The vertical bar represents the erect male organ while the loop and the split horizontal bar represent the fe-

male sexual organ. Together, indicating sexual intercourse, they are a symbol of fertility. With this understanding it is easy to see how the ankh has evolved into a symbol of life, eternal life, reincarnation, and rebirth. Why would the Isis' sandal strap represent eternal life, as some have claimed?

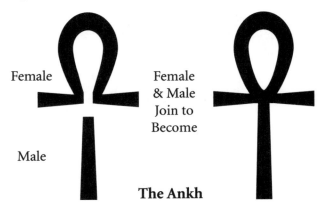

The Ankh

Why, as one group maintains, would the shadow of a person with his or her arms outstretched (which looks like an ankh) represent life after life? This cross is a pre-Christian and non-Christian symbol. Curiously, the ankh is used by Roman Catholics. On their robes (specifically, part of certain forms of the chasuble or possibly a type of rationale worn over the chasuble), some church officials wear two ankhs, one on the front and one on the back, with a common loop. When wearing this outfit, the loop is placed over the head, which gives rise to speculation over sexual symbolism and spirituality. In any event, the looped cross is not a Christian symbol.

The ancient Pagan Europeans also had crosses. One type of cross which was popular was the equal-armed, or solar, cross. Another was the circled or Celtic cross. (Remember, "Celtic" is pronounced "kel-tik" and not "sel-tik." The cross and the people are pronounced "kel-tik." The basketball team is pronounced "sel-tik.")

Another form of the cross that appeared all over Europe, Asia, and both North America and South America was the spinning solar cross, also known as the fylfot ("fill-foh") cross, the hammer of Thor,

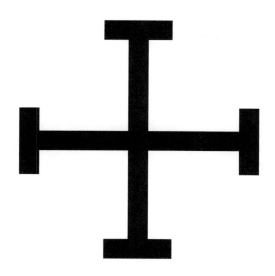

The Equal-Armed Solar Cross

One Version of the Circled or Celtic Cross

In the diagram you can see how the Nazi swastika goes against the Sun, giving the impression of spinning in a counter-clockwise direction. Note, too, that it is on a point rather than horizontal-vertical. Although the Nazis did at times use the true mystical swastika, their official symbol was the perverted version. Today, most people in the West are disgusted with the symbol because it represented the horrors brought upon the world by the Nazis. In places such as India, however, in its standard form it is still hon-

Common Forms of the Mystical Swastika

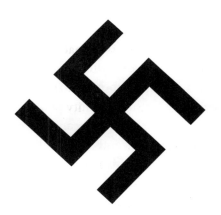

Hitler's Version

ored as a sacred symbol and a good-luck charm.

The purpose of the above paragraphs, besides looking at symbolism, is to firmly implant in your mind that the rituals we do, even though in places they do involve the symbolism of the cross, are not Christian, Nazi, or any other faith or dogma. Nor are they merely de-Christianized versions of Christian symbols and rituals. If anything, it would be more correct to say that Christianity has borrowed the ancient mystical symbols for its own purposes. Thus,

or the swastika. This holy and mystical symbol was most often drawn in a horizontal-vertical pattern with the arms in such a way that the cross appeared to be moving either with the Sun, clockwise, or against the Sun, counterclockwise. It is a shame that this symbol was perverted by Adolf Hitler himself, who chose the full design of the Nazi flag.

Why Did Hitler Choose the Swastika?

Racism, Anti-Semitism, Religion, and Occultism

It was a strange convergence that led Hitler to choose the swastika as a symbol of the Nazi party. It began when linguists began to notice that the ancient language of India, Sanskrit, had many similarities with Western languages. How could this be possible if there was not communication between India and the West in ancient times?

One linguist, Max Müller (1823–1900), hit upon an answer. He came up with a theory that India had been inhabited by a dark-skinned race (known as Dravidians and who, this theory holds, were ignorant savages) and that around 1500 B.C.E. they were invaded by a race of light-skinned "Indo-European" people from northwestern Asia (known as Aryans), who were highly advanced and brought language and civilization. He chose that date because he believed in the theory held by some Christians that the world was created by God in 4004 B.C.E., so this invasion couldn't have happened earlier.

This theory was picked up by German occult groups and nationalists who hated the idea that Western culture came from the Semites (i.e., Jews) of the Middle East. It also, regrettably, was picked up by other occult groups, including the important Theosophical society and its major voice, Madame Blavatsky. Hitler, wanting to link the Nazis with the superior, light-skinned culture, took a symbol of this supposed "Aryan race" and changed it to fit his needs.

There is one major problem with Müller's theory. There is not one bit of proof to support it. The supposedly civilized Aryan people who brought Sanskrit to the Dravidians left no written record, while the "ignorant" people of India produced some of the most amazing, spiritual, and elaborate writings going back many thousands of years. There is no physical evidence for such an invasion. There is no DNA to support this migratory theory. In fact, the word "Aryan" simply means "a noble or honorable person." It was used as a term to describe spiritual leaders and had nothing to do with "races."

Sadly, the British promoted this Aryan invasion theory in India. After all, presenting a racist concept of a superior light-skinned race bringing civilization to the "ignorant" and "uncivilized" people of India mirrored their own domination of the subcontinent and helped their empire control the Indian people.

Even today, with increasing proof that there is no "Aryan race" and there never was an Aryan invasion of India, some people—even people in India—desperately hold on to their belief in the reality of this racist and anti-Semitic myth born out of hatred and silly fundamentalist Christian beliefs as to the time of the birth of the universe.

if you are Jewish, Hindu, Moslem, Pagan, agnostic, or something else, there should be nothing to hinder you from using the holy symbol of the cross as in the famous Celtic Cross Tarot reading, the Kabalistic Cross section of the LBRP, and in other rituals as well. The way we use a cross is not Christian, or perhaps I could say that it is "beyond Christian." Also, symbols currently used by other traditions can be used by those from Christian backgrounds without insult, as they come from our universal mystical source, not a sectarian one.

Another symbol is composed of the letters "INRI." The most famous use of these letters was supposedly on Jesus' cross. They were an abbreviation (again a Notarikon; there are many of these in both the Christian and Jewish versions of the Bible) for "Jesus of Nazareth, King of the Jews."

During the Dark Ages and into the Renaissance, if you did not want to be tortured and burned by the powers of the church, it was a wise idea to hide mystical and political ideas within Christian symbolism. Thus, other meanings of the letters INRI developed. To alchemists, it stood for *Igne Naturae Renovatur Integra*, Latin for "Nature by Fire is renewed in its integrity." In a later lesson I will be discussing certain aspects of alchemy that will make this particular phrase instantly clear and of great magickal import.

Another version of these letters that was also important to the medieval alchemists was *Igne Nitrum Raris Invenitum*. Again, this was Latin, then the language of the learned, and meant "shining (or glittering) is rarely found in Fire." This may be a bit more difficult to comprehend, but once a certain aspect of alchemy is explained, it should become very clear.

Believe it or not, there are many people today who consider the Jesuit Order to be a danger to our way of life. Personally, I don't agree with that thought, even if they do follow a leader known as the "Black Pope." He is called this not for spiritual blackness, but because black is the color of his robes. Also, I am not personally a believer in conspiracy theories of world domination. However, the Jesuits did go through a very political period, much as some clerics

of different faiths express their political views today. When the Jesuits went through that political period, INRI to them stood for *Iusticum* [or *Justicum*] *Necare Regis Impium*, which is Latin for "It is just to kill an impious king."

Kabalistically, the letters INRI represent much more. INRI, which in Hebrew would be Yud, Nun, Resh, and Yud, are also the first letters in Hebrew for the four archetypal elements (according to J. S. M. Ward in his book *Freemasonry and the Ancient Gods*):

English letter	Hebrew letter	Hebrew element	translation
I	Yud	Yam	Water
N	Nun	Nour	Fire
R	Resh	Ruach	Air
I	Yud	Yebeshas	Earth

According to the ancient Kabalistic document the *Sepher Yetzirah*, the Hebrew letters also have astrological meanings:

English letter	Hebrew letter	Astrology name
I	Yud	Virgo
N	Nun	Scorpio
R	Resh	Sol (the Sun)
I	Yud	Virgo

For those of you who may be totally unfamiliar with astrology, let's examine briefly the meanings of these astrological signs on a very simple basis.

Virgo is the pure and virginal sign of nature.

Scorpio is the sign of energy, death, and transfiguration.

Sol (the Sun) is the source of light and life to everything on the Earth. It is central to our lives because it is central to our solar system.

There have been many "savior gods" in the history of our planet. For the Norse it was Baldur. For the Egyptians it was Osiris. For the ancient Celts of the British Isles it was Lugh. To the Hindus it was (and is) Krishna. Just as in the Christian story of the "only" son of God, all of these "savior gods" died and came back to life for the good of humanity. All of these resurrection gods are associated with the Sun. They "die" in winter and are reborn with the warmth and plant and animal life which reappears in the spring. Unfortunately, the topic of savior-resurrection gods is far too extensive to cover in depth here. If this topic interests you, see the books listed in the bibliography.

If we were to use the Egyptian pantheon of gods, Virgo is represented by the goddess Isis, she who is nature and the mother of all things. Scorpio is represented by Apophis (also known as Set or Typhon), who was death, the destroyer. Sol is represented by Osiris, who, slain and risen, was the Egyptian resurrection and vegetative deity. Since the "I" in the "INRI" formula is repeated and represents two of the magickal elements, the three members of the Egyptian pantheon (Isis, Apophis, and Osiris) can repre-

sent the four archetypal elements of which everything on Earth is composed. They can also represent famous thoughts of alchemy, and, if you desire, they can represent some of the basic, albeit "borrowed," ideas used by Christianity.

It is interesting to note that the Notarikon, the abbreviation made of the first letters of Isis, Apophis, and Osiris, "IAO" (pronounced "eeeee-aaaaahh-oooohhh") forms the name of the supreme God of the Gnostics, an early sect of Christianity.

Resurrection or redeemer gods are always associated with Sol, the Sun. The Sun is the primary giver of light to our planet. It follows, therefore, that light is always associated with the idea of a redeemer god. This is why beneficial or "white" occult groups always try to bring light (spiritual light) to humanity.

In Latin, the word for "light" is spelled LVX and pronounced "lux," with the "u" sounding like that in

The Holy Sideburns

I have always been fascinated by etymology, the study of where words came from and how they developed. The word "impious," of course, is the antonym or opposite of "pious." In the *Tanach*, or Jewish version of the Bible, the Hebrew men are told not to trim or cut their sideburns. Today still, orthodox Jewish men can be seen with long sideburns. Sometimes they are even braided. It is considered a sign of holiness or piety. In fact, that's where the word "pious" comes from: "pious" is Hebrew for "sideburns."

The above now makes me think about the word "holy" and where it came from. Etymological dictionaries say its source is unknown and "probably" has to do with the concept of wholeness and health. To me, that seems to be a long reach and more in line with modern beliefs than with those of people from eons ago. I think something else makes far more sense, or at least as much as pious having to do with sideburns.

In ancient times, long before the births of Christianity or biblical Judaism, the type of religion or spiritual system followed by many people was shamanistic in nature. Part of many shamanistic cultures is the idea that a stone with a natural hole in it was considered very sacred. So, too, were other objects with natural holes, from sea shells up to the mouths of caves. From this comes the idea that one sign of a sacred object was its natural hole. A "holey" object was sacred. From this came our word "holy."

Holy moley!

the word "tube." In rituals we represent certain archetypal ideas to our psyches via poses and actions. It is easily possible to represent the idea of spiritual LVX or "light" by spelling it out with various gestures. For example:

V—Both arms straight up over the head forming the letter "V." The palms should be facing each other. The angle between the arms should be about sixty degrees.

L—Left arm straight out to the side, horizontally, with the palm forward. Right arm straight up, palm to the left.

X—The arms crossed on the chest, right over left, head slightly bowed.

These positions are the basis for what are known as the LVX gestures. By knowing the ideas represented by our mystical notion of light, we can use the gestures to aspire to the illumination (LVX) implied by these "gestures of the art."

Here is another interesting thing in regard to the idea of LVX. In Roman numerals, L = 50, V = 5, and X = 10, for a total of 65. In Hebrew the letters Aleph = 1, Dalet = 4, Nun = 50, and Yud = 10. Together, they also total 65. These Hebrew letters spell out the word "Ah-doh-nye"(my Lord), one of the names of God. As you will remember, it is used in the LBRP. If spiritual light (LVX) = 65 and Divinity (in the "Ah-doh-nye" aspect) = 65, then according to Gematria we must assume that there is some relationship between the two. There is such a relationship: they are one and the same! The ultimate Divinity is that infinite spiritual light known in Hebrew as Ain Soph Or (meaning Limitless Light), the third veil of "negative existence" before God begins manifesting at Keter.

Before moving on to the next part of this lesson, there are still a few theoretical things to cover. First is the meaning of the magickal word "ARARITA" ("Ah-rah-ree-tah"). It is a Notarikon, an abbreviation or acronym for the phrase in Hebrew, pronounced:

Eh-chad Rash,
Eh-chu-doh-toh Rash Ye-chu-doh-toh,
Teh-mur-ah-toh Eh-chad.

As always with transliterated Hebrew in this book, the "ch" in this phrase is pronounced like that in the Scottish word "loch."

The above phrase, represented by the Notarikon ARARITA, means "One is God's beginning, one principle is God's individuality, God's permutation is one." This clearly states the Kabalistic attitude that no matter the name by which you call Divinity, there is only one ultimate Divinity, one divine source which can be summoned. Everything is of Divinity, or as is said in a ritual, "There is no part of me which is not of the gods."

There is a short series of hexagrams which you must learn. Actually, I think of them more as being "paired triangles" than hexagrams. Israel Regardie, in his book *Ceremonial Magic*, suggests using Crowley's unicursal hexagram instead of the traditional

four paired triangles. I have learned it both ways and I quite prefer the traditional style. That is what will be given here.

Practice drawing them somewhat large in the air in front of you. They should be similar in size to the pentagrams of the LBRP. Take note of the direction to face when drawing these hexagrams. Also note the archetypal element to which each is associated.

Many people have noticed that the elements associated with the quarters of the circle have changed and are puzzled over this. One author went so far as to "explain" this change by saying it is a trap for the unwary and meant to fool people. I respectfully disagree.

The elemental associations for the LBRP are specifically related to the physical plane, the Earth plane, Mahl-koot. The elemental associations for the hexagrams that you'll see on the next page are associated with a higher plane, specifically the level associated with the zodiac. On the Earth plane, most of us are familiar with the elements as Water to the west, Air to the east, Fire to the south, and Earth to the north. On the zodiacal level, the signs follow a natural order called the triplicities because it repeats three times through the zodiac. The first sign, Aries, is a Fire sign. The second sign, Taurus, is an Earth sign. The third sign, Gemini, is an Air sign. The fourth sign, Cancer, is a Water sign. This structure—Fire, Earth, Air, and Water—repeats twice more for the remaining eight signs of the zodiac, in order. It also forms the pattern for use with the hexagrams on this higher, zodiacal plane: east is Fire, south is Earth, west is Air, and north is Water. All of this changing may seem complex, but with just a little practice the two different systems will be mastered.

Each triangle begins at the apex (even if the triangle is inverted and the apex is at the bottom), and the figure is drawn counterclockwise until it returns to its point of origination. In the diagrams on the next page, start drawing at the point numbered 1 and move in the direction of the arrow until you complete the triangle. Then start at the point numbered 2 and move in the direction of the arrow until you complete the second triangle. Note that the hexagram of the west has a common line, however for clarity it is shown as two separate triangles.

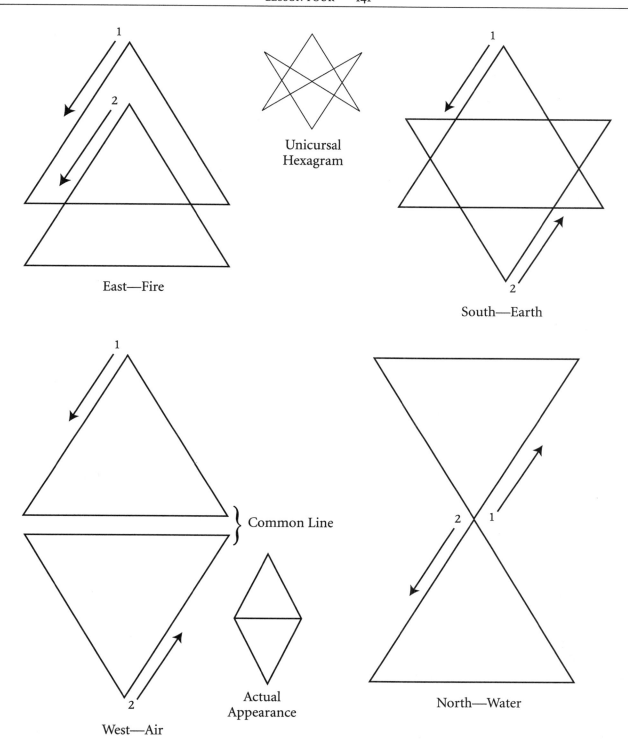

Unicursal
Hexagram

East—Fire

South—Earth

Common Line

West—Air

Actual
Appearance

North—Water

The Banishing Hexagrams

The Advanced Tarot Contemplation Ritual

Before moving on to the next part of this lesson, it is probably time for you to alter the way you perform the Tarot Contemplation Ritual. You should by now be using all of the Major Arcana cards in this ritual. When you choose a card in this advanced version, instead of merely looking at the card, *imagine yourself as the main character in the card*. You may change the gender of the main figure of the card so that the sex of that character matches your own. If there is no main character, or no human character, simply put yourself into the card anywhere. Close your eyes and visualize yourself in the card. Imagine you are there. Once you feel that you are "in" the card, will your eyes to open (not your physical eyes; keep them closed). Rather, allow your astral or psychic eyes to open so you can really look out at the scene from the card. Take a few minutes and really look around. See everything in the card from the viewpoint of yourself within the card. Try to see what is behind the images of which you can normally see only the front. Most importantly, determine if you can see anything *beyond the edge of the card*. Don't do anything, just look. Do not attempt to move or go anywhere. Just observe. Your observation should not be limited to vision. What do you hear? What do you feel? What do you smell? Do you have any sensation of taste? After a few moments of this, will your psychic eyes to close and return to normal consciousness. Record your experience, whether or not you experienced any unusual sights, sounds, smells, tastes, feelings, or sensations, in your magickal diary. Take the next seven days to read over what you have done so far in this lesson and practice this Advanced Tarot Contemplation Ritual. Then move on to the next section.

PART FOUR

The Air Dagger

Earlier in this lesson I mentioned that I was going to discuss the difference between the wand and the dagger. Although the wand has traditionally been as-sociated with the magickal element of Fire and the dagger has been associated with Air, some people, especially in recent years, have reversed these as-sociations. This is largely due to those people who have been using associations from their training in Wicca or Witchcraft. While it is true that Witchcraft is thousands of years old, it is also true that much of what is today called Witchcraft is either a creation of or a reconstruction by the late Gerald B. Gardner and his followers.

This is not meant to belittle anybody who follows a Pagan path. In fact, those who follow one of the various Pagan paths in many cases seem to have regained the link between humanity and nature that many ceremonial magicians only talk about and secretly envy. As you may have noticed, one of the important areas which this course has emphasized is the attunement to the elements, something which has been sadly lacking in most books or courses on High Magick. Part of my goal with these lessons is to bring that link back to the practitioners of ritual magick.

It is clear that Gardner simplified some seemingly complex magickal techniques and philosophy (probably "borrowed," with or without permission, from the ubiquitous A. Crowley). Then, with the help of Doreen Valiente they created the modern Craft.

It does not matter whether or not he received initiation from the New Forest Witches, as he claimed. Nor does it matter that many have gone far beyond his initial researches, training, and techniques. His importance is that he introduced many to a form of spirituality that could not be found elsewhere when he began his work. His contributions, thankfully, will last for many years to come.

However, as I said, some of what Gardner did was a simplification of traditional magickal philosophy. One of these simplifications was the equating of the dagger with the sword. This is understandable, as the sword does appear to be nothing more than a long dagger. And if you had only learned the LBRP, you might know that Me-chai-el bears a sword and stands to the south, the direction of the element Fire. Water, of course, would be associated with the chalice, and Earth with the pentacle. This leaves the wand to the element Air. And Rah-fay-el, the archangel of that element, does hold the caduceus wand. This all seems so logical.

Unfortunately for the above simplification, it is not correct to equate the purposes of any of the several wands used by a magician. The Fire wand is not the same as the lotus wand, the caduceus wand, or the rainbow wand. The wands carried by the initiatic officers of occult groups have different purposes, too. I usually wear casual shoes during the day, but "dress shoes" if I'm going out at night. They look similar—they both cover my feet—but they have different purposes. Similarly, the different wands all have varying functions even though they have the same basic shape. So, too, is the dagger different in design and function than the magickal sword.

If it helps to clear things in your mind, some people like to think of the dagger as being the tip of a spear, which is thrown through the air.

The traditional Air dagger is a simple, double-edged blade with a T-shaped handle, as shown below.

Since the Air dagger should never have been used to cut living things, it should preferably be new. Undercoat the handle and the hilt that forms the "T," but protect the blade from paint. Follow the instruction on the paint concerning the treatment of the wood and/or metal before applying one or more coats. Several light coats look better than one thick, gloppy coat. Then paint the undercoated parts a bright yellow.

On the next page you will find a listing of the Hebrew words and sigils to be painted in bright purple or mauve around the handle and "T" crossbar. As you will see, there are eight groups of these, the same number as for the Earth pentacle. In fact, all of the tools will have eight sets of words and sigils.

I have already discussed the motto (number VIII), so let's look at the others.

I—is the God name associated with the tool.

II—is the name of the archangel associated with the tool (notice that for the dagger the name is Raphael, the archangel associated with the magickal element Air).

III—is the name of the angel associated with the tool.

IV—is the name of the ruler of the element.

V—there are said to be four rivers coming out of paradise. V names the river associated with the element.

VI—is the name of the direction associated with the element and tool in Hebrew.

VII—is the name of the element in Hebrew.

VIII—is the motto.

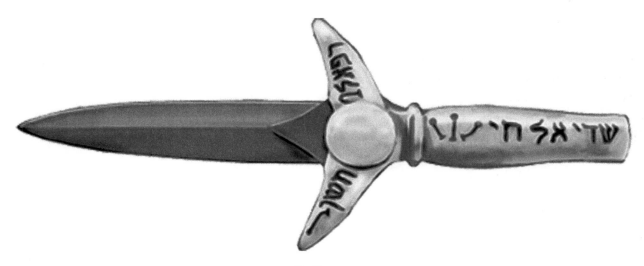

Air Dagger

After completing the painting, coat the handle with a clear plastic such as Varathane. Note that the above numeration will stay the same for all of the tools.

Let me make clear that this course is presenting traditional Western occultism. From this standpoint, other associations are incorrect. However, within their own systems, other attributions may be totally correct and the traditional system presented here would be "in error." The only moral of this paragraph, if I can call it that, is *if you do not totally understand the system you are using, do **not** mix it with other systems.* It will only cause you problems. This is not to say that you cannot blend multiple systems once they are fully comprehended. That was a prime achievement of the Golden Dawn. On the other hand, I am aware of a person who could not get involved in a Western magickal group (although he tried), then didn't like the Wiccan group he became involved with because it did not have the same magickal traditions. One was too complicated and the other too easy. The result is that he has formed his own "Ancient Cabalistic Celtic Coven." My only regrets are for the students he was "teaching" and the problems they may have in the future. It is said that "When the student is ready, the teacher will appear." Unfortunately, this is true even when the student is ready to be mistaught.

Part of your work for this lesson is the construction of the Air dagger as described. It is not expected that your art work will hit the level of a da Vinci or Michelangelo, only that it be done to the best of your abilities. There is also no "law" that says you cannot add to what is given. I added purple gemstones to mine. What will you add to your tools to make them uniquely yours?

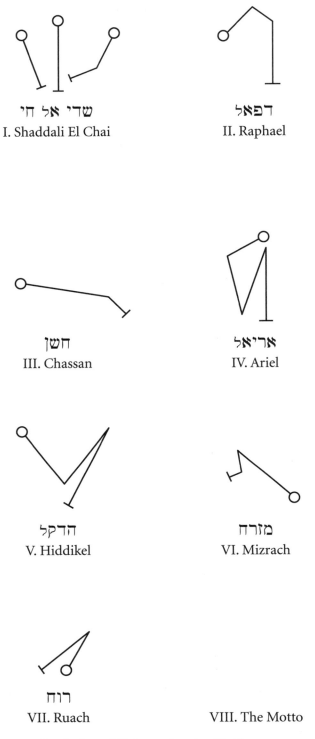

שדי אל חי
I. Shaddali El Chai

דפאל
II. Raphael

חשן
III. Chassan

אריאל
IV. Ariel

הדקל
V. Hiddikel

מזרח
VI. Mizrach

רוח
VII. Ruach

VIII. The Motto

Symbols and Hebrew for the Air Dagger

PART FIVE

Kabalistic Psychology

It is possible to classify the study of psychology into two broad areas: normal and abnormal psychology. Unfortunately, the study of abnormal psychology is beyond the scope of this course. If you are interested in this particular field from an occult viewpoint, you will enjoy the book *The Secrets of Dr. Taverner* by Dion Fortune.

Let us look at normal psychology, starting with Freud. Besides being brought up at the end of the Victorian Age, a fact that colored his entire outlook on life, he also came from a Jewish background. From his writings, it is clear to even the most casual reader that there is a harmony that exists between his thoughts and a rather simple version of psychology as described in the Kabalah. In fact, although the Kabalah and Freud argued for the idea of a subconscious or unconscious, many of Freud's contemporaries did not believe such a thing existed! In his later years, Freud said that if he had his life to live over again he would spend it in the study of parapsychology rather than psychology. I think it is safe to assume that Freud was either consciously or unconsciously influenced by the Kabalah.

As explained in an earlier lesson, Freud divided the mind into three categories: id, ego, and superego. In the 1970s a simplified form of Freudianism known as transactional analysis (as popularized in the book *I'm Okay, You're Okay*) tried to put the abstract Freudian ideas into terms understandable by lay people. Thus, id, ego, and superego were replaced with child, parent, and adult, respectively. And it is true that most people can relate better to the idea of a child wanting its way, throwing tantrums if he or she doesn't get it, than to the word "id" that has no easy picture in most people's minds. But the Kabalah goes so much further in its understanding of the mind, that Freud and Jung seem like beginners.

One of the biggest problems with standard psychological theory is that it begins with birth or slightly before. Thus, it must fail to answer some basic questions such as "What was my mind doing before the inception of my body? If reincarnation is a fact, why do I have trouble remembering past lives? And if it is not a fact, why do I have fleeting memories of past lives?" "Why is there such a desire by people in cultures all over the world to reunite with God, to be more than they are?" (Jung saw this and called it a desire for religion, a basic human instinct which Freud did not acknowledge.) The Kabalah answers this and more. Some of this discussion will have to be saved for later during a section on reincarnation, the most complete analysis of which has been hidden for centuries within the Kabalah. But for now we must merely look at that change known as death.

No matter what you believe, for argument's sake, let us assume the validity and reality of reincarnation. Let us also assume that you have died and have been reincarnated into a newborn infant. According to the Kabalah, the soul enters the body with the first breath the infant takes. Perhaps you want to finish that good book you were reading or see that movie you missed just before you died. Unfortunately, you discover that your muscles do not work the way you remembered they worked. This is not psychological, it's physiological. Nerves and bones have not finished developing. Various muscular activity cannot take place due to this lack of development. You can no longer feed yourself. You can't communicate through speech or writing. You cannot even control your bowels or bladder. After a short while, things that were part of your normal existence are now part of a terrifyingly new world.

In order to cope, you must quickly develop new modes of communication. You learn that cooing brings smiling, happy faces and warm, protective bodies. You learn that crying brings worried looks, your mother's breast, or a needed change of diapers. In order to survive, your real consciousness submerges and a false consciousness arises. Eventually, this false consciousness takes over. It becomes the consciousness or ego. It is a covering that is developed so that we can exist. It is necessary, but it is not our true self.

And what of our true self? It has submerged to a point where most people rarely if ever allow it to come out. This is especially true in so-called civilized societies. Is it any wonder that there is so much rebellion in the world? So many people, instinctively trying to release their true, inner selves, seem like rebels without causes.

But in fact, there is a cause. The true self, the part of us that survives what is called death, is not material. Our true self is spiritual and nonmaterial in nature. It is our higher self, our direct link to the Divine. It becomes hidden compared to our false, outer self. Our true self, our link to the Divine, is part of our unconscious. And there have been so many fights, disagreements, and wars caused by people who didn't know what they really wanted: communion with the Godhead. That is, what is really desired is a link to the unconscious, which is linked to the Divine. They wanted to link their conscious to their unconscious. This is a main focus of our magickal work. It is the very essence of White Magick.

As you have probably guessed, the Kabalah does not divide the mind into the Freudian or transactional analysis' three main categories, but into ten. In the next column you will see how the ten aspects of mind relate to the Tree of Life. The first thing you will notice is the dividing line at *the abyss*, the space between the upper three Sephiroht and the lower seven. The three above are immortal and last for as long as the Divine Source wishes them to exist. The seven below are mortal and cease to exist when the body dies. A quick glance will show that the memory is mortal. Thus, it is obvious that our memory of past lives will tend to be very minimal at best. Here, then, is an easy explanation as to why we tend not to remember much more than hints of our past lives.

The *Yechidah* is our True Self, our Link to the Divine, our transcendental ego. It relates to what Freud called the "superego." The *Chiah* is our True Will. It is the creative and inquisitive inner impulse (from the Divine), which causes us to reach outside and inside of ourselves to become better than we are. It makes us try harder, to want to be the best and

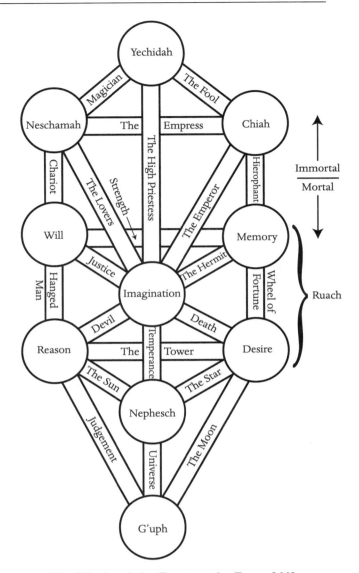

The Mind and the Tarot on the Tree of Life

do better than we have done before. This does not imply competition. We all can advance together. Sometimes this impulse is subdued, but it always comes back in force. This was exemplified by the age of exploration that followed the Dark Ages, and by our current reach into the vastness of space. It also explains the urge to commune with the Godhead, to know the joy and ecstasy of the Knowledge and Conversation of your Holy Guardian Angel, and to practice White Magick.

The *Neschamah* is the intuition. It is the seat of all the psychic abilities of humanity. There is a method of instruction called "the Socratic Method." As you would expect, it is based upon the teaching methods of Socrates. He believed that people did not learn new things. Rather, he thought they remembered things that they had forgotten at death before their current incarnation. By asking questions, Socrates would elicit from the student answers, which would lead the student to the discovery of an idea or principle that the student could not have known. Today, this system of *involving* a student rather than merely telling a student seems to be the most effective way to teach. It allows the student to have a growing, inquiring mind. It also allows for intuitive leaps and bounds, resulting in an individual who is creative rather than a robot only capable of rote repetition.

Part of the definition of magick is that it is a science. As magicians we should understand modern scientific thought. One such canon of science is the theory of evolution. Evolution is not, as many think, a smooth line. Rather, according to some of the latest concepts, it moves in jumps and jerks. Current evolutionary thought calls this "punctuated equilibrium." Likewise, the advancement of mind and humanity has often come in sudden steps. The laser was the accidental result of communications research. Today lasers are used for everything from playing music to dentistry and brain surgery previously impossible to perform even with the sharpest of scalpels. This is an example of a link to the Divine via the unconscious will. This uncontrolled link is an aspect of the Neschamah. A controlled link to the Divine is an aspect of the Chiah. Thus, from our point of view the Chiah is active and outgoing, while the Neschamah is receptive. As always, it is the goal of the Kabalist to blend opposites and bring balance into manifestation. By allowing the Neschamah to be in our awareness, we develop psychic abilities. By being conscious of the Chiah, we are able to perform magick.

The *Ruach* is our consciousness, our intellect, our false self. It equates with Freud's idea of the ego. Notice that it is composed of five parts: memory, imagination, reason, desire, and will. The aspect of will related to the Ruach is different from that of the Chiah. The Chiah is our True Will. As such, it is in alignment with the will of the Divine. The will of the Ruach is that which is moved by our superficial and transitory desires. The True Will of the Chiah is to create, to love, and to seek unity with the Godhead. The will aspect of the Ruach is to have sexual release, to eat good-smelling food although you know that the food is neither good nor needed, and to be better than those around you, even if it means hardships for them or their destruction.

The *Nephesch* is the lower self. It is the most superficial layer of the unconsciousness, wherein dwells the darker side of ourselves. It is usually under the tight control of the Ruach. Earlier I equated the Nephesch with the Freudian id. While correct, it is not precise. The id is really a process, not an aspect of the mind. It is frequently submerged and hidden within the Nephesch, but it is not exactly the Nephesch. The process called the id, when submerged in the Nephesch, is said to be controlled by the Ruach. However, when the Ruach does not control the id and the Nephesch dominates, the id is free to roam the aspects of the mind and come out in sometimes unfortunate places. Part of the techniques of magick that you have been learning include the control of this id energy so that it can be used as you wish under the control of the united Yechidah and Ruach. The Nephesch is also the source of the astral body and the seat of the energy called *Praña* (correct pronunciation: prahn-yah) in Sanskrit. In the Kabalah this energy is also known as Ruach, but should not be confused with the Ruach meaning "consciousness."

Note that there is a difference between the energy called Ruach or Praña and the id. The id is a process, a motion, while the Ruach or Praña is that which moves. Freud's original definition of the libido, as described earlier in this course, would have made it the same as Praña or Ruach energy.

Finally, the bottommost Sephira is related to the *G'uph*, the physical body. Many people wonder how the body can be an aspect of mind. To me, the interrelation is quite obvious on many levels. First, as you incarnate, you "choose" a particular body, depending on the types of experiences you need in life (more on this in the discussion of reincarnation). Also, imagine the different thoughts of someone born with severe handicaps as opposed to a person born physically "normal." There are also differences in the psyches of people who, according to the dictates of society, are considered ugly or are considered beautiful. There are even differences in the psyches of people who tend to be slim and those who tend to be obese. The physical body plays an important role as part of the psyche and should not be ignored.

But after all this information, we are left with a feeling of "That's interesting, but so what?" Actually, once you know the basis for Kabalistic psychology there is much that you can do with it. The two keys to what you can do are:

1. Understanding Kabalistic psychology using the Tree of Life, and

2. Understanding the Tarot and how it fits on the Tree of Life.

Let us say that it has been so long since you have been involved in a relationship that you cannot feel desire for someone, even though that person indicates a desire for you. A possible diagnosis here is that you no longer have the memory of what a loving relationship is like. You need something to trigger the memories. Looking at the Tree we can see that what is needed is an infusion of imagination (which is linked by a direct path to the Yechidah, our link to the Divine). Contemplating the card known as the Hermit will bring imagination back into the memory. Spend a few minutes contemplating the Hermit each day for a week. If the goal of bringing up desire has not been achieved, it is probably not because you have failed, but because you have not brought the memory down to the level of desire. Contemplation of the Wheel of Fortune card for a few minutes a day will help you accomplish this.

Perhaps you feel that you are a very logical person and pride yourself on your reasoning talents. From the standpoint of the Kabalah there is absolutely nothing wrong with this. It is fine to be proud of your talents, and not to do so would be a lie. But perhaps you feel that you are not creative enough in your life. Here, a short period of daily contemplation on the card titled "The Devil" will reward you immensely. It does not mean that you will be satanically inspired. Hopefully it will allow you to learn about and break out of your "satanic" enthrallment to cold logic and reason. Coming from the other side, if you find yourself very creative but with illogical, time-wasting ideas, contemplation of this same card will allow reason to enter your world and guide, but not over-control, your imagination.

Thus, neatly packed into the Tree of Life we have a complete system not only of psychotherapy, but also a system of dealing with day-to-day situations and improving your life. It is also a wonderful way of becoming familiar with the Tree and the Tarot.

Sometime in the future, people will have forgotten that there once was a series of "light bulb" jokes which all began, "How many _____s does it take to change a light bulb?" The answers were frequently blackly humorous. One version of this joke goes, "How many psychiatrists does it take to change a light bulb?" The answer is "Only one, but it has to want to change." The reason I bring this up is that anytime you wish to use magick to change somebody's mind, *you must ask for that person's permission first.* And the person must give it to you. You have no right to change a person even if it is for what you think might be the betterment of that person unless that person wants the change. The reason I say this is to suggest that you do not go up to a friend who you think needs changing and say, "Here, look at this card for three minutes a day for the next week" without telling that person the reason and how it works. That person may not want to change in the way you think he or she should.

Changework of this type is not a power grab or doing "something" to "someone." Rather, it is a co-operative effort to make desired changes. If someone asks for your help, fine. If he or she agrees with you after being informed of what you are doing, fine. But changing a person's mind without his/her permission is nothing but Black Magick, and you will

Freud the Failure?

Although many magicians today seem to want to "psychologize" everything (gods and demons are just aspects of our unconsciousness) and bow in obeisance to Jung with his magickal (but essentially meaningless) idea of synchronicity, if we're looking at psychology we can't ignore Freud. Freud really began what is the modern method of helping to correct the mind. He opened people to new ideas. But ultimately, he was a failure.

Freud began his studies in Paris, where incredible cures were achieved through hypnosis. Freud abandoned hypnosis for two reasons. First, he was lousy at it. He was a failure at hypnosis. He had horrible bad breath. Would you go into trance when someone leaned close to you with breath like that and said "*Sleeeeep!*" Not me, and not many of Freud's patients. So he wanted to come up with something that would get the results of hypnosis, without the use of hypnosis.

Almost.

He also saw that cures using hypnosis were very fast. He wanted something that would take much longer to achieve the success of hypnosis for a simple reason: he wanted to make lots of money. He wanted patients to come back to him for many months or years in order to overcome issues that hypnotists helped within a few sessions. So he developed psychoanalysis to take a long time and cost a lot of money.

Today, although most training in psychology goes into the study of Freudian concepts—and many are still valid—few psychiatrists practice Freudian psychoanalysis. Newer methodologies have placed analysis on the ash heap of time.

Without Freud, modern psychology would not be what it is today. But like the Greek Titans who were overthrown by their children, the Olympian gods, the children of Freud have gone in new directions.

Don't take my word on this. Check it out yourself.

---

be the one to suffer most. Start working on improving yourself before trying to help others who may be healthier than you think.

PART SIX

Egotism

We all have it to a greater or lesser degree. Many people react negatively to hearing this and insist that they are not egotistical. Well, if you don't have a strong ego, something is wrong with you. We all need strong egos, strong senses of self to survive and thrive.

What we need to do is isolate different aspects of ego from one another and eliminate those aspects we no longer desire. That positive aspect of our egos which tells us "I'm great at some things and other people are great at various things too" should be encouraged and built upon. That aspect that says to us "I'm great and everybody else is wrong" needs to be overcome.

I've gone through periods of the latter. Luckily, I have had techniques and teachers that allowed me and still allow me to overcome the problem of negative egotism when I became aware of it. It is unfortunate but true that people who teach metaphysical topics can end up being led to believe in their own (non-existent) greatness as the result of the adulation of students. One of the reasons that I suggest you read at least one other book on the topics of these lessons while you are studying this course is so that you will get other opinions and ideas, some of which may contradict the ideas presented here. Really, I'm just another human.

In Eastern mystical traditions, the physical, phenomenal world is considered an illusion (*maya*) which hides the true spiritual reality behind the phenomenal world. Our higher self can know the true universe, but it is cut off by our dominant egos, which only see the illusion. Thus, our egos "slay" the true, inner reality. We are told that to achieve enlightenment we must "slay the slayer," get rid of our egos and see the inner reality. Crowley wrote about this frequently, yet, although he claimed to have succeeded, it is very questionable as to whether he really freed himself from his ego.

According to Israel Regardie, in the West our goal is not to rid ourselves of our egos, but to perfect our egos so they are in harmony with our higher selves. I doubt if a large percentage of Western mystics have achieved that state. I'm still working on it.

What both Crowley and Regardie seem to imply is a very mechanistic mind. That is, they seem to see the amount of ego reaching a certain level which, by following certain instructions, can be raised or lowered. While I have great respect for these two gentlemen, I disagree with this viewpoint. The mind seems to be far more flowing and changeable than their mechanistic version. We can quickly or gradually change from large to small amounts of negative egotism depending on such things as the weather, our health, our physical environment, and perhaps various astrological influences. What we need to have are techniques to aid us by first allowing us to sense that a problem exists (i.e., an increase in negative egotism) and then give us some ways to deal with it.

You might be asking yourself why I'm giving you this information now. It's because I want to tell you some more about the pitfalls of leading a group, and my worst failure as a teacher.

Several years ago I had a student who I believe had more potential as a magician than anyone I had met before or since. I tried to lead him into becoming a good magician, well grounded in occult philosophy. Unfortunately, due to differences of opinion between myself and this student we ended up going separate ways.

One of the reasons for this was that he did not like the way I did some of my private tutoring. As I discussed earlier, I prefer the Socratic method of teaching. One of my teachers, Dr. Michael Turk, gave me a simple explanation of the method:

Tell me... and I'll forget.
Show me... and I might remember.
Involve me... and I'll understand.

When this student asked me a question, I would answer in a way designed to lead him to a deeper understanding of the implications of the question, and not give just a simple yes or no. He did not like the idea of having to think about the answers. He wanted a "yes or no" answer to complex questions. I refused to give him that which he really wanted: magickal power with no personal work.

About a year after he had stopped being my student, I was asked by an international occult order to start a chapter of that order in the city where I then lived. I knew several people who would be interested and who might make good members, including this former student. Naturally, on the day before I had planned to call him I accidentally ran into him and told him about it. In a short time, he, I, and some others were working together. I soon realized that previous commitments would not allow me the time to lead the group. Because he had more latent magickal talent and charisma than other members of the group, I chose him to be my successor.

This person is very intelligent. He has worked as a secretary for many years and because of it has two problems. First, since many secretaries do what they are told and allow their bosses to have the responsibility for their success or errors, he has the attitude that magickally he can do whatever he wants, and if he errs he can always do it over or use some sort of magickal "white-out" to correct the mistakes. This is a very dangerous attitude to have when doing practical magick of the sort he is doing, and both he and one of his close assistants have told me of the times when he has "summoned up something" and not been able to banish it. Had he been more advanced, the manifestation could have been more physical. The result could have been life-threatening.

Second, as a secretary he does what he is told and thus has a feeling of impotence and lack of power. I did not realize this at the time I turned the organization over to him. It was a big error on my part.

Rather than allowing him to develop more quickly, as I had hoped the leadership role would do, the power of being the local head of a group gave him a feeling that he could do anything and get away with anything. He began to lie and break his oaths left and right. He tried to give away some of the secrets of the order to others so that he might learn the inner secrets of organizations to which they belonged. Finally, although remaining a member of the organization, he decided that this order was not spiritual at all. So he became a de facto member of a well-known, very authoritarian, pseudo-Hindu order.

Since this pseudo-Hindu group tells its "devotees" when to get up, when to go to sleep, what to read, what to think, when to bathe, what to wear, when to have sex, when to eat, etc., it seemed to me that this organization would be perfect for this person who was so used to taking orders anyway. However, he insisted on continuing in the leadership role of the local group. From what I learned, he subtly twisted the teachings and used "politics" to try to get himself into total leadership of the group. He also tried to make this pseudo-Hindu order—a group that has been accused of brainwashing, mind control, gun running, and child abuse by many authorities—look very positive to members of the occult group and make several of the pseudo-Hindu devotees into members of the occult group. Fortunately for the occult lodge I had founded, his attempt failed, although his lack of focus caused the branch that I started with about ten people to fall apart and finally close down.

When the founder of the pseudo-Hindu group died, there quickly were battles to control it, resulting in the formation of new groups, some of which have genuine Hindu interests. Unfortunately, my former student became involved with drugs and prostitution. Eventually he overcame both, but still looking for the "quick magickal fix," he became involved in Satanism. I hope he gets his head together some day. I still wish him well.

One of the little-known facts of teaching is that a teacher must accept the karma of what he/she teaches. If a teacher's students use the teachings wisely, it benefits the teacher's karma. If they use the teachings to do negative things, it hurts the teacher's karma. In this case, I have to accept some of this person's karma (for his using the things I taught him in a negative way). And because he messed up some of his students, I also have to accept some of their karma as well. Needless to say, there are things I am doing magickally to end this karmic link.

The reason I have gone through this long story is to show you some of the problems caused by egotism when forming or being a member of a magickal group. The egotism of S. L. MacGregor Mathers, one-time undisputed leader of the Golden Dawn, helped cause the breakup of that organization. Crowley's egotism caused his O.T.O. and A.A. to shrink in numbers until they were very small by the time of his death. There are far more people who study and idolize Crowley today than there ever were during his lifetime. Egotism and power hunger have broken up more magickal groups, covens, and other such groups than any other single cause.

So how do we avoid the problem of negative egotism in ourselves and others? First, we must acknowledge that if it is not on the surface, it is lurking just under the surface. Second, we have to learn how to recognize it. A simple way to do this is to look at attitudes. The negative egotistical attitude is presented in the book *Krsna (sic) Consciousness, The Topmost Yoga System*, by the late founder of the Hare Krishnas. In it (p. 40) he says, "Give up research—throw it away—just become submissive... [listen only to] authorized sources." Of course, the authorized sources you should listen to and the organization you should be submissive to in this case is the Hare Krishnas. On the other hand, look at the note at the beginning of Crowley's *Book 4*, the first part of the book *Magick*:

> . . . others have said, 'Believe me!' He [Crowley] says 'Don't believe me!'. . . He wants an independent and self-reliant body of students to follow out their own methods of research. If he can save them time and trouble by giving them a few useful 'tips,' his work will have been done to his own satisfaction.

It is with this last viewpoint that I heartily concur.

If you are the head of a group and you find yourself thinking that you have all the answers and any other way is wrong, it is time to get to work on yourself. Also, if you find yourself thinking you know all there is to know about the Kabalah and magick and occultism, it is time to work on yourself.

For most of us, our sense of "self," our ego, is based on the link between consciousness and body. Even those of us who spend many hours in Astral projection still think of "me" as being the mind-body unit. The mind, being non-physical, cannot possess, cannot be superior or inferior, cannot have or do anything other than exist and seek unity with the Divine. But when mind-body are thought of as one, it can have possessions, can be physically, mentally superior or inferior to other mind-body units. Thus, the key to overcoming negative egotism is to realize and accept (not merely understand) that the mind is not the body. The mind is the true self and the body is just a servant for that true self when living in the physical universe.

The following are gentle versions of techniques, some of which are given by Crowley in his books, which will help you in this endeavor.

1. Sit in a chair, back straight, knees together, feet flat on the floor. Your hands should be palms down on your thighs with the thumbs just touching. Now, just hold this position. In a short time your body will start to tremble and your legs will move apart and separate the thumbs. You will soon learn that this simple, basic position can rapidly become very uncomfortable. The body, it turns out, quickly becomes uncomfortable in *any* position. Just try to lie in any position for a short time and you will see for yourself that this is true. It is possible, with practice, to overcome the feelings of pain and discomfort. Since the body becomes painful in any position, it must be that something else overcomes the pain. That "something else" is not part of the physical body. It is the mind.

2. When you start to see negative egotism slipping into your life, make an agreement with yourself not to say the word "I" for at least two weeks. During that time keep a pad of paper with you, and anytime you say the word "I," put a small mark on a dated page. At first the page will be filled with marks, but as you go through the two-week period, the daily number of marks will lessen. The effect of not saying the word "I" for a few weeks is quite astonishing. It tends very nicely to separate the idea of your self from the mind-body unit. To improve and speed up the result, you might wish to give a dollar or a quarter or a dime to your favorite charity for each of your "breaks," that is, each time you say "I." This exercise is a "charitable" version of Crowley's technique; he would have you slash your arm with a razor blade every time you had a break! I find the method given above quite satisfactory and much safer.

3. Do the Tarot Contemplation Ritual twice a day—once using the advanced technique, and once using the original basic technique.

PART SEVEN

I have always found amazing the large number of people who talk magick and the tiny amount of people who practice or live magick. The vast majority of people I have met who claim to be magicians show little knowledge of any rituals other than simple variations on the LBRP. Luckily, this is changing. More and more magicians are really doing magick.

Don't get me wrong, though. I cannot overstress the importance of the LBRP. Becoming proficient in magick is a precarious task, and the LBRP is the rather tiny support:

If you are not proficient at the LBRP, the entire system can fall down around you. This is why the LBRP is taught right at the beginning. In fact, other than initiation rituals, it was the *only* ritual given out to members of the Golden Dawn until they entered the Inner Order. This would take over one year of practice.

Magickal Technique

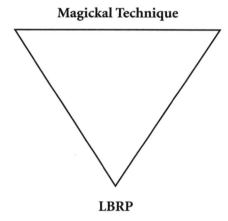

LBRP

Thus, if you start actual practice on a daily basis of other rituals such as the Middle Pillar Ritual and the ritual which is to follow, you will be doing the practical work that so many people who call themselves magicians talk about, but so few actually practice.

Let me reaffirm to you now that magickal practice is not just self-delusion or "mental masturbation." During sexual stimulation the chemistry of the body actually changes. Various hormones are released into the bloodstream, which cause the obvious signs of sexual arousal. Drugs called endorphins are created by the body and released into the blood and eventually arrive at the brain. Endorphins are similar to opiates and increase the pain threshold. As

a result, bites and scratches that at other times would be painful become very pleasurable for some people.

However, the changes due to sexual arousal are temporary. The practice of ritual magick will make longer-lasting changes. These include longevity, youthfulness, increased I.Q., and others. But unless you practice on a regular basis, nothing will happen. Magick is experiential, not mental. It all depends upon what you choose to do or not do.

The purpose of the LBRP, among other things, is to clear your immediate area of physical and non-physical distractions. This especially refers to what might be considered "negative influences."

However, when doing Grey Magick it becomes important to clear your area not only of lower or negative influences, but also of positive or higher influences. This is because when you want to get into contact with one aspect of Divinity, you do not want anything (whether it be positive or negative) getting in the way.

Perhaps at some time in your life you have had some people make very clear that they have a romantic crush on you. They always want to be around you. They want to help you in every way possible and want to touch you as much as possible. Their motivation is completely based on their idea of love, yet they can quickly become a terrible annoyance, a "pain in the neck." Even though they come to you out of love and affection—two things which are undeniably very positive—they can get in the way of your efficient functioning at school, at work, and in your personal and professional life. It may be fun for a short while, but soon it only gets in your way. We try to break our admirer of their obsession and stop the interference into our life. Similarly, it is important to prevent even positive interference into our magickal work. We must clear our immediate area, the area wherein we will work our magick, not only of negative influences, but also of positive influences. In short, we want to have an area for magickal work that has been cleared of *all* influences.

The LBRP clears the area of negative influences. The Banishing Ritual of the Hexagram (BRH) clears the area of positive and negative influences from higher planes. Just as with the LBRP, the Banishing Ritual of the Hexagram must be mastered.

Although I thoroughly enjoy the LBRP, I have always considered it to be on the level of doing my laundry. It is important and must be done regularly, or you can get into trouble. For many years I did it on an average of twice a day. I feel good about doing it, too. But I also think that a ritual done daily should have "more."

When I first learned the BRH, I found that "more." While the Evocation of the Archangels in the LBRP is powerful, and it seems to me to always be increasing in power, the Invocations and physical actions of the BRH are to me quite awe-inspiring. I never cease to get chills when I pause after commanding the Divine Light to descend. And when that section is repeated at the end of the ritual, it is almost overpowering. At times I have wanted to cry over this ritual's magnificent yet simple beauty.

It may surprise you to know that many rituals of groups such as the Golden Dawn are filled with amazing levels of beauty. Is there any more magnificent and beautiful way to "adore the Lord of the Universe and Space" than by the Golden Dawn's:

Holy art Thou, Lord of the Universe!
Holy art Thou, Whom Nature hath not formed!
Holy art Thou, the Vast and Mighty One!
Lord of the Light and of the Darkness!

As I wrote when I introduced the LBRP, the area you are working in becomes a temple of the Godhead. The LBRP is a preparation, a cleansing of that temple. The BRH has aspects which are nothing less than simple, glorious, honest worship along with its already mentioned banishing qualities.

The Banishing Ritual of the Hexagram

Preliminaries

1. Perform the Relaxation Ritual.
2. Perform the LBRP.

3. If you have any questions about the symbolism, reread Part Three of this lesson.

Section One: The Analysis of the Keyword

STEP ONE. Stand in front of the altar (if you have one) with your arms out to the sides so that your body forms a cross. You should be facing east. If you have a ritual wand, you should use it in this ritual. It should be held in the right hand with its point up.

STEP TWO. Say meaningfully:

I N R I
Yud, Nun, Raish, Yud,
The sign of Osiris slain.

As you say the letters in Hebrew (the second line of the above verbalization), draw them, from right to left, in front of you. Use the tip of your wand or your right index finger. The letters are formed from top to bottom. As you draw them, visualize them in bright blue flames. They look like this:

STEP THREE. Form the letter "L" by raising your right hand straight up from the shoulder. If you have a wand, it, too, should still be pointing up. This is similar to the position of the right arm of the magician card in the Rider-Waite Tarot deck, except that the arm should be straight up. If not, your hand should be open and your palm facing the left. Your left hand should be straight out to the side, palm forward. Look at your left hand with your head slightly bowed. Say meaningfully:

L . . . the sign of the mourning of Isis.

STEP FOUR. Raise the arms to a position over your head so that they form an angle of about sixty degrees. This makes the letter "V." The palms should be facing one another. Tilt your head back and look up. Say meaningfully:

V . . . the sign of Typhon and Apophis.

STEP FIVE. Now cross your arms on your chest, right over left. Your finger tips should be just touching your shoulders. This forms the letter "X." Bow your head. Say meaningfully:

X . . . the sign of Osiris, slain and risen.

STEP SIX. Now, reform each of LVX signs, saying the name of each letter as you do so. This is fol-

lowed by the word they spell, which is pronounced to rhyme with the word "boots":

L . . . V . . . X . . . LUX.

STEP SEVEN. At the word "light" in the following statement, spread your arms and look forward. Then recross the arms as before and bow your head while saying meaningfully:

The light . . . of the Cross.

The Sign of Osiris Slain

The Sign of Apophis and Typhon

The Sign of Mourning of Isis

The Sign of Osiris Risen

STEP EIGHT. Again return to the first position, arms out to the sides, looking forward. Slowly raise the arms toward the "V" position, slowly raising your head as you say meaningfully:

Virgo, Isis, mighty Mother,
Scorpio, Apophis, Destroyer,
Sol, Osiris, Slain and Risen . . .

STEP NINE. Continue toward the "V" position. Say meaningfully:

Isis, Apophis, Osiris . . .

STEP TEN. By the time your hands reach the "V" position, you should be looking up at the level of Step Four above. Vibrate:

IAO
[pronounced "EEEEEE-AAAHHH-OOOOHHH"]

STEP ELEVEN. Take a few seconds to aspire to the light (LVX), then through visualization draw it down over your head and down to your feet. When you can feel this beginning to happen, say meaningfully:

Let the Divine Light descend!

Feel it cover you and further purify you so that you become positive enough to exist without negative or positive influences around you. If you wish, you may relax in this state for a few minutes before continuing with the ritual.

Section Two: The Formulation of the Hexagrams

STEP TWELVE. As in the LBRP, go to the east, or if there is not enough room, continue facing east from where you stand. Make the Hexagram of Fire in front of you with the wand or index finger. You should visualize it as a golden flame, just as the pentagrams from the LBRP upon which the hexagrams are overlaid are in blue flame.

STEP THIRTEEN. Inhale, drawing in energy, while bringing your hands next to your ears. As you exhale, take a step forward with the left foot and thrust both hands toward the center of the Fire hexagram (the middle of the base line of the top triangle). At the same time vibrate the magickal word of power: **ARARITA**. (Review the LBRP for exact instructions on inhaling and exhaling energy and the position of the Enterer. Both are duplicated in this ritual.)

STEP FOURTEEN. With your wand or the right index finger, point to the center of the Fire hexagram and move around the circle to the south. This matches what you did in the LBRP. If there is not enough room to "circumambulate," simply turn in place. Coming from the tip of the finger or wand you should see the formation of an intense, bright white line. This goes over the bright white line that connects the pentagrams of the LBRP. When you reach the south, form the hexagram of Earth in bright golden flame. Inhale and exhale the energy as before, and make the sign of the Enterer toward the middle of the Earth hexagram (the center of the interlacing triangles). As you do so, vibrate the word of power: **ARARITA**.

STEP FIFTEEN. In a similar manner, move or pivot to the west, carrying the brilliant white line. At this direction form the hexagram of Air. Repeat the charging process, again pointing to the center of the hexagram (at the middle of the common base lines). Vibrate the word of power: **ARARITA**.

STEP SIXTEEN. Move or pivot to the north, carrying the white line. Here form the hexagram of Water. The middle of the hexagram is where the apexes of the triangles meet. This is where you point when you vibrate the power word: **ARARITA**.

STEP SEVENTEEN. Carry the white line from the north back to the east, completing the circle of white light with the golden hexagrams at the quarters. If you have had room to move about rather than pivoting in place, return to your position in the middle of the circle, in front of the altar (if you have one, otherwise the middle of the circle). Face east.

At this time you should have around you the blue pentagrams from the LBRP connected by a white line that has expanded into a sphere. In the same locations as the pentagrams there should also be golden hexagrams which are also connected by a circle of white light. All of the colors should be incredibly intense, bright and virtually pulsating with energy. They should be just short of blinding in intensity.

STEP EIGHTEEN. At this point there are two options:

a. You may repeat the Analysis of the Keyword. This is especially good when doing White Magick rituals, as you can bask in the glow of the Divine Light for as long as you desire at the end. The intensity of this light is increased by the act of formulating the hexagrams. For general purposes, this is the ending I prefer.

b. You may do the Kabalistic Cross as in the LBRP. This is slightly shorter and has the effect of creating a stronger link between the LBRP and the BRH. It is good for Grey Magick rituals. On a practical level, it will save some time if you are doing a long, involved ritual.

This completes the Banishing Ritual of the Hexagram.

This is as long and as time-consuming as your daily ritual work will get. You may wish to add things (such as meditation), and that is fine. But nothing else is going to be added to your regular work. Here, then, is your daily ritual work. It should be done at least once daily.

1. The Relaxation Ritual.
2. The Lesser Banishing Ritual of the Pentagram.
3. The Banishing Ritual of the Hexagram.
4. The Middle Pillar Ritual.
5. The Circulation of the Body of Light.
6. The Tarot Contemplation Ritual—Advanced Version.
7. Completion of your Ritual Diary.

As with all of the basic rituals, the Banishing Ritual of the Hexagram should be memorized. Until you do so, you will find the summary below helpful.

Remember, there is only one way to succeed in ritual magick. That way is to practice, practice, practice. You will never succeed if you do not do the nec-

essary work. There is no secret key that allows you to bypass the work. Even if you have to fumble around with the summaries included in this book, that is okay! What is not okay is any excuse for lack of practice on a regular schedule.

The Banishing Ritual of the Hexagram as a Ceremony

If you wish to do the BRH in a ceremony with other people, there are a couple of nice ways to do it. It should always be done after the LBRP. One person can do the entire BRH, or it can be divided by having one person do the Analysis of the Keyword and another do the Formulation of the Hexagrams. If you have enough people, a glorious way to do it is by having three people do the Analysis and another four do the Hexagrams:

The Analysis of the Keyword:

Person 1 - **I**
Person 2 - **N**
Person 3 - **R**
Person 1 – **I**

—pause

Person 1 - **Yud**
Person 2 - **Nun**
Person 3 - **Raish**
Person 1 - **Yud**
All: **The sign of Osiris slain.**

(The visual spelling of the Hebrew is not done in this version. In the following section each participant makes the appropriate signs.)

Person 1 – L . . . **the sign of the mourning of Isis.**
Person 2 – V . . . **the sign of Apophis and Typhon.**
Person 3 – X . . . **the sign of Osiris risen.**
Person 1 – **L . . .**
Person 2 – **V . . .**
Person 3 – **X . . .**
All - **LUX. The Light of the Cross.**

The Banishing Ritual of the Hexagram Summary

1. Face east, hands out to sides, say:

   I N R I
   Yud, Nun, Raish, Yud
   The Sign of Osiris Slain.

2. Form L, look at left hand, bow head, say:

   L . . . The Sign of the Mourning of Isis.

3. Form V, head back, look up, say:

   V . . . the Sign of Typhon and Apophis.

4. Form X, head bowed, say:

   X . . . the Sign of Osiris Risen.

5. Form all 3 signs, saying:

   L . . . V . . . X . . . LUX.
   The Light of the Cross.

6. Arms out to the side, gradually raise them as you say:

   Virgo, Isis, Mighty Mother,
   Scorpio, Apophis, Destroyer,
   Sol, Osiris, slain and risen . . .
   Isis, Apophis, Osiris,
   IAO! [EE-AH-OH!]

7. Aspire to the light and draw it down over your head to your feet. Say:

   Let the Divine Light descend! [and FEEL it do so!]

8. Go to the east, make hex of FIRE in Golden Flame, point to center of top triangle's base line, vibrate: **ARARITA!**

9. Carry white line to south. Make hex of EARTH, point at center, vibrate: **ARARITA!**

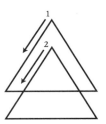

10. Continue to west. Make hex of AIR. Point to common lines' center. Vibrate: **ARARITA!**

11. Continue to north. Make hex of WATER. Point to junction of triangles. Vibrate: **ARARITA!**

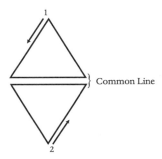

Common Line

12. Complete circle. Return to original position. Repeat steps 1–8 or do Kabalistic Cross as in the Lesser Banishing Ritual of the Pentagram.

Here Ends the Ritual

(All slowly raising arms):

Person 1 - **Virgo, Isis, mighty mother,**
Person 2 - **Scorpio, Apophis, Destroyer,**
Person 3 - **Sol, Osiris, slain and risen.**
Person 1 – **Isis . . .**
Person 2 – **Apophis . . .**
Person 3 – **Osiris . . .**
All – **IAO . . . Let the Divine Light Descend!**

In this section, the three ritualists can stand in a line in front of the altar, with Person 1 to the right or south, Person 2 to directly in front of the altar, and Person 3 to the left or north. They should all be facing east. For the formulation of the hexagrams, you can have one person stand at each quarter. Have the first person do the appropriate part at the east and carry the line to the south. At this corner, the second person forms the hexagram, charges it with **ARARITA**, and carries the line to the west. While this is being done, Person 1 moves quickly clockwise to the north. Here the third person does the appropriate part and carries the line to the north. The person at the north finishes by doing the appropriate hexagram and carrying the line to the east. After Person 2 and Person 3 have finished their appropriate portion and the carrying of the connecting line to the next quarter, they continue in a clockwise direction around the inside of the circle and return to the quarter where they began. Thus, at the end of this section, each ceremonialist is back at the quarter at which he or she started this section of the ritual.

When the formulation of the hexagrams is complete and everyone is back at his/her original station, all turn inward and face the center. Together they should raise their right hands (with wands if they have them) straight up in the air. They should slowly bring them down so that they are parallel with the ground and pointing at the ritualist(s) in the center who will finish the ritual.

As they lower their hands they should start intoning the vowel "AH" quietly and in a low tone. As they move their arms the sound should raise in pitch and volume so that by the time they are pointing straight ahead the "AH" sound should be very high in pitch and quite loud. A preselected person, when he or she feels it is right, should suddenly raise his/her arm, which signals the ritualist to finish and be quiet. Then they should lower their arms (keeping the wands pointing up, though), and return to their seats in the circle.

I have found this ceremonial version of the Banishing Ritual of the Hexagram to be moving, spiritually powerful, and magickally effective.

PART EIGHT

One of the things which I will not be discussing in depth during this course is the subject of astrology. I mention this here so that you do not notice its lack later on and think that I am anti-astrology. Nothing could be further from the truth. I have had the honor of knowing several excellent astrologers who have amazed me with their talents. I even have one friend who insists that magick and astrology are inextricably linked. He has gone so far as to design his own magickal system based upon art and astrology.

The plain fact of the matter is that for the systems of magick taught in these lessons, only a minimal amount of astrological knowledge is necessary. Most of it can be understood by comprehending the Tree of Life rather than recourse to deep study of astrology. On the other hand, the better you know astrology, the better you will understand the Tree of Life. So although a knowledge of astrology is not needed for this course, it is suggested that you do learn something about the subject.

Ah, the easy way. So many people are looking for it. The pages of tabloids are filled with ads offering instant fame, memory, money, love, and success. Other offers include simple "spell kits" designed to allow you to curse your neighbor even if you have had no magickal training whatsoever. Unfortunately, there is no such thing as an instant gift of magickal powers. They must be earned as the result of three things: *practice, practice, practice!* I have said it before and I am repeating it here: to become a magician, to develop psychic-magickal powers requires work and study. If you think there is a shortcut . . . you lose.

As an example of what I mean I would like to describe an ad I saw repeated several times in a national magazine. It was a full-page ad, the center of which showed a drawing of a hand holding a small stick. The ad proclaimed that you could "make good luck your slave" with the "Miracle Stick." This stick could allegedly bring you anything. If you read the small print of the ad you learned that the stick must be burned, and if you examine the drawing closely, you will see that the stick being held by the disembodied hand is just a stick of incense! The price was many times the retail value of the incense.

The distributor of the item would not be putting out full-page ads if people were not sending in their money. Thus, especially with occult items purchased through the mail or over the Internet, I give you this ancient warning: *caveat emptor*: "let the buyer beware!" And from this warning I jump to ancient grimoires.

So far in this course I have hardly touched the subject of the ancient textbooks of magick known as the "grimoires." Some of the famous ones, which are still available, include *The Greater Key of Solomon*, *The Lesser Key of Solomon* including *The Goetia*, *The Grimoire of Armadel*, *The Book of the Sacred Magic of Abra-Melin the Mage*, and *The Secret Grimoire of Turiel*. Some books, such as *The Secret Lore of Magic* by Idries Shah and *The Book of Ceremonial Magic* by A. E. Waite, are nothing but compilations of other grimoires such as the ones mentioned.

If these books are so powerful, wouldn't it have been easier for me just to say, "Go buy them and follow the instructions carefully"? Unfortunately, it is not that easy. That is why so many of the above-named volumes are printed and purchased, but so little real magick is done. There is a little-known key to unlocking their secrets and learning how to successfully use them.

This key is found in the idea behind the word that describes these texts: *grimoire*. It is a French word. The direct translation of it is "black book,"

but it has the meaning "grammar book," which were frequently in black bindings. It was expected that a student of magick would have a teacher to instruct him or her in the subtleties of the various planes of existence, and how to alter them through the knowledge and use of universal laws. Grimoires were not meant to give out every bit of magickal knowledge. They were designed to aid a student's memory. They are, in a sense, nothing more than class notes.

Once this is understood, instead of looking at what is included in these books, notice what is *omitted*. In the grimoires, the knowledge of karma or tee-koon and the need to do a divination before doing any Grey Magick is never discussed. The teacher would have instilled these ideas very strongly into the head of a student.

But more importantly, omitted from the grimoires are what I call:

The Three Necessities of Grey Magick

The Necessity of a Positive Attitude

This is the first of the three necessities. If you don't think that your magick will work, it won't. This should not imply, however, that magick is nothing more than mental techniques. There are many cases of the techniques of standard allopathic (Western) medicine being overpowered by a negative mental attitude. This is not because the medical treatment was nothing more than a placebo. Rather, it is because the mind and body are intimately connected and one cannot be cured if the other is not cured. Similarly, if the mind is not positive toward the magick you are doing, it can defeat your practical techniques. It is impossible to be successful as a magician if you are not positive that your magick will work.

The Necessity of Knowing How to Generate and Control Magickal Energy

This second necessity is just what you have been learning to do in the rituals given so far in this course.

The Necessity of Knowledge

The third necessity is the knowledge of what to do with the energy once that energy has been raised and can be controlled.

The ancient magickal student would learn that he or she must have a positive attitude, and would also do hours of exercises to learn how to generate and control energy (just as you have been doing). But memorizing large quantities of knowledge as to what to do with that energy would be difficult for anyone. This is true even for those who lived in periods where techniques of memory were far more in practice than they are today. Thus, this knowledge aspect of magick was written down to aid the student and help the student avoid possibly dangerous mistakes. It is these workbooks that are known as grimoires. We will deal with some of the methods of these texts in later lessons in this course.

Review

The following questions are designed to help you determine if you have mastered the information in Lesson Four. Please try to answer them without looking at the text. The answers are in Appendix Two.

1. What are the qualities of elemental Air?
2. What was the earliest symbol used to represent Christian belief?
3. Why did Hitler choose the swastika as a symbol for Nazism?
4. What are the differences between a true, mystical swastika and the Nazi swastika?
5. Who is the archangel of Air?
6. Why is it difficult to remember past lives?
7. The LBRP is a support or basis for what?
8. What does the BRH clear from your area?
9. Why do the elements change associations in the BRH when compared to the associations for the LBRP?
10. What is the order for doing your at-home rituals?
11. What is a paired triangle?
12. What does the word "grimoire" mean?
13. Name three things you need to do to succeed at ritual magick.
14. What are the Three Necessities of Grey Magick?

The following questions only you can answer.

1. Are you regularly performing all of the rituals?
2. Are you in control of elemental Air?
3. Have you made your Air Dagger?
4. Do you understand the differences between the Eastern and Western systems of magick described in these lessons?
5. Have you chosen a motto?
6. Could you help someone make personal changes using only the Tree of Life and the Major Arcana of the Tarot? Have you done this on yourself?
7. What can you do to strengthen your ego without becoming egotistical? Are you doing it?
8. How does it feel when you say, "Let the Divine light descend," in the BRH?
9. If you could change one thing in your life right now, what would it be?

Bibliography

For more information on these books, please see the annotated bibliography at the end of this book.

Conway, Flo, and Jim Siegelman. *Snapping*. Stillpoint Press, 2005.

Farrar, Janet, and Stewart Farrar. *A Witches' Bible*. Phoenix Publishing, 1996.

———. *Eight Sabbats for Witches*. Phoenix Publishing, 1988.

Frazer, Sir James. *The Golden Bough* (abridged edition). Oxford University Press, 1998.

Kuhn, A. B. *Lost Light.* Filiquarian Publishing, 2007.

Massey, Gerald. *Gerald Massey's Lectures.* Book Tree, 2008.

Regardie, Israel. *Ceremonial Magic.* Aeon Books, 2004.

———. *The Golden Dawn.* Llewellyn Publications, 2002.

———. *The Middle Pillar.* Llewellyn Publications, 2002.

LESSON FIVE

PART ONE

Stress affects us all. Stress can be caused by hearing or reading about politics or economics, job worries and situations, relationship ups and downs, health issues, and other major concerns. It can also be caused by little things such as a phone call that hangs up just as you answer, or getting stuck in a traffic jam. Although stress generally affects people more in cities, even living in rural or country areas can be stressful. Trying to decide what to make for dinner, trying to deal with increasing prices and decreasing returns on money spent, and trying to get parts for vehicles and having to wait weeks for their delivery are just some minor examples of what can cause stress.

Being "stressed out" can really make life miserable. Symptoms of not being able to deal with stress include lack of focus and the inability to make decisions. It can decrease your ability to tolerate things other people do and prevent you from getting needed rest. Virtually any health problem you have might be amplified by stress, and it can be the direct cause of pain, heart disease, digestive problems, depression, obesity, skin conditions such as eczema, and many other physiological issues.

Actually, stress *per se* has a bad reputation. We experience stress all the time and need some level of stress to function. All of our muscles work through stress and relaxation. The stress of wanting to live in a nice house or apartment and have regular meals keeps some people active and creative in their work. So stress is not the issue. Rather, it is stress beyond our tolerance levels and our inability to deal with and overcome that excess stress that is the problem.

Unfortunately, we often don't recognize (excess) stress or its effects on us. Worse, even some psychological professionals who should be helping people with this may not recognize it. A few years ago a friend of mine appeared very stressed out. She was desperate over a variety of issues (job, friends, family) and didn't know what to do. What shocked me most was that she had been going to a psychologist for over a year. "Has your psychologist given you any strategies for dealing with stress?" I asked. She responded that this had not even been discussed. I should add that she was also under the care of a psychiatrist who was prescribing powerful psychoactive drugs. In spite of all this professional care, she was still stressed out and it was harming her physically, mentally, and emotionally.

Luckily, she was strong and determined. She combined yoga, acupuncture, and hypnotherapy to wean herself from the drugs. She stopped seeing her psychologist. She still gets stressed from time to time, but she has strategies for dealing with it. In fact, she now teaches classes on stress reduction at her place of work.

The relaxation ritual given previously is one of the best ways for getting rid of stress. You could pay hundreds of dollars and learn some version of this technique from a psychologist, purchase CDs or MP3s with something like it recorded on them, or get it out of a book. Don't ignore it, because it *is* powerful and it does work. To perform it well, however, may take more time than you have available. Thus, to remedy this problem, I am presenting here what I call the Instant Relaxation Ritual. It is not meant to replace the relaxation ritual, but can take its place occasionally when you are short of time. It is a good way to get rid of or minimize excess stress in your everyday life.

The Instant Relaxation Ritual

This can be done standing, sitting, or lying down.

STEP ONE. Start by tensing all of the muscles in your feet and ankles.

STEP TWO. Without relaxing the tension in your feet, tense the muscles of your calves.

STEP THREE. In a similar manner, tense the muscles of your thighs, hips, stomach, chest, back, arms, hands, neck and head. In other words, tense every muscle in your body, starting at the feet and ending with the head. Hold your body in this totally tensed condition for five to ten seconds.

STEP FOUR. Take a deep breath and hold it for a brief moment. Then, suddenly, as you let all of your breath flow easily and effortlessly out of your lungs, simultaneously relax all of your muscles. Permit your body to go as limp as the position you are in will allow. Just let go. Completely. Just let go.

STEP FIVE. With your mind, "look" through your body for any tension. Be especially aware of the neck, forehead, shoulders, stomach, and lower back. If there is any tension, immediately send the "golden glow" of the relaxation ritual to that area and allow the tension to fade. Enjoy this very relaxed and stress-free condition.

Caution: Unlike the standard relaxation ritual, this technique is physiological as well as psychological. The sudden change in muscle tension and its sudden release may, in a very few people, cause a muscle spasm commonly known as a "charlie horse." If this occurs, stop immediately and deeply massage the area until the spasm ends. Then do the regular relaxation ritual as soon as possible. If you are a person who gets a charlie horse, do not shy away from using this technique. Once your body becomes used to the sudden change in muscle tension and stress diminution, the spasms should cease and you will have a wonderful and fast system of relaxation and stress reduction. Also, I have found that such a spasm is more likely to occur when sitting or lying, so if you are one of the few to whom this happens, you might practice this several times while standing to acclimatize the body to the sudden physiological change. After several positive experiences with this ritual while standing, change back to a sitting or reclined position.

PART TWO

The Water Element

While becoming familiar with our system of the elements, we have covered Earth and Air. If after working the exercises for those elements you are not satisfied with your sense of unity with them and control of them, continue with the exercises for another two weeks. Then perform them sporadically as you will. Also, please remember that I am just a teacher. If you can come up with some exercises that will help you become more familiar with the elements, feel free to incorporate them into your work. Don't feel limited to the exercises and techniques shared in these lessons. Instead, think of them as a start to your explorations. However, even if you continue working on the previous two elements, you should begin the exercises below immediately.

The element of Water has the qualities of being cool and moist.

Exercise 1. Observe those things around you which have the combined qualities of coolness and moistness. Remember, all of these elemental qualities are relative. If you open an oven wherein something is being baked, you will be greeted by a warm (or hot) blast of damp air. On first consideration, it may not seem to have the quality of coolness along with the moistness. However, it is much cooler and more moist than the heat from a smelting furnace. Therefore, the oven has more of the element of Water than does the smelting furnace. The smelting furnace has more of the element of Water than does the Sun. See if you can determine relative watery qualities as you experience them. Make a note of all of these things and record your list in your magickal diary. Do this exercise daily for one week.

Exercise 2. Remove your clothes and enter a pool or bath where the water is cool. If you have access to a lake or river, this would be best. Also, it would be good if you could get a swimming snorkel so that you can breathe while completely submerged beneath the surface of the water. Obviously, this would be difficult to do in a small bath tub or in a shallow pool, but if you have access to a snorkel and a place where you can be totally submerged, you will have the quickest success.

Once you are submerged as much as possible—and if you are completely submerged, breathing comfortably through the snorkel—do the relaxation ritual. Thanks to the buoyant quality of water you will find that this is quite easy. Next, become very aware of your breath. You don't have to "do" anything, just observe it as you inhale and exhale. As you do this you will find that your respiration will automatically slow down. Notice the way the air feels as it comes in through the nose (or through the snorkel and mouth), down the air pipe and into the lungs. Sense or imagine the interchange of oxygen and carbon dioxide within the lungs. Feel the CO_2-laden air as it leaves your body.

Now imagine that your entire body is nothing but an enormous breathing apparatus. Imagine that every part of your body only has the function of breathing. Know that your skin is a vital part of this system. In this pore breathing exercise, as you breathe in air, imagine that every pore of your body is breathing in elemental Water. Feel it as it washes in and out of you, flushing the impurities from your entire body. Do not confuse elemental Water with physical water or you may get a drowning sensation. If this happens, stop the exercise immediately and try it again another time.

Experiment with this exercise at different times of the day, and if possible, at different locations. Water is not very compressible, but it is very changeable. Try to experience it in its many variations. After a week of doing this exercise go on to the next one.

Exercise 3. Spend a period of up to three minutes (but no more), once a day, *imagining that you are the element Water.* Feel the fluidity, the coolness, the refreshing moistness of the elemental waters. If you study astrology, compare what you learn about the element of Water with those signs that are of the Water Triplicity (Cancer, Scorpio, and Pisces). Become familiar with water in all of its various appearances. Know what water feels like; what water is. Practice this exercise for one week.

Exercise 4. Once you have learned how to "be" elemental Water, the next step is to learn how to consciously control this element. Take a moment and again imagine yourself to be elemental Water. Bring the feeling from the last exercise into your consciousness. Next, hold your hands nine to twelve inches apart with the palms facing each other. Now imagine or visualize to the best of your ability a bottle, cylinder, or small cask between your hands, Next, as you exhale, visualize all of the Water element that is in you going out with your breath and being deposited in the container between your hands. Four to seven breaths should be enough to fill it. Once it is filled, observe it for a short time. Then, with three breaths, inhale it back into yourself and return to normal consciousness. Spend a week performing this exercise at least once daily.

The Test. Once again, here is a simple self-test to allow you to see whether or not you really have become not only in harmony with the element of Water, but also its master. No one else will ever inspect your work, so practice the exercises and take the test as often as you like. To become a good magician necessitates that you are capable of controlling all of the elements.

The next time you feel hardheaded, unwilling to change, and overly tense with your muscles hard as a rock, form the container of Water as described in the previous exercise. Once the container has been filled, inhale the contents with one big inhalation. Bring all of the contents into you. Within five minutes you should be more relaxed and reasonable.

The next time that you are being pushed around or are acting "wishy-washy," again form the container of Water before you. Make sure it is filled. Then visualize a large, black hole in the air before you and throw the container into this hole. Immediately visualize the hole sealing up after you have cast the container into it. In a few minutes you should feel less overly flexible and not as liable to allow others to take advantage of you. It may be necessary to repeat this "black hole" several times to have complete success.

When you have passed both parts of the test to your satisfaction, you will be the master of the element Water. Again, as I have already stated, you may find one or more of the elements easy to master while others may take time. Just keep practicing without "lusting for results" and eventually the outcomes you desire will be yours. Record all the results of your experiments and tests in your magickal diary. This means the successes and the failures.

The Chalice

The chalice is the weapon or tool that represents elemental Water. It is the easiest weapon to construct because all you have to do is buy a stemmed goblet and paint it. It requires virtually no construction. Although most people prefer a silver goblet, the Golden Dawn suggested the use of a stemmed glass. Other people prefer wood or pewter. The choice of material is up to you, although I must say that a glass can be a problem due to a high potential for breakage over time.

Water Chalice

The shape of the goblet above the stem should resemble a crocus flower. Thus, it should flare out (see diagram on the next page) at the top. Take a piece of twine or "kite string" and cut a piece equal to the circumference of the goblet at the point where it begins to flare out. Fold the measure in half and use a felt-tip pen to mark the string at that point. Take the folded string and again fold it in half. Mark both parts of the string at the fold. Repeat this process one more time and mark all four points of the

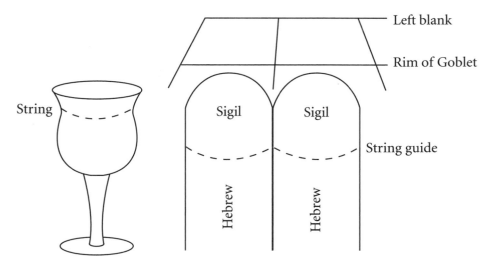

The Hebrew, the sigils, and the outlines are in bright orange. The background is in bright blue. The space between the "curved triangle" petals is left blank.

string at the fold. The result of this will be a length of string divided into eight equal sections.

Prepare the goblet for paint according to the paint's instructions. Make sure the paint is appropriate for the type of material of which the goblet is made. Although it will be rare to drink out of the chalice, you may do so at times. Therefore, *make sure the paint you use does not contain any lead or other potentially poisonous substances.* Take the string and place it around the goblet just below the flare. Using a soft pencil (on wood, a pin will work), make a mark on the goblet over the marks on the string. Using bright orange paint, connect the marks on the goblet to the stem with straight lines. Above these lines, on the flare part of the goblet, connect the lines with a sort of "curved triangle" (see diagram). Fill in these spaces with bright blue paint. On the following page you will find the appropriate sigils and Hebrew words for the chalice. The Hebrew should appear in the rectangular section and the sigil(s) should be drawn within the curved triangle section. Use orange paint to draw the sigils and Hebrew. To protect the finish, use several coats of a clear plastic such as Varathane over your work.

PART THREE

"Security Through Obscurity"

In this section you will learn the Rose Cross Ritual. Although it is not part of the daily work, it is excellent and easy to perform. You will probably find yourself using it frequently.

There are five main reasons for using this ritual:

1. It is an excellent banishing ritual, although its effects are quite different from the LBRP. The LBRP ritual will protect you, but it also lights up the entire astral plane with its lines and pentagrams. It is very powerful. It can also have the effect of attracting the attention of sometimes unwanted astral entities (Little Nasties), as we have already discussed. The Rose Cross Ritual, on the other hand, works like a curtain by containing your aura. It will protect you from unwanted outside influences in a different way. Do not substitute the Rose Cross Ritual for the LBRP. Be sure to do the LBRP before any magickal ritual. Use the Rose Cross Ritual for self-enclosure. As an example, if you feel troubled and cannot focus your attention, do the LBRP to banish any outside influences that may be distracting you. Follow this with the Rose Cross Ritual to regain your peace of mind.

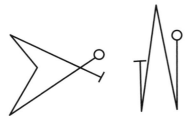

אלהים צבאות
I. Elohim Tzaboth

גבראל
II. Gabriel

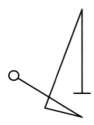

טליהד
III. Taliahad

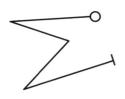

תרשיס
IV. Tharsis

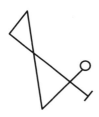

גיהן
V. Gihon

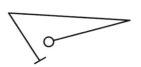

מערב
VI. Maarab

מים
VII. Mayim

VIII. The Motto

Symbols and Hebrew for the Chalice

2. The curtaining effect induces a type of invisibility to the world around you. This is not to say that you become invisible in reality. Nor should you infer that people who are looking closely for you will not find you. But if people are not looking for you in particular you will tend to be ignored. Thus, you have the *effect* of invisibility.

I do not recommend breaking the law to anybody, however I do wish to share this experience with you. One time I was late for an appointment and knew that I would have to speed in my car to get to my appointment on time. I quickly did both the LBRP and the Rose Cross Ritual. I was driving fast . . . very fast. Suddenly a highway patrol vehicle came up from behind and turned on the red light. I thought I had missed some variable in my magick and it had failed, but to my surprise, delight, and relief, they pulled over the car next to me, even though we were going at the same speed. The highway patrol ignored me as if I never existed!

Be careful if you are considering using this technique. If the highway patrol isn't seeing you, then drivers in other vehicles won't be seeing you, either. Be extra vigilant so that you see them.

3. This ritual is a good preparation for meditation. It works by calling forth your higher self. Thus, it can be helpful when doing a problem-solving type of meditation.

4. You can do this ritual with the aim of aiding others who are hurting either physically or spiritually. Simply build up in your mind an image of the person you wish to help. Place that image in the center of the room where you will be doing the ritual. Do the ritual with the image of the person you are aiding as the center of the ritual. Draw down the light upon the image of the person you are aiding. When the ritual is over, command the figure you have mentally created along with its now added peace, serenity, and well-being to return to the actual person for whom the ritual is being done. Tell the figure to go back to the real person and take with it the grace of Divinity.

Of course, before doing this you should get the permission of the person and since this is a type of Grey Magick you should perform a divination to learn if the result will be positive or negative.

5. Sometimes you may find yourself in a place where there are "negative psychic vibrations." As an example, you may feel uncomfortable in a house where very negative people live or where terrible things have occurred in the past. You don't have the right or duty to "fix" the place or the people. In fact, the people there may be unaware of the situation and, even if they were, they might not want you to do magick for them or desire any change. This ritual will not so much banish the negativity in the aether as it will protect you from the "invasion" of your psychic body, your astral self.

At this point, reread the lesson which prepared you for the Banishing Ritual of the Hexagram. Focus on understanding the analysis of the Key Word. It will be used again in this ritual.

The Tetragrammaton and the Pentagrammaton

The Tetragrammaton is dealt with elsewhere in this course, but due to its central importance to magick and the Kabalah it will avail us to go over it again. The Tetragrammaton is composed of four Hebrew letters: Yud, Heh (superior), Vahv, and Heh (inferior). This four-letter name ("Tetragrammaton" means "four-letter name") is considered to be the ultimate name of Divinity. No one knows the correct pronunciation of this word. Some of the letters may have been pronounced differently than they are today. The letters may have been a code for other letters. Some of the letters may have been doubled. Today, Jews do not attempt to say this word. Instead, they say "Ah-doh-nye," which means "my lord." There are no vowels in the original Hebrew. They were added much later in the form of points and lines written above, within, and below the letters. To ensure that no one would try to pronounce the Tetragrammaton by mistake, the vowels for Ah-doh-nye were placed around the holy four letters. If you try to pronounce the four-letter word using these vowels you end up with something like the following: Yahveh, Yahweh, Yehovah, or Jehovah. All of these result from an incorrect understanding of Hebrew.

The secret of the Tetragrammaton is in the meaning of its component letters. The Yud represents archetypal masculinity and the Heh (superior) represents archetypal femininity. The Vahv, which looks like an elongated Yud, represents physical masculinity while the second Heh, the Heh inferior, represents physical femininity. Thus the Tetragrammaton signifies that the ultimate secret that the Godhead is the union of all dualities (i.e., male and female), both physically and spiritually. The Divine is everything, and everything comes from and is of the Godhead.

This does not mean, however, that to know the universe is to know the Divine. Merely because everything is of the Godhead does not mean that the Divine cannot be more than everything that exists or could exist. Divinity is more. The Source of All is beyond comprehension except for the ways in which the Godhead chooses to be comprehended.

Shin and Jesus

The letter Shin (ש) looks like three small flames. This letter represents the flame of Divinity, what is sometimes called Holy Spirit or Ruach El-oh-heem. It is also known as chi, ki, prana, kundalini, mana, Manitou, and many others. If the letter Shin is placed in the center of the Tetragrammaton, we get the Pentagrammaton (five-letter name). This new word (Yud, Heh, Shin, Vahv, Heh) is a symbol representing the union of divine masculinity and femininity with physical masculinity and femininity by way of the Holy Spirit. Biblically, any person who would be a savior or messiah to himself or herself must be able to unite Divinity with physicality and this union of all opposites comes by way of the Holy Spirit. Thus, any savior must *be* this five-lettered name, the Pentagrammaton. If you pronounce the Pentagrammaton in Hebrew, it would be "Yeh-hah-shu-ah" (some people today use "Yeh-heh-shu-ah" or even "Yeh-shu-ah"), which is usually translated as Joshua. However, in Greek it became Yay-su, which in English became Jesus.

Thus, the name "Jesus" isn't a name at all. It's a title or description. *Anyone* can come to hold the title. The process described by the Pentagrammaton is that each of us must find our own union with Divinity. We cannot have a vicarious atonement. Nobody can rid us of our past, present, and future karma or "sins." Each of us must be our own savior, our own messiah. Each of us must become "Jesus." This is a policy of personal responsibility. We cause what happens in our lives. We are not victims of fate or some "Lords of Karma."

This, by the way, is strict Kabalah. It has *nothing* to do with Christian theology. In fact, Christian theology tends to disagree with this Kabalistic understanding of the Pentagrammaton. In orthodox Christianity today, Jesus was a specific human and God, although many Christians didn't believe that Jesus was ever a literal human until it was voted to be part of the accepted belief system in 325 C.E. I know many of you reading this may not believe it, especially if you come from a Christian background. So I say don't take my word for it. Check it out for yourself.

Another form of the Pentagrammaton puts the Shin between the Vahv and the second Heh. This gives the word "Yeh-hoh-vah-shah." It represents the unity of masculine and feminine on the physical plane by way of the Ruach El-oh-heem (Holy Spirit of the Divine) and is presided over by the union of archetypal masculinity and femininity. This is, by the way, one of the secrets of Tantric yoga and sex magick, but that is left for another lesson.

יהושה   יהושוה

"Yeh-hah-shu-ah"   "Yeh-hoh-vah-shah"

I also want to assure you that this is not sexist in nature. If you do not like the terms male and female, masculine and feminine, they can be replaced by such terms as Yin and Yang, positive and negative (as in the sense of the terminals of a battery, not in the sense of good and bad), projective and receptive, electric and magnetic, etc. The reason I use male and female is because it has traditionally been used and also was used by the ancient Kabalists, sometimes in even more anthropomorphic forms. It was their attempt to deal with the dualities which exist everywhere in nature. I am merely following their traditional lead.

Finally, I want to repeat that the symbol known as the cross far antedates the birth of Christianity and should *not* be considered a Christian symbol when used for magickal purposes. I read somewhere that there were over 200 forms of crosses in use before Christianity began. In this ritual it represents the four elements (the four bars of the cross) and the union of physical (the horizontal bar) and spiritual (the vertical bar). The rose, which in the ritual is indicated by a circle, represents the unfolding of the soul and the evolution of consciousness.

The Rose Cross Ritual

STEP ONE. Prepare yourself by doing the Relaxation Ritual.

STEP TWO. If it is appropriate, do the LBRP.

STEP THREE. Your tool for this ritual is a lit stick of incense. Any scent you like will do. Begin in the center of your area (station 1).

STEP FOUR. Go to the southeast corner (station 2) of your area and look toward the southeast, away from the center of your circle. Use the incense to make a large cross and rose (circle), making your stokes in the air in the order indicated at the top of the next column. The image should be about the size of, or very slightly smaller than, the pentagrams or hexagrams of the LBRP and BRH:

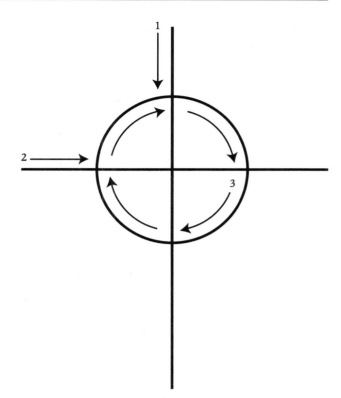

As you form the rose, vibrate the God name

Yeh-hah-shu-ah

You should finish the syllable "shu" as you finish the circle. On the final syllable "ah" you should stab the center of the circle with the lit tip of the incense, at the point where the arms of the symbol meet, at the center of the "rose," and feel the energy going out and charging the symbol.

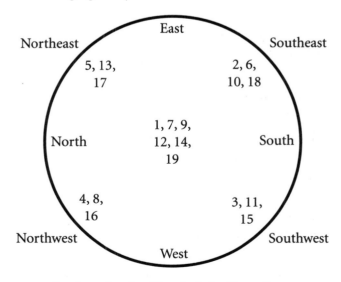

Stations for the Ritual of the Rose Cross

STEP FIVE. Point the incense to the center of the cross. Keeping the lit point of the incense on that level, move to the southwest (station 3). Make the cross and rose and stab the center. As before, vibrate

Yeh-hah-shu-ah

STEP SIX. Repeat the process, only this time move to the northwest (station 4).

STEP SEVEN. Repeat, moving to the northeast (station 5).

STEP EIGHT. In a similar manner, move to the southeast (station 6), completing the circle. Do not reform the rose cross figure or vibrate the word.

STEP NINE. Immediately turn to face the direction diagonally across the room, the northwest. Now bring your incense stick high into the air and walk toward the northwest. In the center of the room (station 7), stop and make the Rose Cross above your head while vibrating the name as before. Point to the center of the figure, and with the incense still high in the air, move to the northwest corner (station 8). Bring the top of the incense to the intersecting arms of the cross that you previously created in this corner. Do not reform the figure or vibrate the name here.

STEP TEN. Now move back to the southeast, but with the incense held at arm's length pointing *down* toward the ground. Stop in the middle of your area (station 9) and form a Rose Cross and vibrate the name below you, still pointing at the ground. Point again with the incense to the center of this cross, and with the stick pointing down, move to the southeast (station 10) and bring the tip of the incense to the interlacing bars of the cross, which you have already formulated at that corner. Do not redraw the rose and cross or vibrate the name in this corner.

STEP ELEVEN. Point to the center of the southeast's cross, then walk in a clockwise direction to the southwest corner (station 11). Do not redraw the rose and cross, but as you point to the center of the cross, revibrate the name.

STEP TWELVE. With the incense held above your head, move diagonally to the northeast. Stop at the middle (station 12) to revibrate the word without reforming that symbol above your head. When you reach the northeast (station 13), point to the center of the figure that is already there, then hold the incense with the lit point down and return the way you came. Of course, stop at the center (station 14) to revibrate the name below you. You will end up in the southwest (station 15).

STEP THIRTEEN. Point to the center of the cross here in the southwest. Keeping the incense on this level, go in a clockwise direction around the circle, pointing to the center of each cross. Do not remake the figure or vibrate the name. Go from the southwest to the northwest (station 16), to the northeast (station 17), and return to the southeast (station 18).

STEP FOURTEEN. When you return to the southeast, rest the point of the incense for a moment at the center of the cross. Then, remake the cross, only do it in a bigger size, as big as you can make it. Make the rose appropriately bigger, too. As you slowly form the bottom half of the circle, vibrate **Yeh-hah-shu-ah**. As you form the top half of the circle, vibrate **Yeh-hoh-vah-shah**, pointing to the center on the last syllable.

STEP FIFTEEN. Now go to the center of your area (station 19), face east, and visualize the six Rose Crosses around, above, and below you. The crosses should be golden in color, and the lines connecting them between the corners and above and below should be brilliant white. The "roses" should be bright red. Thus, you should have a protective "sphere" all around you.

STEP SIXTEEN. Now do the analysis of the Key Word from the BRH. Start from the vibrating of INRI through "let the divine light descend." Be sure to use the appropriate actions as described in that ritual.

Notes: If it feels right, you may omit the analysis of the Key Word, Step Sixteen above. Instead of directing this ritual toward the east, you may face the direction from which you think danger may be coming. As a group working, let one person do this entire ritual while everyone else sits on chairs inside the area where the ritual is performed. Be sure that there is room for the ritualist to make the diagonal, cross-area movements.

PART FOUR

Those of you who have read this far will have learned by now that magick is work and study. After the next lesson we will be moving on to the realm of Grey Magick. By studying the material, performing the rituals, and practicing the techniques you have earned this right. You have become versed in elementary occult philosophy and the Kabalah, as well as many other related topics.

Now, because you have reached this point, I want to give you something special. As I said before, I cannot initiate you. And, as I have described, although initiation is not necessary, it can speed up your progress. Even though I cannot initiate you, there is something *you* can do which can aid in your development. It is a self-dedication, wherein you dedicate yourself to the Great Work: attaining the Knowledge and Conversation of your Holy Guardian Angel (also known as cosmic consciousness, enlightenment, and unity with Divinity) and the bringing of Spiritual Light to a dark world.

If you choose to do this, you must have an altar as described in an earlier lesson. It sits in the middle of your magickal circle at the conjunction of the four elements, which come from the four quarters. It also represents the physical universe, and thus symbolizes the idea that the universe of the magickal circle is far larger than the material plane. If you contemplate the altar, you will surely come up with many more things the altar can represent.

On the top of the altar, besides the magickal tools, should be two additional items. These are a red triangle and a white cross. While they can ideally be made of painted wood or metal, they can also be made out of construction paper or felt. The cross represents our vow to follow the Great Work (our "cross to bear"). The triangle, which should be made so that it looks like three bars rather than one piece with a solid middle, represents all forms of trinities. This includes Isis, Apophis, Osiris; Tao, Yin, Yang; Keter, Hochmah, Binah; body, mind, spirit; and especially Light, Life, and Love. As you face east from behind the altar, these two symbols should rest on the altar with the cross just above the triangle:

Be sure to read the dedication vow below and make sure that you want to keep all of its provisions before actually doing this ritual. At this time, do not change the vow. After you have completed this course, you may wish to add to it. At that time you can repeat this entire ritual with your new vow.

Within the circle you should also have a small cup of water and some burning incense. They should not be on the altar, but to the sides. The incense should be to the south and the water should be to the north. Be sure that the censer is on a fire-proof surface.

The Rite of Self-Dedication

STEP ONE. Do the Relaxation Ritual.

STEP TWO. Do the LBRP.

STEP THREE. Do the BRH.

STEP FOUR. If it suits your Will, do the Rose Cross Ritual.

STEP FIVE. Pick up the water cup in the left hand and dip the fingers of the right hand in the water. Sprinkle a few drops from your fingers to the left, then ahead, then to the right. The center should be lower than the other two sprinkles so you are forming an elemental Water triangle. Redip the right index finger and make a cross on your forehead with your damp finger while saying: **"I consecrate myself with Water!"** Replace the water cup.

STEP SIX. Pick up the incense and wave it to the left, center, and right. The center should be higher than the other two waves so you are forming an elemental Fire triangle. Hold it so that you can smell its fumes while saying: **"I purify myself with Fire!"** Replace the incense.

STEP SEVEN. Hold both hands above shoulder level, palms forward, and bow your head. Say:

Holy art Thou, Lord of the universe!
Holy art Thou, whom nature hath not formed!
Holy art Thou, the vast and mighty one!
Lord of the light and of the darkness!

STEP EIGHT. Now kneel before the altar. (You may need to use a stool so you can reach the top of the altar with your hand. A folded towel on the floor may help if you have sensitive knees.) Place your right hand on top of both the triangle and the cross. Hold your left hand up in the air. Say the following slowly, meaningfully, and with conviction:

I, [state your magickal motto or full name], in the presence of the Lord of the universe who works in silence and naught but silence can express, do hereby dedicate myself to the accomplishment of the Great Work by taking the following vow: I, of my own free will and accord do hereby and hereon most solemnly pledge to keep secret all of my occult knowledge from any and all whom I deem unworthy due to their evil intents or lying ways. I undertake to prosecute with zeal the study of oc-cult sciences for the betterment of myself, the betterment of those around me, and the betterment of all humanity. I will not suffer myself to be placed in such a passive state that any person, power, or being may cause me to lose control of my thoughts, words or actions. I will not use my occult powers for any evil purposes. I agree to these points generally and severally, upon this sacred and sublime symbol, without evasion, equivocation, or mental reservation of any kind whatsoever. I realize that should I willfully break this, my magickal oath, that I shall be known as a perjuring wretch, void of all moral worth, and unfit for the society of all right and true persons. Furthermore, should I break this, my magickal oath, may my weapons turn against me or turn to dust, and may all of my magick and rituals be for naught, so help me the Lord of the universe and my own Higher Soul.

STEP NINE. Do the Middle Pillar Ritual and the Circulation of the Body of Light. When you finish, visualize yourself surrounded by brilliant white light and bask in its spiritual glow.

STEP TEN. Finish with the LBRP.

STEP ELEVEN. Record the results in your magickal or ritual diary.

As you can see, the penalties for breaking this magickal oath are quite severe. You may not wish to take this oath, or you may wish to wait to take it. But if you take it now, the "Powers that Be" will take note of your vow and your dedicated work over the past few months. They will smile upon your efforts and dedication. The result will be faster progress in all of your magickal and spiritual work. But don't take my word for it. Try it out and see what happens.

PART FIVE

Past Lives

A topic that deeply concerns many occultists is the "magickal memory." To Crowley, the magickal memory was an important part of occultism. And, like many aspects of occultism, under another name it has become a popular topic with the general public. Thus, it becomes hard today to discover anyone who is not familiar with some theory of reincarnation and past lives.

Sooner or later you will have a past-life experience as a result of your occult work. It may be in the form of a vision during meditation. Or, perhaps in the midst of a group ritual the appearances of the hall wherein you are working, the clothes and even the faces of the people with whom you are working will alter either subtly or dramatically. You may have the impression that you are in another location and working with other people. These are all signs of a returning magickal memory.

Before discussing the Kabalistic theory of reincarnation, I want to make clear the importance of past-life experiences. To be quite frank, I am not convinced that reincarnation is an *objective* reality. The scientific evidence for it is too scant, too non-repeatable, and at times too silly to take the whole thing seriously. I have met several dozen people who have told me that they were Jesus' disciples in a past life. I do not know where they were hiding in the Christian Bible's accounts, wherein only twelve are mentioned. One lady told me in all seriousness that she and I had "studied Kabalah together at Jesus' feet." I found that very interesting, as I had done some past-life regressions to that time and further back, and according to my experiences had never even been to the Middle East. I even knew two ladies who were lovers, one of whom thought she was an incarnation of Jesus, the other of whom thought she had been Judas! This certainly told more about their present-day psyches than their past lives. In fact, their present-day relationship resulted in them almost destroying each other mentally and spiritually.

I also know of several people who claim to be the current incarnation of Aleister Crowley. I have a letter from one of these self-avowed incarnations that shows a total lack of knowledge of Crowley's philosophy and an even smaller knowledge of the English language. Even if you think little of Crowley, his mastery of English is beyond question. On the other hand, I have a friend who insists that all of the many people claiming to be Crowley actually may be Crowley. He says there must be at least thirty-three people making the claim to be Crowley, and they each have about one thirty-third of Crowley's intelligence, talent, skill, and wit. Dion Fortune, in her book *Sane Occultism* (which should be required reading for all occultists), writes: "To claim greatness in the past does not so much cast reflected glory on a mediocre present life as suspicion on the intervening lives . . ."

Past-life experiences are one of three things:

1. They may be real experiences of actual past lives. This could be individual, genetic, or grouped.
2. They may be fantasies to glamorize a current lifetime in which a person feels irrelevant or insignificant.
3. They may be messages, which your subconscious needs to give to your conscious, but which your conscious refuses to hear. Thus, the subconscious presents them in a way that can be accepted by the conscious: as a symbolic past life.

Point one requires a bit of explanation. It's fairly obvious that an individual past life could be just that. It's the idea that your consciousness is a continuation of the consciousness during a lifetime before the current one. It's what most people think of when they hear the term "reincarnation." Genetic reincarnation is based on the idea that the DNA may carry certain memories. If this is true, a memory of a past life may actually be the memory of an event experienced by your great-great-grandmother or some other close or distant blood relative.

The concept of a grouped memory or "pool of souls" is rapidly gaining popularity. The concept is simple: after death, your consciousness and its memories, along with the consciousness and memories of everyone else, goes into a group or pool. People who are incarnating can take memories from that pool according to what they need for spiritual evolution in the upcoming lifetime. This pool is open to anyone and everyone. Therefore, literally hundreds of people could be having memories of being Napoleon or Cleopatra. And they all could be accurate.

The truth, however, is that it *does not matter* which is the cause of a past-life experience. What matters is what you get out of it *now*, in your current lifetime. If you re-read the section on the soul or personality according to the Kabalah in an earlier lesson, you will see that the memory is mortal; it ceases with the physical end of the body at the change known as death. Thus, if we do have a past-life experience, not only does it tend to be short and incomplete, but it also must be important enough to have made an impression on one of the immortal aspects of our being. And whether it is an actual memory, an important message from our subconscious or an ego-building fantasy, the message we should get out of the past-life experiences is the same: What can I learn from it now?

Frequently, the answer to this question deals with allowing us to learn some way of living better in the present. Sometimes they give cathartic experiences, which can free us from phobias and neuroses that are no longer valuable to our physical and mental well-being. Sometimes they tell us more about our inner makeup and desires.

Past-life experiences are, always have been, and ever must be very personal in nature. To be of any value at all, we must personally experience them. Sooner or later, as a result of doing the Great Work, experience them you will. Once experienced they can make drastic, positive changes in your life. They can also improve your magickal talents by freeing you from problems which might be holding you back. However, they can only do so if you pay attention to the lessons they hold.

Unfortunately, whenever there is something of true value, it seems that there is also either a cold-blooded opportunist trying to make a fast buck or a self-deluded believer who must help everyone . . .

and make a few bucks in the process. These people can be found at "psychic fairs" and giving classes or lectures, the main part of which features them telling you about your past lives. If you accept these people as entertainers, you may get your money's worth. They may actually be tapping into and informing you of real past lives (assuming such exist). But for magickal purposes *they are useless*. As I said, for them to be of any value to you whatsoever *you* must experience your past lives—just hearing about them is magickally valueless. Luckily, there are now teachers who are helping people to relive their past lives, and your participation in such a class is encouraged. There are also many fine books on the market that tell you how to experience past lives. And as I have already mentioned, the magickal work you are doing will probably trigger at one time or another a past-life experience.

In this course our real interest is the Kabalistic theory of reincarnation. The Kabalah, remember, is not a static, unchanging theory, but an *evolving* metaphysical philosophy. The Kabalah has several theories of reincarnation, which have evolved over time. None, however, are as simplistic as W. W. Westcott, a founder of the Golden Dawn, expressed when he said that according to the Kabalah people are limited to three incarnations. This has been copied by some authors who were members of the Golden Dawn and by other writers who don't give their sources credit. Before going on, I must add that in another work Westcott does talk about a more advanced Kabalistic theory of reincarnation. This is the Lurianic theory of metempsychosis, the Kabalistic theory of incarnating as a higher or lower life form.

There are two prime Kabalistic theories of reincarnation. The first relates to the Four Worlds. This theory sees four levels (relating to the Worlds), each of which has a series of lessons to be learned. If you do not learn them in one lifetime, you must reincarnate until you do. Once you have learned all of the lessons in the lowest level, becoming as spiritual as possible in the lowest World, in your next incarnation you will find yourself at the most unspiritual place of the next of the Four Worlds. As you may have guessed, the lessons and experiences are associated with the Tree of Life, and thus have ten basic areas of concern, although there may be many more subcategories. It can be seen that according to this system, there can be innumerable incarnations.

According to this system, the goal is to traverse all Four Worlds and perfect yourself so that you can reunite with the Divine. However, it is claimed that most people only get to the Tiferet level of B'ri-yah. At this point a person has evolved to such a high state that further incarnations are no longer necessary for evolvement.

The second basic theory is the above-mentioned one of Isaac Luria. Luria was a famous Kabalist who never wrote anything, but whose students' writings make him a father of modern Jewish Kabalism. His system has two basic features that would today be called metempsychosis and karma.

Metempsychosis, or the transmigration of souls, is the idea that we can incarnate as a lower life form if our current life is not in tune with the working of the universe. But the Lurianic theory goes much further than other theories of this type. In this system you are not punished for evil by becoming a cow. Rather, your next incarnation is dependent upon what you need to learn. Thus, if you need to learn stealth you might incarnate in your next life as a thief or as that thieving bird, the magpie. As you can see, the reason for incarnating into a "lower" life form is very logical.

The Lurianic system not only features this high level of logic, it also features greater depth. If you need to learn patience, for example, you may incarnate as a rock. If you need to learn flexibility you may come back as a reed by a river.

The ideas that come out of this are fascinating. The implication is that plants, rocks, and animals are alive and have souls. This also implies that all planets and asteroids are teeming with some form of life. In fact, it means that the entire universe is wonderfully alive, and that we are but a small part of it while at the same time intimately connected to all of it.

According to this system, we stay in a "lower" form until we have learned the necessary lesson and we have been of some use to a "higher" life form. Thus, in the example given above, you could stay a rock until you learned patience and until you had become useful, perhaps by providing shade to a snake or an insect, or serving as a stool for a human hiker. It is possible that your stay as a stone could last a relatively short time, or it could last for thousands of years. Likewise, you might stay a reed until you learn flexibility and become the food of an animal or perhaps part of a reed boat. As a side note, Dion Fortune urges non-vegetarianism for Western occultists because giving up animal products in the diet may cause a psychic opening too quickly and bring about psychic or physical damage. Those who believe in the Lurianic theory of metempsychosis would argue that you should eat meat, as it will help those who have incarnated as animals move up the evolutionary scale. Others say you should avoid meat, as it brings down the frequency of your energy, preventing you from evolving as quickly as possible.

To my mind, you should do what's right for you. If you force yourself to do otherwise you will be uncomfortable and unhappy, which is a handicap for psychic development. If you don't want to eat meat, don't; if you want to eat meat, do.

The Lurianic system also features a notion of karma. In Hebrew it is called *tee-koon*. As mentioned earlier, in English and other Romance languages, words tend to have specific meanings. In Sanskrit, this is not so. In fact, some of the earliest works in Sanskrit, the Tantras, frequently use what is called *sandhya bhasa*, or "twilight language," and are filled with hidden meanings that required a key to understand the twilight language code. Hebrew and other Semitic languages are similar in frequently having broad or imprecise meanings for words. Thus, although "tee-koon" means "correct" (as in "to make a correction"), it implies the restoring of the soul to its true identity. Therefore, the reason we reincarnate in other life forms is to correct errors we have made in previous lives. The reason we experience bad things

Auras and Past Lives

There is an old technique that I learned many years ago (a variation of it is used in the evocation of spirits) that can initially be used to see auras and, eventually, be used to see past lives.

The technique is actually very simple. Get a large piece of cardboard that is black, or else paint it black. Many stores selling art supplies have poster-size sheets of cardboard that are black and are perfect for this. As a minimum, about two feet wide by three feet tall is good.

Place this on an easel or some sort of stand with a chair in front of it so that when you look at a person seated in the chair, the black poster is centered behind his or her head. Behind this put an electric lamp so that you cannot see the bulb. Use a bulb with low wattage. Just a fifteen-watt bulb or less will do. People can sit in an audience to look at the person sitting in front of the poster. So, from the side you have:

LAMP   BLACK BOARD   CHAIR   VIEWERS

When you are ready, simply have a person sit in the chair, make the room as pitch black as possible, and turn on the light behind the black poster board. Then, the audience should simply watch.

After a surprisingly short time, you should begin to see a glow around the head of the person sitting in the chair. Typically, it is grey, silver, white, or golden. This is the opening of your astral vision so you can see the aura. After a while, that glow should start to show colors typically described in auras. It may take several sessions for you to see the colors. Be sure to do this with different persons, as you may be able to see colors more easily with one person than another.

Bring your attention back to the face of the person in the chair. Once you have begun to see the aura, it is likely that you will soon begin to see the face alter and change. You may even see images of different hats, hairstyles, gender changes, facial hair, age changes, and different clothes. These may be visual clues into that person's past lives.

Be sure to share your successful abilities with others by describing to them what you see.

It may help to use peripheral vision rather than focused or "foveal" vision. To learn this, simply look at a point on the wall in the center of the far side of a room. Now, expand your vision to the sides. Try to see as far to both sides—simultaneously—as you can. This is sometimes referred to as "soft" vision. Back in the late twentieth century, there were complex pictures that seemed to be a swirl of lines. However, if you softened your vision in this way, an image of a horse or a space ship in 3D would seem to leap out at you. This is the type of vision you should use.

in our lives for no apparent reason is for the working out of this tee-koon process. There is a passage in the Bible which says that God punishes a person for his sins unto the third generation. If you do not believe in reincarnation, this implies an incredibly vicious and vindictive deity. If, on the other hand, you believe that this is a type of twilight language and really means that you have to spend up to three incarnations to learn to "correct" past behavior, it becomes a reasonable and logical statement. Three lifetimes could easily be over 200 years, and that's a long time to spend on correcting errors in your actions. This may also be the source of Westcott's "three incarnations" error.

Let us assume that you have gone through many, many lifetimes and have achieved as much spiritual perfection as is possible for a person to achieve. You have been corrected. What, then, is the result? To answer this question we must first answer the question of where souls come from.

Simply, the Divine created all of the souls before their first incarnation. Thus, unrecognized, we are all imperfect parts of the Divine Source of all. Many have not incarnated as yet. It is possible that some may never do so. These proto-human souls are referred to as "sparks" in Kabalistic literature. These sparks are androgynous. When the soul is ready to incarnate, it is split in two. Each half will go to a member of a different gender. Each "soul half" watches over the forming fetus, but does not join with it until the first breath is taken. Also, note that according to this system you do not start as a lower life form and work your way up. Rather, you start as a human and can work yourself up or down.

Once you have achieved as spiritual a state as possible in each lifetime, the next step in the tee-koon process is for you to find the other half of your soul. The other half will also have gone through a series of experiences and will be waiting to join with you. It may be that one of you achieves the state of being ready to re-unify sooner than the other and will have to wait several lifetimes for the arrival of the missing half. When the time is right, you will be united with your "soul mate." This is the Kabalistic understanding of the term. In the interim you should love, marry, and have children. When the time is right, your true soul mate will appear, will be about your current age, will be of the opposite gender, and will not be a blood relative. (And please do not swallow the "Hey, baby. Don't you know I'm your soul mate?" line. Anyone who says it, isn't.) This obviously is in contrast to the theory popular among some that we have many soul mates.

Once you meet and unite with your soul mate, your divided soul will also unify during the time you spend together. This uniting is especially important during sex; however, that is a topic to be discussed later in these lessons. Once your soul is back in one piece as a result of the tee-koon process, you are fit to reunite with your creator . . .

Who works in silence,
And naught but silence can express.
—Golden Dawn Neophyte Initiation Ritual

PART SIX

I am often amazed at the incompetence of people claiming to be ceremonial magicians. Many of those whom I have met seem to think that the LBRP is the highest level of ritual magick, then wonder why Pagans criticize them for their "complicated rituals." In fact, some self-described magicians drop the "Lesser" so that the LBRP becomes *THE* Banishing Ritual of the Pentagram. This is totally wrong and totally in error. The LBRP was given to the members of the Golden Dawn (remember, they were a non-magickal group) to prepare them for the magickal work to come in the Inner Order of that organization. It is hoped that by this time you have been practicing the LBRP for several months. Time will not wait, and it is important that you are fully competent with the LBRP so that you can start practicing the following rite, the Supreme Invoking Ritual of the Pentagram.

As you probably remember, the points of the pentagram represent the five magickal elements: Spirit at the top, then, going counterclockwise, Air, Earth, Fire, and Water (see diagram on the next page).

In the LBRP you will note that since we start from the lower left we are moving *away* from the point of the pentagram association with elemental Earth. Had we moved from the top *toward* the lower left corner when making the first line, we would be performing the Lesser *Invoking* Ritual of the Pentagram. Some people advise doing the invoking in the morning and the banishing in the evening. In fact, I used to teach this. However, I now do not believe this is effective, as it prevents rapid and thorough learning of the LBRP. I now believe that the banishing *must* be learned and effective first. *Being able to do the LBRP effectively is a prerequisite for the rest of this course.* After a person has become completely effective with the LBRP he or she might wish to do the Lesser Invoking Ritual of the Pentagram (LIRP) in the morning and the LBRP at night. By the time they have achieved excellence with the LBRP they should have been doing enough other work in their magickal training that they can deal with any unexpected energies literally invited in during the day by the use of the LIRP.

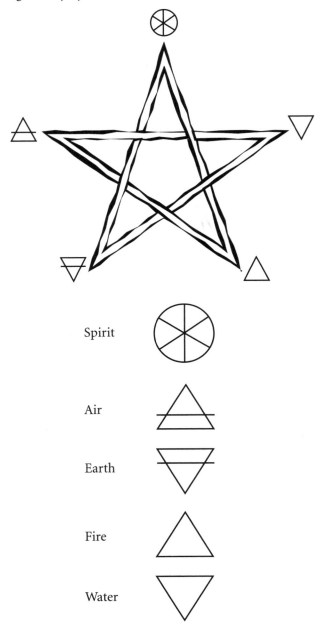

Spirit

Air

Earth

Fire

Water

There are also four pentagrams associated with the element of Spirit. Instead of invoking, two are called "equilibrating." Instead of banishing, two are called "closing." Both Equilibrating and Closing are divided into active and passive, giving a total of four, as shown in the first diagram on the next page.

Along with the four pentagrams of Spirit, there are also eight pentagrams, two for each of the other elements. Each element has a banishing and invoking pentagram, as shown in the second diagram on the next page.

The Supreme Invoking Ritual of the Pentagram is a more powerful version of the Lesser Invoking Ritual of the Pentagram. As you can guess, it can become the Supreme Banishing Ritual of the Pentagram by using the banishing forms of the pentagrams instead of the invoking ones. However, the purpose of this ritual at this time in our work is to bring *into* our lives the forces of all the elements. Later, it will take on even more importance.

At this time, practice this ritual *only in the morning*. When doing this work, at this time in the course, always follow it with the LBRP. Do not perform the Supreme Invoking Ritual of the Pentagram (SIRP) in the evening. This is not because the SIRP is dangerous, but because it can be very invigorating and might cause you difficulty in falling asleep. This is especially true when you are in the learning process and have not perfected the ritual.

Two other things need to be noted here. First, in the center of each of the pentagrams are drawn figures associated with each element. For Spirit is drawn a wheel with eight spokes:

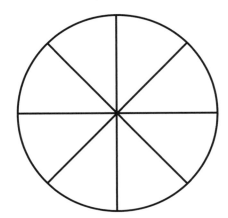

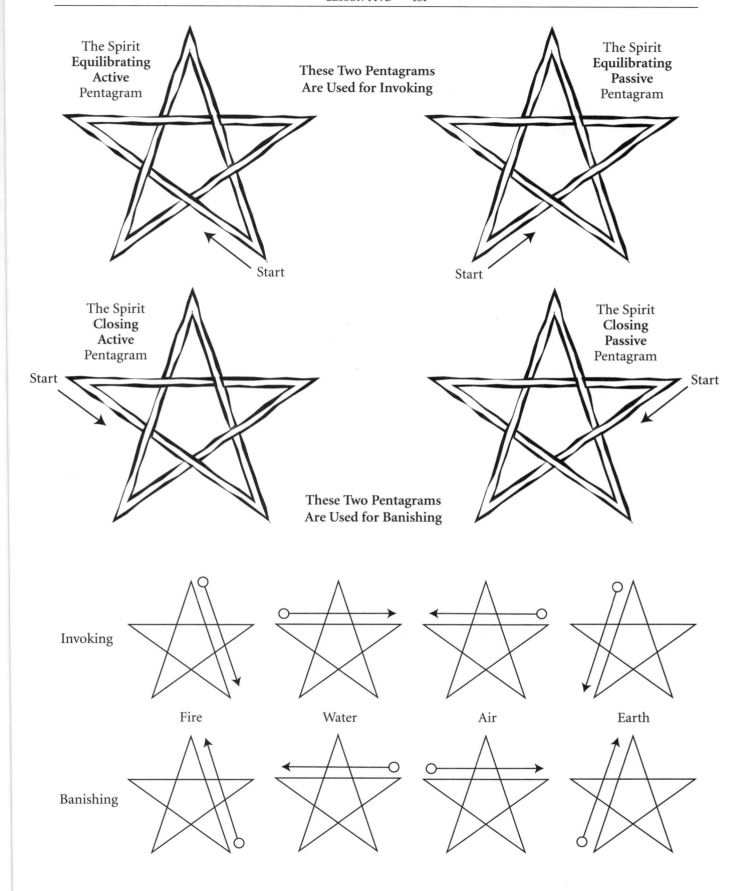

For Air the symbol of Aquarius is drawn, which in spite of its superficial association with Water is actually an Air symbol, as any book on astrology will confirm:

The sign for Leo represents the element of Fire:

The eagle is associated with Water:

As the symbol of Aquarius seems to be related to Water, so, too, does the Eagle seem to be related to Air. But here the Eagle is an alchemical symbol for distillation, a process definitely associated with Water.

The sign of Taurus represents the element Earth:

The other thing you will need to know is that some of the words in this ritual are not from the Hebrew, but from the Angelic or Enochian (pronounced "Ee-noh-kee-un") of Kelly and Dee. They are secret names of Divinity, and I will be discussing this system to a small degree in a later lesson. The pronunciation of the Enochian used here is as follows (the Enochian word is in bold and the pronunciation is in italic):

EXARP
Ex-ahr-pey

ORO IBAH AOZPI BITOM
Oh-row Ee-bah-hah Ah-oh-zohd-pee Bee-toh-ehm

OIP TEAA PEDOCE HCOMA
Oh-ee-pay Tay-ah-ah Pay-doh-kay Hay-coh-mah

EMPEH ARSEL GAIOL NANTA
Ehm-pay-hay Ahr-sel Gah-ee-ohl Ehn-ah-ehn-tah

EMOR DIAL HECTEGA
Ee-mohr Dee-ahl Hek-tay-gah

The Hebrew you should already know. Remember what YHVH represents, and it should be pronounced "Yud Heh Vahv Heh."

The Supreme Invoking Ritual of the Pentagram

STEP ONE. Do the Relaxation Ritual, the LBRP, and the BRH. These are optional and need not be done, but they are good for balancing you and preparing you for this ritual.

STEP TWO. From in front your altar (if you have one) face east and perform the Kabalistic Cross from the LBRP.

STEP THREE (a). Go to the east of your area. Make the equilibrated Active Pentagram of Spirit. As you do so, vibrate **EXARP**. This should be done so that the last syllable (pey) is sounding after you finish drawing the pentagram. As in the LBRP, inhale, feeling energy come into you, but exhale as you make the pentagram. Be sure to save enough breath so that you can thrust your hands forward into the center of the while you vibrate the last syllable "pey."

STEP THREE (b). While making the sign of Spirit, a wheel, in the center of the already drawn pentagram, vibrate **EH-HEH-YEH**, again saving the breath and last syllable to thrust forward with the hands at the center of the wheel. This symbol should be made by first making a clockwise circle, starting and ending at the top. Next, draw the vertical, then horizontal spokes. Follow this with the two diagonal lines. (Reread the instruction for the LBRP if you need to be reminded how to send energy out and thrust forward with the hands and left foot. The only difference is that in this ritual you do it at the end of the word of power you are vibrating.)

STEP FOUR (a). Still facing east, and over the figures you have already made, make the Invoking Pentagram of the element Air. In the same manner as above, vibrate **ORO IBAH AOZP** while making the pentagram, saving the last syllable to thrust forward and charge the image.

STEP FOUR (b). In the same manner, vibrate **YHVH** while forming the sign of Aquarius in the center of the already drawn pentagram.

(In this ritual, all the vibrating of words of power will be done in the same fashion.)

STEP FIVE. Move to the south, carrying a white line as you did in the LBRP.

STEP SIX (a). Make the Equilibrated Active of Spirit while vibrating **BITOM**.

STEP SIX (b). While making the inner Wheel, vibrate **EH-HEH-YEH**.

STEP SEVEN (a). Still facing south, over the figures you have already made, make the Invoking Pentagram of Fire. Vibrate **OIP TEAA PEDOCE** as you do so.

STEP SEVEN (b). Vibrate **EL-OH-HEEM** while making the Leo sigil in the center of the pentagram.

STEP EIGHT. Move to the west, carrying a white line as you did in the LBRP.

STEP NINE (a). Make the Equilibrated Passive Pentagram of Spirit while vibrating **HCOMA**.

STEP NINE (b). Vibrate **AGLA** while making the Wheel of Spirit.

STEP TEN (a). Still facing west, and over the figures you already made here, make the Invoking Pentagram of Water while vibrating **EMPEH ARSEL GAIOL**.

STEP TEN (b). Make the Eagle Head to represent Water in the center of the pentagram while you vibrate **EL.**

STEP ELEVEN. Carry the White Line to the north.

STEP TWELVE (a). Make the equilibrated Passive Pentagram of Spirit while vibrating **NANTA.**

STEP TWELVE (b). Vibrate **AGLA** while making the Wheel of Spirit.

STEP THIRTEEN (a). Still facing north, and over the figures you have already made, make the Invoking Pentagram of Earth while vibrating **EMOR DIAL HECTEGA.**

STEP THIRTEEN (b). Vibrate **AH-DOH-NYE** while making the sign of Taurus.

STEP FOURTEEN. Carry the line to the east, completing the circle. Return to your original position in front the altar, facing east.

STEP FIFTEEN. Do the Evocation of the Archangels and the Kabalistic Cross as in the LBRP.

While you are learning this Supreme Invoking Ritual of the Pentagram, always end by doing the LBRP. Always! And it will be better if you also do the BRH.

NOTES: As in the LBRP, the pentagrams are blue and the lines connecting them are white. The Wheels of Spirit should also be the same brilliant, pure white light as the lines connecting the pentagrams. The Aquarius sign should be yellow to represent Air. The Leo sigil should be red for Fire. The Eagle symbol should be blue to represent elemental Water. Finally, the Taurus sign should be shiny black to represent Earth.

If you were doing this ritual in the form of a banishing ritual you would use the same symbols within the pentagrams. However, the pentagrams would use their banishing forms while the Spirit pentagrams would use their closing forms.

You may notice that I did not mention a particular tool to use in this ritual. At this time, use the dagger. However, as we progress in this course, you will find that one particular weapon is not associated with this ritual as the dagger is with the LBRP.

Of course, conclude the ritual by recording what you did and what you experienced in your ritual diary.

On the following page you will find a summary for this ritual. The SIRP should be learned, and preferably memorized, but it is not a part of your daily work. While you are learning it, you might want to make a copy of the following page and carry it with you. If you need more information, or if it is more convenient, while you are learning it copy it onto filing cards. As they are made of cardboard, rather than paper, they are more stable and easier to handle. Some people like to use the typical 3 x 5 inch cards, however I always found those to be too small. Instead, I preferred 4 x 6 inch cards. They're not that much bigger but have surprisingly more space. As always, however, if you want to use something like cards, try different sizes and see which works the best for you.

The Supreme Invoking Ritual of the Pentagram

1. From in front of your altar, face east and perform the Kabalistic Cross.

2a. While making the Equilibrated Active Pentagram of Spirit vibrate: **EXARP.**

2b. While making the wheel vibrate: **EH-HEH-YEH.**

3a. Make the Invoking Pentagram of Air while vibrating: **ORO IBAH AOZPI.**

3b. Make Aquarius symbol and vibrate: **YHVH.**

carry line to south

4a. Make Equilibrated Active Pentagram of Spirit, vibrate: **BITOM.**

4b. Make wheel, vibrate: **EH-HEH-YEH.**

5a. Make the Invoking Pentagram of Fire, vibrate: **OIP TEAA PEDOCE.**

5b. Make Leo symbol, vibrate: **EL-OH-HEEM.**

carry line to west

6a. Make Equilibrated Passive Pentagram of Spirit, vibrate: **HCOMA.**

6b. Make Wheel, vibrate: **AGLA.**

7a. Make Invoking Pentagram of Water, vibrate: **EMPEH ARSEL GAIOL.**

7b. Make Eagle sign, vibrate: **EL.**

carry line to north

8a. Make Equilibrated Passive Pentagram of Spirit, vibrate: **NANTA.**

8b. Make Wheel, vibrate: **AGLA.**

9a. Make Invoking Pentagram of Earth, vibrate: **EMOR DIAL HECTEGA.**

9b. Make Taurus sign, vibrate: **AH-DOH-NYE.**

carry line to east, completing and closing the circle

10. Return to your original position behind the altar, facing east. Do the Evocation of the Archangels and the Kabalistic Cross as in the LBRP.

11. When practicing this ritual, *ALWAYS* finish by doing the Lesser Banishing Ritual of the Pentagram.

12. Record your experience in your ritual diary

PART SEVEN

I want to return now to a further look at the Kabalistic Four Worlds. These Four Worlds represent four planes or levels of existence. In English we could say that these four planes are the physical, emotional, mental, and spiritual.

The physical plane relates to the lowest world of Ahssiah; the emotional plane is associated with Yetzirah; the mental level equates with the world of B'ri-yah; and the spiritual plane is related to the world known as Atziloot. You might wish to reread the section on the Four Worlds from an earlier lesson at this time.

There are other systems that claim that there are far more planes of existence. Many systems hold that there are seven planes. Others hold that there are thirty-three or more planes. Some believe that there is only one other plane, and the philosophy known as materialism claims that there is only the physical reality we know in our everyday existence and nothing more. Soon we will be studying Grey Magick, and although the practice of White Magick necessitates the knowledge of all of the Kabalistic Worlds (especially the spiritual world of Atziloot), in Grey Magick there is really only one plane other than the physical plane that is of interest. This is the emotional plane, the Kabalistic world of Yetzirah.

As you should recall, Yetzirah is also considered to be the so-called "astral plane." As I said in the lesson discussing the Four Worlds, Yetzirah, the astral plane, is "the basis for everything that exists in the physical universe." You may have passed over this quotation, ignoring it, or you may have wondered

Help for Everyone

Even in the first edition of *Modern Magick* I tried to make clear that what I was sharing was the Western mystery tradition of magick. What I shared had worked for me. It also worked for many of my students.

I also included variations on the tradition and stressed two things. First, merely repeating what others had done wasn't magick, it was hero worship. Second, this is a tradition, and traditions must evolve. If they do not, they become antiquated and obsolete. Magick is a living, breathing, experimental science, not ancient laws carved in stone never to be tampered with. The tradition is a tradition, however, because is has worked for so many people.

Once, I got into an online debate with a person who wrote that the important thing about magick was that you did it, not that it did anything. I responded to him that if that were true there would be no reason to do magick. I preferred the comment in Crowley's *Book of the Law*: "Success is your proof." He replied that I just didn't get it and wouldn't respond to me after that.

Maybe I didn't get it, but the magickal tradition I know is focused around what is successful and practical, not doing something that has no results.

The thing is, I'm just one person. What works for me may not work for everyone. But what works for you might work for someone else. When I was teaching a regular series of classes, as opposed to individual workshops as I mostly do now, there was more time for people to share their experiences.

I love to hear what others are doing! They share ideas that I had never thought of. They add different things and twists that add to their effectiveness. Earlier in this course I suggested that everyone paint a set of Trees of Life, each one in the colors from a different Kabalistic scale. I used to assign that task to my class students. Every one that was turned in was different, but they all followed the scales. It was their interpretation, and sharing them allowed people to see that they can follow the tradition but still have independence and individuality. I think this is an important lesson to learn.

But when the first edition of *Modern Magick* was published, there was no way to share all of the variations within the tradition. So I didn't mention anything about it. Now, however, there is a way for each person to share what they've learned. It's one of the most powerful and most magickal tools ever created. Of course, I mean the Internet.

I encourage you to start your own web page or website. Share your experiences, your tools, your drawings, your adventures. Or, you can do this on one of the social networking websites that are available. When I shared everyone's Trees, I didn't do so with the attitude of one being wrong and another right. Rather, I wanted to show that variation and originality is possible. I hope you approach this in the same light. Share what you have done not to claim that others are wrong but that there can be power in diversity.

That way, by the simple act of sharing, you'll be helping magickal people everywhere.

what was meant by the claim that the astral plane was the basis for everything in the physical universe, including, of course, all people and things in our world. This gives me another chance to urge you to go back occasionally and review past lessons. Each time you read them you will get more out of them. They should not merely be read and forgotten. If you had really thought about it, you might have realized that the quotation from that earlier lesson may be the most important thing you will ever read. In fact, it may indicate a turning point in your life.

This quotation tells, in a simple manner, the basis of all Grey Magick. But to fully understand the importance and meaning of it we have to start by looking again at reincarnation. However, this time we will approach it from a different angle. We need to look at the question we have all asked at one time or another: "Where did I come from?"

Quite obviously, the human being is more than just flesh, bone, and blood. There is also an energy, which animates the body. As already stated, in the Kabalah this energy is known as Ruach. But merely having a piece of meat that is animated by Ruach does not make a human being. The thing that really makes you different from other pieces of animated meat is your personality and what is commonly called your "soul."

The soul and personality are not the same. Rather, the personality relates to your ego, or that aspect of the personality known in the Kabalah as the Ruach (not to be confused with the animating energy of the same name). The soul, in Freudian terms, is the superego; in Kabalistic terms it is the Yeh-chee-dah, your higher self. (Yeah, I know this gets complex and even confusing. Read it a few times and think about it. Make notes. If it still doesn't make sense, just drop it for a week or two. When you come back to it you'll find a new awareness and confidence as it becomes clear.)

According to the Kabalah, when you die, the body immediately starts to decay and should go into "Shee-ool." As an interesting side note, Shee-ool is usually translated when it appears in the *Tanach* or Jewish Bible as "ground" or "earth." However, in some instances (when the translators wished to convey the idea that if you are a "sinner" when you die you will be punished), the same word is translated as "Hell." The Kabalah does not have any such place of eternal punishment. According to both the Kabalah and an accurate translation of the *Tanach*, there is no Hell.

The Kabalistic tradition says that when you go through the change known as death the personality (ego or Ruach) does not realize exactly what has occurred. This is especially true in cases of sudden or traumatic death. The personality of the dead person, suddenly freed from the physical body, tends to wander back and forth between the body (in Shee-ool, the grave) and the previous home of the person for a period of seven days. Traditionally, Jews stay in their home for a week after the death of a member of the household. In Hebrew, the word for the number seven is *sheevah*, and this practice is commonly known as "sitting sheevah." Mirrors are covered so the returning spirit won't be shocked at seeing themselves in a dead state.

What most modern Jews who follow this practice do not know is the purpose of this ritual. The purpose is the same as the purpose of such books as the Egyptian and Tibetan Books of the Dead: to tell the personality that it has gone through the change known as death and that it is free to move on. It is probable that there may be a lost Hebrew text similar in nature to the Books of the Dead. If so, it was probably lost along with most of the texts concerning Merkabah mysticism.

According to the Kabalistic tradition, after about one week the personality begins to realize what has happened and eventually dissolves to nothingness (remember, it is mortal). However, people with extremely strong personalities can will themselves to stay in a shadowy world of semi-existence. This may be one of the causes of what is commonly known as hauntings.

It is not advisable to allow or aid the Ruach-ego to exist for long periods after physical death. This is because there are important links between the Ruach-ego and the Yeh-chee-dah. By keeping the Ruach-ego locked to the physical world, it prevents the Yeh-chee-dah from reincarnating and eventually achieving its far more lofty goal of unity with the Divine. Thus it is that the Kabalists usually frown upon spiritism and spiritualistic practices. Communicating with our deceased loved ones (if that's who it is we really are communicating with) tends to lock the Ruach-ego near the physical plane. It prevents necessary evolution.

As I stated earlier, your Yeh-chee-dah is your link to the Divine. Actually, it is more than that: it is literally a small part of God. That is why it is said we were made in the likeness of Divinity. The Divine is a part of us. God is not a big old man with a beard, sitting on a throne that is on a cloud.

But for some reason unknowable to our mortal minds, most of humanity has lost the conscious awareness of that link. In order to re-establish the fact that there is a part of us that is of the Divine, we must evolve our consciousnesses. This, along with the working out of karma (Tee-koon), is the purpose of reincarnation.

As stated in an earlier lesson, our memories, like the Ruach-ego, are mortal, and most of them die with our physical bodies. But the important things, the lessons we need to learn so that we can again become not just linked with Divinity (Yoga) but actually rejoin the Godhead, are remembered. Unfortunately, one lifetime is usually not enough to learn all of the lessons necessary so that we can become one with the Godhead and need no longer incarnate. Each lifetime on Earth is necessary to learn either one or more lessons. If you do not learn them in this lifetime, then when you reincarnate you will still need to learn them.

Sometimes we are shown the lesson we need to learn but end up flunking the course. Then, after retaking the lesson we flunk it again! As a certified Tarot Grandmaster, a reader of Tarot cards, I used to frequently work at psychic fairs. Usually at least once at each fair a young woman, frequently with a baby, would tell me a story like this:

"When I started living with_____, he was very good to me. We have two wonderful children. But after a few years he started drinking, running around with other women, and beating me and the kids. Well, I took this for three years. Then, I finally picked up the kids, moved out, and got a job. About six months later I met a really nice guy. He moved in with the kids and me. But recently he has started drinking, running around with other women, and hitting me and the kids. What can I do to make him nice again?"

Of course, there are similar situations with men, only they usually tend to allow themselves to be manipulated until they can no longer take the ego bruising rather than being physically abused. Sometimes, people will tell me the same story has happened to them four or five times.

For the woman above, there are many lessons to be learned. Usually such a situation is based upon feelings of lack of worth and the need to develop self-respect, and to treat yourself well. Another lesson illustrated in the above example is to learn what attracts you to these bad situations, and what attracts bad people to you. There are many variations in the exact story, and each reveals more lessons which can be learned.

The Hermetic Order of the Golden Dawn advised you to seek your Holy Guardian Angel and find out the lessons you need to learn so you will not have to learn them again in this or a future lifetime. This brings us (finally) to how you were born.

Obviously, the meeting of the sperm and ovum both produces the physical body and, in most cases where birth is the end result, instills the zygote with Ruach energy. But where does the soul, the real and eternal you, come from?

Since your soul has a direct link to the Godhead, it is obvious that your soul must also have a link to the total knowledge of the all-knowing deity. After the ego ceases to be, the soul is freed from bondage to the ego. It can freely learn through that link to the Divinity and discover exactly what it will need to learn in its next incarnation in order to evolve to

Tanach? What Happened to the Old Testament?

If you read the first or second editions of *Modern Magick*, you may be surprised to see that in this edition I do not use the term "Old Testament." There is an important reason for this.

The Jewish Bible is composed of several parts or books. The most famous section, of course, is the first five books known as the Torah. If you go to a synagogue and see the Torah scrolls brought out, the writings there are the first five books of the Bible and not the entire holy scriptures. To Jews, the technical name for the entire Bible is the *Tanach*.

To religious Jews, the *Tanach* is the lifeblood of Judaism. But Christians refer to it as the "Old Testament," replaced by their wonderful "New Testament." The use of those terms is so commonplace that even Jews now refer to the *Tanach* as the "Old Testament."

But to Jews, the *Tanach* is a spiritual document. It is neither old nor obsolete. They need no "New Testament" and find their religion quite enough, thank you!

To call the *Tanach*, the holy book of the Jews, "Old" is to denigrate what's in it, Jewish beliefs, and Jews themselves. It is basically an anti-Semitic term. Yes, I used it previously. But we all grow and develop and understand more as we evolve. So in these lessons, and for me personally, it's *Tanach* and not the "Old Testament."

Some people may claim I'm just being "politically correct" with this change. I would respectfully disagree. I choose not to be anti-Semitic and I choose to be accurate. If that's being "PC," so be it. It's not my intention to offend any particular group of people, although I realize that some people are going to be offended by the very publication of this course.

Sorry about that, chief!

---

that desired state where incarnation will no longer be necessary. Then, not being bound by the physical laws of time and space, your future soul searches for a "house," a body to inhabit, which will allow it to actually learn the necessary lessons.

According to the Kabalah, the soul joins with the chosen human body when that body takes its first breath, and not before. However, it will watch over and help protect the forming fetus. It may only take hours for the soul to find the appropriate body, but it might take years.

When a woman and man are making love they set up a vortex of energy, which attracts souls waiting to incarnate. If the act of sexual intercourse is done spiritually and with love, it will attract a soul needing a nurturing family and be able to develop spiritually. If the "love" act is done with hatred and anger, a soul needing that type of treatment will be attracted. Is it any wonder that most of the people who physically abuse their children were themselves abused as a child? Is it any wonder that most of the people in prison for serious felonies were abused children? This does not mean that a childhood of abuse necessitates a violent life. In fact, it may be that a person needs to learn to overcome violent behavior and incarnates into a situation where he or she learns violence so that it can be overcome. By the way, an interesting Kabalistic tradition holds that sometimes several souls will actually argue over trying to get into a particular body.

As mentioned before, your soul, or let us say "soul consciousness," descends in superiority and becomes secondary to your emerging ego and personality. In fact, that soul consciousness descends so far that it becomes what is known as your unconscious.

Thus, it is your unconscious that is your link to Divinity. This is why true meditation, which reverses this order and makes the unconscious once again dominant (not the superficial layers of the unconscious as represented by the Freudian id, but the real "soul consciousness"), allows you to know the link between yourself and the Godhead and use that link to all wisdom and all knowledge. It allows you to obtain answers to seemingly insoluble problems. Furthermore, this deep level of your unconscious, your true "soul consciousness," exists on what is called the astral plane: the Kabalistic world of Yetzirah. If you had been born with another soul, you would not be the same person. The part of you which exists in the Yetziratic world, the astral plane, was in existence before your physical body.

In fact, everything that exists in our physical plane, the Kabalistic world of Ahssiah, has an astral or Yetziratic counterpart. This counterpart is usually known as the astral body. Every person has an astral body or astral double. So does every animal, vegetable, or mineral. Everything has a pre-existing astral double. You do not have an astral body because you have a physical body. Rather, you have a physical body because the astral body already existed and wanted to join a new "home." While your soul was waiting to inhabit its physical body with the body's first breath, it was establishing a link between itself and the physical body. This link is the astral body. *For anything to exist on the physical plane it must first exist on the Astral Plane!*

Therefore, in order to create anything and bring it into your life, all you have to do is create it in the astral plane. This is the underlying principle of all Grey Magick. The reason why there are so many different types of Grey Magick is because there are many ways of creating things in the astral plane. Soon, you will be learning a few of them.

At this point in the course, if you have not done so already, I want to urge you to pause and study, at least briefly, a book by another author. It should be about any of the subjects of this course. A true magician does not blindly follow the words of others. He or she is a scientist and investigates any and all possible avenues. A magician is not locked into any form of dogma or conditioning. This is why a magician is a dangerous person. A true magician does not buy the semi-truths and lies told by religious and civic leaders to keep the masses in tow and in fear. A magician is always free, and freedom always frightens totalitarians.

PART EIGHT

In the next few pages I am going to be discussing a very important part of your magickal training: physical fitness and health. Now before you skip this section totally, let me explain that I am most definitely not talking about hours of arduous exercises with weights until you look like a stand-in for Arnold Schwarzenegger! What I will be talking about here is quite different.

First, let us look at the idea of health. What exactly is health? If you ask an M.D., he or she will tell you things about vital signs, blood pressure, cholesterol and triglyceride levels, etc. But what is really being talked about is not health. Rather these are indications of what constitutes both a lack of disease and disease prevention. You could be without disease in Western medical terms but still not be vibrant and full of health.

	2
HEALTH	_____
DISEASE	_____1_____
DEATH	_____

Levels of Health

The diagram above shows that although you could be above the point where a disease manifests (Point 1), you could still be below a really healthy condition. Some people get to Point 1, just above the disease line, so that no disease is manifesting. But just a tiny change in conditions could result in slipping below the line and coming down with, perhaps, a cold or flu, or possibly something more severe.

Do you know anybody who seems to be coming down with a cold every few weeks or months? It is because they only improve their health to Point 1. If, on the other hand, your health stays above the health line (Point 2), minor changes will have little effect upon your health. It will take a major change for you to fall all of the way down to below the disease line, where you leave yourself open for illness. It should be obvious, then, that we would want to achieve a state of high-level health. This is especially true for magicians who may have to spend tiring hours in a magickal circle where the temperature can make sudden and radical jumps. (Yes, I know we haven't done anything like that yet, but we will!)

Ask your doctor what signs of health are and you get responses which show what disease isn't. What, then, are the signs of health?

In the West, we really do not at this time have a good definition, although holistic health practitioners are working on establishing them. That simply hasn't been the focus of Western medicine. For now, to answer this question, we turn to traditional Chinese medicine.

According to my Shiatzu teacher, Dr. Turk, the ancient Chinese believed that there were eight signs of health. The goal of the physician was to maximize these signs in his or her patients:

The Eight Traditional Chinese Signs of Optimum Health

1. *Vitality.* This means having a life full of energy. It should show in the way you walk and in the condition of your eyes. There should be a spring in your step and you should have the energy to do whatever is required for you to do.

2. *Appetite.* This means not only having an appetite for food when you are hungry, but also an appetite for new experiences, new learnings, and even for sex. Perhaps a better expression for this quality would be "a lust for life."

3. *Deep and Sound Sleep.* According to traditional Chinese medicine you should only need four to six hours of sleep a night. This does not mean that a way to health is to start cutting down on the sleep you need. Rather, it indicates that as you get healthier you will need less sleep. If you need ten to twelve hours of sleep per night on a regular basis, however, you may want to see a doctor, as this could indicate a medical problem.

Notice, too, that it is not just quantity of sleep that was recognized by the Chinese, but also quality. In this tradition "sound sleep" indicates a dreamless sleep. This, of course, is a misnomer. Perhaps it means a sleep with dreams that are not disturbing. But I know that I have experienced nights where I slept and awoke feeling tired, haven't you? This is certainly not a sound sleep!

4. *Good Memory.* This is fairly clear and indicates that you should have both a good short-term and a good long-term memory. In a curious reversal of Western thought, the ancient Chinese believed that as you got older your memory should *improve*, not deteriorate. Old age was not seen as a cause of poor memory; disease was. Further, the Chinese believed that you should have a good memory of the past, present, and future. Present memory referred to what we call short-term memory. Past memory is long-term memory. Future memory is the ability to remember the plans, goals, and dreams we wanted for our future and that we made months or years ago. It also means that we should still be trying to achieve those goals.

5. *Humor.* We should have a good sense of humor to be healthy. We should especially be able to laugh at ourselves and the world immediately around us. As a friend of mine said, "Don't take life seriously . . . you'll never get out alive!"

6. *Infinite Giving.* No, this does not mean that you should give away all of your possessions and money. Rather, it means that to be healthy you should be able to give of yourself to your friends and to those in need. Also, you should be able to give time and effort to yourself.

7. *Clear Thinking and Precise Action.* This indicates that a sign of health is the ability to quickly see through a problem, make a decision, and act on that decision without spending an undue length of time considering possibilities and alternatives. Fear and procrastination are seen as types of diseases associated with imbalances in the body's energy system. There is also the implication that part of being healthy is having intuitive and psychic abilities that are correct more often than not, as well as having an awareness of them and an ability to use them. Put another way, a sign of health is the ability to make decisions quickly and have them prove to be effective and successful.

8. *Realization of Oneness.* This is a state of utmost health. It is indicated by having all your dreams instantly realized—sometimes even getting the things you want before you even realized that you wanted them. Perhaps another way of putting it would be that the healthiest person is a natural magician.

Now please don't start thinking that because you don't have all these eight qualities in large amounts that you are sickly and going to die in ten minutes! Put down those pills and stop charging the defibrillator paddles! These eight signs of health are goals to *strive* for. They represent optimum health. It's possible that we may never fully achieve them, but you may wish to aim for them.

For the purposes of these lessons, we are only concerned with the first quality, vitality. This includes physical vitality and vitality of the energies of the body. For this I need to tell you about a strange manuscript known as *The Eye of Revelation.*

I had heard about this mysterious manuscript for quite some time and had been looking for it for several years. Today it is well-known and a cottage industry seems to have grown up around it, but when I first researched it, information was rare.

The exercises in that document are known as the "Five Tibetan Rites" (or sometimes just the "Five Tibetans") and had been passed along in a sort of

occultists' underground for a long time. I knew the rites, but I wanted to find a copy of the original text. Finally, a first edition of it fell into my hands. This small book was written by a man named Peter Kelder and had a copyright date of 1939. It tells the story of an elderly man who visits a lamasery in India and learns some magickal rites (which are more like physical exercises). These rites rejuvenate him to such a degree that he is mistaken for his son.

Quite frankly, I doubt that this story as presented is true because there are many things in it which sound as if they were made up. Further, I more recently found another small book, also with a copyright of 1939, that is even more rare. It is by a man named Emile Raux, titled *Hindu Secrets of Virility and Rejuvenation.* It is practically the same information without the questionable story attached to it. I've checked with some authorities, but nobody will state which came first. My guess is that it was the Raux book, as it includes photographs while the Kelder book only has drawings, and the rites do have some similarities to certain forms of Indian hatha yoga. Besides, to the best of my knowledge, no Tibetans have ever acknowledged the rites as being part of any Tibetan practice, although one lama has claimed they are an authentic part of an Indo-Tibetan Tantric tradition.

Whatever the source, no matter the debate over the veracity of the story attached to the exercises, I know of nothing that can deny the success so many people have had toward improving their health as a result of practicing the Five Rites. It works not only on the physical body, but also on the non-physical energetic system. The instructions for the Five Rites are on the following pages.

As with any exercise program, you should consult an M.D. first and tell him or her that you wish to begin exercising. This is especially true if you have not exercised in a long time or if you are considerably out of shape. You should never strain with these exercises, although you may perspire. Only do as many as you can and advance gradually. Never force anything.

One of the problems with Westerners is the curse of perfectionism. We want everything to be totally perfect. If it is not perfect, then we don't want it at all.

Practice Makes Perfect?
or
Greater Success Through Lowered Expectations

We've all heard the expression "practice makes perfect" hundreds, perhaps thousands, of times. We heard it when we were having difficulty achieving something. We heard it with lessons we didn't want to study. It's driven into us over and over until we accept it as a law. There's just one problem with it:

It's a lie.

Practice has *never* made anything perfect. Practice simply repeats something until it becomes a habit. (This supposedly takes twenty-one days of repetition, remember?) So if you practice something the wrong way long enough, you'll make a habit of doing it the wrong way. In short, the truth is that practice doesn't make perfect. Only perfect practice makes perfect. That's why musicians break down pieces of music and work out the difficult parts until they can get them perfect before moving on to the entire piece.

Only perfect practice makes perfect.

There's another part of this that is important to understand. When you say you're going to do something and succeed at it, your unconscious mind carries that over into all levels of your life. "I'm a success" it thinks, and then it literally drives you to success in all areas. Similarly, if you fail at one thing, your mind carries the "I'm a failure" focus into other areas of your life. People who fail at one thing tend to fail at others, too.

Now obviously, you're a bright person (you bought this course, didn't you?) so you want to bring success to all aspects of your life. A key to that is making appropriate and attainable goals (more on that later in this course). However, an easy way to become a success is to simply lower your expectations.

Since we're about to discuss health, let's say you decide to go to the gym. Maybe you've made a New Year's Resolution of "I'm going to go to the gym five days every week." You probably know people who have done that. My guess is that most, if not all, have eventually failed and given up. Many gyms work on the assumption that most people who sign up will stop attending within a few months, but keep paying "dues."

Let's look at what happens. Well, life happens. Something comes up and before long you've missed a day. You only went four times that week. Well, as a failure, you may as well give up. That's the way most people think.

So let's turn it around. Change the goal to a minimum of twice a week. You start out going five times a week. You're not only a success, but you've exceeded your goal. And success feels really good.

Then a problem happens and you're only able to go to the gym three times a week. You're still an amazing success, exceeding your goals. That's better living through lowered expectations!

In the case of these exercises or rites, do the best job with them that you can. But if you cannot do a rite even one time well, do it one time poorly. Just do it.

The Five Rites should be done once a day, every day, skipping no more than one day a week. If you are setting goals for yourself and can't quite do all the desired repetitions of one particular exercise, do the unfinished number of repetitions later in the day. The full set of exercises should take no more than ten minutes per day once they are learned.

When doing the rites, remember to breathe! You should exhale whenever your body goes through a contracting part of the exercise and inhale at a stretching or relaxation section. Try not to pant.

As a last thought, many people who become involved with ceremonial magick become disappointed rather quickly, because they find that due to a lack of knowledge or talent they are unable to do magick quickly. Or, they find that there is a great deal of study, practice, and work, which will take more time than they wish to dedicate. I think that most people have bizarre expectations as to what magick really is because of the silliness seen in movies and on television. It is also due to the lies fostered by fearful religious and pseudo-occult groups. Some people expect that if you wear a black robe, say a few weird words, and wave your hand in the air, you can do magick. As those of you reading this lesson know, nothing could be further from the truth.

In getting this far in the course you have persevered on the path of magick and occultism when many who have come before you have faltered, failed, or given up. You should congratulate yourself.

The next lesson will be the last to focus on White Magick. Starting in the seventh lesson we will be going into the techniques and practices of Grey Magick. These methods will allow you to make positive changes in your life and the lives of those around you.

What you have been practicing in these five lessons and in the next lesson are specifically arranged to prepare you to do Grey Magick. If you are not competent at doing the rituals given in these lessons, you will have great difficulty succeeding with Grey Magick. This does not mean that the thousands of people who have practiced Grey Magick over the centuries have been fooled because "it doesn't work." Rather, it means that you need more preparation. And practice!

The Five Tibetan Rites

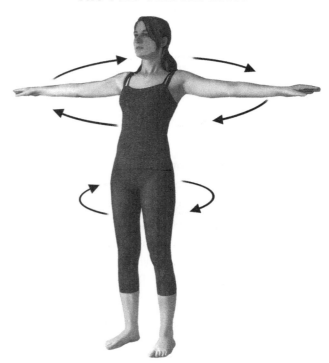

Rite Number One. This is the simplest of the rites, but do not discount its importance. Stand upright with your hands straight out to the sides. Now spin around in a clockwise direction (from left to right) until you become slightly dizzy. When you first try this you may only be able to make three to six turns, but within ten weeks you should be up to twenty-one circles, which is the maximum you need to do.

Rite Number Two. In this exercise you lie down, feet together, on a flat surface. Your hands should be palms down with the fingers together, but slightly turned in toward the center of the body (see illustration above). Raise the legs off the floor so that they are straight up, or, better yet, until they are slightly past center. At the same time touch the chin to the chest. Then slowly lower the legs and head and relax. Do this as many times as possible, but don't strain. Your goal is to get up to twenty-one repetitions. Don't bend the knees, but if you cannot do even one repetition, see how many you can do with your knees bent.

Rite Number Three. This rite should be done immediately after doing the second rite. Simply kneel on a flat surface with your hands by your sides, palms in. Lean forward as far as you can without los-ing your balance. Be sure to touch your chin to your chest. Then lean backward as far as you can, allowing your head to fall back. Repeat this as many times as you can, your goal being twenty-one repetitions.

Rite Number Four. Sit on a flat surface with your arms down at your sides so that the palms are flat on the ground. Now raise the body and bend the knees so that your torso becomes like a table to the supports of your arms and legs. Before pushing up, your chin should touch your chest. As you move up, your head should be allowed to gently move back (see illustration). Return to original position. As with the other rites, your goal is twenty-one times.

Rite Number Five. Lie face down on the floor with the arms about two feet apart. Your legs should also be about two feet apart. Push the body, especially the hips, straight up as high as possible. Touch your chin to your chest. Now allow the body to come down to a sagging position with the head thrown back. Ideally you should not touch the ground, but if you must that is okay. Again, twenty-one repetitions is your goal. As with all of the other rites, allow yourself ten weeks to reach this goal.

Review

The following questions are designed to help you determine if you have mastered the information in Lesson Five. Please try to answer them without looking at the text. The answers are in Appendix Two.

1. What are the qualities of elemental Water?

2. List five reasons for doing the Rose Cross Ritual.

3. When can you use the Rose Cross Ritual to replace the LBRP?

4. Ruach El-oh-heem (Holy Spirit) is represented by what Hebrew letter?

5. What three things can the past-life experience be?

6. What do the triangle and cross represent?

7. Draw invoking and banishing pentagrams for Air, Earth, Fire, and Water.

8. Name a ritual that can impart a type of invisibility.

9. What is "vicarious atonement"? Do kabalists believe in it? Why or why not?

10. What is the Hebrew word for "karma"?

11. What is "sitting sheevah"?

12. Before anything exists on the physical plane, where must it first exist?

13. List the eight traditional Chinese signs of health.

The following questions only you can answer.

1. Are you doing all of the necessary rituals?

2. Are you experimenting with the extra rituals and techniques?

3. Are you in control of elemental Water?

4. Have you made your chalice?

5. Have you dedicated yourself to a magickal way of life and the accomplishment of the Great Work by doing the ritual in this lesson?

6. What are your feelings on reincarnation?

7. Do you do some form of physical exercise?

Bibliography

For more information on these books, please see the annotated bibliography at the end of these lessons.

Berg, Philip S. *The Wheels of a Soul*. Kabalah Publishing, 2004.

Cicero, Chic, and Sandra Tabatha Cicero. *The Essential Golden Dawn*. Llewellyn, 2003.

———. *Secrets of a Golden Dawn Temple*. Thoth Publications, 2004.

Crowley, Aleister. *Magick*. Weiser, 1998.

Kelder, Peter. *The Eye of Revelation*. Booklocker.com, 2008.

Regardie, Israel. *The Golden Dawn*. Llewellyn, 2002.

Shaw, Scott. *Chi Kung for Beginners*. Llewellyn Publications, 2004.

Sperling, Harry, Maurice Simon, and Paul Levertoff (translators). *The Zohar* (5 volumes). Soincino Press, 1984.

Winkler, Gershon. *The Soul of the Matter*. Judaica Press, 1982.

LESSON SIX

PART ONE

The Fire Element

In the last three lessons we have been examining the archetypal magickal elements. In this lesson we will continue the pattern by studying the last of the four elements, Fire. I remind you that there is a fifth element, Spirit. The reason it is not discussed in the same way as the other elements is because it is the source of the four archetypal elements. The way to come to know Spirit is by a thorough knowledge and understanding of Air, Earth, Fire, and Water. The element Spirit is nothing less than the Spirit (Ruach, energy, or Shakti) of Divinity. It is only through those manifestations of Divinity of which the Godhead wishes us to become aware that we can come to know the ultimate deity. The infinitude of the Divine Source of All is beyond the comprehension of our finite minds, save the ways in which the Godhead chooses to be revealed to us.

According to the *Sepher Yetzirah*, Air emanated from Spirit, Primitive Water emanated from Air, and Fire emanated from Water. Earth comes from a division of the Primitive Water into Water and Earth, although some say it is a combination of the other three elements.

If you are not satisfied with your familiarity with any of the three previous elements, continue to work on the exercises for those elements for another week or two, and then as you will. But be sure to begin the exercises for Fire immediately.

The element of Fire has the qualities of being warm and dry.

The following exercises will help you to become more aware of this magickal element in your daily life.

EXERCISE 1. Observe those things around you that have the combined qualities of heat and dryness. Compare the heat and dryness of a fire to that of the Sun. Interestingly, the burning core of the Sun is frequently referred to as "plasma" and is spoken of in terms resembling the way water would be described (such as flowing). Steam has more Fire than does ordinary water. Ordinary water has more Fire in it than does ice. Thus, to a degree, fire and water can coexist. Yet, they are considered to be total opposites, and should be able to cancel each other out. How can they exist together when they should destroy each other? The answer is in the percentage of each. Much water destroys a little fire, and vice versa. But even a small amount of fire changes water and a small amount of water also has some effect on fire. Try to observe fire in its various combinations with the other elements around you. Keep a record of this in your magickal diary. Do this exercise daily for at least one week.

EXERCISE 2. Find a place that is extremely hot, such as a desert or dry sauna (*not* a steam bath). If those are not possible, find a place where a roaring fire is going. Such a fire could be in a fireplace or a barbecue pit or grill. Remove all of your clothes (or as much of your clothes as is reasonable—and legal) and get as close to the heat source as possible without risking a burn. If you are in the desert, make sure that you have a sunscreen with a very high SPF level. Put an even higher SPF-rated sunscreen or protective clothing on any sensitive parts of the body that are exposed. This is especially true for the genitals and, if you are a woman, the breasts. These areas can become extremely painful and hypersensitive if sunburned. This must be avoided.

Once you are in a situation where it is uncomfortably hot (but not painfully or unbearably so) and your perspiration is freely flowing, do the Relaxation Ritual. This may be difficult due to the heat, but it will test you to see how well you can do this ritual. Then focus on your breathing and feel the heat-laden air going in and out of your lungs.

As before, imagine your entire body is nothing more than an enormous breathing apparatus. Imagine that every part of your body only has the function of breathing and nothing else. *Know* that your skin is a vital part of this system. As you physically breathe in air, imagine that every pore in your body's skin is also breathing in heat and dryness: elemental Fire. Feel the Fire course through your body, cleansing and purifying. Then, as you exhale, feel it leave through your pores, taking with it the body's toxins, pains, and sufferings. Repeat the pore breathing until you have mastered it.

Caution: Only do this exercise next to a real fire or in a place like a desert once. Do not, under any circumstances, spend longer than ten minutes doing this exercise in real heat. When doing this type of work it is all too likely that you may lose your sense of time. Have an alarm set to sound after ten minutes or have a friend come and pull you out of the heat. *Immediately* drink one or two large glasses of cool (not cold) water. Get out of or away from the heat. If you have physical problems dealing with heat, consult an M.D. before doing this. This caution is for your health and safety, and neither the author nor the publisher will be responsible for your errors in this exercise.

Remember, the purpose of this exercise is to pore-breathe the magickal element of Fire. It is not to get you burned to a cinder. After you have done this exercise once next to or in a real heat source, you may repeat it by imagining the heat. Do this at different times of the day and at different locations. Try it in the cool of the night and even in a rain. If you start to perspire, you are being successful. Practice this for up to a week initially, then as you will.

EXERCISE 3. Spend a period of up to three minutes, once a day, imagining that *you are the element Fire*. Feel the heat and your ability to transmit that heat. If you have a regular lover, ask him or her if your kisses are "hotter" (more on this later). Feel the dryness and as a result, perhaps, stop your perspiration if you are perspiring. Know what Fire feels like, what Fire is. Practice this exercise for one week.

EXERCISE 4. Now that you have learned to "be Fire," the next step is to learn how to consciously control this magickal element. Take a moment and again imagine yourself to be Fire. Bring the feelings you had in the last exercise into your awareness. Next, hold your hands nine to twelve inches apart with the palms facing each other. Visualize between your hands a bottle, cylinder, or small cask. Next, as you exhale, imagine all of the Fire element which is in you going out with your breath and being deposited in the container between your hands. Three to five times should be enough to fill it. If it gets too hot to "hold" between your hands, move your hands farther apart. Once it has been filled, simply observe it for a short space of time. Then, with three breaths, inhale it back into yourself and return to your normal consciousness. Spend about a week with this exercise.

The Test. Here is the simple self-test that will allow you to learn whether or not you have become not just in unison with the magickal element Fire, but also if you are its master. This test is to prove something to you, not to me or anyone else. If you do not pass the test, that is okay. It merely means that you need to do more work on the above exercises. Then you can take the test again. In fact, take the test as often as you wish. Just be sure to always record the results in your magickal diary.

The next time you feel as if you are bursting with an overload of energy, so much that it is hard to concentrate due to the fiery energy within you, try this: Form the container of fire as described in the previous exercise. Once you have done this, visualize a large "black hole" in the air in front of you. Now, "throw" the container of Fire into the black hole and then see the hole close so that nothing can return. Do this "black hole" three times. Your excess energy should be gone, but you should have enough energy left to do your necessary tasks. *Never do this black hole with Fire more than three times in one day.* Otherwise, you could become so drained that your physical body could be weakened. This could open you up to disease.

The next time you are feeling listless and have a total lack of energy (or for that matter, a lack of

desire to do the necessary things in your life), form the Fire container, but this time inhale all of the contents of the container. Within a few minutes you should feel energized and revitalized. Try this instead of your morning cup of coffee. If you find that you have too much energy, black hole the excess as already described.

When you have passed both parts of the test to your satisfaction, you will know that you are the master of the magickal element Fire. In fact, since this is the last of the four elements, once you pass this test and have passed the other three as well, you will be a master of the elements. To prove this to yourself, here are some suggestions to try.

1. Sit in a room that has no air circulating. Light a candle and place it in the center of the room. Become one with the fire of the candle. Now, move the candle flame by your will, just as you might move your arm. For many people this is surprisingly easy.

2. Become one with the moisture (Water) of a cloud. Now add Fire to it so that it expands in all directions. The cloud should disappear. White "fluffy" clouds of a smaller size when no dark clouds are visible tend to be the best for this experiment.

3. On a windy day, find a high spot such as a hill or the top of a tall building. Become one with Air until you can almost feel yourself going aloft. Then, start to bring some of the slowing power of Earth into you, and expand it into your environment. The wind should slow or cease in your area. Don't try this for the first time during a hurricane! Try it with a light breeze. Later you might want to try a storm.

You can probably come up with many more experiments to test your mastery of the magickal elements. Notice, however, that I am suggesting rather minor phenomena, not major changes in the environment. This is for two reasons. First, the test needs only to prove to you that you are capable of controlling the elements. Second, causing major changes in the environment is Grey Magick. To affect a large area means that you are interfering with the lives of other people as well as the plans of Mother Nature. You may want a dry day for your picnic and work to end a rain shower. To the farmer awaiting rain it could spell disaster and ruin the farmer's livelihood. It might also increase the prices for a grocer and even result in some people having to go on welfare to pay for the increased prices of food. A magician must never take his or her actions lightly, especially when they influence or might influence the lives of others.

PART TWO

The Fire Wand

Now we come to the construction of the last of the elemental tools of the magician. It is perhaps the best-known tool of the magician, too. It is the wand. Even stage magicians use wands in their acts, and perhaps no other magickal tool has caught the attention of the public more than the wand of the magician.

Curiously, many stage magicians dislike the idea of real magick. In England, for many years they did not even call it "magic," but "conjuring." There, a stage magician was called a "conjurer." But even they present a front of real magick. There is a saying among such magicians that they are actors pretending to be real magicians doing real magick.

Just as real magicians use various words of power, calling on higher spiritual entities or working with the strength of vibration, so, too, do stage magicians use such words. Of course, they mistakenly imply that just saying the word will have some sort of effect, and I hope that by this time you realize that's not true; however, that's a different discussion.

One of the most popular of "magical words" among stage magicians is "Hocus Pocus." This is simply a slightly garbled version of the magickal part of the Catholic Mass where the priest holds the sacrament and says in Latin, "*Hoc est corpus*" ("This is the body"). By his initiation as a priest and the authority he holds, combined with his mastery of Latin and of the Mass, the sacred wafer, through a process known as transubstantiation, becomes the body of God. Certainly the transformation of a wafer into a body is real magick at its highest.

The wand is as closely identified with one who practices magick as Dr. Watson is with Sherlock Holmes. Yet, few people have ever seen a real ceremonial magician's Fire wand. This wand is the tool for controlling or directing two things:

1. The magickal element of Fire.

2. The energy of the magician.

Look at the image below. It is the shape of a true magician's wand. Does its outline look familiar? It is quite simply an image of an erect phallus! The energy mentioned above is the psycho-sexual energy that you have been learning to manipulate with the exercises and rituals in the first half of this course. Anyone who denies the psycho-sexual aspect of magick is either not telling the truth, is uninformed, or is not really a magician.

Those who practice magick under the traditions of Paganism, many of whom call themselves Witches, use the dagger as their primary weapon. The name used by many Pagans for this dagger, athame, is likely taken from a Kabalistic book, *The Greater Key of Solomon* where it is called an "arthame." Ceremonial magicians, on the other hand, use a wand as their primary tool. It is not, however, the Fire wand, but an even superior wand, which will be described later in this lesson.

In the meantime, you will need to construct the Fire wand. Make it out of a dowel. Make it any length and thickness you desire, but remember it must fit on

Fire Wand

your altar. Some lumberyards or hardware stores may have a decorative end piece for furniture (known generally as a "finial") called an "acorn." Attaching this to the end of the wand will yield a perfect shape. Otherwise you can carve a block of balsa wood and attach it to the end of the wand with glue and a dowel pin.

If you have access to a lathe, the entire wand can be carved out of a thicker dowel. If you use two pieces of wood joined with glue, use two or three extra undercoats and then give it several coats of bright red paint. The multiple coats of paint will help to hold the pieces together. Let this paint dry very well.

The Story of the Cloudbuster

Remember Wilhelm Reich? He was the follower of Freud who maintained that Freud had been correct when originally considering libido to be an actual energy. Reich called this energy "orgone." He went on to claim that orgone was the basic energy of the universe, the very stuff from which life was made. It could affect anything.

He found that he could make a device that looked like gun turrets on a battleship, only they were telescoping tubes up to eighteen feet long that ran via cables to a deep water source. He called this device a "cloudbuster." He used it on the desert outside of Tucson, Arizona, in the 1950s. The place was so dry, there had been no growth of grass for over fifty years. He used it for several months. The result was not rain, but the water table rose to a level higher than anyone remembered. Grass grew on the desert for the first time in decades. Was he responsible?

In 1953 there was a drought in Maine. Several blueberry farmers brought him in to make rain. The weather bureau forecast no rain. He went and used his cloudbuster. Ten hours after starting it, the rain began. Over the next few days it rained almost two inches. The blueberry crop was saved and the farmers paid him for his services. They credited him with the end of the drought.

Worried that causing rain to occur in one location might cause an absence elsewhere, resulting in a lawsuit, Reich ceased using the cloudbuster to bring rain, using it instead to shoot down enemy UFOs he believed were powered by orgone. But it was his work with the universal energy that got him in trouble with the government.

He made some experimental boxes the size of telephone booths that would accumulate orgone. He believed that by being bathed in this energy he could help people heal. As with many physicians, he leased the devices to cancer patients who were in the last stages of the disease. He said they were for experimental use and admitted that all of the patients who used it had died. The Food and Drug Administration claimed he was falsely telling people he could cure their cancer. Working with the legal system, they had him thrown in jail. Then they went to his headquarters and destroyed all of his accumulators and, like a nightmare out of Nazi Germany, burned his books.

Wilhelm Reich died of a heart attack in prison in 1957. I don't know if he was a kook or a genius, a kook *and* a genius, or a genius who became a kook. But I do believe the actions of the government in his case were an embarrassment to science, research, and freedom.

Paint a bright yellow stripe one-half to one inch wide around the circumference of the wand at the base and at the bottom of the acorn section of the wand. Divide the length of the wand between the two stripes into three equal sections, and separate those sections with two more stripes. Thus, there should be a total of four yellow stripes and three sections of red paint, plus the top of the acorn (see previous diagram).

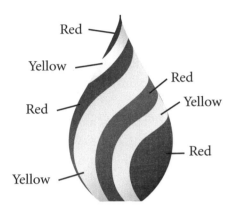

The acorn section should be decorated with elongated yellow "Yuds," the Hebrew letter, as shown below. There should be a total of three Yuds.

Elongated Yud

Finally, in the next column you will find a list of the Hebrew names and sigils, which should be painted on the red parts of the shaft of the wand with bright emerald green paint. If there is not enough room you can also use the red sections on the acorn. When finished, use several coats of a Varathane-like product to protect the finish.

Some people insist that there should be a magnetized wire running the length of the wand. This is exceedingly difficult to do as it requires the drilling of a very long hole or splitting the wand and gluing it back together. If you wish to include the wire you

might try using a hollow piece of cane for the wand's shaft and running the wire through its length. Or you could use a lightweight pipe. Then fill the re-

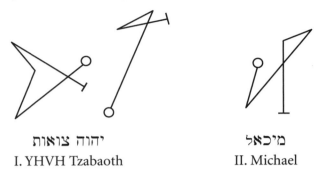

יהוה צואות
I. YHVH Tzabaoth

מיכאל
II. Michael

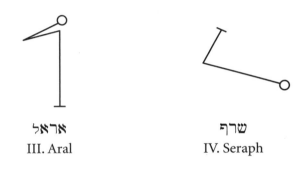

אראל
III. Aral

שרף
IV. Seraph

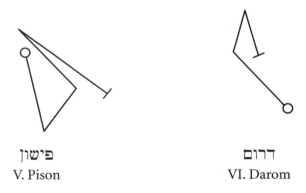

פישון
V. Pison

דרום
VI. Darom

אש
VII. Easch

VIII. The Motto

The Hebrew and Sigils for the Fire Wand

maining space with a combination of glue and sawdust. The north end of the magnetized wire (it repels the north pole of the compass) should be at the plain end of the wand. The wire should extend only one-sixteenth inch from the flat end and through the acorn finial or carved end.

Actually, the wire is not necessary. It represents the "tube of energy," which also goes through the phallus. While it can help direct energy, the shape of the Fire wand itself is more than adequate. For more information on how to construct the wand you can read Wang's *The Secret Temple* or the Ciceros' *Secrets of a Golden Dawn Temple Book 1: Creating Magical Tools.*

PART THREE

So far we have spent much time dealing with the Sephiroht and very little time discussing the *paths* on the Tree of Life that link the Sephiroht. Many books on the Kabalah and the Tree of Life spend almost their entire length covering the Sephiroht and ignoring or at least slighting the paths. This is not surprising, because there is a very logical reason for the paths being so hard to pin down.

The Sephiroht, in a sense, are way stations for the energy of Divinity (Ruach El-oh-heem) as it descends toward the Microcosm, which is our Universe and our World. As this energy travels through the Tree of Life it changes and evolves (although its inner essence remains constant). By the time it reaches Mahl-koot it is at a level where humanity can deal with it on a day-to-day basis.

Just as the current "punctuated equilibrium" theory of evolution proposes jumps in evolution rather than changes at a steady rate, so, too, does the energy traversing the Tree of Life change neither slowly nor evenly. In its path from its ultimate pure form to the physical manifestations around us, it changes until it reaches the utmost point of a certain level or quality. Then it goes in a different direction.

In the diagram below you can see how a form of vibrational energy, color, changes from white to black. It can definitely be said that within the circle labeled "white" it looks white, and in the circle labeled "black" it appears black. But what about in between? Where is it pure grey? Where is it light grey? To complicate matters even more, two people seeing the same shade of grey might label it differently.

This is exactly the problem faced when trying to understand and describe the paths on the Tree. The Sephiroht in some Kabalistic literature are called the "vessels." These vessels hold the energy of Divinity until it reaches a maximum in some direction. As an example, the Sephira Gih-boo-rah represents the ultimate manifestation of the strength of the Godhead as typified by the astrological qualities of the planet Mars. Page after page could be spent discussing the Strength of Divinity. But how does one describe the changing energy between Strength and Beauty, between Gih-boo-rah and Tih-fehr-et? It is far more difficult.

It is for this reason that a good Tarot reading can be given using only the Major Arcana of the Tarot. They are associated with the paths on the Tree and

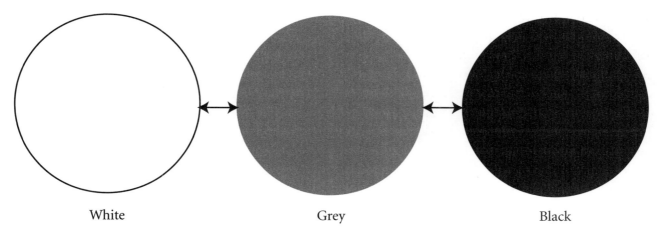

White   Grey   Black

thus demonstrate the changing energies in a person's life. The Minor Arcana are associated with the Sephiroht and are thus more related to static situations. The Minor Arcana adds more details. The Major Arcana gives more information as to the direction of a person's life and the forces in play about that life.

The very fact that the paths represent changing energy patterns makes them difficult to describe. Later, through the process known as Kabalistic Pathworking you will learn for yourself the changing qualities of the paths and how they apply to you. For now, however, we will merely look at some of the important correspondences for the paths on the Tree of Life.

On the next three pages you will find lists of Kabalistic Correspondences for the paths. There are twenty-two paths, numbered from 11 to 32. The first ten "paths" are actually the ten Sephiroht. This, then, points out a preliminary problem in dealing with the paths: their numerations. As I have said, the paths are traditionally numbered from 11 to 32. However, each path is also associated with a Hebrew letter. Since each Hebrew letter also has an associated number, there are, so far, two numbering schemas for the paths. Notice that the unusual numbering system for the Hebrew letters seems to be a mixture between Roman numerals and the Arabic numerals we commonly use.

Spelled out: Three hundred forty-seven

Roman numerals: CCCXLVII (three hundreds [CCC], plus fifty [L], minus ten [X], plus five [V], plus two [II])

Hebrew numerals: Shin, Mehm, Zy-in (three hundred [Shin], plus forty [Mehm], plus seven [Zy-in])

Arabic numerals: 347

Perhaps, then, Hebrew (or its source) is a basis for the numbers we use today.

The ancient Hebrews did not have separate symbols for their numbers in addition to each letter also representing a number. We will discuss more of this in a later lesson.

But for now it is enough to see that the 11th path is also the first or Aleph path. The 22nd path is also the 30th or Lah-med path. The 30th path is also the 200th or Resh path. Note also that the Major Arcana cards, being associated with the paths, also use their numbers to identify the paths. Thus, the 19th path is also the 8th or Strength path. The 30th path is also the 19th or Sun path. We can come up with some rather unusual-looking "equations" which, if you know the secret, make perfect sense. Otherwise they are indecipherable:

Path #		Hebrew		Tarot #
17	=	7	=	6
23	=	40	=	12
32	=	400	=	21

I mention this multiple numeration system here not because it is vital to this course (although we will be making good use of it later), but because so many advanced books throw numbers around left and right, and a beginner could quite easily get lost. Remember, one of the goals of this course is to allow you to read any Kabalistic work and, if it is logical and based on tradition, understand it.

Kabalistic Correspondences

The Paths—Part 1

Path	Value	Hebrew Name	Hebrew Letter	English Meaning	Tarot Number	Tarot Name	K.S. Color
11	1	Aleph	א	Ox	0	The Fool	Bright Pale Yellow
12	2	Bet	ב	House	1	The Magician	Yellow
13	3	Gimmel	ג	Camel	2	The High Priestess	Blue
14	4	Dallet	ד	Door	3	The Empress	Emerald Green
15	5	Heh	ה	Window	4	The Emperor	Scarlet Red
16	6	Vahv	ו	Nail	5	The Hierophant	Red Orange
17	7	Zy-in	ז	Sword	6	The Lovers	Orange
18	8	Chet	ח	Fence	7	The Chariot	Amber
19	9	Teht	ט	Serpent	8	Strength	Yellow (Greenish)
20	10	Yud	י	Hand	9	The Hermit	Green (Yellowish)
21	20	Kaph	כ	Palm	10	Wheel of Fortune	Violet
22	30	Lahmed	ל	Ox Goad	11	Justice	Emerald Green
23	40	Mehm	מ	Water	12	The Hanged Man	Deep Blue
24	50	Nun	נ	Fish	13	Death	Green Blue
25	60	Sah-mech	ס	Prop	14	Temperance	Blue
26	70	Eye-in	ע	Eye	15	The Devil	Indigo
27	80	Peh	פ	Mouth	16	The Tower	Scarlet Red
28	90	Tzah-dee	צ	Fish Hook	17	The Star	Violet
29	100	Koph	ק	Back of Head	18	The Moon	Crimson (Ultraviolet)
30	200	Resh	ר	Head	19	The Sun	Orange
31	300	Shin	ש	Tooth	20	Judgement	Glowing Orange Scarlet
32	400	Tahv	ת	Cross	21	The Universe	Orange Scarlet Indigo

Note: When five of the letters occur at the end of a word they have a different appearance and value. Final Kaph ך = 500; Final Mehm ם = 600; Final Nun ן = 700; Final Peh ף = 800; and Final Tzah-dee ץ = 900. The Final Mehm becomes more square while the other Finals have tails that extend below the baseline of writing. This information is included for completion, but it is not of vital importance during the study of these lessons. Contrary to rumors, there is no evidence supporting the claim that you can tell when a Kabalist dies by his Final Kaph (cough)!

Kabalistic Correspondences

The Paths—Part 2

Path	Astrology Association	Astrological Symbol	Animal	Plant
11	Air	△	Eagle	Aspen
12	Mercury	☿	Swallow, Ibis, Ape	Vervain
13	Luna	☽	Dog	Almond, Mugwort
14	Venus	♀	Sparrow, Dove, Swan	Myrtle, Rose, Clover
15	Aries	♈	Ram, Owl	Tiger Lily, Geranium
16	Taurus	♉	Bull	Mallow
17	Gemini	♊	Magpie	Orchid
18	Cancer	♋	Crab, Turtle	Lotus
19	Leo	♌	Lion	Sunflower
20	Virgo	♍	Virgin, Hermit, Anchorite	Snowprop, Lily, Narcissus
21	Jupiter	♃	Eagle	Hyssop, Oak, Poplar
22	Libra	♎	Elephant	Aloe
23	Water	▽	Eagle, Snake, Scorpion	Lotus
24	Scorpio	♏	Scorpion, Beetle	Cactus
25	Sagittarius	♐	Centaur, Horse	Rush
26	Capricorn	♑	Goat, Ass	Hemp, Orchis Root, Thistle
27	Mars	♂	Horse, Bear, Wolf	Absinthe, Rue
28	Aquarius	♒	Man, Eagle	Coconut
29	Pisces	♓	Fish, Dolphin	Unicellular Organisms
30	Sun	☉	Lion, Sparrowhawk	Snowflower, Laurel, Heliotrope
31	Fire	△	Lion	Red Poppy, Hibiscus
32	Saturn	♄	Crocodile	Ash, Yew, Cypress

Kabalistic Correspondences

The Paths—Part 3

Path	Stones	Scents	Tools
11	Topaz, Chalcedony	Galbanum	Dagger, Fan
12	Opal, Agate	Mastic, White Sandal, Mace, Storax	Wand or Caduceus
13	Moonstone, Pearl, Crystal	Camphor, Aloes	Bow & Arrow
14	Emerald, Turquoise	Sandalwood, Myrtle	Girdle
15	Ruby	Dragon's Blood	Horns, Burin
16	Topaz	Storax	Preparations
17	Alexandrite, Tourmaline	Wormwood	Tripod
18	Amber	Onycha	Furnace
19	Cat's Eye	Olibanum	Disciplines
20	Peridot	Narcissus	Lamp & Wand, Bread
21	Amethyst, Lapis Lazuli	Saffron	Scepter
22	Emerald	Galbanum	Cross of Equilibrium
23	Beryl, Aquamarine	Onycha	Cup & Cross, Wine
24	Snakestone	Benzoin	Obligation, Pain
25	Jacinth	Lignum Aloes	Arrow
26	Black Diamond	Musk, Civet	The Secret Force, The Lamp
27	Ruby	Pepper, Dragon's Blood	The Sword
28	Artificial Glass	Galbanum	Censer, Aspergillus
29	Pearl	Ambergris	Magick Mirror
30	Crysoleth	Olibanum, Cinnamon	Bow & Arrow
31	Fire Opal	Olibanum	Wand or Lamp
32	Onyx	Asafetida, Sulphur	Sickle

The first column of correspondences is the path number. This is followed by the number of the Hebrew letter, the Hebrew letter's name, and the way it appears. This is followed by a translation of the meaning of each of the Hebrew letters. Where I have spelled out the name of the letter, I have done so in a way that you can see how it is pronounced. As an example of this, Zy-in, meaning "sword" is frequently spelled "Zain." This leads to people pronouncing it "Zane," which is incorrect. The next column has the number and names of the Major Arcana cards of the Tarot.

The final column on the first page of correspondences lists the King Scale (K.S.) colors for the paths on the Tree of Life. As you should remember, there are four scales of colors associated with the four Kabalistic Worlds. They are identified with names of the face cards of the Tarot as used by the Golden Dawn: Princess, Prince, Queen, and King. The Sephiroht are, for our purposes, colored according to the Queen Scale. The Paths follow the King Scale colorings. This keeps the inherent gender balance within the Tree. It also points to the moving energy (archetypal male) of the paths and the contained energy (archetypal female) of the Sephiroht. When a Tree is colored according to this combined system it is called the *Minitum Mundum*, or Little World. It will be an important focus of our later work, so you should consider making one in a very large size. When so done it is referred to as "the Temple Diagram." You might also consider purchasing one in poster size from one of the many occult shops, both local and online, that carry them.

Although not vital to the purposes of our course, it would certainly benefit you to color in complete Trees of Life in each of the color scales. A complete list of these can be found in Regardie's *The Golden Dawn*, Crowley's *777*, David Godwin's *Godwin's Cabalistic Encyclopedia*, or Skinner's *The Complete Magician's Tables*.

The second page of correspondences for the paths begins again with a listing of the path numbers. This is followed by astrological listings of the planets and the constellation signs plus Air, Water, and Fire, the three primary elements according to the *Sepher Yetzirah*. The next column consists of various animals, both real and imaginary, associated with the paths. An Anchorite was an early Christian Hermit. The other animal names should be clear. Their importance to you will become obvious in a later lesson. So, too, will the next column of magickal plants. Note that associated with the 29th path are unicellular organisms, which are not animals, but plants.

The third page of path correspondences begins again with the path numbers. The next two columns, which associate stones and scents or perfumes with the paths, should be clear. The final column lists the magickal tools or weapons. Going from top to bottom we find that the girdle is listed as a magickal tool. This is not the modern device made to hold in an oversized stomach. Rather, it is an ornament that surrounds the waist and which is associated with Venus. It can be used for blindfolding and for fascination rituals. The horns are frequently worn in Pagan ceremonies to represent the power of the masculine aspect of the deity. Thus, it shows outgoing, archetypal masculine power. The burin is a tool like an ice pick and is used to carve talismans from wax as well as having other carving duties.

For the 16th path in the Tools column, the term "preparations" means just that. The time you put into preparation for a magickal ritual and the time you put in studying to become a practitioner of the magickal arts is in itself a magickal technique. A tripod was traditionally used to support the incense burner. It was also used by the famous Oracle at Delphi. A tripod suspending a chair was placed over a crevice into the earth from which fumes were escaping. The *Pythia*, a priestess to Apollo, would sit in the chair and be asked questions to which she would respond in an oracular fashion. Her divination abilities may have been caused by the sulfurous fumes altering her body chemistry and affecting her mind. Another explanation would be that the fumes altered her consciousness, allowing Apollo to possess her and respond prophetically. A furnace is used here in alchemical sense. It means a place of work.

The disciplines are those that you must go through to be able to do magick. The Cross of Equilibrium or Solar Cross is a symbol of your balancing of nature. The obligation is the vow you take when you are initiated or in your personal dedication.

The idea of pain being a magickal tool may surprise you, but it is true. I am not talking here about flagellation or other forms of bodily abuse, although some people involve this type of pain in their magickal work. The pain here is more psychological in nature. There will come a time when you will have to decide if the magickal path is correct for you. If you choose the magickal life, you will find that huge vistas of non-physical experience will be opened to you along with the love of Divinity showering upon your head. But most people in this world, no matter their professed spiritual beliefs, are diehard materialists at heart. They cannot keep up with you because they will either fear to do so or refuse to do so. As a result, you may find yourself drifting away from some friends and loved ones. This can be very painful. But those who follow spiritual, magickal paths must go their own way. Choose this path and you may know pain and loss, but the rewards will far exceed the costs. Why else would so many people strive to become magicians?

At this point, spend a few moments studying the meaning of the Hanged Man card from the Tarot before continuing with this lesson.

The secret force is what is commonly known as kundalini or Ruach or chi. An aspergillis is the device used to sprinkle sanctified water. For deeper information on these Magickal Tools, read Crowley's *777* and/or his *Book 4 Part II* found in *Magick*.

At this time it is not necessary to memorize these correspondences—that's why they're listed in books!—but you should become familiar with them. In some instances there are several associations in one category for each path. It would also be a good idea to make up several filled-in Trees of Life, in-

cluding the correspondences with the ten Sephiroht given in an earlier lesson.

PART FOUR

Remember that magick is both an art and a *science*. In this part we are going to be studying the basic preparation for *all* Grey Magick rituals. So, in a sense, this is the equivalent of a scientist preparing to perform an experiment. As you will see, it employs aspects of the Supreme Pentagram Ritual learned in the last lesson.

Let me repeat, what you are learning here will be used in all of the Grey Magick rituals that are to follow.

First, however, you need to make five items. For this, get four pieces of poster board at least 8½ x 11 inches. A bigger size would be better. Paint one bright green, another bright orange, another bright purple, and the last bright silver. Once these have dried, paint a large bright red triangle on the green board and a bright blue triangle on the orange board. On the purple board paint a bright yellow triangle with a line across it parallel to the base line of the triangle. Paint a similar figure on the silver board with *flat* (not glossy) black paint.

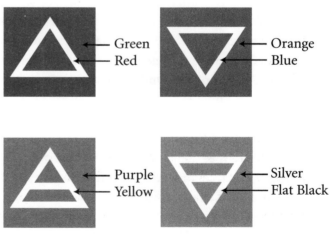

The Elemental Tablets

These are going to be your four elemental tablets. Once dry they should be framed and hung in your temple. The one with the red Fire triangle should be in the south. The one with the blue Water triangle should be in the west. The one with the yellow Air symbol should be in the east. The card with the black Earth symbol should be in the north. Unless otherwise noted, have these on the walls in all future rituals, including your daily rituals.

The last of the five items you will need to make is the Tablet of Union. This comes from the magickal system known as Enochian ("Ee-noh-kee-yan"). This system was discovered by Dr. John Dee (astrologer to Queen Elizabeth I) and his assistant, the mysterious, roguish Edward Kelly. Kelly, who always wore a hat pulled over his head to hide the fact that his ears had been cut off in punishment for a crime, functioned as Dee's seer in a series of magickal experiments in 1581. The result of those experiments is the much talked-about and little understood system known as Enochian.

I do not claim to be anything close to an expert in this particular system, but I do know that certain rituals that incorporate Enochian symbolism and techniques are very powerful. There seems to be a magickal quality to the very sounds of the mysterious words. Some have declared Enochian to be the most powerful magickal system around. Paul Foster Case modeled his own order, the Builders of the Adytum (BOTA), after the Golden Dawn, of which he had been a member. Most of the outer order is focused around the Tarot. The rituals performed for the Inner Order are very close to those of the Golden Dawn. The main difference is that Case seems to have feared Enochian and removed all traces of it from his rituals.

The Tablet of Union represents the fact that your altar functions as the place where the four magickal elements meet, come together, are united. To make it you simply get a heavy piece of paper or cardboard and make a rectangle four units tall by five units wide. I do not specify the size of the units because you need to make it to fit in the center of the altar. Outline the spacings so the card is filled by twenty boxes: five across and four up and down. This should be done with very dark, black ink. The paper should be white. Fill in the card as follows:

E	X	A	R	P
H	C	O	M	A
N	A	N	T	A
B	I	T	O	M

The letters, like the lines, should be as dark as possible. EXARP is the Enochian or Angelic name for the Spirit of Air. HCOMA is the name for the Spirit of Water and NANTA is the name of the Spirit of Earth, which leaves BITOM as the name for the Spirit of Fire. If you can, have the Tablet of Union laminated with a plastic coating or put it in a small frame.

Set up your altar with the Tablet of Union in the center so when you are behind the altar (west of the altar facing east) you can read the tablet. On each side of the Tablet should be one of the elemental tools you have made. To the east place the Air dagger. To the south place the Fire wand. To the west place the Water cup, and to the north place the Earth pentacle. There should be water in the cup.

You will also need another dagger with which to do the LBRP. Candles to light the area are also nice, along with some incense burning. These items can be placed on tables around your area or on the floor. Be sure they will harm nothing nor start a fire. Prepare yourself for this ritual as described for the LBRP, and begin the next ritual.

The Watchtower Ritual

STEP ONE. If you have a bell, sound it ten times. Ring it three times, pause one second, then four times, and then three times. It is indicated this way:

/// //// ///

Each mark (/) represents a striking of the bell. If you do not have a bell, sound the pattern by striking the top of the altar with the end of the handle of the dagger you are going to use for the LBRP. Then, in a loud, commanding tone, say:

HEKAS, HEKAS ESTE BEBELOI!

This is pronounced "Hay-kahs, Hay-kahs, Ehs-teh Beh-beh-loy!" It is a traditional way of announcing that a ritual is about to begin and those (both physical and non-physical) not entitled to witness it should leave the area.

STEP TWO. Sound the bell (or knock) once. Then do the LBRP.

STEP THREE. Sound the bell (or knock) two times. Then do the BRH.

THE OPENING BY WATCHTOWER

STEP FOUR. Sound the bell (knock) nine times: /// /// ///

STEP FIVE. Always walking clockwise, go to the south of the altar. Take the Fire wand and wave it three times, once each to the left, right, then center while facing the south and the elemental sigil you have hanging there. Now hold the wand with the point up over your head and slowly walk once around the room in a clockwise direction, saying:

And when, after all the phantoms have vanished, thou shalt see that holy and formless Fire, that fire which darts and flashes through the hidden depths of the universe, hear thou the voice of Fire.

Time this speech so that when you finish you are back at the south. Facing in that direction, trace a large circle, clockwise in the air. Visualize it golden. In this circle draw a bright blue invoking pentagram of Fire as described in the last lesson. Form the sign for Leo (the Fire Kerub) in the center. Now point to the center with the wand and vibrate:

OIP TEAA PEDOCE

This is pronounced "Oh-ee-pay Teh-ah-ah Peh-doh-kay." The words are three holy names for Fire in Enochian. Now hold the wand up in the air and say:

In the names and letters of the Great Southern Quadrangle, I invoke ye, ye angels of the Watchtower of the south.

Spend a few moments visualizing and feeling the pure elemental Fire-filled energy from this side of your circle. Replace the wand on the altar.

STEP SIX. Move to the west and take the Water cup from the altar. Face the west and sprinkle some of the water with your fingers to the left, right, and middle of the elemental symbol that is there. Hold the cup on high and circumambulate the circle once in a clockwise direction, saying:

So therefore first, the priest who governeth the works of Fire must sprinkle with the lustral water of the loud resounding sea.

The Name's Dee . . . John Dee

John Dee (1527–1608 or 1609) was one of the most interesting figures of the Elizabethan Age. When he died, his home in Mortlake (an area of London) had the largest library in all of England. Beside being a magician, he was also an astronomer and astrologer, a geographer, a world traveler, a mathematician, a scholar, and . . . a spy.

His fame allowed him to be an advisor, on occasion, to Queen Elizabeth I of England. When others advised her to send out the British fleet to attack the Spanish Armada, he used astrology to determine that she should wait, and advised her so. She took his advice, and a storm destroyed most of the Armada, allowing her fleet to finish the job. The result changed the face of the world and began the British Empire.

Because of his knowledge and wisdom, he was welcome in many countries. As a result, he could function as an agent of Elizabeth. He was a spy. When he obtained information he thought valuable, he sent it back to her, often using carrier pigeon. He added a special symbol to indicate that the message was legitimate. The symbol was three numbers: 007.

No, author Ian Fleming, creator of James Bond, didn't know this secret about Dee. At least there's no evidence to support that claim. His idea of giving Bond the number 007 came from another source—it was the last three digits of his agent's phone number.

Time this speech so that when you finish you are back at the west. Facing that direction, use the cup to trace a large golden circle in the air and inside of it draw an electric blue invoking Water pentagram. In the center of this draw the Eagle Kerub. Point to the center, vibrating:

MPH ARSEL GAIOL

These Holy Enochian Names ruling Water are pronounced "Ehm-pay-hay Ahr-sell Gah-ee-ohl." Then, holding the cup high in the air, say:

In the names and letters of the Great Western Quadrangle, I invoke ye, ye angels of the Watchtower of the west.

Spend a few moments visualizing and feeling the pure elemental Watery energy from this side of your magickal circle. Replace the cup on the altar.

STEP SEVEN. Walk clockwise to the east of the altar, take up the Air dagger, and turn outward to where your elemental sigil is placed. Shake the dagger three times, once to the left, right, and center

of the elemental sign. Hold the dagger on high and walk around the circle once, saying:

Such a Fire existeth, extending through the rushing of Air. Or even a Fire formless, whence cometh the image of a voice. Or even a flashing light, abounding, revolving, whirling forth, crying aloud.

Time this speech so that when you finish you are back at the east. Facing east, use the dagger to trace a large golden circle. Inside the circle draw a bright blue Invoking Pentagram of Air. In the space in the center of the pentagram draw the sign of Aquarius, representing the Air Kerub. With the dagger point to the center and vibrate:

ORO IBAH AOZPI

This is pronounced "Oh-row Ee-bah-hah Ah-oh-zohd-pee." Hold the dagger on high with its point up and say:

In the names and letters of the Great Eastern Quadrangle, I invoke ye, ye angels of the Watchtower of the east.

Spend a few moments appreciating the power of pure elemental Air coming from this direction. Return the dagger to its place.

STEP EIGHT. Walk clockwise to the north of the altar. Take the pentacle and, facing north, shake the

pentacle three times, once left, right, and center, toward the Earth symbol outside the magickal circle. Remember to hold it by the black section. Now hold the pentacle on high and say as you circumambulate once:

Stoop not down into that darkly splendid world wherein continually lieth a faithless depth and Hades wrapped in gloom, delighting in unintelligible images, precipitous, winding: A black ever-rolling abyss, ever espousing a body unluminous, formless and void.

On returning to the north, use the pentacle to make a golden circle as before, only place inside it a bright blue Invoking Pentagram of Earth. Inside of that place the image of the Earth Kerub, which is the astrological sign of Taurus. Point to the center with the pentacle and say:

EMOR DIAL HECTEGA

This is pronounced "Ee-mohr Dee-ahl Hec-tey-gah." Again hold the pentacle on high and say:
In the names and letters of the Great Northern Quadrangle, I invoke ye, ye angels of the Watchtower of the north.

Now spend a few moments sensing the great Earthly power, which comes from this direction. Replace the pentacle. Move in a clockwise direction to the west and face east from behind the altar.

STEP NINE. Over the altar and the Tablet of Union, make the sign known as the "Rending of the Veil." This is done by making the Sign of the Enterer (left foot forward as hands thrust out), but do it with the palms together. Rotate your hands so the thumbs are down and the back of the hands are touching. Then separate your hands as if you were parting some curtains (or rending a veil).

Say:

OL SONUF VAORSAGI GOHO IADA BALTA.
ELEXARPEH COMANANU TABITOM.
**ZODAKARA EKA ZODAKARE OD ZODAM-
ERANU.**
**ODO KIKLE QAA PIAP PIAMOEL OD
VAOAN.**

This means "I reign over you, says the God of Justice. (*Three Magickal Names* who rule over the Tablet of Union.) Move, therefore, move and appear. Open the mysteries of creation: balance, righteousness, and truth." It is pronounced in this manner:

"Oh-ell soh-noof vay-oh-air-sah-jee goh-hoh ee-ah-dah bahl-tah.

El-ex-ar-pay-hay Co-mah-nah-noo Tah-bee-toh-ehm.

Zohd-ah-kah-rah eh-kah zohd-ah-kah-ray oh-dah zohd-ah-mehr-ah-noo.

Oh-doh kee-klay kah-ah pee-ah-pay pee-ah-moh-ehl oh-dah vay-oh-ah-noo." The boldfaced and italicized words of power should be vibrated in the usual manner.

STEP TEN. Now say:

I invoke ye, ye angels of the celestial spheres, whose dwelling is in the invisible. Ye are the guardians of the gates of the universe. Be ye also the guardians of this mystic sphere. Keep

far removed the evil and the unbalanced. **Strengthen and inspire me so that I may preserve unsullied this abode of the mysteries of the eternal gods. Let my sphere be pure and holy so that I may enter in and become a partaker of the secrets of the Light Divine.**

Now spend a few moments trying to sense and balance the four magickal elements here at the center of your circle.

STEP ELEVEN. Now move to the northeast corner, facing outward, and say:

The visible Sun is the dispenser of light to the Earth. Let me therefore form a vortex in this chamber that the invisible Sun of the spirit may shine therein from above.

STEP TWELVE. Now circumambulate three times around your circle. Each time you pass the east make the Sign of the Enterer in the direction you are going. That is, you don't point to the east to give the sign, you do it straight ahead of you. As you move around, visualize and feel the building up of a powerful vortex of energy. (Some people like to do this quickly, others like to form these circles of power slowly. Try both and see which is more effective for you.) After you make the third pass of the east, go to the west of the altar and face east.

STEP THIRTEEN. Give the Sign of the Enterer and say:

Holy art Thou, Lord of the universe.

Give the Sign of the Enterer again and say:

Holy art Thou, whom nature hath not formed.

Give the Sign of the Enterer once again and say:

Holy art Thou, the vast and mighty One. Lord of the light and of the darkness.

Now give the Sign of Silence (stamp left foot as you bring your left forefinger to your lips as if telling someone to hush).

STEP FOURTEEN. Do your Grey Magick.

STEP FIFTEEN. When you have finished your magickal work, say:

Unto thee, sole wise, sole eternal and sole merciful One, be the praise and glory forever, who has permitted me who now standeth humbly before Thee to enter this far into the sanctuary of the mysteries. Not unto me but unto Thy name be the glory. Let the influence of Thy divine ones descend upon my head, and teach me the value of self-sacrifice so that I shrink not in the hour of trial, but that thus my name may be written on high and my genius stand in the presence of the holy ones.

(*Note:* "Genius" is a term meaning the Higher Self.)

The Closing by Watchtower

STEP SIXTEEN. Now circumambulate three times *counterclockwise*, giving the Sign of the Enterer in the direction you are going as you pass the east. As you do this reverse circumambulation, feel the energy you have gathered dissipate.

STEP SEVENTEEN. Do the LBRP.

STEP EIGHTEEN. Do the BRH.

STEP NINETEEN. Say:

I now release any spirits that may have been imprisoned by this ceremony. Depart in peace to your abodes and habitations, and go with the blessings of

YEH-HAH-SHU-AH   YEH-HOH-VAH-SHA

(Vibrate the above two names.)

STEP TWENTY. Ring bell (knock) ten times: /// //// ///. Say with finality in a commanding tone:

I now declare this temple duly closed.

Knock (do not ring bell) once.

The ritual is over.

Okay. *Before* you tear these pages into little bits and decide to abandon magick forever because it is so complicated, stop for just a second and notice that this time I have not included a summary. This is because for this ritual you should make up your own summaries. Instead of using regular-sized paper, I used 4 x 5 index cards. I was able to fit the entire ritual on both sides of three cards.

The Watchtower Ritual looks much longer than it really is because of all the added instructions I have given you within the text of the ritual. In practice, it takes little more than ten minutes *if* the LBRP and BRH are memorized.

When you are making up your summaries or cards, be sure to go over how the invoking pentagrams are made. This was described in the last lesson. The Watchtower Ritual is a potent preparation for any magickal ritual.

Some of you may be familiar with the version published by Israel Regardie in his book *Ceremonial Magick*. I must warn you, however, that that book is filled with many errors. This can be verified by checking what is printed in that book against both Regardie's *The Golden Dawn* and Laycock's *Complete Enochian Dictionary*.

For more information on the Enochian system, I suggest looking at the book *Enochian Magic for Beginners* by Donald Tyson or *Practical Enochian Magick* by Jason Augustus Newcomb. As long as you stay with the Enochian material as presented in this course, you will be able to use it safely and effectively. The material, as presented here, has been tested and practiced for over 100 years. If you investigate this form of magick further, I urge extreme caution. Some people claim that the reason Aleister Crowley was unsuccessful in his lifetime was because of errors he may have made when doing the "Enochian Calls" form of this magickal system. In any event, the main thrust of this course is toward the Kabalah and not Enochiana.

At this point in your studies it would be a good idea to practice this ritual at least once a week. Notice that I said *practice* this ritual, not *perform* it. Separate it into sections and go over each section several times until you are very familiar with it. It would be best if you could memorize this ritual, as it will be a major focus of all the practical or Grey Magick work that is to follow. If you can't memorize it, at least become very familiar with it.

It is not necessary to perform it and work with it over and over as you (should) have been doing with the LBRP, the BRH, the Middle Pillar, the Circulation of the Body of Light, and the Tarot Contemplation Ritual. This is because two other things are needed.

First, the instruments or tools need the appropriate preparation. In a sense, they need to be initiated or dedicated to magickal service. Second, a final, ultimate magickal tool is needed. This ultimate tool must have some sort of universality in its nature so that it can virtually be used for any purpose, as opposed to the elemental tools which represent certain singular qualities. It is with this ultimate tool that the four elemental weapons will be energized, charged, and consecrated to their sacred, magickal tasks. More on this tool in a moment.

Meanwhile, it would be a good idea to spend some time thinking about how the Watchtower Ritual could be done with a group. The exact division of parts must be determined by the number of people who will be working with you. If you have at least four people in your group, each person can represent one of the elements throughout the ceremony. If there are five people, four can represent the elements and the fifth can do the other sections of the ritual that are not totally related to one of the elements; that one person should sit in the east when not actively involved in the ceremony. This person can be the leader of the group (at least during the ceremony), and should not take part in the circumambulations. This person represents spiritual wisdom and Light. Light rises, like the Sun, from the east, so this person (representing Light) sits in the east while the others circumambulate. As they pass, they salute with the Sign of the Enterer in the direction they are going, not to the person. The respect is toward the philosophy and the sacred, secret science of Light, not to a person.

PART FIVE

There is virtually no way to make a single tool that can work with the four elemental forces. Water would counteract the energies of elemental Fire, just as Air and Earth are also antithetical to each other. Therefore, to make a truly universal tool, another basis is needed.

A possible thought would be to make a tool based on the Tarot cards. The problem with this is that it would require a minimum of twenty-two and possibly twenty-six (twenty-two Major Arcana plus one for each suit) or more sections. Such a tool would be either too large to be practical or have symbols or sections too small to be useful.

The solution to this problem is to use astrological symbolism. This brings our symbols down to twelve, one for each of the signs of the zodiac. To this we add two more for practical purposes, as you will see. The Golden Dawn associated this with Egyptian symbolism for the design of a fairly difficult-to-construct Lotus Wand. By removing only the Egyptian aspect, the lotus flower, we are left with our main tool for the performance of practical or Grey Magick: the Rainbow Wand.

Construction of the Rainbow Wand

1. Start with a piece of dowel three-eighths to three-quarters inch in diameter. Judge the best diameter by holding various dowels and sensing which size "feels" best in your right hand (even if you are left-handed). Cut your chosen dowel to 36 ¼ inches in length. With sandpaper, round the ends so that the final length is exactly 36 inches. Now lightly sand the rest of your future wand to take off any surface dirt or uneven surfaces. Give the entire wand a white undercoat. Following the directions on your paints, wait the appropriate length of time, then give it a second white undercoat.

2. Measure seven inches from one of the ends. At this point make a dark but narrow black line around the wand. Two inches farther from this line (nine inches from the end), make another black line. Continue making thin black lines until you have drawn a total of thirteen lines. The image of your wand at this point is that you have at one end a space of seven inches, at the other end a space of slightly under five inches, and between these two areas twelve spaces of two inches each. A simple way to get straight lines around your wand is by taking a small card, wrapping it around the circumference of the wand at the appropriate area, and using the edge of the card for a guide.

3. Paint the seven inches the brightest white you can find. Paint the five-inch space the darkest black you can find. Paint the rest of the wand as illustrated in the next column.

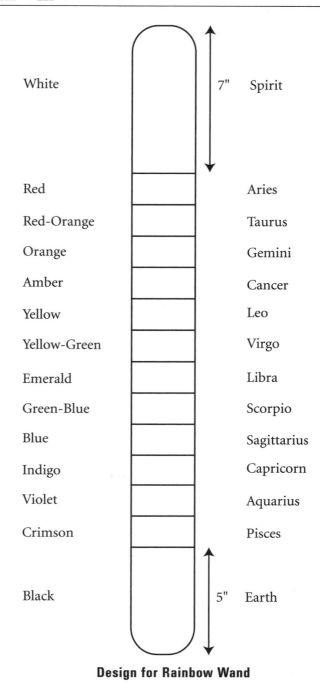

Color		Sign
White	7"	Spirit
Red		Aries
Red-Orange		Taurus
Orange		Gemini
Amber		Cancer
Yellow		Leo
Yellow-Green		Virgo
Emerald		Libra
Green-Blue		Scorpio
Blue		Sagittarius
Indigo		Capricorn
Violet		Aquarius
Crimson		Pisces
Black	5"	Earth

Design for Rainbow Wand

4. Finish by coating the colors with a protective coat such as Varathane. In fact, give it several coats of the clear protective to make it easy to clean away oils and dirt from being held by hand. Also, try to find the brightest colors possible for painting this wand. Each color should positively glow.

Preliminary Preparation of the Rainbow Wand

1. When doing your daily ritual practice, hold the Rainbow Wand by the white section while doing the Middle Pillar Ritual and the Circulation of the Body of Light.

2. At this point, always hold the Rainbow Wand vertically. The white end should be up; the black end should be down.

3. Upon completion of this practice, wrap the Rainbow Wand in white silk or cotton. Do not use wool or synthetics, as they can build up a static charge and disrupt the energy you're putting into the wand. Place the covered wand in a safe place where no one else will touch it.

4. It would also be a good idea to sleep with the Rainbow Wand in your bed next to you. Make sure that the white end of the wand is toward your head.

5. It is in these ways that the wand slowly absorbs the energy you have been controlling and becomes a magickal part of you. Similarly, you become a magickal part of it. Magickally, it more than represents you; it is your magickal counterpart.

The symbolism of the Rainbow Wand is both obvious and deep. First, we can see that white, the color used to represent the element of Spirit, also undercoats the entire wand. It is the basis for everything, even the darkness at the other end of the wand. If there was no light, how could you tell when it was dark?

Second, notice that the color spectrum, the rainbow, only occupies the center part of the wand. In a similar manner, the wand, as a representation of our magickal power, takes us beyond the physical realms represented by the visible spectrum.

Third, the number of black lines is thirteen, the number of unity according to Gematria. As such, it also represents a link to the unitary Divinity, to God.

Once you have spent at least one month working with your Rainbow Wand as described above, you will be ready to fully consecrate and charge it to magickal purposes. Be sure you work with it for at least one month before doing the following consecration.

Tip for the Lines on the Rainbow Wand

Painting straight lines, especially painting straight lines on a curved surface, is difficult to do. The card system I described above worked for me when I made my wand. It's still inexpensive and effective.

Other people have come up with different solutions. My favorite one so far is to simply butt each color against the next. Then, go to an auto supply store and get some of the tape used to make pin stripes. You can get it in metallic gold. Simply cut off a strip and wrap it around the wand every two inches where the different colors meet. When you put a clear coat over everything, you'll have one of the most beautiful wands around!

Shh! Don't tell anyone this secret.

The Consecration of the Rainbow Wand

STEP ONE. Do the Watchtower Ritual up to Step Fourteen. Your Rainbow Wand should be resting on the altar with the other tools. Its white end should be facing the east.

Imagine that you are standing on the face of a clock. Twelve o'clock faces east, 3:00 faces south, 6:00 faces west, and 9:00 faces north.

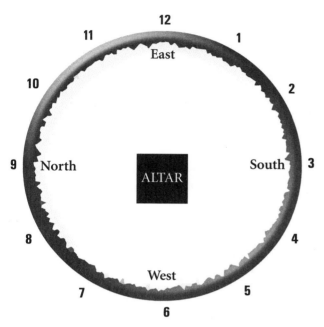

STEP TWO. Facing east, take the Rainbow Wand by the red band in your left hand. Since this belongs to Aries, a Fire sign, take the tool of Fire, the Fire wand, in your right hand. Hold both above you and say (vibrate the words that are all capitals):

> **The heaven is above and the Earth is beneath. Between the light and the dark do vibrate the colors of life. I supplicate the powers and forces governing the nature, place and authority of the sign ARIES, by the majesty of the divine name YUD HEH VAHV HEH, with which, in Earth life and language, I ascribe the letter HEH to which is allotted the symbolic tribe of GAD and over which is the angel MELCHIDAEL, to bestow this present day and hour, and confirm their mystic and potent influence upon the RED band of this Rainbow Wand, which I hereby dedicate to purity and to occult work. May my grasp**

> **upon it strengthen me in the work of the nature and attributes of ARIES.**

STEP THREE. Now, visualize the forces of the nature of Aries descending from all around you onto the Rainbow Wand. When you sense this has occurred, or after three minutes, replace the Fire wand on the altar (consult any basic book on astrology for more on the qualities of the signs).

STEP FOUR. Move your left hand down to the next stripe of color on the Rainbow Wand. It is red-orange. Turn to face the direction of the number 1 on the face of the imaginary clock upon which you stand. Take the appropriate elemental weapon according to the chart on the next page. Now repeat the invocation from Step Two. However, change the capitalized words to the appropriate words from the chart.

STEP FIVE. Repeat step four, turning one number on the imaginary clock, shifting your hand to the appropriate colored stripe, using the proper elemental tool and words from the chart. Once you have completed the twelve invocations to the powers associated with the signs of the zodiac, you should again be facing east. Place the Rainbow Wand on the altar with the white end pointing toward the east. Raise your hands and say:

> **Oh great Goddess of the forces of nature, great one who has been known by a thousand-thousand names since before remembered time, let thy influence descend and consecrate this Rainbow Wand which I dedicate to thee for the performance of the works of the magick of Light.**

STEP SIX. Wrap your charged and consecrated Rainbow Wand in the silk or cotton cloth that you have for this purpose. From this moment on do not allow anyone else to touch it. Do not unwrap it except when you are going to need it for magickal purposes. Should someone else handle it, it would be a good idea to redo this entire ritual.

STEP SEVEN. Now complete this ritual by doing the Closing by Watchtower, Steps 15–20 of the Watchtower Ritual.

Your Rainbow Wand is now ready for magickal usage.

Chart for Rainbow Wand Consecration

	Color	Tool	Sign	Symbol	Yhvh	Hebrew	Letter	Tribe	Angel
1	Red	Wand	Aries	♈	YHVH	יהוה	Heh	Gad	Melchidael
2	Red-Orange	Pentacle	Taurus	♉	YHHV	יההו	Vahv	Ephraim	Asmodel
3	Orange	Dagger	Gemini	♊	YVHH	יוהה	Zy-in	Manasseh	Ambriel
4	Amber	Cup	Cancer	♋	HVHY	הוהי	Chet	Issachar	Muriel
5	Yellow	Wand	Leo	♌	HVYH	הויה	Teht	Judah	Verchiel
6	Yellow-Green	Pentacle	Virgo	♍	HHVY	ההוי	Yud	Naphthali	Hamaliel
7	Emerald	Dagger	Libra	♎	VHYH	והיה	Lahmed	Asshur	Zuriel
8	Green-Blue	Cup	Scorpio	♏	VHHY	וההי	Nun	Dan	Barchiel
9	Blue	Wand	Sagittarius	♐	VYHH	ויהה	Sah-mech	Benjamin	Advachiel
10	Indigo	Pentacle	Capricorn	♑	HYHV	היהו	Eye-in	Zebulun	Hanael
11	Violet	Dagger	Aquarius	♒	HYVH	היוה	Tzah-dee	Reuben	Cambriel
12	Crimson	Cup	Pisces	♓	HHYV	ההיו	Koph	Simeon	Amnitziel

Notes to the Chart for Rainbow Wand Consecration

a. The number refers to the order in which the invocations are performed. Normally, an invocation brings a higher entity into you (more on this later in this book). Here, the energy is invoked into the wand

b. The color refers to the band of color on the Rainbow Wand that you hold while doing each invocation.

c. Tool indicates the elemental tool used in the right hand for each invocation.

d. YHVH shows the permutations of the holy Tetragrammaton. The source of these permutations is the *Sepher Yetzirah*, and they are directly related to the astrological signs. Each "Y" is pronounced "Yud"; each "H" is pronounced "Heh"; each "V" is pronounced "Vahv".

e. The names of the Hebrew tribes and the appropriate angel are fairly clear. Remember, "Ch" sounds like the German "ach."

f. It will probably be easiest to make up twelve cards in advance, each with the appropriate words filled in, for doing the twelve invocations of this ritual.

g. Remember to turn one number on the "clock" for each invocation.

Take a while and make sure that you have the time to do the above ritual correctly. Do not rush it. Also, do not go on to the next section until you have prepared your Rainbow Wand as above, for the next part of the lesson uses the consecrated and empowered Rainbow Wand to charge and consecrate your magickal tools. Complete the ritual by recording the result in your ritual or magickal diary.

On the next page you will find a diagram of the altar layout for the Consecration of the Rainbow Wand Ritual. You will usually have the elemental tools or weapons placed in the same positions for all magickal rituals. The dagger should be to the east; the wand to the south; the cup to the west; the pentacle to the north. Candles should preferably be in the color of their quadrant (yellow to the east, red to the south, blue to the west, and black, brown, or green to the north), or else white.

E	X	A	R	P
N	C	O	M	A
N	A	N	T	A
B	I	T	O	M

Altar Layout for Consecration of Rainbow Wand and Other Magickal Operations

PART SIX

I strongly suggest that the following rituals of consecration not be performed on the same night. Rather, do them on four consecutive nights or one a night on two consecutive weekends. At this point there is no real rush to complete these consecrations, as the next lesson will be centered around mental magick and will not require the tools. However, your tools really will need to be completed and consecrated before the eighth lesson in this course. All four of these rituals should only be performed during the waxing of the Moon.

Consecration Ritual for the Pentacle

STEP ONE. Do the Watchtower Ritual up to Step Fourteen.

STEP TWO. Face north and hold your pentacle in the left hand by the black section. Always remember to move and pivot clockwise within your "tem-

ple" unless told otherwise. In your right hand hold the consecrated Rainbow Wand by the *red-orange* stripe, the stripe associated with Taurus representing elemental Earth. The pentacle should be held horizontally. As you vibrate each magickal word, title, or name, trace in the air above the pentacle the Hebrew letters and sigils that are on the tool. If you have any questions about this, go back to the lesson that showed you how to make the pentacle. The symbols are drawn over the tool with the Earth (black) end of the Rainbow Wand, representing the making physical—that is, the bringing to the physical plane—of the spiritual forces. These spiritual forces are, of course, represented by the white end of the Rainbow Wand. Thus, you are sending pure magickal energy down into the pentacle. Say:

> **O Thou who art timeless, thou who art
> Mother and Father of all things, Thou who
> dost clothe Thyself with the forces of nature**

as we don a robe, by Thy Holy Divine Name (vibrate as you trace the word and sigil) **AH-DOH-NYE where, too, Thou art known in this quarter by the secret name** (vibrate and trace word and sigil) **TZAPHON. I beseech Thee to grant me strength and inner vision as I search for inner wisdom within Thy hidden light.**

STEP THREE. Continue, saying:

I humbly request, as a student of Thy mystic laws, that Thou mayest cause Thy archangel (vibrate and trace) **OH-REE-EL to guide me on my holy journey. Please also direct Thy angel** (vibrate and trace) **PHORLAKH to watch over me and protect me as I traverse the mystic pathways of the universe.**

STEP FOUR. Continue, saying:

May the ruler of the Earth, the powerful prince (vibrate and trace) **KERUB, by the permission of the Eternal One, increase and strengthen the secret forces and virtues of this pentacle so that I may use it to perform those magickal rituals for which it has been fashioned. It is to this end that I now perform this rite of consecration in the presence divine of** (vibrate and trace) **AH-DOH-NYE.**

STEP FIVE. Place the Rainbow Wand on the altar with the white end pointing east. Pick up the dagger you used to do the LBRP and again return to the north. Slowly trace a large Earth Invoking Pentagram (see Lesson 5) in the air over the pentacle in your left hand while saying:

By the secret holy names of God borne upon the banners of the north (vibrate, do not trace) **EMOR DIAL HECTEGA, I summon Thee, oh great king of the north** *(vibrate, do not trace)* **IC ZOD HEH CHAL** (pronounced "Ee-kah Zohd-ah Hay Kah-la") **to be here now, to increase the effect of this ritual whose purpose it is to consecrate this magickal**

pentacle. Give it power enow to be more than capable in all works of Earth so that by it I may find a strong defense and powerful weapon to direct the spirits of the elements as is dictated by the One whom naught but silence can express.

STEP SIX. Replace the dagger on the altar and again return to the north. Hold the pentacle at chest level, facing outward. Say:

Oh mighty princes of the Great Northern Quadrangle, I invoke you and ask that ye hear my petition and be here now! Bestow upon this pentacle the strength and purity whereof ye are masters so that its outward and material form may be a true symbol of its invoked inner and spiritual force.

STEP SEVEN. Circumambulate in a clockwise direction to the south. Hold the pentacle above your head, facing out from the center of the circle toward the south. Say:

O thou glorious angel (vibrate): **NAAOM** (pronounced Nah-ah-oh-em), **thou who rulest the fiery aspects of Earth, I invoke thee. Be here now! Bestow upon this pentacle those magickal powers which thou dost rule that with it I may also govern those spirits over whom thou art Lord.**

STEP EIGHT. Wait in the south for a few moments until you sense that your request has been fulfilled or three minutes have passed. Then move to the west and hold the pentacle in the same way as in the south, only pointing to the west. Say:

O thou glorious angel (vibrate): **NPHRA** (pronounced Ehn-frah), **thou who rulest the watery aspects of Earth, I invoke thee. Be here now! Bestow upon this pentacle those magickal powers which thou dost rule that with it I may also govern those spirits over whom thou art Lord.**

STEP NINE. Wait in the west for a few moments until you sense that your request has been fulfilled or three minutes have passed. Then move to the east and hold the pentacle facing east in a manner as before. Say:

> **O thou glorious angel** (vibrate): **NBOZA** (pronounced "Ehn-boh-zohd-ah"), **thou who rulest the airy aspects of Earth, I invoke thee. Be here now! Bestow upon this pentacle those magickal powers which thou dost rule that with it I may govern those spirits over whom thou art Lord.**

STEP TEN. Wait in the east for a few moments until you sense that your request has been fulfilled or three minutes have passed. Then move to the north and hold the pentacle as before. Say:

> **O thou glorious angel** (vibrate): **NROAM** (pronounced "Ehn-roh-ah-ehm"), **thou who rulest the densest aspects of Earth, I invoke thee. Be here now! Bestow upon this pentacle those magickal powers which thou dost rule that with it I may also govern those spirits over whom thou art Lord.**

STEP ELEVEN. Now do the LBRP with two differences:

a. Use the pentacle instead of the dagger.

b. Trace the *Invoking Pentagram of Earth* instead of the Banishing Pentagram of Earth when drawing the pentagrams.

STEP TWELVE. Replace the now charged and consecrated pentacle in its appropriate place on the altar. Finish by performing Steps 15–20 of the Watchtower Ritual.

The rite is finished.

Before leaving the circle be sure to wrap the pentacle in a piece of material made of cotton or silk. It should be black; however, browns or greens or the universal pure white will do. Be sure to record the result of the ritual in your magickal diary.

Note that in these consecration rituals you should vibrate the names and trace the Hebrew letters and/or sigils when using the Rainbow Wand. When not using the Rainbow Wand you should vibrate the names but not trace the sigils. If you do not sense that your requests for empowering the tool have been answered within three minutes, it does not mean that this has not happened. It only means that you are as yet not psychically aware enough to perceive it. If you continue with your daily ritual work, you will open to impressions from other levels of existence. Be sure to record your results in your ritual diary.

On the following evening, or when you have planned to do it, perform the Consecration Ritual for the Dagger. Note: This is for the Air Dagger, not for the dagger used to perform the LBRP. Also, compare this ritual to the previous one for performance information such as which words to vibrate and when to trace sigils. I will be limiting those notes in this and the remaining two rituals.

Consecration Ritual for the Air Dagger

STEP ONE. Do the Watchtower Ritual up to Step Fourteen.

STEP TWO. Face east and hold your Air Dagger in your left hand. In your right hand hold the Rainbow Wand by the *orange* stripe. This stripe is associated with Gemini and elemental Air. The Air Dagger should be held horizontally. The Hebrew and sigils are traced in the air over it with the black end of the Rainbow Wand. Say:

> **O Thou who art timeless, Thou who art Mother and Father of all things, Thou who dost clothe Thyself with the forces of nature as we don a robe, by thy holy and divine name YUD-HEH-VAHV-HEH where, too, thou art known in this quarter by the secret name MIZRACH, I beseech thee to grant me strength and inner vision as I search for inner wisdom within Thy hidden light.**

STEP THREE. Continue, saying:

> I humbly request, as a student of Thy mystic laws, that Thee mayest cause Thy archangel RAH-FAY-EL to guide me on my holy journey. Please also direct Thy angel CHASSAN to watch over me as I traverse the mystic pathways of the universe.

STEP FOUR. Continue, saying:

> May the ruler of Air, the powerful prince ARIEL, by permission of the Eternal One, increase and strengthen the secret forces and virtues of this dagger so that I may use it to perform those magickal rituals for which it has been fashioned. It is to this end that I now perform this rite of consecration in the presence divine of YUD-HEH-VAHV-HEH.

STEP FIVE. Replace the Rainbow Wand on the altar. Pick up the dagger used for doing the LBRP in your right hand and move to the east. Slowly trace a large Air Invoking Pentagram (see Lesson 5) in the air over the Air Dagger (which is still in your left hand) while saying:

> By the three holy names of God borne upon the banners of the east, ORO IBAH AOZPI ("Oh-row Eh-bah-ha Ah-oh-zohd-pee"), I summon thee, oh great king of the east BATAIVAH ("Bah-tah-ee-vah-hah") to be here now; to increase the effect of this ritual whose purpose it is to consecrate this magickal dagger. Give it power enow to be more than capable in all works of Air so that by it I may find a strong defense and powerful weapon to direct the spirits of the elements as is dictated by the One whom naught but silence can express.

STEP SIX. Replace the dagger used for the LBRP on the altar and return to the east. Hold the Air Dagger, point up, at chest level. Say:

> Oh mighty princes of the Great eastern Quadrangle, I invoke you and ask that ye hear my petition and be here now! Bestow upon this dagger the strength and purity whereof ye are masters so that its outward and material form may be a true symbol of its invoked inner and spiritual force.

STEP SEVEN. Circumambulate to the south. Hold the Air Dagger, point up, over your head. Say:

> Oh thou resplendent Angel EXGSD ("Ex-jazz-dah"), thou who rulest the fiery abodes of Air, I invoke thee and ask that thou mayest hear my petition and be here now! Confer upon this dagger those magickal powers which thou dost rule that with it I may also govern those spirits over whom thou art Lord.

STEP EIGHT. Move to the west and again hold the Air Dagger on high. Say:

> Oh thou resplendent angel EYTPA ("Eh-iht-pohd-ah"), thou who rulest the watery abodes of Air, I invoke thee and ask that thou hear my petition and be here now! Confer upon this dagger those magickal powers which thou dost rule that with it I may also govern those spirits over whom thou art Lord.

STEP NINE. Move to the east and hold the Air Dagger on high, point up. Say:

> Oh thou resplendent angel ERZLA ("Eh-rah-zod-lah"), who rulest the abodes of pure and permeating Air, I invoke thee and ask that thou hear my petition and be here now! Confer upon this dagger those magickal powers which thou dost rule that with it I may also govern those spirits over whom thou art Lord.

STEP TEN. Move to the north and hold the Air Dagger as before. Say:

> Oh thou resplendent angel ETNBR ("Eht-en-bah-rah"), thou who rulest the densest abodes of Air, I invoke thee and ask that thou hear my petition and be here now! Confer upon this dagger those magickal powers

which thou dost rule that with it I may also govern those spirits over whom thou art Lord.

STEP ELEVEN. Now do the LBRP with two differences:

a. Use the Air Dagger instead of the usual dagger.

b. Trace the *Invoking Pentagram of Air* rather than the Banishing Pentagram of Earth.

STEP TWELVE. Replace the now charged and consecrated Air Dagger in its appropriate place on the altar. Finish by performing Steps 15–20 of the Watchtower Ritual.

The rite is finished.

Before leaving the circle, be sure to wrap the Air Dagger in a piece of material made of cotton or silk. It should be yellow, but the universal white will do. Once consecrated, let no one else touch your Air Dagger. Record the result of the ritual in your magickal diary.

Consecration Ritual for the Chalice

STEP ONE. Do the "Opening by Watchtower," the Watchtower Ritual Steps One through Fourteen.

STEP TWO. Take the cup in your left hand and hold the Rainbow Wand by its amber band with your right hand. The amber band is associated with the astrological sign Cancer and elemental Water. Hold the chalice in a normal fashion and again use the black end of the Rainbow Wand to trace the letters and sigils in the air above the cup. Say:

Oh Thou who art timeless, Thou who art Mother and Father of all things, Thou who dost clothe Thyself with the forces of nature as we don a robe, by Thy holy and divine name EL, where, too, Thou art known in this quarter by the secret name MEARAB ("Me-ah-rahb"), I beseech Thee to grant me strength and inner vision as I search for inner wisdom within Thy hidden light.

STEP THREE. Continue, saying:

I humbly request, as a student of Thy mystic laws, that Thee mayest cause Thy archangel GAHB-RAY-EL to guide me on my holy journey. Please also direct Thy angel TALIAHAD to watch over me and protect me as I traverse the mystic pathways of the universe.

STEP FOUR. Continue, saying:

May the ruler of water, the powerful prince THARSIS ("Tahr-sis") by permission of the Eternal One, increase and strengthen the secret forces and virtues of this chalice so that I may use it to perform those magickal rituals for which it has been fashioned. It is to this end that I now perform this rite of consecration in the presence divine of EL.

STEP FIVE. Place the Rainbow Wand on the altar as before and pick up the dagger used in the LBRP. Move to the west. With the dagger, slowly trace a large Water Invoking Pentagram (see Lesson 5) in the air over the Cup while saying:

By the three secret holy names of God borne upon the banner of the west, EMPEH ARSEL GAIOL ("Em-peh-heh Ahr-sell Gah-ee-ohl"), I summon thee, oh great king of the west RA AGIOSEL ("Eh-rah Ah-jee-oh-sell") to be here now; to increase the effect of this ritual whose purpose it is to consecrate this magickal chalice. Give it power enow to be more than capable in all works of Water so that by it I may find a strong defense and powerful weapon to direct the spirits of the elements as is dictated by the one whom naught but silence can express.

STEP SIX. Replace the dagger on the altar, and return to the west. Face outward. Hold the chalice at chest level and say:

Oh mighty princes of the Great Western Quadrangle, I invoke you and ask that ye hear my petition and be here now! Bestow upon this chalice the strength and purity whereof ye are masters so that its outward and material form may be a true symbol of its invoked inner and spiritual force.

STEP SEVEN. Circumambulate to the south and hold the cup on high. Say:

Oh thou powerful angel HNLRX ("Heh-nu-el-rex"), thou who rulest the fiery Waters, I invoke thee. Be here now! Endue this chalice with those magickal powers which thou dost rule that with it I may also govern those spirits over whom thou art Lord.

STEP EIGHT. Move to the west, hold the cup on high and say:

Oh thou powerful angel HTDIM ("Heh-tah-dee-mah"), thou who rulest the pure and fluid Waters, I invoke thee. Be here now! Endue this chalice with those magickal powers which thou dost rule that with it I may also govern those spirits over whom thou art Lord.

STEP NINE. Move to the east, hold the cup on high and say:

Oh thou powerful angel HTAAD ("Heh-tah-ah-dah"), thou who rulest the airy Waters, I invoke thee. Be here now! Endue this chalice with those magickal powers which thou dost rule that with it I may also govern those spirits over whom thou art Lord.

STEP TEN. Circumambulate to the north. Hold the cup on high and say:

Oh thou powerful angel HMAGL ("Heh-mah-gee-ehl"), thou who rulest the dense qualities of Water, I invoke thee. Be here now! Endue this chalice with those magickal powers which thou dost rule that with it I may also govern those spirits over whom thou art Lord.

STEP ELEVEN. Now do the LBRP with two differences:

a. Use the cup instead of the usual dagger.

b. Trace the Invoking Pentagram of Water instead of the usual Banishing Pentagram of Earth.

STEP TWELVE. Replace the now charged and consecrated chalice in its appropriate place on the altar. Finish by performing the Closing by Watchtower, Steps 15–20 of the Watchtower Ritual. When finished, wrap the cup in a piece of cotton or silk. It should be blue in color, but white will do. Allow no one else to touch it.

The rite is finished.

Be sure to record the results of your ritual in your magickal diary.

Finally we move to the last of our consecration rites. While it is true that continual usage of the magickal tools will have the effect of charging and consecrating them, it is also true that doing these rituals, even if you only do them once in your life, will speed up the process many times over. However, it is also suggested that you repeat these rituals occasionally, perhaps once or twice a year. As you develop as a magician, so, too, will your ability to charge, empower, and consecrate your tools.

Another purpose of these consecration rituals is to allow you to see how one basic ritual, through additions and relatively small variations, becomes applicable to other purposes. In this case, a ritual used to consecrate one magickal weapon, by changing a few words and actions, becomes usable for consecrating other tools. In time you will see the importance of this idea.

It is also important to discuss these consecration rituals as they would be performed in a ceremonial situation. That is, how they should be done in group workings. To answer this we again look back to the Golden Dawn. To that organization, the consecrations were a symbol of a person's passing from the Outer, *Mystical* Order (The Golden Dawn) and into the Inner, *Magickal* Order (the R.R. & A.C.). Thus, the person doing the consecrations should either do them privately or only with those who have already done their own consecrations. No one else should watch. Those who do watch should add their visualizations to those of the person doing the consecration. It is important that the person doing the consecration do the entire ritual by himself or herself.

Consecration Ritual for the Fire Wand

STEP ONE. Perform the Opening by Watchtower.

STEP TWO. Take the Fire Wand in the left hand and hold the Rainbow Wand in your right hand by the *red* band. This band is associated with Aries and the magickal element of Fire. The Fire Wand should be held horizontally, and, as usual, the tracings in the air should be done with the black end of the Rainbow Wand. Face south and say:

> **Oh Thou who art timeless, Thou who art Mother and Father of all things, Thou who dost clothe Thyself with the forces of nature as we don a robe, by Thy holy and divine name EH-LOH-HEEM, where, too, Thou art known in this quarter by the secret name DAROM, I beseech Thee to grant me strength and inner vision as I search for inner wisdom within Thy hidden light.**

STEP THREE. Continue, saying:

> **I humbly request, as a student of Thy mystic laws, that Thee mayest cause Thy archangel MEE-CHAI-EL to guide me on my holy journey. Please also direct thy angel ARAL to watch over me and protect me as I traverse Thy mystic pathways of the universe.**

STEP FOUR. Continue, saying:

> **May the ruler of Fire, the powerful prince SERAPH, by the permission of the eternal one, increase and strengthen the secret forces and virtues of this wand so that I may use it to perform those magickal rituals for which**

it has been fashioned. It is to this end that I now perform this rite of consecration in the presence divine of EH-LOH-HEEM.

STEP FIVE. Place the Rainbow Wand on the altar and pick up the dagger usually used for doing the LBRP. Return to the south. With the dagger make a large Invoking Pentagram of Fire (see Lesson Five) over the horizontally held Fire Wand as you say:

> **By the three secret holy names of God borne upon the banners of the south OIP TEAA PEDOCE ("Oh-ee-pay Tay-ah-ah Peh-doh-kay"), I summon thee, oh great king of the south, EDEL PERNAA ("Eh-dehl Pehr-nah-ah"), to be here now; to increase the effect of this ritual whose purpose it is to consecrate this magickal wand. Give it power enow to be more than capable in all works of Fire so that by it I may find a strong defense and powerful weapon to direct the spirits of the elements as is dictated by the One whom naught but silence can express.**

STEP SIX. Replace the dagger on the altar and return to the south. Hold the Fire Wand horizontally at chest level and say:

> **Oh mighty princes of the Great Southern Quadrangle, I invoke you and ask that ye hear my petition and be here now! Bestow upon this wand the strength and purity whereof ye are masters so that its outward material form may be a true symbol of its invoked inner and spiritual force.**

STEP SEVEN. Circumambulate once around the circle until you return to the south. Hold the Fire Wand above your head with the pointed end up. Say:

> **Oh thou mighty angel BZIZA ("Bay-zod-ee-zod-ah"), thou who rulest the four angels of most fiery Fire, I invoke thee. Be here now! Impress into this wand those magickal powers which thou dost rule that with it I may also govern those spirits over whom thou art Lord.**

STEP EIGHT. Move to the west and hold the Wand on high. Say:

Oh thou might angel BANAA ("Bay-ahn-ah-ah"), thou who rulest the four angels of fluid Fire, I invoke thee. Be here now! Impress into this wand those magickal powers which thou dost rule that with it I may also govern those spirits over whom thou art Lord.

STEP NINE. Move to the east, raise the wand, and say:

Oh thou mighty angel BDOPA ("Bay-doh-pay-ah"), thou who rulest the four angels of ethereal Fire, I invoke thee. Be here now! Impress into this wand those magickal powers which thou dost rule that with it I may also govern those spirits over whom thou art Lord.

STEP TEN. In a similar manner, upon moving to the north say:

Oh thou mighty angel BPSAC ("Bay-pay-zah-cah"), thou who rulest the four angels of densest Fire of earth, I invoke thee. Be here now! Impress into this wand those magickal powers which thou dost rule that with it I may also govern those spirits over whom thou art Lord.

STEP ELEVEN. Now do the LBRP, with two differences:

a. Use the Fire Wand instead of the usual dagger.

b. Trace the Invoking Pentagram of Fire instead of the usual Banishing Pentagram of Earth.

STEP TWELVE. Replace the now charged and consecrated Fire Wand in its appropriate place on the altar. Finish by performing the Closing by Watchtower. Use a piece of red or white cotton or silk to cover the Fire wand.

The rite is finished.

Be sure to record the result of your ritual in your magickal diary.

When you have finished performing these rites to your satisfaction (we are harder judges of ourselves than we are of others), you will no longer be a beginner or neophyte in the world of magick. Very few have started down the path leading to a magickal way of life. Even fewer go past the first few faltering steps. It is a miniscule number, indeed, who can claim to be true masters of the magickal art.

No, you are by no means a master of ceremonial magick even if you have really practiced and learned from these first six lessons. But from my experience, if you have practiced and learned, you probably are more knowledgeable and magickally adept than 75 to 95 percent of those calling themselves magicians. This is true even though you have not as yet done any real practical or Grey Magick.

It is not well known, but there were really two "inner" orders in the Golden Dawn. No members of the Outer Order were supposed to know about either of these inner orders or their workings. One of these inner orders only had one degree and taught no magick. It was where people who were judged to have no magickal skills were placed. Even they were not aware of the full meaning of the magickal inner order, the R.R. *et* A.C. The name is a Latin abbreviation for "Red Rose and Gold Cross." To get into the R.R. & A.C., you needed to be invited. Once invited it was your task to make and consecrate your magickal tools.

Entry into a grade of a magickal order was done by initiation, meaning to start. A person did not have the full abilities of a degree when he or she entered that degree, only (theoretically) when it was left or completed.

Therefore, for all practical purposes, if you have done the work, done the study and understand what you are doing, for all reasonable purposes you have attained (entered) the grade of Adeptus Minor.

Furthermore, so long as you do not claim that grade as a result of initiation into a particular group, I see no reason why you should not consider yourself and describe yourself as an Adeptus Minor of the Magickal Arts. Although rarely used, the appropriate title of this grade for a woman is Adepta Minora.

It is therefore appropriate that you take, for yourself, an obligation to the magickal path. Once you have done this you are an Adeptus Minor, a person prepared to be a Wizard and Magician.

The Ritual of Magickal Obligation

STEP ONE. Set up your temple and do the Opening by Watchtower.

STEP TWO. Say the following self-obligation:

I, [state your magickal name or motto], do this day spiritually bind myself to a magickal way of life. I will to the utmost lead an unselfish life and will prove myself a faithful and devoted servant to the Divine Source of All, who works in silence and naught but silence can express, the unity beyond duality, the unity beyond comprehensible unity.

I will keep secret all practical and theoretical knowledge from those who in my judgment are not ready to receive it, for to tell the truth to someone who is not ready to accept it is the same as telling that person a lie.

I will not claim to be anything more than what I am, a student of the magickal way of life, light, love, and freedom. Not being an initiate of an order, I will not initiate anyone.

I will perform all practical magick in a place concealed and apart from the gaze of the outer world. I will not display my magickal implements nor reveal the use of them to those who are not at a level where they need to know of them. I will not make any symbol or talisman for those who are not truly in need of such help. Before those with little knowledge of magick I will only perform simple and well-known techniques, keeping the deeper wisdom and methods for those who are themselves ready to learn.

I further promise and swear that with the Divine permission I will, from this day forward, apply myself to the Great Work— which is to purify and exalt my spiritual nature so that with the divine aid I may at length attain to be more than human, and thus gradually raise and unite myself to my higher and divine genius, and that in this event I will not abuse the great power entrusted to me.

I further most solemnly pledge never to work at any important magickal task without first invoking the highest divine names connected therewith. I especially pledge not to debase my knowledge of practical magick to purposes of evil and self-seeking. If in spite of this pledge I do so, then I invoke the avenging angel HUA that the evil may react on me.

I promise to treat all people with equality, no matter the color of their skin, the religion of their parents, or the gender of their flesh. I will not slander. I will not lie. I will not spread rumors.

I undertake to continue my practice of the magickal way of life whether I work with others or am unassisted.

Finally, if in my travels I should meet a stranger who claims magickal knowledge, I will examine him or her before acknowledging that such is the case. I will reveal to that person nothing of the inner wisdom I have gained, save that which I could give to any man or woman, until I am sure that his or her claim to knowledge is true.

Such are the word of this, my obligation as an Adeptus Minor [Adepta Minora] of the Magickal Arts, whereunto I pledge myself in the presence of the Divine One, and of the great avenging angel HUA. By my own will, and under their watchful vision, if I fail to keep my magickal obligation, may my magickal powers cease until that time when I can rightfully have them once again given

unto me, so help me with my mighty and secret soul!

STEP THREE. Finish with the Closing by Watchtower. Record the results in your ritual or magickal diary.

PART SEVEN

Dealing with Non-Magickal People

One of the rather unique problems of people who spend many hours practicing and studying magick is dealing with other people concerning your interests. Generally speaking, there are four types of people you will be dealing with in relation to your magickal beliefs.

1. *Those who don't care one way or the other.* They just figure that this is something you are involved in and, so what? They think you're a little bit weird, but they also probably think that everybody has a bit of weirdness in them.

   People in this category are usually too concerned with themselves to bother you. If they ask you any questions about what you do, answer them honestly but at their level of understanding. Usually after a few questions they lose interest in that aspect of your life because they find their own life far more interesting.

2. *Religious fanatics.* These people live a life based on fear and/or paranoia. Those who live a life filled with fear are the ones who are constantly trying to convert you from your beliefs and organizations, which they call "cults," to their particular religious sect or cult, which, of course, they think is the sole arbiter of truth. They see everything as black and white, we and they. "Since we are right, you must be wrong. Therefore, I have to convert you to my faith because that way you will be right and there will be no one around to imply that I (horrors!) could be wrong. For if I am wrong about this, then I could be wrong about everything in my life, and I am too fearful to spend

time examining my life." This type of person is frequently (but not always) poorly educated when it comes to religion and philosophy. "It was good enough for Daddy, it's good enough for me" is their operative motto. If it doesn't fit on a bumper sticker, it's too complex for them. If these people question you as to what you are doing, a good answer might be "studying early Jewish philosophy." Then, immediately tell them that they can help you. Ask them if they study the Bible. When they say yes, respond, "Good. I need to talk with someone who is fluent in Hebrew, Aramaic, and Greek." When they hem and haw and finally admit that they really know little if any of those languages, just look at them with surprise on your face and tell them that you hope they will someday really begin to study the Bible. Then walk away. Remember, we are not trying to convert anybody to our magickal point of view. If they are ready for it they will find it. If not, it won't make any sense to them. In this section we are only learning appropriate ways to deal with others who do not share our beliefs.

The other type of religious fanatic is the one filled with paranoia. These people are usually (but not always) poor and in a lower economic class (although being poor does not automatically make you one of them). They accept the responsibility for nothing in their lives. Their problems are always somebody else's fault. They don't have money because "Jews gypped them out of it." ("Gypped" comes from the word "Gypsy." Here is another minority group unfairly depicted in modern English.) Or else "Blacks (or more recently, Mexicans) took all the jobs." It's always somebody else's fault.

As briefly mentioned earlier, those with this mind-set and a more religious (?) bent blame everything on "demons." Demons cause their addiction to alcohol or tobacco or overeating. Demons keep them impotent or frigid. Demons control the bosses so "I can't keep a job." If this type of person asks you what you are doing, the best answer is, "minding my own business and wondering why you aren't doing the same."

Quite simply, these people have a very narrow focus to life and only want to deal with people who share their focus. Therefore, since your focus is wider than their narrow view, it is best to get away from them quickly. These people have the possibility of becoming quite dangerous. People with paranoid personalities may become schizophrenic and commit violently antisocial behavior. These are the people who roast their children in order to burn the demons out of them. These people were the sadists of the various inquisitions. When possible, stay away from them.

3. *The materialist/skeptic/debunker.* This type of person doesn't want to believe in the possibility of something they can't understand in their own terms. These people, if they discover your interest in magick, will primarily try to mock and make fun of you. They don't have to deal with you if you, and what you believe in, are merely jokes. Frequently, these people think they are very scientific. They may call themselves "skeptics." In reality, they have a religion of their own making, usually an untrained belief in partially understood or obsolete scientific theories.

You can ignore these people and they will quickly lose interest in trying to antagonize you. On the other hand, if you are quick to anger, a clever repartee can quiet them quickly. If someone asks you to turn them into a toad (ha! ha! how clever), ask them why? After all, it would be redundant! Although I don't really suggest it, if the person is obnoxious, you could add to this by referring to his or her eating material, flies, and upon what material flies like to sit. Other allusions could be made

to the similarity of the person's appearance with that of a frog, etc. If you go this route, the idea is to turn the topic away from you and on to the other person.

4. *The curious.* Finally comes a more or less logically minded person who is interested in what you have to say, but as yet does not understand. What I like to tell this type of person is that I am studying ancient, little-known metaphysical theories. Two thousand years ago these theories included physics, mathematics, geometry, medicine, astronomy, reading, writing, and many other things. In those days many of these beliefs were far more subjective than objective. Today this is no longer true.

Thus, what I am studying are the subjective philosophies of the present, which are destined to become the objective sciences of the future.

SSOTBME is a small book that was originally published as I first began teaching occult topics. It's a unique book in two ways. First, it was one of the first modern publications of some of the amazing, surrealistic art by occultist Austin Osman Spare. Second, many of the concepts hinted at in this book became incorporated into what would eventually be called Chaos Magick. I'll talk more about that system in Lesson Twelve. The title of the book is not the name of some Enochian spirit. Rather, it is an abbreviation (Notarikon) for "Sex Secrets of the Black Magicians Exposed." This shows a bit of the author's attitude. There are no sex secrets in the book, it has nothing to do with black magicians, and it exposes nothing.

I agree with the author of *SSOTBME*, Ramsey Dukes (writing as Lemuel Johnston), who claims that there are four major viewpoints that we all have to a greater or lesser degree. These are logic, observation, feeling, and intuition. Mix intuition with logic and you get a religious bias. Mix feelings with intuition and you get an artistic bias. Mix logic with observation and you get a scientific bias. I choose to mix feelings with observation. The result is a magickal bias.

From this philosophy, everything is relative. If you have a strong religious bias, science and art would appear in some instances to be forms of magick. A stronger scientific bent would have a person see economics and psychology as being more magickal or artistic than scientific. An artistic bias would have a person thinking that astrology and philosophy are very scientific. Who would be right? All of them—from their own particular points of view. Thus, if we can discover where a person's particular bias lies, we can perhaps present our interests in ways that will be most easily understood by the person confronting us.

Remember, the important part of dealing with people who are confronting you is to quickly gain

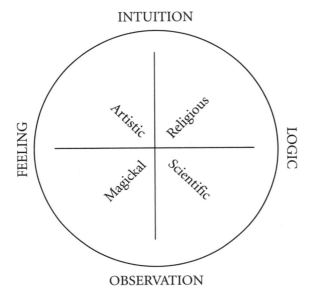

control of the conversation, then turn it around and talk about the other person rather than letting all the discussion be about you.

Review

The following questions are designed to help you determine if you have mastered the information in Lesson Six. Please try to answer them without looking at the text. The answers are in Appendix Two.

1. What are the qualities of elemental Fire?
2. Who is the archangel of Fire?
3. How can 23 = 40 = 12?
4. How was a tripod used by magicians? How was it used by the Oracle at Delphi?
5. What is "the Secret Force"?
6. What is punctuated equilibrium?
7. How do you pronounce the Enochian word "AOZPI"?
8. What plants are associated with Aries?
9. What colors are used on the elemental tablet representing Earth?
10. How many items should be on your altar for the consecration of the Rainbow Wand? What are they?
11. How many colors are on the Rainbow Wand?
12. What are the secret holy names of God borne upon the banner of the south?

The following questions only you can answer.

1. Are you in control of elemental Fire?
2. Are you still doing all of the daily rituals?
3. Are you attempting new rituals?
4. Are you constructing your tools?
5. Have you consecrated your tools?
6. Have you taken, or are you going to take, your magickal obligation?
7. Have you ever had trouble dealing with people who did not like your interest in magick, the Kabalah, etc.?
8. Do you understand the correspondences?
9. Do you think you are on your way to becoming a powerful magician? If not, what do you think you need to learn or develop?

Bibliography

For more information on these books, please see the annotated bibliography at the end of this volume.

Cicero, Chic, and Sandra Tabatha Cicero. *Secrets of a Golden Dawn Temple.* Thoth Publications, 2004.

Crowley, Aleister. *777 and other Qabalistic Writings of Aleister Crowley.* Weiser Books, 1986.

Johnstone, Lemuel [Ramsey Dukes]. *SSOTBME: An Essay on Magic.* The Mouse That Spins, 2002.

Laycock, Donald. *The Complete Enochian Dictionary.* Weiser Books, 2001.

Regardie, Israel. *Ceremonial Magic.* Aeon Books, 2004.

———. *The Golden Dawn.* Llewellyn Publications, 2002.

Shaw, Scott. *Chi Kung for Beginners.* Llewellyn Publications, 2004.

Tyson, Donald. *Enochian Magic for Beginners.* Llewellyn Publications, 2002.

Wang, Robert. *The Secret Temple.* Marcus Aurelius, 1993.

Section Two
The Inner Order

*In magickal organizations such as orders or covens,
the Inner Order is an in-group where the most potent secrets
are taught to and practiced by members who have been through
the trials and ordeals of the Outer Order and proved their worthiness.*

LESSON SEVEN

PART ONE

Back in Lesson Five of this course I shared with you the important occult magickal secret that whatever is created on the astral plane eventually must manifest in our world, the physical plane. This means, of course, that if you can create something in the astral world, it will eventually show up in our day-to-day reality. If you create wealth for yourself on the astral plane, you will become wealthy. If you create a new car for yourself on the astral, you will eventually get that car. Over the past few years there has been a flurry of interest in this technique. Unfortunately, most of the books and movies discussing this well-known "law of attraction" generally leave out the practical techniques necessary to use this "secret."

From the simple, one-sentence description that whatever is created on the astral plane eventually must manifest in our world, it should be obvious that the basis for Grey Magick is the creation of a desired goal on the astral plane. The reason there are many different forms or styles of Grey Magick is that there are many ways to implant a creation into the astral or Yetziratic level of reality. Personally, I have always found ritual or ceremonial magick to be the most effective for me. This is because I find the use of intense symbolism mixed with ritual to be highly evocative. When well performed, a ceremony affects me very deeply. Plus, ritual magick also uses the assistance of spiritual entities from other planes of existence. I can use other forms of Grey Magick successfully, but I find them more tedious and a lot less fun.

However, there is another system that is not ceremonial magick per se, but is important to know. A knowledge of this style of magick can aid you in your understanding of how magick works. Also, this system is very simple and effective. With this system you can successfully work magick with no tools other than a pencil and piece of paper.

As I have said, the major differences between various styles of magick are based upon different ways of getting an idea or thing created in the astral plane, or what is Kabalistically known as the Yetziratic world. So, in this simple system, we must first discover how this can be done.

Earlier in this course I described how there are links between the conscious and the unconscious minds. When our unconscious sends a message to the conscious, it is called "intuition." If the conscious cannot deal with the information given by the unconscious and represses that information, psychological and even physical problems can occur. In some instances this can result in a person requiring psychological, psychiatric, or some form of therapeutic aid. There are also other methods for the unconscious to contact the conscious. If you have forgotten some of these, reread the previous sections on dreams and past-life experiences.

More important for our purposes, however, is the fact that there are also methods that will allow the conscious to contact and send messages to the unconscious. This is important because **the unconscious is our direct link to the astral plane.** This means that whatever we put into the unconscious must eventually become a physical reality.

ASTRAL PLANE

U
N
C
O
N
S
C
I
O
U
S

PHYSICAL PLANE

There are two common ways for this conscious-to-unconscious communication to occur at will. They relate to the modern right-brain, left-brain theories of mentality. The left hemisphere of the brain is said to deal with logic, mathematics, and deductive reasoning. The right hemisphere deals with intuition, inductive reasoning, feeling, and art.

Before going on I am going to interject that I do not believe in the total reality of this theory. Its im-

plication is that the mind, that part of our total self that actually thinks, is nothing more than the few pounds of nervous tissue between our ears. My personal belief is that there is a type of symbiotic relationship that exists between the physical brain and the non-physical mind. An example of this is the fact that the taking of certain drugs and substances can alter the way we think and perceive the universe around us. This has led some people to claim that consciousness and even emotions such as love are nothing more than a chemical state. It implies that introducing those drugs would create an emotion. However, techniques such as hypnosis and biofeedback have shown that it is easily possible to create those chemicals without the associated emotion, and vice versa. Further, some people may remain entirely unaffected by substances that would have an enormous psychoactive effect on most of us. Altering the chemical makeup of the brain does not *necessarily* change the workings of the mind. This invalidates the idea that the mind and brain, even though closely linked in most people, are one and the same.

Furthermore, the right-brain, left-brain theory is an oversimplification of the complex reality of the mind-brain unit. Still, as a theory, it does have some value. It functions as a metaphor for understanding the functioning of the mind. Primarily it shows that the mind has a type of duality. Perhaps it would be more appropriate to say that a part of the mind deals more with the intuitive while another part deals more with the deductive. Further, these parts of the mind are related to what is commonly called the right-brain, left-brain theory. In order to facilitate your understanding of this course's material I will use the right-brain, left-brain terminology as a concession to popular terms.

The system of magick associated with the left brain is commonly known as the "Use of Positive Affirmations." In this system you merely say over and over what it is you desire. This, in a sense, is an attempt to use your conscious to convince your unconscious through reason, logic, and repetition that "this-or-that" is what you want, desire, or need.

The system that is related to the right hemisphere of the brain is known as "Creative Visualization." In this system you consciously put an image (through the process known as visualization) into your conscious mind, knowing that eventually this image will be absorbed into the unconscious.

It should be obvious that people who use either Positive Affirmations or Creative Visualizations are only using half of their mind/brains in order to create a different reality in their lives. Some people are very successful using either system. Most people practicing one system or the other have only a modicum of success. The simple Kabalistic system that I am going to present uses a very effective combination of both Positive Affirmations *and* Creative Visualization. Both I and many of my students have found the Kabalistic system to be far more magickally effective than either Creative Visualization or Positive Affirmation by themselves. Also, there is a Kabalistic secret which will help improve magickal success with these combined systems. But I will get to that in a few moments.

First, let us assume that someone knows how to create something on the astral plane. Does this mean that this person will always get what is created? Clearly, many people attempt Creative Visualization and/or Positive Affirmations and have no successful result. Just ask the vast majority of people who have experienced the futility of trying to use the incomplete principles given in some of the popular books. Perhaps you have tried one of these systems and not achieved the result you desired. Thus, to a casual observer or one who is unfamiliar with the inner secrets of these forms of mental magick, it will seem that the answer to my rhetorical question is "No, a person does not always get what he or she creates on the astral plane." But, once you understand the following information, you will see that the real answer is "Yes, a person *always* gets what he or she creates on the astral plane."

You may see that as a contradictory statement. First I point out that people who try to use the law of attraction via Creative Visualization and/or Positive Affirmations rarely get what they have created on the astral plane through the use of those techniques.

Then I say that they always get what they create. Either I'm being contradictory or something isn't clear. And what isn't clear is that there are secrets that have been left out of some of the books on the law of attraction. Perhaps an example will make this more apparent.

Let us assume that "John Magus" is a man who knows how to create things on the astral plane using Creative Visualization and Positive Affirmations. He spent fifteen minutes this morning creating wealth for himself on the astral plane. He used all of the right words, expressed in the appropriate way. He used all of the appropriate visualizations. Then he spent five minutes worrying about how he was going to pay his bills. Later he spent ten minutes thinking about how little money he had. All day he thought about his crummy, poorly-paying job. When he arrived home from work he saw more bills in the mail and worried about them and about how he was going to raise the money to pay for them. So although Mr. Magus had spent fifteen minutes creating wealth, he spent hours throughout the day thinking about, and thus creating, poverty on the astral plane. To repeat, he is creating his own poverty. That is why he is, and remains, poor.

You see, **we are constantly creating on the astral plane!** Most of the systems of Creative Visualization or Positive Affirmations which you may read about or study do not take this occult fact into consideration. The Kabalistic system I am about to share with you will show you exactly how to be in control of this process.

If you saw what John Magus was doing and didn't know that we are always creating on the astral plane, you might think that John Magus was failing in his attempt to create wealth. But although it is true that he failed to create wealth, he was successful—in creating the poverty he was spending so much time thinking about. Remember, we are always creating on the astral plane **whether or not we are consciously trying to do so.**

There are a few other reasons why Positive Affirmations and Creative Visualization may not appear to be successful. First, there is an important cosmic law that forbids waste. One author refers to the effect of this law as "the Sphere of Availability." If you cannot afford food on which to live, yet you use either or both of the systems so far described in an attempt to obtain a car, you may not achieve your goal. This is because you would really not be able to use the car effectively. If you can't afford food, how will you be able to afford fuel, oil, insurance, tires, brakes, etc.? It would be a waste for you to own a car, and cosmic law forbids waste.

A version of this law is used in physics. Since cosmic law forbids waste, this includes wasted space. Thus it is said that "nature abhors a vacuum." It is important to understand that merely because something may look wasteful to you does not mean that on a cosmic scale it would be wasteful. Don't worry about what somebody else is trying to create. Make sure that what you are trying to bring into your life is necessary for you. John Magus should work to get a job before he works to get a car.

Another reason for apparent lack of success may be due to karmic lessons that you need to learn for your mental and spiritual evolution. If you need to learn a lesson related to poverty, there will be no way for you to break out of that poverty . . . until you have learned the lesson(s) necessary for your evolutionary advancement and poverty is no longer necessary.

The Kabalistic System of Mental Magick

STEP ONE. Start by writing down on a piece of paper the following statement:

"It is my will to use all of my abilities to obtain the following goal: _____."

At the end of the statement fill in whatever it is you want.

    a. Be simple!

    b. Be specific! Most people do not want "money." They want money for a purpose such as a bet-

ter lifestyle, a better car, etc. So put that ultimate purpose in the blank at the end of the statement. If that purpose is a long-term goal, choose the first step toward that goal. If it is your aim to be a teacher, it should be your first goal to get the training necessary for you to teach. If it is your goal to do something noble, such as "to serve," that is very good. But serve in what way? A doctor serves, but so does a garbage collector, a plumber, a hypnotherapist, or a waitress. Each needs a vastly different skill set and each needs different types of training to become successful in their fields.

STEP TWO. Now make a visual picture of yourself *involved* in that goal. If you want a car, see yourself in that car. If you want a better lifestyle, see yourself wearing something that represents that lifestyle, etc. This image will be used for visualization.

    a. Always involve yourself in the image.

    b. Remember, some people cannot visualize to an extent where they can "see" something in their mind's eye. If you cannot thus "see," there is still no problem. But you must *know* that what you are visualizing, if you had better developed astral vision, is really existent on the astral plane; not just believe this to be so, but *know* it to be so.

    c. For help, you can make a "Treasure Map." To do this, simply go through magazines or newspapers and cut out images that represent your goal. Now paste them together on a piece of cardboard or paper to form a magickal collage. If you prefer, you may draw the images rather than cut them out. Be sure to include yourself in the Treasure Map either by putting a picture of yourself in the map or writing the word "me" in the center of your Map.

STEP THREE. Every day, for five minutes in the morning just after you awake and for five minutes in the evening just before going to sleep, repeat the phrase you wrote out in Step One in a firm but quiet

SMART Goals/DUMB Goals

The concept of SMART goals and DUMB goals moved from the mystical to the world of management in 1950s. The concepts were well known to mystics and magicians, but were codified and clarified by Peter Drucker in his book *The Practice of Management*. We can reverse that process and determine the validity and quality of a goal we want to manifest using Grey Magick.

All of your magickal goals should be SMART. In this instance, SMART is an acronym (Notarikon) for five qualities each goal should exhibit.

S—Your goal should be as *Specific* as possible. The more concrete you can make your goal, the more likely you are to achieve it.

M—Your goal should be *Measurable*. You should be able to easily and effortlessly judge when you have achieved the goal. If your goal is to get a car, it is fairly easy to measure when you have it. However, if your goal is health, how would you measure that? I'm not trying to dictate what your measurement should be, only that you should have one. Further, the more *Meaningful* the goal is to you, the more likely you are to achieve it.

A—Your goal should be *Attainable*. If you are a golfer, getting a birdie (one under average or par) on every hole in one round of golf has never previously been attained on a professional course, so there is no reason to assume you can attain it. As a general rule, if someone else has achieved something, there is no reason why you cannot also achieve it.

R—Your goal should be *Realistic*. If you are sixty years old, a goal to get on to the PGA golf tour is unrealistic. Nobody of that age has ever done it. However, it would be realistic to try to get on the seniors golf tour.

T—Your goal should have a *Time frame*. Of course, this time frame should be realistic and achievable. If you want to lose twenty pounds but don't put a time frame on that loss, you will always want to lose it but may never actually attain that loss. Similarly, if the time frame for that loss, say two weeks, is unrealistic or unhealthy, it is also a poor choice for a goal.

Personally, I would add an *E* to this, making it SMARTE. I contend that your goals should also be *Ecological*. By that I mean your goals should be good for you, good for people around you, and good for the planet.

Some people suggest that your goals should be DUMB: **D**oable, **U**nderstandable, **M**anageable, and **B**eneficial. While I agree with the concepts embodied in the acronym, I don't think that focusing on being dumb is positive, and the ideas in the DUMB acronym are implied in the SMART(E) goals system.

voice. *Do this only once in the morning and evening.* Spend the rest of the five-minute period either visualizing the image you made in Step Two, or looking at the treasure map you made in that step. See, smell, taste, feel, and sense the visualization. Remember, you must be involved in the image.

a. Only do this process at morning and at night. However, anytime during the day you realize that you are having thoughts contrary to your goal (as was the case with John Magus), immediately begin repeating your magickal phrase until the contrary thoughts pass away.

STEP FOUR. Silence is also an important factor in this process. Once you have completed your statement and visualization, forget it! Put it out of your mind. Let it go. You are using many cosmic forces in this process. If you talk with others about what you are doing, it sends the energy into the discussion rather than into the manifestation. If you talk to yourself about what you are doing, such as by wondering about how well you are doing with this Kabalistic system, you are doubting your success. Just do it with all of your heart, know that it will work, and be silent about it.

Aleister Crowley wrote about a time he was low on money. He did a ritual to raise the money he needed to pay his rent. He had such a positive attitude about his magick that he went into town and spent some of his remaining meager funds on ice cream. Oh, by the way, he did get the money that was necessary to pay his rent.

STEP FIVE. Here is the Kabalistic secret promised earlier in this lesson. If you reread some of the earlier material given in this course you will notice that in one place it is mentioned that the astral plane, also known as the Yetziratic World, is related to the *emotions*. The secret is this:

The more emotionally involved
you become with your goal,
the greater your chances for rapid success.

"Sort-of" wanting something will not have the success of "gotta-have" something. The more emotionally worked up you get over your desire—especially when stating that desire and doing the visualization—the faster it will manifest. As it says in *The Book of the Sacred Magic of Abramelin the Mage,* "Inflame thyself with prayer."

That, very simply, is the Kabalistic system of mental magick. Practice the system daily until you get what you want. Then *immediately* start anew with another goal. Keep your emotions high and success must inevitably follow. Record results in your ritual or magickal diary.

Some people wonder why the peculiar wording is used for the magickal phrase given in Step One. The choice of words is very important and should always be used. "It is my will . . ." means that you are using your consciousness, and putting that aspect of yourself in charge of the unconscious. Most people tend to allow their unconscious to control them without even knowing it. These four words indicate a change in your life: you are no longer an ordinary person. You are becoming a true magician.

" . . . to use all of my abilities . . ." is important because it is telling your unconscious that all abilities which you possess, whether you are aware of them or not, are to be used in achieving the goal. Thus, even if you are not aware of your innate psychic powers, your unconscious, as a result of being ordered to do so by your conscious, will cause those powers to be put to use to achieve your goal.

" . . . to obtain the following goal . . ." Here the important word is "goal." This is not a light-hearted wish or mild desire. This is a goal toward which you will be directing your entire life at this time. If you cannot direct all of your efforts toward that goal, don't even start this process. Let's say that you want an expensive book on magick and you use the Kabalistic system of mental magick to obtain it. But then, instead of saving your money, you spend it on some CDs or MP3s or going to a club or a movie. This is a message to your unconscious that you do not really want to achieve the goal of getting the book. Your unconscious will comply with this and help you achieve the goal of not getting the book.

Although in this particular instance I am saying that it is important to save your money for the book, I am not saying that it will be necessary to spend all of your money for the book. Nowhere in the magickal phrase of intent does it say *how* you are to obtain the goal. Let it come to you as it will. Don't try to dictate how something should come to you. You must still use all of your abilities to obtain it. In this case, it means saving your money. In the instance of Crowley mentioned earlier, he had done a ritual to obtain all of the money he would need so that he could pay a rent bill. What little he had at that time was not relevant, since he was not going to go out and get work to earn money.

To recap the Kabalistic system of mental magick briefly:

1. Come up with a specific goal and write it down in the given form.

2. Come up with a visualization that involves you. Use a treasure map if it will help.

3. Recite the goal and do the visualization for five minutes when you awake and five minutes before going to sleep. Become emotionally involved with the goal.

4. If something comes to mind that contradicts your goal during the day, immediately recite the magickal phrase repeatedly, as you might do with a mantra, until the contradictory thought is gone.

5. Make sure your goal is a SMART(E) goal.

PART TWO

Magick High and Low

Throughout this course I have described three types of magick: White Magick, which has been the focal point so far in this course; Grey Magick, which we have begun to investigate and which will occupy most of the rest of this course; and Black Magick, which will only be discussed in terms of how to avoid doing it either purposely or accidentally. These definitions of types of magick have used the purpose and outcome of a magickal ritual or act to determine the type of magick we are doing. As an example, any techniques or rituals used to help us achieve a closer relationship with Divinity are defined as White Magick—any techniques. What you *do* doesn't determine the type of magick you have performed. Rather, what you *get* is the basis of the definition. A person could use the same techniques, but depending upon the goal and/or results, the type of magick would be different. The important thing to under-

stand about this, then, is that when using the terms White, Grey, or Black Magick, purpose (or result) determines definition.

You may have heard of other ways of differentiating types of magick. Some people use multiple colors. Others give different definitions for the meanings of White, Grey, or Black Magick. I'm not trying to dictate and say that the definitions given in this course are the only allowable definitions; I'm just saying these are the definitions used in this course. As long as someone defines what he or she means by a term, that's fine with me.

There is another definition of different types of magick I'd like to discuss. These definitions are based upon heredity, the ancient source of the style of magick. There are two major categories based on history. The type of magick we have studied, and for the most part will be studying, is based in the structure of city life. It was in cities where the middle classes first evolved. It was in cities where leisure became possible on a weekly if not daily basis. A merchant who lived in a city could work from "nine to five," whereas those people who lived and worked on farms had to work virtually from before sunrise to after sunset. In the city, people were able to have extra time to learn how to read and study. Thus, the style of magick that has evolved out of city lifestyles tends to include long, precise spells, complicated formulae, and sometimes involved astrological preparations. It is a style of magick that is left-brain, logic oriented.

The city-dwelling middle classes and upper classes had time for leisure and study. They also had enough excess capital—extra and spendable money—to afford ritual items. Some of these ritual tools were made of gold or silver, showing that if some of the magicians were not upper class, then they received support or patronage from a wealthy person or group.

Practically from the beginning of time, many cities were built on high ground near a source of fresh water. Being on high ground was necessary because it was an easy place to defend against attackers. Also such a city would have a natural drainage system thanks to gravity. Such drainage systems, especially after rains, would help prevent flooding and the health problems associated with standing, stagnant water. The style of magick that we have been learning in this course, the style of magick which developed in cities located near high ground, is known as High Magick or Art Magick.

Every culture had, has, and will have its own magick. At the time High Magick or Art Magick was developing in the cities, so, too, were the magickal systems of those people who lived outside of the cities. It was the magick of the farmers and hunters and animal herders that evolved from even earlier magicks of the earliest, prehistoric tribes of hunters and gatherers by way of various religio-magickal systems.

Farming life has always been very difficult. In the Middle Ages there were only basic tools and no real insecticides, fertilizers, or irrigation systems that worked at the turn of a faucet. True, the Nile culture and the Aztec culture did have irrigation systems. And it is also true that people knew that various herbs would keep away certain insects and manure could be used to fertilize the soil. Still, the people of 100–10,000+ years ago had nothing to compare to our modern "green revolution."

These hard-working farmers could not take the time to learn how to read or study arcane magickal texts and lore. Instead, they learned the laws of the universe from the gracious Mother Nature. They saw how the Moon affected their lives and crops. They saw the importance of air, earth, heat, and water. Having little knowledge of writing, their magick was passed orally. They developed their own language and codes. They studied and learned the powers of the plants around them. And some, following the Roman and Greek pantheon, worshipped a beautiful goddess, represented by the Moon, and a strong god of the hunt, represented by the Sun. Although there is no evidence that there was ever a "universal" goddess religion, there is ample evidence of a goddess tradition in virtually every ancient culture. According to one respected author, Raphael Patai, the

ancient Hebrews worshipped a goddess along with their god and even had an altar to her in the first and second temples, up to the year 70 C.E. Today, many Christians hold Mary in very high esteem, to the point where some are accused of "Mariolatry." Jews still honor the "Sabbath Bride" and welcome the coming of the Moon. In Hebrew, the word for Moon is "Levannah," which also happens to be the name of an ancient Semitic Moon goddess.

Perhaps you remember from your study of history the so-called "divine right of kings." This included such things as the pick of the crops and animals raised by those who lived in their kingdoms, the right to ride through the crops of a farmer who lived in a king's domain, even the right to have sex with a woman before her husband on their wedding night! In return, the king was expected to protect the farmer from foreign invaders. In times of such danger, farmers and their families could run to the king's castle for protection. Thus, they did not need to live and work on high ground. Further, the terracing of hilly areas was a terrible chore. It was far easier to live in lower-lying lands where there was both natural irrigation from rains and the washing of fertile soil from the higher areas by that same rain. The magick that developed from these cultures is known as Natural Magick or Low Magick.

It is important to point out that there is no quality judgment or moral judgment based upon the terms High Magick and Low Magick. They are simply different methods of achieving the same goals with the primary differences between them being cultural and technical. As the centuries passed and the cultures of both city dweller and rural inhabitants developed, problems arose for practitioners of High and Low Magick. Organized religion, especially Christianity in the form of the Roman Catholic Church hierarchy and later even more so by the various Protestant authorities, did not want people who either could work or were believed to work "miracles." Only those who were involved with the various churches were supposed to be able to do this. The High Magick practitioners were able to present a façade of Christian worship in their practices and in many instances they were, for a while, able to avoid persecution.

Not so for the people who did Low Magick. Not only could they do things that the organized religion did not like (magick), but they also worshipped deities who were not the same as the ones worshipped by those in power. The organized religions tried to wipe these people out, insultingly referring to them as "people of the heath" or heathens. Similarly, in Latin the expression meaning "those of the earth," *paganus*, became the then-insulting term "pagan." Originally the words "pagan" and "heathen" were just descriptions, but they became virtually a rallying cry for genocide.

Initially, the worst problem was not that these people practiced Low Magick, but that they worshipped different gods and goddesses. In the sixth century the Pope wrote, if "heathen temples are well built they should be purified from the worship of demons . . . In this way the people, seeing their temples are not destroyed, may flock more readily to their accustomed" places of worship. Of course, to the Pope any god that was not his God must be a demon.

But conversion was not enough. The organized Christian religion took an image of the Roman god Pan, horned, hoofed, and tailed, and said that this image was the image of their chief source of evil, Satan (try to find that description of Satan anywhere in the Jewish Bible). Thus, "heathens" and "pagans" who still worshipped their God and Goddess were told they were worshipping evil demons. These people, wanting to worship their own deities, became "Satan" worshippers to organized religion. As such, they lost their human status, and were persecuted, tortured in unbelievably foul ways, and killed in surprisingly large numbers. Some say the number of Pagans tortured and killed by Christians, over the course of hundreds of years, was under 100,000. Other authorities claim the numbers rival or surpass the Jewish Holocaust perpetrated by the Nazis. But the Pagans were not destroyed by the Nazis. They were victims of Catholics and Protestants.

Those Pagans who escaped hid from their persecutors. Their religious aspects went "underground," and those people became known as healers and masters of the herbs. Much of the various traditions was lost. Some of the women who kept up their skills as healers and herbalists also remembered some of the religious aspects that they taught to their daughters and sometimes to others. They became known, quite appropriately, as "wise women." It was said that these people could bend reality to their wills. A word used to describe these people and which means "to bend" is "Wicca" (masculine) or "Wicce" (feminine; pronounced "wee-cha"). In English, this word became "Witch."

This has been a very brief generalized history of Witches. I make no claim to its perfection in any way, and there are many books that can give you a far more detailed history of this subject than I can do in a few paragraphs. What I do want to make clear is that Witches do not worship the devil, do not perform the infamous Black Mass, and do not kiss the Devil's hindquarters. These were all fictions created by organized Christianity to cast a bad light on those who worshipped in a different light.

Every schoolchild in the U.S. knows that "in fourteen hundred and ninety-two, Columbus sailed the ocean blue." What the children are not told is that in the same year Isabella and Ferdinand ordered all Jews to leave Spain, convert to Christianity, or be killed. Remember, the Jews held the secrets of the Kabalah, which is one of the sources for High Magick.

Some Jews converted and some left. Others, known as the *conversos*, pretended to convert. Others hid in the countryside, aided by the people of the countryside, many of whom were Witches. The same sort of thing appears to have happened all over Europe, with Witches protecting Kabalistic Jews, and, in some cases, Jews protecting Witches. At this time there came to be a slight mixture between the High Magick of the Kabalists and the Low Magick of the Witches as each shared gratefully with the other.

Some people have asked me how this could be possible, considering that Jews are given the injunction

"Thou shalt not suffer a Witch to live." Well, first off, that is an incorrect translation from the Hebrew. But don't take my word for this. Find a translation of the Jewish Bible in a Jewish bookstore and look it up for yourself (Exodus 22, v.18). The correct translation, you will find, reads "Thou shalt not suffer a sorceress to live." In context, the Hebrew word refers not so much to a sorceress as it does to a poisoner, and the Hebrew word is so translated in other parts of the Bible. In other words, this was not an injunction against Witchcraft, but against murder. The Kabalists knew this. They would welcome their magickally oriented brothers and sisters. Also, since Rabbinical Judaism came to the forefront after the destruction of the second temple in 70 C.E., religious tolerance has become a Jewish tradition, although some people claim that for ultra-orthodox Jews this is becoming less and less the reality today.

Here is a brief series of important dates in the history of Witchcraft, with a special focus on Britain and the United States. Some of the dates are approximate.

Circa 1500 B.C.E. The Picts, original inhabitants of Britain, built Stonehenge. Their religion was lunar based, with a major emphasis on devotion directed to a goddess.

Circa 500 B.C.E. The Celts settled in Britain and taught the concept of reincarnation. Their religious leaders, the Druids, were solar oriented, and major emphasis in worship was placed upon a god. As the Celts and Picts interrelated and intermarried, the god and goddess became equally adored. From this union evolved traditions that, in a reconstructed form, are today known as Wicca (today commonly pronounced "Wik-ka"). There are other reconstructions that go back to other areas of Europe, especially Norse-Germanic and Italian traditions.

313 C.E. The Edict of Milan made Christianity the legal religion of the Roman Empire. Christian temples were built on the old sacred gathering places of the Pagans.

447 C.E. The Council of Toledo defined the Devil as the personification of evil in Christian doctrine. It was a simple move to equip him with horns and so identify him with the Horned God of the Hunt worshipped by Pagans, or Pan.

553 C.E. The Council of Constantinople declared the doctrine of reincarnation to be a heresy. Prior to this it had been taught by some Christian sects.

Circa 700 C.E. "Liber Potentialis" of Theodore forbade the practice of dancing while wearing animal masks, especially those of horned beasts. This had been a religious practice of some Pagans.

Circa 900 C.E. King Edgar of England regretted that the Old Gods were much more worshipped in his dominions than the Christian God.

1100 C.E. The death of William Rufus (William II of England), who was, it is believed, a Witch.

1303 C.E. The Bishop of Coventry was accused by the Pope of being a Witch.

1324 C.E. The trial of Dame Alice Kyteler in Scotland on charges of Witchcraft. She took refuge in England among her highly placed friends and was acquitted, largely because of her wealth and status.

1349 C.E. Founding of the Order of the Garter by Edward the Third. Many believe that Edward was a Witch and the Order of the Garter (the garter being a Witch symbol) was a Witch order.

1430 C.E. The trial of Joan of Arc for being a Witch.

1486 C.E. The publication of the *Malleus Maleficarum*, or *Hammer of Witches*. This heralded severe and widespread persecution of Witches.

1502 C.E. Pope Alexander's act against Witchcraft.

1542 c.e. Henry VIII's act against Witchcraft.

1563 c.e. Elizabeth I's act against Witchcraft.

1584 c.e. First edition of Reginald Scott's *The Discoverie of Witchcraft,* one of the first books to deny the superstitious ideas concerning Witchcraft and to treat the subject in a rational manner. James I ordered the books to be burnt by the public hangman.

Circa 1600 c.e. Some Witches come to America to escape religious persecution in Europe and Britain. They settle on the East Coast.

1645 c.e. Matthew Hopkins declares himself "Witch-Finder General" in England, spawning numerous imitators.

1647 c.e. On May 26, the first American Witch hanging took place in Connecticut. Three others followed Alse Young to the gallows.

1692 c.e. The infamous Salem Witch trials began. During the summer fourteen women and six men were killed. Trials continued to take place until May of 1693, when more than 150 persons held in prison for the "crime" of Witchcraft were freed upon the order of Governor Phips. A few other trials took place after 1693 in America, but none resulted in death. In all, thirty-six people were executed. None were burned at the stake.

1712 c.e. Jane Wehman was tried as a Witch in England, but after having a jury find her guilty, the judge procured her release, as he did not believe the evidence and disagreed with the jury's verdict. This is thought to be the last trial for Witchcraft in England.

1735 c.e. The Witchcraft Act of 1735, in the reign of King George II, stated that Witchcraft did not exist and that there would be no more punishments for it. However, it did specify that anyone who

pretended to possess supernatural powers would be prosecuted as an imposter.

1921 c.e. Dr. Margaret Murray's *The Witch Cult in Western Europe* sparked a revival of interest in Witchcraft both in scholarship and practice. Dr. Murray presented her thesis that the Witchcraft of the persecutions did, in fact, exist and that Witchcraft was an organized religion descended from ancient fertility cults of the Stone Age Europeans. Many of today's scholars would dispute this claim.

1951 c.e. The Witchcraft Act of 1735 was repealed, and the Fraudulent Mediums Act introduced in England to replace it. The act recognizes the existence of genuine mediumship and psychic powers, and provides penalties for those who pretend to possess such powers for the purpose of making money.

1954 c.e. Witchcraft Today by Gerald Gardner is published, the first book about Witchcraft by a self-avowed Witch. What Gardner describes, valid as it may be, is actually composed from old books, quotations from Aleister Crowley, ideas and poems from Doreen Valiente, and his own genius.

1972 c.e. The U.S. Internal Revenue Service grants the Church and School of Wicca tax-exempt status on the basis of Witchcraft having qualified as a religion.

1974 c.e. Mr. Bob Williams, a Kansas Pagan, agreed to help a staff writer for a Wichita paper with an article on a Pagan group if his (Williams') name was not used nor his occupation listed. However, both were revealed in the series of articles. Williams was fired from his job and evicted from his home. A short time later, his life ruined, he committed suicide.

1975 c.e. Z Budapest was arrested for "fortune-telling" at her occult supply store in Venice, California. She received a 180-day suspended jail sentence, two year's probation, and a $300 fine. Though not technically charged with Witchcraft, she felt her trial was due to her being a self-proclaimed Witch. This trial caused a national sensation among both Witches and non-Witches. (Ms. Budapest had an occult shop on Lincoln Blvd, just down the street from the Fox Venice movie theater that showed art films. I purchased, and still own, a box to hold Tarot cards from her shop. The shop is now gone; the theater is a permanent indoor swap meet.)

1985 C.E. A woman in San Diego lost her job because she was accused of being a Witch. In the same year, a bill was defeated in Congress which would have taken away the tax-exempt status of Witchcraft religious groups.

1987 C.E. A lecture by author and Witch Ray Buckland is cancelled after the sponsors receive numerous telephone threats, many of which are from people calling themselves fundamentalist Christians.

1999 c.e. Congressman Bob Barr (Republican from Georgia) sends letters to military leaders at U.S. bases demanding they cease allowing Wiccan rites on the bases as they are like "Satanic rituals." Senator Strom Thurmond (Republican from South Carolina) states that Wicca is "irreligious" and its practices should not be accommodated by the U.S. military. Texas governor and future president George W. Bush stated that he did not believe Wicca is a religion.

2007 C.E. After a ten-year struggle, the Veterans' Administration finally approves the pentacle, a symbol of Witchcraft, as a headstone symbol in U.S. military cemeteries.

Thus we see a pattern of fear, hatred, and persecution against a religious group, a pattern which exists to this day. I remember a popular occult shop in a tourist area of southern California that closed down after bricks came through the windows, following which the store was firebombed. Unfortunately, the true study of Witchcraft and its history,

not the lies that have been printed about it for hundreds of years, is beyond the scope of this course. Any occult bookstore should be able to recommend some good titles for you to begin with if that is your interest.

Low Magick, the magickal system used by Witches, tends to be simple and direct. It is neither better nor worse than the High Magick of the ritual magician. It is just different. For many people the craft of the Witches is effective, but for others the methods of Kabalistic art magick work better. Many people find that the Kabalah appeals to them because people from Western cultures tend to be very logic and left-brain oriented. Witches frequently tend to be more right-brain and intuition oriented.

It will be valuable for you to learn one typical system of Low Magick. I want to point out that there are literally hundreds of different versions of Witchcraft, and some may do something similar to what will be presented later in this lesson, while others may think it bizarre. Witches are different all over the world in practice, but many of the basic beliefs are similar or the same. On the next pages I will discuss what talismans and amulets are, and a Pagan system for empowering them. Following this I will go into the method of making modern Kabalistic talismans. For this, you will need to have your magickal tools prepared and consecrated in order to make these talismans into powerful magickal engines.

PART THREE

Talismans

The word "talisman" is said to come from the Arabic words *talis ma*, which means "magick writing." However, there is no proof of this. It may come from the Turkish meaning "one who is learned in divinity; a priest." According to Sandra Tabatha Cicero, talisman comes from the Arabic *tilsam*, which comes from the Greek *telein*, meaning "to consecrate," and *tetelesmenon*, meaning "that which has been consecrated." Other sources may be from the Byzantine Greek *telesma*, meaning a "religious rite," *telein*, meaning "perform a religious rite," or *telos*, meaning "completion."

Likewise, the word "amulet," often used as a synonym for talisman, is believed to be of Arabic origin; however, Cicero traces it to the Latin *amuletum*, which, in turn, is derived from *amolior*, meaning "to repel." That, in turn, may have come from the Arabic *amula* (a small receptacle used for healing) or *hamla* (a small object worn for protection). Another source claims it may be related to the Latin *amoliri*, meaning "to avert." Again there is no proof. No one knows exactly where either word came from.

Today, talismans are used to draw things toward you. Their purposes include obtaining money, luck, health, or love. Amulets are used to keep things away. They protect from evil or bad luck, and help keep one from ill health. In this course, "talisman" with a lower case first letter will refer generically to both Talismans and Amulets. "Talisman" with a capital first letter will refer to an object used to draw something to you. "Amulet" with a capitalized first letter will refer to an object used specifically to keep something away.

So far the definitions of these terms has been very general, so let's get into a more precise definition of the term "talisman" from a magickal point of view.

A talisman is . . .
> *any object,*
> *sacred or profane,*
> *with or without appropriate symbols,*
> *which had been charged or consecrated by*
>   *appropriate means*
> *and made to serve a specific end.*

Now let's analyze this definition. First, a talisman is not simply a thought or idea, it must be an object, a physical thing. Second, it can be any object. That means it could be a rock or a seashell, a finger ring, or a piece of paper. It doesn't have to be any form of sacred object, although if you had one you wanted to use, it certainly could be a sacred item. It may have words and/or symbols on it, but that is not necessary. It must be instilled with magickal energy,

either through the process known as "consecrating" or through "charging" it. And finally, it needs to have a specific purpose.

For thousands of years, writing was a magickal art. It was held in secret by the privileged classes and magicians. It was believed that certain symbols had magick power in and of themselves. This tradition has been carried even into modern movies where Count Dracula cringes in fear at the very sight of a cross. Thus, symbols placed upon a rock or piece of parchment were, of themselves, considered to be powerful. This is what I call the "animistic" theory of how talismans work. They have a life of their own.

Today, many magicians do not believe in this theory. Rather, they take what I call the "energetics" theory of how talismans work. They believe that the charging of the talisman is the important part; putting magickal energy into the object chosen to be a talisman. The time taken to carefully put the proper symbols on the object is a good way to create and send energy. Mix this with the energy raised and directed during a ritual to charge the talisman, and it is no wonder that this technique of magick is powerful.

Do not doubt that talismans, if properly made and charged, are powerful. Here are three instances of which I am personally aware.

1. "M" had been divorced and was looking for a new mate for her life. She followed the instructions in this course. Within days a man came into her life who fit virtually all of her desired characteristics in a man. They dated for a while and were married. Two decades later they are still happily married.

2. "N" was taking my course in the southern California area. In the class after the one on talismans she told me she would have to drop the class. When I asked why, she replied that she had been trying to sell her mobile home for six months without luck. She tried making a talisman to help her sell her house. The house sold in a few days and she had to prepare to move.

3. "Q" was studying at a major university while he was also taking my class. He asked how the talismans could help him to study and learn for a test he would be having in two weeks. I gave him advice on what type of talisman to make. Later, however, I had to give more help. He had made a Talisman to gain knowledge and information, but he had charged it improperly and too soon. He found that his head was filled with data that had nothing to do with the test he was going to take. I gave him some more help and he did very well on the test.

As discussed in the previous section of this lesson, practitioners of the art of Low Magick were closer in spirit to nature than most of their High Magick practicing counterparts. Notice that I used the past tense in the previous sentence. Today, many Low Magicians live in large cities and know little of nature's majesty. Many who call themselves "Witches," "Wiccans," or "Pagans" are nothing more than people practicing a simplified form of High Magick. However, this in itself should be considered a small miracle because as recently as a few decades ago most people who considered themselves to be High Magicians did not practice any type of magick. This means that if you practice Magick as described in these lessons you truly will be unique, a real practitioner of Art Magick.

Looking back at the Pagans of an earlier time, we see that most if not all were in harmony and close communication with nature. They easily saw that all things on this planet were composed of four categories. Everything had degrees of hotness or coldness. Perhaps copying the early high magicians and alchemists, they came to call this the element "Fire." Things could also be more or less solid (Earth), have varying degrees of fluidity (Water), and various degrees of compactness or expansiveness (Air).

We have already discussed these four elements. In fact, you should by now not only be in harmony with these elements, but you should also have some degree of success in being able to control them. Al-

though the main focus in this course is High Magick or ceremonial magick, being able to work with the elements is a basis for many forms of magick. To a real magician, terms such as High Magick, Low Magick, Art Magick, etc., are terms used only to help others understand what you are doing and to enable you to better communicate. To a real magician the important question is not whether it is High or Low, but did it work?

With this in mind, I want to discuss another disagreement that magicians have with another set of people. These people have their minds open to new ideas . . . as long as those ideas fall within a surprisingly narrow set of belief patterns. No, I am not talking about religious fanatics. I'm talking about some scientists. As stated before, many scientists tend to scoff at this "simple" fourfold division of matter. Modern science points to its own periodic table of the elements and says, "we can prove the existence of over 115 elements." This, according to the modern scientist, makes the old four-element theory obsolete superstition.

Nonsense!

The four-element (really five-element) theory does not define "element" the same way modern science does. The four elements define the properties of matter, not its chemical makeup. Gold is an element in the modern scientific sense. In the four-element theory (or perhaps four-quality theory would be a better phrase), gold has relative amounts of Fire, Air, Earth, and Water. Therefore, both the ancient four-element theory and the modern scientific theory of the elements can coexist with no problem so long as you understand that the word "element" has a different meaning for scientists and for magicians. I feel that it is important to understand these differences, which is why I have represented this material at this time.

You have probably heard of a person obtaining the lock of another person's hair to use as a basis for casting a "spell" upon the person from whom the lock of hair was taken. The hair does not merely represent the person from whom it was taken, but is actually said to be "in sympathy" with that person. Here the word "sympathy" has the earlier, somewhat archaic meaning of "being closely related" and not the modern meaning of "feeling sorry for someone" or "having similar feeling or emotions as another person." That is the reason that this type of spellcasting is frequently called "sympathetic magick."

Other things could be used to represent and be in sympathy with another person. A picture, a piece of clothing, parings from the person's fingernails or toenails, a drawing, or a doll could all be used to relate to the person. Expanding on this, we can find that there are many things that could correspond to a person. It is in this way that lists of correspondences can be set up, as was the list of Kabalistic correspondences given in an earlier lesson.

The four elements have correspondences, too. Here is a list of some possible correspondences.

AIR: A feather; incense; the colors blue, white, or gold.

EARTH: A rock; pentacles in the Tarot; the colors brown, black, or green.

FIRE: A piece of coal, a match, the color red or reddish-orange.

WATER: A pebble found near or in water; a shell; the colors blue, black, or green.

Notice that in the above short list there is duplication in the use of colors corresponding to the elements. This is not a mistake. Rather, it allows you to choose which system of color correspondences you wish to use.

Just as in the above list certain objects correspond to one of the four elements, so, too, can the elements relate to a variety of ideas, as is shown below:

AIR: Schooling, memory, intellectualism, teaching, tests, divination, communications, travel, writing, organizing and organizations, groups of all kinds, theorizing, drug addiction.

EARTH: Money, jobs, promotions, business, investments, material objects, fertility, agriculture, health foods, ecology, conservation, stock market, antiques, old age, museums, buildings, construction, progress, the home, the physical world, daily necessities such as food and clothing.

FIRE: Success, sex, passion, banishing some illnesses, military, conflicts, protection, courts, law, police and sheriff's agencies, contests, competitions, private detectives, dowsing, treasure hunting, gambling, athletics, strength, good health, war, terrorism, and on a more personal level anything related to the Freudian "id," the lower emotions of absurd desire and lust (that is, too much desire or lust), anger, violent emotions. Also things having speed.

WATER: Higher forms of love and the deeper emotions such as compassion, faith, loyalty, and devotion. Also friendship, partnerships, unions of any kind, affection, contract negotiation, beauty, rest, recuperation, meditation, spirituality, healing wounds, restoring growth, childbirth and children, the home, receptivity, family, swimming, diving, fishing, ancestors, medicine, hospitals, compassion, doctors and nursing, clairvoyance.

Notice that a few of the listings above seem duplicated, appearing in more than one of the four elemental categories. As an example, the home is listed under Earth and Water. Again, this is not an error. Here it allows you to more closely define the terms. Under the element Earth, the home refers to a structure, the building wherein you live. Under the element of Water, the home refers to the qualities of home life: love, stability, support, etc.

You could probably add many other ideas to this list as a result of your working with the elements over the last few months. This is highly advisable. What you might do is start keeping a small book with precise definitions of what the elements represent to you. Use the above list as a starting point and expand upon it. And no, the above list is not written in stone as immutable law in some dank cave in the Himalayas. So, if you want to remove something from the above list or place it under another element, follow the motto of frontiersman, soldier, and politician Davy Crockett (1786–1836): "Make sure you're right . . . then go ahead." With the above information you now have a system for the making of talismans.

Do you need help with a test? Make a Talisman of Air. Do you need more love? Make a Talisman of Water. Is there too much anger and violent emotions in your family life? Make an Amulet of Fire. If you need more money, a Talisman of Earth should do the trick.

Now that you know on which element to base the talisman you wish to construct, the next question is "What is the first step for constructing a Low Magick talisman?" Whether you are doing Low Magick, High Magick, or any other Magick, if you are doing something to affect yourself or someone else on this plane, that is, if you are doing Grey Magick, *ALWAYS begin by doing a divination!* I cannot stress this sufficiently.

One law that everything in our world must live by is the law most commonly called karma, the law of cause and effect. Every action that you take has its own consequences which will come upon you whether you are prepared for them or not. Many practitioners of Low Magick tend to go one step further than the "as you sow, so shall ye reap" idea of karma. They say that whatever you do will be returned to you threefold. This threefold law states that if you do something good, you will be rewarded with a similar amount of good three times over. However, do something negative and you will be "rewarded" with three times as much bad coming your way. And karma is carried over from one life to the next. Suicide or death does not expiate karma.

Suppose you want to leave the country and need lots of money to do so. You make a Talisman to get the money. Then you learn that your parents have been in an accident and died, leaving you a large inheritance. You have done Grey Magick and helped yourself on the physical plane by getting the money. But your Talisman may have been responsible for the deaths of your parents, so your magick was definitely of the blackest kind.

Karma is *amoral*, meaning it has no morality. It is perfectly and totally just. There are no exceptions to the law of karma any more than there are exceptions to the law of gravity. If you do Black Magick, whether or not you originally intended it to be Black, you will, sooner or later, pay for it. I am therefore urging you *never* to do Black Magick. I do so not on any moral grounds (although I am ethically against Black Magick), but for self-protection.

In the above case, the talismanist had no way of knowing whether or not the Grey Magick would become Black. What should have been done first, therefore, was a divination to see whether or not it would be a good idea to do the talisman, and what the outcome would be. By doing this you can protect yourself from accidentally doing Black Magick and having to suffer the consequences.

Before doing any Grey Magick always do a divination!

The next step in making a Low Magick talisman is to find an appropriate object to use for the talisman. Given just before the above correspondences for the four elements are different objects that can be used for the making of talismans associated with the elements. However, any object may be used. A rock painted red can represent Fire. A necklace or ring can also be used.

Put a coin in your refrigerator for an hour. Take it out with your left hand and hold it for a few moments. Now put it in your right hand. You will find, of course, that the coin has gotten warmer than it was when you removed it from the refrigerator. The coin has been infused with energy in the form of heat. Likewise, virtually anything in this world has been infused with various types and quantities of psychic energies. Perhaps you have gone on a vacation and been in an utterly magnificent hotel room. Yet that room may have felt "cold" and uncomfortable compared to your far less luxurious home. This is because your psychic energies have not infused the room as they have your home. This is why, even if

Never Do Black Magick.
Never Ever, Ever. Except . . .

You should never do Black Magick. Not even accidentally. That's what I wrote in the first edition of *Modern Magick*. That's what I believed. That's what I've taught. However, as my understanding of karma (Tee-koon) has evolved, my position on this has had to evolve, too.

As I have described, karma is completely based on actions, not intent. It doesn't matter that an accident resulting in your harming someone else was unintended. You did it. You get the karma for it. It's that simple. Deal with it.

But there is something unique that happens as you grow and evolve as a magician: rules aren't simply rules you follow because, well, because they're the rules. Rather, you follow them because you understand them. You understand karma.

For example, if I violently harm someone, I get the karma for my action. That's simple and direct. But now let me give you a little scenario . . .

I'm walking to my house, and I hear screams. I go to investigate. A man is raping a woman. I tell him to stop. He ignores me. I push him away. He just pushes back and continues his ugly attack on the woman.

I know that the next step will be to stop him through the use of physical harm to him. Causing physical harm will result in my accruing "negative" karma. It's a form of Black Magick (although understood by Western science) that's not even accidental. If I act with violence, I'll be committing Black Magick.

So what should I do? Call for help and avoid the unwanted karmic result of my actions?

Sorry. No chance. I'm just a human and far from perfect. If it's necessary to harm that person to prevent a rape, I would do it without worrying about the karmic consequences for me. I wouldn't give it a second thought. In my imperfect way I would do what I feel I have to do and feel not a single drop of remorse.

So, if you're still around during my next lifetime and I come back as a skunk or a rock, please, take advantage of me and make me useful so I can once again evolve spiritually.

Karma is perfectly just. But sometimes, as a human, I may need to tell karma to go to Hell as I consciously choose to do something that will incur unwanted karma. That's okay. I can live with it. Again and again, if need be.

So in some instances I'll choose to do what I believe right for the greatest number of people and for our planet, even if it's karmically regressive for me.

That's just the way I am.

---

your home is a "dump" and crawling with bugs, it still can feel like home. You would have to live in a place for days, weeks, or even months before a new house or apartment really becomes your home.

Even small objects pick up psychic charges from their environment. Therefore, before using any object as a talisman, it must first be purified and cleansed of any known or unknown charge of psychic energy.

This is easy to do. Hold the object to be used as a talisman under running water. For this purpose you can use water coming out of a sink faucet or a garden hose, or, more traditionally, a stream. Hold it there for about three minutes while you visualize all energies within the object flowing out of it with the water. Do not use the waves of the ocean for this purpose, as the waves keep coming back and would return to the object you have chosen the energies you wished to cleanse.

If the object will not last well under flowing water, bury it in the ground for at least a half hour, preferably overnight. Our Mother Earth has a natural ability to "ground" out energies that are unwanted. We now have an object that has been purified and is ready to be charged. If you so desire you may paint it an appropriate color.

The ancient Pagans were too busy working during the day to do magick during the sunlit hours unless absolutely necessary. Holidays might be celebrated during the day, but Grey Magick was not usually done during festivals. Thus it has become traditional to do Low Magick at night. The best sites to do Low Magick are:

First: . . . . . . Outside, with a clear view of the Moon.

Second: . . . .Outside, without a view of the Moon.

Third: . . . . . Inside, with a view of the Moon.

Fourth: . . . .Inside, without a view of the Moon.

The Moon, representing the Goddess aspect of divinity, was also seen to be a key force in magick of all kinds. The phases of the Moon were guides as to what your magick could do. During the waxing Moon, the period from first sight of the new Moon to the full Moon, magick should be done to draw things toward you. The strength of the Moon will be at its height at the moment of the full Moon. Therefore,

Talismans *should be made during*
the waxing Moon.
Amulets *should be made during*
the waning Moon.

This phase is known as the waning Moon and reaches its strength during the dark of the Moon, that is, when the Moon is not visible.

If someone is ill and you wish to make a talisman to aid the person, you can make a Talisman for health during the waxing of the Moon. If the Moon is wan-ing you can make an Amulet to cause disease to leave. Determine the phase of the Moon and plan whether to make a Talisman or an Amulet accordingly.

If you are not familiar with astronomy or astrology, you may wonder how to quickly determine the phase of the Moon. Even if you do not have an astrological calendar that clearly tells you the phase of the Moon (although you should probably obtain one such *as Llewellyn's Astrological Calendar* or *Llewellyn's Daily Planetary Guide* and learn how to use it, as they are useful tools for a magician), there is an easy source for this information: your daily newspaper. Usually near either the weather section or the sport fishing section you will find some rather silly looking drawings of the "Man in the Moon." These will tell the dates of the full, new, and quarter moons. With this information it becomes easy to determine the phase of the Moon.

Most Pagans, both past and present, do not like the morals and ideals of others foisted upon them. As a sign of their independence and freedom, many practitioners of Low Magick prefer to work "skyclad," that is, wearing only the sky: nude. While this does cut down on clothing bills and cleaning expenses, it can also cause a problem (due to prying neighbors) for those who wish to work outside in their backyard. If you cannot work skyclad, or would feel strange or inhibited working without clothes, then by all means do wear your special magickal clothes or robe.

Set up a small altar. You can use a table, chair, tree stump, or flat rock. But orient it so that when you are behind it *you will be facing north*, not east. On the altar have the object you wish to use as a talisman, plus candles of the appropriate colors and incense if you like. You are now ready to begin the ritual that will charge the talisman and make it a powerful magickal tool.

Before going on, did you remember to do a divination first? If not, do so now. Remember to word the question of your divination in the form of "What will be the outcome of my making a(n) talisman (amulet) for the purpose of _____?"

Pagan Prudery?

Since I originally wrote the comments on going skyclad, a vast change has occurred in Wicca and Witchcraft. Originally, the terms were synonymous. Today, people give them different meanings and have made both subcategories of the term "Paganism." A good way to see this would be using this Venn diagram:

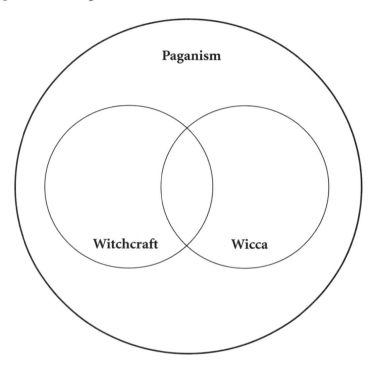

Part of the change that has taken place over the past few decades has been a shift away from a group format to an individual or "solitary" format. In the group format, people seeking membership spent months or longer—traditionally a year and a day—in training. Part of this training was actually the *untraining* of various ideas and beliefs into which people had been indoctrinated throughout their lives. Without this some modern Pagans have simply adopted selections of their old belief systems into their Paganism. One of these sets of ideas was Christian morality, which portrayed the naked body as evil.

Today, a surprisingly large number of people who identify themselves as Pagans have adopted this belief. I've seen some posts online where people boldly declare that Pagans never worshipped skyclad. Others could not conceive of themselves being naked in front of others, showing that they don't understand the concept of being skyclad to honor the Goddess and/or have issues over body image and other insecurities.

While some people who have been Pagans for a long time feel sad about this change, it is what has happened. Trying to fight evolution is like trying to hold back the tides with a bucket rife with holes. The effort may feel good, but the results are nil. Perhaps it's better just to accept a simple truism: **What is, is.**

The following ritual is far more mental than verbal. In fact, in this ritual there is little to say, but many things to do.

Using Low Magick to Charge a Talisman

STEP ONE. First, you should purify yourself and your area. Visualize a brilliant white (some say violet) light coming from the ends of the universe, going through the top of your head and down through your feet into the Earth. As it does so, realize that this pure light is taking with it all problems and impurities that may have been within you and are on your mind either consciously or unconsciously. Next, visualize a bright white light forming a ring about your now-purified self, at chest height. Now see in your mind's eye the expansion of this light of pure white brilliance so that it forms a circle around you three, five, seven, or nine feet in diameter. The size depends upon the space available to you. Finally, this circle should expand up and down so that you are surrounded above, below, behind, and to the front with a sphere of white light. You should be in the center of a brilliant sphere of purification, consecration, and preparation.

If you prefer more ritualism, you may mix the work in the above paragraph with the following. If ritualism is not that important to you, you may ignore the following paragraphs and jump to Step Two.

A. You will need a stick of incense, a small bowl of salt, and a second small bowl containing some water. Light the incense and hold it in front of you. Remember, you should be facing north. Say,

Behold! This is the union of Fire and Air!

B. Place the incense in a holder you have for the purpose. Pick up the water bowl. Put three pinches of salt into the water, or use the tip of your magickal blade to pick up and pour three "measures" of salt into the water. Hold up the mixture and say,

Behold! This is the union of Water and Earth!

C. Put the bowl down and pick up the incense. Move to the edge of the north side of the circle. Hold the incense in front of you and say,

I purify the north with Fire and Air.

D. Walk (clockwise) to the east, hold out the incense and say,

I purify the east with Fire and Air.

E. Continue in a similar manner at the south and west. Complete the circle by returning to the north. Now go back to your altar, replace the incense, and pick up the mixed water and salt.

F. Go to the north edge of the circle. Dip your fingers in the salt and water solution and sprinkle it toward the north three times, saying,

I purify the north with Water and Earth.

G. Continue sprinkling as you move to the east. Stop here, sprinkle three times as you say,

I purify the east with Water and Earth.

H. Continue in a like manner to the south and west. Complete the circle by returning briefly to the north, then return to the altar.

I. Now repeat this entire censing and sprinkling process. Except instead of using the word "purify," use the word "sanctify." Hence, "I Sanctify the north with Fire and Air," etc.

Again, you may mix the two methods of purifying yourself and the area or use either the mental or ritual procedures. You do not have to use both.

As an aside, some self-professed "Pagans" who abhor anything that hints at ritual magick or Kabalism, clear their area with . . . the LBRP! While there is nothing wrong with this practice, it is certainly not part of any ancient Pagan system. Those who practice magick should be open to all possibilities. People who use Kabalistic methods while decrying

Kabalism should seek to enhance their knowledge or discover the motive for their hypocrisy.

STEP TWO. After purifying and clearing your circle, the next step is to "Grab the Moon." What you do is take the essence of the magickal nature of the Moon (the Goddess aspect of Divinity) into your hands and place that nature into the talisman. At the same time you charge the nature of the Moon with the purpose of the talisman. To Grab the Moon we use the gesture known as the "Triangle of Manifestation" which is described earlier in this course. To refresh your memory, this action is made by holding both hands flat with the thumbs extended at sixty degrees from the fingers. Place the tips of the thumbs together and tips of the first fingers of each hand together. This will form a triangle with the thumbs as the base line and the first fingers forming the sides. See the illustration below.

Now hold up this Triangle of Manifestation so that you can see the Moon surrounded by the triangle. If you are in a place where you cannot see the Moon, visualize the Moon within the triangle. In a short time there will seem to be two moons. The real (or visualized) Moon will have a second moon next to it. It will appear slightly to the side or "out of phase" with the original Moon. This second moon is the essence of the Moon's magickal power. It is possible that you may not be able to see this second moon, but *knowing beyond the slightest doubt* that it is there will suffice.

STEP THREE. In this step you do two things at once. While concentrating on that second moon, slowly bring your hands down toward the object you are using for the talisman. Try to keep the second moon's image within the triangle (or know that it is there) and, in your mind, mentally repeat over and over a single word or short phrase that best represents the purpose of the talisman. As an example, the word "health" could be used to represent "I wish to get over this cold and regain my health." Limit any phrase to no more than four words.

As you do these things, bring your hands over, then down around the talisman. The goal is to surround the talisman with the triangle formed by your hands. The energy of the Moon, impregnated by your will for the purpose of the talisman, is now joining with the object.

In a few seconds you should experience a new sensation. Some people describe it as a sudden lightness

in the hands. Others describe it as a rush of energy or a snapping sensation. Everyone experiences this sensation somewhat differently, so I can't give an exact description. However, as soon as you experience the change, clap your hands or snap your fingers. Then, as you separate your hands, say,

It is done!

What has happened here is that the Goddess energies of the Moon, mixed with your will, have moved into the object, empowering your talisman. It is now charged and operative.

STEP FOUR. To finish the ritual use your own words to thank the powers of the universe who have aided you in this ritual and bid them depart to "their homes and habitations." Write the results of your ritual in your magickal or ritual diary.

When you have achieved the goal of the talisman, the object needs to be discharged of any remaining energy. This can be done by holding it under water or burying it as before. It can then be reused as a talisman for another purpose. If possible, and if the object is disposable (and biodegradable), destroy the object by burning it to ash and getting rid of the ash in the air (by throwing it) or into water. Or, just put it into running water or bury it where it will not be found.

You may charge several talismans for the same purpose at one time. However, it is not a good idea to try to energize several talismans for different purposes (even if they're associated with the same magickal element) at the same time or even during the same ritual. Focus on one thing at a time.

When using a talisman it is a good idea to keep it on you or near you. If you are making the talisman for someone else, tell him or her to keep the talisman on or near their body. Of course, you should ask the person's permission before making the talisman or giving it to him or her. Do not, however, tell the person the intricacies of the ritual and of the construction of the talisman. Tell the person to whom you give the talisman to destroy the object or return it to you once the talisman has achieved its purpose.

The unconscious mind does not think in negatives. Don't make a talisman to "stop smoking." Rather, make one to be "free of smoking."

As described in the sidebar earlier in this lesson, it is a good idea to make the goals of your talisman SMART goals. Therefore, it is desirable to put a time limit on your talisman. In your charging have it planned to achieve its goal in one week or one month or by a certain date. Even if you do not achieve the goal by that date, be sure to purify or destroy the talisman at that time. Then wait two more weeks to see if a result is forthcoming. Sometimes talismans get things started but not completed by their time limit. If you don't notice a result two weeks after the functionality of the talisman has ended, go back over your magickal diary, analyze what you might have done wrong, and start over. Chemicals, under the same conditions, always react with each other in the same way. If they do not, the mistake was made by the experimenter. Likewise, magick always works. If not, you have made some error. It is interesting to note that while scientists will readily accept the statement regarding chemistry, some will attempt to refute the similar statement regarding magick. In this case, logic is on our side, not theirs.

Once you have charged your talisman, don't think about it. Your unconscious plays an important part in the magickal process. Constantly bringing the aspect of the mind that connects us to the astral plane down to the physical world will lower the effectiveness of your magickal work. Go back and re-read the section on Creative Visualization.

Making a Magickal Guardian

Be confident that your talisman is charged and will be effective. If you wish, you may recharge a talisman once a month without purifying the object if you are charging it for the exact same purpose and goal.

A small or large statue or objet d'art makes a wonderful protective amulet (technically called a "guardian") for a house or apartment. It should be recharged at least once every six months, although monthly would be better. Keep it by the front door.

If you have several entryways into your home, use several small statues (or even colorful rocks) overlooking each entry. Scott Cunningham used toy dinosaurs for this purpose. He had them by the door and the windows of the apartment. It was in one of the most crime-ridden areas of San Diego. There was never a robbery, crime, or attempted burglary in that apartment while Scott and his guardians lived there.

PART FOUR

Now we turn our attention back to Kabalistic magick. As you have seen from the last section, making and charging a talisman using a Pagan system such as the one just presented is direct and fairly easy. There is little you have to prepare. You will find that the Kabalistic system takes more time and thought to construct a talisman. To me it makes a Kabalistic talisman more precise. I personally enjoy that precision and necessary mind-work. My personal experience indicates that a Kabalistic talisman, once charged, may take a little longer to achieve its effect, but that effect can be far more intense than a Low Magick talisman. I am inclined to believe, however, that this is due to my own predilection for the Kabalah. In all probability, the Kabalistic talisman is neither more nor less effective than one made using Low Magick. The difference is based upon the person who does the actual work. Also note that although the Kabalistic talisman takes more time and effort to create than does a Pagan talisman, it is not more difficult to construct. It just takes some more thought and creativity. If you follow the instructions given here you will have no problem in the construction and charging of a Kabalistic talisman.

A Bit of History

Before the destruction of the second Temple in 70 c.e., many Kabalistic (or pre-Kabalistic) talismans were made of precious metals which could hang as a pendant on a chain or be attached to clothes. But the most common type of talisman from that time was a long, narrow scroll of parchment. Some of these have been found which were about two inches wide and twenty-two inches long. This scroll was literally covered with writing. In fact, the ancient Kabalistic talismanists frequently used abbreviations to allow for more meaning on the strip of parchment than straightforward writing would allow. This was then rolled up and placed in a leather, cloth, or metal (usually silver) container.

In E. A. Wallis Budge's *Amulets and Talismans,* the author describes a "perfect" Kabalistic talisman. Of course, no such talisman ever existed. Budge examined many ancient Kabalistic talismans and listed what was common to most of them. In a similar manner, musicologists examined all of Johann Sebastian Bach's fugues and, with the help of a computer, came up with an "ideal" Bach fugue. However, when comparing the computer's ideal with Bach's actual compositions, they discovered that none of Bach's fugues perfectly matched the ideal.

Budge claimed that the ideal Kabalistic talisman had four sections:

1. The appropriate magickal name.

2. Appropriate Biblical texts.

3. A special prayer that is similar in nature but not identical to types of invocations.

4. The words "Amen" and "Selah" each repeated three times.

Gaster, in the *Hastings Encyclopedia,* claims the ancient talismans were made this way:

1. The parchment must be specially prepared.

2. The magickal name must be written exactly as it appeared in the Hebrew in the *Tanach* (Jewish Bible).

3. The rest of the talisman must be written in "Ashuri" (the square Hebrew) letters.

4. No letter may touch another.

5. The talisman must be made in purity and while fasting.

6. It should be wrapped in leather or cloth (after being coiled into a tight roll).

7. It should be worn on the person or attached to his or her clothes.

8. Prayers should be said while constructing the talisman.

Gaster gives even more information and details, but these are not necessary for our study. The important thing to note is the time, care, effort, and sacredness that are believed to be part of the construction of ancient Kabalistic talismans.

The early Kabalists did not create their mystic system from out of the air, no matter how romantic that idea may seem. Although the ancient Kabalistic talismans were particularly Hebraic in nature, much of what was done was based on earlier Pagan ideas. Thus, early Kabalistic talismans were not as specific as the ones made today. In fact, there were only about six reasons for making ancient Kabalistic talismans:

1. For generally beneficial and benedictory purposes.

2. For promotion of health.

3. For protection against the "evil eye" (curses, black magick, poisoning, etc.).

4. For the prevention of miscarriages.

5. For the promotion of fertility.

6. For the protection of mother and child at the time of birth.

As I have said before, the Kabalah is not something static and unchanging. It has evolved over the past several thousand years. These changes allow us to have a far wider variety of topics and deep precision in choosing the purpose for making our talisman. Also, it allows us to almost "fill in the spaces" according to a simple system once we know the purpose of the talisman we wish to construct.

First, we do not have to worry about the choice of an object to charge. Although precious metals were sometimes used, for eons the object of choice to use as a Kabalistic talisman has been a piece of virgin parchment. Parchment was so strong that it could be washed and used for writing over and over. Thus a used piece of parchment could carry with it various psychic energies that would be unwanted. Virgin

(unused) parchment solved this problem. It was also easy to destroy once it had achieved its goal.

Today, real parchment is very expensive and hard to find. Imitation parchment is readily available at most stationery stores. If you are a purist, some occult stores do carry the real thing, which is made of the skin of sheep or goats.

But why, other than for tradition, should you use parchment? In the ancient Middle East, wood and paper made from wood pulp was a fairly scarce commodity. Parchment was a sturdy and re-usable writing surface. It was an early, standard form of paper. For today's magicians there is nothing wrong with using plain, white, unused, and unrecycled paper, except for aesthetic reasons. So, if you wish, you can use imitation parchment from a stationery store or even real parchment from an occult supply store. In this course I will be referring to the object upon which we will be making Kabalistic talismans as "paper," for paper will do just fine.

We will not be using a long scroll of paper. Modern Kabalistic talismans are much smaller and packed with more symbolism than their predecessors. If you cut out a piece of paper so that it is two inches by four inches and fold it in half, you will find that there are four squares: two on the front and two on the back, each exactly two inches by two inches. Each of these four squares is going to be filled with words and symbols. But where will we find them? Obviously, many will come in some way from the Tree of Life, the main symbol of the Kabalah. But how is this done?

On page 266 you will find a list of possible wants or desires associated with each Sephira. Read over the chart and see how various ideas relate to the ten Sephiroht. If something is not on the list, you can expand on the ideas list for each Sephira. Can you see, for example, how football would be related to Giburah? Or can you understand how poetry is related more to Netzach than to Hode?

Let us say, for example, we wish to create a talisman to obtain a really good friendship. By going over the chart we can see that this would relate to Tiferet. Now check back to your list of Kabalistic correspondences given in Lesson Three. From that page can be

What's A *Selah*?

The word *Selah* has puzzled scholars for over two thousand years. Its meaning is completely questionable, even though it appears seventy-one times in the book of Psalms (and three times in the book of Habakkuk).

Worship in the Temple of Jerusalem was an impressive and joyous event, not some dour and ultra-serious, monotone of rote repetition. Worship included large choirs and even an orchestra. This may lead to a clue as to the meaning of Selah.

The psalms were not meant to be read; they were meant to be sung. Therefore, some scholars believe that Selah was a musical instruction. It may have indicated a dramatic pause or an indication of the volume of the chorus being raised . . . or lowered. It has also been suggested that it indicates when a new melody is introduced or as a signal for an instrumental crescendo or diminuendo, an increase or decrease in volume. So how the heck did that get on to a talisman?

One of the most popular translations of Selah into English is "forever." If that is correct it could have a meaning similar to AMEN, and therefore, because God is a faithful king, he will keep his word and empower the talisman. Another version that might even be closer is that it means "let there be [made]." That makes even more sense to me. It's like saying "Here is my talisman. Let it be made properly."

One scholar simply suggests that it marks a transition from one thought to another. Another suggestion is that it is a cue for people to join in singing, meaning "lift up your voices." Another scholar suggests that it means "this sentence really doesn't belong here." It may also be an abbreviation for several words or a corruption of some word.

A Jewish music expert suggests it simply stresses the importance of what went before it. One commentator said this is where the congregation would prostrate itself before God.

One Christian commentator, Tony Warren, suggests it means "to hang" with the implication of weighing and measuring to determine value. Thus, it means "valued."

Certainly saying that what came before on a talisman is valued makes a lot of sense. Unfortunately, all of these suggested meanings are nothing more than logical guesses. Until something that more clearly identifies the meaning of Selah comes along, we can just live with its sonorous sound.

Talismanic Magick

KETER: Basic inventions. Electronics. Radiations such as x-rays, radar, radio, or television waves, etc. The unusual. Space vehicles. The far future. Ideas.

CHOCHMA: Radio. Television. Film. Extrasensory perception (ESP) and things psychic. Power generators. Magnetism. Static electricity. Rockets. Fireworks.

BINAH: (*Saturn*) Buildings. The elderly. Funerals. Wills. Reincarnation. Destruction of diseases and pests. Terminations and death. Plans. Debts. Real estate. Inheritances. Excavations. Mines. Trees and paper. Smelting. Fertilizers. Antiques. Concrete. Studying for exams. Acquiring the astral plane. The home. Obtaining esoteric knowledge.

HESED: (*Jupiter*) Speculation. Gambling. Acquiring wealth. Abundance. Growth. Plenty. Bankers. Divination of the past. Leadership. Ambition. Career success. Obtaining friendship. Obtaining health. Acquiring honors. Obtaining luck. Law. Materialism. Poverty (the partner of wealth). Money. Expansion.

GIBURAH: (*Mars*) Conflict. Hunting. Military success. Energy. Vitality. Dentists. Surgeons. Surgery. Barbers. Butchers. Police. Soldiers. All things pertaining to war. Aggression. Physical strength. Courage. Politics. Debates. Athletics. Competition. Men. Lust.

TIFERET: (*Sun*) Obtain friendship. Obtain health. Create harmony. Obtain luck. Obtain money. Obtain patronage. Obtain peace. Find missing property. Prevent war. Regain youth. Superiors of all sorts. Illumination. Immediacy. Employees. Promotions. Labor. World leaders. Divine power.

NETZACH: (*Venus*) Beauty. Fostering friendship. Obtaining love. Ensuring pleasure. Art. Music. Parties. Luxury. Jewels. Aphrodisiacs. Scents. Perfumes. Partnerships. Women.

HODE: (*Mercury*) Business and commercial success. Success in exams. Divination of the future. Influencing others. Theatrical success. Authors. Short trips. Writing. Bargain hunting. Schools. Basic medicine. Praxis (putting theory into action). Statistics. Teaching. Predictions. Self-improvement. Celibacy. The mind. Communications. Learning.

YESODE: (*Moon*) Knowledge of astral travel. Safe journeys. Achieve reconciliations. Foods, especially vegetables and flours. Fetuses and infants. Milk and dairy products. Preventing war. The home. The family. Cooking. Clairvoyance. Dreams. The sea. Agriculture. Natural medicine. Herbs.

obtained the following list of items that can be put on the talisman. All of these words and items are associated with the Sephira Tiferet:

Tiferet	Beauty
Gold (or Yellow)	Olibanum (a scent)
Heart	YHVH El-oh-ah V'dah-aht
Breast	Sol (the Sun)
Topaz	Raphael
Divine Physician	Malacheem
Messengers	Ruach
Intellect	Vahv (of YHVH)
Phoenix	Sunflower
King	and others . . .

This is a large list. But there are even more things which we can use. For instance, we can come up with a numerical representation through one or both of two systems of numerology. Here is the most common system used today. It is known as the Pythagorean system.

1	2	3	4	5	6	7	8	9
a	b	c	d	e	f	g	h	i
j	k	l	m	n	o	p	q	r
s	t	u	v	w	x	y	z	

As you can see, the letters "a," "j," and "s" are listed under and equal the number 1; the letters "b," "k," and "t" equal 2, and so forth. For our talisman, let's use the keyword "friendship" and figure out its numerical value according to the chart on the previos page:

f r i e n d s h i p
$6 + 9 + 9 + 5 + 5 + 4 + 1 + 8 + 9 + 7 = 63$ $6 + 3 = 9$

Notice that when the total of a word is greater than 9, the digits of the result are summed to get a single digit answer. This is known as "Theosophical Reduction." In our example, the single digit that can be used to represent the word "friendship" is 9. So let's add this number to our list.

A more Kabalistic system, based on the sound qualities of the letters, is as follows:

1 = a, j, i, y.
2 = b, c, k, r, q. (The "c" is hard as in the word "cat.")

3 = g, l, s, ch, sh. (The "s" sounds like "sh," as in the word "sugar.")

4 = d, m, t.

5 = e, n, h.

6 = s, u, v, w, c. (The "s" sounds like that in "sea"; the "c" sounds like that in "cent.")

7 = o, z, s, x. (The "s" sounds like a "z," as in "scissors"; the "x" also sounds like a "z," as in "xylophone.")

8 = p, f, x, h. (This "h," as in the German "ach," is rare in English, but occurs in other languages.)

9 = th, tt, s. (This is an "s" that comes before a "w" as in the word "switch.")

Now if we take our word, this is the enumeration:

F r i e n d sh p
$8 + 2 + 1 + 5 + 5 + 4 + 3 + 1 + 8 = 37$
$3 + 7 = 10$ $1 + 0 = 1$

Here you can see that Theosophical Reduction must be done twice to reduce the number down to a single digit. The only time this reduction is not done is if your sum yields 11, 22, or 33, in which case you leave it as a double-digit figure. Books on numerology will explain these "master numbers" in detail.

In this more Kabalistic system above we have determined that the value of the word (and idea of) friendship is 1. We can add 1 to our list.

The reason this is a more Kabalistic system of numerology is because the values of the English letters are determined by associating them with the numbers of the Hebrew letters with which they sound identical. Thus, the Hebrew letter "Gimel" is related to the English letter "g." Since the Gimel equals 3, in this system the English "g" also equals 3. The Yud is associated with the English letters "i" and "y," and, according to some people, "j." Thus, these letters are associated with the number 10, the number associated with Yud. By Theosophical Reduction they become related to the number 1. Other possible associations, because they have several possible correspondences with Hebrew, have been moved to those numbers deemed appropriate.

A Spare System

Another system to make up magickal talismans was created by Austin Osman Spare, a contemporary occultist and remarkably talented artist. This derivation of his system is based upon his idea of an "Alphabet of Desire." In this system you take the English letters of a word, delete the vowels (remember, Hebrew has no vowels), and push the remaining letters together to form symbols. Here is how to create a symbol for the word "woman."

Here is how to create a symbol for "friendship":

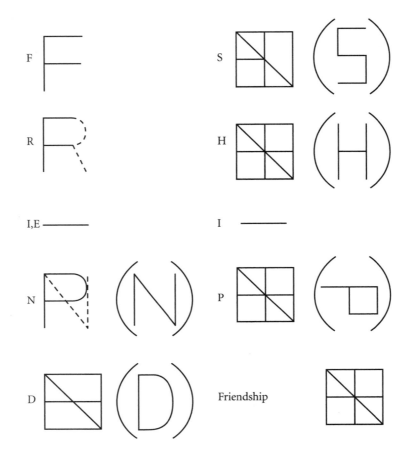

Notice that with the "woman" example, the "n" is forced into an angle so that we can literally get a symbol that looks like an "X" repeated four times and jammed together. Your conscious mind, at some time in the future, might not realize that this symbol means "woman," but your unconscious mind will remember and act on it without the conscious getting in the way.

Note, too, that the letters in the "friendship" example are made angular and may be turned sideways, as with the "p," or exaggerated as with the evolution of the "r." If you use a little imagination you can get a nice, artistic, and somewhat complex symbol to add to our list representing the concept of "friendship."

The System of the Hermetic Rose Cross

Another system you can use to make symbols for use on your talisman is based on the illustration shown on the next page. It is the center of a cross filled with elaborate symbols used by the Golden Dawn and known as the Hermetic Rose Cross. The three circles of Hebrew letters are based on a description of Hebrew found in the *Sepher Yetzirah*. The three letters in the center are called the "mother letters," and the represent the three elements (remember, it has a system where the four elements came from three). The middle circle is composed of seven letters, representing the seven days, the seven lower Sephiroht, etc. They're called "double letters" because each one traditionally had two forms, one of which was used at the beginning or within words, while the other was used at the end of words. The outer circle has twelve letters, representing the signs of the zodiac. They're called "single letters" because they have only one form.

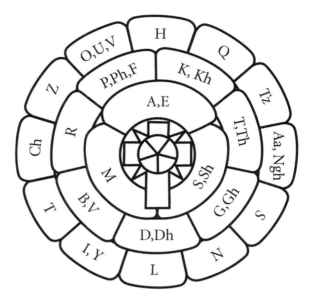

In the version of this glyph shown in the next column, the Hebrew is transliterated into English, making it easier for non-Hebrew readers to use. You will notice that in some of the boxes, there are multiple English letters. This is because there is no direct transliteration between the two languages, and some Hebrew letters have multiple sounds. Thus, the Vahv is transliterated as "V," "O," and "U." The Peh is transliterated as "P," "Ph," and "F." You will also note that some English sounds are associated with multiple letters such as the English "K."

To use this glyph to make mystic symbols, simply lay a piece of thin paper over the figure. Draw a small circle in the section where you find the first letter of the word that you wish to symbolize. From that circle, draw a straight line to the space with the second letter of the word. Continue with this pattern until you have completed the word. Draw a short

line across the end of the figure to indicate the end of the word. If you have any double letters in your word, simply draw a loop back to the same section as indicated in the example immediately below for the word "Happy." When you have a situation where there are multiple locations for a letter on the image, choose whichever design you believe looks most aesthetically pleasing. Remove the tracing paper from the Hermetic Rose Cross and you will have your symbolic design as shown for "Happy."

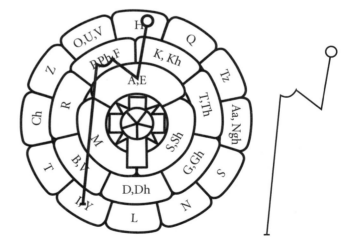

Happy

It is okay to have lines cross over each other. See the example on the next page:

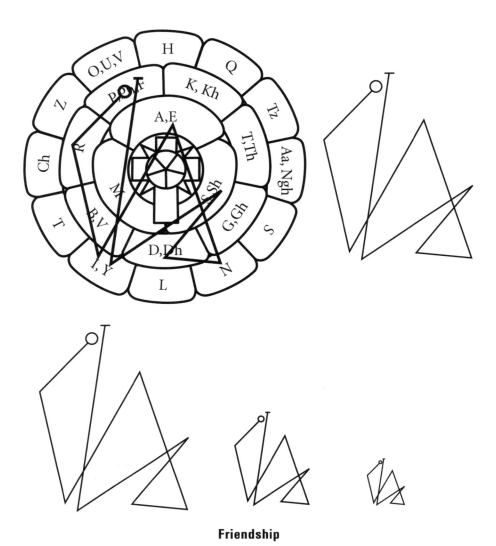

Friendship

Notice that in the above two samples, for the words "happy" and "friendship" I have shown that the symbol, once designed and understood, may have any dimensions. Thus we have another symbol, which can be added to our list of items that can be used to make a talisman.

With what we have thus far it is possible to design quite a nice talisman for friendship. All we need to do is fill up the four squares of our piece of paper with selections from our list. You do not have to use all of the selections from the list, nor should you be limited by the contents of the list.

On the next page is an example drawn from the list we have created. On side one we see a heart, the letter "Vahv," plus the letter name spelled out. We

also see the words "Ruach" and "intellect." Again, all of these ideas are from the list we have compiled.

On the second side we see that the whole side has been shaded golden yellow. In the center is the astrological symbol for the Sun, a circle with a dot at the center. Also on this side is the God name, YHVH El-oh-ah V'dah-aht, and the name of the archangel Raphael, who is the Divine Physician.

On side three is the name of the Sephira, Tiferet, and its meaning, which is "beauty." On either side is found the name of the order of angels, the Malacheem that means "Messengers." In the center is the symbol derived from the system of A. O. Spare.

Finally, on side four are seen the numerological values of the word "friendship" and the symbol drawn from the center of the Hermetic Rose Cross.

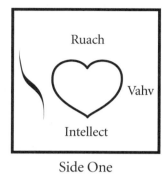

Side One

Shaded Golden Yellow

Side Two

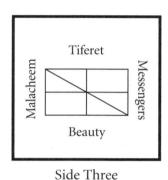

Side Three

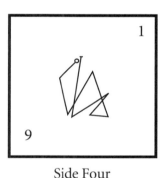

Side Four

It is not necessary to make your talismans absolutely perfect works of art. Merely draw your best and put all of your energies into the construction of the talisman and you will be successful.

In the next lesson you will learn how to make your piece of paper with symbols on it change into a powerful magickal tool. To do so you will also need something in which to place the talisman once it is charged. The easiest way to do this is by getting a felt square of the color appropriate to the Sephira with which you are working. In this case, yellow or gold would be the correct color. Take the square and cut out a piece three inches by five inches. Fold it in half and staple or sew up two of the open sides. You will have a container that is the right size and into which

the charged talisman may be slipped. Don't sew or staple the top until after you have placed the talisman inside! A string may also be attached so that it can be worn as a necklace under your clothes.

Pay Attention to This Secret!

It is important for you to understand that you cannot learn magick by just reading. It takes practice, study, and thinking. If you have not reread, studied, and thought about the previous lessons in this course, you should do so immediately.

As you do so, please remember Dion Fortune's position that there is no room for authority in occultism. As I like to say, "Don't take my word for it. Check it out yourself."

Some writers on the occult will warn you against following instructions in some books because they contain "blinds" with false information to make sure that those who are unwary will not have luck in their magick. So now, I have a secret to reveal. I have purposely included one such blind. It is the only such blind in this book.

The truth is, however, that if you have been reviewing this book as I have consistently suggested, you should have discovered it already. If you paid attention to the information, you would have seen that the Hebrew spelling of the archangelic names used on the elemental weapons *always ends with the letter known as the Lahmed.* Since this has an "l" sound, and archangelic names on all of the tools end with the syllable "-el," this should be obvious. Now look back to Lesson Three where instructions are given on the symbols for the pentacle. The Hebrew spelling of Auriel is missing the Lahmed.

Did you catch this as you studied your lessons and think it was a typographical error? If so, congratulations! You are well on the way to being a thinking, competent magician.

If not, do not feel bad nor despair. If this had been meant to be a trick or a trap I would not have revealed it. Rather, it is a simple lesson that is better learned here than during the performance of a magickal rite! It is important to be certain that everything you are doing and using is correct.

So go over and restudy the lessons up to this point. Don't just read them. Think about them, question them, take the logic presented in them to the limit, and see where it takes you or if it breaks down. In this way you can become an excellent, fearless, powerful magician.

On your pentacle, you should correct your Hebrew by simply adding the additional Lahmed at the end of the name. Auriel looks like this:

Or does it? The Resh and Dallet look very similar. The Zy-in and the Vahv look alike, too. But you've come so far. Don't get paranoid and start doubting yourself. Just remember ol' Davy Crockett: "Make sure you're right . . . then go ahead."

Supplement to Lesson Seven

At this time some of you may be thinking that the information I have presented to you on Kabalistic talismans is incomplete. Why didn't I mention that the numeral 6 could also be used for the friendship talisman, as Tiferet is the sixth Sephira? And what about all those other talismans one can see in books and for sale in occult shops that look nothing like the talismans I have described?

These are fair questions, for which I have two answers. First, the ancient Kabalists made individualized talismans, not mass-produced items. In fact, some were so individualized that various abbreviated Hebrew inscriptions cannot be interpreted even after years of study. Certainly you could copy designs from other sources. But the work and time spent in the designing of your personal talisman is Kabalistically and magickally important. Just the work of designing and creating the talisman adds energy and focus to it. Also, many of the pre-fab talismans have been mutilated and changed over the centuries, making their validity questionable.

Second, and more importantly, this course is meant to be an introduction to ceremonial magick, not the final word. As stated in an earlier lesson, a goal of this course is to allow you to pick up any book on magick, read it, and have enough understanding of it to use what is in the book. (I have to add that over the past several decades some highly advanced magick books have been published that are tremendously difficult for those who do not understand specialized meanings of keywords. But, being very advanced, it would not be a good idea to start off with them, anyway.) I have numerous books on talismans, and to present all of the information in those books, all of the sigils, symbols, and ideas, would take hundreds of pages. If I added the history of those symbols along with their derivation and meanings, it might take up thousands of pages. That simply is not the purpose of these lessons.

However, I think it only fair to present to you in supplement some other symbolic systems for representing planetary influences. Yes, it will be incomplete, but it will show you from where they are derived. If you want, feel free to include them in your talisman making.

The Olympian Spirits of the *Arbatel of Magick*

The book the *Arbatel of Magick* is extremely rare today. It was first published in Latin in 1575 at Basle, and published for the first time in English in London in 1655. It is supposed to contain nine sections, but only one remains (or ever existed). It is known as "Isagogue," or "A Book of the Institutions of Magick." In this work, which is introductory in nature, are given the so-called "Olympian Spirits," each with its own "character" or symbol. There have been a few different versions of symbols associated with the names of these spirits. In the previous edition I gave one of them. After a great deal of research and thought, I have come to the conclusion that the version I gave was not the earliest version, and therefore not what I would consider the most accurate. Below is a version that I now consider to be the most accurate listing of their names, symbols, and the planets to which they correspond:

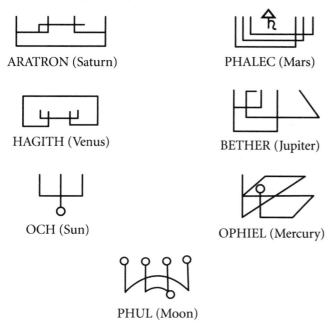

ARATRON (Saturn)

PHALEC (Mars)

HAGITH (Venus)

BETHER (Jupiter)

OCH (Sun)

OPHIEL (Mercury)

PHUL (Moon)

Other symbols you can use on your talisman include the astrological symbols of the planets and their number (which is the same as the number of the Sephira) as follows:

Planet	Number	Symbol
Saturn	3	♄
Mars	5	♂
Venus	7	♀
Moon	9	☽
Jupiter	4	♃
Sun	6	☉
Mercury	8	☿

Notice that there is no planet associated with numbers 1 and 2. This is because the first two Sephiroht are associated with what is called the "first swirlings" (the "Big Bang"?) and the belt of the zodiac. Some modern Kabalists do equate these with the outer planets, but this is debatable and in my opinion there is still too much disagreement to change to anything other than the ancient sources as given here.

You can also see that the "Talismanic Magick" chart does not include the tenth Sephira. This is related to the planet Earth and to the magickal elements of which our planet is composed. It is not needed for our system of talisman making.

Other Designs for the Four-Sided Talisman

It would also be appropriate to cut your talisman into a shape with the number of sides matching the number of the Sephira or planet. The square design is always appropriate as is the circular design with a hinge, as shown below. This design looks like a locket:

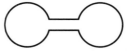

In a similar fashion, an appropriate shape for a Saturn- or Binah-oriented talisman (related to the number 3) is the triangular locket design shown on the next page:

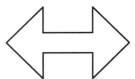

A locket made of nonagons would be associated with the Lunar or Yesodic talisman:

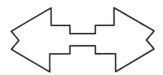

The Geomantic Key to Talismanic Symbolism

Geomancy is an ancient divinatory art with similarities to the I Ching. Originally, dots were made at random with a pointed stick in the soil. The number of these dots was then totaled. If the sum was even, two dots were made to the side. If the number was odd, only one dot was used. A figure made up of four lines of either one or two dots was thus created.

This process was then repeated several times followed by more patterns synthesized from combinations of the original patterns. Finally, all of these figures were placed on a horoscope chart and interpreted according to a set of rules.

When first learning geomancy, it appears complex and difficult. Actually, one becomes quite facile at it with just a few hours of practice. The rules of geomancy are available in several books, including *The Golden Dawn* by Israel Regardie and *The Equinox* by Aleister Crowley.

Each geomantic figure is related to a particular planet. By playing "connect the dots" with the figure you can make a series of designs related to the planets and based on the geomantic symbols. This subject is too complex to discuss fully here, but I want to give you an idea of what the symbols look like so you will recognize them in talismans you may see in various pieces of literature and on pre-fab talismans.

The figure in the next column is the Geomantic figure known as *Carcer* ("kahr-sehr"). It is associated with Saturn in its rulership of Capricorn:

By connecting the dots you can make a variety of designs, including any of these figures:

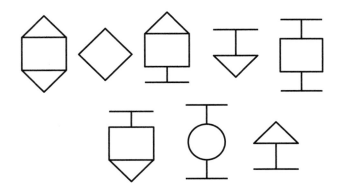

When used on talismans they might be used singly or in groups, as shown in the samples below:

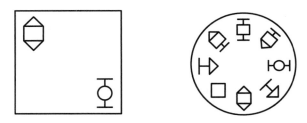

The geomantic figure known as *Acquisitio* ("Akkwih-seet-ee-yoh") represents Jupiter ruling Sagittarius. It looks like this:

A series of more complex figures can be constructed from this figure. Here are some of them:

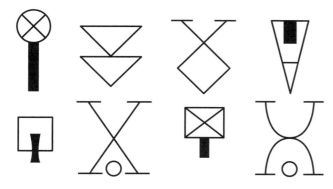

Geomantic symbols used in talismans all have the same style and "feel" as the ones shown above. They are presented here so you can recognize their appearance when you see them. As an example of this, see the book entitled *Raphael's Ancient Manuscript of Talismanic Magic*. It contains many typical talismans that use the above geomantic type symbols. It also uses such things as the written letters of the Enochian or Angelic language (for samples of this language see the Watchtower Ritual).

There are several other books that have examples that you can use as a basis or as a model for your talismans such as *The Black Pullet* and the pseudo 6th–10th Books of Moses.

However . . . you will never be a true magician if all you can do is copy what others have done before you. It is far better to design your own talismans from scratch. This is the way the ancient Kabalists did it, and it is the way you can do it, too. Therefore, I strongly urge you to ignore talismans you have seen presented elsewhere and create your own for now. Later you can copy or borrow as you will.

In many ways the creation of a talisman is like the designing of a magickal ritual. While there are certain rules and patterns to follow, you are allowed a great deal of leeway within those patterns.

Remember, anybody can copy anything or follow a few rules. But magick is more than just copying and learning rules. That is merely the "science" aspect of magick. What you do within the guidelines is the "art" aspect of magick. The best magicians are not mere copyists. They are creative artists of the highest caliber. I hope that by the time you finish this course you will be well on your way to knowing the rules (being a magickal scientist) and being capable of creativity and originality within those rules (being a magickal artist). The person who perfects both of these is a powerful wizard, indeed.

Review

The following questions are designed to help you determine if you have mastered the information in Lesson Seven. Please try to answer them without looking at the text. The answers are in Appendix Two.

1. What is your direct link to the astral plane?

2. To what do the terms "Low Magick" and "High Magick" refer?

3. How is the Kabalistic System of Mental Magick different from Positive Affirmations and Creative Visualization?

4. Give the ways Witches worship Satan.

5. What happened to the first edition of Reginald Scot's *The Discoverie of Witchcraft* and why?

6. What book, published in 1921, sparked an interest in Witchcraft?

7. Why was the book *Witchcraft Today*, by Gerald Gardner, important?

8. Define "talisman."

9. What should you do before performing Grey Magick?

10. What does "skyclad" mean?

11. How many talismans with the same purpose can be charged at the same time? How many with different purposes can be charged at the same time?

12. What is a house "guardian"?

13. What is Theosophical Reduction?

The following questions only you can answer.

1. Are you continuing with your rituals?

2. Is your life changing in any way?

3. What are your feelings about the religion of Wicca? Are you prejudiced against any particular religion?

4. Have you made any talismans yet?

5. Are you keeping your diaries up to date?

6. Can you think of a situation where you would be willing to face the problems of negative karma for doing Black Magick?

Bibliography

For more information on these books, please see the annotated bibliography at the end of these lessons.

Bach, Richard. *Illusions: The Adventures of a Reluctant Messiah*. Arrow Books, 2001.

Buckland, Raymond. *Buckland's Complete Book of Witchcraft*. Llewellyn, 2002.

Cunningham, Scott. *Magical Herbalism*. Llewellyn, 2001.

———. *Wicca: A Guide for the Solitary Practitioner*. Llewellyn, 1993.

Farrar, Janet, and Stewart Farrar. *A Witches' Bible*. Phoenix Publishing, 1996.

Gardner, Gerald. *High Magic's Aid*. Pentacle Enterprises, 1999.

———. *Witchcraft Today*. Citadel, 2004.

Grimassi, Raven. *The Wiccan Mysteries*. Llewellyn, 2002.

———. *Ways of the Strega*. Llewellyn, 2000.

Leitch, Aaron. *Secrets of the Magickal Grimoires*. Llewellyn, 2005.

Patai, Raphael. *The Hebrew Goddess*. Wayne State University Press, 1990.

Regardie, Israel. *The Golden Dawn*. Llewellyn, 2002.

Sheba, Lady. *The Grimoire of Lady Sheba*. Llewellyn, 2001.

Starhawk. *The Spiral Dance*. HarperOne, 1999.

Valiente, Doreen. *An ABC of Witchcraft Past and Present*. Phoenix Publishing, 1988.

———. *Witchcraft for Tomorrow*. Robert Hale, 1993.

LESSON EIGHT

PART ONE

In the previous lesson, as in several other lessons, I have indicated that theoretical perfection is not necessary for successful magickal work. All you need to do is your best. This is an important consideration, as otherwise there would be even fewer real magicians in the world today. Visualization work would be limited to those with textbook-perfect visualization abilities. Vibration of the names and sacred words would be limited to those with a full knowledge of Hebrew, Latin, and Greek (not to mention Egyptian, Chaldean, Enochian, and other languages) and who are also professional quality singers or at least trained in public speaking. Likewise, no talismans would be made, save by artists of the highest rank.

Thankfully, this is not necessary. What *is* necessary is that you do your best—your very best. But what exactly is your best?

Imagine for a moment that you are somebody's supervisor. They turn in a piece of work to you for your approval. Although it is very good, you believe that the worker is capable of better and you tell the worker so. To this the worker replies, "But this is my best work!" You reply that you think the worker is capable of more and want the worker to do the project over. To the pleasure of both of you, the new work is far superior.

This is not just some sort of "strive to do better" philosophy. The fact is that most of us are not even aware of, or awake to, our capabilities and possibilities.

I have a friend who is a novelist. Years ago, when she was starting her career, she asked me to comment on some writing she had done. I told her I would do so only if I could be very honest, and she agreed. I read the pages she sent me and called her on the phone to give her my honest opinion. I dreaded the conversation because I knew her work could be better, much better. Some of the situations were unbelievable. The dialogue was awkward in some places and just inappropriate for the characters elsewhere. As I told her what I thought, I could sense her becoming cold and distant. I knew she was furious with me, and I thought she would never speak to me again after my critique.

A few weeks later I got a call from her. She greeted me with, "You're a mean sonofabitch!" She told me that because I was her friend she valued my opinion and how she couldn't sleep for days, upset over what I had said. Finally, she went to a friend who was a writing instructor and asked for his opinion. He apparently agreed with me on several points. She spent hours rewriting the pages. She read them to me over the phone and I was deeply impressed. She knew that her writing was now much better; I still think it is one of the best things she has ever written. I told her, simply, that I knew she was capable of work as fine as this and I would not let her get away with doing less than her best.

I don't know you as I knew her. I knew what she was capable of and I expected excellence. Because I don't know you, even if I were to watch you practice magick I would have no way of knowing if the work was the best you could do. I have nothing to compare it to. Therefore, the judgment as to the quality of your work cannot be mine or anyone else's. It must be yours. You should objectively look at what you're doing and determine if it is your best work. Just as we are each responsible for our actions, so, too, are we each responsible for doing our best without the prodding of another to excel. This is commonly called "self-actualization." It means that you should not allow yourself to do less than your best. Many times your best is better than you think it can be. Strive to always do the very best you can. Understand what is excellent for you and accept nothing less than excellence from yourself.

If you ever have the opportunity to talk with people who perform and record music for a living, ask them if there is anything they would change on their last album. Having been a musician and knowing many musicians, I will tell you now that to a person they will each tell you that there are many things they would have done differently. They seek perfection, but settle for their best.

Across my room sits a pentacle that I made. Quite frankly, it not only is one of the best things I have ever done, but it is also better than most of the similar pentacles I have seen. Some people have told me that it is incredibly well done. But I see the lines that could be better, the letters, which could be better formed. It came out better than I thought it ever could, but I am still striving for perfection.

Of course, we can never achieve perfection while we are physically alive. I have heard that when craftspeople make Persian rugs they will always put in a wrong thread somewhere because "only Allah is perfect." I am not saying that you should make imperfections in your designs for talismans. Rather, strive for perfection, but accept your best. Remember, though, that your best may be far better than you think.

Let me make clear, then, that the examples of talismans given in this course are just that: samples. You can adjust them as you will, adding or subtracting from them according to what you think is right. Use them as guidelines only. When you actually construct them for use, when they are no longer samples, they need to be your very best.

With this in mind, let's look at another sample talisman:

After being out of work for six months, "Thomas Jones" has just been hired for a new, well-paying job. But over the last several months his debts have piled up. Unless he can get help soon, he may be kicked out of where he lives (the gas, electricity, and phone have already been cut off) and his car will be repossessed. Thomas decides that he would need a thousand dollars to tide him over until his new paychecks start coming in regularly. Notice that in this instance, the desire for money will cover many problems. Thus, in this type of situation, doing a talisman for more money is appropriate.

First, a Tarot divination is done. The results of this divination are very positive, so a list is made of what figures and symbols might be included on the talisman.

A Talisman to Obtain One Thousand Dollars

Keyword: Thousand   Key Symbol: $1,000
Sephira: Hesed   Planet: Jupiter

Perfectionism And Kai Krause

Most people have never heard of Kai Krause. In the 1970s and 1980s he worked on synthesizers, as well as helping on almost thirty movies, receiving an award for his work on the first *Star Trek* film. He moved to computers and especially user interfaces—the way you interact with software. Many of his original concepts—now included in the Windows, Macintosh, and Linux operating system interfaces—revolutionized the approach people have to software design.

In the computer industry he is perhaps most famous for a series of additions or "plug-ins" used in Adobe Photoshop, one of the standard graphics applications, used all over the world. This collection, known as "Kai's Power Tools" or KPT, made it easy for novices to get spectacular graphic effects, so much so that some things that were difficult prior to KPT—such as a corner of a page curling up—became a cliché.

Krause is a true Renaissance man, moving from music to movies to computers to graphic interfaces and some spectacular applications, including one of my personal favorites, Bryce, which allows you to easily create realistic or surreal 3D scenes. Eventually he sold his products and his company to other developers. With the money he purchased a 1,000-year-old castle on the Rhine, which he has named "Byteburg." There, operating under a self-described press embargo, he and a small team are designing software that you and I will be using in the future.

The reason I'm bringing him up is because of a statement he made that impressed me greatly. He wrote, "A true artist never finishes his work, he merely abandons it." *

In this lesson I've really stressed doing the absolute best that you can, adding that often our best is beyond what we think is within our capacity. The problem with trying to do our very best is what I call the "curse of perfectionism."

Perfectionism is more than just wanting to do the best you can possibly do. A perfectionist will work on something over and over and never feel that it is good enough. For the perfectionist, the desire to have something absolutely perfect prevents him or her from finishing anything. I've known some people who have written numerous books but they never even try to get them published or even share them with others because "they're not perfect." This isn't because they're simply writing for themselves. They'd like to see their work published, but no matter what they do, it's never good enough.

Back in Lesson 5, I discussed the concept that one of the traditional Chinese signs of health was clear thinking and precise action. Going over and over a project to try and make it absolutely perfect is the opposite of precise action. In fact, extreme perfectionism can be a symptom of what is called Obsessive-Compulsive Disorder (OCD), something that is not healthy to have, and to overcome it may require years of treatment.

When I write that you should do the best you can, be excellent, and your best may be better than you realize, I'm not talking about being a perfectionist. Yes, do the best you can when you design something, when you do ritual, in fact, when you do *anything*. But I would urge you not to be a perfectionist. Even if you think you could touch up a little here and do a bit more there, a time comes when, as Krause says, you need to just abandon it.

Then make your next project even better!

*Before publication I learned that this concept actually originated with Paul Valéry (1871–1945). He wrote in an essay, "In the eyes of those who anxiously seek perfection, a work is never truly completed—a word that for them has no sense—but abandoned; and this abandonment, of the book to the fire or to the public, whether due to weariness or to a need to deliver it for publication, is a sort of accident, comparable to the letting go of an idea that has become so tiring or annoying that one has lost all interest in it." Other versions have included "A poem is never finished, only abandoned," also attributed to Valéry, but never written by him, and "A painting is never finished, only abandoned," attributed to a variety of people including Picasso.

Selections from Kabalistic Correspondences page:

Sephira number: 4

Sephira meaning: Mercy

Color: Blue

Chakra: Heart

God name: El

Stone: Sapphire; Amethyst

Metal: Tin

Archangel: Tzadkiel

English of Tzadkiel: Justice of God

Angelic Order: Chasmaleem

English of Chasmaleem: Brilliant Ones

Creature: Unicorn

Tool: Wand

Western (Pythagorean) numerology:

for:

T H O U S A N D

$2 + 8 + 6 + 3 + 1 + 1 + 5 + 4 = 30$ $3 + 0 = 3$

In Kabalistic numerology:

Th O U S A N D

$9 + 7 + 6 + 7 + 1 + 5 + 4 = 39$ $3 + 9 = 12$ $1 + 2 = 3$

Interestingly, 3 represents the idea "thousand" in both Western or Pythagorean numerology and Kabalistic numerology.

Here is the sigil for "thousand," taken from the Rose, in various sizes:

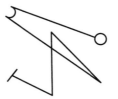

Here is the sigil for the Olympian Spirit Bether:

Here is the astrological symbol of Jupiter: ♃

Here is the system of Spare:

THOUSAND
(without vowels becomes)
THSND

T +	⊤	
add H=		H is on its side
add S=		very angular, stylized letter
add N=		
add D=		angular, stylized letter

Here is the final symbol:

Now, with all of the information on the previous page, let's try a sample talisman to obtain one thousand dollars. Below you will find the sample design. Side one has the symbol from the system of Spare, the number derived from the numerological systems, the number of the Sephira, the name of the Sephira, and its translation.

Side two has the sigil from the Rose, the God name, the archangelic name, and the translation of that name, plus a heart as the symbol of the heart chakra.

Side three has the symbol for Jupiter in the center. Above is an image of a unicorn's horn. Below is a wand and to the left is a tin can. To the right is a gem to represent a sapphire. This whole side is shaded deep blue.

Side four has the sigil of Bether plus the name of the angelic order above and the translation of that name below.

Thus you can see how easy it is to construct a talisman from the information contained so far in this course. I would urge you at this time to try your hand at creating some sample talismans. Try one to help pass a test, to win at gambling or obtain spiritual wisdom. Figure out what your needs are and then try designing some talismans for those purposes.

At this point in your studies I suggest that any talismans you create should be constructed from the information contained in this course. Do not go to outside sources to help you design talismans. This is not meant to hinder you from looking at other sources. I always encourage looking at the works of other writers.

I realize that this sounds like a bit of a contradiction, but it is not. Let me explain why.

The fact of the matter is some books that claim to be showing talismanic symbols give in part or *in*

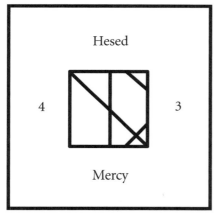

Side One

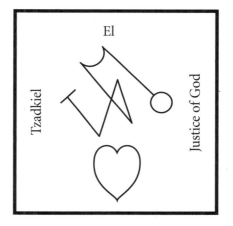

Side Two

Side Three

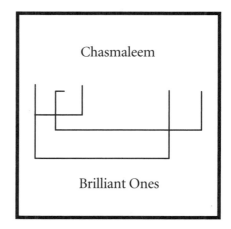

Side Four

toto symbols used to "summon up" spiritual beings, entities, or powers (call them what you will). As an example of this I call your attention to the small book *Secrets of Magical Seals,* by Anna Riva. This book gives a wide variety of symbols with "instructions" on how to use them as talismans. One of the largest sections of this book is dedicated to the "Seals of Solomon" and you are told "an appropriate seal can be found to influence one's special situation or objective."

These "seals" come directly from *The Greater Key of Solomon* and are actually known as "Medals or Pentacles." Their purpose is to strike "terror into the Spirits and . . . [reduce] them to obedience . . . If thou invokest the Spirits by virtue of these Pentacles, they will obey thee without repugnance, and will fear them, and thou shalt see them so surprised by fear and terror, that none of them will be sufficiently bold to wish to oppose thy will."

These are not figures for use on talismans such as we have been discussing. They are protective devices for use in magickal evocations and invocations.

I am not suggesting that you should not look at and study other books. I think I've made it clear that I encourage you to do so. What I am saying is that, for now, follow the instructions in this course. By the end of these lessons you will be able to tell the difference between symbols to be used on talismans and symbols to be used for other purposes. At that time freely choose whatever symbols you wish on your talismans. At this time, I urge you to stick to what is included in this course. Remember, one of the goals of this book is to allow you to pick up and understand any book of magick by the *end* of these lessons, not by the middle!

Let's assume that you have constructed your talisman, after, of course, you have done a divination to discover the outcome of making the device. The next step is to empower it, to charge it, to consecrate it. This brings us to the next section of this lesson.

PART TWO

The charging of a Kabalistic talisman requires more preparation and, to my mind, involvement than does the charging of a Low Magick talisman. This *may* make a Kabalistic talisman more powerful. Remem-

ber, involving the emotions and passion will enhance the power in any ritual. If a ritual is very simple and straightforward, it may not give the practitioner time or direction to deeply involve the emotions, to "enflame thyself with prayer." Note, however, that I used the term "may" rather than "will." All of this depends upon the character of the individual practitioner. If a magician becomes deeply involved in a direct and simple ritual, it can be far more powerful than one where a person simply reads the words and has no passion. In short, whatever you do, whatever appeals to you, perform it with all your heart, spirit, energy, and mind.

In common with the Low Magick talisman, a Kabalistic talisman may be constructed at any time. Another similarity is that Talismans should be charged during the waxing of the Moon and Amulets should be charged during the waning of the Moon. But the *time* for the charging of a Kabalistic talisman is far more precisely defined.

The phases of the Moon each last about two weeks. The Kabalah moves down to a daily structure. Each day is associated with a planet. Monday is a variation for "Moon-day" and is, logically, associated with the Moon. In French, the name of Tuesday is *mardi*, the day of Mars. Tues was the name of a European god who was equated with the god Mars. Similarly, the northern European's Woden's day became Wednesday. In French it is *mercredi*, the day of Mercury. Thor's day became Thursday. Thor relates to the god Jupiter, and in French *jeudi* means "Jupiter's day" and is the name for Thursday. Freya's day became Friday. In French this is *vendredi* or "the day of Venus." Saturn's day and "Sun-day" are obvious.

From this information we see that each day is associated with a planet:

Monday	=	Moon
Tuesday	=	Mars
Wednesday	=	Mercury
Thursday	=	Jupiter
Friday	=	Venus
Saturday	=	Saturn
Sunday	=	Sun

If we are going to make a talisman associated with the Sephira Hesed and the planet Jupiter, it would make sense to charge that talisman on the day associated with that planet, Thursday. But there's more. For the charging of the Kabalistic talisman gets even more precise than moving to a day of the week.

Our numerical system is a decimal system known as "base 10." Practically everything numerical is centered on 10. This, however, has not always been the case. At one time base 12 was very important and may have been the dominant mathematical system. There are still many remnants of base 12. In English there are special names for the first 12 numbers. After that the numbers are combinations such as three-ten (thirteen), four-ten (fourteen), twenty-five, thirty-six, etc. There is no "oneteen" or "two-teen." Furthermore, there are 12 inches in a foot, not 10 inches. There are solar 12 months in a year even though there are 13 lunar cycles. There are 12 constellations in the zodiacal belt, although more or less could have been chosen. As an example, the constellation Cetus, the Whale, is within the zodiacal belt, but is ignored by most astrologers.

The day is split into 24 hours. Dividing this in half, we find that there are two periods of 12 hours each. It is logical to think that there are 12 daylight hours and 12 darkness hours. While this is nice to assume on a theoretical basis, the complicating fact is that this precise 12-and-12 day only occurs twice during the year: on the equinoxes.

The ancient Kabalists did divide the day into 24 hours and associated each hour with a planet. There have been a few variations on the following list, but I have found the one shown on the next page, taken from *The Greater Key of Solomon*, to be the most accurate.

This Table of Magickal or Planetary Hours shows that each hour is associated with a planet. If you go back and look at the page of Kabalistic correspondences in Lesson Three, you will see that there are no planets associated with either Keter or Hochma. If you make a talisman associated with either of these two Sephiroht, it can be charged at any hour. Those talismans associated with the other Sephiroht are most effective when charged during the appropriate magickal or Planetary Hour. Charging them at other times is fine, but may lessen their effectiveness.

It is important that you understand the comments under the Table of Planetary or Magickal Hours. These Magickal Hours are astronomical in nature and are not based upon the ticks or inaudible hum of common clocks. Planetary Hours are *not* the same as our regular sixty-minute hours.

Here are the steps to find out how long a Planetary Hour is:

1. Divide the number of minutes between sunrise and sunset by 12. This gives you the length of a daylight hour.

2. Subtract the number of minutes in a daylight Magickal Hour from 120 (the number of minutes in two regular or "clock" hours). This gives you the number of minutes in a nighttime Magickal Hour that occurs between sunset and sunrise.

Example: Let's say that the sun rises at 5:00 A.M. and sets at 7:00 P.M. This gives us a daylight period of 14 hours or (multiply by 60 minutes per clock hour) 840 minutes. Divide this by 12 and we get a Magickal daylight hour of 70 minutes. This means that the first Magickal Hour will run from 5:00 A.M. to 6:10 A.M. The second will run from 6:10 A.M. to 7:20 A.M., etc.

Subtracting 70 (the minutes in a daylight Magickal Hour) from 120 (the number of minutes in two clock hours) you will see that a nighttime Magickal Hour on this day lasts 50 minutes. Continuing with the above example, we can see that the first evening Magickal Hour will last from 7:00 P.M. to 7:50 P.M. The second evening Magickal Hour will run from 7:50 P.M. to 8:40 P.M., etc.

Obviously, this entire process could be reversed. You could determine the length of time from sunset to sunrise and divide it by twelve to first find the length of a nighttime Magickal Hour. It will work both ways. The important thing to remember is that *Planetary or Magickal Hours are based on the length of time between sunset and sunrise, sunrise and sunset. They are not based on sixty-minute hours.*

For some reason, many students seem to have difficulty working out the Magickal Hours. Usually this

Table of Planetary or Magickal Hours

	Sunday	Monday	Tuesday	Wednesday	Thursday	Friday	Saturday
Sunrise							
1st Hour	Sun	Moon	Mars	Mercury	Jupiter	Venus	Saturn
2nd Hour	Venus	Saturn	Sun	Moon	Mars	Mercury	Jupiter
3rd Hour	Mercury	Jupiter	Venus	Saturn	Sun	Moon	Mars
4th Hour	Moon	Mars	Mercury	Jupiter	Venus	Saturn	Sun
5th Hour	Saturn	Sun	Moon	Mars	Mercury	Jupiter	Venus
6th Hour	Jupiter	Venus	Saturn	Sun	Moon	Mars	Mercury
7th Hour	Mars	Mercury	Jupiter	Venus	Saturn	Sun	Moon
8th Hour	Sun	Moon	Mars	Mercury	Jupiter	Venus	Saturn
9th Hour	Venus	Saturn	Sun	Moon	Mars	Mercury	Jupiter
10th Hour	Mercury	Jupiter	Venus	Saturn	Sun	Moon	Mars
11th Hour	Moon	Mars	Mercury	Jupiter	Venus	Saturn	Sun
12th Hour	Saturn	Sun	Moon	Mars	Mercury	Jupiter	Venus
Sunset							
1st Hour	Jupiter	Venus	Saturn	Sun	Moon	Mars	Mercury
2nd Hour	Mars	Mercury	Jupiter	Venus	Saturn	Sun	Moon
3rd Hour	Sun	Moon	Mars	Mercury	Jupiter	Venus	Saturn
4th Hour	Venus	Saturn	Sun	Moon	Mars	Mercury	Jupiter
5th Hour	Mercury	Jupiter	Venus	Saturn	Sun	Moon	Mars
6th Hour	Moon	Mars	Mercury	Jupiter	Venus	Saturn	Sun
7th Hour	Saturn	Sun	Moon	Mars	Mercury	Jupiter	Venus
8th Hour	Jupiter	Venus	Saturn	Sun	Moon	Mars	Mercury
9th Hour	Mars	Mercury	Jupiter	Venus	Saturn	Sun	Moon
10th Hour	Sun	Moon	Mars	Mercury	Jupiter	Venus	Saturn
11th Hour	Venus	Saturn	Sun	Moon	Mars	Mercury	Jupiter
12th Hour	Mercury	Jupiter	Venus	Saturn	Sun	Moon	Mars

Magickal or Planetary Hours are not the same as regular daily hours. Divide the total time between sunrise and sunset by 12. This will give you the length of the Magickal Hours of the day. Dividing the time between sunset and sunrise by 12 will give you the length of the Planetary Hours of the night. The hours of the day and night will be of different lengths except on the equinoxes.

lasts until they try to work out a set of Magickal Hours for one day. If, therefore, the Planetary Hours are not clear to you right away, try working out a day or two. The sunrise and sunset times are listed in most daily newspapers in the weather section. Many sporting goods stores also have lists of these times. The can also be found in *Llewellyn's Daily Planetary Guide*.

I am aware of a few computer programs that will automatically work out the Planetary Hours for you. These are great timesavers, and if you have computer access and can find such a program, I would suggest you to use it. However, knowing how to determine the Magickal Hours is an easy and quick skill to develop and master. I would encourage you to do so. Besides, what would you do if the power was out or you had no access to computer for your use?

I advise you to become familiar with the technique but use timesavers when available.

Playing All the Bases

Codes such as are used in Gematria, Notarikon, and Temura are an important part of the Kabalah. I find it curious that modern Kabalists have not yet worked with our modern understanding of base systems.

Most commonly, we use base 10. The number just to the left of the decimal point is the "one's place." You multiply the number that appears there by 1 to determine its value. Thus, if you have 7.0, 7 x 1 = 7. The next place is the ten's place, then the hundred's place, etc.

There is a saying that base 12, as used on clocks, the zodiac, etc., is just like base 10 if you had 12 fingers instead of 10. It, too, has a 1's place, but needs 12 numerals to fill it up. Let's use the numerals 0–9 followed by letters "A" and "B." In base 12 the number 7.0 equals 7.0 in base 10. But the number "A.0" in base 12 equals 11 in base 10. The next place over is not the ten's place, it's the twelve's place. In base 10, 32.0 equals (3 x 10) + (2 x 1). In base 12, 32.0 equals (3 x 12) + (2 x 1), or 38 in base 10. The next place over in base 12 is the 144's place (12 squared). 243.0 in base 12 is (2 x 144) + (4 x 12) + (3 x 1), or 339.0 in base 10.

Computers are focused around base 2. This is because modern computers use microprocessors filled with millions of microscopic switches that can be either on or off, represented by the numerals 1 or 0. In base 2, as you move to the left of the decimal point there is the 1's place, 2's place, 4's place, 16's place, etc. However, when you go beyond our modern "high level" programming languages, computers use "machine language," which is often centered on a base 16 system. Since we don't have 16 numerals, machine language uses a combination of numerals and letters in a code know as *hexadecimal*. Instead of using the numerals 0 to 9 as we do in base 10, hexadecimal uses 0, 1, 2, 3, 4, 5, 6, 7, 8, 9, A, B, C, D, E, and F. Programming languages such as C++ have converters so you can use the high-level language and allow it to convert to the low-level instructions, making programming easier.

I built the first real computer I ever used out of a kit I purchased from a company called PAIA. It used an Intel 6802 microprocessor. The computer allowed me to program a music synthesizer, also built from a kit, from PAIA. To use it, I used a keypad to arduously enter sets of numbers and letters. It was incredibly time consuming.

It seems to me that some enterprising Kabalist will work out a coding system using a base system such as this. Maybe you can come up with something? Try it out and use a web page to let people know how it works.

And yes, base 16 is just like base 10 . . . if you have sixteen fingers!

Times for Charging Kabalistic Talismans

BEST: On the day and in the hour associated with the planet appropriate to your working.

EXCELLENT: On any day, in the hour of the appropriate planet.

LEAST ACCEPTABLE: Other times.

EXCEPTIONS: Keter and Hochma, which are not associated with planets.

Phases of the Moon should be observed.

In the last lesson we designed a talisman for friendship that was associated with the planet Sol, the Sun. First let me say that I do know that the Sun is not what we would today consider a planet. However, the word "planet" means "wanderer." Those bodies in the skies, which moved faster than the slow turn of the stars, were considered to be wanderers or planets. Since the Sun and Moon appear to move faster than the backdrop of stars from our Earth-centered point of view, for magickal purposes they are considered planets.

The best time to charge this talisman would be on the day associated with the planet, Sunday, in the Magickal Hour of the Sun. But let us assume that today is Monday and we do not wish to wait for Sunday to come around to charge the talisman. Let us further assume that, because we work all day, we wish to charge the talisman in the evening.

We can see from the previous chart that on Monday the Sun is related to the seventh Magickal Hour after sunset. If we also go by the example given earlier of 50-minute magickal evening hours and sunset is at 7:00 P.M., we can develop the following chart:

After Sunset	Planet	Time
1st Hour	Venus	7:00–7:50 P.M.
2nd Hour	Mercury	7:50–8:40 P.M.
3rd Hour	Moon	8:40–9:30 P.M.
4th Hour	Saturn	9:30–10:20 P.M.
5th Hour	Jupiter	10:20–11:10 P.M.
6th Hour	Mars	11:10 P.M. to Midnight
7th Hour	Sun	Midnight to 12:50 A.M., etc.

So on this particular Monday the evening Planetary Hour of the Sun does not come until the midnight hour. It may happen that this would not be a good time for us to do the ritual. Perhaps we may have to arise early in the morning and do not wish to stay up quite that late.

On Tuesday evening, however, the Planetary Hour of the Sun comes only four Magickal Hours after sunset. Since the times would be very close with only a day difference, this would mean that on this particular Tuesday the evening Magickal Hour of the Sun would last from about 9:30 to 10:20 P.M. with perhaps a few minutes' difference at most. In this theoretical example, the Tuesday evening hour works out fine, so we decide to charge the talisman during the hour of the Sun on Tuesday evening.

Remember, a talisman itself is nothing but inert material. It must be activated by the forces of higher planes and guided by our Will. Even if you go to an occult store and buy an expensive (and frequently poorly or incorrectly made) talisman, it is still inert until it is charged. The effect of the following ritual is to endow an inert and impotent "thing" with balanced motion in a given direction.

The Simple Talisman Charging and Consecrating Ritual

Part One

1. Set up your altar as per your regular ritual practice.
2. Put on your altar the talisman, ready to be charged.
   a. It should already have been designed and constructed.
   b. According to the Moon's phase it should be deemed a Talisman or Amulet.

c. A bag to hold it, such as already described, should lie next to the talisman on the altar.

d. A divination should have been done to determine the outcome of the magickal operation. A decision to perform the rite, based on the divination, should have been made.

e. A word or short phrase should be determined to represent the talisman.

3. You should take a ritual cleansing bath as previously described in this course.

Part Two

At the appropriate hour (in the case of our example, the hour of the Sun) begin the ritual with the following:

1. The Relaxation Ritual.

2. The Lesser Banishing Ritual of the Pentagram.

3. The Banishing Ritual of the Hexagram.

4. The Middle Pillar Ritual (do *NOT* do the Circulation of the Body of Light).

Part Three

1. Change the energy flowing through you as a result of the Middle Pillar Ritual by the use of your imagination and Will to the color of the appropriate Sephira. In the case of our example you would use pure gold or yellow.

2. Pick up the talisman and hold it between your hands. Direct the energy controlled in the Middle Pillar down your arms, into your hands, and thus into the talisman. Feel it flow!

3. Say:

a. **Come, oh** [vibrate name of the Angelic Order], **servants to God. Surround, Consecrate and charge this talisman!** [Re-vibrate name of Angelic Order.]

b. **Oh** [vibrate name of Archangel], **help thy humble servant and consecrate and charge this talisman!** [Re-vibrate name of Archangel.]

c. **I invoke the power of** [vibrate God name]**!!! Charge and consecrate this talisman for thy name's sake!** [Re-vibrate God name.]

In our example, the name of the Angelic Order is "Malacheem" and the Archangel is "Raphael." The God name is "Yud-Heh-Vahv-Heh El-oh-ah V'dah-aht." These can be found on the first list of Kabalistic correspondences. I hope you are beginning to see just how important that page of information is.

4. Using the predetermined word or short phrase, say, out loud, the purpose of the talisman.

5. Hold the talisman flat in your left hand. Pick up the Rainbow Wand by the band of color associated with the planet with which you are working. To do this you must know which planet is said to rule which sign.

Sign	Planet
Aries	Mars
Taurus	Venus (loving security, luxury)
Gemini	Mercury
Cancer	Moon
Leo	Sun
Virgo	Mercury (more practical than Gemini)
Libra	Venus
Scorpio	Mars (energy and instability)
Sagittarius	Jupiter
Capricorn	Saturn (outgoing, seeking change)
Aquarius	Saturn (erratic, revolutionary energy)
Pisces	Jupiter (easily changeable, kind, receptive)

As you can see, some of the planets have dual rulership over signs. In the above chart you are given the information necessary to decide which band of the Rainbow Wand to hold. In our example, you would hold the yellow band, the band associated with the sign of Leo, which is ruled by the Sun.

Holding the Rainbow Wand by the appropriate band, make an Invoking Earth Pentagram over the talisman. This pentagram should not be made horizontally, but vertically, like the pentagrams in the LBRP, but smaller. You will find that your wand is horizontal, parallel to the earth. The black end of the Rainbow Wand should be slightly lower than the white end. It should never be higher than the white end.

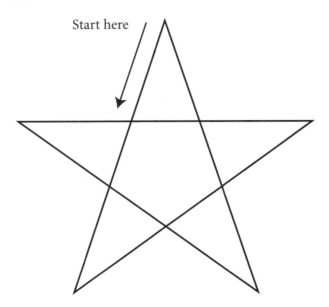

Start here

The Invoking Earth Pentagram

If you have not as yet constructed your Rainbow Wand, or if it is an emergency and you do not have your Rainbow Wand handy, you can use the blade with which you perform the LBRP or your right index finger.

6. Now, inhale, and thrust the black end of the Rainbow Wand (or dagger or finger) at the center of the pentagram you have formed while you exhale and vibrate the appropriate God name. In the case of our example it is Yud-Heh-Vahv-Heh El-oh-ah V'dah-aht.

7. Repeat steps 5 and 6 to total the number of the Sephira with which the talisman is associated. In our example we would perform steps 5 and 6 for a total of six times, six being the number of Tiferet.

8. Say firmly and meaningfully:

SO MOTE IT BE!

9. Place the talisman in the container you have prepared for it.

Part Four

1. Perform the Banishing Ritual of the Hexagram.

2. Perform the Lesser Banishing Ritual of the Pentagram.

3. Record results in your magickal or ritual diary.

The ritual is complete

Notes

1. Before doing any Grey Magick, such as talismanic magick, always do a divination, such as with Tarot cards, to learn if it is a good idea to do this magick.

2. You can charge several talismans for the same purpose at the same time, but you should not try to charge several talismans for different purposes at the same time, even if they are associated with the same Sephirah or planet.

3. Keep the talisman on your person or very close to you at all times. With a string you can make the bag that contains the talisman into a pendant on a necklace. If you are giving the talisman to another person:

   a. before doing anything, ask their permission to do the magick.

   b. have that person keep the talisman near or on his/her body.

4. Destroy the talisman (burn and throw the ashes to the wind or place them in running water or bury them) once it has achieved its intended purpose. If you set a time limit on the talisman, destroy it at the end of that period even if it does not seem like it has achieved its goal. It may have only started the motion to the desired end.

This form of magick is quite solitary in nature. Obviously, nobody else is necessary to allow you to perform the charging and consecration of a talisman. However, this Simple Talisman Charging and Consecration Ritual does make a wonderful and powerful group rite.

Rather than repeating the entire ritual, I am just going to give you notes on how this ritual magick can be turned into ceremonial magick.

Keys to Performing the Simple Talisman Charging and Consecrating Ritual with a Group

STEP ONE. Everyone in the group should be informed of the purpose of the talisman. They all should be together when the divination is performed. Everyone should agree on performing the ritual.

STEP TWO. All present should take ritual baths.

STEP THREE. If there is a leader, that person should sit in the east unless the leader is the person charging the talisman.

STEP FOUR. The LBRP and BRH should be performed by the group as described earlier in this course.

STEP FIVE. All present should do the Middle Pillar Ritual.

STEP SIX. When the person doing the charging feels everyone is together (hint: try to synchronize breathing), he or she should tell everyone to change the pure white energy of the Middle Pillar to the color associated with this talisman.

STEP SEVEN. Let the person doing the charging direct everyone else to send the energy down his or her arms and into him or her, the person doing the actual charging. When the person doing the ritual senses the energy, that person should recite the invocations. However, all present should vibrate the names of the Angelic Order, the Archangel, and the God name.

STEP EIGHT. This idea is continued when doing the Invoking Earth Pentagram. All present should vibrate the God name. By the way, the purpose of

this part of the ritual is to bring into the Earth Plane (hence the invoking earth pentagram) the energies from higher planes.

STEP NINE. All present should be inside the magickal circle. No interested bystanders remaining outside the circle should be allowed.

STEP TEN. Either the BRH or the LBRP may be repeated at the end of the ritual or the leader of the group (not necessarily the one doing the ritual) may come before the altar and say:

I thank all ye creatures who have watched and joined in our ritual. Return now to your abodes and habitations and harm none on your way. Let there be peace between thee and we. And may the blessings of [vibrate] YEH-HAH-SHU-AH YEH-HOH-VAH-SHA, as you are able to receive them, be upon thee.

The leader then taps the altar or ground with the bottom (black) end of the rainbow wand ten times in a 3-4-3 pattern (/// //// ///) and says:

I now declare this temple duly closed.

STEP ELEVEN. If desired, the BRH and LBRP plus the leader's closing may be used, but unless the leader feels there are unusual circumstances (such as the atmosphere feeling very "crowded" with energy or entities), doing both is not necessary.

PART THREE

One of the famous stories concerning S. L. MacGregor Mathers, a founder and driving force behind the Golden Dawn, concerns peas. It seems that he had some enemies within the order and he wished to get rid of them. So he took some peas and, according to the story, he "baptized" them with the same names as the people of whom he wished to be free. Then he swirled them in a sieve with the idea being that as the peas went down the sieve, so, too, would his enemies have a downfall.

Several people I know who claim to be occultists have made fun of Mathers over this. They felt that Mathers, the head and guide of the Golden Dawn, should have used ceremonial magick techniques and not what seems like Low Magick. It is certainly possible that the exact details of Mathers' actions were incorrectly reported or misinterpreted, because I doubt that Mathers would have let any uninitiated person watch him perform the ritual. Isn't it possible that Mathers or the initiated person reporting this episode used expressions such as "peas," "baptize," and "sieve" as a "blind" to non-initiates? Initiates would be able to figure out that these were code words for other ideas, and non-initiates would have a small idea of magickal processes at best, and not be able to understand the codes. I think that this may not only be possible, but is likely.

I have talked before about the meaning of initiation, and wish to bring it up again. In most initiations the candidate is blindfolded, brought into a new and unfamiliar situation, and then taught about his or her new surroundings. This is similar in nature to the birth process. First, everything is dark. Then you are thrust into a new situation about which you need to learn. Initiation is a type of rebirth. In fact, some occultists claim, much to the consternation of Christian fundamentalists, that when the Bible discusses being "born again" what is really being discussed is the idea of initiation. What is baptism if it is not an initiation into a particular religion with its accompanying belief system? Did not, according to the Bible, Jesus tell his inner group that some things they would understand, but to the masses he must speak in parables? (Hmm. That inner group had twelve disciples/initiates. Twelve plus one is the number typically associated with small groups such as covens. And that total, thirteen, could just be symbolic of unity—remember that thirteen is the numerological value of the Hebrew word *echod*, which means "one"—and is therefore a metaphor for God. Lots of fascinating possibilities here.) One function of initiation is that of being born a second time into a new, more spiritual way of life. Any valid initiation ritual has this quality. You may wish to look at some books with initiation rituals in them to see whether or not this is correct.

I feel that it is possible that in the story about Mathers, "peas" were used as a code name for "talismans." "Baptize" could be a code word for "initiate" and "sieve" a code word for the process of focusing mind power. Admittedly, this is just speculation. But if it is correct, what Mathers was doing would be *strict* Golden Dawn-style ceremonial magick.

An initiation (or baptism) can give a person a new or second life. Does it not follow that something inert, something without a life force, can be given a life force, can be born for the first time and given life by the initiation process? The Golden Dawn believed so, and as a result of my personal experience, I agree.

On the next few pages I will be giving a Complete Ritual for Charging and Consecrating a talisman. It will be your longest ritual so far and may take up to two hours to perform, although one to one-and-a-half is more the norm. So, before starting, I want to show you how it works and describe the various sections of the ritual.

The first phase, of course, is the preparations. This means planning out the ritual, gathering all necessary tools, designing and constructing the talisman, doing the divination, preparing the area and yourself (cleansing), setting up the temple, etc. This should all be finished just before the start of the appropriate Magickal Hour.

The second phase of this ritual is the Watchtower Ritual. This should take at least fifteen to twenty minutes by itself.

The third phase is not done in the Simple Talisman Charging and Consecration Ritual. In this phase you enliven, you actually give a form of life to the talisman, via an abbreviated initiation ritual.

Phase four includes charging the talisman by the names and symbols of the appropriate cosmic forces or beings.

The fifth phase is the empowering of the talisman, by force of Will, charging it to achieve a specific goal.

Finally, phase six concludes the ritual with the Closing by Watchtower as described earlier in this course.

Most rituals reach their highest peak of effectiveness when they are memorized. You can focus on the ritual rather than reading. Memorizing the LBRP, the Middle Pillar and Circulation of the Body of Light, the BRH and Rose Cross Ritual can make them better and more effective. For most forms of Grey Magick, memorization is impractical, as there are so many changes. Thus, it is a good idea to make up note cards with writing big enough so that you can read the words of the ritual. I use a music stand to support 8½ x 11 inch cardstock sheets for the purpose. Thin sheets of paper tend to slip and fall down. You may wish to do something similar. Years ago, I used a marker pen so that the words would be bold enough for me to read in dim light. Today, I use my computer and printer, making the text large and clear. This also allows me to edit the text easily.

If your Magickal Hour is only fifteen or twenty minutes long, how can you fit a two-hour ritual into it? The answer is that phases one, two, and three can be done just before the start of the Magickal Hour. Parts four and five should occur within the designated Planetary Hour for greatest effectiveness. Part six may occur after the end of the Planetary or Magickal Hour.

As you follow through this ritual you will find nothing difficult nor unusual, with perhaps one exception. At various times you will see the words "ad-lib." This is an abbreviation for the Latin *ad libitum*, the exact translation of which means "at one's pleasure." However, it is generally taken to mean that you should improvise and do something that is spontaneous and without any sort of specific advanced planning. Of course, all of the training and practice you do is a form of general advanced planning, and the more ritual you do, the easier such ritualistic ad-libbing becomes. The important aspect of this is that the specifics of what you do should be both spontaneous and from the heart with only the form being practiced. In these sections you are to freely add whatever words or actions you deem appropriate for the purpose of that section of the ritual.

If you have been practicing the teachings of this course, such ad-lib work is not as hard as you might think. It's funny—surveys have shown that the number one fear of most people is speaking in public. That means people are more afraid of public speaking than they are of becoming crippled, facing a debilitating disease, or dying! The more you practice, however—and in this case that means the more you do the rituals of these lessons—the easier it becomes. And when it's easy to do by yourself, it becomes easier when in front of a group. Confidence is the key, and confidence comes from knowing that you can ad-lib ritual sections easily and effortlessly. The only way you can know this is by doing it, first by yourself, and then with others.

For example, let us assume that there was an invocation followed by the word "ad-lib." Here is an example, just pulled off the top of my head, which would be appropriate:

Oh my Lord AH-DOH-NYE, Thou hast permitted me to venture this far into Thy temple of the mysteries. By Thy glory, do not deny your servant now. Fill this talisman with Thy presence for *Thy* name's sake, not mine. For to Thee is the kingdom and the power and the glory until eternity fades to nothingness. So mote it be!

It does not have to be long, although it may be. In the previous editions *of Modern Magick* I wrote:

It may seem stilted or artificial, yet it is still a good idea to dress it up with pseudo-Old[e] English. This serves the same function as does the putting on of the [magickal] robe. The robe indicates that you are not doing everyday things. The affected speech shows that you are not talking with your next-door neighbor.

For me this still holds true. There is something about the "thees" and "thys" that affects me on a very deep level. However, this section I'm describing is meant to be ad-lib, so it should be at *your* pleasure, not mine. Try using the pseudo–Olde English and, if you desire, try modern English. If you know it, try other languages. See what works best for you and which is the most effective.

Finally, the most important part of these ad-lib sections is that they must be from your heart and be meaningful and deeply felt. They should also be filled with passion—enflame thyself with prayer! Otherwise they are useless phrases, about as attractive to the gods as are dead flowers to us mortals.

The Complete Ritual for Charging and Consecrating a Talisman

Part One: The Preparations

Begin by physically cleansing your working area. If it has a hard floor, mop it, or at least vacuum. If you have an air filter that rids the air of dust particles, leave it on in your working area for a few hours before cleansing with vacuum and/or water. Wash and polish all of your magickal tools, too. If you have some nice music you can play in the background while you do this physical preparation it would be nice. Gentle "New Age" music, especially those pieces without strong rhythms or standard Western harmonies, are appropriate.

The whole of these preparations should not be thought of in terms of "work." Rather, you should think of these things in the terms of getting dressed up to go out on a Saturday night. While doing this physical cleaning, you should direct your thoughts to clearing the area of all unwanted or negative influences.

Once this physical cleaning has been completed, set up your working area so that it becomes your temple. Place appropriately colored candles around so that you will have enough light. However, since you will be leaving the area for a while, if there is even a remote possibility of flame or dripping wax starting a fire, don't light them yet. (It would be wise to have a fire extinguisher handy when rituals include flames.) Have all of your tools on the altar and, most importantly, have your already constructed talisman and a holder-bag for it on the altar, too. Make sure you have your instructions for the ritual close by.

When you have completed the above work, go to the doorway of the room that contains your prepared temple and look the room over. If it is as perfectly prepared as possible, spend a moment congratulating yourself on a job well done. Then, take a deep breath, and as you exhale, say:

Thank you, O Lord, Grand Architect of the Universe, for Thy permission to construct this temple as a tiny, pale echo of Thy greater creation. May Thy blessings fall upon it for Thy name's sake. So mote it be!

Then close the door so that nobody else can enter the room. Lock the door if necessary. Note that besides asking for the grace of Divinity upon the temple, we are also calling the temple a small version of the entirety of the Universe; the microcosm to the macrocosm of the cosmos. As above, so below. In this way the altar becomes the exact center of the universe, the meeting place of balance and harmony for all elemental and planetary forces, all spiritual and physical powers.

The next step is to turn off the telephone or cell phone so that its ring will not disturb you. If you live with other people and cannot do this, tell them you do not wish to be disturbed for the next few hours, and should the phone ring and be for you, ask them to please take a message.

Finally, take a ritual cleansing bath as already described. When finished, put on your ritual robe or special clothes reserved for ritual work. If you have any special magickal jewelry, now is the time to put it on, too. As you put on your garments and jewelry, say:

Blessed art Thou, O Lord, Maker of the Universe, who usest Thy universe as but a footstool: for Thou hast allowed me to don the robes of the magickal art [or say something similar ad-lib].

Upon completion of your ritual bath and donning of the robe, it should be the time to enter your temple. By this I mean it should be the start of the appropri-

Another Approach to Prepatory Work:
The *Mitzvah*

Work. Generally, people think of work as, well, *work*. It's something you gotta do. It's appropriate that "work" is a four-letter word as are some other powerful swear words. If you're a creative person, having to work to pay rent, taxes, bills, etc., takes you away from your creative endeavors. Work, well, sometimes work just sucks. Big time.

So when you think of the preparatory work you do with your ritual space and tools, you may sigh and grudgingly do it. In the body of these lessons I suggested that you consider it work in the sense of the work you do on yourself to get ready to go out on a Saturday night. You know—any shaving you might do, taking a shower, picking the right clothes, getting dressed, changing clothes when you don't like the way the ones you picked look on you, driving to where you're going, etc. That's real work.

Of course, maybe you don't think of it in that way. Maybe this metaphor doesn't work for you at all. After all, vacuuming a room is *not* the same as blow-drying your hair.

Let me present another approach. It's based on the Hebrew word *mitzvah*.

Mitzvah is a curious word in that it has two contrasting meanings that are both valid. First, it means "a commandment." In the Bible, it's something you are commanded to do by God. Normally, when we think of something we have to do we think of it as work. If your parents tell you to do your homework, or if your boss tells you to finish a report, those are more than just requests, they're commandments. You have to do them, and doing them entails work.

However, mitzvah has a second meaning: a blessing. Specifically, it is a blessing—and you receive blessings from God—when you do the work. So yes, some task may be work, but you'll be blessed and honored for doing it.

Perhaps this is the metaphor that will work best for you. Instead of thinking of the preparatory tasks before a ritual as work, think of them as a blessing. The blessing you'll receive is greater ritual success.

Remember, magick takes place all the time, 24/7. Although the ritual per se supercharges and focuses the magick, what you do before and after is also important. If your cleaning is second-rate and perfunctory, your actions will be countering the effects of the ritual. So if you want the blessing of a highly successful ritual, approach the pre-ritual work as if it a mitzvah. Yes, it's something you have to do, but it's also a blessing leading to greater magickal success when you do it.

ate magickal Planetary Hour, or early enough so that the important body of the ritual will take place during that time frame. If it is too early, it is okay to enter the temple but you should not begin the ritual. Rather, you should sit in quiet contemplation until the correct beginning time. Think about what you are going to do in a few minutes. Consider the months and hours you have put in practicing the rituals, doing the spiritual exercises, and earning yourself the right to do the ritual you will be performing shortly. And, of course, also think about the awe and majesty of the Divine Source of all.

Wax On, Wax Off, Wax Watch Out!

When I give warnings concerning being careful about open fires, I'm serious. An unattended lit candle can cause a fire that can literally change lives.

Many years ago, there was an occult shop in Hollywood, California, sponsored by a group known as "The Brotherhood of the Ram." Some people have alleged they were a cult that may have been involved with another group, which, again, some have called a cult, known as "The Process," which, it has been alleged, may have been loosely associated with Charles Manson and his "family."

The shop changed hands over the years, including changing names. It became the Ram Occult Center in 1971. Some of the people who ran it were also involved in a collection of carnival sideshow exhibits and presented them next door (and upstairs) to the shop in a "Weird Museum." This theater of the bizarre displayed such things as the supposed bones of Vlad Tepes the Impaler, who was fictionalized as Dracula; the supposed head of "Landru," known as Blackbeard, who murdered his wives; and a boy with two heads. The latter was a malformed fetus that had spontaneously aborted and was now in a bottle of formaldehyde. Years ago, sideshows at carnivals frequently used fetuses in formaldehyde with overstated claims about the exhibit in order to bring in the "rubes." Between themselves, the carneys who operated the exhibits referred to them as "pickled punks."

The group also used the upstairs rooms for doing rituals. In July 1984, someone left some candles burning after a ritual. The result was a fire that caused a lot of destruction. Investigators found the exhibits and demanded explanations for human bones, fetuses, and the like. Naturally, the result ended up in the newspaper, along with all sorts of bizarre and incorrect guesses and rumors as to the uses for these odd items. The fact that they were sideshow exhibits was ignored.

The shop eventually moved and changed its name, becoming Pan Pipes. In 1995 the shop was purchased by actress and star of such movies as *The Craft*, Fairuza Balk (who, it turned out, lived just two blocks from my apartment in Venice Beach). She sold it and is no longer associated with the shop.

Today, the shop is called Panpipes Magickal Marketplace, and since the original shop opened in 1961, they claim they are the oldest occult shop in the U.S.A. Although the physical size of its "bricks and mortar" store is rather small (they do a large online business), it has been used as a set in numerous films and TV shows.

The point of this story is that if people who are experts with candles can still make errors resulting in serious fires, so can you. When fire is involved, be extra careful. To repeat what I wrote: "It would be wise to have a fire extinguisher handy when rituals include flames."

Finally, everything will be ready. You will have already done a divination. The temple is prepared. The talisman is prepared. The phase of the Moon is correct. The ritual you will do is written down so you will not err. And most importantly, you are ready to begin.

Part Two: Banishing and Balancing
Perform the Watchtower Ritual Opening.

This ritual has the effect of spiritually purifying the temple. It is the astral equivalent to your earlier physical cleansing. It also has the purpose and effect of balancing the magickal elemental forces. Thus, upon completion of the Watchtower Ritual, your altar becomes the focus of a perfectly balanced influx of energy from all of the magickal elements. Therefore, take your time and do this ritual well.

Part Three: Enlivening and Consecrating the Talisman
STEP ONE. While keeping yourself inside your magickal circle, place the talisman outside the circle between the south and west. Go to the altar and pick up the Rainbow Wand by the colored stripe appropriate to this magickal working with your left hand. Take the dagger used in the LBRP in your right hand. Go to the southwest side of the circle. (Always remember to walk clockwise in your temple unless there are specific instructions to do otherwise.) Face outward toward where the talisman lies and cross your hands in front of you so that your magickal tools from an "X," blocking entry into the circle. Say:

Before I entered this magickal circle I was alive yet not alive. Once inside I have been born anew. So too are all things outside this circle without true spiritual life. Hear, now, O Talisman [Amulet if appropriate] that thou mayest enter but may not move on. [If you prefer, this declaration may be done ad-lib.]

STEP TWO. Using the tip of the dagger, draw the talisman into the magickal circle. Say:

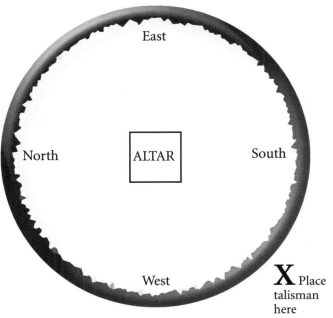

East

North   ALTAR   South

West   **X** Place talisman here

Now, O creature of talismans, become a dwelling place of [purpose of talisman] **and be thou a body for the magnificence of** [name of Sephira associated with this talisman].

STEP THREE. Pick up the talisman and place it at the foot of the altar so that it is between you and the altar when you face east. Both you and the talisman are west of the altar. Say:

In the name of [vibrate appropriate God name], **and by all the powers and forces invoked here this night (day if done during daylight), I proclaim that I,** [say your magickal name], **shall invoke thee to form a true and potent link between my human soul and that spirit of** [give word telling purpose of talisman] **summed up in the name of** [vibrate name of appropriate Sephira]. **To this end I have formed and perfected this Talisman (Amulet if appropriate) bearing the necessary seals, sigils and symbols. I proclaim that this Talisman (Amulet) shall be charged in order that** [state purpose of talisman] **may be mine so that I may be enabled to perform the Great Work and be better able to assist humanity. May the**

powers of [vibrate appropriate Sephira] **witness this my solemn pledge.**

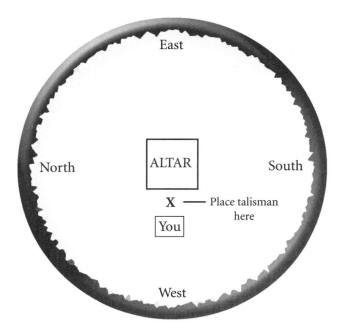

STEP FOUR. Pick up the talisman and place it in the center of the top of the altar. Put the dagger on the altar and hold the Rainbow Wand by the white band of color. Say:

> **I now invoke the powers of** [vibrate name of Sephira] **into this temple. In the name of** [vibrate God name], **be here now! Know that all is in readiness to consecrate this Talisman (Amulet). Aid me with thy power that I may cause the great archangel** [vibrate name of appropriate archangel] **to give life and strength to this creature of talismans in the name of** [vibrate God name].

STEP FIVE. Put the Rainbow Wand down on the altar and pick up the dagger used in the LBRP. Now move east of the altar and face west. As you go through the following speech, draw the appropriate figures (as you drew them on the talisman) in the air with the dagger. They should be drawn over the talisman. Visualize them in bright blue, flecked with shimmering gold. Say:

> **I invoke the powers of** [vibrate God name and draw it in the air]. **Bring** [state purpose] **to this Talisman** [Amulet].

> **By the powers of** [name planet and draw symbol of it] **I invoke** [state purpose] **into this Talisman** [Amulet].

> **By this symbol** [draw a symbol you used such as from the system of A. O. Spare] **I invoke** [state purpose] **into this Talisman** [Amulet].

Repeat this type of invocation ad-lib until you have drawn each and every symbol that is on your talisman. Feel free to turn the talisman over and open it up so that you can see the symbols and words as you draw them in the air over the talisman. Now move back to the west of the altar and face east.

STEP SIX. Put down the dagger and the talisman. Pick up the cup and sprinkle the talisman with a few drops of water after dipping your fingers in the cup. Say:

> **I purify with Water.**

If the ink might run, sprinkle toward the talisman, but not on it. Now pick up the incense and wave it over the talisman. Say:

> **I consecrate with Fire.**

Now pick up the talisman in your left hand and the dagger from the LBRP in the right. Tap the talisman three times with the tip of the dagger's blade. Next, hold the talisman and dagger (point up) above your head and stamp your left foot (/) between the following spoken words:

> **So (/) mote (/) it (/) be (/)!**

Finally, knock slowly three times on the altar with the hilt of the dagger.

STEP SEVEN. Still holding the talisman and dagger, move in a clockwise direction, and walk around (circumambulate) the altar once and continue until you just go past the south (but not all the way to the west). Say:

Unpurified and unconsecrated, thou canst not enter the gate of the west.

Put the talisman on the ground and, always moving in a clockwise direction, go to the altar. Place the dagger down and bring the cup to the talisman. Dip your finger in the water and sprinkle a few drops of water on (or toward) the talisman while saying:

I purify the Water.

Go to the altar and replace the cup. Take the incense and bring it to the talisman. As you wave it over the talisman say:

I consecrate with Fire.

Go to the altar and replace the incense. Pick up the dagger and return to the talisman, which you also pick up (in your left hand). Say:

Creature of Talismans (Amulets), twice purified and twice consecrated, thou mayest approach the gateway of the west.

Now move to the west and look out in that direction. Tap the talisman once with the tip of the blade of the dagger and say:

Before thou canst come into the light, thou must first come out of the darkness. Yet fear not the darkness of the west for there is no place that God and the light of God are not. Therefore, take on manifestation before me without fear. For in the west is he in whom fear is not. And now that thou knowest this truth, pass thou on.

STEP EIGHT. Circumambulate the circle once. Then go around again until you just pass the north (but not all the way to the east). Say:

Unpurified and unconsecrated, thou canst not enter the path of the east.

As in Step Seven, purify with Water and consecrate with Fire, saying the appropriate phrases. Then, pick up the talisman in your left hand (your right hand has the dagger) and say:

Creature of Talismans (Amulets), thrice purified and thrice consecrated, thou mayest approach the gateway of the east.

Move to the east and face outward in that direction. Hold the talisman and dagger on high and say:

To become a Talisman (Amulet), strong and true, thou must pass from darkness into light, from death into life. To do this requires the light which shines from within the darkness, though the darkness comprehendeth it not. By the will of God I can control a speck of that light which ariseth in darkness. I am the exorcist in the midst of the exorcism. Therefore, take on manifestation before me for I am the Wielder of the Forces of Balance. Now pass thou on unto the double cubical altar of the universe.

STEP NINE. Return to the west of the altar and face east. With the dagger used in the LBRP, redraw all of the symbols and sigils drawn on the talisman as done earlier. Repeat, too, the ad-lib invocations, only end by saying:

Thus do I potently conjure and exorcise thee . . .

Quickly put down the dagger and pick up the rainbow wand by the appropriate band in your right hand. Hold both the wand and the talisman on high and cry out:

Creature of Talismans: Long hast thou dwelt in the darkness of unlife. Quit the night and seek the day!

STEP TEN. Place the talisman back on the altar and hold the rainbow wand vertically over it. Say:

By all the names, powers, and rituals already rehearsed, recited, and performed, I conjure upon thee power and might irresistible,

Khabs Am Pekht. Konx Om Pax. Light In Extension. As the light hidden in darkness can manifest therefrom, so shalt thou become irresistible.

STEP ELEVEN. Now hold the Rainbow Wand in front of you and perform the Middle Pillar Ritual. Begin to cycle the energy through you, down the front as you exhale and up the back on the inhalation as in the Ritual of the Circulation of the Body of Light. When you feel the energy flowing and reaching its apex, make the Sign of the Enterer, as in the LBRP, but toward the talisman resting on the altar. Your right hand should hold the Rainbow Wand on the appropriate color with your index finger pointing along the wand so that the wand becomes an extension of your arm and hand.

As you give this sign, look down your arms directly at the talisman. Know that this ritual gesture is also known as "the Projecting Sign" and that you are projecting the energy raised in the Middle Pillar and controlled in the Circulation of the Body of Light. Feel it flow down your arms and out of you. Sense it congeal within the talisman. At the same time, watch the talisman. When you see a twinkle of light or a slight movement of the sigils on the talisman, it will be charged.

STEP TWELVE. Immediately stand straight and tap the black end of the rainbow wand three times on the floor. Say:

It is done!

STEP THIRTEEN. Now hold your hands in the air (the Rainbow Wand is in your right hand) and say:

Let the white brilliance of the Divine Spirit descend upon this creature of Talismans (Amulets) and fill it with the glory of thy majesty that it may be unto me an aid to aspire to the Great Work.

Draw an Invoking Earth Pentagram with the rainbow wand in the air over the talisman. See it in bright blue. Say:

Glory be unto thee, Lord of the land of life, for Thy splendor flows out rejoicing, even to the ends of the universe.

STEP FOURTEEN. Pick up the talisman in your left hand and hold it so it can be seen from outside the circle. Circumambulate around the circle while saying:

Behold all powers and forces that are here in attendance. I am pure. I am pure. I am pure. Take witness that I have duly exorcised, purified, initiated, enlivened, consecrated, and empowered this creature of Talismans (Amulets) by the power of [stop, vibrate name of planet, and form sign of the planet in the air with the Rainbow Wand, then continue on], **with the aid of** [stop, vibrate and draw the God name] **and by the exaltation of my own higher nature.**

STEP FIFTEEN. Return to the west of the altar and face east. Place the talisman in the center of the altar. Put down the Rainbow Wand, pick up the Air dagger, and touch the tip of the blade to the talisman and say:

By the powers of Air . . .

Replace the dagger and hold an edge of the Earth pentacle to the talisman. Say:

and of Earth . . .

Replace the pentacle and touch the Fire wand to the talisman and say:

and of Fire . . .

Put down the Fire wand and sprinkle some water from the elemental cup on (or toward) the talisman as you say:

and of Water . . .

Put down the cup and pick up the Rainbow Wand by the white band. Hold it on high and say:

And by the secret names of the divine presence who works in silence and whom

naught but silence can express, I declare by my rights earned by my practice of the arts magickal that this Talisman (Amulet) is charged and consecrated. So mote it be!

STEP SIXTEEN. Put the talisman in the bag that you have prepared for it. Place it on your person (whether it is for you or not) and say:

Not unto me, but unto thee be the power and glory forever and ever and even beyond the ends of time. I thank thee for allowing me to enter even thus far into the temple of thy divine mysteries. [Or, you may ad-lib appropriately.]

Part Four: The Banishings
Perform the Closing by Watchtower.

This ritual is now complete.

Record the results of this ritual in your magickal or ritual diary. All of the rules concerning what to do with talismans after they have achieved their goal or have exceeded their time limit apply to those talismans charged with this ritual.

Until you "break down" all the trappings of your area, it is still a temple and should be treated as such. Until you put everything away be sure to walk clockwise in your temple. The end of the ritual does not end the spiritual qualities of the area.

You will have noticed that the "phases" of this ritual as mentioned earlier do not easily match the parts of this ritual. This is because the phases overlap and do not occur in seclusion and isolated from the other phases. Part of the preparation for a Grey Magick ritual is total understanding of that ritual. Before performing this ritual, you should study it so that you can spot where each of the phases takes place and how they interpenetrate each other.

Before going on to the next lesson in this course I strongly urge the following:

1. Design and create at least two talismans. Charge and consecrate one by way of the Sim-

ple Ritual and one by way of the Complete Ritual. You can do more if you like.

2. Spend some time reading at least one book on the Tarot. Look especially for philosophical books rather than "how to give a reading" books. The bibliography for this lesson lists several of my current favorites.

In the next lesson I will explain how to work with the "grimoires." These are some of the most famous of magickal texts. Unfortunately, many of them are either incomplete, such as *The Arbatel of Magic*, are questionable, such as the *Necronomicon*, are too time consuming, such as *Abramelin*, or are too rare and expensive.

Therefore, I will be basing the lesson on two texts that are reasonably priced and available at many occult bookstores. The books are *The Greater Key of Solomon* and *The Goetia*, which is a section of *The Lesser Key of Solomon*. Both are available in more than one edition, and any edition will work. If you wish to be a ceremonial magician, I strongly urge you to obtain these two books.

I have talked often about how most self-professed "magicians" talk a great deal but do nothing. I know many people who have the Lesser and Greater Keys and have looked through them, but have never practiced the rituals or techniques that are within them. There are many reasons for this, but the three primary reasons are based on fear and egotism:

1. They don't have enough knowledge to do them. They are afraid that if they seek out that knowledge they will learn just how little they know and expose themselves for not being the "great occultists" they claim to be.

2. They fear the rituals and don't even wish to try them. Even worse, they are afraid of what might happen if they *are* successful and cannot control the powers they summon.

3. They're afraid that if they try them and fail it will show that they are not as good as they claim to be. Or, it will prove to them that

magick is fake and they have wasted years of their lives in its study.

Again, if you do not own these books, I urge you to obtain them. It would be better for you to spend a few weeks obtaining them while you study this and the previous lessons rather than going ahead. Versions may even be available online, but you should print them out.

Everything you will need to try out some of the rituals will be printed in the next lesson, but these books give advanced information along the lines of the Kabalistic correspondence charts. They give lists of powers or entities who are appropriate to deal with when seeking to obtain certain items or qualities.

If you have these books, or if you obtain them soon, do not try any of the rituals before going through the next lesson. You can't get hurt like so many seem to fear, but you may be wasting your time. The next lesson will include the information you need which makes the grimoires workable. Furthermore, these books deal with magickal evocation and the bringing to visible appearance entities from higher levels of reality.

Back in the beginning of this course I told you that you would not be "summoning" anything up. How, then, can something be evoked to visible appearance without summoning it up?

I promise you that you will learn all this and more. You will learn the true secrets of magickal evocation. And you will see that the rituals in the grimoires are the first ones in these lessons which are easier to do in groups and more difficult (but not impossible) to do by yourself—virtually pure ceremonial magick!

Review

The following questions are designed to help you determine if you have mastered the information in Lesson Eight. Please try to answer them without looking at the text. The answers are in Appendix Two.

1. What planet is associated with Thursday?

2. What is a term for doing your best without the encouragement of others?

3. What are the Planetary or Magickal Hours based on?

4. When are the Planetary or Magickal Hours exactly 60 minutes in length?

5. What is a talisman before it is activated by the forces of higher planes and guided by our Will?

6. What might Mathers have meant by "baptize" in the infamous peas-and-sieve incident?

7. Why should you break down and put away your temple, altar, and tools after a ritual?

8. What two books should you have for the next lesson?

9. What are three reasons that some self-professed magicians don't really do any magick?

The following questions only you can answer.

1. Are you still practicing all of the rituals?

2. Are you keeping your diaries?

3. Do you understand the idea of Magickal Hours? Can you easily figure out the Planetary Hours for any day?

4. Do you think the rituals to charge talismans in this lesson are more or less effective than the one in Lesson Seven?

5. Do you think it is okay to use magick to manipulate other people?

6. Have you read another book on the subjects of this course?

7. Do you have a good collection of books on magickal subjects?

8. Can you do your best without the encouragement of others? That is, do you think you're self-actualizing?

Bibliography

For more information on these books, please see the annotated bibliography at the end of this course.

Crowley, Aleister, and Samuel Mathers. *The Goetia.* Weiser, 1995.

Mathers, Samuel. *The Greater Key of Solomon.* Digireads.com, 2007.

Regardie, Israel. *The Golden Dawn.* Llewellyn, 2002.

———. *How to Make and Use Talismans.* Thorsons, 1983.

Philosophical Tarot Books

Crowley, Aleister. *The Book of Thoth.* Weiser, 1988.

Jette, Christine. *Tarot Shadow Work.* Llewellyn, 2000.

McCoy, Edain. *Past-Life & Karmic Tarot.* Llewellyn, 2004.

Pollack, Rachel. *Rachel Pollack's Tarot Wisdom.* Llewellyn, 2008.

Sterling, Stephen. *Tarot Awareness.* Llewellyn, 2000.

Wang, Robert. *The Qabalistic Tarot.* Marcus Aurelius Press, 2004.

LESSON NINE

PART ONE

The Secrets of the Magickal Evocation of Spirits

Magick works! We can assume that this is true until a time when experience allows us to say not that we assume magick works, not that we believe magick works, but that we *know* magick works. If this is not true, then you are wasting your time reading this course and I've wasted my time writing it.

Obviously, I do not think that this is so. For, as a result of over twenty years of experience, I know that magick works.

To briefly repeat some information from an earlier lesson, the magickal tradition holds that the Source of All created laws under which we all must live. One such law is gravity. We cannot jump high enough to escape gravity's grip. However, once we understand gravity we can build rockets with enough thrust to lift us beyond gravity's hold.

There are many laws that were unknown only a hundred years ago. This includes the laws concerning the weak and strong atomic forces, laws that are a basis of modern physics. Similarly, there are other laws that are still not commonly known. Among these are the laws of magick.

Either these laws are valid and true or they are not true natural laws. Either there is gravity or there is not gravity. There is no in between. Likewise, either the laws of magick are valid or they are not. There cannot be any type of rule saying that sometimes they are valid and other times, under identical conditions, they are invalid. Remember, magick is an art and *science*, and a basic tenet of science is that under the same conditions an experiment will always have the same result.

Now put this idea on the "back burner" for a moment while I discuss art—not the art of magick, mind you, but the art of motion pictures, fictional novels, and short stories. You've read them or seen the films. The wizard casts a spell and out of the mists appears a demon to do the wizard's dirty work. One of the best examples of such a film is a 1957 black-and-white movie called *Night of the Demon* (also known as *Curse of the Demon*) starring Dana Andrews and directed by Jacques Tourneur. (The evil magician, Dr. Julian Karswell, played by actor Niall MacGinnis, was supposedly modeled after Aleister Crowley.) Also look at *Doctor Faustus* with Burton and Taylor. Read some of the stories by H. P. Lovecraft, who makes Poe sound like Erma Bombeck. Look also at the Dr. Strange comic book.

I'm sure you can think of many more films and stories that have a hero or villain summoning up creatures from some astral netherworld. And, in all honesty, wouldn't you like to do that? Wouldn't you like to have the power to summon up some ghastly beastie to control people, help your friends, and punish those who have hurt you?

In all honesty, the *possibility* of doing that is one of the reasons my interest in magick was maintained over my first few years of study. I didn't want to actually do such things, but I wanted to know if such things were possible. At least, that's what I convinced myself. If only I could find the right book or teacher, I could have the powers of the universe in my grasp! Needless to say, had such a thing happened to me my karma would be in an awful state! Further, my mystical leanings have led me far away from the desire to control others. But still, wouldn't it be nice to evoke a being to our plane of existence who will take revenge on bad people?

The movies and books and stories I had read greatly influenced me. Taking that influence and combining it with my understanding that magick works initially led me to totally ignore a very useful grimoire, that part of *The Lesser Key of Solomon* published as the *Goetia*.

In the *Goetia*—at the end of the first conjuration to "call forth" any of the spirits listed in the book—it advises, "if the Spirit come not yet, say as followeth." Then the book gives another summoning or evoking conjuration, at the end of which it says, "If He come not yet at the rehearsal of these two first conjurations (but without doubt he will), say on as followeth." This is followed by commands rather than requests for appearance, commands that are filled with and followed by a series of rather nasty curses.

To me, this just did not make sense. If all entities in the universe follow certain cosmic laws, they must appear when they are called. Otherwise, magick would not be a science and there could be no such thing as a magickal system. Obviously, something must be missing.

In my studies of this and other ancient grimoires, I learned that virtually none of the grimoires, the ancient texts on magick, were complete. I decided to think about this from a more historical point of view.

As recently as a century ago, students of magick didn't just pick up a book and start practicing. Rather, they would train under the guidance of a teacher or mentor, someone who learned magick in this same teacher/student method. So if a student was not expected to learn magick from a book, what exactly were these "grammar books" of magick? It became clear to me that these books were meant to be guidelines and tips for the students. They were meant to give in written form those items that could not be quickly memorized nor repeated so frequently that rote memorization would occur. That means *the real secrets of magick consist of what was **not included** in the ancient texts!* Whatever those things are, combined with what is in the grimoires, form the real workings of practical magick. So what is it that every student of magick needs to know in order to work with the grimoires?

After years of study, practice, and analysis, I came to the conclusion that there were just three primary things a student of magick had to memorize, internalize, and be able to do. These three things are:

1. **The development of a positive attitude about success with magick**

2. **The ability to generate or raise magickal energy**

3. **The ability to manipulate and direct the raised energy**

Let's examine each of these concepts. The idea of a positive attitude about magick is that you must know (not hope or wish) that the magick you are doing is going to work. This does not mean that magick is nothing more than a mental practice. If you are ailing, a doctor can give you medicines, but unless you really wish to get better, there will be a much longer healing period and, in fact, you might not heal at all. This is a mental "will to live" which can affect you on the physical plane. The mind has effects on all planes. Likewise, the knowledge that your magick will succeed will alter all planes. Simply knowing your magick will work doesn't cause the magick to work—it merely allows it to do so. But if you think magick won't work, it won't! Part of being a ceremonial magician is having the right mental attitude.

The second part of the needed skills a magician must learn is the ability to generate magickal energy. This you have been doing when you practice the Middle Pillar Ritual. The third part of magick to learn is the ability to manipulate and direct the energy you have generated. This you have been practicing with the Circulation of the Body of Light and the LBRP. In fact, your work with all of the rituals has helped you develop the abilities to generate, manipulate, and direct energy.

The development of these three skills has always been a major focus of magickal training, and a student would have practiced for hours and would learn where in a ritual the energy should be raised and how it should be directed. With all this training, there was no need to include these concepts in any book on magick. The student was supposed to know these things. That is why all ancient grimoires are purposefully incomplete.

Earlier in these lessons I pointed out how a simple sentence was the key to Grey Magick. However, when I first wrote it earlier in these lessons you may have glossed over it because I didn't specifically draw your attention to it. In a similar way, it took me several years to realize something to which I had never paid attention. There is a translation of the *Sepher Yetzirah* by Phineas Mordell (*Origin of Letters and Numerals According to the Sefer Yetzirah*, Weiser, 1979, now out of print) which states that the Yud Heh Vahv Heh of the Tetragrammaton may be a code for duplicated or other letters. Also, a friend pointed out to me that Witches (she is a Wiccan) frequently used codes in their Book of Shadows, books that contain their rituals and instructions. As an example, "baby's blood" was a code for strawberry juice. Thus, if a Witch's Book of Shadows fell into the hands of an uninitiated person that person might be too scared or too offended to try out any information in the book. Unfortunately, the books sometimes fell into the possession of people who actually believed a literal interpretation of what they read. A history of torture and death is one of the results of this. In retrospect, I would say the decision to use some of those codes might not have been the wisest choice.

I don't remember the exact day, but I suddenly had a flash of intuition and realized that the grimoires had codes so that idiots (like myself some years ago) wouldn't get into trouble doing things for which we were not prepared. I realized that the secrets of magickal evocation were not in the grimoires, or if they were, they were in code. I had to solve this mystery!

I had so many questions. Why did grimoires call for more than one person to do an evocation? Why is there a circle drawn inside the triangle where the entity manifests? How do the pentacles for magickal evocation work? Why does incense of a particular scent draw entities from other levels of existence to the physical plane? If it is because they like the astral form of the incense as some claim, they could stay on the astral plane and enjoy it without having to materialize. There were too many questions and no answers.

Then one day a friend who is a very knowledgeable occultist made a passing remark about the foolishness of those who thought that magickal evocation rarely happened. He said that some magicians wrongly believed that entities were only drawn to the local area of the astral plane so that they could be more easily dealt with. Naturally, he had never done any evocations of any sort himself.

I laughed with him about this. How absurd! I, who up to that time had never done an evocation, knew that such a concept was ridiculous.

I continued working on my own magickal and spiritual development, only dealing with the concept of evocation when it came up in books and in conversations with people who were actually performing evocations. I discovered that three Crowley-oriented groups I was aware of believed and practiced magickal evocations only to the astral plane. I found a self-published book, *Secret Magick Revealed*, by two excellent occultists, Nelson and Anne White, who agree with this idea (the book has gone out-of-print following his death in 2003). Finally, really making my understanding sure, I read in *Aspects of Occultism* by Dion Fortune:

> *In the great majority of cases of evocative magick, the form is built up on the astral and can only actually be seen by the clairvoyant, though any sensitive person can feel its influence.*
>
> *The initiated magician is usually, unless engaged in some special experiment or research, content to evoke to visible appearance on the astral, depending upon his psychic powers for communication with the entity evoked. He does not go to the trouble to evoke to visible appearance on the physical because, if he is an adequate psychic, astral appearance serves his purpose just as well; in fact better, because it is more congenial to the nature of the beings . . . and places less limitation upon their activities.*

Certain substances can be used to induce physical manifestation. Fortune adds that of these substances, "the principal [one] is fresh blood; excreta can be used for the same purpose." However, their ability to give off "ectoplasm" from which these entities can create a physical appearance wears "off by the time the body heat has departed." This corresponds with the Tantric belief that semen loses its magickal potency with fifteen minutes after ejaculation.

Since this course is an introduction to ceremonial magick we will not be going into the study of evoking entities to the physical plane, and there will be no instructions for blood sacrifices—usually a few drops of one's own blood—on these pages. But will the idea of evocation only to the astral plane answer the questions we have? Let's go through some of them and see:

1. *Are the grimoires lying or in code when they say that by using the rituals in them you can evoke a being or entity onto the physical plane?* Neither, because they don't say that! They merely say that you can evoke an entity to physical appearance—you can see them. Certainly this can and does include seeing them on the astral plane.

2. *Why are there usually at least two people present when doing a magickal evocation?* This is so that one can perform the ritual and the other can act as a seer into the astral plane.

3. *Why, in the* Goetia, *is a circle drawn within the triangle wherein entities are supposed to manifest?* Because this is where a circular magick mirror is placed. The seer may look in this mirror to aid in being able to see on the astral plane. It is a physical doorway to the astral plane.

4. *How do the pentacles for magickal evocation work?* The seer contemplates them during the ritual. The pentacles help put the seer's mind in a state receptive to a particular entity.

5. *Why do entities like a particular incense?* Whether or not the enities enjoy it is irrelevant; the scent affects the seer and helps put the seer in a psychically receptive state.

6. *Finally, what is the need to call an entity over and over? Shouldn't they obey on the first call if our magick is correct?* Yes, if our theory of magick is correct, they need only be called once. Unfortunately, the minds of humans are not so easily controlled. The seer may need large doses of incense, many minutes of contemplating the pentacles, and frequent repetition of the evocations to open his or her psychic vision to that level of the astral plane where they can see and communicate with an entity that has come to do the magician's bidding.

The fact of the matter is that if we assume magickal evocation brings entities to communication with us on the astral plane rather than on the physical plane, it virtually solves all of our questions. It will also answer the question you may have had as to how I could teach you how to evoke entities (to visible appearance) without summoning up anything (onto the physical plane).

I have spent several pages sharing how I learned this magickal secret and how it answered all of my questions. When you first started taking this course, you may have thought if you said a few words or waved a magick wand something you desired would instantly occur. By now you should know (hopefully by experience) that magick takes time and occurs through totally natural means. Similarly, it is time to disabuse yourself of the false notion that if everything is done correctly, demons will rise out of the haze to do in your enemies. It is time to learn to ignore the fantasies of those who write or make films of occult fiction but have never practiced even one magickal ritual. In all likelihood they do not even believe in the possibility that magick works.

Before going on with this lesson, go back over this first part and read it again, understand how this sane and logical explanation of magickal evocation reasonably resolves all questions concerning the theory of this subject.

The material that is going to be presented in this lesson will not take you into someone else's fantasy.

Rather, it will send you on your own adventure, an adventure that will lead you to the deepest levels of magick and the highest levels of spirituality.

PART TWO

Invocation and Evocation

As you have noted, I have consistently used the term "evocation" in the discussion of the type of magick being presented in this lesson. In your readings you may have noticed that there are some authors who use "invocation" as a synonym of evocation. This error is never made by real magicians, and is only presented by writers who either have no practical magickal experience or by those who wish to blur the distinctions of different types of magickal practices. This blurring is usually done in an attempt to make all forms of magickal work seem the same in order to cast negative aspersions on all magick.

If you have been doing the work of this course you will find evocative magick very safe. Its purpose is to allow you to communicate with other intelligences, powers, or entities that do not exist on our physical plane. Some people contend that we are only communicating with aspects of our unconscious minds that are normally hidden. Whether or not this is so I do not know or care. This is because evocative magick functions as if one is dealing with other entities and no matter the source, is treated as if one is dealing with external intelligences.

I have seen many serious problems develop after the use of invocatory magick by those who are not competent in magick. Invocation is the magickal act wherein you allow your body to be temporarily shared by another entity. The modern name of this process is "channeling." As long as your banishings are properly done and the magician chooses whom to allow to join in the use of his or her body, there is no danger. It is when there is little thought or control in the magickal act that problems occur.

I have been to many Wiccan rituals where the aspects of Divinity, generically called the God and the Goddess, have been successfully and safely invoked.

Magickal Wars

One of the challenges with magick comes with the development and attempted perfection and control of the ego. Unfortunately, no matter how much people work on this (or profess to work on this) it is not always achieved. And let's face it—if you're running a magickal order (or even if you just think you know enough to write a book on magick) you're going to have some level of ego . . . and egotism.

It is this egotism that has resulted in the "I'm right, you're wrong, no alternatives" attitude that has resulted in what can only be called "magickal wars." There have been magickal wars between groups that called themselves the "real" Rosicrucians, both of whom called the other "black sex magicians." Crowley and Mathers warred with each other. Witchcraft groups have warred with each other. And the silly warring—taking people away from doing the work—continues.

I had been the member of a magickal order that a woman and her followers tried to take over. I stood with the founders, creating more than a little anger on her part against me. When *Modern Magick* was first published, she had one of her surrogates attack it for such things as using a different form of Hebrew transliteration. I had stated twice that I was using modern Hebrew and why I had made that choice. In fact, I simply answered the false claims about the book so stridently that she said nothing for some time. After *Modern Magick* became popular she started to claim that she had been my teacher (I had taken one class from her, which consisted of each student doing a book report—there was almost no input from her).

More interesting—and the reason I bring it up here—was an attack on this lesson in previous editions of *Modern Magick* by another person. He claimed I gave no sources although I listed in this lesson all of the sources I had for this section. He claimed I "stole" it from him even though I had never read anything by him on the subject (I don't know if he wrote anything). He kept saying that he talked about it on a TV show that was on at 1:00 A.M. Sorry, but in those days I was either out playing music or already asleep.

He didn't talk about how he cheated me out of a small sum of money and wouldn't respond when I wrote to him about it. He didn't talk about how his lawyer threatened to sue me. He did, in a message, claim that he thought I was working with one of his enemies. He did, repeatedly, demand that I change my book to list him as a source. I told him that I listed all of my sources, and if he had influenced those sources, he should have them change their books. He spent a lot of time—and I mean *a lot of time!*—blasting me in various areas of the Internet such as the newsgroups on Usenet.

Such wars are nothing but a colossal waste of time, energy, and effort! When you see magickal wars starting or continuing—and if you continue studying and practicing magick you eventually will—I would encourage you to ignore them and just do your work. To my attackers: good luck on your future magickal work. I honestly wish you well and hope you can find peace.

It is quite a remarkable transformation as the facial characteristics of the people into whom the God and Goddess are invoked (usually the High Priest and High Priestess) and even the body's carriage sometimes seems to alter and give a far more regal appearance than the normal, daily appearance of these people. Done properly, this magickal procedure is quite safe and quite thrilling. It should always be done with positive entities (or, if you prefer, positive aspects of our unconscious) and never with unknown or "negative" entities, i.e., those who might give suggestions, which, if followed, would increase our burden of negative karma.

There are two instances when invocation or channeling can be dangerous or at least very antiproductive. The first is when you perform no banishings and invite absolutely any entity to share your body. Certainly from your readings and practice and thoughts about magick you can see just how dangerous this could be. Yet, a whole religion has developed based on this magickal act. This religion is known as Spiritualism or Spiritism. Most practicing occultists tend to frown on the practices of Spiritism because it allows virtually any entity to communicate with the living. Just because something (usually a very low-astral entity, more on this in a later lesson) says it is Uncle Charlie doesn't mean it's so. There have been instances of damage in séances caused by these low elementals and some mediums have ended their lives as alcoholics.

Furthermore, just because Uncle Charlie died doesn't mean he got any smarter! Yet many, many people change their lives because of messages given by entities claiming to be deceased relatives or friends. Please understand that I am not condemning the religion of Spiritism nor its philosophy. Certainly everyone is entitled to his or her own religious beliefs. Nor am I condemning invocatory magick such as that from which séances borrow. What I am condemning is lack of preparation, lack of protection, and blind acceptance of frequently wrong or valueless information. If you think that this is unjust, look at the hundreds of books published by channeled writers (not all of whom are Spiritists, but who have taken their techniques from Spiritists) who claim to have the real writings of people such as Einstein, Tesla, Nurmi, and Edison. In thousands of pages and millions of words, not one thing has ever been presented that has revolutionized life or could not be learned from previous information.

And I have not mentioned the self-deception and outright fraud which has been a part of modern Spiritism since its inception in the middle of the nineteenth century.

The second instance of danger occurring in this type of magick is if a "negative" entity is invoked. One of the most fascinating stories concerning Aleister Crowley is how he allowed the "demon Choronzon" to be invoked into his body. Once invoked, the "demon" tried to attack Crowley's assistant using numerous ploys. Some people believe that Crowley's successes began to diminish after this, perhaps because Choronzon was never properly banished.

Invocation is a very important part of magick, but for safety it must be done correctly. This will be covered in another lesson.

After this discussion on the difference between evocation and invocation, we turn our attention back to the former and see how it is done. This will show us how to use two of the most commonly available grimoires, the *Goetia* and *The Greater Key of Solomon*.

On the following page you will see a diagram of a magickal circle and Triangle of the Art wherein entities appear. It is derived from a commonly available edition of the *Goetia*. Why is there a circle within the Triangle of the Art? Understand that this drawing is actually a neatened-up version of the original for publication. This was done either by the translator, Mathers, the editor, Crowley, or the original publisher.

On the page following the elegant version is a copy of the drawing as it appears in the original manuscript now in the British Museum. Other than being much sloppier (my guess is that it is a page from a student's notebook), the important thing to notice is that the circle within the triangle of the art could easily be filled in as shown. It indicates the presence of a magick mirror.

Constructing the Triangle of the Art with a Magick Mirror

Magick mirrors are not shiny silver. Rather, they are dark black. Here are the instructions for making a magick mirror for use in evocative magick.

1. Although heavy cardboard can be used, a better idea would be to use three-eighths to one-half inch plywood and cut out an equilateral, equiangular triangle. That means, as in the diagram below, the length of each side

is equal and each angle of the triangle is exactly sixty degrees. Undercoat it and paint it *flat* (not glossy) white. Using *flat* (not glossy) black paint, paint in the Greek names of God along the border of the wood (not outside as misdrawn in the diagram). Using *flat* (not glossy) red paint write in the archangelic name MI-CHA-EL (pronounced "Mee-chai-ehl"). To seal and protect this work, use a *flat* (sometimes called "satin" or "matte") clear finish such as a Varathane.

Notice that I did not specify a length for each side of the triangle. This is because the size will depend upon the amount of room you have available. About the smallest size you

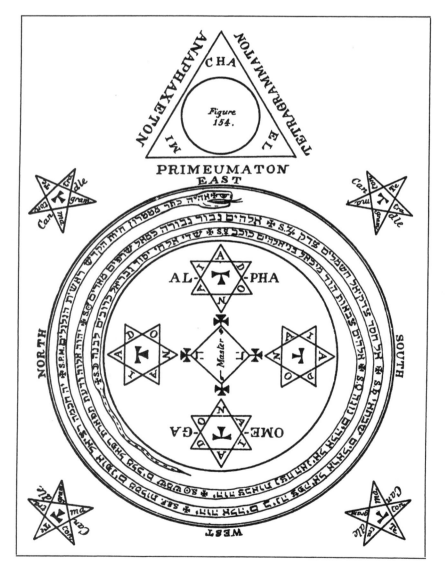

Figure 154.

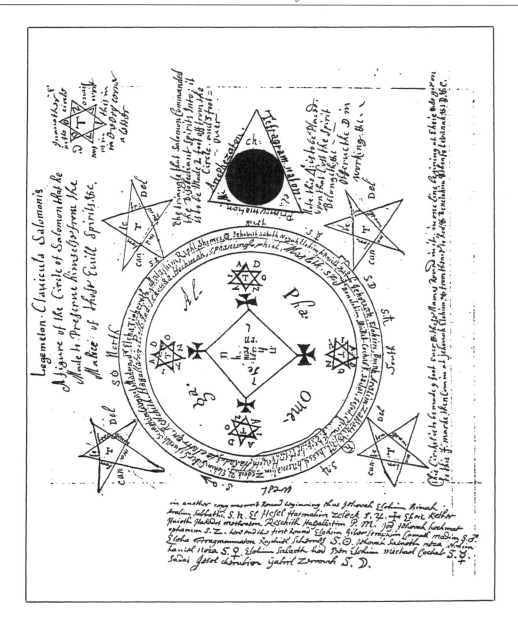

would want to use is one and one-half feet per side. Over about four to five feet wide there will be too many light-caused reflections in your magick mirror. This, as you will see, is an undesirable situation.

2. Unless you are good at glass cutting and have a circular cutter, go to a store that sells glass and have them cut a flat disc of it for you. The diameter of this disc will depend upon the size of your triangle. It should not cover any of the lettering, although it can be smaller than the

diagram indicates. About four inches is the smallest that is easy to use. On the big end, one and one-half to two feet in diameter is about maximum.

Warning: Be very careful when handling cut glass! It will have some edges that are rather sharp and could seriously cut you. Until it is mounted I urge that you wear protective gloves when handling it. This is true even if you can find a store that has precut circular pieces of glass with fused edges which are not sharp.

When you have your glass disc, place it under running water and purify it as was done with talismans. If it is small enough this can be done in a sink. Larger pieces will need the use of a stream, bathtub, or shower. *Be very careful!* Next, dry the piece of glass thoroughly with a clean, soft cloth. Place the glass down on several sheets of newspaper or a drop cloth. Make sure that the topmost side is totally dry and free of lint and water spots. Spray-paint this side with *flat* black paint. In my experience the best paint to use for this is paint designed for making blackboards, however any flat black paint that will adhere to glass will do. Apply several light coats according to the instructions on the paint. On the last magick mirror I made, I used thirteen coats of paint. Excess paint will not hurt it, but too little paint will. Allow plenty of time for the paint to dry. Then, turn your mirror over and see if there is any paint on the other side. If so, remove it with paint remover, a paint scraper, or a razor blade. Again, be careful not to cut yourself or scratch the surface of the glass. Wearing soft gloves, now hold the glass up to a bright light source and see if any light at all can pass through the magick mirror. If it cannot, you have been successful.

3. The final step of the construction is to mount the mirror on the triangle of wood. The best way to do this is to get "mirror mounts" at a hardware store. These are "L" shaped pieces of metal or plastic with a screw or nail going through one of the bars of the "L." Once screwed into the wood it can be pivoted so that the other bar of the "L" is toward the center of the glass. This holds the mirror in place. If the mounts are turned away from the center the mirror may be removed.

You will need to use at least three of these mirror mounts with one toward each corner of the "Triangle of the Art." However, the bigger the glass,

the more mounts you should use for safety. Once mounted, paint the mounts flat black using a small brush. If you cannot find these mounts, nails driven into the wood at various points along the circumference of the mirror will do. Of course, the nails should be painted flat black also.

It is important to make very clear that the side of the glass that is painted black should be against the wood of the triangle. In other words, if you are looking at the triangle with the mirror mounted, the unpainted side of the glass should be toward you and the painted side should be the far side of the glass, next to the wood. This will have the effect of making the black paint, seen through the glass, appear quite shiny. Once mounted, your construction of the magick mirror within the "Triangle of the Art" is complete.

Now look again at the diagram from the *Goetia*. It appears that a complete circle is drawn on the ground. It also appears that outside of the circle the triangle is drawn on the ground.

I am sure that this will upset many "grimoire purists," but the fact of the matter is that there is no need to draw a physical circle. Should you draw one if it gives you more confidence or makes you feel more secure? Sure, go right ahead. But if you are good with your banishings, as the many months of practice while taking this course should have made you, it is enough. My personal experience and the experience of others proves this to be true. Why, then, are there complex instructions and figures in the diagram? Of course, the writer or copyist of the diagram is not here so there is no way to be sure, but it appears to be merely a cover, a blind to deceive any person into whose hands the document might wrongly fall. And considering the small number of people who have ever attempted the magick of this book against the large number of people who own it, this blind has been very successful.

To repeat, if you wish to draw the complete circle on the ground, go ahead. Those who do this usually use chalk. Some have painted it on a hardwood floor and, when not being used, cover it with a carpet. Others have painted it on a large cloth which can be laid out when needed, but rolled up and put away at other times. I've even seen some people who make a circle out of wood with several sections, and lay those sections on the floor when it is time to do the ritual. But if you have been following this course, doing one lesson a month, and have been doing the daily rituals, it is not necessary.

Another consideration is that using the Triangle of the Art with its magick mirror while having it flat on the floor outside of your circle is absurdly difficult. However, placing it in this position assumes that the original artist was an expert at three-dimensional representation. If you look at the copy of the original page, it clearly shows that the artist had trouble with proportions and lines. Is it not possible that the Triangle was not meant to be flat on the floor?

Early drawings of Christian figures frequently show a disc behind the head of the religious figure. It is believed that this is meant to represent a halo. Since the artist did not have the skills to show it surrounding the head, it is shown behind the head.

In a similar manner, the artist who made this sketch may have wished to show the correct shape and lettering of the Triangle. However, he or she did not have the necessary artistic knowledge or skill to show it in its proper position.

The Triangle of the Art should be placed outside the area of where the circle will be formed. The Triangle should be raised up so that the center of the mirror is at the eye level of the seer (more on the seer, later). Obviously, if there is a chair for the seer the Triangle will be at a different height than if the seer stands. Although the Triangle may hang straight up and down (vertical), more commonly the top is made to lean back so that it is at an angle. To achieve this tilt, the Triangle may be rested upon a chair, an artist's easel, or a music stand. Make sure that the Triangle is firmly supported and will not fall over. The Triangle should be placed east of where the circle will be formed, but quite close to the edge of where your circle will be. With this, and your regular preparations, most of your physical preparation for using the magick of the *Goetia* is complete.

PART THREE

As I have shown, most forms of magick can be done by yourself. Indeed, traditionally most Grey Magick group workings have the group merely observing and adding their visualizations to that of the operator, the magician actually doing the work.

But with the magick of evocation, everything changes. Although it is *possible* to do evocations solo, it is much more difficult. Many people trying this type of solo work achieve little if any success. Therefore, I suggest that you have another person, a *seer*, help you with the evocation. Or, if you are going to act as the seer, you will need another person to perform important parts of the ritual.

It is the seer's task to look into the magick mirror and see the being evoked. The seer then functions as an intermediary between the ritualist and the evoked entity. The ritualist or operator recites the callings and evocations that not only call the desired entity to the mirror, but also aid the seer in obtaining the vision necessary to see something in the mirror.

If you are working with a group of people, your first trial at evocative magick should involve as the seer the person who has the most psychic sensitivity. Clues to this are ease at doing divinations, divinations that go far beyond the inherent limitations of the system used (i.e., extreme precision), divinations that prove correct on a very regular basis, a very detailed dream memory, a very strongly emotional or overemotional person, a daydreamer, etc.

Because of societal influences, the fact is that the best seers are frequently women. If you have a person such as has been described in your group, be that person male or female, use that person as your seer in your first experiment. If not, try a volunteer. If you follow the directions given here, the worst thing that could happen is that your seer will see, hear, or sense nothing. This would not necessarily be due to failure of your experiment, but rather because the seer may not have an adequately opened psychic vision.

For those of you who have been working solo, here is some very practical advice on how to find a seer. I am giving this advice here simply because placing an advertisement in your local paper or on the Internet for a seer (e.g., "Wanted: mystic with open astral vision interested in evoking spirits") is not advisable.

Perhaps the best place to seek out a seer is at your local occult bookstore or supply shop. Simply "hang out" there for a while and look for people coming into the store who are interested in magick and divination. When you meet such a person introduce yourself and eventually ask such things as, "Do you do divinations? Are they usually correct? Do you have vivid dreams? Do you daydream frequently?"

If you are shy about meeting people, remember that you are not trying to "pick someone up" for a romantic rendezvous. You are looking for a co-worker. This should be clearly explained to the person if they are interested in working magickally with you. If the person is interested, perform your daily work with him or her sitting in your circle and see how the person responds. If there seems to be a good working relationship possible between you, if your selected seer seems appropriate, it is time to tell the person what his or her preparations will be.

On the next page you will see a drawing attributed to Saint-Germain. On the left there is a male seer peering into a goblet that is being used as a magick mirror. The woman ritualist on the right holds a knife and wand. There is a fire burning directly below the face of the seer.

The inhalation of the smoke from the fire, which probably has incense, will cause a change in the blood chemistry of the seer. Also notice that it is possible that the ritualist is using the wand to strike the seer. This combination of pain and lack of oxygen combines to alter the consciousness of the seer and allow him to more easily observe the sights within the magick mirror.

As the illustration indicates, and as my personal experience and the experience of my students shows, an altered state of consciousness is a necessity for the seer. This can be accomplished in a number of ways. A mild hypnotic trance, perhaps induced via self-hypnosis, will suffice. If a person is not an alcoholic nor allergic to liquor, that person may be allowed to drink to a state of mild intoxication—no sloppy drunks, please.

There are many natural and synthetic drugs that will alter your consciousness. Although I do not advocate the use of any drug that is not specifically prescribed for you by a licensed doctor, it would be foolish of me to think that none of my students use what are known as "recreational" drugs. I am not going to describe their usage to alter your consciousness for magickal purposes because if you don't already know how they affect you, I am not going to suggest that you try them to find out. I will say that some people have told me of great success when they have chemicalized themselves.

Ritualized induction of small amounts of pain, such as implied in the drawing, can also affect your consciousness. The small amounts of pain cause various hormones to flow throughout the bloodstream, and these hormones affect the brain-mind complex. There are drawings at least as far back as Pompeii showing ritual scourging. Some Wiccan groups use this as part of certain rituals. Pain is part of spiritual practices in some shamanistic cultures. Even some very mainstream Christian sects have used and use hair shirts and self-flagellation. I personally have not found such techniques useful, but there are those who have found them effective.

It is believed that many of the visions experienced by seers have been induced by the "Demon CO." Here, CO is the chemical name for carbon monoxide, the result of fires or incense using up the oxygen in a room. When using incense always be sure to have fresh oxygen coming into the room through an open window or door. Still, the odor of the incense, especially if burned near the seer, can have a remarkable effect on the consciousness of this person. Sexual activity is another means of changing hormonal balance and affecting the brain-mind complex, but that will be discussed in another lesson. Still another way to alter the consciousness is by denying sleep for several days. There are other methods, too. You can probably think of several. In any event, allow the seer the choice of which method(s) he or she wishes to use, and with which you are both comfortable, to

The Magick Mirror

alter his or her consciousness. If there is any possible concern, the seer should have a medical exam first to be sure that nothing done could possibly damage the seer's health.

Please note that none of the methods mentioned, if done with care, will hurt a healthy person. Further note that these practices have been done for thousands of years safely, and are still being done in shamanic cultures. However, also note that nobody is forcing you to do anything. If you try to actually perform evocative magick, using methods that are illegal or legal, neither the author, publisher, nor distributors of this course assume or will have any responsibility for your foolishness or disregard for the law and your health. The following rituals and explanations are presented as educational so that you can see what many people have done and what many people are doing. Should you decide to attempt such a ritual, all responsibility for your health is yours. Further, neither the author, publisher, nor distributors in any way condone the use of illegal substances or the abuse or wrongful use of legal substances or drugs. With this word of warning, we will move into the study of how to do rituals from the *Goetia*.

PART FOUR

Preparing for the Evocation

There are two other things that you need to obtain for this ritual other than your normal tools and the triangle of the art. The first is a set of two candle-holders with stems long enough that they may be held by the seer while he or she looks into the magick mirror. Alternatively, you may obtain candle stands which reach the floor and are about three to four feet tall or more, depending upon the height of the seer. Needless to say, the latter are far more expensive. If you do get the ones that can be hand held, make sure that they have wide enough drip protectors so that the seer is not shocked by hot wax suddenly falling on his or her hands. This will also help prevent you from having to scrape wax off your floor or ironing it out of your carpet. As another alternative, two small tables can be used on which the smaller candle stands may be placed.

The second necessary item is the seal of the entity you wish to evoke. For this you must get a copy of the *Goetia*. Each seal represents and gives power to deal with an associated entity called a "spirit." To determine which spirit to call and which seal to use you will need to look through the book and see which powers each spirit offers.

Let us say, for example, that you have reached a point in your life where you do not wish to be bothered by other people and their problems. You want to be alone. This is the true meaning of invisibility when described in the grimoires. Invisibility does not mean that you will become transparent, but that others act as if you are not there. So, looking through the descriptions of the spirits you find the name Bael (pronounced "Bah-ehl").

Bael is said to have the power to "maketh thee to go Invisible . . . He appeareth in divers shapes, sometimes like a Cat, sometimes like a Toad, and sometimes like a Man, and sometimes all these forms at once [!]. He speaketh hoarsely." Furthermore, we are told that the seal must be worn like a necklace by the seer "or else he [Bael] will not do thee homage." The seal of Bael is shown on the next page.

It may be drawn on paper as per the lesson on talismans. A string needs to be attached so that it may go around the seer's neck, but it must be long enough so that without removing the string from around his or her neck, the seer may pick it up and look at it.

Set up the temple as usual. Place the triangle of the art outside the circle in the east. A chair may be placed in the east within the area of the circle for the seer if you feel that the seer may need it. Both of you should be robed and the seer should wear the seal. The two candleholders should be in the east on either side of the chair (if there is a chair) or to either side of the space where the seer will stand. The candles in them should not be lit. You will also want a pencil or pen and some paper to write down any message the seer may give you.

The Seal of Bael

The seer should be in the east of the circle, facing east. There should be incense near the seer so that he or she will inhale much of the smoke.

Perform the Opening by Watchtower. As you do so the seer should pay no attention to the ritual. It is the seer's task to stare at and contemplate the seal. The chosen method to alter the consciousness of the seer should already have begun with the exception of self-hypnosis, which should wait until after the opening. If you have enough people participating in the evocation, one should be assigned the task of making sure that incense is always flowing toward the seer. Make sure that when casting the circle you walk outside the seer so that the seer is definitely within the magickal circle.

After the Opening the operator should stand behind the seer and light, or have someone light the seer's candles. Put the candles in the seer's hands. This will force the seer to drop the seal. Make sure that when it hangs down the seal is facing out. If you are using floor-standing candleholders, or ones on tables, tell the seer to let go of the seal and stare into the magick mirror. Speak to the seer in a smooth, comforting voice, saying:

> "Stare deeply into the mirror. Do not look at it, but *into* it. Move the candles so that you can see yourself, but so that you do not directly see the reflection of the candle's flames. Stare deep … deeper … deeper …"

Now it is time to do the first conjuration. When a spirit's name is mentioned and is in parentheses, you should use the name of the spirit you are actually evoking. In this example, you will see (BAEL), but if you are evoking Botis, you would vibrate BOTIS instead of Bael. All capitalized names/words of power should be vibrated.

Ritual for the Evocation of a Spirit

The Opening Conjuration

I do evocate and conjure thee, O spirit (BAEL): and being with power armed from the Supreme Majesty, I do strongly command thee, by BERALANENSIS, BALDA-CHIENSIS, PAUMACHIA, and APOLOGIAE SEDES; by the most powerful Princes, Genii, Liachidae, and Ministers of the Tartarean abode; and by the Chief Prince of the seat of apologia in the ninth legion I do evoke thee, and by evocating conjure thee.

And by being armed with power from the Supreme Majesty, I do strongly command thee, by Him who spake and it was done, and unto whom all creatures be obedient. Also I, being made after the image of God, endued with power from God and created according unto God's will, do exorcise thee by that most mighty and powerful name of God, EL, strong and wonderful, O thou spirit (BAEL).

And I command thee by all the names of God AH-DOH-NYE, EL, EHL-OH-HEEM, EHL-OH-HY, EH-HEH-YEH AH-SHAIR EH-HEH-YEH, TZAH-BAH-OHT, EHL-YONE, YAH, TETRAGRAMMATON, SHA-DYE, Lord God Most High. I do exorcize thee and do powerfully command thee, O thou spirit (BAEL), that thou dost forthwith appear unto me here before this circle in a fair human shape, without any deformity or tortuosity. And by this ineffable name TETRAGRAMMATON YUD-HEH-VAHV-HEH, do I command thee, at the which

being heard the elements are overthrown, the air is shaken, the sea runneth back, the fire is quenched, the earth trembleth and all the hosts of the celestials, terrestrials, and infernals do tremble together and are troubled and confounded.

Wherefore come thou, O spirit (BAEL), forthwith and without delay from any or all parts of the universe wherever thou mayest be and make rational answers unto all things that I shall demand of thee. Come thou peaceably, visibly, and affably, now and without delay, manifesting that which I shall desire. For thou art conjured by the name of the living and true God, HELIO-REN, wherefore fulfill thou my commands and persist thou therein unto the end, and according unto mine interest, visibly and affably speaking unto me with a voice clear and intelligible without any ambiguity.

You may repeat this as often as you wish. Pause after the conjuration and ask the seer if he or she sees anything in the mirror. If, after a short pause, the seer has no vision, you should repeat the conjuration. Although you may repeat it as much as you like, I have found that after three or four times *my* interest wanes. Then you should move on to the next conjuration. If the seer interrupts and claims to see something in the mirror, finish the conjuration before going on to *The Questionings*. However, if there is no appearance after the above first conjuration, go on to the second one as follows:

The Second Conjuration

I do evocate, conjure, and command thee, O thou spirit (BAEL), to appear and to show thyself visibly unto me before this circle in fair and comely shape, without any deformity or tortuosity by the name and in the name YAH and VAHV, which Adam heard and spake, and by the name of God AH-

GLAH, which Lot heard and was saved with his family, and by the name EE-OHT, which Jacob, who was delivered from the hand of Esau, his brother, heard from the angel wrestling with him, and by the name ANN-AH-PHAX-EH-TOHN, which Aaron heard and spake and was made wise.

And by the name TZAH-BAH-OHT, which Moses named and all the rivers were turned into blood, and by the name AH-SHAIR EH-HEH-YEH OHR-ISS-TONE, which Moses named and all the rivers brought forth frogs, and they ascended into the houses destroying all things. And by the name EHL-YONE, which Moses named and there was great hail such as had not been since the beginning of the world. And by the name AH-DOH-NYE, which Moses named and there came up locusts which appeared upon the whole land and devoured all which the hail had left. And by the name SH'MAH AH-MAH-TEE-YAH, which Joshua called upon and the Sun stayed its course.

And by the name ALPHA and OMEGA, which Daniel named and destroyed Bel and slew the dragon. And in the name of EE-MAN-YOU-EHL, which the three children, Shadrach, Meshach, and Abednego, sang in the midst of the fiery furnace and were delivered. And by the name HAH-GEE-OS, and by the throne of AH-DOH-NYE and by ISS-KEER-OS, AH-THAN-AH-TOS, PAH-RAH-CLEE-TOS, and by OH THEOS, EEK-TROS, AH-THAN-AH-TOS and by the three secret names AH-GLAH, OHN, TETRAGRAMMA-TON, do I adjure and constrain thee.

And by these names and by all the other names of the living and true God, the Lord Almighty, I do exorcise and command thee, O spirit (BAEL), even by God who spake the word and it was done and to whom all creatures are obedient; and by the dreadful

judgments of God, and by the uncertain sea of glass which is before the divine majesty, mighty and powerful; by the four beasts before the throne having eyes before and behind; by the fire around the throne, by the holy angels of heaven and by the mighty wisdom of God, I do potently exorcise thee, that thou appearest here before this circle, to fulfill my will in all things which shall seem good unto me, by the name BAS-DAH-THE-AH BAHL-DAHK-HEE-AH and by this name PRIME-UU-MAH-TAHN, which Moses named and the Earth opened and did swallow up Kora, Dathan, and Abiram.

Wherefore thou shalt make faithful answers unto all my demands, O spirit (BAEL), and shalt perform all my desires so far as in thine office thou art capable thereof. Wherefore come thou, visibly, peaceable, and affably, now without delay, to manifest that which I desire, speaking with a clear and perfect voice, intelligibly, and to mine understanding.

Again, ask the seer if he or she sees anything in the mirror. If the answer is yes, proceed to *The Questionings*. If not, you may repeat this second conjuration or any of those that follow in the grimoire. You may also chant the name of the spirit you are trying to contact over and over as if it were a mantra. This is especially effective if you have a group of several people participating in the ritual; the more the better.

Although there are more conjurations in the *Goetia*, it has been my experience that the first two will more than suffice. If after reciting them three times there is no result, it is fair to conclude that you are not going to have any luck and that the seer is not capable of learning anything from the spirit at this time. If the seer informs you that he or she does see something, but it is unclear, everyone should chant the name of the spirit until the seer says the vision is clear. Once it is clear, proceed to *The Questionings*.

The Questionings

1. The first question to ask is directed toward the seer. Simply ask, "What do you see in the mirror?" If the seer says, "Nothing," or gives no reply, repeat one of the evoking conjurations.

   If the seer describes a scene, write down what is reported with the paper and writing implement, which was put into the circle for this purpose. If the seer describes an entity, see if it matches the description in the grimoire you are using. In the case of Bael, he normally appears as a cat, toad, man, or all three at once. Remember, however, these may be metaphorical descriptions and (gulp!) say nothing about *size*.

   If the entity appears in a shape so unusual or weird (as will sometime happen) that the seer is frightened or upset, say loudly, and in a firm voice:

   I do evocate, conjure, and command thee, O thou spirit (BAEL), to show thyself in a fair and comely shape, without any deformity or tortuosity, by the name and powers of EH-HEH-YEH AH-SHAIR EH-HEH-YEH and YUD-HEH-VAHV-HEH EHL-OH-HEEM!

   When recited, the figure should change appearance. If it does not, immediately give *The License to Depart* (which is given later in this lesson) and thoroughly banish the area, for the wrong entity has somehow appeared as a result of your magick.

   If the spirit is of pleasant appearance, or takes on such an appearance at your command, move on to:

2. Ask the spirit, "What is thy name?" The seer should respond by saying, "I feel his name is _____" or "He says his name is _____" followed by the spirit's name.

   You will find that the entities we deal with do not answer with outright lies (a lie of commission). However, they may not always give a full answer (a lie of omission) or one that is unintelligible (a lie of obfuscation) to you. As an example of this, they may give another name by which they are known or may simply refuse to answer. If this should happen, say:

By the power of [vibrate and spell out the letters with your LBRP dagger in the air and visualize the letters in bright blue—remember, they should go from right to left] **YUD-HEH-VAHV-HEH, I command you to tell us your true name without hesitation or equivocation!**

At this time you should get the correct reply. If the spirit gives its name as being the one you are seeking to contact, continue to *The Welcome* below. If not, give *The License to Depart* and thoroughly banish the area.

The Welcome Unto the Spirit
Welcome, O most noble spirit (BAEL)! I say thou are welcome unto me because I have called thee through God whom hast created heaven and Earth and all that is in them contained, and because also thou has obeyed the will of God and mine own will by appearing here now. By that same power by the which I have called thee forth I bind thee for a time that thou remain affably and visibly here before this circle and within this triangle, so long as I shall have occasion for thy presence, and not to depart without my license until thou hast duly and faithfully performed my will without any falsity.

The Purpose of the Ritual
Now, standing behind the seer, point the dagger used in the LBRP directly at the triangle outside the circle and say:

By the power of God have I called thee! Give unto me a true answer!

Now state what it is you desire of the entity you have summoned. In the case of this working with Bael you would ask:

What are the secrets of invisibility?

Have the seer tell you anything and everything the spirit says, points toward, or does, and copy what the seer says on the paper you have brought for that purpose. If there is a group, another person may act as the secretary and record this information. Once this part of the evocation is complete, give out loud:

The License to Depart
O thou spirit (BAEL), because thou hast diligently answered unto my demands and hast been very ready and willing to come at my call, I do here license thee to depart unto thy proper place. Go now in peace to thy abodes and habitations, causing neither harm nor danger unto humans or beasts. Depart, then, I say, and be thou very ready to come at my call, when duly conjured by the sacred rites of magick. I charge thee to withdraw peaceably and quietly, and may the peace of God be ever continued between thee and me! So mote it be!

Finish the ritual with the Closing by Watchtower. Transfer information to your ritual diary.

Additional Information
It is not necessary to have a seer; you can act as the seer yourself. However, it is much easier to have a seer so that one of you can perform the ritual while the other concentrates on the magick mirror.

Also, you will have probably noticed that I did not tell you the appropriate incense to use, nor the appropriate time to do this ritual, nor the appropriate color symbolism. There is an important reason for this. The purpose of this course is not to make you "sort of" familiar with magick. It is not to have you read and be somewhat familiar with stacks of books on the subject. It is the purpose of this course to make you a practicing magician. Should you merely be able to follow books, you will never be more than what a "hack writer" is to literature. And frankly, a few Joyces, LeGuins, and Kerouacs are worth a thousand formula novelists. This is not to say that there isn't a place for numerous romance novels or comic book magicians—there is. But it is not what I hope this course will produce.

Yes, the time this ritual is performed is important, the color symbolism is important, the choice of incense important. But at this time I leave it to you to figure out the details. Go back over these lessons and you should have no problem doing so. As a hint, compare what the spirit can offer you with the Talismanic Magick chart. From there you should be able to get the planet and Sephira. The rest should be obvious. If it is not, start this entire course over, for you have not really understood the information presented to a level where you are ready to do evocations. Go through these lessons again and I'm sure you'll understand the concepts and be able to effortlessly figure these things out.

The *Goetia* has the seals, names, and descriptions of seventy-two different spirits, each having various talents and powers that can be shared with you. Much of the book, it is sad to say, has picked up the junk and excrescences of centuries of repression and stupidity. Some sections of the *Goetia* refer to other books of *The Lesser Key of Solomon* (of which the *Goetia* is but one). When I originally wrote *Modern Magick*, I wrote, "Unfortunately, there is only one known source for the Complete Lesser Key, and it is rather expensive and of poor quality." Thankfully, new versions have appeared and are valuable contributions to magickal literature.

However, with the instructions in this course and the commonly available editions of the *Goetia*, you can have virtually years of practical work and experimentation. See the bibliography at the end of this chapter for suggested versions of the grimoires used for Solomonic evocations.

One of the most commonly available editions of the *Goetia* also refers to itself as "the Book of Evil Spirits." This, however, is quite misleading, for in this book you are dealing with energies or forces that take on a type of personality. But they are no more "evil forces" than electricity, another force, is good or evil. Electricity can be used to kill people or light up the night. It's the same energy, but can be seen as good or evil depending upon the use that the energy is put to. Similarly, the spirits in the *Goetia* are neither good nor evil. In fact, they have no free will and can only do what is in their nature.

Even though evil is not an issue here, karma is. Even something that superficially seems to be positive may lead to karmically negative results. So before acting on the advice of any Goetic spirit, be sure to do a divination in order to be positive that you will not be performing any magick or action that would unknowingly lead to deleterious results. Remember, it won't be the spirits who experience karma from your actions, it will be you who acquires karma.

Since this is not a course in Goetic magick I will not be giving you seventy-two examples, one for each spirit. Rather, at this time I again urge you to obtain a copy of the *Goetia* and simply follow the pattern given in the ritual above. Replace the name of BAEL with the name of the spirit from the book you wish to evoke. Use the appropriate seal as given in that text.

Until you can obtain a copy of the book, or if you merely wish to try out some Goetic magick and see if it appeals to you, on the following pages are a few samples of Goetic spirits, their seals, description, and purposes.

The Seal of Amon

Above is the seal of the spirit **AMON**. Amon is great in power and is also said to be very stern. He looks like a wolf with the tail of a serpent and breath of fire. At the command of the magician, Amon will change to look like a man with a raven's head. Sometimes there are "dog's teeth" (i.e., fangs) in the head of this raven. Amon will give you information on all things past and things yet to be. Having a neutral nature, he can help reconcile differences between friends. However, he can also cause feuds. Needless to say, care must be taken in asking for what you desire of Amon!

The Seal of Buer

Above is the seal of the spirit **BUER**. Buer should only be evoked during the astrological sign of Sagittarius and appears as the Sagittarian centaur. He

teaches science and philosophy, including such things as mathematics, ethics, logic, and physics. His specialty is teaching the secret magickal and medicinal powers of herbs and plants. He also has healing powers, especially over psychological pain.

Below is the seal of the spirit **BOTIS**. At first he will appear as an ugly viper, but on the command of the magician changes into the shape of a man with "great teeth" (fangs, again), two horns, and carrying a sword of exquisite sharpness and brightness. When evoked, he can offer things similar to Amon (note the similarity with the change of appearance and the fangs). Botis is said to tell all things from the past and those things yet to be. He can also reconcile disagreements between friends and foes.

The Seal of Botis

As a historical document the *Goetia* is fascinating. Several "spirits" are clearly nothing more than deities of earlier cultures. Thus, the spirit Astaroth is nothing more than a form of the goddess Astaroth, also known as Astarte and Isis. Revealing a Christian masculine bias, the spirit Astaroth changes gender and becomes a male! This certainly helps to validate the sociological theory that the gods and goddesses of any culture become the demons of the following culture. And even goddesses became male demons.

I recently saw a program on television wherein the studio was decorated to appear as a cave. The speaker was putting forth some bizarre hysteria about how a fantasy role-playing game was resulting in demon possession and people leaving Christianity. Since this program was on a "religious" (i.e., Protestant Christian Evangelical) network, the purpose of this program had to be only to appeal to the paranoia of those who already believe in one form of Christianity. However, another Christian writer, theologian, and radio personality says that Christians cannot be "demon possessed." Therefore, this TV program presented a philosophy not even in accord with other Christian apologists. Of course, one good way to keep large numbers of people under your control is to keep instilling fear into them. This seems to be a major function of "Christian" broadcasting. In any event, I disagree totally with the TV program's content as being nothing more than irrational, fear-inducing, paranoid superstition.

To be fair, much of occultism is also hidden in the stupidity of paranoia and superstition. A book I read on occult topics used the *National Enquirer* and a Hare Krishna magazine as sources for information. And even if the author did not understand that the *National Enquirer* is not necessarily considered an example of journalistic excellence, he should have checked for other sources, too. He also should have realized that the Hare Krishna magazine would present things in order to make their organization look good, truth and reality notwithstanding. So I repeat here,

*Don't take my word or anybody else's word
for anything in occultism!*

Check it out and research it for yourself. Before workshops I give these days I write on chalkboards or whiteboards (or have my laptop and projector spell it out on a screen) the letters: T.F.Y.Q.A. This, I explain, stands for "Think For Yourself. Question Authority."

By now you might be thinking, "What does all this have to do with magickal evocation and the *Goetia*?" Well, I want to tell you that I like to think that I am not paranoid, but I have in my possession something that scared me. Although I doubt demon possession is the result of playing simple fantasy role-playing games (RPG), I have a RPG from several years ago that features evocations from the *Goetia*, and playing pieces which are nothing less than miniature versions of the Seals of the Spirits from that book! Although this game had a rather small circulation and certainly gives no danger to trained occultists, it could have been a problem for a person who has latent magickal abilities and spends a lot of time looking at the game pieces. That type of person, with no magickal training or protective preparations, could be quite shocked upon seeing a weird figure in a reflective surface. Such a scare could hurt an unknowing person's psyche and grasp on reality. It could be possible that a few people may become obsessed with certain thoughts and ideas, whether they be along occult, magickal, or other lines. For a person who is magickally trained—such as you are becoming by following the teachings of this course—obsession or possession is not a problem. For untrained, easily influenced people, care is needed. That is why I'm glad that copies of the game I possess received little circulation. In fact, I recently went into a store that specializes in selling RPGs and even has tables set up for people to play. Nobody, not even the owners, had heard of the game. With this, we end our study of the *Goetia*.

PART FIVE

Before moving on to discuss material from a second book of evocation, I'd like to pause and share another ritual of protection. The theoretical and philosophical focus of this course has been on modern Kabalistic theory, what I have somewhat facetiously called the "WASP Kabalah." This system is based on earlier mystical Judaic traditions, which, in turn, had been based on even earlier Semitic, pre-Semitic, and non-Semitic sources.

In contradistinction to the WASP Kabalah is what I have called the "Kosher Kabalah," a Kabalistic philosophy that has eschewed many later influences that had de-Judaified Kabalistic traditions. I am personally delighted to see a growing Jewish Kabalistic resurgence in both the West and the Middle East. It is hoped that as a result many previously rare and untranslated or poorly translated texts will become available to imperfect students such as myself. As an example of this need, one of the most important Kabalistic magickal texts, a book on talismans known as the *Sepher Ratziel*, to my knowledge has not been translated into English. I searched out and found a Hebrew copy of it at the University of Judaism in Los Angeles, California. It was about sixty years old and in poor condition. The type used was somewhat dissimilar to the style most commonly used today. That, along with printing that cut off portions of letters, made the book impossible for me to try and translate.

Another important book not yet translated is by the famous Rabbi Isaac Luria. It is called *The Revolution of Souls* and is about reincarnation. Much of his theory has been presented in these lessons, which I learned from second-hand sources. Perhaps some true scholar of a mystical bent will try his or her hand at the necessary task of translating these two books, as well as many of the others which sit in waiting for a time when they may illuminate the world.

Another book often talked about is the *Picatrix*. It has a great deal to do with talismanic magick. It was finally translated into English in two volumes, the second volume appearing in October 2008.

The reason I am again talking about the Kosher Kabalah is that many people have asked me if there are any uniquely Kosher Kabalistic rituals. Of course there are, and just before the publication of the first edition of *Modern Magick* I found a good protective ritual of this sort. It is based totally on Jewish sources, specifically on the *Sepher Yetzirah*.

In the *Sepher Yetzirah* we are told that God sealed the directions of space with various permutations of three letters of the Ultimate Name, those three letters being Yud, Heh, and Vahv. Using this as a basis I present a ritual that can be used in place of the Rose Cross Ritual. I call it:

The Yetziratic Sealing Rite

This rite requires only a candle of purest white, a stick of incense, and a match or lighter.

STEP ONE. Face east, and light the candle on the table or altar, which is before you. Now, hold the fingers of the hands in three groups each: the little finger and ring finger are together, the middle finger and index finger are together, and the thumb is by itself. The right thumb should just touch the left. It is the traditional hand position of blessing used by the Jewish high priests (see figure below):

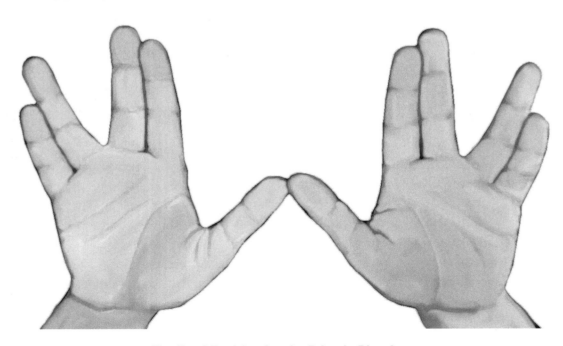

The Hand Position for the Priestly Blessing

Hold your hands in a position to indicate that you are blessing the candle and say:

Blessed art Thou, O Lord [vibrate] **YUD-HEH-VAHV-HEH, Ruler of the Universe, Who hath consecrated and commanded us to kindle the sacred lights.**

STEP TWO. Take the incense in your right hand and light it from the flame of the candle. While it is still flaming, say:

Let the whole universe know that the one God who is my God is [vibrate] **YUD-HEH-VAHV-HEH!**

Then blow out the incense so that it only smokes.

STEP THREE (a). Look up and say:

I seal the heights with [vibrate] **YUD-HEH-VAHV!**

As you vibrate the name, spell it out in Hebrew above you with the tip of the incense. Remember, the letters go from right to left (יהו).

STEP THREE (b). Look down and say:

I seal the abyss with [vibrate] **YUD-VAHV-HEH!**

As you vibrate, spell the letters with the tip of the incense pointing down (יוה).

STEP THREE (c). Looking forward (to the east), say:

I seal the east with HEH-YUD-VAHV!

While vibrating, spell the letters with the tip of the incense in front of you, pointing to the east (היו). In a similar manner, vibrate and spell the words in the following actions.

STEP THREE (d). In a clockwise direction turn 180 degrees so you are looking to the west and say:

I seal the west with HEH-VAHV-YUD! (הוי)

STEP THREE (e). Turn clockwise 270 degrees so you are looking to the south and say:

I seal the south with VAHV-YUD-HEH! (ויה)

STEP THREE (f). Turning clockwise 180 degrees to the north, say:

I seal the north with VAHV-HEH-YUD! (והי)

STEP FOUR. Turn clockwise 90 degrees back to the east. Put down the incense and reassume the position of priestly blessing as in Step One. Say:

In this way does the microcosm
repeat the macrocosm,
and the whole world is blessed.
Hallelujah! Hallelujah! Hallelujah!
Selah! Selah! Selah!
Amen! Amen! and Amen!

STEP FIVE. You may now abide in the peace for as long as you wish.

The rite is ended.

Be sure to record the results in your magickal diary.

PART SIX

The Greater Key of Solomon is readily available at metaphysical bookstores and occult shops. It is fascinating that many "occultists" claim that the *Lesser Key* deals with evil spirits and the *Greater Key* deals with good ones. This is merely a repetition of what other ill-informed writers have claimed. There is not one bit of proof that one *Key* deals with evil spirits and the other deals with good ones.

The *Greater Key* is divided into two major sections or "books." The second of these books describes the various tools or "weapons" of the magician, including several that do not seem appropriate for the practice of High Magick at all. But this is necessary, as the first book of the *Greater Key* is a combination of High and Low Magick methods. As an example of the later, the *Greater Key* includes a method of making oneself invisible using "a small image of yellow wax, in the form of a man." This type of image magick, sometimes called poppet magick, is not in the repertoire of most Kabalistic magicians. This is far more in the realm of natural or Low Magick.

The Oldest Part of the Torah

In the Israel Museum is a fragment of parchment that has been dated to 700 B.C.E. and is considered the oldest piece of text from the Torah, the first five books of the Bible. It only contains fifteen Hebrew words, which are found today in the book of Numbers 6:24–26. They contain the beautiful priestly blessing, which in English reads:

May the Lord bless you and keep you.
May the Lord cause His countenance to shine upon you and be gracious to you.
May the Lord lift up His countenance toward you and bring you peace.

During the giving of this blessing, the priest—or in modern Jewish synagogues, the rabbi or cantor—is supposed to have his hands in the position of blessing shown on a previous page. Many synagogues don't include the use of the hand position any more, and I can understand why. As I discussed earlier, most modern Jewish traditions are not involved in mysticism and magick, and this is a very magickal technique.

In this position, the hands are supposed to be—not merely represent—windows into heaven. There are five points this way: the grouped outer fingers on each hand, the grouped inner fingers on each hand, and the touching thumbs. This is supposed to indicate a lattice-work and references a passage in the "Song of Songs" (often mistakenly called the "Song of Solomon") 2:9 that reads, "My beloved . . . standeth behind our wall, he looketh in through the windows, he peereth through the lattice." It also can be seen as the letter "Shin," an abbreviation for Sha-dai, one of the names of God. And it even represents the four "corners" where Asherah, the female half of God and who was later thought of as God's bride, is said to rest.

Returning to the quotation from the "Song of Songs," you might ask who is this "my beloved," who "peereth through the lattice"? It is, of course, none other than God Himself. And it is believed—well, it used to be believed—that during this blessing God looked through the hands of the priest toward the congregation! Now that's magick, indeed. That is one reason that during this benediction many Jews will bow their heads. It's not proper to look back at God. In fact, there's a superstition that if you do so, you will be blinded.

In the Hebrew of the blessing, there are thirteen instances of the letter "Yud." As you remember, thirteen equals unity and love. Therefore, the use of this blessing indicates God's love for the people. According to one of the great Jewish rabbis, known as the Rambam, the blessing is not dependent upon the priests, but rather on God. So feel free to use it as a blessing.

In Hebrew this brief prayer has two names. The most common one is the Birkat Koh-hah-neem or "Priestly Blessing." It is also known as the Nes-ee-yaht Kah-pai-yeem or the "Raising of the Hands." In Hebrew this prayer is pronounced as follows. Remember, the "ch" is that gutteral sound and "ay" rhymes with "say."

Yih-vah-rech-cheh-cha Ah-doh-nai vih-yeesh-muh-reh-cha
Yah-air Ah-doh-nai pah-nahv ay-leh-cha vee-choo-neh-cha
Yee-sah Ah-doh-nai pah-nahv ay-leh-cha vih-yah-saim lih-cha sha-lohm

If you remember, "Ah-doh-nai" is what is said instead of the Tetragrammaton, YHVH.

It is because there are natural magickal methods in this grimoire, along with the lack of appeals to Jesus and the Trinity, which gives internal evidence of an earlier date for the *Greater Key* than the *Lesser Key*. In fact, the earliest written versions of the *Greater Key* date from the fifteenth or sixteenth centuries, while the earliest copies of the *Lesser Key* are from the seventeenth century. Of course, oral versions of both of the books may go back much further, and earlier manuscript forms of these books may still be discovered. This did happen with a grimoire called the *Picatrix*, which was only translated into English in 2008. It was thought to be a typical example of writing from the Middle Ages. Recent discoveries show it to be a translation of a much earlier Arabic work.

As with our study of the *Lesser Key*, it is not my purpose to recopy the entire *Greater Key of Solomon* here. However, the evocational conjurations are similar in form to those of the *Lesser Key* as given earlier in this lesson. Thus, you could use the evocations from the *Lesser Key* by changing the phrase "spirit Bael," as in the earlier example, for "angel So-and-So." I know that this may infuriate some purists, but the technique and philosophy are the same. If you want to drag yourself through five, single-spaced pages of evocations, such as are given in the *Greater Key*, you may be my guest!

In the *Greater Key* we are again confronted with a puzzle to our understanding, a puzzle obviously created to fool those without training. Between Books One and Two of the *Greater Key* is a section filled with "pentacles" and how they can "bring" you various powers and abilities. This seems to imply that they are actually talismans. However, if you go through Book One and actually study the evocations, you will see that the magician is told to show the pentacles to the spirit that appears and "demand all that he shall wish from the King of Spirits." As you can see, implying that these symbolic figures are talismans is a blind to prevent their true potential from falling into the hands of the untrained and unprepared.

Below is a pentacle associated with the Sun. Its purpose is to free you from the thought patterns that keep you from achieving your desires. The evocation should be done on the day and in the hour of the Sun. If so done, the entity that appears will tell you how to break your (mental) bonds and be free. In your evocation, use the term "Lord Yud-Heh-Vahv-Heh" instead of "spirit Bael."

Below is a pentacle for controlling the spirits of Venus. It would be good for any of the purposes listed under Venus on the Talismanic Magick chart. You would want to use the name of the appropriate archangel instead of "spirit Bael." Evoke the spirit of Venus (the archangel, amongst others) and ask of it what you will as is appropriate to the planet. Of course, do the evocation during the hour of Venus, and, if possible, on the day of Venus.

Below is another pentacle associated with Venus. Its purpose is to invoke the spirit Yohn-ehl to give you information on how to obtain grace and honor. "Yohn-ehl" comes from the Hebrew outside the central figure: Yud, Vahv, Nun, Alef, and Lahmed.

Finally, the pentacle below is another one of Venus. Its purpose is to learn from the angel Monachiel how to attract love.

I wish to reiterate here that magickal evocation is not just working with your fantasies and imagination. Neither is it a type of Spiritism that seeks contact with any dead souls or entities that happen to be nearby. Rather, it is a very real method of making contact with entities on a higher level of existence. They are always there. It is usually we who are not aware of them. In magickal evocation we not only become aware of them, but also choose with whom of the myriad of entities available we desire contact.

In the *Greater Key*, we obtain some specialized information that is not in the *Lesser Key*, and we can assume that it is specifically for use with *Greater Key* entities. When doing evocations from the *Greater Key* there is a slightly different method for employing the pentacle. After using the pentacle to focus your attention (don't confuse this with your magickal tool—the Earth pentacle), cover the pentacle so that it cannot be seen. Usually a piece of black silk is used for this purpose. Then, when the entity appears in your magick mirror, show the pentacle to the entity. The result is that the entity will be bound by your will. We will use this technique in a similar way, but for another purpose, in a later lesson.

Before going on to another aspect of evocative magick, there is another book I wish to mention in passing. This is a book that was apparently used as a source book by a branch of the Golden Dawn known as the Alpha and Omega. The name of the book, which was translated by Mathers, is *The Grimoire of Armadel.*

This unusual book, though still in print, is mostly ignored by "magicians" because they do not understand, or dare not try, the magick of evocation. Its internal structure (references to Jesus throughout the book) indicates a later work than the *Greater Key.* In fact, some of the names of spirits in this book seem to be similar to those of both the *Lesser Key* and *Greater Key* and another work known as *The Arbatel of Magick.*

The seals or sigils in *The Grimoire of Armadel* are far more involved than most other works of this genre. Unless you buy the book and work to understand it, they are rather unusable. This book does not even bother to give outrageous methods to draw a magick circle. Rather it merely says to "see that the Circle be [correctly] formed according to the instructions we have [elsewhere] given."

The meanings of the seals, and the purposes for using them, are hidden in abstruse language. After reading this lesson you should be able to discern the meanings and see through the veils to the uninitiated. If you do buy (or already have) this book, simply remember that the purpose of evocative magick is to allow yourself to see into the astral plane and communicate with entities who can answer questions and give instructions according to their nature.

Although *The Grimoire of Armadel* does not have instructions on how to make the magickal circle, it does have the same kind of protection rituals and conjurations as given in other grimoires of this nature such as the *Greater Key* and *Lesser Key*. Curiously, this book also has some heavily disguised information on sex magick toward the end. (There will be more on sex magick in the next lesson.)

PART SEVEN

Elementals and Artificial Elementals

Unless you are totally new to magick and occultism, you have probably heard of entities known as elementals. And, if you have a little more knowledge, you probably know that there are different types of elementals. Each type is associated with a different element:

The elemental spirits of Earth are the Gnomes.

The elemental spirits of Air are the Sylphs.

The elemental spirits of Water are the Undines.

The elemental spirits of Fire are the Salamanders.

These natural elementals are quite unique. Here, on the physical plane, everything is made of a combination of the elements, but the elementals are totally composed of only one element. Thus, they can rarely be seen on this plane except within their element. Salamanders can sometimes be seen weaving around a roaring fire. Sylphs can occasionally be seen as sparkles in the air on a clear day.

The proper place for describing entities whose main appearance is on other planes will come in another lesson. Further, the length of this course does not allow time for learning to do magick with the aid of the elementals. However, there is something that uses a creation similar to elementals and which forms an important part of your magickal curriculum. It is known as the creation of *artificial* elementals.

An artificial elemental is something that you, by force of will and magickal techniques, create to do your Will. In a sense, this is a type of evocation. Another way of looking at artificial elementals is that they are a type of talismanic magick without the talisman. And . . . you already know how to make artificial elementals.

An artificial elemental combines the force of a particular element with a temporary will or a direction created by yourself. Thus, if two of your friends were having a disagreement, you might wish to send them a bit of elemental Water to cool them off. Here you are combining an element (Water) with a purpose (calm friends).

Perhaps you have a boyfriend or girlfriend who to your mind is not amorous enough. Sending that person some Fire (element) to increase their ardor (purpose) might do the trick. Similarly, if you are a manager with a lazy employee, sending some Fire (element) to increase the employee's productivity (purpose) could be exactly what is needed to encourage the employee and enhance his or her work.

An artificial elemental also has a type of rudimentary consciousness or sense of purpose. This is what you instill in it, as will be explained. Much as a cruise missile will move around objects in order to find its target, so, too, will an artificial elemental discover ways of achieving the goal you give it.

This means that the amount of elemental energy you give it may not be equal to the task you assign it. If the energy is too little, the artificial elemental will not succeed in achieving its goal. If you give it more elemental energy than it needs, and do not tell it how to discharge that excess energy once the goal has been reached, an artificial elemental can become an unthinking (and sometimes uncontrollable) elemental force, sending out its undirected energy at anything and anyone, including its creator. Therefore, when making an artificial elemental for a particular purpose, you should pay close attention to the following concepts:

1. You should have firmly in mind what you want the artificial elemental to do.

2. You should not have the artificial elemental affect another person without that person's permission. In the above situations (a) employees tacitly give approval for managers to affect them to encourage their productivity; (b) the person was already a boyfriend or girlfriend and thus what you would be doing would be to strengthen something already in existence—you are not affecting a new or unknown person; (c) you are not affecting the outcome of the argument, merely calming the emotions associated with it so that the two can more easily settle the differences between them.

3. Since this is a type of Grey Magick, it would be good to perform a divination first to see if the outcome of the magickal act would be positive or negative.

4. As part of the magickal process, the artificial elemental must be given the command to disperse all energy with harm to no one when it achieves its goal or by a certain date and time.

Ritual for the Creation of an Artificial Elemental

STEP ONE. Decide on the purpose and do a divination to determine the outcome. If it is positive, proceed to Step Two.

STEP TWO. Perform the Opening by Watchtower.

STEP THREE. Imagine that you are the element that you wish to form into an artificial elemental (instructions for this are in earlier lessons of this course). Hold your hands nine to twelve inches apart, palms facing each other. Now imagine a bottle or box between your hands. Next, as you exhale, visualize all of the element you are working with going out with your breath and being trapped in the container between your hands. Do this until the container is literally bursting with elemental energy.

STEP FOUR. Take your hands away and let the container float in front of you. Pick up the magickal tool associated with the element with which you are working. Put the end of the tool against the visualized container. Say:

I hereby name thee _____.
   Go thou and do (such and such).
   When you have completed this task, disperse and reunite with (name of element) **everywhere and harm none on your way.**
   If thou hast not completed thy task by (date and time), **then disperse nonetheless and reunite with** (name of element) **everywhere and harm none on your way.**
   So mote it be!
   Be on thy way!

STEP FIVE. Perform the Closing by Watchtower.

The rite is ended.

Notes

1. For a name you can use anything. It can be a common person's name or totally made up. However, it should apply to the purpose of the artificial elemental. Calling an artificial Fire elemental "Water-bearer" is not appropriate.

2. You can add the name to the words of the rite above. Thus the above ritual can be expanded to include "*Go thou* [name of artificial elemental] *and do* [such and such]."

3. In the space marked "such and such," name the purpose of creating the artificial elemental. Examples include "*Go thou and bring peace to my friends,*" or "*Go thou and bring greater ardor to my lover,*" etc.

4. When giving a date and time for dispersion, it is best to give astronomical dates instead of dates invented by humans. So, rather than saying "Tuesday at 4:00 P.M.," it would be better to say, "When the Sun is at its highest on the day of the next full Moon." Even more precise would be, "On the next day of Mars when the Sun is halfway between its highest point and its setting." This last phrase means Tuesday (the day of Mars) at some time between 3:00 P.M. and 5:00 P.M., depending upon the time of year.

5. Although an artificial elemental has a type of consciousness, it is no more alive than a computer with which you play chess. Therefore there is nothing ethically wrong with creating an "imprisoned artificial elemental." These are frequently used as protective devices. They may be put into something solid or something that is hollow but sealed. This may be the source of the genie-in-the-bottle myth.

To do this you would change the second line of the evocation above to say, "*Go thou into this* [statue, vase, rock, etc.] *and do* [such and such]." If you are using a vase or bottle that can be sealed, leave it open until after you see or sense that the artificial elemental has entered the bottle. Then quickly and securely seal the container. An example of such a protective artificial elemental would be based on the element Fire and would have the purpose of creating the fiery emotions of fear and paranoia in any who would seek to intrude in an area such as your home without permission or honorable intent. Be sure to give it a dispersal date and time. And if your container is hollow, open it on that date and at that time to allow the imprisoned artificial elemental to disperse.

PART EIGHT

The Magick of Invocation

I have already discussed the differences between evocation and invocation, and how invocational magick is the basis for Spiritism. With what you have learned, the way a Spiritist does an invocation (becomes a "medium" for an entity claiming to be the spirit of someone deceased) may be surprising to you:

1. The magician protects himself or herself with appropriate banishings, etc. The Spiritist does not use magickal protections.

2. The magician prepares to allow one particular entity to unite and control the magician's consciousness. The Spiritist allows anything that is hanging around to enter.

3. Magicians tend to doubt what they are told by non-physical entities. It took Crowley years before he fully accepted the *The Book of the Law.* Many Spiritists tend to accept anything that "comes from the other side."

Invocational magick, as done by ceremonial magicians, follows a straightforward pattern:

1. Banishings and purifications.

2 & 3. Calling on a particular entity and using words that have the dual purpose of loosing (not "losing") the control of the consciousness and allowing this other entity to "take over" for a time.

4. The identification of the entity.

5. Comments of the entity and questioning the entity.

6. Release of the entity and return to normal consciousness.

7. Final banishings.

Ceremonial magick invocations are actually too advanced to spend the space fully explaining a ritual invocation in this introductory course. But although I am not going to actually give a ritual for invocation, I will be showing you how to do one according to the pattern given above. With study and practice you should be able to construct your own invocational rituals.

Keys to Magickal Invocation

1. For banishings and purifications, the best method I know of is the Opening by Watchtower.

2 & 3. To call on a particular entity requires knowledge of that entity. The more you know about the entity, the more likely you will have success. Very frequently the entities chosen are gods from various pantheons, archangels, or spirits from various grimoires. As a *general* rule—and one that works well for safety— "invoke the higher and evoke the lower." That is, invoke deities, archangels, and angels. Evoke lower spirits. You must learn all you can about the particular entity you will be invoking, including the physical position (if any) in which the entity is most frequently described. Physically assuming that position, as well as visualizing yourself in this position is known as "assuming a God-form." Appropriate colors and scents should also be around, and poetry or songs and even dances dedicated to the entity should be performed. Sometimes, words that are fairly meaningless to us are repeated over and over, like a mantra. These are frequently (and wrongly) called "the Barbarous Names of Evocation." Together, this combination of calling a particular entity and using devices to alter the consciousness of the magician produces a condition that allows an entity to temporarily displace the consciousness of the magician.

4. Next, the magician will identify himself or herself as the entity. At this time, the speech pattern and appearance of the magician may change to match the entity's characteristics.

5. The invoked entity may give comments to those assembled. As with evocational magick, invocational rituals are group acts. Others are needed to take notes or ask questions of the invoked entity. It will later be up to all the people present whether or not they wish to follow the advice of the entity. The group may also wish to ask questions of the entity in order to prove the identity of the entity. This method was explained earlier in this lesson. Sometimes, however, magicians will do an invocation by themselves not for communication, but in order to obtain qualities of the entity invoked. For example, a soldier might invoke a warrior deity before going into battle.

6. Since the chosen entity is from a non-physical plane of existence, it will not wish to stay for long. Sometimes an additional rite is added here. This rite will be discussed in the next lesson. Then the entity will freely choose to go and the magician's normal consciousness will automatically return. During the entire ritual, from after the Opening by Watchtower, the Earth pentacle—a symbol of the physical plane—should be covered with a opaque black cloth, preferably of silk. If the entity does not leave as quickly as desired, or (as I have seen happen) if people in the circle start to have a bad reaction from the extraterrestrial contact, unveil the pentacle and show it to the eyes of the magician/invoked entity. It will depart to its own abodes. Also, give the license to depart as in evocational rituals.

During the time when the non-physical entity is invoked, the consciousness of the magician is not simply gone. Rather, one of two things happen. It may stay on the astral plane near the body of the magician. Otherwise, it may go throughout the astral plane. Sometimes the consciousness of the magician may meet other entities on the astral plane, and the report of experiences by the magician during this period may be of more value to the group than the actual invocation.

7. Do the Closing by Watchtower.

There are many beautiful versions of this type of ritual given in sources both Pagan and ceremonial. One of my favorites is an invocation to a deity that came before creation, and thus, was not created. In the words of the invocation, the entity is "bornless."

This is Crowley's poetic version of an earlier invocation. Listen to the words of the calling:

Thee I invoke, the Bornless One.
Thee, that didst create the Earth and the Heavens;
Thee, that didst create the Night and the Day.
Thee that didst create the Darkness and the Light . . .
Thou hast distinguished between the Just and the Unjust.
Thou didst make the Female and the Male.
Thou didst produce the Seed and the Fruit.
Thou didst form Men to love one another . . .

This is followed by a long section of "Barbarous Names," which is meant to be repeated over and over (although it is not mentioned that you are supposed to do so) until the Bornless One takes over. The best way to allow this to happen is to "enflame thyself with prayer!"

Finally, the magician's personality leaves and the Bornless One identifies himself:

I am He! the Bornless Spirit! having sight in the feet:
> *strong, and the Immortal Fire!*
I am He! the Truth!
I am He! who hateth that evil should be wrought in the World!
I am He, that lighteneth and thundereth.
I am He, from Whom is the Shower of the Life of Earth:
I am He, Whose mouth ever flameth:
I am He, the Begetter and Manifester unto the Light:
I am He: the Grace of the World . . .

Is that not beautiful? Versions of it can be found in some editions of *The Lesser Key of Solomon: Goetia* and in Crowley's *Magick*.

The reason I am not presenting an invocational ritual in full is not because it is dangerous. If you have practiced the rituals given so far in this course and follow the instructions given, you will have no problem. What I wish to present to you is the idea that rituals are not static and unchanging. Is there an entity you wish to invoke? Do the research on that entity, learn all you can about the entity. Find poetry dedicated to that entity or write some yourself. To be successful you must become totally involved with that god, archangel, or spirit. And then you must truly want the entity to come to you. To do this you must "inflame thyself with prayer" aimed toward that particular entity.

I want to give you as much information as possible in this course. With evocation and invocation, this task is rather incomplete. This is because the very nature of magickal evocation requires the use of other books, and the nature of invocations requires a great deal of work on your own.

Although these types of magick are very dramatic, you can be a successful magician and never use them. If you do desire to practice these techniques you will have to obtain the appropriate books and do the necessary work.

Remember, one of the goals of this course is to allow you to pick up any book on magick and be able to understand it and work its system. Had I not told you the inner secrets of magickal evocation and invocation, several books might not have been as clear to you as they could be. Thus, this lesson serves its purpose.

The instructions on how to create an artificial elemental are a more complete set of magickal instructions. You now know how to create an artificial elemental for any purpose you desire. Although the ritual looks short, in fact it requires much time and effort. It requires that you know the material in the eight previous lessons of this course.

You needed to know the correspondences with the elements. You needed to know the Watchtower ritual, which means that you needed to know the Pentagram and Hexagram rituals.

You needed to know how to generate elemental energy, which also requires the knowledge of elemental pore breathing.

In short, this course is cumulative. I cannot stress this too much. To achieve success in magick requires dedication to study and practice. If you want to talk about magick, I think you will enjoy this entire course. If you want to be a magician, a real practicing magician, you must practice the exercises and techniques and rituals given in these lessons. There is no secret pill or formula to become a wizard overnight. Now is the time to get to work if you have not already begun.

Review

The following questions are designed to help you determine if you have mastered the information in Lesson Nine. Please try to answer them without looking at the text. The answers are in Appendix Two.

1. According to Dion Fortune, entities are evoked to what level and who can see the evoked entities?

2. According to Tantric belief, for how many minutes does semen retain its magickal value after ejaculation?

3. What is the difference between invocation and evocation?

4. What type of magick is difficult to work by yourself?

5. Who is the "Demon CO" and why is this demon dangerous?

6. In an evocation, what is the first question to be asked?

7. In an evocation, what is the second question to be asked?

8. What does the spirit Amon look like?

9. Who is the ultimate authority in magickal matters?

10. How many directions are "sealed" in the Yetziratic Sealing Rite?

11. What are the names of the four types of elemental spirits and why are they unique?

12. List the seven steps in magickal evocations.

The following questions only you can answer.

1. If you have been doing magick for some time before studying the lessons in this course, did the information on the truth about evocations surprise you?

2. Are you still doing your rituals and keeping your diaries?

3. Do you go back and occasionally study earlier lessons in this course?

4. Have you ever attempted an evocation? Will you in the future? Do you have some of the other source books (such as the various grimoires) needed to do evocations? If not, do you plan to get them?

5. Can you do the Watchtower Ritual by heart yet?

6. Have you ever done an invocation? If you did, and if it was successful, what did it feel like to you?

Bibliography

For more information on these books, please see the annotated bibliography at the end of this course.

Crowley, Aleister, and Samuel Mathers. *The Goetia.* Weiser Books, 1995.

Fortune, Dion. *Aspects of Occultism.* Weiser, 2000.

Konstantinos. *Summoning Spirits.* Llewellyn, 2002.

Kraig, Donald Michael. *The Truth About the Evocation of Spirits.* Llewellyn, 1994.

Leitch, Aaron. *Secrets of the Magical Grimoires.* Llewellyn, 2005.

Mathers, S. L. M. (translator). *The Greater Key of Solomon.* Digireads.com, 2007.

———. *The Grimoire of Armadel.* Weiser, 2001.

Peterson, Joseph. *Arbatel.* Ibis, 2009.

———. *The Lesser Key of Solomon.* Weiser Books, 2001.

Skinner, Stephen. *The Complete Magician's Tables.* Llewellyn, 2007.

———. *Veritable Key of Solomon.* Llewellyn, 2008.

Skinner, Stephen, and David Rankine. *The Goetia of Dr. Rudd.* Golden Hoard Press, 2007.

LESSON TEN

Prefatory Comments:

"Magick is not something you do, magick is something you are." I have said this over and over to students and I have tried to make it clear in these lessons. True magicians realize that since they can work magick and affect (and effect) their lives, they are really free to do anything they wish. True magicians also realize that they are responsible for their actions. Thus freedom and responsibility are signs of a magickal lifestyle. This attitude is also the basis for a magician's view of sex.

As a magician, I believe that every adult is entitled to have sex any way he or she desires, as long as it does not involve the coercion of anyone else. If you are straight, gay, celibate, or polyamorous; if you are into BD/SM or just about anything else, that's fine with me . . . as long as you and your partner(s) are adults and you do not coerce someone else into something they do not wish to do. Freedom, responsibility, and honesty should be a magician's guide. For that matter, these ideas should guide any person's actions.

Unfortunately, numerous organizations of dubious worth coerce people into various sexual situations. One organization I am familiar with had the leader determine sexual partners. This included having to be in an adjacent room while your "significant other" had intercourse with another person. This allowed you to hear every sound.

Another organization I know of preaches strict celibacy. Married members are only allowed to have sex once a month, and that is only for the purpose of procreation. However, I know that several leading members of this organization do not follow this rule. In fact, one of the vice presidents of this organization, a man who taught celibacy, had a torrid affair with a woman I know. The organization is aware of his extracurricular activities and moves him from so-called temple to temple but does not expel him.

Another organization's leader told several members to get divorces, which they did. This leader also encouraged romantic affairs but was against marriage. The leader's actions destroyed several families.

Why do these organizations and their leaders try to control people's sex lives?

Brainwashing, You Say?

Lots of people talk about brainwashing. They claim that somebody or some group brainwashed them or another person. Often, when used as an accusation against a group or individual, it is about as realistic as one magician calling another a "black magician" simply because they do something the first magician wouldn't do. In most cases the claim of brainwashing is just hogwash meant to emotionally manipulate people listening to the claims.

Some people claim that brainwashing isn't really feasible. However, according to military studies, brainwashing is real and possible. The U.S. military has studied this in order to prepare American soldiers to resist brainwashing attempts used against them.

Real brainwashing is far more complex than simply hypnotizing someone. There are five things necessary for brainwashing, and to be successful all must be used. To make you aware of what is required for brainwashing, and through this information help you avoid it should someone or some group attempt it in your life, here are the five elements of real brainwashing:

1) *Removal from environment of influence.* You are normally in an environment with friends, family, coworkers—people you know and who give you mental and emotional support. Removing you from this supportive environment is usually the first part of the brainwashing process. Forced sexual activity may be a part of the new environment.

2) *Sleep deprivation.* This is a change of routine and the lack of sleep keeps you tired and lowers inhibitions.

3) *Pain with disagreement.* If you disagree in some way with those attempting to brainwash you, you receive a punishment out of proportion with the disagreement. For example, if you refuse to move at the speed they want, you are kept in a dark room for three days.

4) *Pleasure with agreement.* The amount of reward for agreement is also out of proportion to the agreement, but opposite to the way you are treated when you disagree. For example, agreeing to give some secret gives you a small, extra serving of food or the chance to go outside for a few minutes.

Lots of pain for disagreement and a tiny amount of pleasure for agreement results in justification of behavior along the lines desired by the brainwashers.

5) *Change in biochemistry.* Although this can be caused by sleep deprivation, physical punishment, or the use of drugs, it's most often induced by a change of diet.

Brainwashing will change your attitude and point of view. Contrary to popular belief, however, it's not always negative. For example, militaries use these techniques to turn ordinary people into erstwhile soldiers willing to charge into a barrage of bullets when common sense would say (to quote Monty Python), "Run away! Run away!"

The most personal and private thing we possess is our sexuality. It is impossible to get physically closer to another person than during sexual relations. Romeo Void's 1982 song, *Never Say Never*, exemplifies this idea with the repeated lyric, "I might like you better if we slept together." Sex is totally involved in our psyches. Control a person's sex life and you can control the person's psyche; you control the person. Control of a person's sex life is part of what has been called brainwashing.

Perhaps you remember Patty Hearst. In 1974 she was kidnapped by a group with whose philosophies she did not agree. She later became an active member of the group. One of the means used to accomplish this change was the control of her sex life. She was forced to have sexual intercourse with several people, including having group sex. This was one of the ways her will was broken down until she lost her own ideals and adopted those of her captors. This is not an attempt to philosophically side with Ms. Hearst or her captors, it is only to show how control of sex can be a part of brainwashing techniques.

In the case of the first group I mentioned earlier, controlling the sex life of the members allowed the control of the members' minds. Thus, although the organization is supposed to teach each member how to be an unique, independent individual, everyone tended to freely accept the commands of the leader. Also, the members gave large amounts of money to the organization, much of which went to the leader. Eventually, the leader gained enough money and property. He retired from the group. It split into smaller groups—one of which tried to link itself to the philosophy of the *Star Wars* movies!—and, to the best of my knowledge, eventually disappeared. Some small offshoots may remain.

Concerning the second group, when its leader died, various temples and their leaders, in spite of claiming advanced spirituality, fought for power, control, and the group's money. The group split up. Some of the resulting groups still have power/money/sex-oriented leaders. Others actually have developed into very spiritual groups.

The desire for celibacy by the members, combined with the inability to be perfect at it, results in some of the members feeling guilty over their failure. They end up working harder to raise funds for the organization in an attempt to make up for their perceived failure. It quickly becomes easy for them to believe the "truths" of some of the leaders who proceed to teach the members how to lie and steal. In fact, this group was convicted in court of "wrongful death," libel, and kidnapping. A spiritual organization, indeed!

The third organization was totally in thrall to its leader. The leader dressed up in bizarre clothes with built-in light bulbs and she made incredibly amateurish videos of the group's (i.e., her) theories. These videos are so bad that they are unintentionally hilarious. Yet, like controlled robots, none of the leader's followers seem to care or realize how foolish they look. The more people laugh at them when they dress up in clothes that are half Renaissance, half science-fiction, the more they become dedicated to the leader who controlled their lives. The leader died in the mid-1990s, and I lost interest in observing the group after her death.

The reason I am giving you these prefatory notes is to point out that there are organizations that attempt to control your sex life as a means of controlling your will. On a lower level, there are groups that use a guise of spirituality or learning in order to obtain people for sexual exploitation. These types of groups exist in all fields of endeavor, including the study of magick. Some "magickal" groups are nothing more than a cover for one of two things: gaining sexual partners and gaining power over others.

It is indeed a shame that some people feel so weak and helpless that in order to overcome these feelings they must seek to have power over, and control, other people. It is also a shame that some people need "spiritual" façades in order to gain sexual partners.

If you are working with a group of people and it seems obvious to you that sex is going to become a part of that group's activities, *stop!*

Ask yourself if you really want to become involved with these particular people in this particular way. If these are not people you wish to become sexually involved with, get out before they make a strong effort to possibly take control of your life and will.

And please do not think that you are immune to brainwashing or too smart for it. Many cults get a large percentage of their recruits from college campuses. I have seen very bright and intelligent people go and "investigate" cults only to become trapped in cultic double-think and end up as pawns of a ruthless leader.

It is because the control of a person's sex life can be used to get control over that person's life in general that I am taking so much time discussing brainwashing and cults. For the true sign of a magician is freedom of thought and freedom of will. You will never be a magician if you are under some cult's mind control.

Further, brainwashing may not be what you think. You do not have to be tortured and berated day after day, although that is part of one method. Most groups today use a gradual process that induces you to ignore logic and accept the group's "double-speak." In the bibliography that comes with this lesson I am listing a few books that describe the signs of cults and their brainwashing techniques. I urge you to study them before joining any group that uses sexuality as part of its teachings.

PART ONE

Sex Magick

There are several different aspects to sexual magick, and it is difficult to divide them into categories, as they overlap a great deal. Even so, it is necessary to make loose categories in order to discuss the subject. Please understand that these divisions are just for communication's sake, and other writers may not follow them.

I divide the types of magick that use the sexual energies as a fundamental source into three groups:

1. *Thought Control.* This is a method of controlling sexual energy via the mind during sexual excitation and orgasm. This may not sound difficult, but it actually requires you to concentrate on something while you are in a state of consciousness where directed thinking is very difficult. This will be explained later, including how to overcome the problem.

2. *Inner Alchemy.* This is a type of White Magick that could be called White Sex Magick. It is an important part of Taoist alchemy (also called Taoist yoga) and Tantric sexual yoga. Some purists may be upset that I am introducing Oriental elements into this course. However, I'm very eclectic. Even before the writings of Blavatsky, Oriental mysticism has been incorporated into Western mystical philosophy and practice. Even the Golden Dawn took much from the East. This includes both the ideas of karma and the "Tatvic Tides," a system that can help in understanding and working with the magickal elements. Also, it is unfortunately true that with the denunciation of sex for anything but procreation as taught by the Christian church for over 1500 years, much of Western sex magick had to be deeply hidden. This was not the situation in the East, and thus there is much more material, even if it is, in many instances, heavily disguised.

3. *Outer Alchemy.* This is more along the lines of Grey Magick. It uses sexual fluids, which have been magickally charged for the purpose of achieving a magickal goal. Note that this uses tangible elements as opposed to the sexual energies that are the basis of Inner Alchemy. Outer Alchemy is frequently associated with Western Hermetic alchemy, as much Western alchemical literature, once you know the code, is simply disguised instructions for sex magick.

None of these three systems is easy to learn or master. Further, one hundred years ago the techniques were deep secrets and only spoken of in hushed whispers. But we are in a new era, and with the knowledge that may now be shared, along with sincere and dedicated practice, anyone may become proficient at any of the techniques of sex magick.

Many magicians believe that sex magick entirely traces its heritage back to the Tantrics of India and Tibet. While Tantra has influenced much of modern sex magick, there are aspects of sex magick that are from traditional Western sources, even if they do have similarities with Eastern practices. An example of this is that sex, and concomitantly sex magick, is a basic part of the Kabalah.

Even stodgy A. E. Waite (with blushing face, no doubt) admits in *The Holy Kabalah* that "the Supreme Wisdom [of the Kabalah] is a Mystery of Sex." He also reports that the *Zohar* makes clear that the best time for a man and woman to have intercourse is on the holiest day of the week, the Sabbath. It is also stated there that if a man travels away from his wife for a time in order to study the Kabalah, on his return home his first duty and obligation is to make love to his wife.

Of course, there is a difference between sex and sex magick. But by understanding that the sides of the Tree of Life are masculine and feminine, and even the Tetragrammaton is composed of masculine and feminine letters, one can see the inherent sexuality of the Kabalah.

There is a Hebrew book called the *Iggeret ha-Kodesh*, which translates as *The Holy Letter*. This book dates from around the end of the thirteenth century, and on the surface is a type of medieval Jewish "marriage manual."

Today's marriage manuals are nothing more than sex books giving various positions for sexual intercourse and other sexual activity. In ancient China these were known as "pillow books." But marriage manuals were not always such. A century ago, many marriage manuals hardly even mentioned sex, limiting discussions to philosophy and simple psychology. This was primarily due to the cultures wherein

these books were written and to the censorship rules of that society.

Judaism and Kabalists did not cringe from sexuality as did many cultures. One of the holy books of the Jews, found in the *Tanach*, is the *Sheer Ha-Sheer-eem* or *Song of Songs* (often called the *Song of Solomon*). On the surface it is nothing more than an erotic love poem. Yet, Rabbi Akibah, a famous mystic (one of his disciples, Simeon Ben Yochai, is said to have written the *Zohar*) said of this work, "The whole universe is not worth the day that book [*The Song of Songs*] has been given to Israel." Further, he said that "all the scriptures are holy, but the *Song of Songs* is the most holy." Certainly there is more to the sex of the *Song of Songs* than mere eroticism!

The Holy Letter discusses sexuality in all of its aspects. This includes mystical and magickal aspects of sex. Thus we read, "when a man unites with his wife in holiness, the Shechinah is between them in the mystery of man and woman." Since the Shechinah (pronounced "sheh-chen-ah," "ch" as in the German "ach") is equivalent to the idea of God's Holy Spirit or the Tantric "Shakti" (note the similarity in the sounds of the words), we can see that the author of this book is talking about something special. Indeed, the author is discussing what is commonly called kundalini yoga (more accurately *Laya Yoga*). This will be discussed more when I talk about Inner Alchemy.

The Holy Letter also describes the aspect of sex magick that I term Thought Control. This type of sex magick may be the most palatable for people from Western cultures. *The Holy Letter* simply states, "According to the thoughts you have in intercourse, so will the form come upon the seed." Superficially, this means that if you are thinking spiritual thoughts when having intercourse you will have a spiritual child; if happy thoughts, a happy child, etc. As we all know, however, every act of sexual intercourse does not result in the birth of a child. *Or does it?*

Certainly I could not deny that the number of times sexual intercourse leads to the birth of an infant human is small compared to the number of times sexual intercourse is performed. But think back to my comments on creative visualization. Remember that whether you realize the fact or not, you are constantly going through the visualization process. Likewise, every time you have sexual intercourse you give birth to what Crowley called a "magickal childe," even if no human child is the result. Or, to put it another way, the key idea behind the Thought Control form of sex magick is that *the thought held at the instant of orgasm comes to pass.* Unfortunately, this is not as easy as it might sound. To understand why this is so we need to look at the theories of Dr. Wilhelm Reich.

Reich, Energy, and Sex

Many professionals in the field of psychology dismiss Reich's concepts of Orgone and his ideas about the orgasm. They claim that one of Reich's basic theories, that people who were psychologically disturbed could not have an orgasm, is false. It is clear that many people with psychopathological problems are capable of having an orgasm such as in the instance of violent rape. And, since this is a basis of many of Reich's theories on orgasm and Orgone, he must be wrong.

Well, it is obvious to me that none of these "experts" on Reich ever bothered to read Reich's works or else they are purposely misrepresenting it in order to further their own agendas. Reich *never* claimed that people with psychological problems were incapable of having an orgasm. Reich knew that such a person could have an orgasm. He must have been aware of the important psychological text *Psychopathia Sexualis* by Krafft-Ebbing. He was an M.D., and that book had been the physicians' resource on sociopathic sexuality for many years. What Reich said was that a person who was psychologically disturbed could not have a "potent orgasm."

Reich believed that during sexual excitation an energy, which he called Orgone, built up in the body. For full mental health this energy needed to be discharged during orgasm. You could compare this to blowing up a balloon. As the sexual excitation in-

creases, more air is blown into the balloon. If you lose control over your consciousness, the air will be safely discharged through the valve on the balloon. If you do not lose mental control, the balloon increases in size and pressure until it explodes.

Similarly, the natural and healthy in-and-out flow of Orgone energy does not occur, according to Reich, in a person with a psychological disturbance. This type of person would have an unhealthy emotional, psychological, and/or physical control of him or herself at the moment of orgasm. They can't let go.

This controlled behavior at the moment of orgasm, according to Reich, is not healthy. To be healthy, a person needs to be orgasmically potent. This means that during the convulsions of the orgasmic experience a person should not be thinking, "Am I doing this right? Is my partner enjoying this?" Rather, a person should be so caught up in the very animalistic enjoyment of sex that nothing can be thought of. There should be only pure, thought-free experience.

Does this idea of "thought-free experience" sound familiar to you? It should, because going into such a state is exactly what true meditation is! Reich discovered that the moment of orgasm can be identical to true meditation.

Reich believed that being orgasmically potent, being able to achieve the thought-free, sense-oriented state described above, was the only way to release Orgone energy. If this was not done, the human "balloon" would explode from over-inflation of Orgone energy. This explosion would be in the form of psychological or even physiological problems. While it is true that this is *one* way to release the Orgone energy, I must disagree with it being the *only* way. Tantrics have methods of controlling this energy at will. This will be covered in the section on Inner Alchemy.

Further, it is not true that a person experiencing an orgasm that is orgasmically potent is without thought. In fact, such a person is only without *conscious* thought. The act of sexual intercourse (or other sexual activity wherein a person is brought to orgasm) can be so primal that it may mentally take us to a period before our rational consciousness ruled our selves. Thus, it is our unconscious that holds sway over us at the moment we experience an orgasmically potent orgasm.

As I've written previously, the unconscious is our link to the astral plane (also called the Yetziratic World). When you create something in the astral plane as a result of your thinking procedures, it must come into existence on the physical plane. Whatever thought is in our mind at the point of orgasm goes directly to the unconscious and into the astral plane. It must manifest. That is why the thought held in the mind at the instant of orgasm must come into existence.

But that is also the difficulty. To open up the unconscious we must be orgasmically potent. This means we must, temporarily, lose our sense of self, our ego. Unfortunately, that aspect of our being is locked up with our logical, reasoning self. If we lose that, how can we keep an idea in our mind when having an orgasm?

Luckily, there is a way. The unconscious does not think in words, it thinks in symbols or images. You see the word "tree," but the unconscious (and your memory) keeps an image of a tree you have seen or imagined at one time or another. Therefore, all you have to do is make up a symbol to represent what you want. Symbols, shapes, and objects can stay with you through an orgasmically potent orgasm while words will not. Simply keep the symbol in mind when you have an orgasm. And though this is not difficult, it does require practice.

A Sex Magick Ritual for a Couple

Let both participants be aware that a magickal act, *a spiritual act*, is about to be performed, not just a common act of sexual intercourse resulting from romance, passion, or being "in love."

STEP ONE. Let both participants know the purpose of this act. A divination should be done, with both persons present, to ensure the "karmic correctness" of the magickal act.

STEP TWO. Let a suitable sigil, representing the purpose of the magickal act, be designed. Although a sigil taken from a grimoire will do, designing an original sigil is a better idea. The system of A. O. Spare is quite good for this.

STEP THREE. Let multiple large versions of the sigil be made and placed around the room. This must include the ceiling so that no matter which way you look you will see the magickal sigil.

STEP FOUR. A "Place of Comfort" should be established in the center of your area. Most commonly this is a small mattress or pad of some kind. If there is room, place your altar at the head of the Place of Comfort. If there is not enough room let the Place of Comfort be your altar.

STEP FIVE. Both participants should take time now to shower and/or bathe. Do this separately. Use appropriate scents, perfumes, and oils on your body after you dry yourself. Oils are especially good for this, as different oils can be used on different parts of the body. Robe yourselves, realizing that you are about to perform a sacred, magickal act. As you come into your temple, remember that this is a holy place. Perform the Opening by Watchtower.

STEP SIX. Now move to the Place of Comfort and begin to caress and adore one another. Slowly remove each other's robes. If you wish, apply lubricating body oils to each other as you continue to caress each other freely. Explore each other totally with eye, ear, mouth, voice, hand, foot, tongue, etc. At this part of the ritual, think not of the rite. Rather, think of yourself and your partner. Let your sexual imagination run free.

STEP SEVEN. When both people are ready, begin actual sexual intercourse. As you continue caressing, for a few moments there should be no thrusting motions on the part of either participant.

STEP EIGHT. Begin very slow thrusting motions. As you both become more involved in this part of the rite, observe the sigils around you. *Do not concern yourself about their meaning.* Your unconscious already knows the meaning. Just look at the symbols.

STEP NINE. Allow your passion to dictate the speed of your movements until the intercourse is quite rigorous. If you wish, change the position of your ritual lovemaking. That is why it is necessary to post copies of your sigil all over the room. No matter where you look, no matter what position you are in, you must be able to see a copy of the sigil. Place as much concentration as possible on the symbols. Continue to orgasm. If the couple has been together for a while and both know each other's sexual responses, it would be best if both could orgasm at about the same time, although the so-called "mutual orgasm" is not necessary.

STEP TEN. Stay coupled (maintain penile insertion) for as long as possible, to a maximum of fifteen minutes. During this time the ritualists may caress each other, but refrain from much speaking.

STEP ELEVEN. Re-robe and perform the Closing by Watchtower.

The rite is complete.

Notes on this ritual

1. The length of time of actual insertive intercourse is not critical, but there must be enough time allowed to build up the energy that is released with the symbolic thought at the moment of the active participant's orgasm. A minimum of ten minutes is appropriate, but over half an hour is unnecessary. Certainly women will not have a problem with this, except possibly soreness due to prolonged intercourse with insufficient vaginal lubrication. This can happen to women who are not used to extended periods of intercourse, and can easily be remedied by the use of a *high quality* sexual lubricant.

   Men, on the other hand, might have one of two difficulties: staying erect with minimal physical sensation or having an orgasm too quickly. Masters and Johnson say that the average period for men between insertion of the penis and orgasm is about two and one-half

   minutes. Since this is an average, the implication is that some men will have an orgasm within seconds of insertion. Later in this lesson there are instructions on how a man may delay his orgasm.

2. This ritual may be done with partners of the same sex. It may also be done heterosexually with the penis inserted in the anus or mouth of his partner. (*Note:* After anal intercourse the penis *must* be washed thoroughly before vaginal intercourse.)

3. The sexual position held by the couple at the moment of orgasm is important. Here are some tips:

   Missionary Position (man on top) is good for situations where magick is done to positively affect the man's environment (i.e., allow him to get a raise, get a better job, etc.)

   Woman Superior (woman on top) is for situations where magick is done to positively affect the woman's environment.

   Male Behind (laying like spoons, with the man behind his partner, also kneeling with the male behind his partner) is for sending energy such as healing to a friend of the man. For a friend of the woman it can once again be with the woman on top, but with her back to her partner's face.

4. This ritual may also be done as an act of oral sex, as mentioned. In this instance, there is not a Place of Comfort, but a chair called the "Throne." The person who will have the orgasm sits in the Throne while the partner kneels or sits at the foot of the Throne and performs cunnilingus or fellatio. The King or Queen on the throne needs to hold the symbol in his or her hands and look at it intently while the partner performs the sexual stimulation. The person fellating a King should swallow all of his semen. The person performing cunnilingus on the woman should lick and swallow all of her sexual fluids.

5. This rite may also be done solitarily. The male may masturbate himself. If this is done he should catch the semen in a small vase which has a copy of the symbol in the vase at the bottom. The vase should then be sealed. Alternatively, he may catch the semen on a dish or plate and consume it. A partner may stimulate the man to orgasm by hand and consume the semen.

   Similarly, a woman may stimulate herself by hand or with the aid of a partner or even artificial devices such as vibrators. After orgasm she should clean herself with a small amount of pure water, all of which should be saved, mixed with wine or juice, and consumed.

6. Sexual experimentation and variation can be very enjoyable. But ritual is not the time to try new things. If you feel a sexual position that you have not performed previously with the partner of this ritual is appropriate, it should be practiced beforehand (or at least discussed) so that both of you know the most comfortable way for you to hold the position for several minutes.

7. Although both the Kabalah and the Tantras disagree with him on this point, those who like Crowley may agree with him that you should choose anyone to do the rite with and they need not know the purpose of the rite. Personally I feel that this is a type of sexual abuse, and experience has shown that it is not as successful as when both partners are aware of what is happening. I mention it here so that if you like to follow Crowley, you will know a difference to his system.

Divinatory Sex Magick

This ritual is done the same way as the ritual above; however, the purpose is strictly for divination. It can also be used as part of the evocation rites of the previous lesson. Read in the previous lesson the characteristics of a person who will make a good seer. It is this person upon whom the technique will be performed.

There are three aspects involved in any divinatory technique. The diviner must:

1. Turn off the outside, turn on the inside.

2. Alter the state of consciousness.

3. Increase the blood flow to the brain.

In this ritual, turning off the outside involves the use of what is called the *Yoni Mudra*. This is a position wherein the hands actually close down the other senses. It is done this way:

Put your hands in front of your face so that the fingertips touch and the palms are toward your face. Seal the mouth by locking the lips between the little fingers and ring fingers of both hands. This holds the mouth shut. Seal the nose by pressing against the nostrils with the middle fingers of both hands. Seal the eyes by holding the eyelids closed with the pointer (index) fingers of each hand. Finally, use each thumb to seal the ears by closing the little flap of flesh in front of the ears, technically known as the tragus, over the entrance to the ear canals.

The Yoni Mudra

Pinky and ring fingers seal the mouth;
middle fingers close the nostrils;
index fingers gently hold eyelids to shut the eyes.
Unseen: the thumbs seal the ears closed.

This position closes most of the external senses and allows the inner senses to come through.

In a previous lesson I gave instructions on how to alter the state of consciousness. Methods include the use of alcohol to produce mild intoxication, lack of sleep, etc. In this rite the method used to increase the flow of blood to the head is to have the head below the rest of the body during intercourse.

If you have a mattress for the Place of Comfort, the seer may dangle his or her head over the side of the mattress. If the seer is in very good health, pillows may be placed so that the hips and legs are elevated. In fact, if oral sex is used, the position on the throne can actually be reversed so that the person's legs are over the back of the chair and the person's head is at the foot of the chair. The partner stands behind the throne and performs oral sex on the genitals, which are near the top of the chair's back.

Important: This should *not* be done if the seer has high blood pressure.

When the seer has achieved orgasm, he or she should be questioned in a manner similar to the techniques in the previous lesson. If information about a particular subject is desired, during sexual stimulation the seer may look at a symbol that the partners created.

Before moving on, a final point about the Yoni Mudra. Students have told me that they have trouble breathing in this ritual pose. I really don't understand how anyone could merely have difficulty breathing in this position because when you have the mudra locked in place, breathing shouldn't be difficult, it should be *impossible!* Separate the middle fingers and slowly inhale through the nose. Replace the fingers and hold the Yoni Mudra and your breath for as long as it is comfortable. Then separate the ring fingers from the little fingers and exhale very slowly through the mouth. After the lungs are fully empty, replace the fingers and hold the mudra for as long as it is comfortable and repeat during the use of this position. When I explained this to students, some of them complained that it takes some of the spontaneity out of lovemaking. Remember that this is *not* lovemaking.

It is highly ritualized and formalized. It is for a purpose; any pleasure that results is a wonderful bonus.

Another divination technique that uses sexuality is definitely not for all practitioners. Most will not wish to do it, and that is okay. It is called "Eroto-Comatose Lucidity" and does not involve a coupled pair. Rather, this ritual involves one ritualist-seer and several aides who are usually of the opposite sex. After the opening as above, the aides (and the more sexually experienced they are, the better) attempt to exhaust the ritualist sexually by every known means, and arouse the ritualist sexually by every known means. Every device and technique known may be used by the aides. If some of them tire, they should be replaced by others.

Finally the ritualist-seer will sink into a deep sleep as a result of utter exhaustion. Now the goal of the aides must be altered. They must try to awaken the ritualist through sexual stimulation alone. But, upon the first signs of the ritualist awakening, all stimulation must cease. This should continue indefinitely until the ritualist is in a state that is between waking and sleeping, "and in which his [or her] Spirit, set free by perfect exhaustion of the body, and yet prevented from entering the City of Sleep, communes with the Most High and Most Holy Lord God of its being, maker of heaven and earth."

The rite is over when the ritualist falls into total sleep, or awakens, has a final orgasm, and falls into an undisturbable sleep. Upon rising after this sleep, the ritualist-seer should immediately write down his or her remembrances.

This ritual of Eroto-Comatose Lucidity is from Crowley's works, although it is said that the technique was devised by and given to him by one of his woman students. Another example of sex magick of this Thought Control type is novelized in Crowley's book, *Moonchild*.

There is one more position for divinatory sex magick, which I will share with you. Let me make clear, however, that it is designed primarily for people who are slender, athletic, and strong. It involves a Tan-

Was Crowley Really Wrong?

As I wrote, I consider it virtually sex abuse to use someone for sex magick and not let him or her know what you are doing. The question is, was Crowley really wrong when he suggested it?

Well, on one level he certainly was. If you inform partners you're going to do sex magick with them and they object, to go ahead and do it anyway is a form of abuse. By not telling your partner that you are doing sex magick you avoid this possibility but are being dishonest (through omission of information) and unethical.

On another level, though, he may have had a point. If you say, "I want to do sex magick with you," to a partner who is interested but untrained in magick, that person may agree, but then go on to ask things such as "Am I doing this right? Should I be doing something differently? Is the magick working? How should I help?" and so on.

All of these questions are legitimate. All of them are reasonable. But they also have one thing in common: they're going to take your attention away from the magick and direct it toward this person's questions. It will have a similar effect to simply thinking that your ritual was not effective and won't be successful.

So, if you have a willing sexual partner and want to do sex magick without instructing him or her in the fine points of magick, what Crowley was saying really does make sense . . .

. . . *if you were living when Crowley lived, more than sixty years ago!*

Previously these lessons discussed the concept that working magick with more *trained* people increases magickal energy exponentially. In my opinion, getting someone to work with you and help you, or spending the time to train them to do so, is far better than using them to work sex magick without their knowledge.

Spend a few weeks sharing magickal concepts with them. Better yet, work through *Modern Magick* with that person. Help your partner become an excellent magician rather than simply using them.

The night of using others has passed. The light of daybreak, of working *with* others instead of using them, is rapidly dawning. As it says in the Neophyte Initiation ritual of the Golden Dawn:

> *Long hast thou dwelt in darkness—*
> *Quit the night and seek the day.*

tric sexual position known as "The Crow." After the usual opening and much sexual stimulation, the man, while standing, lifts the woman so that she is upside down and facing him. In this position they may have mutual oral sex. Usually, the woman will lock her legs behind the man's neck or head, depending on the length of her legs. The man will usually support the woman by holding her around her waist. This position can cause the man to tire physically quite easily unless he is in very good shape and/or the woman is quite slender. The woman, who is completely inverted, will have a great deal of blood flow to her head. This can lead to seership and divinatory experiences.

The only technique that I have not tried nor any of my students confessed to is Eroto-Comatose Lucidity. But I can say from personal experience and from the reported experiences of some of my students, that these types of sex magick techniques are some of the strongest and most effective magickal techniques available.

PART TWO

Outer Alchemy

The next technique I wish to talk about is called Outer Alchemy. Of the three techniques of sex magick, it is the easiest in that it requires the least amount of self-discipline.

Sex magick of Outer Alchemy, unlike the other two forms of sex magick, requires the use of a partner of the opposite sex. Thus it is by its very nature not a technique that can be adapted to male or female homosexual practices. This must lead us to a brief discussion of magick and sexuality.

Anybody can do the Lesser Banishing Ritual of the Pentagram. It does not matter if you are Jewish, Christian, Moslem, Buddhist, atheist, or anything else. All that matters is your ability to perform the ritual.

When I perform the ritual I may visualize God as a concept that exists before the gods and goddesses of creation. Others may see God as the Christian Trinity. Still others may view the source of the energy in the LBRP as Jah of the Rastafarians (or even the Flying Spaghetti Monster of the Pastafarians!). If it works for you it does not matter. The point I am trying to make is that although our magickal practices are spiritual, they need not follow any particular religious viewpoint. True, the Kabalah has an intrinsic Jewish flavor to it, but this is because it has been safeguarded by the Jews for the past few thousand years. One of the things I have tried to do in this course is make the procedures general in spiritual nature, and thus applicable to any religious belief (or lack thereof).

Just as it is possible to separate spirituality from religion, so, too, from a sex magician's point of view, it is possible to separate sex from love. Please note that I am not saying sex *should* be separated from love, only that it can be. But the fact of the matter is that for some people sex is not about love and romance. Rather, it is little more than a form of exercise with a pleasurable ending.

I am not taking the point of view that sex should be based only on desire, lust, enjoyment, etc. Sexual intimacy can be based on the relationship, which can develop between two loving people. In fact, the most valuable sex magick experiences I have had have been with partners whom I truly loved. But what I am saying is that just as spirituality can be separated from religion, so, too, can the sex of sex magick be separated from the sex experienced in a love relationship.

This does not mean that it's okay to have sex with a person other than your regular partner using sex magick as an excuse for cheating. In fact, I would suggest that you do not do so unless you have told your partner about it and have your partner's approval. And this approval should not come through gritted teeth and pursed lips due to anger and jealousy. Remember, honesty and integrity are vital to a magician.

This means that if you do not have a regular romantic partner or if you have your partner's willing permission, it is allowable to work with another person or multiple persons when doing sex magick.

Please note that what I am saying here is *not* meant to be a license to have sex with anybody because you are doing magick. Rather, I am saying that certain forms of magickal ritual, including sex magick rituals, can be done with a partner other than one you are involved with in a love relationship.

I personally consider love and established relationships to be very important in a person's life. If your participation in a ritual, including a sex magick ritual, will create a hardship on your relationship, I urge you to reconsider your choice to perform such a ritual. Or, perhaps you can help your partner learn magick and have him or her participate in sex magick rituals with you.

So if you happen to be a male or female homosexual, and both you and your partner believe that sex can be separated from love, you can perform Outer Alchemy. This will depend on your nature and the nature of your relationship. Perhaps the best way to conceive of a sex magick ritual is as just another ritual, one that happens to use genitals instead of a chalice or a wand.

It is the belief of many magicians that the classic texts of Western Alchemy are coded information for the performance of sex magick. The basic idea is that the sperm of the male and the ejaculatory fluids of the female have natural magickal qualities as a result of mental direction and sexual stimulation. The alchemical instructions are simply ways to make these magickal fluids stronger and more powerful.

Although I will be giving a type of Outer Alchemy ritual shortly, I will try to limit some of the precise alchemical terminology. Full alchemical practices, interpreted through the ideas of sex magick, are far too complicated to discuss in a course of this type.

If you decide to investigate traditional alchemical texts as a source for sex magick rituals, it is important to understand two things:

1. Some of the practices given in the alchemical texts are merely chaff to hide the true nature of the techniques and its hidden wheat.

2. Several words commonly used in alchemy are codes for sexual ideas.

Examples:

The *Athanor* is usually described as a special type of oven used to slowly heat the material with which you are working. According to sex magicians it means the penis.

The *Serpent* is said to be a result of heating a substance in the Athanor. To a sex magician it is the semen.

The *Blood of the Red Lion* is also semen.

The *Curcurbite*, a type of alchemic container, is the vagina. So, too, is the *Retort*, which is usually described as another type of alchemical container.

The *Menstruum* or *Menstruum of the Gluten* is the result of the slow heating of a substance in the Athanor. Sex magicians believe it to be either the female lubricating fluids or ejaculatory fluids or both, depending upon the sex magician you talk with.

The *First Matter* is described as a mixture of the Serpent and the Menstruum. While this is a rather hazy type of substance to the physical alchemist, its meaning is clear to the sex magician.

Finally the *Amrita* or *Elixir* is defined as "the transmuted First Matter." How it is transmuted and how it is used is the secret of Outer Alchemy.

One of the traditional secrets of alchemy is that the process of taking your basic material and heating it must be very slow and take days or even weeks to accomplish. To a sex magician, this means that the best way to work with the male and female fluids is to take a great deal of time in their preparation, possibly hours. This involves having sexual intercourse without orgasm or ejaculation for a very long period. The mental technique used to accomplish this is known as *Karezza* (pronounced "kahr-etz-ah" with the accent on the second syllable).

In previous editions of *Modern Magick* I traced Karezza back to a man named William Lloyd. He was a fascinating person who did write about Karezza, but only in 1931 and not the late 1800s as I incorrectly stated. In actuality, the idea was created by a woman named Alice Bunker Stockham (1833–1912).

She was the fifth woman made a doctor in the U.S.A. and got into trouble for promoting birth control. Her interest in birth control was not so much to stop births of children (she was against abortion), but to save lives. At that time, the primary cause of death among young women was giving birth.

She ended up going to India and learned about the physical actions of Tantra. She brought back the technique of prolonged intercourse without orgasm as a means of birth control. Side effects included improved relationships. Her book, titled *Karezza*, was published in 1896.

Metaphysical thought in many places at this time believed that every drop of semen was equal to ten or more drops of blood. Therefore, having fewer ejaculations would be better for the man, while the increased intimate contact would be good for the couple and their relationship.

The problem with this, as already stated, is that according to Masters and Johnson, the average length of time for intercourse, from the time of the insertion of the penis to the man's ejaculation, is two and one-half minutes. Since this is an *average*, it means that for every man who can last a mere five minutes without having an orgasm, there is another man who can last barely thirty seconds. Fortunately, there are a variety of techniques available to allow a man to delay his orgasm up to several hours.

The basic Karezza technique for delay of orgasm is to concentrate on the purpose or goal of the intercourse rather than on the physical sensations. In what we are doing here it would mean focusing on the purpose of the magick rather than obtaining sexual gratification, i.e., orgasm. If the man or woman comes too close to an orgasm, he or she should stop the physical motions, and if necessary the man should withdraw his penis from the vagina.

Unfortunately, this primarily mental technique of ejaculation control is not enough for many men who, from adolescence, have trained themselves to have ejaculation as a goal of their sexual activities. Many men believe the lie that they can have physical problems if they do not ejaculate every time they are involved in lovemaking. One woman told me that

her boyfriend always insisted that he have an orgasm with her or he would get sick. And while it is true that after many periods of sexual excitation without an orgasm a man may feel some minor discomfort, colloquially known as "blue balls," this is not a dangerous condition and is alleviated by having an orgasm or by the mere passage of time.

The point I wish to make here is that most men will need a combination of mental and physical techniques to be able to control their orgasm. This is especially true considering that some men, such as the boyfriend of the woman just mentioned, believe that orgasm must be their immediate goal in every sexual experience.

Of the physical methods, the most well-known technique, and the one that causes the most problems while you need to practice it, is the Masters and Johnson "squeeze" technique. In this technique, when the man feels that he is about to have an orgasm, but has not yet passed what is called the point of ejaculatory inevitability (when he can't stop the ejaculation), he must withdraw his penis from the vagina. Then, either he or his partner must literally grab the penis and apply heavy pressure on the bottom of the penis, just behind the head of the penis until the need for ejaculation passes. After a few weeks of such practice the man can develop good control over his orgasm.

Unfortunately, this is not the most pleasant experience for the man or his partner! Certainly the partner would need to be very understanding while the man trains himself with her help. The following Tantric system is much better.

The advantage of the Tantric technique is that it uses several physical techniques simultaneously, and your partner need never know you are doing them. First, just before you reach the point of ejaculatory inevitability take a very deep breath and hold it for a slow count of sixteen. While you are doing this, look, with both eyes, at the tip of your nose.

Second, begin to breathe slowly. As you do so, roll your eyes in a counter-clockwise motion. First up as high as they will go, then straight to the left, then down, then to the right, then up, and finally back to where your eyes started. Thus, you are not making a circle, but a large square or rectangle. As you do this, tense the anus muscle (the sphincter) as hard as you can. Once you have completed the counterclockwise motion three times, release the anus muscle as you slowly exhale.

Repeat the above steps three times, even if the feelings of ejaculatory need have faded. Note that it is totally possible to use this technique without withdrawing from the vagina, and your partner need never know what you are doing.

But the technique that is probably the best for control of orgasm is a Taoist technique and is primarily physical in nature. At the point just before ejaculatory inevitability, stop the thrusting motions and take three deep breaths. Then, using the first two or three fingers of either hand, apply firm pressure on the perineum, the point midway between the testicles and the anus. This point, known in acupuncture as Conception Vessel One, is important to the energy flow of the body's reproductive system. Applying firm pressure here changes the energy pattern, which has a resultant effect on the physical organs. This actually causes a change in the valves within the reproductive system of the male with a suction-like effect. Ejaculation cannot occur.

Using one or another of these techniques you should be able to control your orgasm. The Taoist technique has an unusual side benefit, which I cannot go into too deeply here for this technique controls ejaculation only. Practicing with this technique

until you learn how to exert mental pressure on the Vessel of Conception Point One will yield a change in the body's energies so that the man can have an orgasm without an ejaculation. Since the result of ejaculation is de-tumescence in the male, the result of this technique is not only prolonged intercourse, but also the almost legendary male multiple orgasm. The feeling is much like small orgasms without ejaculation followed by an incredibly huge orgasm when the male does allow ejaculation to occur. Your experimentation with this technique is invited.

Now let us assume that the man has the ability to control his orgasms. The next part to understand is the idea of the Amrita, or Elixir. As I said, it is the *transmuted* or changed First Matter, the First Matter being the combination of the sperm and female fluids. Shortly I will discuss how the transmutation is done, but first I will discuss what is done with the transmuted First Matter, the true magickal elixir.

The basic idea of this type of Outer Alchemy is that the combination of the sexual fluids of a man and a woman (the First Matter) is magickal in nature (becomes the Elixir). The Elixir must then be reabsorbed by the magicians performing this type of sex magick. The easiest way to do this is to simply allow the now flaccid penis to remain in the vagina for a period of fifteen minutes. According to some Tantric traditions, sperm loses its magickal powers after fifteen minutes, so a longer period is not needed. These fluids, to a minor extent, and/or the energies they

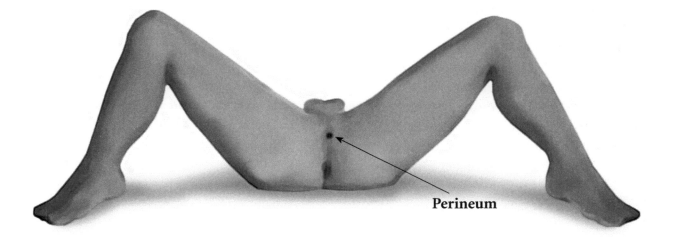

Perineum

contain will be absorbed through the thin tissues of the vagina and the head of the penis. However, not all of the fluids are absorbed in this manner.

Although many people raised in Western cultures may find the following idea disagreeable, a large number of sex magicians have overcome this phobia and treat the Elixir as a magickal Eucharist. As a friend of mine likes to poetically say,

First 'e loves 'er,
then Elixir! [he licks her]

In other words, after his orgasm the man performs oral sex upon the woman, taking the combined fluids into his mouth. He may then keep the fluids under his tongue, allowing them to be absorbed, for the most efficacy. Alternatively he may kiss his partner and share the Elixir. Another possibility is to put the Elixir into a small cup of wine and share the Elixir. It is this idea of swallowing the sexual fluids that may turn some people off. However, over the past forty years there has been an increase in the popularity of oral sex, so this taboo is quickly being overcome. In some cases, just a small drop of the elixir is used as a way to "charge" the wine, just as a small amount of "starter" is used to create an entire loaf of sourdough bread.

It should also be noted here that this type of ritual can be done with others present when the cup of wine is used. The Elixir-charged wine may be passed among those present. In fact, in some groups another man or woman is chosen as the "cup bearer." It is his or her duty to obtain the Elixir instead of the woman's sexual partner.

Obviously, there are many possibilities for Outer Alchemy. The next question is duration of the magick. As a result of personal experience by myself and by students who have reported back to me, as well as through research in various books, it is my belief that that the intercourse of sex magick should last a minimum of forty-five minutes to be effective, and after about three hours, depending upon the magicians, a point of negative returns is reached. So, as they currently abbreviate on the Internet, YMMV: "Your mileage may vary."

The final point before giving a ritual is the procedure of transformation, which turns the First Matter into the Elixir. It is done simply by prolonging the act of intercourse while focusing on a particular goal rather than for mere physical gratification. This can be accomplished by means similar to those already discussed, i.e., by will power or concentration on sigils.

There is also a system that aligns sex magick practitioners with the forces of nature and strengthens the transmutation.

Women have a natural menstrual cycle of approximately twenty-eight days, matching the cycle of the Moon. According to occult science, on each one of the twenty-eight days, a woman will secrete a different fluid when she is sexually excited and/or has an orgasm. Therefore, a sex magick ritual can be performed on a specific day of the month for a particular purpose. By combining the spiritual forces of humans with the forces of nature, the Elixir becomes an unbelievably powerful magickal fluid.

Here is a copy of a published list of the magickal abilities of the fluids of the twenty-eight days, starting with the new Moon *of the woman*. That is, beginning with the day after the end of her menstrual cycle (from a list by Sariel):

1. Good Fortune
2. Separation and ill will
3. Gaining official favor
4. Love
5. Material well-being
6. Victory in battle
7. Overcoming illness
8. Maintaining health
9. Spirituality
10. Misfortune in love
11. Harmony in marriage
12. Separation and divorce
13. Friendships
14. Material wealth
15. Keeping thieves away
16. Keeping venomous creatures away
17. Aiding births
18. Aiding hunters

19. Dealing with enemies
20. Dealing with fugitives
21. Destruction
22. Domesticated animals
23. Vegetation
24. Gaining love and favor
25. Liquids and containers
26. Water creatures
27. Destruction
28. Reconciliation

Notice that some items on the list are very broad topics. They can be affected by the magicians' contemplation during the magickal rite. As an example, the magicians may choose to help or hinder a fugitive from a bully by doing an Outer Alchemical sex magick ritual on the twentieth day of the cycle. Of course, since this is a type of Grey Magick, a divination should be done before a ritual of this sort.

I must note here that there are many lists of the magickal qualities associated with each day of the lunar cycle. Sometimes each day is referred to as a "digit of the Moon." If you find other lists you may wish to compare them to the one above. However, the only way to determine what is accurate for you is through personal testing.

In his book *The Tree of Life* by Israel Regardie, the author gives an outline of a ritual called "the Mass of the Holy Ghost." This is, pure and simple, an Outer Alchemy sex magick ritual. Here are his instructions translated into common terms.

1. After the usual preliminaries, the couple should begin their ritual sex.

2. "Through the stimulus of warmth and spiritual fire [intercourse] to the Athanor [penis] there should be . . . an ascent of the Serpent [sperm] into the Curcurbite [vagina]."

3. The mixture of the sperm and the fluids of the woman is charged by "means of a continuous invocation of the spiritual principle conforming to the work in hand."

4. The ritual is concluded by treating the Elixir as the magickal Eucharist or by using it to anoint and consecrate a talisman.

As you can see, there is some overlap with the earlier type of sex magick described in this lesson. At the end of the "Mass" is described a technique of charging a talisman by simply applying some of the Elixir to it. This is a very powerful technique, as your experience will come to show.

From what you know it should not be too difficult to create your own sex magick ritual. First do the Opening by Watchtower. Then do the actual sex magick. Follow with the Closing by Watchtower. If there are other people present, they may sit, holding hands, in a circle around the pair practicing the sex magick. In some groups they watch the proceedings, their own excitation enhancing that of the two magicians directly involved. Other groups have the people sitting with their backs toward the center of the circle so that the couple will have a modicum of privacy. Those sitting in the circle should concentrate on the purpose of the ritual. This can be very difficult, as watching two people have sex (even if it is sex magick) for a few hours can become very boring. Thus, learning to concentrate on a desired subject or goal becomes very important. Then, as stated before, the Elixir can be mixed with wine either by the male ritualist or a cup bearer. The wine–Amarita mixture can then be passed around the circle. The couple actually involved in the sex magick should be the last ones to drink so that they get the final drops of the magickal mixture. The pair can each take a small sip, passing the cup back and forth until the fluid is gone. Then, together, they should hold the cup upside down and say,

It is finished.

The two systems of sex magick described so far in this lesson are traditionally Western in nature, although there is ample evidence that both have been used by the ancient Tantrics and Taoists. Similarly, the third form or Inner Alchemy is more traditionally associated with Eastern systems, although it also has a firm foundation in the West.

PART THREE

The reason the previous form of sex magick is called "Outer Alchemy" is because it works with the energy systems of the body and magickally charges substances that are outside of the body part of the time. Inner Alchemy keeps all of the forces within the body and uses the force of magickally directed sexual excitation to strengthen and empower the psychic energies of the body. This Inner Alchemy may be the easiest to work for a magician who has diligently practiced the rituals of this course.

Inner Alchemy, sometimes called "Tantra yoga" or "kundalini yoga," involves the taking of the sexual excitation and energy and channeling it to purposes other than sexual gratification. When you are quite sexually aroused and stimulated, send the energy up from the groin toward the head. This is sort of a reversed version of the Middle Pillar Ritual.

Important: Until you have mastered the Middle Pillar Ritual, do not try this technique of causing the energy to rise from the sexual center.

Everything You Know Is Wrong

Now that I have given the standard introduction on the subject, and you're satisfied that you know as much or more about it than I do, I want to tell you that it's all a bunch of garbage!

I could use stronger words, but I have tried to avoid the scatological slang that so many people have as part of their daily speech. However, let me reiterate that 90 percent of what you hear about Tantra is just plain wrong, and most of the rest is garbled at best. Let me start by breaking down some popular notions that are totally incorrect.

*Tantra yoga is the yoga of sex. **False!***
Tantra is a widely varied set of spiritual traditions that have evolved over thousands of years. Some Tantric traditions do not look at sexuality at all.

Most of those that do look at sexuality are very encompassing, and the sexual studies are only a small part of the whole. To call Tantra the "yoga of sex" (as one author has done) would be like calling reading the yoga of staring at paper.

*More books are being published that explain the secrets of Tantra. **False!***
The secrets of the Tantrics, especially the sexual secrets, have gone underground and are now kept within various occult orders. Most books coming out now are not written by initiated Tantrics. They are either compilations (cut and paste jobs) of earlier works, or the author's errors and fantasies. Remember, many of the early Tantric texts were written in code, a "twilight language" similar to the alchemical code described earlier in this lesson. If you don't know the code, you can only guess at the true meaning of the words.

*Kundalini yoga is the ancient technique of causing the energy to rise up the spine until you achieve enlightenment. **False!***
First, while the concept of kundalini is ancient and established, the expression "kundalini yoga" is a relatively new term, invented by Westerners. The ancient term was *Laya Yoga* (pronounced "Lie-oh-gah") and was first described over a thousand years ago. The Tantric who described it also explained that it was only symbolic, and not to be taken as reality. Furthermore, do you know anyone who has achieved enlightenment as a result of kundalini yoga? In your readings do the authors tell of anyone who has achieved enlightenment as a result of kundalini yoga, or do they merely tell what is supposed to happen? Have the authors of those books experienced it themselves? The answer to all of these questions is "No."

*The kundalini serpent is coiled three and a half times at the spine's base. **False!***
All forms of yoga, to be valid, are true sciences. If proven false they are discarded. Have you ever seen a snake coiled up in the entrails of a human body? Of

course not. It's not there. Again, this serpent is symbolic—it's a metaphor—not actual.

Some Initiated Truth about Tantra

Now that I have dismissed some of the lies about Tantra and Laya Yoga, let's start rebuilding from the ground up.

There are a large variety of psychic power centers throughout the human body. They are not limited to the five, six, seven, or eight you usually hear about. As an example, there are several in the head and others in the palms of the hands and the soles of the feet. This will become important later in this lesson. In the meantime, it is absolutely *unimportant* to worry about whether or not the heart chakra or the brow (third eye) chakra is "open." What *is* important is to learn how to make the energy flow up from the base of the spine.

What I am about to present to you is not some theory that you are meant to visualize, but scientific fact. It is repeatable and verifiable under laboratory conditions. If I did not have to explain it to you in this course, I would have you experiment first and discover for yourself what thousands of people know. Further, I do not say this as a result of reading, but rather as a result of my own experience as an initiated Tantric. Of course, there are certain things which I cannot divulge as a result of my initiation vows, but by making slight alterations as well as coming up with techniques based on secret methods, I will be able to give you more real information on Inner Alchemy than has ever been published in one place.

In order to learn about the energy you must first learn about the breath. According to the ancient Tantric manuscripts (which may be the oldest spiritual writings in India), a breath lasts about 4 seconds. This means that in a day you breathe 21,600 times. (Calculate: 15 breaths per minute times 60 [number of minutes in an hour] times 24 [number of hours in a day] equals 21,600.) Of course, when sleeping or resting you breathe slower, and when exerting yourself you breathe faster. Therefore, this number cannot be taken as a real or even average figure. Rather, it is symbolic. And since these ancient Tantrics thought enough about the breath to figure out how many times we supposedly breathe in a day, it is logical to assume that the breath was very important to them.

And, in fact, it is. The oldest and original mantra, the repetitious chant, is not that of "OM," but is the sound of the breath.

Put down this lesson and just listen to the sound of your breath for a few seconds. Can you hear the mantra you recite 21,600 times a day? When you inhale, can you hear the sound "Hahm"? And on the exhale can you hear your breath say "Sah"? This mantra, Hahm-sah, is repeated unconsciously 21,600 times per day. By controlling it we can learn to control its power.

"Hahm-sah" is a Sanskrit word, which means "swan." It is important to understand that *you do not say or chant this mantra*. Instead you simply breathe and hear it on your breath. Try it for a few minutes. (Note: Buddhists tend to reverse this with the mantra "so-aham.")

> Inhale . . . *Hahm*
> Exhale . . . *Sah*
>
> Inhale . . . *Hahm*
> Exhale . . . *Sah*
>
> Inhale . . . *Hahm*
> Exhale . . . *Sah*

The less you *try* to do this, the easier it is to do. Just let it happen. Once you can hear the mantra in your breath, you are ready to move on to the next exercise.

Kriya (pronounced "Kree-yah") is a Sanskrit term that means "action." It also has the meanings of "to make an effort" and "to transform." By making the effort to do the following exercise you will experience the "action" of the psycho-sexual energy or kundalini force that can be mentally, physically, emotionally, and spiritually transformative.

1. Begin by finding a comfortable posture, either sitting or lying down, and doing the Relaxation Ritual.

2. Once your body is deeply relaxed, begin a slow breathing and listen for the "swan."

3. As soon as you hear it, on the inhale/Hahm part of the mantra, visualize your breath traveling up your nose, through the top of your head (just inside the skull), and down your spine to the lowest tip of the coccyx.

4. Hold your breath for as long as it is comfortable, then begin to exhale.

5. Focus on the exhalation and make it as slow as is comfortably possible. As you do, visualize the breath and energy going back up your spine, around the top of your head (just inside the skull), and out the nose. As it moves, hear the "Sah" part of the mantra.

6. Practice this for ten to twenty minutes. Then return to your normal breathing pattern.

Once you can do this comfortably, instead of holding your breath on the inhalation, just pause for a second. Then use your stomach to help give you several short exhalations. This is accomplished by repeatedly jerking in or tensing the stomach muscles. You should hear your mantra saying, "Sah, Sah, Sah, Sah," etc. Repeat until you are out of breath and need to inhale. When this happens, again take a long, slow, deep, breath, hold for a second, then repeat the "Sah, Sah, Sah, Sah" exhalation pattern. Keep up the visualizations, as above. Repeat the process for up to twenty minutes.

The first time I did this exercise I had phenomenal results. After about five minutes my body started to jerk about for no apparent reason. It was as if I suddenly got "the chills" or the "heebee jeebees" in a small part of my body, and that part just had to shiver or jerk about. This shivering and shaking is called *Shaktipat* and is a common part of the process. Then, the shaking suddenly stopped and my body seemed to change. I felt as if my body was tak-

ing the shape of a long tube and the sides of my head began to spread out. My body began to sway and my head turned jerkily and irregularly from side to side. At first I got the feeling that I was doing this to see to all sides as a form of protection. But then I realized that what had happened was that I had allowed the kundalini serpent, the *true* kundalini serpent, to become one with me. My body had spiritually assumed the shape of a serpent and my head had opened into a serpent's hood. I was that snake.

Then, suddenly, I buckled over, almost in pain, from the most intensely erotic feelings I have ever experienced. Needless to say, it took quite some time for my breathing to return to normal!

All of these experiences can happen to you. The only real danger is that you may not expect the sensations you receive. Normally, a teacher would not tell you what could happen and would allow you to experience it and then "rescue you" from these unknown experiences. Since I cannot be with you, I am telling you what you may feel and what type of experiences you should expect. You may not feel the sensation of becoming one with the kundalini serpent or the intense erotic feelings with your first few tries at this Hahm-sah exercise, but you should eventually feel Shaktipat, the jerky motions. If you do not experience them, re-read the instructions for this exercise. Nothing is left out.

Once you have experienced Shaktipat within yourself, it is important to learn how to experience both Shaktipat and the movement of the kundalini energy in another person. To do this you need a willing partner. Your partner should preferably already have experienced Shaktipat within himself or herself.

The best position for this exercise is sitting on the floor or on pillows, or possibly on low stools of equal heights. You and your partner should sit, back-to-back, preferably naked, with your backs touching along their lengths. If you prefer not to have nudity, the wearing of thin cotton shirts is fine. Both of you should perform the Relaxation Ritual, then begin the Hamh-sah exercise. You should both breathe at the same time. Feel your energy and your partner's energy go up and down the spine. Although the energy does flow within the spine (it is the spiritual essence of the cerebrospinal fluid), it also emanates beyond the physical body. The result of this exercise should be that both of your experiences should be intensified.

It is important to realize that all of the forms of working with the breath and working with mantras are *nothing but substitutes for sexual activity*. The reason they have been presented here is to simply and safely familiarize you with the feelings and sensations associated with the energies you have stimulated and are working with. The next step is to repeat the last exercise by using sexual activity as a prod for Shaktipat.

To do this, once again sit back-to-back. In the previous exercise it would have been best if you both were naked. In this exercise it is a necessity. Here the breath no longer holds the same import as you move to tactile stimulation leading to the energetic sensations. After doing the Relaxation Ritual, both you and your partner should begin sexual self-stimulation. I hesitate to use the term "masturbate" as to many people this implies only penile or clitoral and vaginal stimulation. Rather, begin by caressing yourself. Feel your face, hair, and ears. Touch your hands, arms, chest, and breasts. Caress your feet, legs, and thighs. Learn to sexually stimulate your entire body. However, do not touch your partner except with your back.

Once you are both aroused, both of you should begin intense genital stimulation. This means not only stimulating the penis and clitoris, but also, if you like it, your scrotum, perineum, and anus or inner and outer labia, vagina (and G spot), perineum and anus. In fact, you can stimulate any part of your body that gives you the greatest excitation. However, neither of you should reach orgasm.

Stop the genital stimulation before orgasm is inevitable, but continue to stimulate other parts of your body. When the feeling of the immediate need for orgasm fades, return to genital stimulation. Continue this process until you experience Shaktipat and can sense the motion of energy in your partner.

Once you have done this you may either have an orgasm via self-stimulation, make love with your partner, or choose not to have an orgasm.

The next step is to vastly increase the flow of energy. This requires the uniting of the energies of both partners in a special way. It is a physical technique, which automatically increases the energy flows. For this first technique, both the man and woman should at least be wearing undergarments. Although more clothes may be worn, the genitals of both members of the couple and the breasts of the woman should have some covering. Swimsuits or tights and leotards also work well.

The man sits cross-legged on the floor, on a pillow, or on a very low stool or bench. The woman should sit on his lap, facing him, so that they can look at each other. She should wrap her legs around him. Pillows may be arranged to make this position easier to maintain for a period of time. If it becomes difficult, the man may extend his legs. Support for the back may be achieved by sitting next to a wall, a sturdy chair or sofa, or through the use of a special chair for sitting on the floor, commonly known as a "backjack."

Once you have both become comfortable in this position, it is the time for small talk. Ask if your partner is comfortable, is there anything your partner wants to say, are there any feelings or emotions that you or your partner wish to let go. Tell each other your fears and dreams, hopes and disappointments, successes and failures. This will help you develop deep rapport, uniting mentally and emotionally with each other.

Next, start adjusting your breathing patterns. The closeness of the position will make it easy for each of you to breathe *at opposite times*. When the woman breathes out, the man breathes in. When the man breathes out, the woman breathes in. It should only take a few moments for both of you to become comfortable with the mutual breathing pattern. If you have a break in the pattern, don't worry about it, just relax and start again.

As a result of your practice performing the Middle Pillar Ritual and working with the mantra

Hahm-sah as outlined earlier, you will have very strong effects as you go through the next part of this exercise. However, even if you have not done so, the physical actions will have an effect on you.

The man should look into the *woman's right eye* and the woman should look into the *man's left eye*. As she exhales and he inhales, she should sense the energy rising up her spine and leaving through her right eye, while he should feel the energy coming out of her right eye, in through his left eye and down his spine.

As the man exhales and the woman inhales, he should feel the energy continue down his spine and out through his penis. She should feel the energy coming out of his penis, into her vagina and up her spine. This is represented diagrammatically in the figure below:

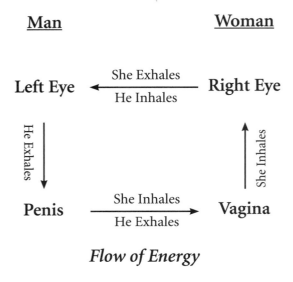

Flow of Energy

Before moving on to the next technique, you must be able to maintain this posture for a minimum of twenty minutes, although forty minutes is preferable. If it is too difficult to remain in this posture, there is another easier alternate, which will also work well. The major difference is that both partners simply stretch out their legs. He can lean back and use his arms to support himself or may even lean up against a wall or some pillows if there is room for his partner's legs. She may choose to leave her legs out or wrap them around her partner below her.

Feel the motion of the energy and how it builds to a level even higher than you have achieved alone or back-to-back. As you practice you may find yourselves shaking from Shaktipat. That is a good sign. However, because of the closeness due to the linked breathing and the circulation of energy between both of you, intense sexual excitation and desire may occur. While this, too, is a good sign, wait until you have finished the exercise (twenty to forty minutes) before engaging in intercourse or other sexual activity. You may find it to be some of the most ecstatic lovemaking you have ever experienced.

The next step is to repeat the above exercise while unclothed. At this time the penis should not be in the vagina. As the experience of Shaktipat intensifies with this technique, you may be tempted to fiercely hug and caress one another. Resist this temptation! Keep clear and open eye contact with each other. You will quickly learn that the energy field is broken—or at least reduced—when eye contact is broken. The result is a loss of built-up energy, and it may take many minutes to rebuild the energy level that existed before the break in eye contact.

After you have practiced this technique without clothes to a point where you can maintain the eye and breath contact for a minimum of twenty minutes, you may add physical caresses. Since you do not want to break eye contact, this cannot include kissing and will be limited to the use of the hands. Pay special attention to the parts of the body that are not generally considered highly sensitive to touch. Caress the face and ears (don't block the eye contact), the arms, legs, chest, and stomach. The woman can reach under herself to caress his penis and scrotum while he can also caress her breasts, clitoris, and labia. Although neither of you should have an orgasm, it will be a good sign if her lubricating fluids make both of your genitals quite wet. If either of you feels an approaching orgasm, you should tell your partner so he or she will change the method of stimulation. Continue this practice until it can be done for a minimum of twenty minutes, although lasting forty minutes would be better.

When the caressing is added, the amount of energy cycled between you should again increase to a higher level. The Shaktipat quivers and jerks may be enough to shake you apart from one another, in which case you should start the exercise over. Once you have completed this exercise, intercourse or other sexual activity may take place if desired.

As you have read, and I hope have experienced, the more intimate the contact, the greater the amount of psycho-sexual energy. The greater the amount of intimate contact, the more powerful are the Shaktipat jerks and shakes. Also, they are greater in number. The intensity of the energy increases.

If you have accomplished all of the above exercises to your satisfaction, you are ready to proceed to the next ritual. All that I have described in this section has only been preparation for the next rite.

The Tantric Ritual of Inner Alchemy

(adapted to Western traditions)

STEP ONE. Have your room dimly lit, preferably with candles. Let there be many sticks of incense burning, primarily of sandalwood, patchouli, or musk. Be sure to keep them lit. In the center should be your Place of Comfort, and within arms' reach of it should be some water, wine, cooked or dried meat or dry cereal, fish or ginger, and sensual "toys" such as feathers, gloves of fur or faux fur, scented and/or flavored oils, etc. Most definitely not to be included are vibrators, penis-desensitizing creams or sprays, or anything which could inflict pain or punishment. Gentle background music is also appropriate. Once the room is set up, close the door as you leave the room until the next part of the ritual. Remember to make sure that candles and incense cannot start a fire. Take the telephone off the hook or turn off the cellphone. Tell anyone not involved that you and your partner do not wish to be disturbed for the next few hours.

STEP TWO. Together, you and your partner should take a long, leisurely bath if at all possible. Scent the water with sandalwood or musk. Light the bathroom with candles. As you wash each other, talk out any problems you had during the day and let the emotional charge associated with these problems fade away. As the problems and their associated emotions fade, feel free to play with one another. Although sexual contact is encouraged, do not have intercourse. If you do not have access to a bath, shower together, then apply a light amount of scented oil or talc to each other. Finally, put on your magickal robes and enter your magickal temple.

STEP THREE. Perform the Opening by Watchtower, or at the very least, do the LBRP.

STEP FOUR. Sit together, the woman to the left of the man, and hold and caress one another. Feed each other with small amounts of the foods and drinks. Caress each other both physically and with words until the sexual excitation becomes so intense that the robes must be removed. Do so. Although you shouldn't have any clocks showing in the room, if it seems like this step took less than what you figure to be half an hour, slow down! You are going too fast. There is no rush.

STEP FIVE. Continue in the same manner. Use the toys you have brought. If either of you nears orgasm, slow down!

STEP SIX. Once the excitation has reached such a state that the man is very erect and the woman is very lubricated, they can assume either position already given in the exercises. However, this time the woman should take the penis and insert it into her vagina.

There is another position, which many couples seem to prefer, and this can be used as an alternative to the previously described positions. The man lies flat on his back and brings his legs up so that they almost touch his chest. The woman, with her back toward his face, literally sits on his exposed penis, making sure that she achieves a deep penetration into her vagina. At this time the man can relax his legs. If the woman pivots to either side slightly, he will find that he will be able to place one foot on the floor and rest the other leg over her hip and leg.

Tantra in Unexpected Places
Is It Really in Those Movies?

Although there are movies that are supposed to be about Tantra, few really manifest the MahaTantra experience. However, there are two that seemingly have nothing to do with Tantra yet brilliantly portray it. And you're not going to believe what they are.

The first one is *Star Trek: The Motion Picture*. In it, a god-like being, V'ger, manifests as Ilia, a female. For the ultimate deity to evolve, this female (goddess?) must join in total unity with a man, Commander Decker. At the climax, they hold each other as energy swirls around them. They merge, and the deity (V'ger), the god (Decker), and goddess (Ilia) evolve and move off to a higher plane.

The second movie was Natalie Wood's last film, *Brainstorm*. The basic concept is the invention of a device that lets you record the experiences, including thoughts and feelings, of a person. When another person plays it back wearing special headgear, they can experience everything that was recorded, including sensations and emotions. Originally, when someone was playing back a recording, the image on the screen in the theater would suddenly get much wider, and the film, traveling at a faster speed, was more realistic. It was an intense sensation for its time.

For fun, one of the experimenters makes a recording of himself having sex with a willing partner. A scientist named Gordy Forbes—overweight, fed up with his job and his life—gets the recording and makes a loop, so he can experience orgasmic sex over and over and over . . .

When they find him he is quivering in a trance-like state! Of course, they think it is something terrible and rush him to a hospital where he recovers. He tells the main characters (played by Wood and Christopher Walken) that he can't do his job any more. He's been changed by the experience. Later, when we see him, he looks healthier and is exercising.

His entire life was changed for the better by the MahaTantra experience.

This is a bit difficult to describe, but very easy to achieve. The man can reach up and caress the woman from behind and the woman can easily caress his genitals.

STEP SEVEN. If you have done the practice, you will find that by now you should have reached a stage where eye contact is no longer necessary. But you must keep up the linked breathing pattern. And, most importantly, don't move! That is, there should be no thrusting motions by either the man or woman. The only motions should involve the woman contracting and relaxing the muscles of her vagina and the man flexing the pubic muscles so that the penis will move within the vagina without thrusting motions.

STEP EIGHT. Now, as you do the linked breathing, feel the energy move through and around you. As you will learn, it is the intimate contact that is important. Therefore, since there is no thrusting, it is unimportant if the woman ceases to lubricate or the man loses his erection. Stay still except for the inner genitalia motion described in the previous step.

STEP NINE. If the woman achieves one or more orgasms, fine. If the man approaches orgasm, let him use the control techniques given earlier in this lesson.

STEP TEN. When you start to experience Shaktipat jerks and shakes, surrender to them and allow them to increase until you have a MahaTantra experience (more on this later) or until a minimum of forty minutes have passed.

STEP ELEVEN. You may then have regular intercourse or engage in other sexual activity. The alchemical Elixir produced will be very strong for a period of fifteen minutes, and although consumption of it is not necessary for this ritual, you are urged not to waste it.

STEP TWELVE. Do the Closing by Watchtower, or at least the LBRP. Record results in your ritual diary.

The rite is over.

About the only thing I haven't covered is what I call the MahaTantra experience. "Maha" means "great," and the MahaTantra experience is great indeed! It is nothing less than the experience of Shaktipat magnified a millionfold.

For most people, orgasms tend to be a brief climax, which only resolves the immediate buildup of sexual energy. Only rarely is it a true, total release. The MahaTantra experience is that ultimate, desired super-orgasm wherein your entire body seems to release the pent-up tension of years. Generally it lasts for only twenty seconds to two minutes, but it may seem like it lasts for hours. During it you may experience feelings of joy, power, release, excitement, contentment, unity with all; of being one with the Divine Source of All That Is. It is enlightenment. It is an altered state of consciousness that makes LSD, mescaline, ayahuasca, *Salvia Divinorum*, and other *entheogens* (from the Greek, literally "becoming divine within"), psychoactive substances used for religious or spiritual purposes, seem like a grain of sand compared to an indescribable desert of ecstatic experience.

You may have an orgasm when you experience MahaTantra and if the man does so he may or may not have an ejaculation of sperm. And although this technique is a form of Inner Alchemy, as was suggested in the ritual, do not waste the Elixir.

Of the MahaTantra experience I can tell you no more. Not because of vows or anything like that, but because there are no real words to describe intensely personal and subjective experiences. Until you have experienced MahaTantra, no words can describe it. Once you have experienced MahaTantra, no words can express it.

This ritual can be used to create intense spiritual experiences that can last hours, days, or longer. It requires no special mental work or direction. It is the equivalent of what many people spend years in meditation in order to achieve. But don't take my word for it. Do the work necessary to be able to do this ritual and try it for yourself. It is a high form of White Magick.

If desired, you could also focus on a magickal goal or use techniques similar to those described earlier in this lesson so your unconscious mind is filled with a symbol representing your magickal goal. Both partners should be aware of the goal, and naturally, it should be SMART. And imagine the energy if several couples worked this together!

PART FOUR

Once again I would like to remind you that this course is only an introduction to ceremonial magick. Just as in the last lesson I could not give you all of the names and powers of the spirits you could evoke, so, too, in this lesson I cannot give you all of the forms and rituals of sex magick. In fact, the ideas and rituals have been rather schematic in nature. This is because I do not want you to be incapable of original magickal thought. True, the various banishings stay the same, but other parts of the rituals can be added to or subtracted from as you see fit. The only judge in this must be your success or failure.

With your knowledge of the three types of sex magick, Inner and Outer Alchemy, and Thought Control, you should be able to pick up any book that covers sex magick and understand what is written there. I say "should" because most magicians who

LGBT Issues

Sex magick is not about love and romance, it's about magick. It uses arousal and the linking of sexual polar energies to create massive increases in magickal power.

Unfortunately, since the birth of the concept of "romantic love" in the late Middle Ages, sex and love have become linked in our minds. As a magician you might ask yourself if that link is true and genetic or simply societal. If you come to the conclusion that it is genetic, you will only want to do sex magick with your romantic partner. If you come to the conclusion that it is societal and can free yourself from the belief that sex and romantic love must be linked, you can partner with anyone who wishes to partner with you. I repeat, this is not about love, romance and attraction; it's about magick. Some people will have difficulty dealing with this and that's fine. You don't have to deal with it. In fact, you can be a successful magician and never do sex magick at all.

Further, just as a straight person or a gay person can work with the tools of a magician, there is no reason why a person cannot do sex magick with members of the same sex (even if you're straight) or opposite sex (even if you're gay). This may shock both straight and gay people but remember—this just uses sexual activity to do the work. It's not about love and romance and personal desire. I have to admit, however, that some people simply cannot respond to members of their own gender or the opposite gender. For these people *some* aspects of sex magick won't work, but others will. I would respectfully focus on what you can do rather than what you can't or won't do. And remember, you don't have to do sex magick at all.

If you notice, one of the things I mentioned was the concept of polar energies. Previously I have discussed the idea of our understanding of things by way of opposites—up and down, electric and magnetic, positive and negative, male and female. If you think about the information I've shared on the Tree of Life and the way it manifests within us, you can see that every person is capable of manifesting both the left and right pillars, the feminine and masculine pillars of severity and mercy.

This means that although I have used the classical terms of male and female, man and woman in describing the workings in this chapter, many of the exercises and techniques can easily be refocused toward people of the same sex. Use your imagination and work on the concept of balancing polarities of energy, not gender.

This chapter is about the way most people practice sex magick today. If you are interested in more information on Western sex magick, please see my *Modern Sex Magick*, which is both traditional and forward looking, as well as appropriate for people of any and all ethical sexual directions.

perform sex magick try to keep their secrets under the cover of coded or "twilight" language. Others hide it in archaic or obsolete wordings that make A. E. Waite seem clear and simple!

It is claimed by some that the wandering minnesingers, golliards, and minstrels of the late Middle Ages practiced some form of sex magick. This was coded into their music. For example, the word "die" in those songs meant "to have an orgasm." By understanding this, such lyrics as "I die, I die in sweetest agony" become clear in meaning. Later, this tradition was carried on in Victorian Age erotica wherein an orgasm was frequently described as "the little death."

Aleister Crowley, being no stranger to erotic literature, continued with the same allegorical idioms. In *Magick* he claimed to have made a sacrifice of "a male child of perfect innocence and high intelligence" 150 times a year between 1912 and 1928. Of course, he was not admitting to the murder of 2,400 children! Some Crowley commentators claim that this refers to magickal masturbation of the Outer Alchemy tradition. Others claim that he was "taking away" the virginity of another person. If this latter is true, I am inclined to believe that Crowley did more than a bit of leg-pulling concerning numbers!

In a ritual printed in Crowley's massive work *The Equinox*, there is an instruction for one of the participants in a ritual to take a sword "and slit his throat therewith." This probably refers to magickal masturbation. In context, it occurs while watching another couple engaged in ritual sex magick.

There are a variety of positions for ritualized sexual intercourse, but since they are already printed in many sources, I will not repeat them here. I urge you to investigate them from the books listed in this lesson's bibliography.

Let me repeat that the threefold division of the types of sex magick are quite arbitrary. I have used them merely as a way to make communication of the various techniques easier. In actual practice, those divisions tend to blur. That is why in the technique of Inner Alchemy, a useful result is the Outer Alchemy Elixir.

Some of you may have read that a man should not have an ejaculation at all, or at least as seldom as possible. Different sources have different attitudes toward this, usually depending upon the attitude of the group of which they are a part. So whether or not you decide to totally or partially withhold sperm is a matter of choice. Certainly the withholding of the sperm negates some forms of Outer Alchemy. I will make several points on the matter, which may help you to decide.

1. The longer a man is sexually excited without having an ejaculation, the more magickally powerful the elixir will be.

2. Even some of those traditions that do not believe a man should withhold his orgasm teach that the sperm should be quickly reabsorbed by the man. This can be done by keeping the elixir under the tongue and allowing its energy to enter the mucous membrane there, by eating the sperm, or through a special hatha yoga technique, which causes a suction within the bladder and allows the man to suck the elixir up his penis and into the urinary bladder where it is absorbed.

3. One of the reasons the withholding of sperm is suggested is for birth control. Modern birth control methods are quite effective for this purpose.

4. One of the reasons Karezza was practiced was because it saved the lives of women. A major cause of women's deaths has been complications of the birthing process. While the death rate due to giving birth has dropped remarkably in economically advanced countries over the last 100 years, it is still a problem in many places in the world. However, I dare say that most of you reading this have access to modern birth control methods and birthing procedures. Karezza at this date should not be held as important for saving women's lives.

5. Many ancient (and some modern) Chinese texts believe that as a man gets older, his ability

to have an erection and produce sperm diminishes. Thus, while a man is young he may have an ejaculation more than once a day. But as he ages he should lessen this number until, in old age, he may ejaculate only once every few months. This does not mean that he should in any other way limit his sexual pleasure. Those of you who are interested in Chinese and Taoist philosophy may wish to consider this attitude. (However, a 2008 study from the University of Nottingham shows that frequent ejaculations by men in their twenties and thirties increased the chance of prostate cancer, while frequent ejaculations by men in their fifties reduced the chance of the same type of cancer.)

6. A long period of lovemaking can help lovers become closer. However, there is something that I have noticed and would like to draw to your attention. There was a period of time when men only considered their own sexual pleasure. More recently, men have become interested in the pleasure of their partners. With the onset of the modern women's movement, many women have decided to become responsible for their own orgasms, even if they are with a partner. In a sense, this is like the period when men were only interested in themselves, although it is nowhere near as selfish. But more recently I have met several women who really enjoy sex and want their partners to prove that they are also enjoying sex. In other words, they want their male partner to have an orgasm and ejaculate. And if their partner doesn't have an orgasm, they want to know why or what is wrong. Several women have also told me that even if they have one or more orgasms, they feel the act of sex is incomplete until their male partner has also had an orgasm.

While I make no claim to my researches being final or even scientific, I certainly believe that the day when Crowley said you can use any woman for sex magick, and not tell her what you are doing, is past. If your partner asks you why you did not have an orgasm, you had better be prepared to say why.

God Eating

There are many people who firmly believe "you are what you eat." In some primitive tribes, the heart of a valiant enemy might be eaten to gain his courage. The hunter who slew an animal would have the first choice of what part of the animal to eat in order to absorb those qualities of the animal that he wished to possess.

The ultimate form of this belief comes with "god eating." This was a pre-Christian tradition, which was eventually adopted by the Christians, and especially by Roman Catholicism. The idea is simple: bring the essence of a god or goddess into something edible and then allow the worshippers to eat that food and thus eat that god or goddess. The result of this would be that those who ate the deity would absorb the qualities of that deity.

I find another similar idea far more enticing. If the essence of a deity can be invoked into food or drink, why not invoke that god or goddess into a person and have sexual relations with that god or goddess? Certainly the myths of Greece and Rome are filled with such ideas. There are some Wiccans and witches who practice this, calling it the "Great Rite."

The technique is twofold. First, the appropriate god or goddess must be invoked into a man or a woman. For this see the instructions in Lesson Nine of this course. Second, the other person should first worship the embodied god/goddess and consider what he or she is about to do: make love with a god or goddess! The worshipper should take that attitude and demeanor and realize how privileged he or she is. The worshipper should really be in an almost constant state of awe! Any sexual fluids from the embodied god/goddess are holy and should be considered as a sacrament.

A Taoist Alchemical Sex Magick Ritual

The ancient Taoists had a ritual similar to Laya Yoga. It usually took place outside, on a hill, and required the person seeking enlightenment, a sensitive assistant, and usually one or more sexual helpers.

First, through sexual activity and breath control the main participant would reach a state before orgasm and seek to maintain that state with the help of his or her sexual helper(s). The result of this, of course, would be the physical twitches the Tantrics call Shaktipat. The sensitive assistant would watch and detect the energy as it begins to move up the spine. To prevent the energy from leaving the body, the assistant would plug the anus with material dipped in wax.

The assistant would watch as the energy moved up the spine. If it seemed to stop, the assistant would pinch and poke the body to make the energy continue to rise. As it approached the head, the assistant would make sure that the head's orifices, as with the anus, were plugged up at the right moment so that the energy could not escape. The result would be that the energy would end up "exploding" out the top of the head, through what the Tantrics called the "lotus of 1000 petals," and the final outcome would be Nirvana, or Enlightenment.

PART FIVE

When I first wrote *Modern Magick* the U.S. culture was moving into what was called the "Me Generation." I wrote that in my observations of culture over the years I had noticed a strong change in society. Back when I was first learning magick and before the Me Generation, it seemed like most people cared more about one another and the environment than they did when *Modern Magick* was originally published. Granted, this was a generalization, but I found through interactions with correspondents and students that although people were talking about community and ecology, their main interests seemed to be how much money they could earn and where the party was that they're going to attend that night. From a magickal standpoint those selfish attitudes were a necessary outcome and response to the previous cycle of caring about society and the world. I certainly do not, therefore, condemn what I saw, though I was saddened. It seemed a "media event" had to be scheduled before anyone would show how much they claimed to care.

No, I couldn't condemn the people who had that attitude. If anything, I must condemn the members of the previous generation who were too directed toward society and could not see the underlying nature of the universe. Every action does have a reaction. In one cycle people try to change society, in another people try to improve their personal wealth. And so it goes . . .

As I write these pages for the third edition of these lessons, things are changing once again, but this time out of necessity rather than choice. Economies of countries around the world are shaky and many people are losing their jobs. They have to depend upon their neighbors and loved ones. As a result, thoughts move from acquiring wealth to mere survival—survival of the individual, the family, the community, and the planet. The wheel continues to revolve. And so it goes . . .

I have yet to meet any group that is perfect. But one group which I have always supported is the loosely knit women's liberation movement, now more commonly known as the feminist movement. Certainly it had (what I consider to be necessary) excesses in the beginning. But one thing that was very important was their insistence that each woman should be viewed as a unique individual and not as an object. Unfortunately, sexism towards women has not decreased. It may be less overt, but it is still strongly in existence.

To top this off, there is a new prevalence of sexism toward men. In the past I have heard men talk about their dates not in terms of a woman being interesting, intelligent, fun to be with, stimulating, erotic, etc. Rather, they talk about the size of her "boobs" or the shape of her legs. Recently I have heard more and more women, when discussing their dates with men, describe them not as fun, intelligent, gentle, kind, generous, stimulating, etc. Rather, they talk about how he was cute and had "tight buns" or "good pecs."

Far be it from me to criticize beauty. It is a marvelous gift from the Divine, although the Divine is often helped at the spa and by the plastic surgeon. Still, to judge a person only on their appearance is nothing less than vicious and cruel. It turns people who don't match some imagined norm into sad, unfulfilled, and lonely people. And since most of appearance is a gift of birth, it is clearly but a step away from racism.

It is not only those who are oppressed who experience loss as a result of "appearance-ism." Those who do the oppression suffer, too, for they never interact with others who may have an amazing amount of wisdom, knowledge, cleverness, and humor that is so bright it far outshines their physical appearance. In truth, the oppressed might be able to add to the life of the oppressor more than the oppressor could even imagine.

I freely admit that I like to be in the company of what I consider to be beautiful women. However, some of the most beautiful women I have ever met have not stepped out of a magazine centerfold. In fact, the women who have been my favorite (and most erotically exciting!) lovers have not fit the Miss America/Playboy/Penthouse mold. Those who have studied Crowley's life know that he took exceedingly ugly women for lovers on purpose. But what does all this have to do with sex magick?

Perhaps the most racist and sexist society that ever existed was in India during the Middle Ages. Everyone had strict rules to follow dependent upon parentage. This "caste" system existed for hundreds of years. If you were in an upper class you could be "defiled" by having the even the shadow of a member of the lowest class, an "untouchable," pass over you. It was a racist, sexist society that makes ours look like pure equality by comparison. But there were freedom fighters then as now.

During the day they obeyed all the rules. But at night, when the curtains were pulled, things were different. Rather than trying to change society, they tried to change themselves. Outside, they acted like anyone else. But in their temples, within the KalaKakra or "magick circle" these Kaula Tantrics treated everyone equally. Caste, appearance, skin color, or shade made no difference.

Inside the Tantric temples all men were gods and all women goddesses. And these Tantrics developed a whole philosophy of beauty, love, understanding, sensitivity, science, and art while western Europe went through the Dark Ages, a period of hate, filth, superstition, ignorance, prejudice, and selfish egotism. Naturally, when the Westerners conquered India with their better weapons, they tried to destroy Tantrism for being "evil."

You may have heard of the KalaKakra and its group sex magick ritual. If you and some friends have been practicing the material in these lessons and wish to try the ritual I will present next, you may want to adopt the attitude of the Tantrics. It is very unlikely that all of you will appear to have stepped from the pages of *Playboy* or *GQ*. You must be able to see the beauty, the Divinity, the "likeness of God or Goddess" within us all. Due to society and the impact of film and television, it is doubtful that a group of ten men and women could do this. Therefore, I suggest starting with this preliminary exercise.

This exercise should be done with a minimum of three men and three women. Five or more of each sex would be preferable. In a large room let there be one of the women and all of the men. There should be a comfortable chair in the center wherein sits the woman. The men sit on cushions in a circle around the woman. Everyone should be naked. The other women should sit outside the circle in darkness and may or may not be dressed.

By predetermination, let one person do the LBRP and another do the BRH. Similar rituals, although with a Hindu flavor, were done by the ancient Tantrics. Now, one at a time, let each man worship the woman in the center of the circle. For she, like all women, is the embodiment of the feminine aspect of the Divine. Each may worship her in his own way.

You may dance or sing in her honor. You may wash her hands and feet or caress her. And yes, this does imply touching or kissing the breasts and genitals. However, it must be treated in the form of worship and awe, not mere sex. Other ways of worship would include chanting her name over and over, giving her gifts, giving her food, rubbing her with scented oils, etc. If she becomes sexually aroused, this must be seen as a sign of favor of the goddess that she is. Close with the LBRP.

Now, without saying anything, repeat the entire exercise with one of the men in the center and all of the women, now nude, in the circle. He should be worshipped as the male aspect of the Divine. The rest of the men may wait in the darkness outside the circle as the women did before. The man should not be the boyfriend, regular lover, mate, or husband of the woman who was previously in the middle of the circle.

Once this is completed, let everyone dress and then gather in a circle and discuss his or her feelings. Special attention should be paid to the feelings, expressions, and actions of both the people who were in the chair, acting the roles of the goddess and god, and their regular romantic partners (if any). Is there any jealousy or anger? Are such emotions hidden just below the surface? If so, these people either must work out their feelings or accept that currently they are not meant for this type of magickal work. The following week this ritual exercise should be repeated with a different man and woman. Eventually, this should be done with each of the women and men of the group.

The ancient Tantrics had nothing exactly like this, but they did have years of training under the watchful eye of the Tantric master teacher. Only when the teacher decided that a pupil was ready to participate in the KalaKakra ritual would that student be allowed to join. Since you probably do not have a Tantra master on your block, the above exercise will help weed out those who are not emotionally ready for the group working. This does not make them bad or immature. It merely means that at this

time they are not psychologically and/or emotionally ready to perform this type of magickal work. If one member of a couple is not ready to participate, both should be excluded.

Let us assume that you have five men and five or more women ready to do the KalaKakra ritual. There may be more women as they are seen as initiatrixes and instructresses and can help the couples in the ritual. Have a room with no furniture but filled with pillows and throws. If it is winter, be sure that the room has plenty of heat. Let there be incense and candlelight and flowers, food, wine, and cool water. Let there also be erotic playthings such as scented oils, feathers, and soft, furry things. Let all the foods be in bite-size pieces. Let gentle music fill the air.

Let there be two other rooms, one a changing room for the women, and one for the men. Let each change into special outfits. For the men, big, loose peasant shirts and drawstringed or loose, elastic-wasted pants are excellent. Rings and necklaces are appropriate, as are small bells on the clothes and jewelry. The same is true for the women. Sheer or transparent clothes are also appropriate. Men and women can apply make-up and even exotic body paints to exaggerate their sexuality. An example of this might be adding some red color to the areolas around the nipples. Today, many men and women shave or trim their pubic hair and you may wish to do so. Also use small drops of different scented oils at various spots on the body so that a traveling nose can find different scents wherever it may wander. All of the women should wear soft shoes which are easily identifiable from each other.

Let the men go into the main room first and do the LBRP and BRH. Once this is done one man should take the knife used for the LBRP and touch its point to the floor just to the right of the door through which women will enter. He should then pick the blade straight up as high as he can reach and move it over the top of the door and down to the floor by the left of the door. He has thus "cut a doorway" in the magick circle to allow the women to enter. A knock on the door will be a signal for them

Uh, Excuse Me . . . *What* Did You Say I Should Shave?

When *Modern Magick* was first published, it put forward lots of ideas and concepts that many people were talking about or doing, but about which nobody had written. As far as I know, it was the first major occult work to deal with AIDS. It was the first occult volume that looked for harmony between ceremonial magicians and Pagans. It was the first set of lessons to reveal the blinds in the grimoires. It was the first occult work that really did give a useable, progressive education in magick without being dogmatic. It was the first major occult volume to give specific and explicit instructions in sex magick. There were a lot of other minor firsts in the first edition of *Modern Magick*.

And now, some people have been shocked not because I have insisted that something they didn't like was necessary, but only that if you wish, you might want to trim or shave your pubic area. *"Oh. Mah. Gawd. Did he <u>really</u> say that?"*

Although it may surprise many people reading this, the shaving or trimming of pubic hair has a long history. The ancient Egyptians did it, as did the ancient Greek women (but not the men). The Roman women also did it, as did the British Celtic men (according to Julius Caesar). Both male and female Muslims did this and the returning Crusaders (eleventh to thirteenth centuries) brought the practice to Europe. Special shaving rooms were included in some castles, but the practice slowly died out. It started to regain popularity in the mid to late 1970s.

The modern popularity of women shaving legs and underarms only dates to 1915. It was due to an advertising campaign for razor blades, which implied that women's underarm hair was not hygienic. In fact, it could be considered a tertiary sexual organ, as it holds pheromone scents secreted by glands under the arms. Unfortunately, this can also be a problem area, as the hair under the arms can also hold undesired bacterial odors.

The same is true with pubic hair. Some find pubic hair attractive while others find the trimmed or shaved look more revealing and sensuous. Increasingly, men are starting to shave their pubic area. There are even electric shavers made for men specifically for "manscaping." One major razor manufacturer claims shaving the pubic area adds a "visual inch"—that is, it makes the penis appear longer—as part of its sales pitch.

If you choose to shave, trim, or use other forms of hair removal such as waxing, depilatories, etc., be very careful. Cuts and razor burn or allergic reactions can be very painful and distressful.

There is a myth among a small segment of feminists that women shouldn't copy actresses in adult films who shave their pubic areas as it supposedly appeals to pedophilic desires in men. Considering many of the same women have surgeries to make their breasts larger—sometimes impossibly large—this doesn't make sense. Prepubescent girls generally don't have breasts the size of basketballs.

Actually, there is a very simple reason that women in adult movies (and men) shave or trim their pubic areas: it makes it easier for the camera to capture the intimate action. How do I know this? For several years I worked as a writer for an advertising agency that specialized in ads for adult entertainment. We often took photos of models and that's the exact reason we asked models to be trim or hairless in the pubic area.

to do so, and once they come into the circle, the actions of the man with the knife should be reversed so that the circle is closed.

The men should sit toward the rim of the circle. The women should walk or dance in a clockwise manner around the circle. They may laugh, talk, or sing—whatever they desire. The men may not use their hands in any way. The women may feed the men, kiss them, give them wine or water to drink, but the men may not use their hands. This usually leads to much laughter and frivolity, a pleasant gift of the gods of Tantra. The women should not stay too long with any one man.

This can last for as long as you like, although the smaller the number of participants, the shorter it will be. Usually there is a minimum of a half hour. Then, the women should remove one of their shoes and place it in the center of the area. Other articles may also be used, such as earrings, bras, etc. Just so long as a woman can identify it as her own and that all of the women put in the same type of object: i.e., one should not put in a shoe if all the others are going to put in earrings. When doing this, the women should form a small circle about their collection of items so the men would have difficulty identifying which women put in what. Then all the items should be mixed. When finished, the women should find places to sit by the edge of the circle while the men get up.

Now that the women have had their fun, it is the men's turn. They also go around the circle feeding the women and giving them wine or water to drink. When this is finished, the men go to the center of the circle and face outward while holding hands. One woman claps her hands while the men walk in a circle clockwise around the items left by the women (more on the woman who claps the rhythm, later). When the clapping stops, each man reaches behind himself and, without looking, grabs one item from the collection. Then, once again, the men go around the circle trying to determine whose item they possess. The women may playfully try to hide the fact that an item belongs to them, and the men may playfully try to discover if an item belongs to a particular woman. This can be especially fun if the item is a woman's bra or panties. But there should be no force or violence. Finally, when the man discovers whom the item belongs to, he should sit to her right.

Thus are the couples formed. They should now, as pairs, feed each other, talk, joke and laugh, and eventually kiss gently and lovingly, though not very passionately. After some time at this, the man finally says to his partner,

**Goddess, thou art mine tonight.
Thou art my wife 'till it be light.**

To which she replies,

**God, thou art mine tonight.
Thou art my husband 'till it be light.**

Now the kissing and caressing and use of erotic toys can increase and the clothes can gradually come off. From here there are two alternatives:

1. When intercourse begins, the couple should take a comfortable posture and not thrust. They should synchronize their breathing until they have the MahaTantra experience and reach Nirvana.

2. Realizing that the deities of Tantra appreciate the energies of love, the couple may have prolonged active intercourse (with much thrusting) in honor of the gods.

3. When finished, each couple may sleep or rest together and may repeat option 1 or 2 until it is light outside. When the first light of dawn is seen, the LBRP and BRH should be repeated and everyone should return to the dressing rooms, dress, and return to their homes.

Notes on this ritual

1. It should start at midnight and end at daybreak.

2. Unless you happen to pick your regular partner for the KalaKakra ritual, you should not seek out your husband/wife-for-the-night for future sexual encounters unless you are both unattached.

3. Traditionally, there may be extra women in the circle. They may guide things (one of them may be the woman who claps to keep time for the men) and also aid the couples by bringing them food, drink, and erotic toys. They may also caress and kiss the couples while the couples are engaged in intercourse. However, they do not actually have intercourse with the couples, nor should the couples seek to caress or kiss these women. In the beginning of the ritual they are treated like the other women as the men go around the circle, feeding the women and playing with them.

4. The method of picking partners given here is a traditional one. Another way is to have the women form a standing circle inside a circle formed by the men. Then one woman claps while the circles move in opposite directions—the women move clockwise and the men move anti-clockwise, or vice versa. When the clapping stops, each person becomes a couple with the member of the opposite sex nearest him or her.

5. It was illegal for a person in India to have sex with another person who was not their spouse. To get around this and still have a random and free choice of partners, they would declare themselves wed for the night.

6. Although this is based on an ancient Tantric ritual, not all Tantrics practiced it. Similarly, most Protestants don't worship in the same way Catholics do. So if someone tells you that he or she is a Tantric and they don't do that sort of ritual, it may be true. But find out the Tantric tradition they belong to and who initiated them into Tantra. Chances are they speak with little knowledge.

This is a very dangerous ritual! Many good relationships have broken up because of it. Or, more appropriately, many relationships that *seemed* good have broken up after this ritual because the relationship was not really stable nor secure nor ready to handle the freedom of the KalaKakra. Because of this possible danger, should you or any reader attempt this ritual, neither the author, publisher, nor distributors of this course will be responsible for the outcome.

If you have any doubts at all after trying the preliminary exercise, don't do this ritual! The ritual of the KalaKakra has been included primarily for purposes of completeness and for people who are capable of dealing with this much freedom.

But just as those of you who have practiced ceremonial magick in a group have no doubt discovered that increased numbers do increase the power of the ritual, so, too, will those who practice this version of the KalaKakra ritual find the nearness of others doing sex magick will increase their own abilities and successes.

Postscript to Lesson 10

As I described at the beginning of this course, I did not merely sit down and write this set of lessons. Rather, they began after years of study and personal practice followed by over ten years of giving lessons and writing. But times have definitely changed.

When I began, the sexually transmitted diseases (STDs) of the time were controllable through drugs. Later came genital herpes, a disease that at the time of the first edition of these lessons was still untreatible. Even so, it would frequently go into remission, staying that way either permanently or for years at a time. Today the symptoms are somewhat treatable but still incurable.

But a few years before the first edition of *Modern Magick* was published, a new disease appeared, seemingly from out of thin air. Acquired immune deficiency syndrome (AIDS) is transmitted through the sharing of bodily fluids, primarily blood. Some suspect other modes of transmission, but evidence of this lessens over time. A really dangerous part of this disease is that it may take five or more years after infection to become aware of it. If left untreated, it is currently almost always fatal. Today there are treatments but no cures.

Throughout this course I have stressed the idea that a magician takes responsibility for his or her actions. Therefore, if you decide that you wish to have more than one sexual partner, you must accept the responsibility for that action. If you choose to share bodily fluids with your partners, you and your partner must also accept the responsibility for that action. I would suggest being tested frequently for communicable diseases including HIV (which seems to lead to AIDS) and various STDs. If you have any diseases, from a communicable STD to "just a cold," it is your responsibility to share with partners and potential partners the information about which diseases you have *before* having sex.

If you choose to have multiple partners, you do so at your own risk, at least until cures for AIDS and other STDs are discovered. My best friend for many years died from an AIDS-related condition, and he is still missed by myself and many of his friends. It is my deepest hope that a cure is found for those who are currently afflicted, and for those who feel angry because they must alter their actions in fear of this disease, that an effective preventative vaccine, or method to induce complete and extended remission, is soon discovered.

Review

The following questions are designed to help you determine if you have mastered the information in Lesson Ten. Please try to answer them without looking at the text. The answers are in Appendix Two.

1. What level of intelligence do you need to have before you are immune to being brainwashed?

2. What five things are necessary for brainwashing?

3. What are three major divisions of sex magick as described in these lessons?

4. What happens to a thought held in the mind at the moment of orgasm?

5. What did Reich discover about the moment of orgasm?

6. According to Masters and Johnson, how long is the average duration of intercourse before a man has an ejaculation?

7. What three things are involved in any divinatory technique?

8. Many people believe that books on alchemy are simply codes for what?

9. What, according to sex magicians, is the Menstruum, or Menstruum of the Gluten?

10. How many people achieve enlightenment by reading books on kundalini yoga?

11. Working with breath and mantras are substitutes for what?

12. Why is the ritual of the KalaKakra dangerous?

The following questions only you can answer.

1. Are you still doing the regular rituals and keeping records? Have you experimented with other rituals and techniques? Do you meditate?

2. Would you do sex magick? Do you find it fascinating or repulsive?

3. Do you think you could ever be brainwashed? Why or why not?

4. If you wouldn't do sex magick, is it okay for others to do sex magick, even with people who are not their spouses or significant others?

5. Since beginning this course, have your feelings about life in general changed? How?

Bibliography

For more information on these books, please see the annotated bibliography at the end of this course.

Avalon, Arthur. *Mahanirvana Tantra: Tantra of the Great Liberation.* CreateSpace, 2008.

Conway, Flo, and Jim Siegelman. *Snapping.* Stillpoint Press, 1995.

Douglas, Nik, and Penny Slinger. *Sexual Secrets.* Destiny Books, 1999.

King, Francis. *Sexuality, Magic and Perversion.* Feral House, 2002.

Kraig, Donald Michael. *Modern Sex Magick.* Llewellyn, 2002.

Lloyd, William J. *The Karezza Method.* BiblioBazaar, 2008.

Mumford, Jonn. *Ecstasy Through Tantra.* Llewellyn, 2002.

Reich, Wilhelm. *The Function of the Orgasm.* Farrar, Straus and Giroux, 1986.

Saraswati, Swami Janakananda. *Yoga, Tantra, and Meditation in Daily Life.* Weiser, 1992.

Stockham, Alice. *Karezza.* Forgotten Books, 2008.

LESSON ELEVEN

PART ONE

Finding Your Own Way

As I have previously described, there is an old legend that when Moses first ascended Mount Sinai, God gave to him the secrets of the Kabalah. This told humanity what it *could* do. Moses, upon seeing the worship of another deity—the Golden Calf—when he descended, destroyed public knowledge of these secrets, saving them only for his brother Aaron and the High Priests of Israel. When Moses again returned to the top of the mountain, he came back with the Decalogue, the Ten Commandments. These were filled with "thou shalt nots," telling people what they *must not* do. The people were truly "children" of Israel. Children are not responsible for themselves and do not have the freedom that adults have. The children of Israel were not yet able to accept the freedom that is inherent in the Kabalah. They needed to become adults first.

Today, most people are still not able to be free. They are infected with the mental disease of insecurity resulting in the symptom of needing to follow various "-isms" rather than accepting their own excellence and thinking for themselves. Sometimes they follow these "-isms" to their death or cause the persecution or deaths of people following different "-isms." People follow the doctrinal line of religious groups, political groups, and peer groups, or blindly follow one or more political, religious, military, or economic leaders. *Most common people are unable to think for themselves, or actually choose not to do so.* This is a result of the level of spiritual advancement in the current Piscean Age, and I fear it will be with us for many years to come.

But there is hope. There are some people who are beginning to think, who are beginning to wake as if from a long sleep. These are the people who are the advance guard of the coming Aquarian Age. These are the people who either are not members of various dogma-filled organizations or stay part of them as long as the group does not ask for blind obedience or unethical behavior. For the most part they work by themselves or in very small groups of like-minded persons. They are the wave of the future and the hope of tomorrow.

371

Is this an elitist attitude? Absolutely yes . . . and absolutely no. For while there is an Aquarian Age elite, it is not limited to those with money or political power—or those with parents who had money or political power—as were previous elites. No, it is an *open* elite that anyone can join at any time, and make eddies, ripples, and waves in the ocean of our coming world.

If you have been studying and practicing the lessons of this course, you are well on the way to becoming a full-fledged member of this Aquarian Age elite—if you are not a member already. However, this does not make you better than others, just different. You should not, you must not, look down on others who have not advanced as far as you have. They may one day jump into the future at a rate accelerated even above your own.

It is said that the true deep secrets of magick cannot be told. It is said that the true secrets of magick are hidden and shown only to initiates of secret occult bodies such as the true Rosicrucians or Illuminati, and then only after the student has spent years of study and practice and has passed serious and even life-threatening tests.

All of this is true.
From this point on I can show you no more.
I can teach you no more magickal secrets.

Yet, there are still many more pages in these lessons. How can this be? To answer this question I have to teach you what I consider to be *the ultimate secret of true magick.*

But first, a bit of a review. There are three things needed to work any magick:

1. The ability to raise, control, and direct magickal energy.
2. The knowledge of what to do with this energy (ability does not equal knowledge).
3. A positive attitude of self-assurance.

In the past lessons I have described these things and given you exercises and rituals to help you develop all three of the above talents. It is interesting to note that no books on magick ever clearly state all of the above three points. The famous magickal texts or grimoires of the past at best only discuss the second point. This is because they were meant to be used as workbooks by experienced mages or magicians-in-training who already know these things from personal lessons and experience.

If you have been practicing the rituals given in this course you have been following a logical, tested system. This system has taught you to have a good attitude. I only briefly discussed this topic because I didn't need to focus on it. Developing a positive attitude is a natural side effect of working with the Tarot cards and doing the Middle Pillar Ritual.

These lessons have also taught you many ways to raise and control the psycho-magickal energy needed to perform magick. And, if you have been studying and practicing the techniques and rituals of these lessons, you will also be prepared to take the next step in your magickal advancement.

The ultimate magickal wisdom cannot be communicated to you by any person or group.

Let me be blunt: any person or group that claims to give you the ultimate magickal secrets is lying. Each person must seek it individually. The so-called "lost word" or secret name of God can never be communicated to you by another person. You must learn it by yourself. One way to do this is by following various systems or schools of magick. You are encouraged to find one that particularly fits your needs. However, if you have been doing the rituals of this course, you should be prepared to discover that information, and take the next step in learning the true, innermost secrets of magick.

If you have been *regularly* practicing the techniques, exercises, and rituals, you, at the very least, should have achieved or be beginning to achieve good control of magickal energy. The LBRP, BRH, Middle Pillar Ritual, and the Circulation of the Body of Light are all techniques that train a person in the ability to raise and control magickal energy. If you have made a talisman that has achieved its goal, you have proved to yourself the successfulness of your ability to raise and control Willed magickal energy.

The important part of this is your ability to use your conscious and unconscious Will to control magickal energy and put it to the uses you desire. Perhaps you have seen books with other exercises on how to raise and control magickal energy. Some are very good. But it is my feeling that repetition of a few basic exercises with millennia of development will work much better than spreading out your personal energies by memorizing large numbers of practices with fewer repetitions of each exercise.

A positive attitude, as mentioned, should be being developed as a direct result of the Tarot Contemplation Ritual. Its development will also be aided by the study of the harmony of the universe as indicated by the balance of nature and shown on the Tree of Life. The more successes you have in Grey Magick, the more confident you will become in your own magickal abilities and the more positive your attitude will be.

There are many books with spells, rituals, ceremonies, philosophy, theory, and information that could help add to your knowledge of how and where to direct the raised and controlled energy. In fact, I could share much more. But I feel no need to do so, as it is intermediate information at best. Instead, I will share with you how to obtain more advanced information, the knowledge of true magickal secrets, for yourself.

**This knowledge is not available
on the physical plane of Earth!
It can only be learned from entities
on higher planes.**

Sometimes these "entities" are called aspects of the higher self, the Yeh-chee-dah. Some people call these entities manifestations of God. The process of how to reach and communicate with these "entities" will be discussed later in this lesson. I wish to stress that there is nothing to fear from the beautiful, natural techniques that you will soon be learning. The best is yet to come.

There Is Only Magick

If you look over the hundreds of pages of these lessons that you have followed so far, you will know that we have covered a tremendous amount of material. Perhaps most importantly I have tried to show you how to be a magician; how to think, act, and feel like a true wizard or wizardess. With this knowledge you should be able to construct your own rituals and ceremonies rather than being locked into the printed words of dead hands.

One of the most important topics I have covered in these lessons are the applications and methods of White and Grey Magick, and how to avoid falling into the pit of Black Magick. Remember, too, that I have always maintained that not all authorities agree with my three divisions of magick. I gave them only so that we could communicate better. Those definitions were only a convenience. For in spite of what any authorities say, *there is no such thing as White, Black, or Grey Magick.* This is important to understand, so I'll repeat some earlier concepts about this in a different way.

Part of the process of becoming a magician is learning to discern "reality" from "actuality." Occultists have always maintained that everything is made up of vibrational energy. Modern scientific thought has finally come to the same conclusion, calling it "wave theory."

Yet, a wall is still a wall. A desk is still a desk. Both are really, truly solid. They support the weight of objects. I cannot place my hand through them without damage to the wall, the desk, and my hand. That is their reality. Still, both science and occultism insist that the wall and desk (and my hand) are only vibrational energy. That is their actuality. What is actual may not appear real. What is real may or may not be actual.

Likewise, some things may appear to be true, and may in reality be true. But their actuality may be false. It is really true that the Sun rises every morning even if the clouds prevent me from seeing it. That is the reality. But the actuality is that the Earth spins, giving the appearance that the Sun rises. In actuality, the Sun never rises.

Most of us will agree that killing is bad and evil. But people who believe this is so go to war and kill. Are these people hypocrites or just evil? From a magickal point of view I would have to say "no."

For a true magician there is no universal, predetermined good or evil. There is no morality from external sources. Yet, a true magician is usually far more "moral" than his or her non-magician friends and neighbors, especially those professing to be highly moral. How can this be so?

It is because a true magician understands the underpinnings of universe, including the laws and workings of karma. A magician realizes that he/she is totally free to choose to do whatever is desired. However, the true magician will invariably choose the path of light, what is called by non-magicians the "morally correct choice." The true magician chooses the path of light not for moral purposes. Rather, this path is chosen because the magician realizes that whatever is done needs to be for the best of himself or herself, the local community, and the world. And further, any action they do will come back to him or her. Such is the universal law of karma.

For the true magician there is no such thing as White, Grey, or Black Magick. There is only . . . magick. Period. It so happens that because of the understanding of the law of karma, a true magician will assiduously avoid what non-magicians or beginning magicians would call Black Magick.

People who are not aware of the law of karma behave "morally" because they are given a code of morals or a set of laws to follow. They look to a book or leader rather than seeing the results of their actions. Therefore, there is always the possibility that they will break their dogmatic code. As a result, people who claim to be "moral" based on a human-designed set of rules are far more likely to break their own moral code than is a magician who follows one rule, that of karma, and does not believe in a set of human laws to govern morality.

Are there people who do evil? Most definitely yes. A few who do evil and are trained in magick, and then use magick to harm others, are called black ma-

gicians. But they should never be considered true magicians any more than a child performing a magic trick with a ball or coin is at the level of one of the performing magicians you've seen on TV or in the theater. Such black magicians can perform petty tricks but do not understand the functioning of the laws of karma. If they did, they would not do "Black Magick."

There is still another aspect to what some people might call Black Magick. If you were dying of a painful, incurable disease, might there not be the possibility that you would commit suicide? Some of you reading this will say, "Yes, it is a possibility." Others will think, "Nope. No way." But there are some "moralists" who would consider it wrong to commit suicide under any conditions. I am not trying to encourage suicide. I am merely saying that it is impossible to consider an action "good" or "bad," Black Magick or otherwise, unless we know the karmic result of the action.

Most of us would agree that it would be bad for us to cut off the arm of a good friend. But suppose the arm was gangrenous and the friend would die if the arm was not removed. It would be karmically bad for us *not* to help by removing the arm and saving our friend. Of course, it might be the karmically correct time for the friend to go through the transition known as death. Then it would be karmically bad for us to save the friend's life! As you can see, there are many complexities in determining the karmic "correctness" of an action. This is why doing a divination is so important before performing a magickal act which will affect you or your environment.

In the Biblical story, Jonah was told by God to go and preach. He chose not to do so and the karma of that action put him in the belly of a "great fish." The karmically correct decision would have been to preach. Had a thousand people barred his way and he had to fight his way through them, it still would have been karmically bad for him not to preach.

If you communicate with a higher, spiritual entity and decide to follow or not follow the advice of that entity, you will be responsible for the karmic result of your actions (or lack thereof). If you decide to do something which agrees with instructions from higher entities, and someone tells you "No," it is karmically correct for you to disagree with that person and even push him or her out of the way if need be. But remember, you will be karmically responsible for whatever happens. Especially because you are a magician, you must accept responsibility for all of your actions. What you are now is a direct result of what you did yesterday. What you are tomorrow is a direct result of what you do today. As you sow, so shall you reap. It is the law of karma.

Discovering things from higher, spiritual entities on other planes of existence and deciding to do them is called "finding your True Will." And, as St. Augustine, Rabelais, and Aleister Crowley said, "Do what thou wilt shall be the whole of the Law."

This is not a license for hedonism and what some people may call immorality. In fact, just the contrary is true. In reality it is a call to become responsible for your own actions, to become united with Divinity and to make God's Will your Will. Your actions will require that you ever tread the path of Light. And the guide on that path is love. For as Crowley added, "Love is the law, love under will."

Every once in a while, the sensationalistic press will tell the story of a man or woman who did something terrible such as beating a spouse or child to death because their victim "was possessed by the devil." Some add, "God told me to do this." The training in this book does not increase the possibility that you may become demented enough to do such a thing. In fact, it helps prevent it. We are not dealing with mediumship or possession. We will be dealing with communication.

Furthermore, there is always a simple way to decide if something is correct for you. You should have noticed that over the past few months, as you have been practicing the rituals and techniques of this course, your intuition has improved. This is a natural result of the rituals and exercises that you have been doing. So if something doesn't seem right or feel right to you, *don't do it!* It's that simple.

If you have a feeling that someone you know may be "possessed by the devil" and you have a desire to make that devil leave by doing bodily harm to the person "possessed," *don't do it!* It may be you who needs help.

The systems that I will share with you are quite safe. Since some people are concerned about direct communication with higher, spiritual entities, as opposed to the somewhat indirect communications of magickal evocation, let me repeat here:

If you follow instructions
nothing in this or any other lesson
will be dangerous
or could cause danger to you or others.
Nothing taught in these lessons could lead you
to what general morality might consider evil.

Non-Physical Entities

I have written on other pages about the "Little Nasties" and how they can be bothersome. I discussed earlier in this lesson that when you come into contact with higher spiritual entities, you should listen to what they have to say. As you may have guessed, I did not mean that you should obey the Little Nasties! Little Nasties, being denizens of what some people call the lower astral plane, are not higher spiritual entities. What I mean by higher spiritual entities are three things: direct manifestations of the Divine (the gods), the Archangels, and the Orders of Angels. Furthermore, you may need to make tests to see if these entities are the spiritual beings they claim to be. How to do this will be explained shortly.

But first, let's look at entities that, though ethereal and existing primarily on other planes, are not higher spiritual entities.

Etheric Body: This is an emanation of all created things. It is not the true astral double and is something like "halfway between astral and physical." It sometimes can take on the appearance of a person on a higher plane, but is always attached to a living being.

Astral Body: This is a manifestation of the spiritual aspect of a living entity. Again, it is always attached to an incarnate being. When detached, it quickly moves to higher planes of existence in order to reincarnate. In this disattached condition they are too busy to occupy your time. When attached to some individual ego, they can be seen as such. Higher spiritual entities are not linked to a particular ego.

Azoth: This is also known by the Sanskrit term "Akasha" (correct pronunciation: "ah-kash") or the astral light. It appears as brightness and is changeable according to a person's will. The past, present, and future can be seen within the Azoth, but it does not have an independent personality. Since futures are only possible futures, getting lost in the astral light can lead to your ignoring the present. This can lead you to the home for "Space Cadets." Remember to keep your feet firmly planted in the present.

Artificial Elementals: These are entities created by human forces and are composed of only one element. They are focused toward one purpose, so if you leave them alone they will ignore you. Depending upon the strength of the will of their creator, they will appear more or less gaunt when seen on the astral plane.

The Empty Ones: If you live in a large city, these entities can be seen in physical form in the "skid row" section of town. They look human, but they have no soul and no hope for the future. They can sometimes show great humor and daring, but quickly fade into the depths of despair. Their eyes show either madness or emptiness. These poor creatures also exist on higher planes. Their touch brings despair and fear.

Elementaries: These are the Gnomes of Earth, Undines of Water, Sylphs of Air, and Salamanders of Fire. They are usually called "elementals," and although that isn't exactly accurate, I have used that term in these lessons. Although composed of only one element, they have their own will and usually do not bother humans. In fact, they prefer it if humans ignore them.

Larvae: These are also known as lemures. It is believed that they live off the essence of blood. They "feed," so to speak, on sick or injured people. They can be dispersed easily by a projection of pure spiritual white light.

Ghosts: When the astral body separates from the ego, it normally moves to a position where it can reincarnate. Sometimes a strong desire for the physical world (or something in the physical world) keeps an astral body in the lowest of the spiritual planes. In this condition they are known as ghosts. They tend to be quite sorrowful or angry and even filled with rage causing their refusal to evolve. Encouraging their evolution may or may not be successful, but it will give you karmic "brownie points."

Pseudo-Ghosts: These are not related to true ghosts. They're closer to the Little Nasties. They "feed" off any energy given to them and will imitate the actions of ghosts in order to get people to pay attention and give them energy. By reading the Astral Light they can know your past and probable future, and thus may appear at séances under the guise of a deceased loved one. They are more bothersome on the physical plane than on any higher plane.

Poltergeists: The poltergeist phenomenon often gives the appearance of being a ghost. However, it is actually a manifestation of the unconscious of a human, most frequently (but not always) a girl entering puberty. The word itself is German for "noisy spirit" and that's what occurs—the poltergeist makes noises, knocks things off shelves, and has even been known to attack people. It is rare for a poltergeist to directly harm someone, but they can push over bookcases, cause people to trip at the top of stairs, etc. Thus, they can indirectly cause harm. The best way to deal with poltergeist phenomena is to get children in a home where it occurs into some form of therapy. Most often, poltergeist phenomena cease as the child matures, but it can return at unexpected times.

These and other entities exist on the higher planes. Those of a single mind will not harm you unless you try to stop them from achieving their goals. Those connected to entities on the physical plane are usually too involved with the physical plane to bother you. There is one type of entity that exists on higher planes that can be problematical: your own thought forms.

Here, "form" is the keyword. On higher planes thoughts take on various forms representing their nature, and, unfortunately, you do not have to consciously create them. This was fictionalized in the famous 1956 science-fiction movie *Forbidden Planet*, where machines created a horrendous attacker, a "monster from the Id."

Thus, on higher planes you may come into contact with ugly, foul monsters of hideous appearance who attempt to stop you from achieving your goals. They are only your own fears, angers, prejudices, etc. They will not harm you themselves, for to harm you would cause harm to themselves. They *are* you.

Most people are unwilling or too frightened to examine or even peek at their *shadow*, the Jungian term for the darker side of themselves, so they'll run in terror at the sight of their own negative thought forms. This can keep you from accomplishing your goal of direct communication with higher spiritual entities.

Visualizing a pentagram of bright blue light specked with brilliant gold flecks and "shooting" it out at them as in the section of this course on psychic self-defense will keep them away. Through banishings, the attack may be temporarily stopped, but it will not end until the magician has dealt with and conquered the inner source of the negative thought form. So if you find yourself frequently thinking you are under psychic attack, even though you have used the techniques described earlier in these lessons to

rid yourself of such attacks, you may have to look at yourself as the cause. The only way to really get rid of them is to face them and your fear, and overcome the negative aspect(s) of yourself that created them. Few magicians are ever really psychically attacked.

Please understand that I am not encouraging you to stay and face the monsters of your own inner self, monsters that we all have. In this type of battle it is a wise person who runs away and "lives to fight another day." Rather, I am suggesting that at a future time you may need to deal with those self-created beings through some sort of focused introspection or professional therapy. Sooner or later you will have to face and conquer your own demons, and you will be happier for it.

PART TWO

In Part One of this lesson I explained that I would share with you how to learn the ultimate secrets of magick, although I cannot share the actual secrets themselves. This is because each person must learn these secrets for him/herself and prove his or her worth and readiness. Also, the secrets are of a very subjective nature. What may be the ultimate secrets of magick for you might not be for another aspirant.

However, if you think that you will begin to learn the techniques for this discovery in this lesson you will be wrong. You will not *begin* to learn the techniques here because you have already begun to learn them from the very first lesson of this course!

Up to this time, without dwelling on it, I have been directing you in the method of how to obtain the desired information and secrets. I have not brought your attention to it because some people seem to fear what is represented by two small words. Frankly, I cannot understand this fear because the process named by those two words is something these same people do every day of their lives. However, they do it without control. When this process is controlled by a firm Magickal Will (something you have been developing by following these lessons and doing the rituals and exercises), however, it seems to scare some people. This is foolish, as there is nothing to fear from something you ordinarily do so easily. It is quite common. And the two words that describe it are ...

... astral projection.

Don't feel uncomfortable with the idea of astral projection. You do it every time you daydream, and very frequently when you dream in your sleep.

Astral travel, which is what you may do after astral projection, is also very common and natural. In fact, you probably had to *unlearn* how to astral travel when you were a child. It is very common for parents to tell their children not to play in invisible scenes and with invisible play-friends. Some children—especially in our MTV world with colorful and fast-moving toys—simply grow out of using their astral vision (and their imagination) where they saw these characters and vistas. These were scenes and entities on and from the astral plane.

You may remember some of this type of childhood experience in a very superficial way. Very few people remember their extreme youth in detail. Because elders would tell you "Come back to reality!" and "Don't play foolish games!" and, perhaps worst of all, "Quit pretending!" it was eventually impressed into your conscious to forget those invisibles which are "see-able" on the astral plane. This process of causing yourself to forget those things that would be uncomfortable or unacceptable to your current state of consciousness is what psychotherapists call "motivated forgetting." It is one of the reasons why most people remember little of their infancy; it was so childish and embarrassing not to be able to walk, communicate, take care of yourself, or even control your bowels that you *want* to forget.

As you may recall, I said at the beginning of this course that your daily ritual practice would become shorter. Part of that is because you would memorize the rituals and be able to be effective more quickly than when you started. Now, however, it will also be because you will be able to do all of your regular daily ritual work totally astrally. Remember, the physical actions of a ritual work to impress the unconscious and reinforce the conscious with what is being done in the astral plane. All of the work you have been doing for many months has created memory and habit patterns in your unconscious mind. That means you can accomplish the same goal *without* physically performing the ritual. Of course, if you wish you may continue with your regular daily rituals—you can do them for the rest of your life and they will get better and help your life become more positive and more successful. However, starting today, you can move to the next level, begin bypassing the physical and go directly to the astral plane by doing the following ritual:

Astral Lesser Banishing Ritual of the Pentagram

Preparation: Until you have practiced this form of the ritual at *least* twenty times and are sure of its effectiveness, begin by doing a regular, physical LBRP. If time allows, also do the BRH.

STEP ONE. Sit in the center of your circle and relax with some steady deep breathing and the Relaxation Ritual. You should be facing the east. Your eyes should be closed and your arms and legs should not be crossed.

STEP TWO. Visualize yourself (or, if you prefer, an idealized image of yourself) standing, facing you. Take some time and get the best image possible in your mind. Remember, even if you can't see the visualization with your astral vision, you should know beyond any doubt that it is there and if your vision were open you would see it.

STEP THREE. Once your double (frequently called a doppelganger) is complete, use your will power and have it turn to face the east, the same direction in which you are looking. This procedure should take no special ritual techniques. Simply use your mind to tell it silently to turn about and it will do so. Of course, it should still be standing.

STEP FOUR. Now, without audibly saying anything, will your twin to do the entire Lesser Banishing Ritual of the Pentagram. Your physical body should be in the center of the area, the position where your physical altar would normally be located. Try to hear, feel, smell, sense, and visualize everything your double does. Keep your physical eyes closed.

STEP FIVE. Once you have completed this astral performance of the LBRP, have your double sit in your lap and allow yourself to reabsorb it. Take some deep breaths to unite yourselves. Clap your hands loudly three times. The sound will help bring you back to normal consciousness. Now you may open your eyes.

Postscript: After you have done the astral Lesser Banishing Ritual of the Pentagram, be sure to again perform the LBRP *physically*. Do this until you have performed the astral version at least *thirty* (not twenty) times. If you are not satisfied that the astral LBRP was effective after those thirty times, continue doing a physical LBRP after the astral version until you are convinced that the astral version has been effective.

As usual, be sure to record the results of the ritual in your magickal or ritual diary.

The astral LBRP may sound quite easy to do from the description above. "Hey, all I have to do is sit on my behind and think it out. No tools or robes. That's easy!" Actually, although it may sound or seem a great deal easier than other rituals you have performed, this ritual takes as much or more concentration than *any* rituals you have done so far in this course. If you find yourself getting lost or falling asleep, just stop where you are and perform the LBRP physically. Simply follow the directions and add nothing to them. Nothing "bad" can happen to you.

If you have trouble concentrating to a level where you can do the entire LBRP in this above astral fashion, try practicing the following concentration exercise:

Exercise to Improve Concentration

Needed: a timer and four cards. The cards should be pure white with no lines. On the first card place a large black spot, and on the second place two spots side by side. On the third card make a row of three

spots and on the fourth card, a similar row of four spots. A black marker is perfect for making such cards, although if you are comfortable using graphic programs on your computer, you may wish to create your cards that way.

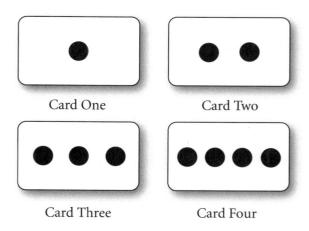

Concentration Exercise Cards

Set the timer for five minutes. Look at Card One until you have a very good idea of that single spot. Burn it into your mind. Now close your eyes and only think of that spot. You will see in your mind's eye an image of the card. It may not be perfect. It may be reversed or a shade of what you saw. That's exactly what it should be.

This is not some magickal power, it is physiological. The mind records an image and holds on to it as an "afterimage." In this exercise we are working with it to attune your mind to improve its visualization abilities. If the image in your mind begins to drift to a side, just let it return to the center of your focus. If any other thoughts come into your mind, simply bring back your focus to that one spot. Cease the exercise when you can no longer see the spot or when the timer goes off. Your goal in this exercise is to keep that single spot visualized in one location for five minutes while you allow nothing to interfere with your concentration. Practice once or twice daily.

When you have very few breaks in your concentration, move on to Card Two with the two spots and repeat the exercise. Continue this practice until you can keep the two spots in your mind for the full five minutes. When you can do this with Card Three and then Card Four and its four dots, you will have excellent concentration abilities.

Although this exercise sounds easy, it is not. The first time I tried it, I broke out into a sweat and was drenched within five minutes. Do not underestimate its difficulty.

On the other hand, you may find that the Astral LBRP is easy for you to do. You may be able to mentally see your doppelganger perform every action and hear it sound every vocalization. If this is the case, or after you increase your concentration and visualization abilities until you reach this level, add to it an astral version of the BRH, the Middle Pillar Ritual, and the Circulation of the Body of Light. Eventually you should be able to do *all* of these rituals astrally. Then, even a few minutes with your eyes closed should equal what is now taking you much longer on the physical plane. Although your daily ritual work should still be done every day, you will reach a time when you will rarely have to do them physically. You will, of course, do most of the so-called Grey Magick rituals on the physical plane, and also those rituals wherein you delve into the deepest realms of the Magickal Arte.

Some of you who have read about or practiced astral projection and astral travel may be thinking, "Wait a minute, what you described as the Astral LBRP doesn't involve real astral projection at all!" Yeaaah. Okay. I confess. You're right. This is true.

There are two techniques that are frequently called astral projection. The first one is often mistaken for astral projection but is nothing of the kind. It is actually *mental projection*. In mental projection you send your mind and senses away from your body by force of will. You still will retain your consciousness and some sense awareness in your physical body. Another name for this is *bi-locationality*.

In true astral projection the consciousness almost totally leaves the physical and joins the astral double. The physical body appears to be sleeping or in a coma. If you have forgotten about how the astral plane works, and how everything has an astral double, now is the time to re-read Lessons Five and Seven.

In the astral LBRP just described, all you are doing is using your powers of visualization and your imagination. You are not doing astral or even mental projection. But look again at Step Four: "Hear, feel, smell, sense, and visualize everything your double does." By doing this, eventually, and quite naturally, you will experience bi-locationality. This will occur when you are open and ready for it. You will have an awareness of both your physical self and your astral body. Another possibility is that your consciousness may seem to jump back and forth between the two forms.

Then, quite naturally and without any sort of force, you will realize that for some time, when doing the ritual you have not been aware of your physical body. It is at this time that you are experiencing true astral projection. When you have this realization my advice to you is the same as the words of Douglas Adams in *The Hitchhiker's Guide to the Galaxy*: "Don't panic!"

Some people, when realizing that they are on the astral plane, really don't know what to do and seek to return to their normal condition as quickly as possible. I suggest that instead you use your mind to take a few deep (astral) breaths, relax, and try to get comfortable in your astral form and get used to the way it feels to be out-of-body. This will make the projection of the astral body easier as time goes on. It's also exhilarating and liberating if you simply allow yourself to revel in the feelings.

If you would like to try some other methods for projecting your astral body and traveling on the astral plane, here are some good ones. They are based on some practical techniques by the author Ophiel (*née* Edward Peach). Remember, however, to always perform the LBRP (and BRH if time allows) before doing any projection. This cannot be overemphasized. Remember, you're a magician now, not a dilettante.

Method One

Step One. Start off by placing some markers around your room or home. These markers could include such things as a rose, a bowl of cold water, a shoe, etc. They should be things that can be appreciated by all of your senses: touch, hearing, taste, smell, and sight. Now lie down on your bed. Next, get up and make a circle, going from one marker to the next before returning to your bed. Involve your senses with each of the markers. Smell the rose. Feel the softness of the petals. Feel the cool wetness of the water. Taste it and pay attention to how it feels in your mouth, throat, and stomach. Feel the texture of the rubber of the sole of the shoe. Smell the rubber. After you have completed the circle, experiencing each item, lie down on your bed in your original supine position. Repeat this several times. In fact, you may wish to make this a multiday exercise, repeating this first step for several days.

Step Two. While lying in the bed, visualize above you a cloud of purest white. It may remain as a cloud or you can form it into the shape of your own body (idealized if desired). You may notice a connection between your physical body and your double in the form of an umbilical-like cord at your navel, solar plexus, third eye area, or at the top of your head. People experience this cord in different places, although you may not notice it at all. In your mind's eye, make this cloud or figure and fill it with as much detail as possible.

Step Three. Now, will the cloud or double to circle around the markers following the same path that you had taken earlier. If you noticed the cord, you can see that it will stretch indefinitely. Have the double or cloud interact with each item as you had physically done earlier. Smell and touch the rose, feel and taste that water, feel and smell the shoe, etc.

Eventually this imaginary tour will change to bi-locationality and finally to astral projection. Once you have attained these states, there is no need to limit yourself as to where you can go. Feel free to visit a friend's home. Remember that you are learning a new skill, so don't try to go too far until you are very comfortable with the experience.

Step Four. No matter what level you are at, even if you are only using imagination, always re-absorb the double or cloud back into your physical body when

you have completed your journey. Also, always end with a banishing ritual and record your results in your diary.

Method Two

Step One. This is similar to method one. Either lie down or sit in a chair. Begin by visualizing a cloud in front of you (or over you if you are lying down). If you wish, you may form it into a double of yourself.

Step Two. Now, firmly desire to transfer your consciousness to the double. If you feel a sudden change in your body, described by some as a lightening or vibrating feeling, will yourself to open your eyes. Do not try to physically open your eyes by using your muscles. Just will yourself to see. Do not be surprised when you see your physical body in front of you.

Step Three. Spend no more than three minutes concentrating on trying to cause your consciousness to leave your body and join your astral self. If it works, fine. If it doesn't work in about three minutes, that is fine, too. Relax, take some deep breaths, and try again tomorrow.

The key to succeeding with this system (and with all of the methods, really) is that you must establish within yourself *the urgent desire to leave your physical body.* When you finally succeed—and with dedication, desire, and regular practice you certainly will succeed—be sure to re-absorb the double into your physical body when you conclude the projection. Of course, do banishings before and after and record your results.

Method Three

Step One. Lie naked on a bed. Have a friend, relative, or assistant put a folded heavy bedspread on your feet. Now, have your aide *slowly* drag the folded spread up your body until it reaches the top of your head. Then the person helping you should quickly lift the spread up and away from you and quietly leave the room.

Step Two. Now duplicate the process in your mind's eye. Only instead of a bedspread, feel your astral body rising up. First your feet rise, then your ankles, calves, knees, and so forth to the top of your head. At the point where the bedspread was lifted from your physical body, imagine your consciousness going with the astral body. When finished, reabsorb the double into your body.

Step Three. Do banishings and record results.

Method Four

This method is ideal for musicians and music lovers. It was the method I used to achieve my first out-of-body experience.

Step One. Hear the musical note D natural above middle C in your mind. A little practice with a piano, pitch pipe, or a friend with a musical instrument will make this pitch familiar to you. Now, double the frequency of the pitch in your mind so that you hear a pitch an octave higher than the first note. If you are not a musician, a friend with musical knowledge can help you with this.

Step Two. Again hear the tone, only an additional octave higher, then hear it an octave above that. Continue this process until you are far above a piano's range.

Step Three. You will notice that you are feeling lighter as the note goes up in pitch. You may sense a vibration in your head. Let the sound rise higher and higher as you feel *the sound* rise toward the ceiling of your room. When you sense that the sound is as high as it can go, both as a pitch and within the confines of the room, will your eyes to open. Again, don't be surprised if you see your physical body below. When finished, allow the double to be re-absorbed into the physical body.

The methods of astral projection and astral travel presented here are enough for anyone to learn from. If you desire more information, look at some of the books in this lesson's bibliography. But be aware that each of the books are limited by preconceived notions of the authors. Set yourself no limits and you will have none. And besides, I believe it is far better to learn by doing than by reading. As I wrote earlier in this course:

> *Tell me and I'll forget.*
> *Show me and I might remember.*
> *Involve me and I'll understand.*

It is my goal to involve you with exercises and techniques so you'll understand.

Some students have expressed concerns about "being lost in the astral" and not being able to come back to their physical bodies. If you follow the instructions given in this lesson, it simply cannot happen. You have a direct link to your body via the cord mentioned earlier. This is true even if you, like some people, are not aware of the existence of the cord. The only time "getting lost" can occur is if you stray too far from your physical body. The relative expression "too far" is not a question of yards or miles. For lack of a better comparison, I like to say that it refers to hundreds of light years. Simply stay near your body while you are learning and you will have no such problem whatsoever.

In fact, the biggest problem for most people is getting out of the body in the first place. The next big problem is staying out. Getting back is not a problem at all. To initially get out you must truly desire to leave your body and approach the entire idea of the astral by knowing that it is beautiful, stimulating, safe, exciting, and fun!

There is one problem, rarely mentioned due to its lack of seriousness. It can occur to beginners and longtime veterans of astral projection and travel. It is what is known as "astral whiplash." Sometimes, when you are out-of-body, something can jar your physical body enough to suddenly draw your astral body back into your physical self. This can be from a knock on the door, a phone ringing, a car backfiring, or a friend nudging you and asking you, "Hey, are you asleep?"

The result of this whiplash back into your physical body is that you may feel groggy, sore all over, tired, and you may get a headache. When you project, astral "substance" (it has gone under many names) comes out of your physical body and unites

My First Time

Although it happened many years ago, I still remember my first experience with astral projection. I was in my girlfriend's dorm room. "Let's try something," she said. Being a typical horny young man, ready to try just about anything, I, of course, agreed.

She had me lie down on her bed, face up. Then she had me close my eyes and take some deep breaths to slowly relax. "Now, listen to this sound." She gently blew into her pitch pipe (we had met in a music class). I heard the familiar, reedy sound, and it was comforting.

"Think of an octave higher," she said. "Focus on it and go with it." That was easy. I just thought of an octave higher and was there.

"Now go an octave above that." I nodded when I had done that.

"Now go an octave above that . . . and an octave above that."

This continued a few more times and I realized that I was hearing a pitch in my mind that was above the human vocal range. In fact, the tone I heard was above any instrument I knew. This was getting really weird.

Somehow, she picked up on this and had me take a deep breath. As I exhaled, she pressed gently on my shoulder. It calmed me.

"Now go an octave higher . . . and an octave higher." Going so high, beyond hearing, was confusing and yet oddly freeing and liberating.

"Okay. Don't open your physical eyes, but just will your eyes to open."

Huh? What the heck did that mean? How can you open your eyes without opening your eyes?

"Just will your eyes to open and let your physical eyes rest."

Okay. I'll give it a try. Slowly, I willed my eyes to open. At first there was a blur. Then there was a clear focus. I could see myself on the bed directly below me. My girlfriend still had her hand on my shoulder. I was at the ceiling of the room.

"I'm doing it!" I thought. "I'm really astral projecting! This is incredible." I willed myself to fly around the room. It was a feeling of total freedom and liberation.

And then I thought, "Wait a minute. *I'm really doing this*—I'm really astral projecting! Aaaaaghhhhh!!!"

Bam! I was suddenly back in my body, jerking up. My girlfriend's hand gently pressed me back down and I caught my breath. In a few moments I developed a headache from the astral whiplash, but it was worth it. Astral projection is an incredible experience, and this just began my future astral adventures.

Thank you, C.G., for giving me my first taste of the astral planes.

with your astral body by way of the aforementioned cord. Coming back too quickly can result in leaving some of this "substance" still out on the astral plane. It is this loss that causes the minor physical problems mentioned above. This is one reason why you should always allow the double to be absorbed by the physical body after you finish your projection.

I experienced astral whiplash on my first successful attempt at astral projection. When I willed my eyes to open, I suddenly realized that I was floating at the top of the room and could see my body below me. The excitement and exhilaration was too much, and, wham, I was back in my body. Luckily, I had not gone too far and I only ended up with a headache and feeling a little groggy. Some deep breathing and a drink of cool, fresh water fixed that.

If you ever have a problem with astral whiplash, and you were not really close to your body when the whiplash occurred, there is a simple remedy for any of the symptoms associated with it. Re-project yourself to the same place to which you went when you were interrupted. Then return to your physical body in your normal fashion, generally by retracing the way you came. You will automatically collect whatever substance was lost. If you do not have a chance to re-project, the feelings resulting from astral whiplash will fade in a few hours or after you have a good sleep.

Perhaps the best solution to astral whiplash caused by an interruption from an outsider would be prevention. Before attempting any projection, turn your phone off and tell anybody else in your home that you are not to be disturbed for the next hour.

At this time there is no need for you to travel far once you have the knack of projection. However, it is important to include in your Tarot Contemplation Ritual the aspect of imagining yourself in the chosen card and looking beyond the edge of the card if you are not doing so already. This and astral projection come together in the next part of this lesson. You may wish to practice both the advanced Tarot Contemplation Ritual and astral projection for a few days or weeks until you have at least a minimal efficiency with both before moving to the next part of this lesson.

PART THREE

The Magickal Value of Astral Projection

So far I have explained techniques for mental and astral projection plus the very beginning techniques of working magickally while in the astral plane, what is commonly known as astral traveling.

I have also advised you to spend some time—days or even weeks—before going on to this section. I remember how excited I was when I first projected and how I quickly wanted to move on with my practices. So if you are quickly going ahead there is no need to apologize.

You are not expected to have achieved immediate success with the techniques. Very few people I have talked with do, and I know that it took me quite some time to get any real control. It may take you weeks or even months of daily work to perfect. It is better to practice for fifteen minutes, or even only five minutes, every day, than it is to practice for one hour once a week. *Persevere and you will succeed.*

But, so what? Once you are able to freely project your consciousness into your astral body and travel around in that state, what good will it do you? Why even learn how to astral project in the first place? Sure, it is fun and exhilarating, but going to a movie can be fun and going dancing can be exhilarating. And moviegoing and dancing take a great deal less preparation and practice.

There are many books that discuss how wonderful it is to be out-of-body. But once you achieve the ability of projection, few of the books discuss what to do with it. Some say you can contact friends or visit the Moon or any other of a variety of more or less mundane things.

Why bother? I can call my friends on the phone or drive over and visit them. And although visiting the Moon might be interesting, it is not at the top of my "things to do" list. And why, if the goal of astral projection is so relatively mundane, have occult schools and fraternities from the earliest dates of recorded history stressed the importance of learning how to project?

As I have made clear, the purpose of this course is to introduce you to various magickal topics so that you can direct yourself in your lifelong study of the occult. This lesson is specifically focused toward being a guide for your future study of metaphysics. In this lesson you are learning techniques that can give you *every magickal secret known and unknown to humanity!*

With these techniques you can achieve whatever you want in life, both spiritually and materially. Few people know about it because real magicians have tried to keep it a secret from mere dabblers in the occult sciences.

It has been necessary to withhold this ultimate secret of magick from you until now for two reasons:

1. You had to prove your readiness to receive the information by sticking through this course. You don't have to prove it to me or to anyone else. You needed to prove it to yourself. You needed to develop a justifiable sense that you have earned the right to move on. And just to help you in your recall, I want you to know this: right now, if you study not one more word of this course, nor read any other book, you probably know more about the theory and practice of real, traditional Western magick than 99.99 percent of the people in this world. In fact, you probably know more about the theory and practice of real, traditional Western magick than most of those who claim to be ceremonial magicians. You have earned the right to have this information by your diligence. This is especially true if you have been practicing the exercises and rituals.

2. According to Eliphas Levi, telling the truth to someone who cannot accept it is tantamount to telling that person a lie. I could have given you this information in the first lesson of this course, but you would not have been able to use it. Thus, it would have been meaningless or a lie to you. In order to make use of this knowledge, you needed to develop all of the techniques and talents you have worked with in these lessons. This course is cumulative.

The technique I will be sharing involves the use of the Tarot, Kabalistic correspondences, and understanding how to do ritual magick plus having the ability to raise, control, and direct the magickal energy and project to the astral plane. In fact, this technique is the reason for learning astral projection. It has long been kept a secret. It is called *Kabalistic Pathworking.*

Before discussing how to do Kabalistic Pathworking, there is some preliminary information that you must have. One of the best writers on magick and the Kabalah, Israel Regardie, at one time claimed that the Tree of Life is a convenient tool for memorization and categorization. While to an extent this is true, it does not go far enough, for the *Tree of Life is also a map of the astral planes.* Magicians can use this map to chart their ways to meeting with higher spiritual entities, non-physical consciousnesses capable of giving any information needed. This is why the study of the Tree of Life is so vitally important to all Western ritual or ceremonial magicians.

Kabalistic Pathworking, quite simply, is the process of using this map to go to the location of some higher spiritual entity. In a sense it is the exact reverse of evocation. Rather than bring a spirit to you, you go to it.

On the astral Tree of Life road you may encounter any or all of the appropriate Kabalistic correspondences for a particular path or Sephira. You may also encounter any of the lower non-physical beings described earlier in this lesson. Each journey up and down the Tree of Life will be unique, although it may have similarities with other such journeys. Therefore, you cannot depend upon what others have written. "*There is no room for authority in occultism*" (Dion Fortune). What you can depend upon is your own Kabalistic knowledge and magickal ability. Now, perhaps, you can see more clearly one of the reasons I have had to wait until this lesson to describe this technique.

I think that the best way to show you what Kabalistic Pathworking is like is to give you an example of a Kabalistic Pathworking experience. Please remember that merely because someone else has done this does not mean that it will be correct for you. Kabalistic Pathworking, like our physical world, is real, and like the physical world, it is interpreted through our senses and our minds. Therefore, it becomes highly subjective. True, for the person experiencing it, the Kabalistic Pathworking is real. Merely because something is real does not mean that it is actual. It only means that it is our present interpretation of what is actual.

Because Kabalistic Pathworking is so intensely personal and important, none of my students have ever told me that they were willing to have their magickal record of a Kabalistic Pathworking published. I feel the same way about my own Kabalistic Pathworking experiences. Therefore, as an example of a Kabalistic Pathworking, I am going to present to you a version adapted from a rare book from 1968 titled *The New Dimensions Red Book*. Although this was a group working, it has some valid points which make it very similar to the Kabalistic Pathworking I will be describing. I have altered it greatly to make it more similar to a Kabalistic Pathworking you might have.

An Example of Kabalistic Pathworking

It is a bright night. The Moon is full and the air is clear and cold. The date is _____. I have relaxed and performed the LBRP, the BRH, and the Ritual of the Rose Cross.

My temple is lit with nine purple candles and I am using the general-purpose incense of combined myrrh and frankincense. My four consecrated tools, the wand, chalice, knife, and pentacle are on my altar, which is in the center of my temple. I am sitting in a chair behind the altar, facing east. I have already drunk some comfrey tea and I hold a piece of quartz crystal in my hand. I am excited, but feel prepared.

I form a body, which is a duplicate of myself standing in front of me. I project my consciousness into my astral double and will my astral eyes to open.

I realize that I am now looking around at my astral temple, a duplicate of my physical temple on the astral plane. Everything is here, but it is more intense, more glowing, and yet also more ethereal. The walls of the room, however, are nowhere to be seen, as they seem to be shrouded in mists. This room may be the same size as my physical room, or it may be infinitely large. I have no way of knowing. Frankly, this scares me a bit and to calm myself I perform the LBRP. I see new and very bright blue stars and luminescent white lines going over those which I had already created. Then I perform the Rose Cross Ritual. It gives me a feeling of quiet calmness.

To the east, from out of the mists, I see three doors appear. The door to my left is a huge card of the Tarot, card 20, Judgement. To the right the door is card 19, the Moon. Due east, between the other card-doors, is a door upon which is card 21, the Universe. Ahead also is an enormous figure. It is my personal temple's guardian, whose name is _____. I know that I can leave both my temple and my physical body safely entrusted to my guardian's care.

This night I have chosen to work up the path of the Universe. It will take me from Mahlkoot, our Earth and my temple, to Yesode, the Sphere of the Moon. I step toward the middle door. The door seems to grow until it is all that I can see. Instead of opening it, I will myself to become the figure in the card. Instantly, we are one.

I find myself floating in a cloud-filled void, but I feel no fear, only joy. I am surrounded by a huge green wreath, and the only other entities I can see are the kerubic creatures of Ezekiel's Revelation: a Bull, an Eagle, a Lion, and a Man. I look around and eventually a path becomes clear. I walk away from the wreath and the four creatures, and move down the path.

The path is straight, but to either side it is very dark. Every so often I see an image, a tableau of great interest, on either side of the path. But rather than waste time, observing what is going on, I continue along the straight and narrow.

After a long walk, I come to a sort of ocean or lake. There is something shimmering in the distance, but I cannot make out what is there. In front of me is large, flat-bottomed boat. Its oarsman is the strongest-looking person I have ever seen. He would make almost every bodybuilder hide in shame. He beckons me onto the boat, so I enter and carefully sit down. He rows swiftly toward the glittering in the distance.

When we arrive, I see that it is a brilliant, white island. I tell the oarsman to approach, but instead he stares at me as if expecting more from me. I do not know what he wants. Rather than approaching the island, he rows around it. Quickly coming into my vision is the most beautiful young woman I have ever seen. She looks like she is perhaps twenty years old. Her body has not yet fully matured but is still excellent to behold. About the only thing whiter and more pure than her skin is her unusual white hair. Her blue eyes look questioningly beyond me, as if trying to learn the mysteries of the universe. She is both virginal and sexy at the same time. I am virtually breathtaken at her youthful beauty.

As we move further around the island, another woman comes into view. I can't guess her age, for she could pass as any age between her late twenties and late fifties. She is magnificently beautiful, too, but her beauty is not that of a young girl. Everything about her says "woman."

Her body is full with large but firm breasts and hips jutting out from a slender waist. Her skin is incredibly pure, and her white hair is puffed out to form a huge halo about her face. Her eyes are of the deepest azure. Almond shaped, the eyes turn down slightly at the outside giving an impression of knowledge, wisdom, and insight; and also sheer eroticism. This lady is by no means a virgin, but few have dared to love her except from afar. Even her posture breathes sensuality and eroticism, unlike the mere sexiness of her younger neighbor. She is surrounded by many animals and she stands on a highly fertile plane filled with grains and ripe fruits and vegetables. As the oarsman rows on I begin to weep,

as I do not wish to ever leave this Lady of Light. I start to sing a song to her . . .

> *Lady of Magick,*
> *Lady of Light,*
> *Breaker of gloom*
> *In the midst of the night . . .*
> *In your heart, in your soul*
> *A part of me lives.*
> *A part without which I'm alive—but don't live.*
> *Alive—but don't live . . .*

Soon, as the boat moves on, I can see her no more.

I feel sad, like a part of me is missing now that she is not there. But this sadness doesn't last long. Soon, another woman comes into view. She is much older, and at first glance her appearance is hag-like. But as I look at her I see a hidden sense of vitality, which shines from within her eyes. I see that she has lived a full and meaningful life. Even though her time grows short, she regrets not one day of her existence. In my mind I can almost see her beauty when she was young, and the exuberance that accompanied that youth. As I look at her, I see what I at first considered to be a hag-like appearance now has a beauty of its own. A beauty of time and experience. A beauty of age. She also has a sort of majesty about her, which gives her a beauty that transcends her physical appearance.

We continue around the island, and I realize that what I have seen are the faces of the threefold lunar Goddess of Paganism. This is natural, since I have studied Wicca or Witchcraft for a long time. We finally return to the first spot where we came upon the island. I bid the oarsman to cease his labors and wait here for a few moments. He stops the boat.

In my heart I say, "Oh Diana, Goddess of the Moon and beyond, I beg that if you have a message for me that you will grant me thy favor and let me now receive it." A beautiful figure approaches from somewhere on the island. She stands with one foot in the water and speaks to me. Although we are separated

Time for a Rant about Language

Okay, I admit it. I'm angry. For over fifteen years I was teaching classes on pathworking. I taught people how to do it and what they would experience. I led them on traditional path-workings up and around the Tree of Life. And lo, it was good.

Right now I am typing at my desk surrounded by glass-fronted barrister bookcases that are filled with occult books and manuscripts. In fact, if you visited my home you might be inclined to think that I lived in a library equipped with a bed. The point I'm making is simply that I've got a lot of books.

For those of you who are also heavily involved in buying (and, I hope, reading) occult books, you may have noticed that over the past decade or so, several books have been published dealing with pathworking. They seem to make pathworking into a mythologized journey through any archetypal images in the imagination. I had experienced this type of visualized journey in numerous classes for many years, but it is only recently that it has begun to be called pathworking instead of "guided visualization." I guess that phrase isn't "sexy" enough.

Well, for a while, I got on a metaphoric soapbox, crying out that they were doing guided visualized journeys, not pathworking. Hey, you writers and teachers! Pathworking is a specific practice. It's not what you're teaching! I tried. I wrote articles. I gave workshops. But my message was met with blank stares and total apathy. Nobody cared that a word with a specific meaning was having its meaning destroyed.

Sometimes, as a result of popularization, words end up developing their own meanings. In fact, the new meanings may actually be contradictory to their original meanings. For some people, "That's bad" now means "That's good."

My favorite example of this is the expression "quantum leap." If you ask most people what this means, they'll tell you it's a giant step forward from the past. In actuality, quantum leap (or quantum jump) originally meant a tiny step (an electron unexpectedly changing instantaneously from one quantum state to another) where you could see a differentiation from what existed before. In both cases there can be something revolutionary as a result, but in the original it was caused by a tiny change and in the popular sense it was caused by an enormous change. So the expression can mean both tiny and large. How can you communicate when the same expression means opposite things to different people?

Well, I discovered that trying to change people's minds about this is like trying to hold back the ocean tides with a bucket that's filled with holes. It's just not going to happen. I decided to stop wasting my time fighting what is.

Therefore, in this lesson (and in my workshops and classes), if I use the term "pathworking" by itself, I'm talking about a guided visualized journey. When I'm discussing or teaching the ancient system of taking a journey up and around the Tree of Life, as I'm sharing with you in this lesson, I'll call it "Kabalistic Pathworking."

by about one hundred feet of water and she speaks quietly, I am able to hear her perfectly. She says:

_____.

She backs away, and I bid her farewell. Now the oarsman takes us back the way we came. I notice things that, in my excitement, I had not noticed on the trip out. I see at the dock where I met the boatman a huge structure of rock, which forms the last Hebrew letter, Tav. I see distantly in the sky the planet Saturn, clearly discernible by its spectacular rings. As I walk back down the path by which I had come, I see trees of ash and yew, along with cypresses. Leaning against a yew I see a large sickle, and I get a small whiff of what smells like rotten eggs. Thankfully, the scent quickly dissipates. I walk back down the path until ahead I finally see the wreath and the four mystical creatures. I enter the wreath and immediately see my temple and its guardian. I walk into the temple and sit in the lap of my physical body. I open my eyes and say a silent prayer, thanking both Diana and my temple's guardian. I once again perform the banishing rituals. When I look at a clock, I am surprised to see that only thirty-seven minutes have passed. It has seemed like several hours.

The important thing to notice in the above story is that the astral traveler could not enter the island. The island, of course, was Yesode. You will be given the secret of how to enter the higher Sephiroht in the next part of the lesson. However, once again I urge you to wait for a few days or even a week and experiment with the simple methods of astral projection as presented so far. If you wish, you may even work with going into the last three cards of the Major Arcana and see what is on those paths, the three lower paths on the Tree of Life. However, I suggest that you:

1. Do not attempt to enter a higher Sephira at this time.

2. Do not stray from the paths.

3. Return to your temple the same way you came, following the same path.

4. Will your astral (or mental) double to be absorbed by your physical body upon your return.

5. Record your results in your magickal diary.

Be sure to always absorb the doppelganger. This is usually done by having the double sit in your lap, or, if you are lying down, by having it lie on top of you and sink into you. Also, notice the symbols mentioned at the end: Saturn, certain types of trees, a scythe, and the Hebrew letter Tav. These are all associated with the 32nd path, the path of the Tarot card "the Universe." It is impossible for me to list all of the appropriate correspondences here. Besides, they have already been listed in the book *777* by Aleister Crowley, *Godwin's Cabalistic Encyclopedia* by David Godwin, and *The Complete Magician's Tables* by Stephen Skinner. These dictionaries of occultism contain information that is a vital for all practicing magicians, and if you wish to improve your magickal knowledge, I suggest you obtain a copy of one or more of them.

The way the Tarot fits onto the Tree of Life is, as you can see, very important. It is the key for moving from one Sephira to another. You should become familiar with the pattern—it's given out in Lesson Three—if you have not already done so.

If you experiment with Kabalistic Pathworking as in the example above, you may use either mental or astral projection. Again, your experience in Kabalistic Pathworking may be quite different from the example above. It was provided only as an example of the types of things that may occur.

PART FOUR

The purpose of Kabalistic Pathworking is primarily one of information gathering. By questioning higher spiritual entities it is possible to learn new rituals, new magickal techniques, and new mystical information. It is important to remind you that this information is for you and you alone. Although rituals so obtained may require others to help you in performing a ceremony, it might not be appropriate for anyone else in the universe to perform such rites for him- or herself.

This presents an opportunity to repeat Dion Fortune's important point yet again: "There is no room for authority in occultism." Merely because someone reports that he or she had success with an originally devised ritual does not mean anyone else will have success with it. Similarly, a great many books on supposedly occult topics are nothing more than the fantasies of the authors. I know of one book that has been through a great many printings and claims that the reason you can hear other people's thoughts (clairaudience) is because when those people think of something they actually "speak" their thoughts through their ears! The idea makes perfect sense to the author, but it seems ridiculous to me. I know of another well-respected author who wrote a book concerning a lost civilization. The author made up the book and used his real name (with a "Dr." added) for an important character. He also used his wife's magickal name in the text. For the pseudonym listed as the author of the book, he switched around the letters of the words "not really" to make up a name! And this book was successful enough to warrant the publishers taking it into a second printing.

But what I have talked about in the previous paragraph refers particularly to what you or anyone else might learn from higher spiritual entities as you work your way around the Tree of Life. What I want to share with you now is how you get to a location where you can meet those entities.

This technique uses virtually all of what you have learned so far in this course. It is what all of the information and techniques, the exercises and rituals have led to. It's called,

The Ritual of the Paths

This ritual is composed of eight basic steps:

1. Purifications.
2. Banishings.
3. Projection and Kabalistic Pathworking.
4. Verifications:

   a. of your location(s).
   b. of the identity of entities.
5. Request for magickal aid or information from the higher spiritual entities.
6. Payment.
7. Return.
8. Banishings.

The only other thing that you will need to know is the key to gaining entrance into the higher Sephiroht, which is the password. Since each Sephira is overseen by an archangel, you need to know that archangel's name in order to enter. This is similar to the idea of having to give the name of a friend in order to get into a private club. In other words, the name of the archangel of a particular Sephira is the password for gaining admittance into that Sephira. Knowing the appropriate passwords (archangelic name associated with the Sephira) will allow you to enter any Sephira.

Preliminaries

First, with the help of the Talismanic Magick chart, decide what the purpose of the Kabalistic Pathworking is to be and which Sephira you are going to visit. As an example, let us say that we feel low on vitality and wish to increase our energy. The Sephira involved is Giburah, and it is to Giburah we must go. Next, as before any act of Grey Magick, do a divination to see what the probable outcome of the ritual will be. Let us assume that the divination indicates that the outcome would be very positive. The next step is to decide the proper time to do the ritual. Let's choose the fourth Magickal Hour after sunset on a Thursday during the waxing of the Moon. This was determined from the table of Magickal Hours.

It may be that your purpose would be only to communicate with a higher spiritual entity and become "friendly" with that entity. In this case it is not really Grey Magick and does not require a divination. However, performing a divination first will indicate the probability of success and could save you a great deal of wasted time.

The next step is to prepare the area. It is a good idea to give the temple area a good cleansing. Dust, wash, vacuum—whatever is appropriate. Then, you must also have an altar and the magickal tools or weapons. These include the four elemental tools and the Rainbow Wand. You will also need a piece of black material, suitable for covering the pentacle. The material should preferably be made of silk, but natural fibers such as cotton or wool will suffice. Stay away from nylons and polyesters. Also needed is a "road map."

A road map simply lists everything that you will need to know for the ritual. For this ritual we will need to know the correspondences for Yesode, Tiferet, and Giburah. We will also need to know the correspondences for the paths on the Tree of Life, which link these Sephiroht. This includes knowing the Tarot cards that are associated with the paths we are going to traverse. For this example the cards are the Universe, Temperance, and Justice. Make sure your writing is large enough and clear enough to be seen in a dimly lit room. Also, I prefer to use heavier card-stock rather than paper, as it holds its shape and is easier to control than flopping, thin paper.

Note that the path we are taking is from Mahlkoot (Sephira number 10) to Yesode (9), to Tiferet (6), to Giburah (5). We could have gone from Mahlkoot to Yesode to Hode (8) to Giburah, which would go up the Left Pillar. Or we could have chosen to go from Mahlkoot to Yesode to Netzach (7) to Tiferet to Giburah. This would be a longer way, but one which would still get us to the goal. In any event, for Grey Magick always begin by going first to Yesode from Mahlkoot. This is because Yesode is associated with magick. Since our example is Grey Magick, we first proceed to Yesode. Had the goal of the ritual simply been to gain knowledge and not ask for either a change in the physical world, or information that would allow us to create that change, we could have followed a path directly up the Left Pillar without first stopping at Yesode.

STEP ONE. Purifications

Begin with cleaning your area if you have not done so. Then cleanse yourself with a ritual bath or shower as has already been described. Robe yourself.

Next, purify your tools. True, their use in ritual work along with their dedication to the magickal arts has purified them, but a little extra never hurts.

Facing east, take the Rainbow Wand and hold it by the white band with the black end facing down. Visualize pure, white, light-filled energy coming from above your head, down through the Rainbow Wand, and out through the black end and into the ground. Say meaningfully,

**By the power of Ah-Doh-Nye, be pure! be pure!
I exorcize thee, Creature of Will!**

Place the Rainbow Wand back on the altar.

Now take the Air Dagger and hold it in your hands. Generate energy as you would in the Middle Pillar Ritual, but feel the energy run down your arms into your hands and into the Dagger. As you visualize all the impurities leaving the Dagger, say meaningfully,

I exorcize thee, Creature of Air!

Replace the Air Dagger on the altar.

Take the Fire Wand in your hands and face south. Generate energy as you did for the Air Dagger, and as you visualize all impurities leaving the Fire Wand say meaningfully,

I exorcize thee, Creature of Fire!

Replace the Fire Wand on the altar.

Take the Water Chalice, which should be filled with wine or water, in your hands and face west. Again generate energy, visualize all impurities leaving the chalice, and say meaningfully,

I exorcize thee, Creature of Water!

Take a sip from the Chalice and replace it upon the altar.

In a similar manner treat the Earth Pentacle. However, you should be facing north when you say meaningfully,

I exorcize thee, Creature of Earth!

Wrap the Pentacle in the black cloth that you have for the purpose and replace it on the altar.

If you have not done so already, at this time light the appropriate number and color of candles. In this example ritual you might wish to use five red candles, five being the number and red being the color of the Sephira to which we wish to travel. Incense should also be lit. Tobacco is commonly used for this Sephira. Other sharp, acrid scents will do, and, of course, you can always use frankincense and myrrh.

STEP TWO. Banishings
Perform the Opening by Watchtower.

STEP THREE: Projection and Kabalistic Pathworking
Using the system described in earlier parts of this lesson, either mentally or astrally project out-of-body. Look around your temple until you find the Universe door. Enter the card as described and look for a path ahead of you. Will yourself to move along this path, which will move you up the Tree toward Yesode. Because your intention is different, your trip may be different from the one previously described.

Eventually you will come to a blocked door or pathway. There will be a guardian or several of them at this point. They are the Order of Angels associated with this Sephira. In the case of Yesode, they are the Kerubeem. To pass them and enter Yesode, use the password "Gabriel" (pronounced "Gahb-ree-ehl"), the Archangel of Yesode.

Once you are allowed to pass into this Sephira, look around and make sure that you are in Yesode (part of Step Four) by comparing what you see, smell, experience, etc., with the known correspondences for this Sephira. As an example, if you see elephants, you are in Yesode. However, if you see a hermaphrodite you have somehow gotten into Hode. If you run into any problems or uncertainties, simply go back the way you came.

Eventually you will come to a door (or perhaps a curtain or painting) that appears to be a huge version of the card Temperance. Project into this card and look for its largest and most apparent path. When you eventually see this path, begin to travel along it. Soon you will find a blocked door or gate or path or entry of some kind. It will be blocked by the Malacheem, the angels of the Sephira Tiferet. To pass, use the password "Raphael" (pronounced "Rah-fah-ehl").

In a similar way to Yesode, now get used to Tiferet. Make sure you are here by the use of correspondences. Next, look for the Tarot card Justice. Project into this card, look for the path, and move until your way is blocked. Here the guardians are the Serapheem and the password is "Khamael" (pronounced "Kah-mah-el"). Again, make sure you are in Giburah by correspondences and by Gematria.

STEP FOUR: Verifications
To verify that you are in the appropriate Sephira, you can use the correspondences as already described. However, an even better way to do the verifications is via Gematria. This can only be done if you come into contact with entities capable of communication. Ask who they are. Since you are above the lowest astral levels, you do not have to worry about the creatures here having egos and thus being liars. Spiritual creatures on these levels have no true will of their own and cannot lie, but they do not have to spell out their answers in plain language. They may test you.

According to the Kabalah, Hebrew is the true language of the angels, and they may reply in Hebrew. On the next page you see a chart with the Hebrew letters. You will also see that each Hebrew letter is associated with a number. Therefore, each Hebrew word has a numerical value. Since 5 = 5, according to the Kabalah and Gematria, any Hebrew word whose letters equal a certain value is related to any other Hebrew word whose letters have that same total.

As an example of a test, perhaps when you think you are in Tiferet you might come upon an entity and you ask whom that entity is. The entity says, "Shavat." This means "rod" in Hebrew, and the letters come to a total of 311. The number of Raphael is also 311. Therefore, you are in Tiferet and are before

Hebrew for Gematria

Hebrew Letter	English Equivalent	Numeration	Hebrew Letter (Final)	Hebrew Letter
א	A	1		Aleph
ב	B, V	2		Bet
ג	G	3		Gimel
ד	D	4		Dalet
ה	H	5		Heh
ו	O, U, V	6		Vahv
ז	Z	7		Zay-in
ח	Ch	8		Chet
ט	T	9		Teht
י	Y, I	10		Yud
כ	K	20, 500	ך	Kaph
ל	L	30		Lahmed
מ	M	40, 600	ם	Mehm
נ	N	50, 700	ן	Nun
ס	S	60		Samech
ע	A	70		Ay-in
פ	P, Ph	80, 800	ף	Peh
צ	Tz	90, 900	ץ	Tzah-di
ק	K	100		Koph
ר	R	200		Resh
ש	Sh, S	300		Shin
ת	T, Th	400		Tav

Notes to Hebrew for Gematria Chart

The first column shows the way the Hebrew letters appear when printed.

The second column gives the sounds associated with each of the letters. Notice that some English sounds and letters are not included. There is no "E." Nor is there an "F," although the Peh does have a "Ph" sound, which for all practical purposes equates with the "F." Although the letter "A" is traditionally given as the sound for Aleph, the Aleph really has no sound. It is merely a placeholder for vowels, which in ancient days were understood and in modern Hebrew are indicated by points and lines written above, within, or below the letters when needed. The Koph is sometimes spelled "Qoph" and is said to be represented in English by the letter "Q." However, it is always pronounced like a "K." The "Ch" of the Chet is pronounced like the "ch" of the Scottish word "loch."

The third column contains the number value of each letter. Note that after 10 it goes to 20, 30, etc. Likewise, after 90 it goes to 100, 200, etc. Eleven is made by the combination Yud-Aleph or Aleph-Yud. Twenty-two is made by the combination Kaph-Bet or Bet-Kaph. Three hundred forty-seven is made by any combination of the letters Shin, Mem, and Zayin.

The second number, when it appears in column three, and the Hebrew in column four show the special enumeration and appearance of five letters known as "finals." The letters in column four show how these letters look when they appear at the end of a word. Their values at the end of a word are given in column three, and follow the commas in that column.

Column five gives the name of each letter in transliteration. The best books currently in print for use by magicians that are specifically on the subject of Gematria include *Godwin's Cabalistic Encyclopedia* by David Godwin, published by Llewellyn, and Crowley's *Sepher Sephiroth* found in some versions of *777*. Both books are really vital to a practicing magician.

the Archangel Raphael. You have been tested by way of Gematria and know how to pass the test. *If you are unsure at any time, simply return the way you came.*

STEP FIVE: *Request for magickal aid*

Once you are positive you are in the correct Sephira, request (by willing) the presence of the Archangel of the Sephira. In the case of this example, it is Khamael. When an entity appears, make sure that it is Khamael via Gematria. If, for example, the entity gives its name and identifies itself as "91," you will know that you are communicating with the correct entity because, by Gematria, Khamael equals 91.

Next, request what it is that you desire. Keep it simple. In the case of this example, you can use the words "energy and vitality."

STEP SIX: *Payment*

Nothing can be obtained without some sort of payment in return. Here, the payment is energy. There are several ways to give this spiritual energy:

a. Raise energy via the technique of the Middle Pillar Ritual and send the energy out your arms toward the archangelic figure.

b. Repeat a word or phrase over and over. In this example the word "energy" would be good. Or, perhaps you could use the archangel's name.

Let it speed up as you repeat it. You should feel energy increase within you and around you as you repeat the word or phrase. When it reaches a peak, say it one more time, but do it slowly and "loudly" toward the figure. Feel all of the energy raised leave with your "breath" and go into the entity. This technique has similarities to what is called mantra yoga in Eastern systems of magick. Of course, your astral or mental body does not really "breathe" nor speak "loudly." However, the sensation is the same as if you did these activities physically.

c. If you are familiar with martial arts, any method of raising and sending ch'i, qi, or ki, etc., will work.

d. If you are using mental projection you can use Inner Alchemy sex magick, and when you have the MahaTantra experience, direct the energy to the archangel. Do not worry about having a physical orgasm.

e. If you are mentally projecting you can run or dance in a circle and feel the energy build as a result of the physical exertion. When it reaches a peak, release it in the direction of the archangel. This, of course, needs the close cooperation of the physical and mental bodies as it is the mental body that directs the energy taken from the physical body. If you choose to use this system, be sure to stay within your protective magickal circle while you run and/or dance.

The energy given, while called a "payment," must really be given freely. The archangel may or may not choose to accept the energy, and whether or not the energy is accepted has no bearing on whether or not the archangel will aid you in your magick. However, nothing can be had for free, and even if the payment is not used, it is still a payment.

It may also seem odd that in this case energy is given in order to receive more energy. This is a secret of the alchemists who said that you must have gold

in order to make gold. In the same way, any energy given here can be returned a millionfold if need be.

STEP SEVEN: *The Return*
Using your own ad-libbed words, thank the archangel kindly for any help that it may choose to give, then start back down the Tree. If you go back the way you came you will not find any guardians blocking your way. Why should they stop you from entering a place to which you have so recently proved that you are entitled to be admitted? Besides, their purpose is to block unentitled people from going *up* the Tree of Life toward Divinity, not from *leaving* the Tree.

It is possible to go down the Tree in a direction other than that by which you arrived. If you do so, you will run into new guardians who may want to hear a password for a Sephira that you have not entered on this pathworking. As you can see, it is easiest just to descend the way you came. Unless you have a deep, memorized knowledge of the correspondences on the Tree of Life, I suggest you leave searching around for later Kabalistic Pathworking experiments.

When you make your way back into your temple, rejoin your physical body.

STEP EIGHT: *Banishings*
Give the "License to Depart" by saying the following, or something ad-libbed that contains all of its ideas:

Because you have been obedient and obeyed the commandments of the Creator, feel and inhale this grateful odor, and afterwards depart ye unto your abodes and retreats. Be there peace between thee and me. Be ye ever ready to come when ye shall be cited and called. And may the blessings of God be upon ye as ye may receive them. And now, let any and all spirits called by this rite return to their abodes and habitations, and harm none on thy way. Be ye all obedient and prompt to come unto me without undue difficulty on my part when thou art called upon according

to the traditions given by the Divine to us. Amen.

Of course, the "grateful odor" is the incense that you have been burning. Thus, if you are alone, you would add some more incense to the burner at this time. As you probably realize, non-physical entities do not have noses and cannot "smell" incense. But by tradition spiritual entities supposedly enjoy the astral double of the incense.

Clap your hands together loudly three times. This helps bring you "down to earth" quite literally. Finish by doing the Closing by Watchtower. Make a record of the ritual in your magickal diary.

The rite is finished.

If at any time you feel uncomfortable or "watched" or anything else which gives you an unpleasant feeling while performing this ritual, work your way down the Tree immediately and rejoin your physical body. Then, take the cover off the pentacle and, starting in the east, show it all around the circle while you move in a clockwise direction. Follow this by doing the usual closing. Then open all of the windows and air out the room. This will protect you from any unknown problems that might have developed as a result of performing this interrupted ritual. If you follow the instructions given, you have all of the help you need right at your fingertips.

This ritual also points the directions that you must study for the future. To successfully perform this ritual do you need to work on Gematria? On correspondences? On familiarity with the Tree of Life? On the Tarot? On astral projection? There are virtually months' or even years' worth of study and development ahead. By coming back to this lesson you will always know exactly what you need to study. You will always have a focus for future development.

One of the things I like to say is that "the beginning of wisdom is the realization of ignorance." You can't know what you need to learn until you realize that you are ignorant in some area. With this ritual as a guide you will always know exactly what you need to study, exactly what you need to learn. And that will continue until you reach your ultimate goal, until you are no longer just a student of the magickal arts, but are indeed a true, successful, and accomplished magician.

PART FIVE

From Ritual to Ceremony

There are two more considerations that need to be met concerning the previous ritual. One of these is how to perform the ritual as a ceremony—a group working. The other is how to find your personal temple's guardian.

If you have reached a state where astral projection is either possible or even easy, you already have a guardian. Before I explain this I have to give a bit of background information.

You may have read of organizations that claim to speed your psychic development or of exercises that can do this. No matter how many exercises you perform or organizations you join, you will not be able to project under the control of your will until you are ready to do so. A necessity for this is becoming totally aware of the physical plane. That is a reason why early in these lessons you were given exercises to develop your control of the elements, for the magickal elements are the very basis of the physical plane. Once you are aware of the ins and outs of the physical plane, you become ready to explore other areas and projection becomes simple—well, at least relatively so. Also, things start to "flow" more positively for you. This is in part due to your harmony and "friendship" with the archangel of the physical plane, Sandalphon.

As one function, Sandalphon oversees the "temples" of all astral travelers. Note that I put the word "temples" in quotation marks. This is because not everyone who projects has a clearly established temple. For most people who project, the temple is nothing more than the place from which they start. And most people have no map of the astral plane such as you have with the Tree of Life. Have you ever been lost in a big city with no map and no friends? It is no wonder that some of these people return from their astral wanderings with absurd tales of terror.

What they see is nothing more than their own fears brought to astral life.

For those people who are aware of the nature of the universe, such as I hope you are learning to be, astral travel becomes a fun and liberating experience. Guarding your temple and your physical body so that neither will come to harm on the physical plane is Sandalphon. The astral duplicate of your temple is protected by your banishing rituals.

Sandalphon is an archangel, and frequently does not do things "in person." Rather, Sandalphon can send one or more members of the Order of Angels under "his" command (actually, angelic beings are genderless except for our convenience). Thus, rather than Sandalphon, your guardian may be one of the Asheem, the Angelic Order whose name means "Souls of Fire." The next question is, "How do you find out this angel's name?" The answer: Just ask!

When you project, you will see your guardian angel. Ask this being by what name it wishes to be called. Ask for the best way by which it can be called. Ask for any special rituals that can help in this. Sometimes, call your guardian just to "say hello" and give gifts of energy (see previous ritual) or incense. Build a bond and your guardian angel will never let you down. Don't forget to thank Sandalphon for sending or assigning you this particular angel.

Changing the Ritual of the Paths to the Ceremony of the Paths is quite easy, but there is an important warning. For a final time in these lessons I repeat it. I'm sorry if you find this redundant, but I really want to urge you to begin thinking for yourself. Merely because someone said something doesn't make it so. The best way to learn Kabalistic Pathworking is by doing it. I know of at least two "teachers" who advise not to try Kabalistic Pathworking unless you are under their supervision, and then all they do is lead you through some guided imagery. Real teachers can start you in this work, but you must do the work yourself. Nobody can do it for you.

So, is a group working possible? Yes, but it may not be the same as what you have read or heard. The beginning is done much the same as any other cer-emony, with the parts divided as has been suggested in past lessons. When this is finished, all must sit in a circle holding hands. This holding of hands is very important, as it links you together both physically and psychically. You must have decided beforehand to which Sephira you will all be going and by which paths. Everyone must go by the same directions.

If a member has trouble projecting, the physical and spiritual link within the circle will help that person achieve projection. Also, if one person is slower than the others, he or she will automatically be pulled ahead to keep up with the group. If one or more persons would exceed the speed of the group on their way up the Tree, they will be slowed down by being part of that group. This happens automatically. The path for each person will seem shorter or longer depending upon their natural speed in the astral plane and the average speed of the group.

Once the journey is complete and everyone is back in their respective bodies within the physical temple, a leader should ask each person what he or she experienced. This may be done orally or each person can write the experience down and the journals can be compared.

Listen and look for similarities. Differences should not be thought of in terms of being wrong. They are simply items that an observer experienced due to his or her personal psychological and magickal makeup. Information that is identical among several people should be considered important. Information that is similar between people should also be thought of as significant. The inconsistencies are simply personal variations on a basic reality.

If this is a first time for a group working together, it may be beneficial to have one or more persons who are experienced with astral projection and Kabbalistic Pathworking as observers within the circle. The observer(s) can watch out for any unknown problems, and, if need be, summon everyone back by calling in a loud voice:

I summon all back from the Tree to their home
in this magickal temple.
Come home now!

If you have a group leader, he or she should hold the Rainbow Wand if there is only one such Wand in the group. If everyone has such a Wand, each should be held between the clasped hands of the people in the circle. The fingers should primarily be on the band of color associated with the Sephira to which they are going.

If you have a member of the group who is functioning as an observer, he or she should keep the candles lit and the incense burning. When energy is to be sent to a higher spiritual entity, it can be the duty of this person or persons to raise and direct the energy. Thus, they may dance or run to raise the energy and then direct it up through the top of the Rainbow Wand while holding the appropriately colored band of the Wand. If sex is to be used as a means of raising energy, the sex magick may be performed by one or more couples who are not going on the pathworking rather than having to break the circle. Direction of the energy is again controlled by holding the Rainbow Wand as above.

Although I personally have not participated in such a ceremony, I have it from a student that if you have a group of people, only one person may choose to do the pathworking while the rest supply the raised and directed energy. This, it is claimed, can be very powerful magickally.

The point I am trying to make with this discussion of group workings is that within certain limitations (the schematic or order of the ritual), nothing is necessarily dictated or set. Feel free to experiment and see what works the best for you and your group.

You may have noticed that as this course has progressed, instructions for rituals have become skimpier and more schematic in nature. I have tried to give you the forms and the background information so that you can fill in the details and make up your own rituals and ceremonies based on, and in harmony with, traditional Western ceremonial magick. At the same time, I have attempted to show you how to be original and thoughtful.

I have tried to give you the basics of Western ceremonial magick so that you can think, act, and be a magician. If I have done this and move you along the path of the Great Work, then I have succeeded.

Review

The following questions are designed to help you determine if you have mastered the information in Lesson Eleven. Please try to answer them without looking at the text. The answers are in Appendix Two.

1. Where can the highest magickal secrets be obtained?

2. To a real magician, what is the true difference between White, Black, or Grey Magick?

3. What is a simple way to decide if a certain ritual, style of magick, or magickal group is right for you?

4. What are pseudo-ghosts?

5. What is "astral whiplash"?

6. What common mystical symbol is also a map of the psychic planes?

7. What is the major difference between the Ritual of the Paths and the Ceremony of the Paths?

The following questions only you can answer.

1. At this time, what do you need to study more of in order to be a Kabalistic pathworker?

2. Have you been able to astral project? If so, what does it feel like to you? If not, what do you think you need to do to succeed at this art?

3. What five things would you like to accomplish by traveling up the Tree on Kabalistic Pathworkings?

4. What is the best thing you've learned so far in these lessons?

5. What did you hope to learn that you've not learned from these lessons? Is there something in these lessons that can lead you to that knowledge?

6. Do you know someone who would make a good seer for evocations?

Bibliography

For more information on these books, please see the annotated bibliography at the end of this course.

Crowley, Aleister. *777 and Other Qabalistic Writings of Aleister Crowley.* Weiser Books, 1986.

Denning, Melita, and Osborne Phillips. *Practical Guide to Astral Projection.* Llewellyn, 2001.

Farrell, Nick. *Magical Pathworking.* Llewellyn, 2004.

Godwin, David. *Godwin's Cabalistic Encyclopedia.* Llewellyn, 2002.

Ophiel (pseud. of Peach, Edward). *The Art & Practice of Astral Projection.* Red Wheel/Samuel Weiser, 1976.

Regardie, Israel. *The Golden Dawn.* Llewellyn, 2002.

Weed, Joseph. *Wisdom of the Mystic Masters.* Prentice Hall Press, 1971.

LESSON TWELVE

Prefatory Comments:

Modern Magick has been an important part of my life. It took ten years for me to learn enough to teach these concepts and more years teaching and practicing before I put it into writing. And now, after being in print for over two decades, it is considered by many to be a "classic" and has sold more copies than any other book of its kind. I've been very fortunate and want to thank all of the people who have read and used earlier editions.

The first and second editions ended with Lesson Eleven. The reason is that with those lessons it is possible to achieve any magickal goal and learn any magickal system. *Modern Magick* is not the alpha and omega of magick, but it does give you the tools so you can discover your own magickal alpha and omega. There quite literally was nothing more to give you because the goal was to let you move ahead on your own. Since the initial publication of these lessons, nothing has changed in that regard.

However, there are new technologies and new paradigms of magick that have appeared. In fact, there have been a surprising number of such new technologies and theories as to how magick works. Several authors have written books claiming that their understanding explains all of magick and makes it easy. You may not be familiar with those books because they have come and gone. I believe the reason they vanished is because the authors failed to understand that magick is both a science and an art. Their revelations were simply personal artistic interpretations of magick and the authors confused it with the science. They made the error in formal logic of going from the specific to the general ("What works for me must work for everyone") without any reason for doing so. This error, unfortunately, is made in many fields of endeavor.

Unless you have some desire to do so, there is no need to learn those neo-magickal systems. Quite frankly, in *Modern Magick* you have everything you need either as a self-contained magickal system or as the basis for understanding other systems. Besides, they may be hard to find, as most of those other systems vanished with their founders. However, the title of this volume indicates that this course of lessons is "modern," and it would be remiss of me not to include new systems that have either stood a test of time or could possibly be the direction that magick in the future is headed.

Therefore, I have added this new chapter for the third edition of these lessons. I think that in some ways nature has directed me to do this, as I always felt that eleven lessons (even though in numerology eleven is a "master number") wasn't right and there should be twelve, matching the months of the year, the signs of the zodiac, etc.

So what are the systems that will be covered here? The first one I'll be sharing is one aspect of the system known as Neuro-Linguistic Programming, or NLP. The original books that were written on the subject by the founders of the system were titled *The Structure of Magic* (Volumes I and II), so it's clear that they considered the ease at making changes in your life and the lives of others virtually magickal in nature. One website I read even defines NLP as a science and an art, just like our definition of magick.

Today, there are many people who have heard a bit about Neuro-Linguistic Programming but don't know much about it. Most people who are NLP IROBs ("I Read One Book [and now I'm an expert!]") or who have seen entertainers who *claim* to use NLP (often misleadingly so) think that NLP is a set of techniques that can be used to manipulate people against their wills. In fact, an entire industry has developed that claims to teach men how to seduce unwilling women using Neuro-Linguistic Programming. When you actually look at the methods of the PUA (pick-up artist) industry you see that they don't really use anything but the most superficial levels of NLP and, in fact, teach that picking up women is simply a "numbers game" (the more women you try to pick up, the more likely you are to succeed with one) and give encouragement and self-assurance techniques. These methods have been taught under different names for at least eighty years.

Many of those people who actually are trained and certified in Neuro-Linguistic Programming tend to think of it in terms of being some form of therapy. Indeed, the techniques of NLP can be used for eliminating the effects of limiting beliefs and decisions, as well as quickly ending problems that in the past took months or years to only create minor improvements in behaviors.

But NLP is much more. Perhaps a simple definition of NLP would be "a set of techniques for modeling excellence." A basic belief is that if someone else can do something, and if you can model or duplicate their way of behaving and thinking, you can accomplish it, too. For example, although I studied martial arts years ago, I did not achieve a level where students produced some of the phenomena that have made certain forms of martial arts so dramatic. And yet, with no further martial arts practice or training, after about two weeks of training in NLP I was able to use my open palm to break a solid wooden board, twelve inches to a side and one inch thick, with a single blow. My fellow students in the workshop were all able to accomplish this feat, too. We did it by modeling someone who was trained in the practice and knowing that if he could accomplish it, so could we. I still have the broken board as proof of my training.

Just as it is impossible to cover all aspects of magick in one book, it is also impossible to cover all aspects of Neuro-Linguistic Programming in part of one lesson in a course of lessons. NLP can be used to help improve writing; enhance public speaking abilities; increase sales; improve relationships; help settle disagreements; overcome phobias, bad habits, and unwanted behaviors; and much more. It covers too wide of an area, and besides, NLP is actually intended to be installed though in-person trainings, not taught in books. I know there are books and DVD courses that claim to teach you NLP, but in reality all they do is teach you *about* NLP. To really use it requires being trained by a qualified instructor, as much of the training occurs on an unconscious level. The skill to do this is installed in certified trainers. Be that as it may, I believe I can adequately teach one aspect of NLP, and you can learn it. It is a form of mental magick that allows you to create whatever you want in your future. It's powerful, simple, and direct.

The second system I'll be describing in this lesson may be the most popular neo-magickal paradigm today: Chaos Magick. I have been studying and practicing this system of magick even before it received that name. I still have the first book on the subject, *Liber Null*, which I had to order from a small shop in the U.K. This was published a decade before the U.S. edition (which was combined with another book, *Psychonaut*) was printed. In 1990 I wrote articles for a small, early U.S. journal, "Thanateros," which was focused on Chaos Magick.

There are some problems with writing about Chaos Magick because, as one of the most popular expressions in Chaos Magick goes: "Nothing is true. Everything is permitted." This expression is attributed to Hassan-i Sabbah, the founder of an Islamic mystery cult that smoked hashish and allegedly committed murders to further their cause. They were known as the *Hasheeshin*, and that name is the source of our word "assassin." The quotation was used by Friedrich Nietzsche in his classic book, *Thus Spake Zarathustra*. Nietzsche is one of the influences of Chaos Magick. The expression means that since everything we know of the outside world comes through our limited senses, there can be no objective truth. Therefore, everything is true and possible. That makes Chaos Magick filled with incredible possibilities. Unfortunately, it also means that some people think their way is *the* way and only way. So whatever I write, I'm sure, will get me in trouble with someone. But that's okay. Read and practice the techniques in this section and decide for yourself.

Finally, the third system I'm going to be sharing is one that has thoroughly attracted my attention. This is the interpretation of magick presented by author Patrick Dunn in his two books (as of this writing), *Postmodern Magic* and *Magic, Power, Language, Symbol*. This system relates the very essence of magick to language (linguistics) and symbol (semiotics). It a modern understanding of the way the mind and even computers work. Can you see where this is evolving? In my view, Dunn's vision of magick actually unites concepts of NLP (with its focus on using language effectively) and Chaos Magick (with its practice of using symbols effectively) into

a system that is ideal for the twenty-first century. He turns age-old beliefs on their head and presents new ways of looking at magick. Of all the systems I've seen, this one—if it catches on—is the most ideal for the iPod-listening, online-game-playing, computer-phillic generation that will be leading the world for generations to come.

The first edition of *Modern Magick* had many firsts, and if the third edition helps drive people to learn more about Neuro-Linguistic Programming, Chaos Magick, and Postmodern Magick, then the title of these lessons will remain accurate for generations of magickal students to come.

PART ONE

Although many people—especially "NLPers" (pronounced "nehl-pers"), people trained in and very enthusiastic about the value of NLP—will say that the concepts behind NLP as well as its many techniques are new, I have to disagree. I had learned many of the methods and ideas years before Neuro-Linguistic Programming was codified, and I'm sure they were around long before I learned them. What is new is the way they are presented and grouped, as well as the terminology used to separate NLPers from non-NLPers.

For example, if someone sees something as negative, often they are so involved with the situation that they can't see it in any way other than negative. By just presenting that person with a new way of interpreting things, it can literally change that person's life:

"I lost my job and now my life is falling apart!"

"Wow. Most people are so locked into the things they're doing that they can't improve their lives. Now you have a chance to restart your life and finally do everything you have always wanted to do. You're really lucky."

"Hmmm. I never thought of it that way."

I had always called that "looking at things in a different light." Some people refer to that as "making lemonade when given lemons." NLPers call it "re-framing."

The things that makes NLP special, in my opinion, are not the concepts and techniques, but the grouping of them into a whole. These groupings and they way they're used have a symbiotic effect—the result is greater than the sum of its individual parts.

As an example of this, let's look at time. Many cultures see time in a cyclical pattern. Modern Western cultures generally view time as linear. That is, we see time as moving in a straight line from the past, through the present, and going into the future. More than that, we each have a concept of personal time: Event A happened in our past, we are experiencing Event B now, and if things keep going along the same path, it is likely that Event C will happen in the future. Mapping out certain events over time is something that is common to history books all over the world. It is known as a *timeline.*

Discovering Your Timeline

While it is easily possible to map out events over time, it is interesting to note that we each have a personal timeline. Even though we don't constantly think about it, when asked we can see our lives as a linear series of events. Interestingly, this is not merely philosophical. There is actually a physical location to our personal concept of time. The first exercise in this lesson is the discovery of your personal timeline.

STEP ONE. Think of a happy event from five years ago. Now, going with your first thought, point to where you hold that memory. It may be to your left or right, above or below you, in front of you or behind you. There is no right or wrong here, it's just a location. If you can't quickly determine where that past event is located in space, try to locate another event earlier in time, perhaps your birthday party from when you were five years old. If, after a few tries, you cannot locate a past event in space, ask yourself, "If I could locate this past event in space, where would it be?" Point to it quickly. Go with your first thought.

STEP TWO. Now imagine something taking place in the future. Going with your first thought, point to where you think it will be. If this doesn't come quickly and easily, try a different event you hope will occur in your future. If its spatial location still doesn't come quickly and easily, ask yourself, "If I could locate this future event in space, where would it be?" Again, point to it quickly. Go with your first thought.

STEP THREE. Imagine a line going from that past point in space to the future point in space. This is your personal timeline.

Notes: For most people, the line is straight. It may go from right to left or left to right. It may go from your front to your back or vice versa. The present may be within you. That is, you may see the past behind you, the present going through part of your body, and the future being ahead of you. This may be on a diagonal. It may go from a lower height (relative to your body) in the past to a greater height in the future. Others may discover that the entire timeline is outside of them. They can see it in front of them or turn to see it behind them, running from side to side. Or perhaps it runs along either of your sides, going from back to front or front to back, but never touches you.

There is no right or wrong position for your personal timeline. Wherever it is located is perfect for you. If it doesn't feel "right" to you, try locating some more points of past events and future events. You may find that your timeline is a curve or a "V" shape. For some people it may be wavy. It doesn't matter. We're just finding out the location of your timeline.

Location, Location, Location

If we look at the shape and location of different people's timelines we can see lots of differences. There are two major grouping factors. For some people, their timeline is completely outside of their bodies. They can see the entire line—past, present, and future—to their sides, in front or behind them, above or below them, etc. At no time does this imagined timeline go through their bodies. Most often, however, the timeline for people in this group forms a line in front of them, going from left to right.

To be a member of the second group, the timeline goes right through you with the present being within you. My personal timeline goes from a past that is below the center of my back, to a present that is within me at my heart, and on to a future that extends up and ahead of me. The most common form of timeline is like this, going from back to front with the present being within the body, but unlike my timeline it is level.

Are you in group one, where you can see the entirety of your timeline, or group two, where part of your timeline goes right through you? Both are fine. Neither is better than the other. But here's a surprise: you can do a psychological analysis based just on whether a person is a type one or type two!

If you experience your timeline as completely outside of you, NLP describes you as being a *Through Time* person. The characteristics of a Through Time person include:

- You are very aware of the value of time.
- You are very good at planning.
- You are precise at meeting deadlines.
- Once you plan something for the future, you can quickly lose interest in it.
- You may have little connection with the present and often ask what day it is.
- Problems from the past can bother you for a long time.
- You're great at remembering past events.
- You're great at remembering birthdays, anniversaries, Moon phases, etc.
- You're a great researcher.
- You probably like "oldies" music.
- You are punctual. If you're late, you know it and may feel guilty.
- You may often look at a watch or clock to check the time, although you probably have an internal clock that very accurately knows the time.

- You have little patience for people who delay you.
- Perhaps the most important question in your life about anything is, "When?" Answers that involve the past or future are far more interesting than those that involve the present.

If you experience your timeline as going through you, NLP describes you as being an *In Time* person. The characteristics of an In Time person tend to be the opposite of those of a Through Time person and include:

- You are the life of a party.
- You only look at a watch or clock if you have to.
- You get engrossed in what you're doing and tend to lose track of time.
- Being late to meetings and appointments is common.
- You may keep an appointment book (or have a secretary do it for you).
- You may look at your appointment book and be shocked at everything you have planned.
- You're not good at planning.
- If asked what you're doing next weekend, you either haven't planned it or can't remember what you've obligated yourself to do.
- You tend not to plan ahead.
- You like to keep your options open.
- You focus on the present and "live in the now."
- You enjoy whatever comes your way.
- In the future, you may regret things you did in the past, but you don't worry about it.
- "Get over it" and "Put it behind you" are two of your favorite types of expressions.

If you look above, you'll see that I am an In Time person. When I was taught the concept of In Time and Through Time, I was surprised at just how uncannily accurate these descriptions were. Not only that, but by determining whether a person is In Time or Through Time I can communicate with them and understand them more easily.

It's important, however, not to think dogmatically. While learning about a person's timeline and whether they are an In Time or Through Time person can give you important information, remember that everyone is an individual. Most people will have some qualities of both groups, although they will *primarily* be an In Time or Through Time person.

Working with Your Timeline

The timeline is not something that is static and simply there. It can be used as a powerful tool for magick and change. In order to use it, however, you'll need to learn how to work with your timeline, a learning that will be the basis of the magick in this section. Working with your timeline is the purpose of the next exercise:

STEP ONE. Perform the Relaxation Ritual.

STEP TWO. Imagine yourself floating above your body and high enough so you can see your timeline either next to your body or running through your body. Just observe. Stay in this position for a few moments.

STEP THREE. Imagine yourself floating higher and higher, so that the timeline is only an inch long. Stay in this position for a few moments.

STEP FOUR. Float down until you are just above the timeline and it stretches far into the distance to the past and the future. If you can see either end of the timeline, imagine the scale of the timeline changing so that it has more detail and you can no longer see either end. Stay in this position for a few moments.

STEP FIVE. Think of a time in the past that has a pleasant memory. Perhaps it was a birthday, a prom, or your first date. Make sure it is a *pleasant* memory. Float back over your timeline until you are above that point in time and look down at it.

This is important: for this exercise *you should be an observer.* You should be able to see yourself having a great time within that memory. Technically, this is known as a dissociated memory. If you start experiencing the memory as if you are in it (technically known as an associated memory), immediately float up above the timeline so you are an observer and return to the present. It is important that in this step you are an observer only, not a participant.

STEP SIX. After you have observed the pleasant past memory for a few moments, return to the present. Allow your consciousness to float back down and rejoin your body. Take some deep breaths. If you feel disconnected, walk around in a circle stomping your feet on the ground to bring yourself back to your normal consciousness.

As I stated in the prefatory comments, the technique you're going to learn is a form of mental magick. It requires no wands or robes and no complex rituals. What you have learned in the exercise above are all of the basic techniques necessary to work with your timeline and do magick.

You may wonder if this entire timeline concept is merely subjective and nothing but a metaphor with no basis in objective reality. Frankly, I don't know if it's objectively real, but I do know that it's easy to prove that it functions in a very real way. The easiest way to prove this is by changing your timeline from In Time to Through Time, or the opposite way around. This changes the way you approach life and time and will make you feel uncomfortable or perhaps just really weird. If it were not real, how could it do this? Experiencing this change is a great way to learn about the reality of the timeline. It's the purpose of the next exercise.

Changing Your Timeline

It is not "better" to be an In Time person or Through Time person. Those are just terms to define how you process time on both a conscious and unconscious level. They are descriptions, not qualifiers. The advantage of knowing whether someone is an In Time or Through Time person is that it allows you to communicate with them better. The advantage of knowing whether you are an In Time or Through Time person is that it allows you to understand how you function in relation to time.

In my experience, these understandings are very real. Perhaps the best way to discover the reality of

Floating and Observing

In this lesson the terms "float" and "observe" are meant to be taken in the widest possible sense. For example, the term "float" could mean that you should get the feeling of floating on an air mattress on the surface of a pool, floating like a leaf on a gentle breeze, floating with your only support being a fluffy cloud, or floating like a waft of smoke from a cigarette through the currents of air. However you choose to actualize the concept of floating above yourself and your timeline, whatever feelings you get and however you do it, is perfect. There is no single correct way to be floating.

Similarly, don't take the term "observe" to only mean a visual sense. Observing in these exercises can be done with any and all of your senses. You may use your hearing or feeling (sensing) as well as your visual sense. We actually use all of our senses when we observe something, so don't let your limiting beliefs result in a limiting decision that prevents you from easily and effectively working magick with your timeline.

The point is, however you float about yourself and your timeline, and however you observe what is going on, is exactly perfect for you.

---

these two ways of processing time is by experiencing how the other half lives.

I want to repeat that the experience of changing your timeline can be very disconcerting. Therefore, I urge that you do not, under any circumstances, allow this change to stay in effect for more than a day. When you first try this you may not want to allow the change to stay in place for more than a few minutes or a few hours. When I first did this I literally felt dizzy. However, nothing will let you see the reality of the timeline better than this experience.

STEP ONE. Perform the Relaxation Ritual.

STEP TWO. Allow yourself to float up until you can see yourself and your timeline. Make sure you float high enough that you can observe the entire length of your timeline and see both ends. Pay close attention to this position of your timeline so you can return it to this position at a later time.

STEP THREE. Using your imagination, allow your timeline to rotate. That is, if it's going left to right, allow it to rotate so it is going back to front. If it's going back to front, allow it to rotate so it is going

from left to right or right to left. Most importantly, if it is going through you, when you rotate the timeline allow it to be completely outside of you. If the timeline is normally completely outside of you, when you rotate it allow it to run through you.

STEP FOUR. Float down into the present, right into yourself, and allow your timeline to organize time according to its new position. You don't have to "do" anything else. The new position will allow this reorganization to occur naturally.

STEP FIVE. Imagine the sound of a large padlock as it clicks closed. Lock in this change so it clicks in place the same way.

STEP SIX. Take some deep breaths. If you feel disconnected, walk around in a circle stomping your feet on the ground to bring yourself back to your normal consciousness.

STEP SEVEN. Spend some time doing ordinary things and observe the way you feel. You have switched from being In Time to being Through Time, or vice versa.

Be sure to repeat this exercise and return your timeline to its original position.

Besides proving the reality of the timeline and the concept of being In Time or Through Time, there can also be a practical use for changing your timeline. A person who is In Time is not as good at planning things as is a person who is Through Time. If you are an In Time person and need to plan an important meeting or party, you might want to temporarily change the direction of your timeline for this purpose. A person who is Through Time may have more difficulty in getting over past occurrences and dwell in anger over events that happened years ago. By switching to being an In Time person this person may be able to make positive breakthroughs in his or her life and move on before switching back to their normal Through Time approach.

By the way, for further information on the differences between In Time and Through Time, you might look at Carl Jung's book *Psychological Types*. An In Time person compares to Jung's concept of the "Judger," while a Through Time person relates to his idea of the "Perceiver."

Timeline Magick

The previous two exercises, along with the information presented, has allowed you to understand the concept of the timeline, work with it, experience the reality of the concept and see how it effects you. The next step is to learn how to work with the timeline to create a desired change in your life. That is, this next part of the lesson will show you how to use the timeline to achieve a desire or goal.

Many of the concepts presented here can be directly related to your other Grey Magick practices. For example, I've already described how the goals of your practical magick should be SMART goals. By that I mean they should be specific, measurable, attainable, realistic, and have a time frame. I've also suggested that they should be ecological—good for you, good for those around you, and good for the planet. Let's look at some other keys to making successful goals:

1. Your goal should be what you want, not what you don't want. If your goal is vibrant health, describe it in a concrete and specific form: "I want to be able to run a marathon, be able to bench press 150 pounds, and fit into size 32 pants." That's specific and positive, as opposed to something like "I don't want to be sick and I want to be stronger."

2. You should know your present situation in comparison to your goal. This will allow your unconscious mind to design a map to achieve your goal. Picture yourself in the present situation. What does it feel and sound like?

3. Determine how you will know when you have achieved your goal. One way to do this is by using the "last step" model. This is by concretely knowing exactly what is the last thing that has to happen for you to know you have achieved your goal. In the example given above, the last thing may be crossing the finish line of a marathon or slipping easily and comfortably into a pair of pants that is the desired size.

4. Make sure that your goal is only dependent upon you. You can't change other people—only they can do that. You can, however, change yourself. Therefore your goals should not be dependent upon others. "I'll be happy when I'm popular" not only isn't very specific (what is popularity?), but it depends upon other people liking you. Instead, goals should be things that are entirely based on what you can achieve. "I'll know I have achieved my goal when I finish a marathon" doesn't require the help of anyone else.

5. Make your goal as explicit as possible. When will you achieve it? Who will be there? How does it sound? How does it feel? What will you see?

6. Turn it up! In NLP this is known as "adjusting the submodalities." Here, the idea is to turn up your senses when creating the magickal goal. Make the sound crisper. Make the colors you

Neuro-Linguistic Programming

How does a person become an expert at something? Why is one person amazingly successful while others barely succeed?

In the 1970s, a college student, Richard Bandler, realized that he might have uncovered the secret. He was transcribing recorded therapy sessions of the famed Fritz Perls and noticed that patients were more likely to accept suggestions from Perls when the therapist used certain words and patterns. Could that be the key to Perls' success?

Bandler got in touch with linguistics instructor John Grinder. Together, they analyzed the work of another psychiatrist, Virginia Satir. The results of their work became the book *The Structure of Magic*, published in 1975. As a result of their work they ended up meeting and modeling Dr. Milton Erickson, a man who revolutionized the approach of psychologists to their patients and legitimatized the use of hypnosis as a therapeutic tool.

By the 1980s, Neuro-Linguistic Programming—"neuro" because they felt it altered people's neurology, "linguistic" because it used language, and "programming" because computer programming was an up-and-coming field—was being hailed as a great advance in the fields of counseling and psychology. However, due to disagreements between the two founders, and the failure of anyone to trademark or register the name, many people started to add concepts to an ever-broadening field. NLP expanded to be used for such things as resolving business conflicts, improving sales abilities, personal growth, enhanced communication skills, and much more.

Curiously, the breadth of what is capable with NLP has caused questioning over its legitimacy. People are so busy using its techniques (and making money from it) that thorough scientific testing of the many techniques used by NLP practitioners has never been done. Still, practitioners can attest to its success with innumerable anecdotal stories and evidence.

The creators of NLP have clearly stated that it has been designed so that people need to be trained in its use. Certified trainers of NLP will explain that they have learned how to embed various aspects of NLP in the unconscious minds of students taking the trainings. This comes from the way the material is presented during the trainings combined with the use of certain words, word patterns, the tone of voice, inflections, etc. None of this can ever be done through a book.

Still, people will try to learn through books. Some people who may have had some training (or who read some books) will try to share NLP ideas, although without the depth and fullness that a real training includes.

If you are interested in improving your life and perhaps helping others by using NLP, I would strongly urge you to consider taking an actual, in-person training. In the meantime, the many books and DVDs available on NLP will teach you a great deal about the techniques and technology of achieving excellence.

visualize sharper, brighter, and more intense. Make the joy you feel flow through every cell of your body. Turn it up!

Don't be afraid to write things down. Writing down what you want is a form of creating a talisman. Once you have done all of these things, you're ready for the magick.

STEP ONE. Perform the Relaxation Ritual.

STEP TWO. In relationship to your goal, focus on where you are now. For example, if your goal is to run a marathon, focus on how far you can run now. Adjust the submodalities by turning up the sharpness, clarity, brightness, intensity, etc., on what you see, feel, and hear when you focus on where you are now.

STEP THREE. Become aware of how you feel with the adjusted submodalities.

STEP FOUR. Float up above yourself so you can see yourself and your timeline from above. Bring the feelings of the adjusted submodalities with you.

STEP FIVE. Take three deep breaths. With each exhalation, charge the feelings of the adjusted submodalities so they are sizzling with energy.

STEP SIX. Allow yourself to float forward along your timeline until you come to the time (or where you think the time should be) where you want to have achieved your goal (part "T" of the SMART goal system). Using all of your senses, visualize yourself having achieved that last step (see point 3 above) of your goal. You are an observer.

STEP SEVEN. Allow the energized feelings you brought with you to flow down and enhance your visualization.

STEP EIGHT. From your position above your timeline, turn back and look down your timeline toward the present. Now just observe. You may notice or sense how all of your conscious and unconscious actions are automatically modifying to inevitably lead you from the way you are in the present to the achievement of your goal in the future. Take as long with this step as you need.

STEP NINE. Float back to the present and merge with your physical being.

STEP TEN. Take some deep breaths. If you feel disconnected, walk around in a circle stomping your feet on the ground to bring yourself back to your normal consciousness.

And that's it. I know this sounds incredibly simple. If you've done the exercises you may think it's incredibly easy, too. The truth is, this method *is* simple and easy. But that doesn't mean it's not powerful and effective.

As mentioned previously, one of the people modeled by the founders of NLP was psychiatrist and hypnotherapist Dr. Milton Erickson. If you want to learn Erickson's techniques from Ericksonians, you must spend months or years studying through observation of what Erickson was doing. You should also have training in psychology or psychiatry and already be a professional in that field. With NLP you can learn the basics of all the techniques of Erickson, known as the "Milton Model," in a few hours. It may take much longer to be able to quickly put all of those techniques into practice and be able to effectively use them, but NLPers believe it can be done.

What happens is that people discover something in their own way and add ideas, concepts, and techniques to "make it their own" even though these additions may have nothing to do with the effectiveness of the discovery. So it could be claimed that the NLP Milton Model includes only the essential aspects of Erickson's techniques. It strips away all of the excesses that really aren't needed.

This aggregation of non-essentials exists in many fields, not just those that have been stripped to their core by NLP. Many would claim that this has occurred in the area of traditional ceremonial magick, too. So what would happen if you could strip away all of the aggregated non-essentials in magick and limit yourself to only those things that are really necessary to magick, resulting in a system that focuses on results? Some people claim that has been done, and it's called Chaos Magick.

PART TWO

As I mentioned earlier in this lesson, it's difficult to pin down exactly what Chaos Magick is and isn't simply because it has no hard and fast rules, no *Tome of Wisdom* ®™© passed down for hundreds of years that have becomes tombs of dogma limiting what can and cannot be done. In an article for *The Llewellyn Journal*, Andrieh Vitimus answers the question of what Chaos Magick is by saying that "possibly no two chaos magicians would agree" on an answer.

As is often the case, a good way to look for answers is to look for beginnings. To really understand the system it would help to understand the milieu in which it developed. One of the most important elements was . . . punk rock.

An Incomplete History of Chaos Magick

It was the middle 1970s. The war in Viet Nam had finally ended. The music world was filled with brilliant musicians, often playing elaborate, stylized music that was much more for the mind than it was for the heart, soul, or beat. Don't get me wrong, I still like what has come to be called "progressive" rock ("prog-rock") or "orchestral" rock. The problem with it was that you had to be an expert to play it and it often lost its core—it didn't encourage listeners to get up and dance. Young people didn't have music to dance to nonstop nor a major political cause to use up their energy. Something had to come up. A revolt had to brew. The industry knew it and promoted . . . disco. Disco wiped out numerous music venues that had previously played live music. Plus, kids saw their parents and grandparents dancing to disco. Yuck! This wasn't their music; it was the music of corporate America. A revolt still lurked. That revolt manifested as punk rock.

The musicians weren't great. The singing wasn't always on key. It didn't have elaborate musical structure or harmonies. But it had power, energy, and a nasty attitude. It changed rock music and what people were doing. It made musicians look at themselves and ask if they needed all of those keyboards and effect pedals and massive drum kits.

By this time, the world of magick had become fairly solid. Ceremonial magicians were actually doing magick. People such as Chic and Sandra Tabatha Cicero and Patricia Monocris, under the guidance of Israel Regardie, were working the Golden Dawn system and running legitimate Golden Dawn temples, although schisms, the bane of many established groups, would eventually develop. Meanwhile, Wicca was becoming a strong tradition and recognized as a religion. Sectarianism, the bane of many religions, would begin to develop and this, combined with Wicca's very success, would eventually lead to the explosive growth of solitary Wicca.

It was amid this environment that Peter J. Carroll and Ray Sherwin had a meeting. I have no idea what exactly was discussed there, but I'm going to assume that they asked questions similar to those of the punk rock musicians: Is religion (Wicca) necessary for magick? Is a belief in gods and goddesses necessary for magick? Are all of the complex robes and wands and rituals necessary for magick? If not, what *is* necessary?

Two years later, Carroll and Sherwin formed a new magickal order, the Illuminates of Thanateros (IOT), and Sherwin published Carroll's *Liber Null* and his own *The Book of Results*. *Liber Null* presented many of the basic theories for Chaos Magick (a term coined by Carroll) and Sherwin's book gave a practical approach to its use based in part on the use of sigils as described by Austin Osman Spare and described elsewhere in these lessons. The IOT allowed the system to grow and evolve within a magickal order. Everything was in place except for one thing.

Wicca had started in England, but exploded in popularity in the U.S.A. Punk rock started in England and took over the music world there. Here in the U.S., the music world was controlled to a far greater extent by the corporations, so punk really only caught on in larger cities where live music was still being played. Chaos Magick also started in England, but without the support of American publishers of books, magazines, and journals, it wasn't developing in the U.S. at all. A full decade went by before the first book on Chaos Magick was published in the U.S. Magazines with information on Chaos Magick were almost entirely British. Very little was getting over to the U.S. (this was pre-Internet), and just as punk rock appealed to younger people, such was also the case for much of Chaos Magick in the U.S.

There is a saying in various arts such as painting and music that you must learn the rules in order to break them. There is no doubt in my mind that the originators of Chaos Magick were (and are!) expert and experienced magicians. While there were certainly some people like that in the U.S. who were involved with Chaos Magick, many, perhaps most, were not. In fact, many were young boys with the attitude of "You mean I don't have to study or practice and I can be a magician? Woo-hoo!" In fact, to be successful with Chaos Magick, as with any form of magick, requires study and practice, but saying this to some of the early U.S. "Chaotes" (practitioners of Chaos Magick; some Chaotes dislike the term, preferring "Chaoist") resulted in disdainful "You're just an old fogey" responses.

I once got into an online debate with a self-professed Chaote who said that (contrary to the importance of results as put forward by Sherwin) the important aspect of magick was simply doing it and that it didn't matter if you got any results. I replied that if it didn't matter whether you actually got any results, why not just sit back, do nothing, and merely claim you had done magick since the results—or lack thereof—would be the same. He responded that I just didn't get it and he would no longer correspond. Well, maybe he was right, but here's what I do get:

Although Carroll and Sherwin can be considered the fathers of Chaos Magick—and perhaps more credit goes to Carroll because he's had more published—the grandfathers are certainly Spare and Crowley. Since Crowley was heavily influenced by his training with the Golden Dawn, it could certainly be said that Chaos Magick is an offshoot (or an evolution) of traditional magickal practices. However, they were not the only influences.

The writings of Robert Anton Wilson were also an influence, as were those of Ramsey Dukes. The ideas of Discordianism and its "don't take life too seriously" attitude play a part, as do the writings of Dr. Timothy Leary. Shamanism influenced Chaos Magick, as did the (then) new science of chaos theory, quantum physics, and science fiction.

What Does Chaos Have to Do with It?

I've already mentioned one of the basic concepts of Chaos Magick, that "Nothing is true. Everything is permitted." This is based on the concept that everything we perceive comes through our senses and is therefore subjective, not objective, reality. We can easily change our subjective reality, so we can achieve anything we want; we can successfully work magick.

But if this is a basic belief, a tenet of Chaos Magick, how is it chaotic? The answer is actually rather simple. At the time Chaos Magick was being originated, chaos science was also developing and was a fascinating subject. It would be easy to say that Carroll just took the name because it was popular, but there's more to it than that.

One of the consistent questions of magick is "Where does the power of magick originate?" Over time, the answer to that question has changed. Anciently, it was with the gods and goddesses. Over time it became spirits and for many it was a manifestation of our inner power. According to chaos science, before the universe formed, there was only chaos. Carroll suggested that since this chaos was the source of everything in the universe, it must also be the source of the energy used for magick. Thus, Chaos Magick wasn't so named because it is chaotic, but because it taps into the primal source of energy, which is pure chaos.

Personally, I think this is simply renaming God or the gods and calling them "chaos." It's a different name for the same thing (please put away your torches and pitchforks!).

This brings up another popular Chaos Magick concept: there are no gods and goddesses, or if there are, they're not involved with us. What we call gods are simply manifestations of our own minds. However, for doing magick, the concept of gods can be very effective. Therefore, we can use any gods from any pantheon and pretend they are real until they develop a subjective reality for us. That is, you "fake it 'till you make it." Personally, I think that's an awful lot of work just to follow the dogma of "There are no deities but pretend they're there 'cause it's useful." Either don't work with deities or use them. But that's just me.

Other Chaos Magick Concepts

One of the important concepts of Chaos Magick has its origins in a combination of two concepts: results are what matters and everything is permitted. Thus, a practitioner of Chaos Magick is likely to work with any appropriate deities from any pantheon in one ritual. A ritual might involve an ancient Sumerian deity, a Voudoun Loa, and an Old One from H. P. Lovecraft's fictional Cthulhu mythos. Of course, they're only representations of concepts and energies, and they're not objectively real, but they make great metaphors to direct the energy and the ritual. Cross-cultural adoptions are fine, and you can just pretend they're real and fake it 'till you make it.

In fact, a practitioner might go one step further, doing what is called *paradigm shifting*. Take a deity from one pantheon and include that deity in a ritual from a completely different paradigm. This paradigm shifting can have a powerful effect on a practitioner, opening him or her up to potentials that are not limited to their normal worldview. It can literally shake things up and break down limiting beliefs.

A Chaote might even go back further, borrowing from shamanic practices to induce an altered state of consciousness called *gnosis*. Those of you reading this who are familiar with various gnostic concepts but are not familiar with Chaos Magick concepts might be unfamiliar with the use of the term "gnostic" in this sense. This altered state, also known as a

Gnostic Trance, is based on becoming totally focused on one thing. The use of extreme focus induces a trance state. Often the focus of such a trance is a sigil designed in a fashion similar to the system of Austin Osman Spare. There are many methods for achieving the Gnostic State and Chaotes will often come up with their own method for achieving it. There is no limitation placed on the technology for achieving Gnosis.

As described previously in these lessons, the goal is to focus the energy (in this case by achieving the Gnostic Trance) and then forgetting what you are doing. This has the effect of sending the purpose of the ritual (as made concrete through a sigil), combined with energy to manifest it, directly to the unconscious mind (rather than the conscious). The unconscious mind puts everything into action, bringing to bear whatever is needed to bring about the goal. This is true even if you don't know what the goal is.

Huh?

Some Chaos magicians will make up a bunch of sigils for various purposes and put them aside. After a while, the conscious mind won't remember the purpose of the sigil. Still, a ritual can be performed to achieve the goal as indicated by the sigil. This makes even more important the old saying "Be careful what you wish for. You just might get it."

Who Are You?

"Who are you?" is the question posed by the caterpillar to Alice during her adventures in Wonderland. Her answer would be applauded by any Chaos Magician: "I know who I WAS when I got up this morning, but I think I must have been changed several times since then."

The ancient statement considered so wise, "Know Thyself," makes a powerful assumption that is so built into our very beings that we usually don't even notice it. Specifically, it assumes that there is a "self" to know.

But what if who you are is infinitely malleable? Had you been brought up differently, every aspect of your being might be different. The way you think about things might be totally different. A person who is loving and tolerant might be hateful and racist. A person who is a fundamentalist Christian might be a Buddhist. This implies that who you are—your soul—is not a reality. Rather, it is something that we create as we develop and is capable of changing and becoming whatever we want. This attitude has some incredible benefits, but also leaves us with a question: if you can change to be whatever you want whenever you want, what is the "real you?"

The answer for Chaos Magicians goes back to A. O. Spare. Unfortunately, Spare was so much against doctrines that he really didn't give a clear definition of the term: *Kia*. He describes it similar to the way Lao Tzu described the concept of the Tao: "The Tao which can be expressed in words is not the eternal Tao."

Carroll refers to the Kia as a unity that exerts will and perception. That was unclear to me (perhaps appropriately so), but luckily, Carroll also describes it as the Spirit or Life Force.

That takes me back to my days as a member of AMORC, the Rosicrucian Brotherhood, which, at the time, was headquartered in San Jose, California. Many people equate the terms "soul" and "spirit." I equated them until I studied with AMORC. They differentiate between the soul and the spirit. To them the spirit is another term for the life force and not the soul. Thus, each person would have both a Spirit and a Soul. With Chaos Magick, people have that animating Spirit, the Kia, which has some of the functions of the Soul, but is not the Soul. Spare wrote in *The Book of Pleasure* that the exuberance of the Kia gives us existence.

Since you can choose to be anything you want, it is likely that you will find a few paradigms that are your favorites. Thus, each Chaos Magician finds structures to work within, structures that may be completely different from those of any other practitioner. Everything is permitted. How do you know there isn't a better paradigm, worldview, or methods of magickal practice for you? You don't. So it is common for a Chaote to experiment and try different things.

So Where Are We?

With Chaos Magick, then:

1. Everything is permitted.
2. Getting results is central to magick.
3. The methodology frequently involved achieving the Gnostic Trance.
4. The concept of gods, at best, is similar to that of Jungian archetypes.
5. Experimentation is encouraged.

I imagine that a great deal of other ideas about Chaos Magick could be stated. They're all right. And they're all wrong. There is no objective truth. "Nothing is true. Everything is permitted."

Dion Fortune stated that we should try to use the magick of the land in which we live. She did not foresee the ease of transportation and communication we have today. Aleister Crowley discussed the concept of Aeons and how old-style magick (such as the magick of the Golden Dawn) belonged to the old aeon, which ended in 1904 and now, in the new aeon (of the Crowned and Conquering Childe), his system of Thelemic magick should be practiced. Chaos magicians would laugh at that (in fact many do a lot of laughing at dogmatic beliefs). It's time to bring about the next cycle, the *Pandamonaeon*. And to the Chaoist, the practice of Chaos Magick and the understanding of the concepts behind it will bring about this next cycle in human evolution.

Or not.

A Chaos Magick Banishing

When the first books on Chaos Magick were published, there was nothing in them about banishings. This was obvious to me. The people who created the concepts behind Chaos Magick were experienced magicians and would know enough to do some sort of banishing. Unfortunately, some of the people in the U.S. whom I saw hadn't figured this out. Perhaps that was the cause of some of their unfortunate egocentrism. Or not. Eventually, however, banishing rituals were published.

I was first introduced to a version of this banishing by Ms. Lola Babalon. She was the first person to bring Chaos Magick to the U.S., and I was privileged to have her write a section in my *Modern Sex Magick*.

The technique of this banishing is very simple, but requires a bit of explanation, as it uses what are commonly called the "European vowels." These are the vowel sounds in alphabetical order, but pronounced a certain way:

A   is pronounced as in "water"

E   is pronounced as in "wet"

I   is pronounced as in "we"

O   is pronounced as in "hoe"

U   is pronounced as in "moo"

However, instead of using them in alphabetical order, try pronouncing them in this order: IEAOU. If you do, you will see that the sounds begin in the middle of the mouth, move to the back, and then to the front. In fact, it seems to be an extension of IAO. However, IEAOU is the key to this ritual.

This is my description of a ritual from Peter Carroll's *Liber Kaos* called "The Gnostic Pentagram Ritual."

STEP ONE. Face any way you like.

STEP TWO. Visualize a glow of energy around your head. Inhale. As you exhale, intone an extended "I." Remember, it should sound like the "e" in "we."

STEP THREE. Repeat, but visualize the energy at the throat and intone "E." Remember, it sounds like the "e" in "wet."

STEP FOUR. Repeat, but visualize the energy at the heart and intone an extended "A." Remember it should sound like the "a" in "water."

STEP FIVE. Repeat, but visualize the energy at the solar plexus/stomach area and intone an extended "O." It should be pronounced like the "o" in "hoe."

STEP SIX. Repeat, but visualize the energy surrounding the genitals and intone "U."

STEP SEVEN. Repeat steps Two through Six in reverse order, going from the genitals to the head.

Use the same vowels, but in the reverse order: UOAEI.

STEP EIGHT. Draw a pentagram in the air in front of you while intoning IEAOU in one exhalation.

STEP NINE. Turn 90 degrees counterclockwise. Repeat Step Eight in this position.

STEP TEN. Repeat Step Nine twice more, then turn so you are facing the original direction.

STEP ELEVEN. Repeat steps Two through Seven.

That's it. Does it sound like a mild variation to the LBRP to you? It sure does to me. In fact, if you've been practicing these lessons, you should have no trouble being wildly successful with this ritual.

Is this disappointing? Where's the newness? Where's the Chaos? I would contend that Chaos Magick isn't new, it's simply a new way of looking at magick. It's a new paradigm with different names. Does it offer some new things? Experimentation? No. I've been urging you to try that from the beginning of these lessons. It's a different approach. Like High Magick and Low Magick, it is no better or worse, it is just different. I would urge you to try it out and see how well it works for you.

A Practical Chaos Magick Ritual

Part of this new paradigm is its directness. The following ritual was taught to me many years ago. I've found it effective and fun. Give it a try.

STEP ONE. Develop a goal for the ritual. Go back to Lesson 7 and make a "sigil" on a piece of paper (no more than 3 x 3 inches) according to the system of Spare that represents your goal. Be sure that the final image gives no impression as to what the goal of the ritual is.

STEP TWO. Perform The Gnostic Pentagram Ritual.

STEP THREE. Hold the sigil in your left hand. Fully extend your left arm in front of you with your wrist bent inward so you can see the sigil in your hand. Focus intently—and I mean *intently*—on the sigil.

STEP FOUR. While still focusing intently on the sigil, begin to turn to your left, spinning in place.

STEP FIVE. Continue with your focus and your spinning in place. Speed up, going faster and faster. If you get dizzy, great. If you get nauseated, even better! Continue spinning and focusing until you are so dizzy or nauseated that you have to fall down.

STEP SIX. Banish with laughter. Laugh loud and long.

That's it. Put away the sigil. Forget about it. Let the magick happen on its own.

As I wrote earlier, I'm sure some people will attack this section (Chaos Magick has some practitioners who support their understanding of the paradigm *very* strongly) as being incomplete or wrong. Or they will say I'm an old fogey and don't get it. But how can you say that if nothing is true and everything is permitted? Chaos Magick is wonderful in its emphasis on experimentation, individuality, and the removal of unneeded excess. But in the end, it is simply a paradigm, a way to understand how magick works. It is every bit as accurate as the interpretation of the ancient shaman, the medieval sorcerer, the traditional ceremonial magician, or the contemporary Wiccan. It's not better or worse than any of those approaches to magick, just different.

If you like it, use it. Perhaps, like me, rather than limiting yourself to only one type of magick, you can work efficiently within any magickal paradigm, including that of Chaos Magick. For example, you may find that Chaos Magick can be used as an addition to the system you most commonly use. To me, being able to work any magickal system is the way of the modern magician. Or not. After all, to a Chaote nothing is true and everything is permitted.

Let's assume, however, that Chaos Magick is really the best *current* paradigm for understanding how magick works. Where will magick go tomorrow? How will we understand magick in the future? Perhaps the answer to these questions will be found in Postmodern Magick.

PART THREE

From the Enlightenment to Postmodernism

From the late 1940s through the early 1960s, the philosophical leaders of the new generation rebelled against the very character of the previous generation, adopting an ethos with new forms of art, music, philosophy, etc. One of the founders of this new movement, Jack Kerouac, described these people as the "Beat Generation," and they became known as beatniks. Of course, following the concepts already described as the Hegelian dialectic, the movement didn't radically change society, but it did alter it. In fact, some people saw that there was a lot of money to be made from the new generation and it was co-opted until many of its aspects became part of the mainstream.

This process seems to constantly repeat itself. In the early 1960s, the next generation took the rebellion against what went before to a new level. Instead of going on road trips as did Kerouac and his friends, the new leaders formed their own communities. The name eventually taken by this culture—based on the concept of them being hipsters—was hippies. Eventually, they too were co-opted by business, media, and their own naiveté and excesses.

Such rebellion against what went on previously can extend over longer periods. For example, at the end of the nineteenth century a movement began that was known as "modernism." Modernism could be called "anti-Enlightenment." There is a great deal of disagreement over when the Enlightenment began, but most people agree that it overthrew concepts such as the rights of aristocracies, control of society by religious structures, and the divine right of kings. The Enlightenment brought in reason and science as opposed to religious control, and self-governance rather than rule by royalty. Certainly the Declaration of Independence by the American colonies was influenced by Enlightenment thought. The document that founded the U.S.A., the Constitution begins not with an appeal to kings or gods, but by saying that this new country was created by "We the people." How could anyone be against such principles of the Enlightenment?

It's true that the Enlightenment freed people from certain beliefs and dogmas, but it introduced many of its own. It still had certain religious beliefs, although by now it has shifted to Deism rather than religious orthodoxy. The Modernists rejected the concept of a loving God. They rejected old styles of music, art, architecture, and belief. Poet Ezra Pound (1885–1972) published a set of essays in 1935, with a title that exemplified Modernism, *Make It New.*

Postmodernism developed after people became disillusioned with Modernism following WWII. It recognized that Modernism (indeed, any paradigm) has its own sets of beliefs, ideologies, and theories. Unfortunately, most people involved in a particular paradigm don't recognize that what they have are a set of beliefs, etc. People assume that what they do is "normal" and everyone else is off base. As a comparison, I live in California and I notice that when people from other areas of the U.S. and the world speak English they have accents while we Californians don't have one. I'm sure that people from London, England, or Atlanta, Georgia, think they don't have accents but we Californians do.

So rather than simply denounce anything old, like the Modernists, the Postmodernists tried to look beneath the ideologies and beliefs of previous generations and discover underlying truths. The result was the adoption of things and concepts that did work combined with the abandonment of old theories and assumptions as to *why* they worked.

The idea of Postmodern Magick follows this concept. It abandons all beliefs about why any form of magick works while acknowledging that it does work. So if you started out with this Postmodern concept, where would you look to understand how magick works from a twenty-first-century point of view?

As I pointed out in the beginning of this lesson, Patrick Dunn, in his two books, uses a thoroughly modern understanding of language (linguistics) and how words work, and the understanding and use of symbols (semiotics). In a sense, then, Dunn's concept of Postmodern Magick is both a direct outgrowth and an intensification of NLP and Chaos Magick.

Magick and Semiotics

The study of symbols has been incredibly important for magicians throughout history. The ancient shamans had systems using symbols in the form of drawings. Ancient Kabalists used, and modern Kabalists still use, symbols—such as the Hebrew alphabet or the Tree of Life—to represent various concepts. And Chaos magicians, of course, use sigils, often in the manner of A. O. Spare, to represent a focus for their magick. So for more than 10,000 years, the use of symbols in magick has been valuable.

The problem, of course, is getting across what the symbol means. Recently, a person asked me about the meaning of the symbol that looked like a skull. It might mean "poison." It might mean "pirates." It might represent the concept of mortality. It could even represent the concept of reincarnation.

Dunn gives the example of the word "tree." If I were to say "Imagine a tree" to ten people it's quite likely that they'd have ten different images, ranging from an oak or yew to a sort of universal tree that looks like a green ball at the end of a brown stick as drawn by young children.

If a word or symbol has different meanings for everyone, how can we say that it has any meaning at all? The solution to this for Postmodernists is easy yet clever. They simply say that *everything* is a symbol. Understanding this is a very powerful tool. If somebody cuts you off while driving, that may be a symbol to you that the other driver is rude and thoughtless. But to the person driving the other car, their action may be a symbol of needing to get someone to the hospital to save their life. By understanding this is all symbolic, we can accept that *someone else's symbolism may not be ours.* This can result in a better understanding of that person. It also compares to the NLP concept that people are not their behaviors.

Since everything is symbolic, it follows that the way we communicate is also symbolic. Indeed, words are simply symbols for concepts we are trying to communicate. We put symbols together in certain ways. For example, the way I've put words together in these lessons forms a pattern known as the English language.

We don't only put symbols together. The mind also eliminates things it deems unnecessary. For example, use your peripheral vision and allow your sight to spread out to both the left and right. Even if you can only go a small amount beyond either side of these pages, you will see things that you didn't notice just a moment before even though they were always there. Your vision is actually taking in those things outside these pages through your peripheral vision. Our unconscious minds eliminate those symbols deemed unnecessary to the immediate tasks at hand. Without this natural ability we'd go crazy from information overload, or TMI: "Too Much Information."

Dunn gives the example of finding a flat place to walk, then keeping your eyes straight ahead as you move forward. You'll notice that your vision, especially at the edges, actually bobs and jerks up and down with your steps. When we're not focusing on this, however, like some magickal form of image stabilization, our minds ignore the gyrations from our motions and eliminates them from our consciousness. We seem to be moving smoothly. In NLP this unconscious process is known as "deletion." Dunn describes this ability to delete the bobbing in our vision as a "code."

We have many such codes. According to Dunn, a code is "a set of assumptions about symbols that aid interpretation." We each have codes that are associated with money. We have codes that are related to time (see the discussion earlier in this lesson on In Time and Through Time). We have codes about sex. So what does a set of codes and filters have to do with magick? According to the tenets of Postmodern Magick:

Magick gives us the ability to modify, alter, and change our codes.

So let's try and codify (pun intended) these linguistic concepts:

1. Everything is symbolic. This includes language.

2. We interpret what we experience through the filters of our conscious and unconscious codes.

3. Codes allow us to understand behaviors. For example, our code that allows us to understand gravity allows us to predict how it will function. A code that allows us to understand how a person behaves allows us to predict how they will react to a new situation.

4. The more inaccurate or incomplete the code, the more inaccurate will be our ability to predict behaviors. For example, if our code of how our friend Jean will behave is inaccurate or incomplete, we won't be able to predict how she will behave and may even make wrong predictions of her behavior. This can lead to unhappiness or shock over her failure to fulfill our expectations of her behavior.

5. Some codes can be detrimental to our well-being. For example, if our code is that eating foods high in calories and low in nutrition is good for us, the result could be any of a wide variety of harmful diseases.

6. The codes allow us to live in the "real world," but they are only a "semiotic web," an interlocking group of symbols. Dunn defines a semiotic web as "a metaphor for the way in which symbols refer to each other."

7. If our current codes don't allow us to obtain what we desire, changing the codes is likely to help us get what we need. Changing the code changes reality.

8. Magick is a means to change our codes.

The Practical Use of Semiotics for Magick from a Postmodern Perspective

You're familiar with the use of sigils from earlier in this lesson and previous lessons. You've also understood their use (I hope!) from the worldview of the Kabalistic and Chaos Magick traditions. What about from the Postmodern tradition?

You begin, as with any form of practical magick, by understanding that you have a want or desire. But let's look a bit deeper. Specifically, *why* do you have that want or desire? The answer would be that your interpretation of reality, as controlled by your codes, no longer meets your conscious needs. You have to get rid of the old codes and introduce new codes.

Unfortunately, this takes more than one step. If you were simply to introduce new codes (by contemplating a sigil, for example), the result would be modified by the Hegelian Dialectic problem. That is, if you're functioning under code A and want to get to a reality represented by code B, because you still have code A operating, you won't get all the way to B, but only to C, somewhere between A and B:

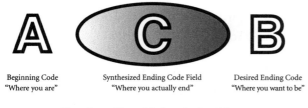

| Beginning Code | Synthesized Ending Code Field | Desired Ending Code |
| "Where you are" | "Where you actually end" | "Where you want to be" |

The Hegelian Dialectic Problem
(Thesis-Antithesis-Synthesis)

To get around this difficulty, also known as the Thesis-Antithesis-Synthesis problem, you can't simply insert the new code. First, you have to obliterate the old code. This leaves you open to the insertion of something new, completely reprogramming you with the new code. This obliteration requires an altered state of consciousness that frees you from your old code.

It is not uncommon to experience such states. They can occur during intense trances, from the use of mind-altering substances, as a result of orgasm, etc. So why don't we change our codes automatically? Because with nothing to trigger our minds in new ways when the altered state is over, our old codes simply fall back into place.

This is where the use of the sigil comes in. As Dunn writes in *Magic, Power, Language, Symbol*, "the sigil acts as a seed . . . The first thing we see when our conscious mind returns is the sigil, and we use that as the framework for rebuilding our codes."

Then, as we've described before, you just forget about the process and let the mind work. The new code goes into action, re-creating reality and bringing into your life the thing, behavior, or emotion that you want.

By eliminating the old code and establishing a new one, you have literally created a new reality that replaces the previous unwanted reality.

Is it really this easy? Do you just need to change the code? Well, if you're a Postmodern magician, the answer is, "Yes." Of course, that also means it's just as easy to change the code back to what it originally was, preventing the magick from occurring. In fact, it's quite possible to say that the new code, even though it's in place, may not be fully embedded in your unconscious. You could end up picking away at the new code you've put into place until there's nothing left and the old familiar code finds its way back. This goes back to what has been described earlier in these lessons. The aim is to forget about the techniques and let the magick happen. If you worry about whether you did it right, will it work, etc., you take the focus away from the new code, allowing the old code to fall back into place. (Dunn calls worry "the great enemy of magic.") Are their any solutions to this?

Dunn mentions three ways to overcome this problem. First, you can work on establishing an attitude of indifference. This matches Spare's frequently quoted comment, "Does not matter. Need not be." It also matches the previously described idea of accepting that "what is, is." Of course, the fact that I'm repeating this should imply that adopting this attitude and really believing it isn't as easy as it may sound. I've known many people who talk about this attitude but who don't "walk their talk." Dunn suggests meditating on this concept and trying fasts to show that it doesn't matter whether you get your daily dose of food or sex (or, I would add, of being online or text messaging).

The second method is replacement. If you start thinking about anything to do with the new code or old code, change your thoughts to focus on something entirely different. For example, if your new code has you much better off financially than your old code, and you start thinking about problems making money, replace the thoughts with something else such as thinking about a new movie, reading a new book, going to a club, playing a game, etc.

The third method is to assume that the new code is firmly embedded and to act in accord with that assumption. Thus, if your new code is to become a musician, you think and act as a musician would think and act. Turn off the TV, move away from the computer, and start practicing your instrument.

Evoking the . . . Symbols?

In the previous section I gave an example of how to use a symbol—in this case, a sigil—to change our inner codes. This alters our reality, providing us with a new reality that incorporates our desired state. But what about something entirely different? For example, instead of trying to change our reality to a new state, what if we want to communicate with a non-physical entity, what is commonly called evocation? I described the traditional interpretation used by many thousands of people in an earlier lesson. How would a Postmodern magician make sense of it? The key is an understanding of what is meant by communication.

The usual idea of communication is that one person is giving information to another. If you think the world is flat and I tell you, "The world is round," I'm giving you new information. You would then choose to ignore or incorporate that new information.

However, this model of communication is making some assumptions. Specifically, it assumes that we both have the same understanding of three words: world, flat, and round. In this particular situation, you might think about what I said and come to the con-

clusion that I'm trying to communicate that the world is flat but the *edge* is round, making the Earth appear to be a disk. You could agree with me completely and we would both be happy even though we both had different conclusions. Even though I said, "The world is round," what I actually meant—and assumed you understood—was that the Earth was spherical (and for this discussion let's ignore the fact that the world is not a perfect, ball-like sphere).

Another way of looking at communication, one that might more accurately reveal what is actually taking place, is that communication means throwing symbols to each other in order to make our symbolic systems correspond and match up. The more our symbolic systems match, the more we are communicating accurately. When they're not close we're not communicating well. When you consider how many symbols we all deal with it makes sense to assume that there will be difficulties and inexactness when attempting communication.

If we accept this postmodern interpretation of communication, the act of evocation involves trying as much as possible to match your symbolic system with that of the spirit you wish to evoke. You use incense the spirit "likes." You say words the spirit understands. You look at the spirit's signature or sigil. All of this is part of the spirit's codes. What you're doing is matching your codes to those of the spirit being evoked. The more your set of codes matches that of the entity, the better your communication with the spirit will be.

Earlier I wrote that the major danger of evocation is not possession, but obsession. The fact that you (and/or the magician's seer) spend so much time making your (or his or her) codes match those of the entity being evoked makes this problem obvious to a Postmodern magician. That's also why a magician will make symbolic anchors that link them to their own codes. These consist of word symbols (banishments and words of power), physical symbols (talismans, the Earth pentacle, magickal swords), etc.

With these understandings, it's possible to use concepts of Postmodern Magick to improve evocations. Since you want to make your codes as close to those of the spirit you'll evoke, you can prepare for this by trying to match your codes to the spirit's for several days prior to the formal evocation. Dunn, using the name of one of the spirits from the *Goetia*, Buer, refers to this process as "What would Buer do?" or WWBD.

During the time before the actual evocation, no matter what you do, ask yourself, "WWBD?" Of course, change this for the name and qualities of any spirit you wish to evoke. So if you're watching TV or reading a book or exercising or having lunch, ask yourself, "WWBD?" Would Buer be watching this show or TV at all? Is this a book Buer would read? Is this how Buer would exercise? Is this what Buer would eat? By following this process you make your codes closer to those of Buer (or whatever entity you're evoking), and the actual communication with the spirit becomes easier and more accurate.

Practice: The next time you are preparing to do an evocation, spend at least two days before the actual evocation practicing "WWBD?" for whatever entity you are going to evoke. This does not include the time spent searching for information about the entity so you can come to understand its codes, making it possible to match yours with its.

The Abstract Sigil

Earlier in these lessons, I gave a method to create a sigil based on the concept of automatic drawing. In *Postmodern Magic*, Dunn gives another version of this process, which I consider excellent. It is especially good for bringing desired qualities into your life.

It is impossible to draw an image of "love" or "courage" or "wealth" or "calm." Remember, however, that in this system everything, including words and ideas, are simply symbols that make up your codes. We've also learned that one of the most important tools in a magician's armory is the knowledge of correspondences. Currently, the most popular books on correspondences remain Aleister Crowley's *777* and *Sepher Sephiroth*. As I've pointed out, I question some of his correspondences. This

means that when it concerns the correspondences I disagree with, Crowley's codes and mine are not in harmony. There's nothing wrong with that. I would hope that you will have differences with Crowley and with me. As individuals, we each have a unique set of codes, making our beliefs and our reality different from everyone else's. Taking it one step further, this means we can create our own correspondences.

So you could make your own correspondences for love, courage, or calm. For love, perhaps your symbol would be a couple staring into each other's eyes. For courage you might choose the image of a soldier or perhaps a lion. For wealth you could choose a pile of money. For calm you might choose a quiet stream or a delicate rose. Perhaps you'll choose other images.

No matter what images you associate with these concepts, draw the image to the best of your ability. Next, draw it several times as fast as you can. As you move faster and faster, the image will become less and less like the original and most lifelike drawing. Eventually, the image won't even look like the original. It will look like some sort of abstract piece of art.

Practice One: For the next talisman you make, use this system to create an abstract sigil for your purpose. Charge the talisman following the techniques given previously.

Practice Two: Create a sigil using this method. Charge it by following the Chaos Magick system given earlier in this lesson.

All three of the systems described in this lesson present new ways of approaching material that has been described previously—including earlier in these lessons—using other paradigms. Some of you reading this may be wondering, "Why bother?" After all, what I described in previous lessons has worked for hundreds and thousands of years. As the saying goes, "If it ain't broke, don't fix it."

Well, yes. What I presented in the previous lessons in this book is a modern explanation of the practices of magick as they are used today by tens of thousands of people. And in most cases, when people are doing something that isn't a simple variation on what I've presented, you should be able to understand what you're seeing or hearing.

However, each generation develops its own "voice." Over the past fifty or more years, terms meaning "good" have included: gear, fab, cool, kewl, hot, bad, phat, awesome, alvo, excellent, the bee's knees, bitchin', the bomb, bumping, businawreck, butter, capitol, cherry, choice, dope, far out, fierce, fly, fresh, gnarly, hip, horrorshow, ill, kickass, killer, off the hook, peachy, primo, rad, sick, slammin', spiffy, stellar, sweet, tight, wicked, and many more. Besides being different voices, they are also symbolic of the paradigm by which a person lives. Someone saying, "That's capitol, old fellow," will have a different worldview than someone who says, "Dude, that's slammin'!" Similarly, this lesson has given you three of what I consider to be the most important paradigms for the future of magick. NLP comes from a different field. Chaos Magick is currently popular among many magicians. Postmodern Magick could be the future paradigm we'll all be using twenty years from now when we discuss magick. Or, perhaps there will be something else that develops.

What I want to make clear is that the purpose of this lesson has been to give you a taste of these three paradigms. There is no way I could thoroughly explain every aspect of each one. Already, there have been hundreds of books published on NLP, and a couple of dozen that either are directly related to Chaos Magick or refer to it. As of this writing there are only two books on Postmodern Magick as described by Patrick Dunn.

If you are fascinated by any of these systems, I encourage you to get some of the books listed in the bibliography of this lesson. That would be a good start.

I must repeat, though, that NLP was not designed to be taught through books, DVDs, or mail-order courses. It was designed to be taught in trainings and in person. A good trainer will be speaking to your conscious and unconscious minds, giving you far more than you could ever get from reading a book or watching a video. Reading books on NLP is a great way to learn about it, but to learn the techniques I would suggest getting trained.

Conclusion

Earlier editions of *Modern Magick* didn't conclude so much as they just stopped. I always had the feeling that it felt as if I had sort of run out of things to say, so rather than blather on I just shut up.

To be honest, I didn't like the way those earlier editions ended. As a result, I have, quite literally, spent years looking for a good conclusion, a way to end these lessons that would let someone close these pages and go, "Ahh. That's it!" I wanted readers and students to have a very satisfied feeling. A currently popular expression would be that I wanted people to have a "sense of closure."

I was wrong.

I've come to realize that if these lessons leave you with a satisfied "Now I know it" feeling, these lessons have failed.

I've come to realize that *there is no conclusion to the study of magick.* There never can be such a conclusion. I want people who read and study these lessons to feel unsatisfied and hungry for more. I want people to realize that magick is a practice and a study, and to move forward it's important to put down the pages of any lessons or book and actually do the work.

There is no conclusion to the practice of magick. As long as people live and breathe and hope for something better in their lives, there will be new approaches to magick and new things to discover. I hope some of you reading this will be the ones who make those discoveries. I hope you share them with others as I have shared my ideas with you.

There is no conclusion to the evolution of magick as long as children wonder why the sky is blue and as long as people want to find out what is on the other side of the mountain, or the ocean, or the galaxy, or the universe. To paraphrase the words of the late Robert Kennedy (certainly in a way he never expected), some people see things as they are and say why. I dream things that never were and say why not.

I hope you will dream with me. Magick isn't something you do. Magick is something you are. Magick isn't a goal, it's a path. It's a path to the other side of . . .

Review

The following questions are designed to help you determine if you have mastered the information in Lesson Twelve. Please try to answer them without looking at the text. The answers are in Appendix Two.

1. What has changed to necessitate the addition of a new lesson as part of *Modern Magick*?

2. What is an IROB?

3. What was the first book published about Chaos Magick?

4. What is NLP jargon for looking at things in a different light?

5. How would Carl Jung identify In Time and Through Time people?

6. What is the name of the person who helped legitimize hypnosis as a tool for therapy?

7. What does Chaos Magick have to do with chaos?

8. What is a meaning of the expression "Nothing is true. Everything is permitted"?

9. What is the Gnostic Trance?

10. What is the meaning of the term "Kia"?

11. Who introduced Chaos Magick to the U.S.?

12. Who created the the Gnostic Pentagram Ritual?

13. What does the word "semiotic" mean?

14. What is a semiotic web?

15. What does the acronym "WWBD?" mean?

16. How do you make an abstract sigil according to Postmodern Magick?

17. What gives us the ability to modify, alter, and change our codes?

The following questions only you can answer.

1. Have you ever acted like an expert in some area when you knew you where not? Why did you feel it was necessary to do so?

2. Where is your timeline?

3. Are you primarily an In Time or Through Time person?

4. Did you try changing the direction of your timeline? What were the results?

5. Do you think the source of magickal power is the original chaos from which the universe was formed, deities, spirits, your own energy, or something else? Why?

6. Will you try a Chaos Magick ritual such as described in this lesson? Why or why not? Have you performed such a ritual? What do you think about it?

7. Do you agree with the expression "Nothing is true. Everything is permitted"? Why or why not?

8. Do you work with trances? What do you think of the Gnostic Trance? How do you enter a trance?

9. Do you understand the concepts of Postmodern Magick as presented in this lesson?

10. Do you think that communication is more than the exchange of information? What do you think it is?

Bibliography

For more information on these books, please see the annotated bibliography at the end of this course.

NLP

James, Tad, and Wyatt Woodsmall. *Time Line Therapy and the Basis of Personality*. Meta Publications, 2008.

Jung, Carl. *Psychological Types*. Princeton University Press, 1976.

Ready, Romilla, and Kate Burton. *Neuro-Linguistic Programming for Dummies*. For Dummies, 2004.

Chaos Magick

Carroll, Peter J. *Liber Kaos.* Red Wheel/Weiser, 1992.

———. *Liber Null & Psychonaut.* Weiser, 1987.

Dukes, Ramsey. *SSOTBME Revised.* The Mouse That Spins, 2002.

Hine, Phil. *Condensed Chaos.* New Falcon Publications, 1995.

Sherwin, Ray. *The Book of Results.* LULU, 2005.

Spare, Austin Osman. *The Writings of Austin Osman Spare.* NuVision Publications, 2007.

Vitimus, Andrieh. *Hands-On Chaos Magic.* Llewellyn, 2009.

Postmodern Magick

Dunn, Patrick. *Magic, Power, Language, Symbol.* Llewellyn, 2008.

———. *Postmodern Magic.* Llewellyn, 2005.

APPENDIX ONE

A Ritual to Vastly Increase Personal Magickal Power

The following is a ritual that you may wish to attempt. I introduced this ritual in the first edition of *Modern Magick*. Although I didn't realize it back then, having never heard of NLP, it actually follows many NLP principles and concepts based on the timeline. In Lesson 12 I gave a ritual using the timeline that can help you create your desired future. Here, without using a formal timeline but using the concepts behind timeline work, you literally re-create your past to enhance your present, changing what you are rather than what you will become. The end result of working this ritual will be an increase of your magickal abilities and talents many times over. If you think about this ritual, you don't have to limit it to magickal power.

STEP ONE. Make a sigil representing magickal power.

STEP TWO. Perform the Opening by Watchtower.

STEP THREE. Sit down and work on visualizing a calendar in front of you. See the pages turn so that you go back in time, back into your past.

STEP FOUR. When you go back a minimum of ten years or half your age, see the pages stop turning. Now visualize yourself, as you looked at that date. Take time to make the visualization as complete as possible. Allow your consciousness to merge with your younger self.

STEP FIVE. Now concentrate on the image of the sigil that you created. When it is as strong as it possibly can be, visualize it going onto the forehead of you as your younger self. See it virtually tattooed on your forehead.

STEP SIX. Once it is firmly tattooed on your forehead, immediately cease the visualization and return to the image of the calendar. Now see the pages moving the other way so that you move forward to the present day.

STEP SEVEN. End with the Closing by Watchtower.

This ritual will have the effect of causing a sudden and notable increase in your magickal abilities. By altering the design of the sigil you may affect exactly how this ritual increases your magickal abilities. Although this ritual will not change your level of magickal knowledge, it will make you more receptive to magickal information. It may increase your ability to memorize and your understanding of that material.

APPENDIX TWO

Here are the answers to the self-tests at the end of each lesson. Please try to answer the questions without looking back through the lesson and *before* you check the answers here.

Lesson One

1. The "Negative Golden Rule" is "Don't do unto others if you would not have them do the same unto you."

2. The four things that can occur when you dream are astral work, psychological messages, play, or a combination of the three.

3. Sturgeon's Law is "Ninety percent of everything is crap."

4. Your personal, secret, magickal text is your ritual diary.

5. You should read other books on subjects such as the Kabalah or magick in order to get different views of the material and in order to get a more in-depth study of a particular subject.

6. You should keep track of your emotional state in your magickal diary because it is a variable, and as a scientist of the future, you want to keep track of how variables such as the emotions affect/effect your experiments (rituals).

7. Arthur C. Clarke believes "any sufficiently advanced technology is indistinguishable from magick."

8. White Magick is the science and art of causing change to occur in conformity with will, using means not currently understood by traditional Western science, for the purpose of obtaining the Knowledge and Conversation of your Holy Guardian Angel. Black Magick is the science and art of causing change to occur in conformity with will, using means not currently understood by traditional Western science, for the purpose of causing either physical or non-physical harm to yourself or others, and is done either consciously or unconsciously. Grey Magick is the science and art of causing change to occur in conformity with will, using means not currently understood by traditional Western science, for the purpose of causing either physical or non-physical good to yourself or others, and is done either consciously or unconsciously.

9. You can avoid accidentally doing Black Magick by doing a divination before doing any Grey Magick.

10. The first historical mention of the Tarot was in 1332.

11. Fortunetelling says that something must happen. Divination indicates what will probably happen if you continue on the path you are currently traversing.

12. When doing a Tarot divination you should not form your questions to ask "Should I do _____?" because this would put the responsibility for your decision on the cards rather than on you, removing personal responsibility. Instead, form your question along the lines of "What will be the effect of doing a ritual for _____?" Then, you can choose to do the ritual or not.

13. Three reasons for doing the Lesser Banishing Ritual of the Pentagram are to know yourself, to expand your aura, and to remove from your immediate area any unwanted influences.

14. When you draw a pentagram for the LBRP you should visualize it as being a very bright and pure blue. It is the same color as you can see in an electric spark, the flame of a gas stove, or when a small dish of lighter fluid or alcohol is set ablaze.

15. The top of your altar should have a heavy protective coating or be topped with a sheet of glass to protect it from spilled melted wax and to make clean up easier.

Lesson Two

1. The four parts of the LBRP are the Kabalistic Cross, the Formulation of the Pentagrams, the Evocation of the Archangels, and the Repetition of the Kabalistic Cross.

2. The Hebrew words of the Kabalistic Cross mean "Thine is the kingdom and the power and the glory forever, amen." "Amen" actually means "God is a faithful king."

3. AGLA is an abbreviation for "Ah-tah Gee-boor Lih-oh-lahm Ah-doh-nye," which means "Thou art great forever, my Lord."

4. The Archangel of the north is Ohr-ree-el.

5. The "Great Voice" means speaking silently, but having the same effect as with loud vibrations.

6. It is false to say that Kabalists have ten gods because the ten names of God on the Tree of Life are names of one deity, just as any person may be called by many names.

7. The sign of Water is made by forming a downward-pointing triangle with the hands held in front of the stomach.

8. The three "literatures" of the ancient Hebrews were the Torah, the Talmud, and the Kabalah.

9. It is incorrect to use "Jehovah" as the name of God because it is actually a combination of the letters of the Tetragrammaton, YHVH, which has an unknown pronunciation, mixed with the vowels of Adonai, meaning "my lord." This was to remind native Hebrew readers to say "Adonai" rather than try to pronounce the Tetragrammaton. Kabalists prefer to use the names of the letters Yud-Heh-Vahv-Heh.

10. It was Eliezer ben Yehudah who made Hebrew into a modern language.

11. Vibrate words by fully inhaling until there isn't room for one more drop of air. Then use the entire exhalation to vibrate the word. Thus, the word you vibrate is elongated. It can be directed toward a part of the body or to the outside world.

12. "Vahv" was probably originally pronounced like the English "w." Today it is pronounced like a "v," "o," or "u."

13. The earliest form of Hebrew mysticism was known as Heh-cha-lot, or Merkabah mysticism.

14. Eliphas Levi (born Alphonse Louis Constant) began the French Occult Revival. By the way, his full pen name was Eliphas Levi Zaed.

15. The four main branches of the Kabalah are the Dogmatic Kabalah, the Practical Kabalah, the Literal Kabalah, and the Unwritten Kabalah.

16. Three signs indicating potentially good teachers are that they are willing to sing, willing to dance, and are quick to laugh, especially at themselves.

17. "Ain Soph" is Hebrew for "without limit."

18. "Little Nasties" are entities from a higher plane which become visible as your magickal work allows your astral vision to open. They cannot harm you, but they may surprise you.

Lesson Three

1. The element Earth is dry and cool.

2. The Three Pillars are the Pillar of Severity, the Pillar of Mercy, and the Pillar of Mildness.

3. The Three Triangles are the Celestial Triangle, the Moral Triangle, and the Mundane Triangle.

4. The Four Worlds are Ha-oh-lahm Atziloot, Ha-oh-lahm B'ri-ya, Ha-oh-lahm Yetzirah, and Ha-oh-lahm Ahssiah. These are, respectively, the World of Emanations, Creation, Formation, and Action.

5. The goal of true meditation is to silence the inner voice and link with the Divine: White Magick.

6. The three steps of true meditation are relaxation, contemplation, and negation.

7. During scanning, you intensely focus on a visual image, having the effect of linking your consciousness to that image. When you de-scan or eliminate the visualization, the consciousness goes with it, leaving you open to the unconscious/higher self, and the true meditative state.

8. The four colors associated with elemental Earth in the Queen Scale are black, olive green (a blend of violet and green), russet brown (a blend of orange and violet), and citrine (a blend of orange and green).

9. You will never become a real magician if all you can do is blindly follow obsolete patterns. Tradition should only be your guide, not your master.

10. According to the Kabalah, the heavenly order is the unknowable divinity, the ten aspects of divinity (as represented by their names), the archangels, and lastly the Orders of Angels.

11. It is never permissible to heal a person who has not given you permission to do so.

12. Rituals are not failures if you sense no immediate change within yourself or outside of yourself. It is not necessary that you have any weird experiences or unusual sensations as a result of the practice of this course's rituals. If the rituals are done properly, the desired results must inevitably occur.

13. The expression "four magickal elements" is popular but incorrect because there are actually five such elements. The fifth element, Spirit, is the source of the other four: Air, Earth, Fire, and Water.

14. The Chinese and Western elements correspond in this way:

CHINESE	WESTERN
Fire	Fire
Earth	Earth
Metal	Air
Water	Water
Wood	Spirit

15. It's a good idea to create a concave pentacle as such a device will return all energy from any source back toward the direction from which it came.

16. Three benefits of joining a magickal group are camaraderie, the ability to specialize, and increased levels of magickal power.

17. Any language can be used for the magickal motto. Popular languages include Latin, Hebrew, English, Greek, and Enochian.

18. I.O.B. means "identify, objectify, and banish." It is a powerful method of ridding yourself of unwanted habits or problems.

Lesson Four

1. Elemental Air is warm and moist.

2. Probably the first Christian symbol was the fish drawn with one continous line:

3. Hitler chose the swastika because he wanted Nazism to be thought of as a descendent of the mythical "Aryan race" of civilized light-skinned northern foreigners who supposedly brought civilization to India.

4. A true, mystical swastika looks like a square with horizontal and vertical lines. It may appear to spin in either a clockwise or counter-clockwise direction. The official Nazi swastika is on a point and appears to rotate in a counter-clockwise direction.

Common Forms of the Mystical Swastika

Hitler's Version

5. The archangel of Air is Raphael.

6. It is difficult to remember past lives because the memory is mortal and lost at physical death.

7. The techniques necessary to do the LBRP effectively are the basis for all magickal techniques.

8. The BRH clears unwanted influences from your area, both positive and negative, that might come from higher planes and are not dealt with by the LBRP.

9. The LBRP deals with the elements on the physical plane. The BRH deals with elements on the next higher plane that corresponds with zodiacal associations. These include the triplicities that direct the order of the elements for the BRH.

10. The order for doing at-home rituals is: the Relaxation Ritual, LBRP, BRH, Middle Pillar, Circulation of the Body of Light, Tarot Contemplation Ritual (advanced version), and the completion of the ritual diary.

11. A paired triangle consists of the two parts of a hexagram.

12. The word "grimoire" is French for "black book," with an implication of being a "grammar book."

13. The three things you need to do to succeed at ritual magick are practice, practice, and practice.

14. The three necessities of Grey Magick are a positive attitude, knowing how to generate and control magickal energy, and knowledge.

Lesson Five

1. The element of Water has the qualities of being cool and moist.

2. Five reasons to do the Rose Cross Ritual are: it is an excellent banishing ritual, it gives you a type of invisibility, it is a good preparation for meditation, you can use it to aid others

who are hurting physically or spiritually, and it will help protect you from negative psychic "vibrations."

3. The Rose Cross Ritual should never be used to replace the LBRP.

4. Ruach El-oh-heem is represented by the Hebrew letter Shin (pronounced "sheen").

5. Past-life experiences may be real past lives, fantasies to glamorize a currently bland lifetime, or messages from your unconscious to your conscious which your conscious does not want to hear. (*Note:* Some people think past lives may also be a tapping into a sort of universal or race memory, what the psychologist Jung called the collective unconscious. That is why many people may have "memories" of being the same historical character. This loosely fits in the last category, since it is the conscious tapping into a level of the unconscious.)

6. The cross represents our vow to follow the great work (our "cross to bear"). The triangle represents all forms of trinities. This includes Isis, Apophis, Osiris; Tao, Yin, Yang; Keter, Hochmah, Binah; body, mind, spirit; and especially Light, Life, and Love.

7. To draw an invoking Air pentagram, start at the upper right and move horizontally to the left. Reverse this for the banishing. To draw an invoking Earth pentagram, start at the top and move to the lower left. Reverse this for the banishing. To draw an invoking Fire pentagram, start at the top and move to the lower right. Reverse this for the banishing. To draw an invoking Water pentagram, start at the upper left and move horizontally to the right. Reverse this for the banishing.

8. The Rose Cross Ritual can impart a type of invisibility.

9. Vicarious atonement is the belief that someone else can atone for your sins. Kabalists do not believe in this concept, as they accept the doctrine of personal responsibility. You are responsible for your beliefs and actions.

10. The Hebrew word for "karma" is "Tee-koon."

11. "Sitting sheevah" is the Jewish practice of staying in the home for a week after the death of a member of the household. It is based on the Kabalistic idea that a soul will move between the grave and the home for a week before it realizes that it has died. This is especially the case in situations of sudden death.

12. Before anything exists on the physical plane, it must first exist on the astral plane.

13. The eight traditional Chinese signs of health are vitality, appetite, deep and sound sleep, good memory, humor, infinite giving, clear thinking and precise action, and realization of Oneness. These names are a simplification, and you are urged to study this section of the lesson to understand the eight signs of health in their fullness.

Lesson Six

1. Fire has the qualities of being warm and dry.

2. The archangel of Fire is Michael.

3. The 23rd path on the Tree of Life equates with the Hebrew letter Mehm, which has a numerical value of 40. On this path is the Tarot card the Hanged Man, which is the twelfth card. Therefore, 23 = 40 = 12. Note that if you do not include the ten Sephiroht when counting the paths, you would get the number 13, making the equation 23 = 40 = 12 = 13.

4. A tripod was traditionally used to support an incense burner. The Pythia, the woman priestess functioning as the Oracle at Delphi, would sit in a chair suspended by a tripod over a crack in the earth through which various gasses vented. The gasses induced an altered state of consciousness, allowing the Pythia to make oracular pronouncements.

5. "The secret force" is the same as kundalini, Ruach, or chi.

6. "Punctuated equilibrium" is the concept that things do not evolve smoothly. Rather, they go through slow changes interrupted or "punctuated" by sudden bursts of change.

7. AOZPI is pronounced "Ah-oh-zohd-pee."

8. Plants associated with Aries are the tiger lily and the geranium.

9. The colors on the elemental tablet representing Earth are flat black on a silver background.

10. On the altar for the consecration of the Rainbow Wand are the four elemental tools, the Tablet of Union, and the dagger used in the LBRP for a total of six, plus possibly a lit candle and incense, for a total of eight. Of course, you should also include the Rainbow Wand itself, for a grand total of nine.

11. The Rainbow Wand has fourteen colors, including the white and black.

12. The secret holy names of God borne upon the Banner of the South are OIP TEAA PED-OCE (pronounced "Oh-ee-pay Tay-ah-ah Peh-doh-kay").

Lesson Seven

1. The unconscious is our direct link to the astral plane.

2. "Low Magick" refers to the magicks practiced by people who lived in lower lands and who were typically farmers. It's also called "natural magick" and is typically practiced today by Pagans, Wiccans, and Witches. "High Magick" refers to the magicks practiced by people who lived in cities that were typically located in higher areas for protection and drainage. People in cities developed excess capital and more free time, resulting in more elaborate forms of magick. It's also called "art magick" and "ceremonial magick." High and Low Magick are different, but neither is inherently superior to the other.

3. Not only does the Kabalistic System of Mental Magick include the best from Positive Affirmations and Creative Visualization, it also energizes the techniques by using the emotions.

4. Witches do not worship Satan in any way. They do not even acknowledge that Satan exists. The common concept of Satan is a Christian invention.

5. The first edition of *The Discoverie of Witchcraft* was burned by the public hangman because it denied superstitious ideas concerning Witchcraft.

6. *The Witch Cult in Western Europe* sparked a revival of interest in the craft of the Witches.

7. *Witchcraft Today* was the first book about Witchcraft by a self-avowed Witch.

8. A talisman is any object, sacred or profane, with or without appropriate symbols, which has been charged or consecrated by appropriate means, and made to serve a specific end.

9. Always do a divination before performing Grey Magick.

10. "Skyclad" means wearing only the sky, i.e., nude. Some Witches prefer to do rituals and magick skyclad, but increasing numbers do not.

11. You can charge as many talismans with the same purpose at the same time as you desire. As a general rule, you should not charge talismans having different purposes at the same time. However, as you become a better and better magician, you may well be able to do this. I suggest that you wait until you have charged many talismans at separate rituals before trying to charge different talismans at the same ritual.

12. A house Guardian is a powerful protective amulet, usually in the form of a statue or objet d'art.

13. "Theosophical Reduction" is the process of adding the digits of a number together until you get a single digit. For example, 195 (1 + 9 + 5) becomes 15, which becomes 6 (1 + 5). This can be used as a technique for coming up with symbols used on talismans.

Lesson Eight

1. Jupiter is associated with Thursday.

2. A term for doing your best without outside encouragement is "self-actualization."

3. Planetary or Magickal Hours are based on the length of time between sunset and sunrise, sunrise and sunset. They are not based on sixty-minute hours.

4. The Planetary Hours are sixty minutes long on the equinoxes.

5. Before it is activated by the forces of higher planes and guided by our Will, a talisman is nothing but a piece of inert, lifeless material.

6. The expression "baptize," when used concerning the peas-and-sieve incident involving Mathers, may have meant "initiate."

7. Until you "break down" all the trappings of your area, it is still a temple and should be treated as such. The end of the ritual does not end the spiritual qualities of the area.

8. The two books you should have for the next lesson are *The Greater Key of Solomon* and the *Goetia*, which is a part of *The Lesser Key of Solomon.*

9. Three reasons some self-professed magicians don't do magick are (1) they don't have enough knowledge to do magick; (2) they fear the rituals and don't even wish to try them; and (3) they're afraid that if they try them and then fail it will show that they are not as good as they claim to be. Or, it will prove to them that magick is fake and they have wasted years of their lives in its study.

Lesson Nine

1. According to Dion Fortune, entities are evoked to the astral only, and can only actually be seen by a clairvoyant, though a sensitive person can feel the presence of the evoked entity.

2. There is a Tantric belief that semen loses its magickal potency within fifteen minutes after ejaculation.

3. "Invocation" is the magickal act wherein you allow your body to be shared temporarily by another entity. "Evocation" is the magickal act where an entity is communicated with, but stays outside of your body.

4. Evocations are difficult to do by yourself.

5. The "Demon CO" is a name for carbon monoxide. Too much burning incense in a closed room can result in too much CO and not enough oxygen. Needless to say, a lack of oxygen can be highly dangerous!

6. The first question asked of the seer in an evocation is, "What do you see in the mirror?"

7. The second question asked in an evocation is directed toward the entity. It is "What is thy name?"

8. The spirit Amon looks like a wolf with the tail of a serpent and breath of fire. At the command of the magician Amon will change to look like a man with a raven's head, sometimes having fangs.

9. There is no ultimate authority in magick except experience. Don't take anybody's word for anything in magick. Experiment yourself. Think for yourself. Question authority.

10. In the Yetziratic Sealing Rite six directions are sealed.

11. The spirits of Earth are Gnomes, of Air are Sylphs, of Water are Undines, and of Fire are

Salamanders. They are unique because normally on the physical plane everything is a combination of elements, but the elemental spirits are totally composed of only one element.

12. The seven steps in a magickal invocation are (1) banishings and purifications, (2) calling the entity and "loosing" the control of consciousness, (3) allowing the entity to "take over" for a time, (4) identification of the entity, (5) comments by the entity and questioning the entity, (6) release of the entity and return to normal consciousness, and (7) the final banishings.

Lesson Ten

1. There is no proof that any level of intelligence can protect you from brainwashing.

2. The five things required for brainwashing, according to military studies, are removal from environment of influence, sleep deprivation, pain with disagreement, pleasure with agreement, and change in biochemistry.

3. Three major divisions of sex magick are Thought Control, Inner Alchemy, and Outer Alchemy.

4. The thought held at the instant of orgasm comes to pass.

5. Reich discovered that there can be a thought-free experience at the moment of orgasm. This is identical to true meditation.

6. Masters and Johnson say that the average duration of intercourse before the man ejaculates is about two and one-half minutes.

7. Three things involved in any divinatory technique are the turning off of the outside and turning on of the inside, altering the state of consciousness, and increasing the blood flow to the brain.

8. Many people believe that books on alchemy are codes for sex magick.

9. The Menstruum, or Menstruum of the Gluten, is either the female lubricating fluids, her ejaculatory fluids, or both, depending upon the sex magician you talk with.

10. Very few people, if any, ever achieve enlightenment by reading and studying books on kundalini yoga. These books are usually written by non-initiates who have never done any practice themselves.

11. Working with the breath and mantras are substitutes for sexual activity.

12. The ritual of the KalaKakra is dangerous because some people and/or relationships are not able to handle the freedom of the KalaKakra.

Lesson Eleven

1. The highest magickal secrets can be obtained from entities on higher planes.

2. To a real magician there is only magick; the notion of White, Grey, or Black Magick is simply a way of communicating with those who are not magicians. A true magician would not do what is thought of as Black Magick because of the karmic result. Nobody shoots himself or herself in the foot on purpose unless they have mental problems.

3. The simple way to determine if it is right for you to do a certain ritual or a certain style of magick, or join a particular magick group, is by listening to your feelings. If it doesn't feel right, don't do it!

4. A pseudo-ghost is more like a "Little Nasty" than a true ghost. Pseudo-ghosts "feed" off energy given to them and they will imitate the actions of ghosts in order to get people to pay attention to them and give them energy.

5. "Astral Whiplash" is the name of what happens when your astral body, while traveling on the astral plane, is suddenly jerked back to the physical body by a disturbance in the area of the physical body. It can easily be fixed by

astral projecting to the place you were when you were disturbed and slowly returning to the physical body in a normal fashion.

6. The Kabalistic Tree of Life is a map of the psychic planes.

7. The major difference between the Ritual of the Paths and the Ceremony of the Paths is that the ritual is performed individually while the ceremony is done with a group.

Lesson Twelve

1. The twelfth lesson was added to explain some important new technologies and paradigms of magick that have developed since *Modern Magick* was originally published.

2. An "IROB" (I Read One Book) is a person who has done very little study or practice and now thinks he or she is an expert.

3. The first book published about Chaos Magick was *Liber Null* by Peter Carroll.

4. The NLP jargon for looking at things in a different light is "reframing."

5. Jung would compare an In Time person to his idea of a "Judger" and a Through Time person to his idea of a "Perceiver."

6. Dr. Milton Erickson is the name of the psychiatrist who helped legitimize the use of hypnosis as a powerful therapeutic tool.

7. Chaos Magick wasn't so named because it is chaotic but because it taps into the primal source of energy, which is pure chaos.

8. One meaning for the expression "Nothing is true. Everything is permitted" is that since everything we know of the outside world comes through our limited senses, there can be no objective truth. Therefore, everything is true and possible.

9. The concept of the Gnostic Trance is based on becoming totally focused on one thing, inducing a trance state. Often the singular focus of the trance is a sigil designed in a fashion similar to the system of Austin Osman Spare.

10. Spare, who first made use of the term "Kia," was so much against doctrines that he really didn't give a clear definition it. He describes it similar to the way Lao Tzu described the concept of the Tao: "The Tao which can be expressed in words is not the eternal Tao." Peter Carroll refers to it as a unity that exerts will and perception. He also describes it as the Spirit or Life Force.

11. Lola Babalon introduced Chaos Magick to the U.S.

12. Peter Carroll created the Gnostic Pentagram Ritual.

13. The word "semiotic" means "the study of symbols."

14. A "semiotic web" is an interlocking group of symbols that form the codes that allow us to live in the "real world." It is "a metaphor for the way in which symbols refer to each other."

15. "WWBD?" literally means "What would Buer do?" Buer is a spirit from the *Goetia* and in this case is a stand-in for any entity to be evoked. "WWBD?" represents the concept of harmonizing your semiotic web with that of the entity to be evoked by asking yourself "WWBD?" in virtually every daily situation you encounter.

16. To make an abstract sigil, come up with an image to represent a non-physical concept you wish to acquire. For example, for courage, you might draw a lion. Then repeatedly draw the symbol as fast as you can. Eventually, it will no longer look like a lion at all. This is your abstract sigil for courage.

17. Magick gives us the ability to modify, alter, and change our codes.

APPENDIX THREE

The *Modern Magick* FAQ

Over the years since the publication of *Modern Magick* I have received thousands of letters and emails from dedicated, aspiring magicians living in virtually every populated area of the world. While many of them fall into the category of "fan mail," a large number of communications also had another purpose.

No matter how well anyone explains a topic, there are always people who will either want to dig deeper or to whom a comment or idea is unclear. This is the "other purpose" resulting in the many letters and emails I just mentioned. The letters consisted of questions about *Modern Magick* and magick subjects in general. I was surprised to discover that many of these questions asked amazingly similar things. In fact, many of them were so similar that they used the same words and expressions to ask identical questions.

There is an "area" of the Internet, which used to be popular, called the Usenet. This is the part of the Internet known for having newsgroups. The Usenet is like a huge bulletin board. Each newsgroup is a section of that bulletin board dedicated to a particular subject. Within each newsgroup you can read messages posted by anyone or post your own comments. Since the time this appendix was first published for the second edition of *Modern Magick*, the Usenet has largely been superseded by forums, personal websites, and text messaging.

When people first investigate a newsgroup they are urged to watch and read only—known as *lurking*—until they are familiar with the subjects. (This is still a common request when people join forums, but regrettably, it is often ignored.) Sometimes, in order to help these people better understand a particular newsgroup or subject, the archives of the newsgroup will have a FAQ, a document that answers "Frequently Asked Questions." Again, this has carried over to modern Internet forums.

This appendix, then, is what I call "The *Modern Magick* FAQ," because it answers those questions on which I have been most frequently queried. The following are in no particular order.

On the Magickal Elements and Associated Directions

Question: In the LBRP, the elements associated with the directions (starting at the east and going clockwise) are Air, Fire, Water, and Earth. In the BRH, however, they are Fire, Earth, Air, and Water. Is this a mistake, a trap for the unwary, or is there some reason for the change?

Answer: The LBRP deals with the physical plane and the lower astral. The BRH deals with the upper astral plane, which relates more to astrological or planetary influences. Thus, when a magician performs the LBRP, he or she associates and links the magickal elements with the traditional physical associations. When the magician performs the BRH, however, these associations must change. For it is here that the magician should associate the directions linked to the magickal elements with the order of the astrological elemental attributions. The following charts may clarify this for you:

The Physical Directions and Their Traditional Associated Elements

PHYSICAL DIRECTION	ASSOCIATED ELEMENT
East	Air
South	Earth
West	Fire
North	Water

The First Four Astrological Signs and Their Associated Elements

ASTROLOGICAL SIGN (IN ORDER)	ASSOCIATED ELEMENT
Aries	Fire
Taurus	Earth
Gemini	Air
Cancer	Water

The Elements and Directions of the LBRP and BRH

DIRECTION	LBRP ELEMENT	BRH ELEMENT
East	Air	Fire
South	Fire	Earth
West	Water	Air
North	Earth	Water

On the Missing Archangel

Question: In the LBRP the archangels are Ra-Fay-El, Gahb-Ray-El, Mih-Chai-El, and Ohr-Ree-El. But the correspondences on the Tree of Life don't include Ohr-Ree-El. Why not?

Answer: The Tree of Life is a wonderful map for understanding everything in the universe. But we should never equate the map with reality.

Although the Tree of Life is a map of the workings of the universe, it does not include everything. There are many archangels. Some are included on the Tree of Life while others are not. Many archangels are not associated with the Sephiroht. Ohr-Ree-El is one of those.

According to Davidson in his excellent book *A Dictionary of Angels*, Ohr-Ree-El (also spelled "Oriel," "Auriel," and "Uriel," and meaning "the Light of God" or "the Fire of God") is also an "Angel of Destruction," and helped the magicians in the courts of the Egyptian Pharaoh. Other sources quoted by Davidson make Ohr-Ree-El either equal to the Roman Hades or the archangel of salvation. Ohr-Re-El is the angel who held the fiery sword which kept Adam and Eve from returning to Eden. It was also Ohr-Ree-El who wrestled with Jacob and was sent by God to warn Noah of the flood that was to come.

In some ways Ohr-Ree-El is also like Thoth, who brought wisdom, language, and magick to the Egyptians. Ohr-Ree-El is said to have spoken to Ezra (a Jewish patriarch) and given him the secrets of the mysteries of heaven. Ohr-Ree-El also brought the secrets of alchemy and the Kabalah to earth.

Ohr-Ree-El has (or had) all of these tasks and responsibilities (as well as being the archangel associated with the element of Earth and the direction north), yet there is not a place for this archangel on the Tree of Life. This is because a map only shows what it needs to show. A map of Denver, Colorado, does not also show the streets of Geneva, Switzerland! Likewise, the map of the workings of the universe known as the Tree of Life only shows its view of the universe, a view in which Ohr-Ree-El is not a major player. That does not mean that Ohr-Re-El is unimportant. It only means that Ohr-Re-El does not play a part on the Tree of Life.

On Determining if a Ritual Worked

Question: *I don't feel anything when I do rituals. Does that mean that they are not working?*

Answer: You cannot determine if your magick has worked by anything you may feel or experience during a ritual. The success of any magickal ritual is only determined by your result. Some people feel (or think they feel) a great deal in a magickal ritual. Others may feel nothing. Either person may have success with magick.

Failure may occur if you feel nothing out of the ordinary but believe you are supposed to feel something. If you don't feel something that indicates to you that your ritual was a success, you may become sure that your magick didn't work. This assumption of failure, mixed with a continued belief that your ritual failed, will virtually assure that your magick, in fact, will fail.

Magick does not take place only during a ritual. It occurs all the time. By believing that your ritual failed, you, quite literally, are working magick to cause that failure. If your ritual took ten minutes to perform, and then you spend the next two weeks thinking it has failed—in a sense doing magick to see that it will fail—you will overpower your ritual with the magick that followed. That is one reason why, when you finish a ritual, you should forget about it. That way you cannot accidentally work against yourself. If you do happen to think about the ritual and the magick, you would be well advised to develop the attitude that you know the magick will be successful.

This is not to say that you will never experience signs or indications of some magickal effect during a ritual. In my personal experience I have found that there are two indicators that something magickal has taken place. The first is "Δ C" or the Delta C factor, also known as time displacement. Specifically, you may think that the ritual has taken several hours when it only took twenty minutes. Conversely, you may think that the ritual only lasted thirty minutes when, in fact, it lasted several hours.

Another sign that some magickal effect has taken place during your ritual is "Δ T" or the Delta T factor: a change in the perceived temperature. If this effect occurs, the temperature of the area will seem to become either quite warm or cold.

On Advice for Young Magicians

Question: *I want to do magick and join a coven or magickal group, but my parents won't let me. I'm only fifteen and can't move away. What should I do?*

Answer: I do not advise you to go against your parents' wishes. You may think that they are unfair, but their life experience means that they have had experiences you have not had. It is likely they are trying to protect you from what they see as harm. If your parents were magicians, they might be helping you to learn magick safely.

I regret to tell you that you may simply have to wait until you're older before becoming more active with magick. Most magickal groups won't accept people under eighteen unless both parents are members or without both parents' written permission.

If you really want to make magick your life, here are some things you can do now to *prepare* to be able to learn more and work magick:

• *Magicians need to have sharp minds and be able to communicate well.* Stay in school and learn as much as you can. Study everything—English, foreign languages, history, math, computers, and the sciences. The more you know on a wide variety of subjects, the more you will be able to bring to your magickal training.

• *Magicians need to be creative.* Study some "artistic" things—sculpture, drawing, painting, woodwork, music, creative writing, acting, computer graphics, etc. Not only will these practices help your creativity (excellent when trying to figure out how to make a talisman or construct magickal tools), but it will also make you a more interesting, well-rounded person.

• *Magicians need strength and agility.* Be sure to get plenty of exercise. This should include aerobics for your heart and lungs, resistance training for muscles and stretching for flexibility. Also study martial arts, fencing, dancing, or a similar activity for agility and grace. Be sure to get the okay from your doctor before beginning an exercise program.

• *Magicians are popular.* Contrary to the popular impression, most magicians today are sociable—sometimes *very* sociable—people. There are several reasons for this. First, humans are social creatures by nature. We need input from others to stay healthy. Second, the knowledge by some people that you are interested in magick might lead them to mock you. As you get older it could prevent you from getting desired jobs. By being able to determine what you can tell somebody of your interests, you can, as it were, "hide in plain sight." Everyone can see you but they won't know your real interests unless they are open to them in a positive way. Finally, by being sociable you are able to meet people and hear what they have to say. It's possible that some of them have interests similar to yours, and an eventual friendship, as well as a circle of friends, may develop.

Many people have trouble meeting and talking with other people. If this describes you, try out one or more of the following:

• Join one or two school clubs with subjects you enjoy.

• Observe people around you and see what they like. Then, ask them questions about those subjects. You'll find that they'll love to tell you all about it.

• If you have trouble talking with people, listen intently to what they say. Then ask them questions based on what they said or ask for more information. You will find that they will go out of their way to talk with you because you listen.

• *Magicians have a strong will.* Make up your mind to do something on a regular schedule and then keep to that schedule. Remember, however, that no one is perfect. Instead of using a missed activity as an excuse to stop, make it a reason to try harder!

There are multiple levels of keeping on schedule. The first is physical. So, for example, make up your mind to do a particular physical action. You might choose to always open a door with your left hand. If you err by using your right hand to open a door, simply make a mark in a small notebook that you carry for that purpose. Or, you could keep a rubber band around your wrist and snap it so that it slaps you for going against what you wanted to do.

The next level is verbal. Make up your mind that you will not use a specific word. For example, you might decide that you will not use the word "I" for a week. Make marks or snap the rubber band when you go against your will.

The most difficult level is thought. Make up your mind that you will not think of something specific for a week. For example, you might decide to not think of watching television for a week. Use the rubber band snap or book marking when you think about watching TV.

You will notice that the first day of each level will be filled with snaps or marks in your book. But as you go through the week your control will become greater and the marks or snaps will decrease. This is tangible evidence that your control of your will is increasing.

On What to Do if You Don't Have a Magickal Tool

Question: I can't find a good dagger. What can I do without this tool?

Answer: The Air dagger can be replaced by anything that represents Air to you. This could include a fan, a feather, or something else. As a standard tool, such as the dagger used for the LBRP, you can use your index finger or both the index and middle finger. Extend one or both of those fingers, as if pointing, from the other fingers that are curled back toward the palm. Any cup can function as the magickal chalice. You could even use the twist-off top from a bottle of soda. Earth could be a small stone and fire could be a match, matchbook, lighter, or a red object.

Don't let the inaccessibility of magickal tools prevent you from doing rituals. Don't wait until you have that perfect Air dagger to do a ritual. Use a butter knife or a fan. I have a delightful fan made of sandalwood for this purpose (I bought it at Disneyland!). If you don't have a water chalice made of glass, get one of pewter. Or stainless steel. Or silver plate. Or wood. Or use a large seashell. Or use a paper or Styrofoam cup.

All magickal tools are helpers. The magick is not in them; it is in you. As I've written before, "Magick is not something you do, magick is something you are."

On the *Necronomicon*

Question: What do you think of the Necronomicon?

Answer: Which one? There are many books that claim to be THE *Necronomicon*. I have several books with that name and several articles that are supposed to be excerpts from the "real" thing. They all have just one thing in common: they are nothing but inventions of contemporary authors.

The most popular version is loosely based on Sumerian religion—very loosely. In fact, much of it appears to be taken from *The Beginnings of History and Chaldean Magic* by François Lenormant.

This version is also based on some of the writings of Aleister Crowley and the works of horror writer H. P. Lovecraft and others who wrote in what is known as the Cthulhu Mythos, stories which used the fictional entities created by Lovecraft (and later, others).

Lovecraft invented the entire idea of an evil book called the *Necronomicon*. In January of 1934, Lovecraft wrote a letter where he says that the *Necronomicon* is nothing but a figment of his imagination. And in August of 1934, Lovecraft wrote that not only was the *Necronomicon* his own invention, but so, too, were the entities from the Cthulhu Mythos including Azathoth, Yog-Sothoth, Nyarlathotep, Shub-Niggurath, and others.

But even though the different versions of the *Necronomicon* that have been published are all fakes, does that mean that they are also ineffective? Not necessarily. The Cthulhu Mythos, as part of the current magickal world, has caught the imagination of a surprisingly large number of people. I believe that their mental beliefs and repeated rituals have created *thought forms* that function, to an extent, along the lines of the entities described in the various versions of the *Necronomicon*.

I would point out, however, that the entities of traditional Western magick have been invoked and evoked for many hundreds, even thousands, of years. My experience indicates that in practice they are much stronger than the *Necronomicon* entities.

So can the entities of the *Necronomicon* be used in magick? Absolutely. Just as any mental creation can be used in magick. But why would you want to use them? If you follow the writings of Lovecraft and other fiction writers, the entities of the *Necronomicon* are evil, intent on enslaving humanity and controlling the world. Frequently (in the stories, at least), the entities of the Cthulhu Mythos are uncontrollable and destroy (or attempt to destroy) those people who call them. Are you willing to chance that? Are you prepared to chance that?

Note: I had read all of Lovecraft's short stories and novellas before I even started to work on the first form of *Modern Magick*. After years of personal study and practice, *Modern Magick* began as a series of lessons I taught in southern California. After that I wrote it out as a series of fifty-two short lessons as I wanted to teach it via mail order. They were never published or printed and I no longer have copies of them. A publisher of mail order courses contacted me through my friend, Scott Cunningham, and asked to see them. After reading them, he asked me to rewrite them in longer lessons for him to publish. I did so, but within six months the company folded. I still have copies of those lessons that were published. I rewrote them into the format that would appear several years later as the first edition of *Modern Magick*. I'm describing this to point out that I was very familiar with the original concept of the *Necronomicon* years before any published version of *Modern Magick* appeared. Further, *Modern Magick* was created *before* the most popular version of the *Necronomicon* was published.

Long after versions of *Modern Magick* were complete, I began to receive letters asking me about the *Necronomicon*. The number of letters gradually increased, so much so that I set up the above message to be a standard response to the letters I received.

In 1999, I was invited to the Starwood festival in upstate New York to give some workshops. While there, I attended a workshop titled "Magick and the *Necronomicon*," given by John Gonce and Daniel Harms. It was a wonderful and humorous workshop.

About a year later I was invited by Llewellyn to add a section to *Modern Magick*. That added section was this FAQ. It first appeared in 2001 and included the previous response concerning the *Necronomicon*.

Harms and Gonce have written a wonderful book titled *The Necronomicon Files*, and I would encourage anyone interested in the *Necronomicon* to read it. In the book they point out, correctly, that I did not publish this FAQ, with the above copy of letters I sent out, until after I attended their workshop. They suggested that I didn't think the *Necronomicon* was a "problem" worth comment upon until "somebody" talked about how people were taking it seriously. I'm going to assume that by "somebody" they meant themselves.

While the dates are correct and my attendance at their workshop is absolutely true (I had a great time), I had been writing the above message to individuals long before I attended their workshop and

did not need "somebody" to tell me that some people were taking the *Necronomicon* seriously. It wasn't mentioned in the first edition of *Modern Magick* because it didn't exist when I was writing it. My comments about the *Necronomicon* written above were originally written long before I attended their workshop. I added the comments in the FAQ to *Modern Magick* because I was asked to write some more material by Llewellyn.

On Joining Groups

Question 1: Will you send me the name of a group in my area I can join?

Question 2: What do you think of the group known as XXXXXX?

Answer: I'm sorry, but as a rule I don't recommend groups. Why? Well, when I meet people involved in a group they may be excellent and doing good work, but in the following months or years they might change and not be as good as they once were.

If I had recommended a group to you several months or years ago but you waited until recently to join, you might have fallen into a bad situation. If they changed between the time I knew them and the time you became involved with them, the same might be true. The direct cause of your involvement with a negative situation would have been my remarks. I do not want this to happen. Therefore, I don't recommend any groups. So what can you do?

My suggestion is to go to local metaphysical bookstores and occult shops and ask questions. Perhaps you'll meet somebody who is part of a good group. You could also do some searches on the Internet.

I would also add that when considering joining a group you should listen to your heart. Does it feel okay or does the group or its leaders (or some of its members) make you feel uncomfortable? Do you feel that something is wrong? Do you feel like they are trying to use psychology to "encourage" you to join or stay a member? Are they charging what you consider to be large amounts of money? Do they tell you how special and powerful you are (or can be) but that you need them to help you manifest this power? Do they offer "astral" or "proxy" initiations? For Western groups all of this is very questionable, and you might wish to stay away.

There is another alternative I'd like to suggest. Why not get a group of friends with similar interests together to form a study and practice group? Several groups have written to me and told me that they are using *Modern Magick* as their training text. There is no reason that you cannot do that, too. Once you've worked your way through *Modern Magick* you can then move on and explore other systems and techniques. Good book titles are given in the bibliography found later in these lessons.

The question of my opinion of various groups is a bit more difficult. You see, I could say that a group didn't have much value while another person might find the information the group presented to be of inestimable value. One student may find my analysis of a group accurate while another may find it completely wrong. In fact, somebody may find that a group is exactly what they need at this time for their spiritual and magickal development. If I discourage a person from joining that group, I may be slowing that person's spiritual evolution.

So rather than commenting on the value of a particular group, I would, instead, urge you to investigate in every way you can. Talk to a wide variety of people. Find out if there are any former members who will talk with you. Talk to current members.

Then, if you decide to join, I urge you to take what I call "baby steps." Go into a group slowly, not participating fully with that group for months or longer. As long as you are ready to exit a group if they turn out to be inappropriate for you at this time, you should not have any trouble. And as I said above, listen to your heart.

On Ceremonial Magick and the Kabalah Being Patriarchal

Question: I'm a Wiccan. Aren't ceremonial magick traditions and the Kabalah patriarchal?

Answer: Although some groups and individuals, both ancient and modern, are patriarchal, that is

more a sign of the times and the individuals involved than of the tradition itself. The Kabalah, for example, sees deity both as androgynous and in the forms of male and female, similar to the relationship of Shiva and Shakti in Tantric traditions. Further, any name (or more appropriately, title) of deity, archangels, or angels ending in "-ah," "-aht," "-ath," "-oth," "-os," or "-oht" is feminine. El-oh-heem, one of the most-used names of deity, is female singular (El-oh-ah, meaning "goddess") with a male plural suffix (-eem). Thus it refers to deity as neither patriarchal nor matriarchal in nature but as having qualities of both male and female.

While there are some very patriarchal organizations, such is rarely the case with magickal groups. Several important ceremonial magick groups have, in fact, been led by women. The first initiate of the Hermetic Order of the Golden Dawn was a woman, Moina Mathers. For many years women led the Golden Dawn. After Paul Foster Case, founder of the Builders of the Adytum (BOTA) died, a woman became the head of the order. Women today lead groups that claim to be the Golden Dawn. Various OTO groups are run by women. At least one current of the AA, Crowley's replacement for the Golden Dawn, was passed through a woman.

Most spiritual traditions are neither patriarchal nor matriarchal. They become so as a result of the people who are involved in the organization. I would suggest, therefore, that if you are interested in a non-patriarchal, ceremonial magick group, all you need do is keep looking. They're out there.

On Chaos Magick

NOTE: This part of the Modern Magick FAQ has been superseded by the section on Chaos Magick in Lesson 12. I decided to leave this in for historical reference and to show what I was thinking on the subject almost a decade prior to the third edition of these lessons.

Question: What is Chaos Magick?

Answer: While many would say that Chaos Magick is entirely new, as far as I have been able to tell it is simply a new way of looking at something old; it is a new paradigm.

For example, most magicians today believe that magickal power (other than any that is inherent in objects such as plants, holy stones, etc.) comes from within oneself and/or from the Divine, the source of everything. Chaos magicians say that chaos is the source of everything. As a magician, you attempt to tap into this source of power. For Chaos magicians, instead of believing all such magick power comes from the Divine, they tap into "chaos." In both instances the results can be the same. Even the concept is the same. The major difference is the name and the approach.

Perhaps the one really new idea in Chaos Magick is the desire to break through many centuries of accretions that surround magickal traditions and see what is the minimum necessary to do magick. Their attitude is that it makes sense to do the minimum necessary to achieve the maximum results.

On Joining Several Magickal Groups and Covens

Question: I've just discovered magick and I'd like to join a bunch of groups and a coven or two. However, some of my teachers have said I should only study one magickal system. Is this correct?

Answer: This does not have a simple, single answer. In some instances, such rules are used by a group (or a leader of a group) to have power and control over members. However, there are some good reasons why it might be better for a person, especially one who is just starting out in the study of magick, to only participate with one group.

First, let's look at why being a member of only one group might be the best for the group. When a magickal group works together, after a time they develop a group spirit known as an "egregore." If you mix one group's philosophy, training, techniques, and beliefs with those of another group, it blurs the egregore and weakens it. This can end up wrecking the unity and cohesion of the group.

There are also problems students can have if they are studying different magickal systems or with several groups simultaneously. Sometimes a person is not capable of keeping a multiplicity of systems separate in his or her mind and actions. Rather than learning from each system, he/she becomes confused and does not advance as quickly as she/he should in any of those systems. Also, there is an idea among some students, especially beginners, that all magick is the same but the rituals have variations. This is simply not true. Although there are similarities between systems, there are also stark or subtle contrasts. The desire to blend systems without a thorough knowledge of them can have negative results on the student and the groups.

I suggest that in most instances it is most effective for a student to learn one system very thoroughly first. Then he/she can study with other groups and learn other systems. Even after the student has done this it is important that he/she be able to keep different systems separate when working with various groups.

Once an intermediate student has determined that he or she can keep different systems separate and grow in both (or more) systems, I see no reason why such a person should not work with more than one group. This is assuming that such a student is also able to divide his or her attention among the groups and still advance within those organizations.

As an alternative, if a student feels confined by the limitations of any one (or even several orders), he/she might wish to develop his/her own system. In my opinion, the thing to keep in mind is that magickal orders should challenge members to grow spiritually and magickally. That means study and practice with things that may not be of immediate interest to you but are of immense value in your development. When given the opportunity to work with multiple systems, some students will focus on what they like and ignore other aspects. This slows their spiritual and magickal progress.

The More Things Change . . .

. . . the more they really do stay the same. More than fifteen years after I first received a question about joining multiple groups and studying many topics, I saw this on an Internet forum:

"I have recently been considering the Kabalah as part of my studies, especially the Tree of Life. I just picked up a copy of *The Mystical Qabalah* by Dion Fortune. It's my study of magick that has brought me here. I am not one for completely following tradition or staying at one point of study for too long . . . The only problem with this is that I spread myself way too thin, I don't dig deep enough. This is probably because everything that has to do with the occult fascinates me. I like things that are hidden away, that are secret. I have even given thought to enrolling in an online school of magick."

I responded this way: "A lot of people express your feelings. I know because at one time I was there, too. I wanted to know everything, I wanted to know it NOW, and I wanted to be able to use it all, this afternoon.

"Unfortunately, it didn't work that way. What I ended up with was a superficial understanding of a variety of topics and areas. I always felt like something was missing and I needed to learn more, MORE! There's nothing wrong with that, of course. One of my personal beliefs is that you don't die when you stop breathing, you die when you stop learning. But all I was learning wasn't getting me anywhere. I had to take a step back and discover why.

"I decided that I needed to study one system in depth and I'm glad I did. What I found was I needed a grounding, a firm base, a place to start and to which I could compare other concepts.

"I thought that this might box me in—and I was willing to accept that (grrrrr) for a while. Surprisingly, just the opposite occurred. My in-depth study of one system left plenty of room for looking at other systems because my time was spent more effectively. Instead of being locked in I found that I was going beyond mere learning all the way to understanding on a very intuitive level. I was able to comprehend, as I studied new things, X is based on Y, Z is a latter addition, M is irrelevant, Y is just wrong, P is a great idea so I'll incorporate it, etc.

"Instead of locking me into one system, an in-depth study of one area resulted in opening me up to the potential in all areas. Therefore, I would respectfully suggest that you consider taking a breath and choose to study just one system for a period of time. Wicca claims a year and a day is a good length of time, and I would agree. However you might want to choose to try this out for just six months . . . or even just three months, and see how it goes."

On Spirit Communication

Question: *When doing an evocation, how do the various spirits communicate with you?*

Answer: The spirits communicate in a variety of ways. In the work I have done this has included everything from hearing a voice in English (from quiet whispers to loud singing), to hearing an internal voice (some sort of telepathy), to just a feeling or "knowing" what the message from the intelligence is.

This brings up another point that is frequently asked. Are the spirits objectively real? Are they separate entities having lives of their own or are they simply aspects of our inner selves? Many magicians today, inculcated with various psychological theories of the mind (especially those of Jung), believe the latter view. As I have stated before, I refer to this as the "psychologization of magick." Personally, I believe, and my experience has shown, that the former is a better representation of reality. It certainly functions as if the spirits are real.

Notice that in both versions I have said that the people supporting the differing views *believe* a certain way; it is subjective. We may never know which is the objective reality. Frankly, to me it doesn't matter. What matters is the result of the magickal operation.

On Inertia of the Will

Question: For some reason I've stopped doing regular rituals. It's not that I don't want to; it's just that I never seem to have the time, interest, or desire. Why is this happening and what can I do about it?

Answer: I have received this question many dozens, if not hundreds of times. I want you to know that not only are you not alone, you are actually experiencing something that is very common.

Newton's first law of motion states that a body at rest tends to remain at rest. This property is known as inertia.

Although the main focus of this law is the physical world, it also happens on the non-physical.

When you do rituals, you are beginning to change your life and put your higher self in charge of your being while overcoming the common, everyday ruler of your body, what I call the magickal ego. But since you are used to being controlled by this aspect of your being, your body, mind, and spirit try to keep it in control. They resist change. They create reasons not to change. It is they who prevent you from doing ritual.

Newton's first law also states that a body in motion tends to continue in motion. That means if you simply use willpower to force yourself back into doing rituals, and keep at it, those feelings of not wanting to do rituals will fade and doing ritual will become a pleasurable joy. It will become uncomfortable *not* to do regular rituals.

So if you are feeling resistance to doing rituals, know that you're doing things right! Now get yourself up and force yourself to do it. Put down these lessons and do it right now. Then set a time to repeat the rituals tomorrow. Within a few weeks of regular repetition you will notice a change and practice will become a habit.

On Having Time

Question: I have to work at odd hours and my sleeping schedule is even more erratic. In your book you talk about regular performance of the Four Adorations at specific times. How can I do that when I might be either at work or asleep?

Answer: Many years ago there was the idea that magicians might have to wait until a certain date in a future year in order to perform a specific ritual. While that may be the optimal time for doing a specific ritual, it does not mean that it is the only time.

If you are doing a ritual that is solar in nature, let's say for finding missing property, the optimal time to perform it would be during a summer month, during the waxing of the Moon or, even better, on the full Moon, on a Sunday during the hour of the Sun.

If you can't wait until the summer, the next best time to do the ritual would be during the waxing of the Moon or full Moon on a Sunday during the hour of the Sun.

If you can't wait until the full Moon, then the best time to do it would be during the waxing of the Moon on a Sunday during the hour of the Sun.

If you can't wait until the waxing of the Moon, then the best time to do it would be on a Sunday during the hour of the Sun.

If waiting until Sunday would be too late, then the next best time would be today, during the hour of the Sun.

And, if for some reason you cannot perform the ritual during the hour of the Sun, the time to do the ritual is now.

Concerning the adorations, however, there are timing functions which do need to be observed. After all, greeting Ra at sunset instead of sunrise would not only be insulting to Ra but would also put you out of synchronization with forces of nature around you.

So, in my opinion, the key is to do each of the adorations as close as possible to their appropriate times. Example: Assume that you must go to sleep at 10:30 P.M. and rise at 6:30 A.M. You are going to sleep before the optimal time to do the midnight adoration and rising before or after the optimal time of doing the sunrise adoration, depending upon the time of the year. Do the midnight evocation before going to sleep. Do the sunrise adoration immediately upon rising or, if the Sun rises after you wake up, at the appropriate time.

If you don't think you have the privacy you would like to do the adorations, re-read the information on the Great Voice. If you are working at noon or sunset, take a break and go outside, or to a private office, or even go to the restroom. There, using the Great Voice, perform the adoration. If need be, you can also visualize your movements instead of physically acting them out.

On Tarot Decks

Question 1: I've been using a Tarot deck that is different than the ones you recommend. Is that okay or do I need to use one of the decks you suggest?

Question 2: I have a deck with more [or fewer] cards in the Major [or Minor] Arcana [or fewer or more suits] than "standard" decks. Are you saying that I can't use it?

Question 3: I love the Crowley Thoth Tarot Deck. Why are you saying that I shouldn't use it?

Answer: I've linked these questions because they can be answered together.

What I have called a "standard" Tarot deck consists of four suits of Minor Arcana cards. Each suit represents one of the four magickal elements: Air, Earth, Fire, or Water. Each suit has ten cards num-
bered from one to ten (often called the "pip" cards) and four face cards often based on European royalty (and therefore known as the "court" cards). Traditionally, the numbered cards do not have images on them other than a collection of symbols representing the number of the card and its suit. For example, the Four of Cups would simply show four cups. The Major Arcana has twenty-two cards numbered from zero to twenty-one. Each one has a symbolic image on it.

Although some people have claimed that the Kabalah and the Tarot have been linked for thousands of years, it has only been relatively recently that this "ancient link" has been established. Even so, that link is incredibly workable and usable, and the binding of the Tarot and the Tree of Life has become widely used among magicians. It is part of the system I teach in *Modern Magick*.

That is why using a "standard" Tarot deck is important with this course. Over the past several decades there has been an incredible increase in the number of Tarot decks available. Most, of course, are nothing more than a reinterpretation of the so-called Rider-Waite-Smith Tarot (itself a variation on the deck used by members of the Golden Dawn). As such, they will have images on even the previously numeric Minor Arcana cards. Although use of such cards is fine, I would remind you that the uses of the Tarot in this course are primarily for meditation and Kabalistic Pathworking rather than for giving readings. The extra images on the numeric Minor Arcana cards are of no benefit or handicap for this. Meditation is done with the Major Arcana cards.

Of the vast number of Tarot decks available, most will work just fine with this course. Some decks change the names of the Major Arcana cards or the court cards of the Minor Arcana. As long as you can relate them back to the standard terminology, they should present little problem when you use them with these lessons.

Other decks add or subtract cards. In some instances the resolution of this problem is easy. For example, in *The Golden Dawn Magical Tarot* by the Ciceros, a second version of one of the Major Arcana cards is included. To use this deck with *Modern Magick,* simply remove either of the duplicates.

Unfortunately, this method cannot work in all cases. I've seen some decks that are so unique that they barely relate to the traditional pack and I would question even calling them a Tarot deck. For example, I have seen a Minor Arcana composed of eight suits of eight cards each for a total of sixty-four. This deck is simply not applicable for work with the system presented here.

One of the most outstanding and remarkable decks is the one designed by Aleister Crowley and realized by Lady Frieda Harris. The painting style has multiple levels. Change the focus of your eyes and you can see something entirely different from what you saw moments ago. It is for this exact reason that I love to use the *Thoth* deck for meditation.

Unfortunately, many people will be surprised at the multiple levels revealed by the art on this deck. As a result, I have suggested that people just starting with the Tarot as part of this course avoid the Crowley *Thoth* deck. This is not because the deck is "wrong," but because its depth may initially confuse. (Recently, a deck published by Lo Scarabeo and called the *Initiatory Tarot of the Golden Dawn* has been released. It has absolutely brilliant art. I've seen several Golden Dawn decks, and this has the finest art of any of them. However, it includes a pictorial Minor Arcana, which can cause problems. Also, surprisingly, the art is so brilliant that it leaves little room for imagination. As a result, this deck is great for doing Golden Dawn and other types of divinations, but not as good for Kabalistic Pathworking and meditation. It's not ideal for beginners with Tarot who wish to use a Golden Dawn style of deck for this course.)

If you are already familiar with the Crowley *Thoth* Tarot, then go ahead and use it. Be aware, however, that Crowley switched the numbers on two of the Major Arcana cards, so for the purpose of this book either reassign them according to the associa-

tions I have given or study his works so you can understand exactly why he made the changes.

On Satanism

Question 1: What do you think about Satanism?
Question 2: What should I do for my friend who has been part of a generational Satanic family?

Answer: When people talk about Satanism, the very name is so filled with emotion and "baggage" that they forget to define what they mean by the very term. Most of the people who argue against Satanism tend to equate all forms of Satanism with an imaginary organization of baby-killing, insane-eyed sociopaths. Those who defend Satanism frequently equate "real" Satanism with a type of self-centered, Ayn Randian philosophy that exalts the individual.

In actuality there are two major types of Satanism. One type is what I call "religious Satanists." They view what they're doing as a religion. Some of them don't believe in Satan as an entity but use the idea of Satan as an analogy for the supremacy of the individual Will (which, unfortunately, is usually interpreted as whatever desire the person has). Others view Satan as a misunderstood deity. One group traces Satan back to an Egyptian deity. The thread that runs through most of these religious Satanists' beliefs is a type of Nietzscheism or Ayn Rand Objectivism where the individual, being superior to others around him or her, is not bound by conventional ideas of right and wrong. In fact, I read some of the semi-secret documents of one of these groups and found that their "ancient" deity actually quoted Nietzsche. (Nietzsche's idea of the "superman" was quite similar to the notion of a superior being who rules over inferiors.)

In practice, most of the people in these groups are law-abiding citizens. Often, the leaders of such groups have to be very careful because various law enforcement agencies, filled with paranoia and religious propaganda from certain Christian fundamentalist organizations, are looking at them to make even the slightest wrong move. Arresting a bunch of

Satanists will help politicians get re-elected even if the accused committed no crimes.

In most cases, religious Satanists are as upstanding as people in any selected group. But with the majority of the Western world having such negative emotions surrounding the very term "Satanism," why would anyone want to identify with a so-called Satanic group, especially when many of them don't even believe in Satan as an entity?

I can only guess (and my limited experience with Satanists has shown this to be accurate) that it is because they are looking for attention or want to spit in society's eye. Some of them seem to think that there is some sort of power in Satanism because so many people hate/fear it. It may stem from some sort of feeling of personal powerlessness and the belief that Satanism will give them that desired power.

Because there is so much negativity associated with Satanism, deserved or not, I suggest that people simply avoid it. That way you will not be drawn into the negativity. If you like some of Nietzsche's ideas, perhaps you'd be better off looking at Rand's Objectivist philosophy. It is very similar to the self-over-all philosophy of some religious Satanists. Curiously, it is also popular among some political conservatives who love it if you call it Objectivism but would denounce it if you called the same beliefs Satanism.

There is another type of Satanism, what I call "Self-Styled Satanism," which is a different story. Such Satanic groups usually are small in membership (often only being one or two people), don't advertise and have a leader or leaders who are highly charismatic. They attract people who tend to have low self-esteem and are usually highly manipulatable. Why? Because the leaders don't want a strong personality that can stand up to them.

Their "theology" or philosophy varies wildly from group to group. Even within a group it may change from day to day at the leader's whim. These beliefs are frequently made up of information culled from cheap movies, bad novels, and a few textbooks. Unfortunately, some of these books are ones written by members of other religions and are filled with wild lies in an attempt to vilify an imagined Satanism. The Self-Styled Satanist assumes that the impossibly absurd and lurid tales from these books are accurate and may actually try to duplicate them, thus proving that the tales were right.

Over the past few decades, there was a growing, then waning, belief in the notion of families of Satanists, existing for generations, who have committed horrible crimes. The only problem with this is that there has never been any evidence that such groups exist. Supporters of the existence of such groups have held on to the stories of various writers even though the tales have proven to be total fabrications. Children have been traumatized and families destroyed by politically and/or religiously oriented government officials who, according to an FBI agent who investigated the matter, seem more interested in ending heresy than solving crimes.

I have no doubt that a person may think that he or she has either been part of a generational Satanic family or a victim of one. There is also ample evidence of books, therapists, and law enforcement officers who see such activities in situations where it does not exist. Experiments have shown that people's memory of events may be easily altered and people will believe the altered versions with all their being.

If you have a friend who believes that he or she has been part of a generational Satanic family, I would urge extreme caution on your part. This supposed problem, no matter how much the person may believe it accurately reflects an actual past, is merely a symptom of other problems that exist in the person's life. Part of it may be true. None of it may be true. If you get sucked into it, you may get pulled into a whirlpool of experiences about which you have incomplete information. This can only lead to problems for you.

On the Ouija Board

Question: *Some friends and I have started to work with the Ouija board. We've been getting all sorts of interesting information from it. But recently somebody told me it was dangerous. What do you think about it?*

Answer: The Ouija board is a simple plank with letters and numbers on it. A three-legged device, known as a *planchette*, is capable of pointing to the figures on the board. In use, two or more people rest their fingertips lightly on the planchette, ask a question, and the device seems to move of its own accord, pointing to the letters and numbers, spelling out words and giving information.

This type of device has been known for a long time, although it specifically grew out of a method where people would invert a stemmed goblet on a table and use the goblet like a planchette. The use of the goblet, in turn, was an advance on table tipping, where people put their fingertips on a table and it would lift up and down, tapping out answers to questions.

Skeptics claim that the motion of the planchette, if not fraudulent, is caused by "unconscious micro-motor motions" of the muscles of the hands and arms. In fact, that is exactly how the planchette moves. No spirit is pushing it around. Unanswered by the skeptics is how the Ouija was able to produce information that none of the participants previously had knowledge of.

I think there is evidence to indicate that people can tap into their unconscious, or that other entities can work through the unconscious of one or more of the people present, to produce messages on the Ouija board. But frankly, I don't care what the source is. The real questions are, "What is the content of the message and what are you going to do about it?"

This goes into the very nature of the difference between occultism and some adherents of the New Age. Some "New Agers" will listen to a message from an unknown source—what is commonly called "channeling"—and simply because it was channeled they will accept it as truth. Occultists, on the other hand, will listen to what the message has to say and then examine it for truth. How does the message compare to other information which has previously been verified? Can you confirm the identity of the entity claiming to deliver the message via Kabalistic or other means?

When I give lectures I usually begin by writing the following letters on a board:

T. F. Y. Q. A.

These letters stand for "Think For Yourself, Question Authority." Merely because I or another lecturer says something, or you find something in a book, does not make it a fact. Indeed, as self-publishing becomes more prevalent, look for more and more books that are filled with opinion not supported by history, tradition, or facts. Currently, one of the most popular purveyors of information on the Internet is Wikipedia. Most people don't look at their disclaimers. For example, as of this writing, they say this about the information on their site: "Please be advised that nothing found here has necessarily been reviewed by people with the expertise required to provide you with complete, accurate or reliable information . . ." No matter the source—even *Modern Magick*—check everything out for yourself.

Consider what will happen if you act on information obtained through a Ouija or any other source. If you get a message from the Ouija telling you to do something, I can assure you that it is you who will face the consequences of that action, not the force behind the message!

Is there a potential problem with using a Ouija board? The answer is "yes." While I was editor-in-chief of *FATE* magazine I personally did some investigation into a case where a Midwestern college dormitory had actually forbidden the use of Ouija boards in the dorm! The reason for this, I was told, was because students became so fascinated by the Ouija that their schoolwork suffered.

And that is the real potential problem with the Ouija: not possession by an evil entity, not following the words of some demon that lead to damnation, but obsession with the seemingly inexplicable movement of the planchette and the messages received.

Therefore, if you want to work with the Ouija, I suggest giving yourself limits to the amount of time you spend with it—perhaps just an hour or two per week. And I also suggest that you perform banishing rituals such as the LBRP and BRH before and after its use.

On Talismans

Question 1: Will a talisman made by someone else and charged by me have as much usefulness as one both made and charged by me?

Question 2: Once charged, should a talisman be kept away from other people's hands?

Question 3: How do you cleanse an old talisman or amulet to prepare it for reuse?

Answers: All over the world there are talismans made by other people that are meant to be charged by the user. Unless that talisman has been charged, it is nothing but a lifeless piece of inert material that probably has some pretty symbols on it. When you charge it, however, you are making it into a living thing, ready to do the magick for which it has been charged.

The actual process of making a talisman has some magickal benefits. You would know everything that goes into the making of the talisman, the purpose behind every word and symbol. The time you take to create it is, in and of itself, a magickal process that can certainly enhance the effect of the talisman. Perhaps, if you have put a great deal of time and energy into the creation of a physical talisman, it would be more appropriate to say that the charging or consecrating of the talisman is like turning on a light switch. The electricity is always there, but until you complete the circuit by doing the ritual, the light bulb doesn't glow.

The difficulty of answering the first question is that it really depends on the capabilities of the magician. An excellent magician could turn a dirty rock into a powerful talisman that would overpower anything made by an inexperienced mage. So part of the answer is that it depends on who is doing the charging of the talisman.

In most instances, however, the process of cleansing and charging a premade talisman will about equal the effect of constructing a talisman from scratch. The important part is that you do the magick.

A Talisman will bring things to it and an Amulet will keep things away. If you have charged one of these devices, having somebody else handle it means that it has been taken away from you, weakening its effect on you. Furthermore, the influence of another's energy pattern, as represented by their aura, can also have an effect on your magickal device.

Therefore, as a general rule, after a magickal tool such as a talisman has been charged, it should primarily be handled by the person for whom it was created. Obviously, the magician charging the talisman will need to handle it to some extent. However, if it is meant for use by someone other than the magician, the less the magician handles it after it has been ritually charged, the better.

The easiest way I've found to cleanse old talismans and amulets is the same as the preparation for new ones. The object can be held under running water and you can visualize all of the residual energy flowing away with the water. Another method for cleansing a talisman is to bury it for a few days where our gracious Mother Earth can naturally neutralize and absorb all of the object's energy. Be sure to mark where you've buried it so you don't lose it!

How do you tell if the talisman has been cleansed? If you have been following the course of study and practices given in these lessons, it will have been weeks or months before you attempt to make a talisman. During that time you should have been practicing numerous exercises and rituals. One of the side effects of doing this is that it enhances your psychic abilities.

By the time you are ready to charge a talisman your psychic abilities should allow you to detect the condition of the object you have chosen for your talisman.

After you have performed the cleansing, hold the object in your hands and "feel" it—not just with your physical hands, but with your spiritual senses. Does it feel clean to you or does it make you feel that something is lurking just under the surface? If the latter, you will want to repeat your cleansing. If the former, the object(s) is (are) clean and ready for charging.

On the Six-Rayed Star

Question: In your description of the Lesser Banishing Ritual of the Pentagram (LBRP), you write that one line should be said, "Within me shines the six-rayed star." In The Golden Dawn *by Israel Regardie, he says to use "Behind me shines the six-rayed star." Why the difference and what is the significance of the six-rayed star?*

Answer: Regardie's The *Golden Dawn* is an invaluable resource tool for the practicing magician. Like the grimoires that came before it, however, much of the book is only notes intended for a student's use. In *The Golden Dawn*, the LBRP is "explained" in a page, while in the first edition of *Modern Magick* I took almost fifteen pages, spread over two lessons, to explain the ritual. Why is this?

If you had received the notes for the ritual of the LBRP, such as are printed in *The Golden Dawn*, it was expected that you would be instructed in how to use them by another member. Regardie's book does not explain why they use those particular words. Neither his book nor these lessons went into great depth on this subject.

The reason I didn't go into detail is that I hoped people would use *Modern Magick* as both a study guide and resource tool. As such, it could be used as follows:

Look on the Kabalistic correspondence chart from Lesson 3. You will see that the number 6 corresponds to such things as the Sun, the Sephira Tiferet, and the heart. In a very real sense, this is the "love" center on the Tree of Life, the source of spreading warmth from our hearts, our internal suns. That "warmth" is the strength of love.

As I also explained, if you want to relate the Tree of Life to the human body, you must imagine yourself backing into it.

When you verbalize the phrase "the six-rayed star" while you perform the LBRP, you hold your body such that the spine is straight and the arms are extended out to either side. It physically makes you the center of the universe: a blending of the physical (the outspread arms reaching to the elements of our universe) and the spiritual (the vertical body receiving power from the Divine). It all meets in the love center, Tiferet, the heart. Later, you will fold your hands directly over this power center.

Thus, this passage is an acknowledgment and recognition that the representation of the Tree of Life on Earth is the physical body of every human being. Where is the central point of that Tree? If you are backing into it, that central point is behind you: "Behind me shines the six-rayed star." If you can recognize that you and the Tree are one, then that star is inside you: "Within me shines the six-rayed star."

I used the term "within" rather than "behind" because I believe it provides a stronger, more accurate, and intense image. I have seen another version that says, "Above me shines the six-rayed star." You might find the Golden Dawn's version, or any other version, more effective for you.

Magick, in order to survive and grow, needs to evolve as humanity evolves. However, I do not support change for change's sake. If you have a logical and emotional reason for making a change, go ahead. Because I had a good reason to change it on psychological, mystical, and image-oriented grounds, I feel that the version I provided in these lessons is valid.

Will You Do Magick for Me?

Question: I just started reading Modern Magick *and it's wonderful. My problem is [fill in the blank here] and I know my life will turn around if you do magick for me. I have no money but I'll be eternally grateful.*

Answer: While I thank you for your kind comments, I regret to inform you that no, I will not do magick for you. My goal in writing *Modern Magick* has been to empower people who practice the techniques in the lessons. It is my hope that it will help to change ordinary people into powerful, independent, self-actualized magicians.

If I were to do magick for you, I would be abandoning everything these words represent. You would be giving me power over your life. You would be dependent on me and not an independent individual.

You would not be self-actualized. You would not be a powerful magician.

It may very well be that magick will be able to help you. Start at Lesson One and work your way through these lessons, taking about a month for each one. I have no doubt that if you do this you will find the solutions to your situation and its resolution yourself.

APPENDIX FOUR

Course Glossary

A

ACHAS B'TAY-AH: A form of Biblical interpretation and the making of codes. See TEMU-RAH.

ADEPTUS MINOR: A term used to describe a magician. In the Golden Dawn you were taught ritual magick once you were initiated into the degree of Adeptus Minor, which was the first degree of the Inner Order, the R.R. et A.C.

AD LIBITUM: Latin for "at one's pleasure," it means to make things up as you go. Once you know the basic concepts of rituals and magick, it is possible to make up parts of rituals "on the fly" rather than depending upon repeating memorized scripts or reading written instructions. Often shortened to "ad-lib."

AGLA: A Notarikon for "Ah-tah Gee-boor Lih-oh-lahm Ah-doh-nye," or "Thou art great forever, my Lord."

AIK BEKAR: A form of biblical interpretation and a system for making codes. See TEMURAH.

AIN SOPH: "Without limit." A description of the ultimate, unknowable divinity.

AIR: One of the five magickal elements. It has the qualities of being warm and moist.

AIWASS (AIWAZ): The name of Aleister Crowley's Holy Guardian Angel. Crowley spent many years trying to determine if Aiwass was his higher self or a non-physical being objectively separate from him.

AKASHA: See AZOTH. Also, the records of all that has occurred, is occurring, and will occur in the universe.

ALCHEMY: A form of magick with the goal of turning a base metal, such as lead, into gold. This can be seen as a literal idea or as an allegory. Another goal of alchemy was finding health and eternal youth.

ALEXANDRIAN: A system of Wicca devised by Alex Sanders combining the Wiccan system of Gerald Gardner with more ceremonial magick than used by Gardner.

AMEN: A Notarikon or acronym for the Hebrew phrase "El Mel-ech Neh-eh-mahn," which means "God is a faithful king."

AMRITA: In alchemy and sex magick it is the magically transmuted First Matter.

AMULET: Similar to a talisman but designed to keep things (usually bad luck, illness, etc.) away from you.

ANGEL: An entity in the hierarchy of heaven. Each has no free will and a solitary purpose. Angels are under the command of an Archangel.

ARARITA: Word of power used in hexagram rituals, it is a Notarikon stating that the ultimate divinity is unitary in nature.

ARCHANGEL: An entity in the hierarchy of heaven. They are more powerful than angels and have free will. They are obedient to divinity and are each associated with an aspect of divinity represented by a God Name.

ART MAGICK: Another name for High Magick.

ARTIFICIAL ELEMENTAL: Like an elemental, but created by a magician for a specific purpose related to the qualities associated with a particular magickal element.

ASSOCIATED MEMORY: A memory that you experience by reliving an event. The opposite of a dissociated memory.

ASTRAL BODY: A manifestation of the spiritual aspect of a living entity. It is always attached to an incarnate being.

ASTRAL PLANE: A non-physical level of existence, which is the basis for the physical plane, and the place where many non-physical entities exist.

ASTRAL PROJECTION: The ability to separate your astral body and consciousness from your physical body.

ASTRAL TRAVEL: Exploring the astral plane after astral projection.

ASTRAL WHIPLASH: The result of your astral body and consciousness being suddenly drawn back into the physical body by a disturbance near the physical body. Symptoms can include headache, dizziness, grogginess, muscle soreness, etc. Reprojecting and returning at a normal pace will quickly overcome this problem.

ASTROLOGY: The provable science of interpreting meanings in what astronomers see.

ATHANOR: In alchemy, a special type of oven. In sex magick, the penis.

AURA: An emanation of energy which people with psychic vision can see or sense around physical objects, including the body.

AZOTH: A word composed of the first and last letters of the Hebrew and Greek alphabets. Also known by the Sanskrit term "Akasha" or the Astral Light. It appears as brightness and is changeable according to a person's will. The past, present, and future can be seen within the Azoth, but it does not have an independent personality. Since futures are only possible futures, getting lost in the Astral Light can lead to your ignoring the present.

B

BABY'S BLOOD: A code term used by ancient Pagans to mean "strawberry juice." It was placed in code so people could not understand secret herbal formulas. In retrospect, this choice for a code was not a good one.

BANISH: To send away. Banishing rituals clear your working area of unwanted entities and influences.

BI-LOCATION: Another name for mental projection.

BINAH: Understanding, the 3rd Sephira on the Tree of Life. It is at the top of the left or feminine pillar.

BITOM: Pronounced "Bee-toh-ehm," it is the Enochian name for the Spirit of Fire.

BLACK MAGICK: The science and art of causing change to occur in conformity with will, using means not currently understood by traditional Western science, for the purpose of causing either physical or non-physical harm to yourself or others, and is done either consciously or unconsciously.

BLAVATSKY, HELENA PETROVNA (1831–1891): A Ukrainian Russian woman who was the guiding force behind the founding of the Theosophical Society. Many members of the Golden Dawn were also members of this society. Her importance is also due to two large books she wrote, *Isis Unveiled* (1877) and *The Secret Doctrine* (1888). Many mystical and occult writings or so-called "channelings" are directly or indirectly based on these two books.

BLOOD OF THE RED LION: An alchemical term, which, in sex magick, means semen.

B.O.T.A.: The Builders of the Adytum. Founded by Paul Foster Case (1884–1954), a member of the Golden Dawn, it was the first organization to present a deck of Tarot cards that revealed the Golden Dawn correspondences of Hebrew with each Major Arcana card. In his rituals he removed all mention of Enochian magick.

BREAKS: Refers to interruptions in concentration. Crowley gave techniques to develop concentration and overcome these breaks.

BRUJERIA: Although based on Afro-Caribbean magickal traditions, Brujeria in the U.S. has a distinctly American flavor, being the spiritual/magical system of Latino barrios.

C

CABALA: See KABALA.

CARROLL, PETER (1952–): A founder and leader in the Chaos Magick movement, he was also the co-founder of the Illuminates of Thanateros.

CELESTIAL TRIANGLE: When looking at the Tree of Life as if composed of three triangles, it is the uppermost triangle, with one point up.

CEREMONIAL MAGICK: A magickal system involving rituals performed by several people. Many Westerners find that this style of magick is most appropriate to their consciousness.

CEREMONY: A ritual involving more than one person.

CHAKRA: Pronounced "kahk-rah," or "chak-rah" with a hard "ch" as in the word "chalk," these are power centers in the aura related to organs or glands in the body. The chakras are not in the body per se; they are actually whirls, vortices, circles, or lotuses, which psychics can see in the aura.

CHALICE: A stemmed goblet used as the tool of elemental Water. Also one of the suits of the Tarot's Minor Arcana.

CHAOIST: Term for a practitioner of Chaos Magick.

CHAOS MAGICK: A paradigm for understanding magick. It seeks to eliminate the excesses that have been added to magick over the centuries and get back to the minimum in order to achieve the maximum. It sees the source of magickal energy as the primal chaos that preceded the "big bang" of creation. Other aspects include influences from A.O. Spare and the concept of the Gnostic Trance.

CHAOTE: Term for a practitioner of Chaos Magick.

CHIAH: Our True Will. Corresponds with the 2nd Sephira on the Tree of Life.

CIRCULATION OF THE BODY OF LIGHT: A ritual developed from the Middle Pillar Ritual wherein you move spiritual energy throughout and around your body.

CIRCUMAMBULATE: Go around a circle once. A description used in magickal rituals.

CODE: In Postmodern Magick, a set of filters through which we deal with any aspect of life. We have a set of codes for money, health, sex, learning, etc. Magick allows us to change our codes.

CONTEMPLATION: Focusing your attention on something. The second step in true meditation.

CONVERSOS: After the expulsion of the Jews from Spain in 1492, those Jews who still remained in Spain and pretended to convert to Christianity but continued to practice Judaism in secret.

CREATIVE VISUALIZATION: A process of using visualizations to affect your unconscious. This will have an effect on the astral plane, leading to changes on the physical plane.

CROW: A physically difficult position for sex magick in which one partner stands and holds suspended the other partner who is inverted, allowing for mutual oral-genital contact. The person who is upside down has blood flowing to their head, which, combined with the sexual activity and flow of magickal energies, allows for oracular potential.

CROWLEY, ALEISTER (née Edward Alexander Crowley, 1875–1947): Many claim he was the most important magician of the twentieth century. After training within the Golden Dawn he developed his own system based on O.T.O. sex magick secrets, Golden Dawn techniques, his own channeled writings, and his own practical experience.

CUP: See CHALICE.

CURCURBITE: A type of alchemical container. In sex magick, the vagina.

D

DAGGER: The tool of elemental Air. A knife sharp on both edges.

THE DEMON CO: A humorous reference to carbon monoxide. When charcoal for incense is burned, it can exhaust the air of oxygen and replace it with carbon monoxide (chemical formula: CO). A magician should always have plenty of air in a room when burning incense.

DEOSIL: Clockwise. The usual direction of movement in a magickal circle.

DISSOCIATED MEMORY: A memory where you observe yourself experiencing an event rather than directly reliving it. The opposite of an associated memory.

DOGMATIC KABALAH: The study of books of the Kabalah such as the *Torah* and the *Sepher Yetzirah*.

E

EARTH: One of the five magickal elements. Its qualities are coolness and dryness.

ELEMENTAL: A non-physical entity composed entirely of one of the magickal elements. They should more accurately be called an "elementary," but most people use this term.

ELEMENTARIES: The more appropriate group name for elementals.

ELEMENTS: There are five magickal elements, Air, Earth, Fire, Water, and Spirit, although usually Spirit is ignored and they are described as the four elements. They relate to relative levels of moisture and heat and should not be confused with the Western scientific concept that uses the same term.

EMPTY ONES: Entities who personify despair on a physical or non-physical level. Physical empty ones have no soul, no hope for the future.

ENOCHIAN: A system of magick channeled by Dr. John Dee, advisor to Queen Elizabeth I, and his assistant Edward Kelly. It was attributed to Enoch by them, and is sometimes called "Angelic." The system was further developed by the Golden Dawn.

ETHERIC BODY: An emanation of all created things. It is not the true astral double and is something like "halfway between astral and physical." It sometimes can take on the appearance of a person on a higher plane, but is always attached to a living being.

EVOCATION: To evoke.

EVOKE: To bring an entity from the higher planes into your field of awareness.

EXARP: Pronounced "Ex-ar-pay," it is the Enochian name for the Spirit of Air.

F

FIRE: One of the five magickal elements. It has the qualities of being warm and dry.

FIRST MATTER: A mixture of the Serpent and the Menstruum. Used in alchemy and sex magick.

FORTUNE, DION (née Violet Firth, 1890–1946): Famous occultist, author, and founder of the Fraternity of the Inner Light. She followed three magickal paths: ceremonial magick (as represented by her classical books such as *The Mystical Qabalah*, 1935), Paganism (as represented in her novels such as *Sea Priestess*, 1938), and mystical Christianity combined with Arthurian myth.

FOUR WORLDS: A traditional way of looking at the Tree of Life as being composed of four divisions or Worlds. There are many variations on this theory. See HA-OH-LAHM.

G

GAHB-RAY-EL: Gabriel. Archangel of the west and elemental Water.

GARDNER, GERALD B. (1884–1964): His book in 1954 titled *Witchcraft Today* was the first about Witchcraft by a self-proclaimed Witch. He is considered the father of modern Wicca.

GEMATRIA: A method of the Literal Kabalah, which assigns numbers to each of the Hebrew letters. Words of equal value are believed to have an important relationship with each other.

GEOMANCY: A form of divination that began by randomly making marks on the earth with a pointed stick. Today it is more common to use a pencil on paper or replace it by taking a random number of stones in the hand from a group of stones kept for this purpose. The result is a number of symbolic figures placed on a type of astrological chart and interpreted. The geomantic symbols are often used in other magickal situations.

GHOSTS: When not caused by psychokinetic activity in a living person (as is usually the case with a poltergeist), they are the astral bodies of people stuck in the lowest of the spiritual planes after the death of the physical body.

GIBURAH: Strength. The 5th Sephira on the Tree of Life.

GNOSTIC TRANCE: In Chaos Magick, an altered state where you are totally focused on one thing. Such an intense focus induces trance.

GOETIA: Howling. A popular grimoire with instructions for evoking non-physical entities. A part of *The Lesser Key of Solomon.* Often mistakenly thought of as that entire book.

GOLDEN DAWN: See HERMETIC ORDER OF THE GOLDEN DAWN.

GREAT VOICE: Silently. In some situations it is impossible to vibrate words out loud. In these instances you can say them to yourself, thus using the "Great Voice." However, they should still cause the universe to vibrate (see VIBRATORY FORMULAE).

GREAT WORK: The work of achieving enlightenment and unity with Divinity (some people would say unity with your Higher Self).

GREY MAGICK: The science and art of causing change to occur in conformity with will, using means not currently understood by traditional Western science, for the purpose of causing either physical or non-physical good to yourself or others, and is done either consciously or unconsciously.

GRIMOIRE: Literally a "black book," but meaning a grammar book. A text on magick. The famous old ones are all incomplete and should serve as guides only.

G'UPH: The physical body as an aspect of the mind.

H

HAHM-SAH: The oldest known mantra, it is the sound of the breath going in and out. It literally means "swan." In some traditions it is reversed, being So-Aham.

HA-OH-LAHM: The World or Universe. In particular, one of the Four Kabalistic Worlds:

> *AHSSIAH:* The fourth of the Four Kabalistic Worlds in descending order. It is the World of Action.

ATZILOOT: The uppermost of the Four Kabalistic Worlds. It means the World of Archetypes or Emanations.

BRI-YAH: The second of the Four Kabalistic Worlds in descending order. It means World of Creation.

YETZIRAH: The third of the Four Kabalistic Worlds in descending order. It means World of Formation.

HCOMA: Pronounced "Hay-coh-mah," it is the Enochian name for the Spirit of Water.

HEATHEN: A person who comes from the heaths. This word has a history similar to Pagan.

HEGELIAN DIALECTIC: See THESIS-ANTITHESIS-SYNTHESIS THEORY.

HEH-CHA-LOHT: Ascent. See MERKABAH.

HERMETIC ORDER OF THE GOLDEN DAWN: A secret society organized in the late 1880s, often referred to simply as the Golden Dawn or the G.D. It was able to synthesize several forms of magick and occult philosophy into a coherent but complex whole. Most books on magick written in the twentieth and twenty-first centuries have been written by people who were members of that order, or who were directly or indirectly influenced by that organization.

HESED: Mercy. The 4th Sephira on the Tree of Life.

HIGH MAGICK: Ritual or ceremonial magick. It is called "high" because it was first developed in cities, which were at a higher elevation than where farming was done.

HOCHMA: Wisdom. The 2nd Sephira on the Tree of Life. It is at the top of the right or masculine pillar of the Tree.

HODE: Splendor. The 8th Sephira on the Tree of Life.

HOLY GUARDIAN ANGEL: An expression meaning your Higher Self to some, a more knowledgeable non-physical entity to others. Contacting the H.G.A. is known as "The Knowledge and Conversation of Your Holy Guardian Angel." Establishing this relationship is considered to be the same as achieving enlightenment or cosmic consciousness.

I

IAO: The supreme godhead in Gnosticism. Also associated with the deities Isis, Apophis, and Osiris.

IGGERET HA-KODESH: A medieval Jewish "marriage manual" dating from around the end of the thirteenth century. In English it is known as *The Holy Letter*. It contains many of the secrets of sex magick.

ILLUMINATES OF THANATEROS: Magickal group founded in 1978 by Peter Carroll and Ray Sherwin, the IOT is focused around the practice of Chaos Magick. In 1991 the IOT morphed into an Inner Order while the Outer Order became known as the Pact.

INFLAME THYSELF WITH PRAYER: Advice given in the grimoire *The Book of the Sacred Magic of Abramelin the Mage*, explaining that for success in rituals you must become exceedingly passionate—inflamed—about achieving your magickal goal.

INNER ALCHEMY: A method of controlling the psychic energies of the body as they are raised during sexual excitation for the purposes of working magick and achieving enlightenment.

INNER ORDER: In magickal organizations an in-group where the most potent secrets are taught to and practiced by people who have been in the Outer Order and proved their worthiness.

INRI: Letters supposedly written on Jesus' cross, they have a multiplicity of meanings to different people and organizations.

IN TIME: A person is said to be "In Time" when they experience themselves as being at the center of time, with their timeline going through them.

INTUITION: A message sent from the unconscious to the conscious.

INVOCATION: To invoke.

INVOKE: To allow an entity to use your body as a temporary vehicle for communicating with the physical world.

I.O.B.: A powerful method of getting rid of negative things in your life, based on Golden Dawn techniques mixed with methods of exorcism. It means "Identify, Objectify, Banish."

IROB: Acronym for "I Read One Book." A description of people who have little knowledge or training but set themselves up as experts.

J

JESUS: A title known as the Pentagrammaton.

K

KABALAH: A spiritual system that forms the mystical underpinnings for the three major Western religions as well as for modern Western ceremonial magick. The word is transliterated Hebrew, and is spelled in English in various ways, including Qabala, Cabala, etc.

KABALISTIC PATHWORKING: Astral projecting through the Tree of Life in order to meet and communicate with non-physical spiritual entities.

KALAKAKRA: Tantric magick circle.

KAREZZA: A male technique for delaying orgasm, it is said to have beneficial effects for both members of a loving couple.

KARMA: Sanskrit for "action." It is the law of cause and effect, or getting back in response to what you give out. It may take multiple lifetimes to work out your karma. The Hebrew term for this is "Teekoon."

KETER: Crown. The 1st Sephira on the Tree of Life. It is at the top of the Middle Pillar on the Tree.

KIA: In Chaos Magick a loosely defined term similar to the sense of Spirit as the body's animating force. It has some of the functions of the soul but is not the soul.

KRISHNA: Although only the sixth avatar, or incarnation, of Vishnu, Krishna has developed into one of the most popular Hindu deities due to his representing unbridled sexuality. Some would downplay the reason for his popularity.

KUNDALINI: An energy said to lie dormant at the base of the spine, ready to rise through the spine to the top of the head and bring enlightenment. Actually, this was an allegory. In reality, the energy is controlled by the mind.

KUNDALINI YOGA: Allegedly a method of exciting the kundalini energy at the base of the spine and causing it to rise up to the head, bringing enlightenment.

L

LARVAE: Non-physical psychic vampires said to "feed" on the energies of the sick and injured.

LAYA YOGA: Pronounced "Lie-oh-ga," it uses breath and visualization to re-create the changes that the physical and spiritual bodies go through during sexual activity. This is usually presented as an allegory of causing the kundalini energy to rise. Laya Yoga is the source idea for kundalini yoga.

LBRP: The Lesser Banishing Ritual of the Pentagram. A powerful technique popularized by the Golden Dawn to rid your area of unwanted negative influences. Also good for psychic self-defense.

LEMURES: See LARVAE.

LEVI, ELIPHAS (actually Eliphas Levi Zaed. Née Alphonse Louis Constant, 1810–1875): Famous nineteenth-century occultist whose writing helped begin the "French Occult Revival" that led to the founding of the Golden Dawn in the late 1880s.

LICENSE TO DEPART: Granting an entity permission to leave an area to which it was summoned.

LINGUISTICS: The study of language and how its use impacts all persons involved in a communication.

LITERAL KABALAH: The interpretation of codes found in Hebrew words, especially words found in the *Torah* and other mystical books. Methods include Gematria, Notarikon, and Temurah.

LITTLE NASTIES: Non-physical dwellers on the astral plane that can be shocking when first seen. This happens when the practice of magick opens up the ability to see onto the astral plane. Little Nasties may be surprising, but are harmless.

LOAS: Deities in Afro-Caribbean religions such as Voodoo, Santeria, etc. They enter their devotionaries, and the worshippers act like the deity and are treated as the deity by other worshipers.

LOW MAGICK: The magick of Paganism, which was developed in the low lands where farming was performed.

LURIA, ISAAC (1534–1572): Famous Jewish Kabalist. His prayers form part of standard Jewish prayer books today. One of his major interests was reincarnation and transmigration of souls.

LUSTING FOR RESULTS: Being focused on results rather than on the ritual to obtain the results. It uncenters you, diminishing your focus and chances for success.

M

MAGICK: The science and art of causing change to occur in conformity with will using means not currently understood by traditional Western science. The use of the letter "k" at the end of the word was reintroduced by Aleister Crowley to differentiate real magick from what a trickster or conjurer does on stage with hats, handkerchiefs, and rabbits. To some, the "k" also stands for *kteis,* a Latin word for the female genitals, thus indicating sex magick to those who practice that form of magick.

MAGICKAL DIARY: Also known as a Ritual Diary, a place to store records of the rituals you perform and the results of those rituals.

MAGICKAL HOURS: See PLANETARY HOURS.

MAGICKAL MEMORY: The memory of past lives.

MAGICKAL RITUAL: Repeated actions for a magickal purpose.

MAHATANTRA: Great Tantra. An orgasmic experience that results in an altered state of consciousness commonly known as enlightenment.

MAHLKOOT: Kingdom. The 10th and last Sephira on the Tree of Life. It is at the bottom of the central pillar and relates to our physical plane.

MAJOR ARCANA: The twenty-two picture cards of the Tarot that are considered to be of vital importance by occultists. They relate to the paths on the Tree of Life and are used in Kabalistic Pathworking.

MANTRA: A sound, word, or phrase of spiritual importance. They are frequently used with extensive repetition. Although some say that any phrase or sound can be used, certain special mantras of mystical import can make profound changes in a person mentally, physically, emotionally, and spiritually.

MARIOLATRY: The veneration of Jesus' mother, Mary. Some say this is a form of pre-Christian goddess worship hidden within the guise of Christianity.

MATHERS, S. L. MACGREGOR (1854–1918): A founder of the Golden Dawn who became the leader and guiding light of the group until schisms developed and the group divided.

MAYA: Illusion. A Sanskrit word which does not mean, as many people believe, that the world is an illusion. Actually, it means that our interpretation of the world around us is an illusion.

MEDITATION: The act of quieting the inner voice of the conscious so that you can commune with your Higher Self and the universe.

MEDIUM: A person who lets the consciousness of an entity, allegedly a dead person, take over his or her consciousness. Also, a person who communicates with the dead or other spirits.

MEE-CHAI-EL: Michael. Archangel of the south and of elemental Fire.

MENTAL PROJECTION: The ability to send your mind to a location distant from your physical body. Not true astral projection. Bi-location.

MENSTRUUM (also MENSTRUUM OF THE GLUTEN): In alchemy, the result of the slow heating of a substance in the Athanor. In sex magick, the female sexual lubricating fluids and/or female ejaculatory fluids.

MERKABAH: Throne. Merkabah Mysticism was a system of pre-Kabalistic spirituality where one would (astral?) travel through seven palaces with a goal of seeing God on His Throne.

MIDDLE PILLAR: The central column on the Tree of Life. Also a ritual designed to help move the body's energy throughout the "Middle Pillar" of the spine, similar to Laya Yoga.

MINOR ARCANA: The fifty-six cards of the Tarot comparing to the modern-day deck of playing cards, but having an extra court card for each of the four suits. Traditionally numerical rather than pictorial, they relate to the Sephiroht on the Tree of Life.

MITZVAH: Hebrew word that means both "blessing" and "commandment."

MORAL TRIANGLE: When looking at the Tree of Life as if composed of three triangles, it is the central triangle, with one point down.

MOTE: An Old English word meaning "must." Frequently used at the end of rituals or spells in the expression "So mote it be."

MOTIVATED FORGETTING: A term used in psychology for the process of causing yourself to forget those things that would be uncomfortable or unacceptable to your current state of consciousness. It is why we remember so little of infancy and very early childhood.

MOTTO: A magickal name or expression. Today, magicians and Pagans choose one for themselves as a representation of what they magickally represent. This has been the practice of many magickal orders, the most famous known examples being from the Golden Dawn. However, most of their mottoes were simply family mottoes or taken from a book of family mottoes.

MUDRA: A Tantric positioning of the hands with mystical import.

MUNDANE TRIANGLE: When looking at the Tree of Life as if composed of three triangles, it is the lowest triangle with one point down.

MURRAY, MARGARET (1863–1963): British anthropologist whose controversial book *The Witch Cult in Western Europe* in 1921 sparked a revival of interest in Witchcraft.

N

NANTA: Pronounced "En-ah-en-tah," it is the Enochian name for the Spirit of Earth.

NATURAL MAGICK: See LOW MAGICK.

NEGATION: Erasing from your consciousness something you have been concentrating on. The third step in true meditation.

NEGATIVE GOLDEN RULE: Don't do unto others if you would not have them do the same unto you.

NEOPHYTE: A beginner. Literally, a new plant. In many magickal orders people in the first or earliest degree are known as neophytes.

NEPHESCH (or NEPHESH): The most superficial layer of the unconscious. The Lower Self. Corresponds with the 9th Sephira on the Tree of Life.

NESCHAMAH: The intuition. Corresponds with the 3rd Sephira on the Tree of Life.

NETZACH: Victory. The 7th Sephira on the Tree of Life.

NEURO-LINGUISTIC PROGRAMMING: A set of techniques involving the use of language, observation, and understanding the functioning of the mind that allows practitioners to achieve excellence.

NLP: See NEURO-LINGUISTIC PROGRAMMING.

NOTARIKON: An aspect of the Literal Kabalah that works with acronyms or abbreviations.

NUMEROLOGY: The attribution of meanings to numbers. Numbers are determined by certain systems (such as translating a name into a number) or by chance (such as by throwing dice), and divinations are given as a result of those numbers and their meanings.

O

OCCULT: Hidden or secret. "Occult" wisdom means "secret" wisdom. It does not mean "evil."

OHR-REE-EHL: Oriel. Archangel of the north and of elemental Earth.

OLYMPIAN SPIRITS: Planetary entities described in the grimoire, the *Arbatel of Magick.* The sigils of the spirits are often used in magick, especially on talismans.

OPENING BY WATCHTOWER: A powerful ritual to begin any magickal operation.

ORGONE: A name used for prana, ruach, qi, or chi, the universal life force, by Dr. Wilhelm Reich.

O.T.O.: Ordo Templi Orientis. A well-known and still existing occult order which has become the primary promulgator of the teachings of Aleister Crowley, who at one time was the head of the order.

OUTER ALCHEMY: Making use of the magically charged sexual fluids for magickal purposes.

OUTER ORDER: In magickal organizations such as orders and covens, a wider membership wherein people are taught the basic theories and concepts of the group. If people last through this training and prove their worthiness and dedication, they may move to the Inner Order.

P

PAGAN: From the Latin *Paganus,* "those of the earth." Originally it was a derogatory term used to describe people of the land and their simplicity. Later, it focused on their choice of Pre-Christian deities. Today, many Witches and Wiccans consider themselves to be Pagans or Neo-Pagans.

PAGANISM: Although most people today use this as a derogatory term, occultists simply equate it with people following non-Jewish, non-Christian, or non-Islamic religions.

PANDAMONAEON: According to Chaos magicians, the coming aeon of human evolution.

PARADIGM SHIFTING: A concept from Chaos Magick where a practitioner uses a deity from one pantheon in a ritual from a completely different paradigm. For example, using a deity from Lovecraft's fictional Cthulhu Mythos in a ritual based on a Kabalistic paradigm or a Wiccan paradigm. Paradigm shifting can have a powerful effect on a practitioner, opening him or her up to potentials that are not limited by their normal worldview.

PATHWORKING: A visualized journey, or guided visualization, usually for some spiritual purpose.

PENTACLE: Any device that has a pentagram or five-pointed star on it. Also, the tool of elemental Earth.

PENTAGRAM: A five-pointed star. It is used to represent spirituality (Spirit over the four elements) when it has one point up. With two points up it is said to represent materialism or "evil." Some forms of Wicca, especially in the U.K., use the pentagram with two points up as a symbol, and for them it has no evil or negative connotation.

PENTAGRAMMATON: Five-letter name YHShVH or YHVShH, which is pronounced "Yeh-hah-shu-ah" or "Yeh-ho-vah-sha," respectively. It adds the Shin to the Tetragrammaton, indicating the addition of the Spirit of God to the formula of the ultimate divinity. Sometimes represented in English as "Jesus."

PHYSICAL PLANE: Our physical world.

PILLAR OF MERCY: The right-hand column on the Tree of Life. It is composed of the 2nd, 4th, and 7th Sephiroht, and said to be masculine in nature.

PILLAR OF MILDNESS: The central column on the Tree of Life. It is composed of the 1st, 6th, 9th, and 10th Sephiroht. Also known as the Middle Pillar.

PILLAR OF SEVERITY: The left-hand column on the Tree of Life. It is composed of the 3rd, 5th, and 8th Sephiroht and is said to be feminine in nature.

PLACE OF COMFORT: A special place within a magickal circle for a couple to engage in sex magick.

PLANETARY HOURS: A division of the day and night into sections ruled by the energies of the planets. To determine the length of each Planetary Hour, divide the daylight hours by twelve. They will be different in length than the night hours (to discover the length of which you divide the total time of darkness into twelve equal periods) except on the equinoxes, when the Planetary Hours are all sixty minutes in length.

POLTERGEIST: The poltergeist phenomenon often gives the appearance of being a ghost. However, it is actually a manifestation of the unconscious of a human, most frequently (but not always) a girl entering puberty. The word itself is German for "noisy spirit."

POSITIVE AFFIRMATIONS: The use of phrases, repeated over and over, as a means of influencing your unconscious in order to cause a change on the astral plane which, in turn, will result in a change in the physical plane. Although a popular technique, *by itself* it is of little use to practical magicians.

POSTMODERN: A reaction to Modernism, it views every paradigm as having its own sets of beliefs, ideologies, and theories, and attempts to reject them.

POSTMODERN MAGICK: It abandons all previous beliefs about *why* any form of magick works while acknowledging that it does work. It replaces them with concepts based on linguistics and semiotics.

POTENT ORGASM: A concept popularized by Wilhelm Reich, it is the idea of being so caught up in the very animalistic enjoyment of sex that nothing can be thought of. An aspect of sex magick.

PRACTICAL KABALAH: Refers to Kabalistic methods of making talismans and amulets.

PRACTICE: What you must do to become a magician.

PRANA: Pronounced "pran-yah," it is a Sanskrit word referring to psychic energy that is triggered by breathing practices.

PROJECTING SIGN: A physical action used in magick to project raised magickal energy that is within the body toward a local or distant location, such as to charge a talisman. Step forward with the left foot and thrust the arms forward with the fingers together and the fingertips pointing forward. Look down your arms and past your thumbs. The energy flows out of you through your eyes and arms.

PSEUDO-GHOSTS: Entities similar to the Little Nasties. By reading the Astral Light they can tell you about your past and future, giving the appearance of being the ghost of a loved one. They "feed" off the energy given to them by those thinking they are the spirits of deceased relatives.

PSYCHIC ATTACK: An attack on a person using magickal or psychic methods. In reality they are very rare, almost non-existent. When they do occur they are usually caused by a current of anger or rage and hit you at your "weakest link."

PYTHAGOREAN NUMEROLOGY: Name given to a system of numerology that associates the numbers 1–9 to the English alphabet in its natural order. Hence, A = 1, B = 2, etc. After you reach I = 9, the process is cycled back to one so that J = 1, K = 2, etc. Numbers thus obtained are used for numerological divinations.

Q

QABALAH: See KABALAH.

R

RAH-FAY-EL: Raphiel, Archangel of the east and elemental Air.

RAINBOW WAND: A central tool for use by a magician, based on the Lotus Wand as used by the Golden Dawn. It is not associated with any one element, being more directed toward planetary energies.

REGARDIE, FRANCIS ISRAEL (née Israel Reguty, 1907–1985): After serving as Crowley's secretary, he joined the Golden Dawn under the sponsorship of Dion Fortune. He found the group almost moribund, so in order to save the order's secret teachings from oblivion, he broke his vows and revealed them in the four-volume (now one-volume) book, *The Golden Dawn.* As a result, more people than ever have studied the teachings of that group.

REICH, WILHELM (1897–1957): Psychiatrist who originally followed Freud, and then departed from Freud's orthodoxy. Introduced the concept of Orgone or universal life force and noted how it was related to sexuality. His books were burned by the U.S. government.

RELAXATION: The first step in true meditation.

RETORT: In alchemy, a type of container. In sex magick, the vagina.

RITUAL: A group of practices that is repeated.

RITUAL DIARY: Another term for Magickal Diary.

RITUAL MAGICK: Although this could refer to any type of magick where a pattern or ritual is followed, it usually applies to those styles of magick where more complex rituals are used. It is also used synonymously with ceremonial magick, although a ritual can be performed by one person while ceremonial magick requires several people.

ROSE CROSS: A symbol of the Golden Dawn and a ritual of protection and invisibility.

R.R. ET A.C.: Roseae Rubeae et Aureae Crucis. The Second or Inner Order of the Hermetic Order of the Golden Dawn. The R.R. et A.C. practiced ritual and ceremonial magick, while the Golden Dawn Outer Order, the one with which most people are familiar, did not. In English it means "Red Rose and Gold Cross."

RUACH: (1) The psychic energy, similar to prana and kundalini. (2) The conscious, consisting of the will, memory, imagination, reason, and desire. Corresponds with the 4th–8th Sephiroht. Also corresponds to the psychic center at the solar plexus.

RUACH ELOHEEM: The spirit of Divinity. Similar to Ruach, but on a cosmic scale. Corrupted into the Christian notion of the Holy Ghost or Holy Spirit.

S

SATAN: Hebrew for adversary. In Jewish tradition, Satan was a title and not a personal name. The Satan would question God (what today is called a "devil's advocate") but could only do God's bidding. In Christianity, Satan became a single entity who is the source of evil.

SATANISM: The supposed worship of Satan. There are generally two types of Satanists. Religious Satanists either see Satan as a misunderstood god or as a symbol for the supremacy of ego, leading to a philosophy similar to that of Ayn Rand and Nietzsche. There are a small number in the second type who are Self-Styled Satanists, usually focused around a charismatic leader with a philosophy based on fictional movies, novels, and random sources. Satanism in any form has no relationship to Wicca, although many have tried to make that association for reasons of power, politics, or lack of understanding.

SCANNING: A method used in meditation where you memorize small strips of a figure or diagram.

SÉANCE: (Pronounced "say-ahns") French for "meeting," a type of religious ritual practiced by Spiritists wherein a medium supposedly makes contact with dead relatives of those in attendance and shares what the dead have to say with the living. The rare physical séance includes paranormal activities ranging from disembodied voices to the appearance of small objects known as "apports," supposedly from the astral plane.

SEER: (Pronounced "see-ur") A person who does a divination. During evocation, the person who is in direct contact with the entity evoked.

SEMIOTICS: The study of the meaning of signs and symbols, their use, and how they relate to the objects or ideas to which they refer.

SEMIOTIC WEB: In Postmodern Magick, an interlocking group of symbols that form the codes that allow us to live in the "real world."

SEPHER YETZIRAH: The Book of Formation. Considered to be one of the first Kabalistic books.

SEPHIRA: An untranslatable word that seems to mean something akin to "numerical emanation." Usually pictured as way stations in the form of circles on popular diagrams of the Tree of Life. Because of their shape and the sound of the term, they are often referred to as "spheres."

SEPHIROHT: Plural of Sephira.

SERPENT: In alchemy, the result of heating a substance in the Athanor. In sex magick it is the semen.

SEX MAGICK: The ability to use the powerful energies raised during sexual activity for magickal purposes.

SHADOW: The "darker" side of your unconscious that includes such things as fears, angers, prejudices, etc. The Shadow can influence our thoughts and actions, leading from minor issues to major personal issues including obsessive-compulsive disorder and dangerous external behaviors ranging from irrational prejudice and xenophobia to various mob activities. Most people are unwilling to examine or even peek at those darker aspects of themselves. It is rare for individuals to integrate the Shadow, thus mastering it, without therapeutic intervention or focused introspection.

SHECHINAH: Pronounced "Sheh-chen-ah," it personifies the energy known as Ruach Eloheem as feminine. Similar to the Tantric notion of Shakti.

SHEE-OOL: A word from the *Tanach* meaning "ground" or "earth." In some instances it was translated as "Hell," probably for theo-political reasons. There is no Hell in the Kabalah because reincarnation is a part of the tradition.

SHERWIN, RAY: British occult author and publisher. One of the founders of Chaos Magick. His *The Book of Results* (1978) is considered one of the first books on Chaos Magick.

SHIN: Pronounced "sheen," it is a Hebrew letter symbolic of the Ruach Eloheem. When inserted into the Tetragrammaton it forms the Pentagrammaton, showing how we can purify ourselves by bringing the Spirit of Divinity within ourselves.

SIGIL: Sign or signature. A simple drawn symbol representing something else, usually a spirit, angel, archangel, aspect of divinity, other entity, or magickal goal.

SKYCLAD: A term used by Wiccans to indicate ritual nudity.

SMART GOALS: Codified and clarified by author Peter Drucker (1909–2005) in relation to management concepts in the 1950s, the concept of SMART goals is also associated with determining the most effective and attainable goals for magickal rituals. SMART is an acronym indicating that your goals should be specific, measurable, attainable, realistic, and given a time frame in which to occur.

SPARE, AUSTIN OSMAN (1886–1956): Acclaimed artist, occultist, and contemporary of Aleister Crowley. His ideas were ignored for years but have come to heavily influence modern magickal systems, especially Chaos Magick.

SPHERE OF AVAILABILITY: A concept first described by the occultist Ophiel (née Edward Peach, 1904–1988). The idea is that things you can achieve or gain through magick must be usable by you. If you cannot use them you are prevented from obtaining them, as they are outside your sphere of availability.

SPIRIT: (1) The animating life force. (2) A synonym for the soul. (3) A synonym for ghost.

SPIRITISM: Also known as Spiritualism, a religion of which a major aspect is the belief in communication with the dead during a ritual event called a séance.

STOCKHAM, ALICE BUNKER (1833–1912): The fifth woman made a doctor in the U.S.A., and a friend of Tolstoy, she got into trouble for promoting birth control. She ended up going to India and learned about the physical actions of Tantra. She brought back the technique of prolonged intercourse without orgasm as a means of birth control. Her book, titled *Karezza*, was published in 1896. The concepts have influenced many sex magick practitioners.

STURGEON'S LAW: Attributed to the famous science-fiction author Theodore Sturgeon (née Waldo, Edward Hamilton, 1918–1985). When asked if 90 percent of science fiction was crap, his response was that 90 percent of everything is crap.

SYMPATHETIC MAGICK: Using an item said to be "in sympathy" (using the archaic meaning of "being closely related") to focus a ritual, linking it to the source of the item. An example would be to focus a ritual on a lock of a person's hair to affect that person.

T

TALISMAN: Any object, sacred or profane, with or without appropriate symbols, charged or consecrated toward the achieving of a specific end. For occultists today, a talisman is a device that will draw something (health, money, wisdom) toward you.

TALLIT: A prayer shawl used by male Jews during certain prayers and rituals.

TALMUD: A huge commentary on the *Torah*.

TANACH: The Jewish Bible, commonly—and anti–Semitically—referred to as the "Old" Testament.

TANTRA: The warp and woof of all creation. A mystical philosophy from ancient India (and later Tibet) which sees the physical world as spiritual. Also, several ancient books about Tantric philosophy. As a complete spiritual philosophy, it looked at all aspects of existence, including sexuality. Today, many people think that Tantra is only about sex.

TAROT: A mystical set of cards having an uncertain origin. Although these cards, covered with images, are most commonly used for divination, they have much more spiritual purposes. Today a standard Tarot is composed of two main sections: the twenty-two picture cards of the Major Arcana and the fifty-six cards of the Minor Arcana consisting of four suits, each with ten numbered or "pip" cards and four images of European royalty or "court" cards.

TAU: Greek for the letter "T," and a cross with the horizontal bar at the top of the vertical line. The shape of the traditional magician's robe.

TEE-KOON: A Hebrew word meaning "correct." It is synonymous with the Sanskrit word "karma."

TELESMATIC IMAGES: A system used by the Golden Dawn to develop images for visualization based on the letters of the name of the entity to be given an image.

TEMURAH: A system of the Literal Kabalah that transposes letters of the Hebrew alphabet, especially words of the *Tanach*. The new words thus formed are said to be important.

TEPHILLIN: Small boxes containing scrolls with prayers written on them. They are worn by male Jews during certain prayers being held on by leather straps in a symbolic fashion.

TETRAGRAMMATON: The four-letter name of Divinity, YHVH. It indicates that the Divine is unitary and has united all opposites within itself.

T.F.Y.Q.A.: An abbreviation used by the author. It means "Think For Yourself. Question Authority," and indicates that just because someone writes or says something doesn't mean it will work for you. Each person should investigate everything for themselves. Dion Fortune meant the same thing when she wrote that there is no room for authority in occultism.

THEOSOPHICAL REDUCTION: A method used in numerology where the digits of a number are added together to form a new number. This is repeated until the sum is one digit (or is one of a few special two-digit "master" numbers).

THESIS-ANTITHESIS-SYNTHESIS THEORY: If you have one condition (A), and wish to change to a different condition (B), you usually get a mixture of the old and new (AB) rather than the new condition (B) you wanted.

THOUGHT CONTROL: A form of sex magick that is a method of controlling sexual energy via the mind during sexual excitation and orgasm.

THOUGHT FORM: Similar to an artificial elemental, it is a magically created non-physical entity formed to accomplish a specific task for its magician creator.

THREE TRIANGLES: A way of looking at the Tree of Life as if composed of three triangles. These triangles are the Celestial, Moral, and Mundane.

THREE VEILS OF NEGATIVE EXISTENCE: Descriptions of the ultimate unknowable deity, beginning with Ain, or no-thing understandable, then the Ain Soph, or the quality of limitlessness. The third veil is the Ain Soph Or, or limitless white light.

THROUGH TIME: People are said to be "Through Time" when they experience their timeline as existing completely outside of themselves.

TIFERET: Beauty. The 6th Sephira on the Tree of Life.

TIMELINE: How a person experiences and interacts with time.

TORAH: The first five books of the *Tanach*, or Jewish Bible. Mystics believe that much of it is in Kabalistic codes.

TRANSMIGRATION: The idea that when we reincarnate we can go up or down the evolutionary ladder.

TREASURE MAP: A drawing or collage used to help you with creative visualization.

TREE OF LIFE: A glyph that is a central symbol of the Kabalah. It can help you memorize a vast amount of material by working as a sort of card file. It is also a way of understanding the Tarot, psychology, the creation of the universe, astrology, and more. It is also a map of the astral plane.

TRIANGLE OF THE ART: A large figure wherein non-physical entities appear to those trained to see them.

TRIANGLE OF MANIFESTATION: A positioning of the hands which forms a triangle. Used in Grey Magick.

U

UNWRITTEN KABALAH: That part of the Kabalah that deals with correspondences on the Tree of Life.

V

VÉVÉ: A symbol drawn on the ground in Voodoo ceremonies as a talisman or device to attract the loas or gods.

VIBRATORY FORMULAE: In ceremonial magick certain words are meant to be vibrated. This means that when loudly sounded they should cause not only you but all of existence to vibrate along with the sound.

VISUALIZATION: Seeing an image in the mind's eye. This is a willed image, and should not be confused with a hallucination, which is an unwilled picture in the mind's eye.

VOODOO: A religion mixing Roman Catholicism and African religion. Magick is an important aspect of the religion. A full discussion of Voodoo is out of the range of this book.

W

WAITE, A. E. (1857–1942): A member of the Golden Dawn, he broke it into pieces by demanding that they cease doing magick and that advancement in the order not be due to knowledge and work but mere time in the order. He wrote several books that were basically compilations from other sources with his comments. His writing style is not considered modern, and whatever wisdom he may have wished to share (suspect as some hold it to be) is often hidden beneath turgid prose. Perhaps his most important accomplishment is the production of a Tarot deck (drawn by Pamela Colman "Pixie" Smith, 1878–1951) based on the Golden Dawn deck, which has become the model or standard for Tarot decks over the past 100 years.

WAND: The tool of elemental Fire.

WANING: The Moon from just after full Moon until it disappears.

WATER: One of the five magickal elements. It has the property of being cool and moist.

WAXING: The Moon from when the new Moon can just be seen to the time of the full Moon.

WHITE MAGICK: The science and art of causing change to occur in conformity with will, using means not currently understood by traditional Western science, for the purpose of obtaining the Knowledge and Conversation of your Holy Guardian Angel.

WICCA: Although properly pronounced "wee-cha," most people today pronounce it "wick-kah." It is the word from which the term "Witch" evolved. It meant "to bend," and implied that people could bend reality to their wills. There is also some evidence showing that it means "wise," indicating that those of the Wicca are the "wise ones."

WICCE: Feminine form of "Wicca."

WIDDERSHINS: Counterclockwise. Occasionally the direction moved in within a magickal circle, but rarely so.

WITCHCRAFT: Popularized by Gerald Gardner and many others, it is a peaceful religion based on the worship of the generative forces in nature. Witches worship the Horned God of the Hunt and the threefold Goddess of Life. They are not Satanists; in fact, they don't believe in Satan.

Y

YEH-CHEE-DAH: Psychic center just above the head, it is also the deepest level of the unconscious. The Higher Self.

YESODE: Foundation. The 9th Sephira on the Tree of Life.

YETZIRATIC WORLD: Kabalistic name for the astral plane.

YHVH: An English representation of four Hebrew letters, Yud Heh Vahv Heh. A code for the ultimate name of Divinity, indicating that the Divine is a blending of everything physical and spiritual. Mistakenly pronounced "Jehovah" or "Yahweh" by some ill-informed people.

YI KING: An ancient book of wisdom from China commonly called the *I Ching*. Like the Tarot it has many spiritual purposes, but is popularly known for giving divinations.

YOGA: Union. Especially a union between a person and Divinity.

YONI: A Sanskrit term for the female genitalia.

Z

ZOHAR: A huge, mystical commentary on the *Torah* first written down in the fourteenth century by Moses de Leon (1250–1305).

APPENDIX FIVE

Annotated Bibliography

(*Author's Note*: When I created this bibliography, and the bibliographies for each lesson, during the writing of the first edition of *Modern Magick*, I tried to be as thorough as possible, giving the dates and publishers for the editions of books I owned. As a collector of occult books, I knew that many people would be unable to obtain the editions I listed and some of the books I included were long out-of-print and difficult, expensive, or impossible to obtain. I have to admit that in some ways it was an egotistical attempt to show off my personal library and I am glad to say that I have grown beyond that. In order to be more practical and truly useful, this bibliography, and those at the end of each lesson, now include the most current publishers and publication dates at the time this is being written rather than the dates and publishers of the editions in my library. I have also tried to eliminate most books that are out-of-print at the time of this writing. Any books that are out-of-print and are included have been listed because of their importance, and thanks to the Internet, obtaining such books is much easier than when *Modern Magick* was originally published. And before anyone asks, sorry, but my collection is not a lending library.)

Achad, Frater (pseudo. of C. S. Jones). *The Anatomy of the Body of God*. Kessinger Publishing, 1977. Fascinating attempt to show that the Kabalistic Tree of Life is the basis of atomic structure. Amazing illustrations take the Tree into multiple dimensions.

———. *Crystal Vision Through Crystal Gazing*. Kessinger Publishing, 1942(?). Examines the idea of crystal gazing from a ceremonial magick point of view. As far as I know, this is the only book like this.

———. *Egyptian Revival or the Ever-Coming Son in the Light of the Tarot*. Kessinger Publishing, 1992. Achad's version of Crowley's version of the Kabalah.

———. *Liber Thirty-One*. Luxor Press, Inc., 1998. Explains the secret meanings in Crowley's *Book of the Law* and made Crowley think Achad was his magickal son.

———. *Q.B.L. or The Bride's Reception.* Weiser Books, 2005. Achad's version of the Kabalah that made Crowley disown him as a magickal son.

Agrippa, Henry C. *Three Books of Occult Philosophy.* Llewellyn Publications, 1992. The granddaddy of modern magick books and the source upon which many are based, usually without credit. Made better by the notes and clarifications of Donald Tyson.

Andrews, Ted. *Simplified Qabala Magic.* Llewellyn Publications, 2003. This small book gives a very simple and basic introduction to the Kabalah with a bit of practical information.

Ashcroft-Nowicki, Dolores. *The Ritual Magic Workbook.* Red Wheel/Weiser, 1998. One of the better books with practical instructions on magick by one of the most important living teachers of occultism.

Avalon, Arthur (pseud. of Woodroffe, Sir John). *Mahanirvana Tantra: Tantra of the Great Liberation.* CreateSpace, 2008. A key Tantric text presenting many of the important ideas and practices of Tantra as is commonly focused on by Westerners today.

Bach, Richard. *Illusions: The Adventures of a Reluctant Messiah.* Arrow Books, 2001. A groundbreaking book on the nature of reality, life, and spirituality. You will probably be able to get through this in one sitting. Very enjoyable, and if you read between the lines during the "vampire" scene, you'll see the difference between Crowley's motto and the Wiccan Rede.

Bardon, Franz. *Frabato the Magician.* Merkur Publishing Co., 2002.

———. *Initiation Into Hermetics.* Merkur Publishing Co., 2001.

———. *The Key to the True Qabbalah.* Merkur Publishing Co., 1996.

———. *The Practice of Magical Evocation.* Brotherhood of Life Books, 2001.

The above four books compose the major corpus of Bardon's works. He has his own theories which are not totally in line with most of traditional Western occultism. Still, many authors "borrow" from Bardon without giving him credit. See, for example, his concept of "fluid condensers." *Frabato* is primarily a loosely disguised autobiography and is well worth reading. Unfortunately, these books are translations from the original German, and can be difficult to wade through, but the effort to do so will be well rewarded.

Berg, Philip S. *The Wheels of a Soul.* Kabalah Publishing, 2004. Kosher Kabalah explanation of reincarnation. I liked some of Berg's earlier books, but I do not recommend many of them today, nor his more recent ones, because some people consider his organization, The Kabalah Centre, to be cultic. When I visited their Los Angeles site, a woman who greeted me spent most of her time trying to get me to spend hundreds of dollars on books in Hebrew. She told me it didn't matter if I couldn't read Hebrew because they'd send me information on how to simply look at the pages to get benefits.

Bonewits, P. E. I. *Real Magic* (Revised Edition). Red Wheel/Weiser, 1989. A famous modern history of magically oriented groups in the U.S. The revised edition shows a great maturity over the first edition. Bonewitz has gone on to become a leader in the Druid tradition and occultism.

Brennan, J. H. *Astral Doorways.* Thoth Publications, 1996. Astral projection taught from a ceremonial magick perspective.

Bruce, Robert, and Brian Mercer. *Mastering Astral Projection.* Llewellyn Publications, 2004.

———. *Mastering Astral Projection CD Companion.* Llewellyn Publications, 2007.

Most books on astral projection have an orientation on achieving projection within a few days. This book and CD set slows the process down to let you achieve and master astral projection over a three-month period. If other systems didn't work for you, this one might.

Buckland, Raymond. *Buckland's Complete Book of Witchcraft.* Llewellyn, 2002. This is probably the best practical guide to the modern practice of Witchcraft ever published. Perfect as a guide for individuals and covens.

Carnie, L.V. *Chi Gung.* Llewellyn Publications, 2002. Although a Chinese system for generating and directing inner (magickal) energy, the techniques can easily be applied to the work found in *Modern Magick.*

Carroll, Peter J. *Liber Kaos.* Red Wheel/Weiser, 1992. More of Carroll's ideas about Chaos Magick.

———. *Liber Null & Psychonaut.* Weiser, 1987. The two books responsible for popularizing Chaos magick in the U.S. Basic reading for all occultists.

Case, Paul F. *Tarot, The.* Tarcher, 2006. A semi-Kabalistic introduction to the Tarot by this one-time member of the Golden Dawn and founder of the Builders of the Adytum (B.O.T.A.).

Cicero, Chic, and Sandra Tabatha Cicero. *The Essential Golden Dawn.* Llewellyn, 2003. Regardie wrote *The Golden Dawn* just before WWII. This book by the Ciceros brings it up to date and makes the ideas and practices clear and easy to understand. An important book and a valuable resource.

———. *Secrets of a Golden Dawn Temple.* Thoth Publications, 2004. Simply the best book with instructions for building the tools and accoutrements of a Golden Dawn temple.

Cohen, Seymour. *The Holy Letter.* Jason Aronson, 1993. A little-known but excellent book on Kabalistic sex magick.

Conway, Flo, and Jim Siegelman. *Snapping.* Stillpoint Press, 2005. How do intelligent and psychologically balanced people end up becoming part of a cult? This is the book that explains how it can happen. I don't agree with all of their ideas, but by knowing what can happen, you can be prepared and prevent it.

Cooper, Phillip. *Basic Sigil Magic.* Weiser Books, 2001. More detailed information on working with sigils. While good for talismanists, it will be of special interest to those focusing on Chaos magick.

Crowley, Aleister. *777 and Other Qabalistic Writings of Aleister Crowley.* Weiser Books, 1986. At one time this was *the* must-have dictionary of Western Occultism. It's been superseded by other, more complete books by Godwin and Skinner, but it is familiar to so many magicians that it is still a popular resource.

———. *The Book of Lies.* Weiser Books, 1986. A delightfully playful exploration into the theories and practices of magick, often highly disguised. An advanced book not because of the content, but because you need to be able to see through the codes and blinds to understand it.

———. *The Book of Thoth.* Weiser, 1988. Crowley's last book published while he was alive, it shows that contrary to the claims of those who dislike him, his mind was still sharp, his memory fine, and he was highly creative. More than an exposition of the Tarot in general and his *Thoth Tarot* specifically, it's also a great introduction to Kabalah and Thelema.

———. *The Confessions of Aleister Crowley.* Penguin, 1989. Whether or not you are interested in magick, his autobiography—he called it an *autohagiography*, the autobiography of a saint—stands as one of his most readable and enjoyable works. Crowley went through various phases in his life, and was always writing. It can be misleading to pick up a book by Crowley and assume it is the essence of his writings on a subject without knowing how he was evolving when it was written. I would contend that it is impossible to understand Crowley without knowing his life. Get this book, the "Hag" as he called it, or a biography of his life.

———. *Eight Lectures on Yoga.* New Falcon Publications, 1992. Simply the best introduction to the theory of yoga ever written. Also known as "Yoga for Yahoos."

———. *Gems From the Equinox.* Weiser Books, 2007. From 1909 to 1913, Crowley published eleven enormous volumes of a "journal" called "The Equinox." Each was the size of a large book.

Most of each was written by Crowley, often using numerous pseudonyms. They included poetry, book reviews, and other bits of snarky contemporaneous comments that are irrelevant today. Within that, however, were incredible amounts of important spiritual information and magickal ritual. Israel Regardie collected, for magically oriented people, the important parts of those books in this one volume. An important addition to any occultist's library.

———. *The Goetia: The Lesser Key of Solomon the King.* Weiser Books, 1995. Although Crowley generally gets the credit for this, he actually did little work on it. Mathers is called the "translator," which is weird because the originals are in English! Crowley is listed as the "editor," but he didn't do much at all. He wrote a brief introduction (minimizing Mathers' work), added a few footnotes, and at the end, added a section with an interlinear translation of the evocations into Enochian. After it was published in England the book pirate L.W. de Laurence printed an unauthorized version in the U.S. He included the added section in the back, but instead of having the Enochian below the English, he simply put the same English under the English. When I first saw this, not knowing the history, it confused me to no end. There are more complete versions and ones with more notes and explanations, but this is the version that has been used by more magicians than any other. It's a basic and good resource.

———. *The Law is for All.* Thelema Media, 1996. For those into Crowley, his most important work. Contains *The Book of the Law*, the key work for Thelemic thought, and two commentaries on it.

———. *Magick.* Weiser, 1998. Although episodic, disconnected, and occasionally having blinds, still an excellent introduction to ceremonial magick ranging from beginning to advanced. Also includes Thelemic concepts interwoven in the text. Not a book to be read so much as studied. A brilliant exposition of *Magick in Theory and Practice.*

———. *Magick Without Tears.* New Falcon Publications, 1991. Crowley's most simple and clear book on magick. Although episodic and disjointed, it attempts to respond to questions he was asked. Explains topics not covered in his other books.

Crowley, Aleister, and Samuel Mathers. *The Goetia.* Weiser Books, 1995. One of the basic books for the practice of magickal evocation.

Cunningham, Scott. *Earth Power.* Llewellyn Publications, 2002.

———. *Cunningham's Encyclopedia of Crystal, Gem & Metal Magic.* Llewellyn Publications, 2002.

———. *Cunningham's Encyclopedia of Magical Herbs.* Llewellyn Publications, 2000.

———. *Magical Herbalism.* Llewellyn Publications, 2001.

These four books are a wonderful introduction to natural magick. The encyclopedias are a virtual must in the same way as Crowley's *777* and can assist in helping you develop your own lists of correspondences.

———. *Wicca: A Guide for the Solitary Practitioner.* Llewellyn Publications, 1993. Gerald Gardner is given credit for restarting (or starting) modern Wicca as a social, coven-oriented form. When this book originally appeared in 1988, it shifted into high gear a revolution resulting in the primary form of Wicca today, a religion followed by solitary practitioners who are not part of a coven structure. My friend Scott played his last joke on me when passed to the Summerland on my birthday in 1993. Now, I can't celebrate a birthday without thinking of him. He needn't have worried—I'll always remember my good friend. He is greatly missed by me and by many tens of thousands of his fans. He may be the most beloved writer on Wicca ever.

Denning, Melita, and Osborne Phillips. *Practical Guide to Astral Projection.* Llewellyn Publications, 2001. A clear and easy-to-follow method for learning to get out-of-body. For additional assistance get their *Deep Mind Tape for Astral Projection* (1979).

APPENDIX FIVE   475

———. *Practical Guide to Creative Visualization.* Llewellyn, 2002. If you have read these lessons, you know I am not a fan of exclusively using creative visualization. Rather, I think it should be a part of Kabalistic Mental Magick. Still, it's a good idea to learn this aspect of the more complete system, and to that end this is one of the better books on the subject.

———. *Practical Guide to Psychic Self-Defense.* Llewellyn, 2002. One of the best books available on the subject, period. There is none of the usual paranoia found in other books of this sort and it has usable, practical techniques for the magickal practitioner.

Douglas, Nik, and Penny Slinger. *Sexual Secrets.* Destiny Books, 1999. This book is held in high esteem by many as an introduction to Tantric and Taoist sexuality. I find this curious, as it has relatively little information but lots of illustrations. The illustrations are beautifully done, but I find it odd that I didn't see any credits for the original photos on which they were based.

Dukes, Ramsey (originally published using the pseudonym Lemuel Johnstone). *SSOTBME Revised.* The Mouse That Spins, 2002. This book had a powerful impact on me as a young man when it first appeared in 1975. It seemed like a magickal drug trip, where the words seemed to go round and round but took you to new concepts and ways of thinking. No wonder Dukes influenced the Chaos Magick movement.

Dunn, Patrick. *Magic, Power, Language, Symbol.* Llewellyn Publications, 2008.

———. *Postmodern Magic.* Llewellyn Publications, 2005.

These two books are the starting points for Postmodern Magick, a system which blends all of the latest concepts in magick into a theoretical and practical whole. If they catch on, they are clearly the future of magick moving into the twenty-first century. Popularity, however, is fickle, and only time will tell how important these books are. People doubted me when I raved about *SSOTBME* and *Liber Null.* I hope you won't feel left behind if you don't discover the concepts behind Postmodern Magick.

DuQuette, Lon Milo. *The Chicken Qabalah of Rabbi Lamed Ben Clifford.* Weiser Books, 2001. A wonderful and intuitive introduction to concepts of the Kabalah presented in DuQuette's inimitable humorous style. Great for beginners and filled with insights for more advanced students.

———. *The Magick of Aleister Crowley.* Weiser Books, 2003. Crowley's books are sometimes difficult to understand. This book brings a modern introduction to his presentations along with examples of Crowley's thelemic rituals.

Farrar, Janet, and Stewart Farrar. *A Witches' Bible.* Phoenix Publishing, 1996.

———. *Eight Sabbats for Witches.* Phoenix Publishing, 1988.

These two books form a complete system of Witchcraft, combining ancient traditions with Alexandrian Witchcraft.

Farrell, Nick. *Magical Pathworking.* Llewellyn Publications, 2004. One of the few good books on pathworking and Kabalistic Pathworking.

Fortune, Dion. *Aspects of Occultism.* Weiser, 2000. Good introduction to many occult topics. Not important as a primary source, but good additional reading to fill out your knowledge.

———. *The Mystical Qabalah.* Lulu.com, 2008. Another must-have book. The classic text concerning the Golden Dawn's interpretation of the Sephiroht. Clear and easy to understand.

———. *Sane Occultism and Practical Occultism in Daily Life.* Aquarian Press, 1995. Two of Fortune's books in one volume. *Sane Occultism* gives good advice on how to prevent yourself from becoming a "space cadet," or how to bring yourself down to Earth. The second, like Crowley's *Magick Without Tears,* answers questions raised in letters to her on topics like past lives, karma, divination, etc. Not one of my favorites by her, but still valuable for extra study.

Franck, Adolphe. *The Kabbalah.* Forgotten Books, 2008. An excellent introduction to the Kosher Kabalah. Shows similarities between that and WASP Kabalah, and thus is liked by Western occultists.

Frazer, Sir James. *The Golden Bough* (abridged edition). Oxford University Press, 1998. A classic study of ancient myth and legend used by many Pagans as a resource. It's an important book, but unless you're an in-depth researcher, get the abridged edition.

Gardner, Gerald. *High Magic's Aid.* Pentacle Enterprises, 1999. An excellent and exciting comparison of Witchcraft and ceremonial magick in the form of a novel.

———. *Witchcraft Today.* Citadel, 2004. When originally published in the early 1950s, it helped to start the modern Witchcraft movement.

Garrison, Omar. *Tantra: The Yoga of Sex.* Three Rivers Press, 1983. An introduction to Tantric sexuality that has been very popular over the years. It is good, but it doesn't reach a level of excellence as Garrison was not initiated into any Tantric traditions and didn't understand the inner concepts and secrets. Still, in my opinion it's better than most on the subject.

Godwin, David. *Godwin's Cabalistic Encyclopedia.* Llewellyn Publications, 2002. The first book to really supersede Crowley's *777* with lots more information in an easy-to-use format. Truly a must for all occultists as an encyclopedia of correspondences.

González-Wippler, Migene. *A Kabbalah for the Modern World.* Llewellyn Publications, 2002. An absolutely wonderful introduction to the Kabalah. Don't let her light style deceive you—this book is filled with modern and historical information from both the Kosher and WASP Kabalah.

Grant, Kenneth. *The Magical Revival.* Skoob Books, 1993.

———. *Aleister Crowley & The Hidden God.* Skoob Books, 1995.

———. *Cults of the Shadow.* Skoob Books, 1995.

———. *Nightside of Eden.* Skoob Books, 1995.

———. *Outside the Circles of Time.* Holmes Publishing Group, 2008.

———. *Hecate's Fountain.* Skoob Books, 1993.

———. *Outer Gateways.* Skoob Books, 1995.

———. *Beyond the Mauve Zone.* Skoob Books, 1996.

———. *The Ninth Arch.* Starfire Publishing, 2002.

These books by Grant are listed in the order they were originally published because to understand them requires knowing what he previously wrote. These books claim to be an expansion on Crowley's works. Certainly they take sex magick and the concept of dealing with non-physical entities far beyond anything in this course. It's advanced work and, to some people, downright weird and even frightening. Many people, including F. I. Regardie, disagree with Grant's theories and the techniques he hints at. His use of language is precise but often as difficult to understand as his seeming pride at "tangential tantrums," physical results of rituals that go horribly wrong. Is this fiction? Metaphor? Reality? Whatever these books are, they have influenced many contemporary occultists, although I find more people talk about his books than have actually read them.

Gray, William G. *The Ladder of Lights.* Red Wheel/Weiser, 1981. Although it is somewhat dated, it is still a good introduction to the Tree of Life.

Greer, John Michael. *The Art and Practice of Geomancy.* Weiser Books, 2009. In these lessons I have described the use of geomantic symbols on talismans. The symbols, however, are part of a larger system primarily used for divination. This book explains the ancient system in detail.

———. *Inside a Magical Lodge.* Llewellyn Publications, 1998. Information on and how to set up and run a magickal order. A great resource, especially if you're thinking of starting a group to work the teachings of *Modern Magick* or another ceremonial magick tradition.

———. *Paths of Wisdom.* Thoth Publications, 2007. An introduction to the Kabalah and Kabalistic magick. A good book to read in order to get another interpretation of the material presented here.

Grimassi, Raven. *The Wiccan Mysteries.* Llewellyn Publications, 2002.

———. *Ways of the Strega.* Llewellyn Publications, 2000.

Raven has been one of my teachers and continues to be my friend. *The Wiccan Mysteries* is an excellent exploration of Wicca today. *Ways of the Strega* is an introduction to an ancient system of Italian Witchcraft updated for modern practitioners. Both books are filled with information, and I highly recommend all of Raven's books.

Harms, Daniel, and John Wisdom Gonce. *The Necronomicon Files.* Red Wheel/Weiser, 2003. A fantastic collection of factual information about the *Necronomicon* and the Cthulu Mythos. Simply a must for Lovecraft lovers and magickal truth seekers. Will sadden those who so hoped there were any objective historical facts to the *Necronomicon.* This book shows that it really is fiction . . . but *wonderful* fiction.

Hine, Phil. *Condensed Chaos.* New Falcon Publications, 1995. One of the best books on Chaos Magick around.

Hoeller, Stephen A. *The Royal Road.* Quest Books, 1995. A Kabalistic interpretation of the Tarot. Includes some fine guided meditations.

Howe, Ellic. *The Magicians of the Golden Dawn.* Red Wheel/Weiser, 1978. Scholarly but negative view of the Golden Dawn Order and its history. Still, if you want to know something about the membership of that pivotal group, this is a good resource.

Hulse, David Allen. *The Eastern Mysteries.* Llewellyn Publications, 2002.

———. *The Western Mysteries.* Llewellyn Publications, 2002.

These two books are phenomenal resources that focus on language as a key to a variety of spiritual systems.

James, Tad, and Wyatt Woodsmall. *Time Line Therapy and the Basis of Personality.* Meta Publications, 2008. A wonderful book based on NLP and the key to understanding the concept of the timeline and how to work with it. Still, the best way to learn about working with timelines is to take a training in the subject. This will probably be your textbook.

Jette, Christine. *Tarot Shadow Work.* Llewellyn, 2000. One of the keys to being a powerful magician is to fearlessly examine yourself. In this book the author shows you how to discover your dark side in order to heal and integrate it. This seems simple, but it is powerful magick.

Judith, Anodea. *Wheels of Life.* Llewellyn Publications, 1999. There are lots of books on the chakras. Most of them are by channelers, IROBs, or people who studied with channelers and IROBs. This book is different. It goes back to classic sources, and is well researched and very practical. In short, if you want to know about the chakras and don't want to wade through a bunch of books from India or questionable Western titles, this is the book to study.

Jung, Carl. *Psychological Types.* Princeton University Press, 1976. One of the key books used in psychology, counseling, and business, it has heavily influenced culture since it was first published in 1921. If you want to learn ways to understand people and communicate with them better, this is one of the most used sources.

Kaplan, Aryeh. *The Bahir.* Red Wheel/Weiser 1980. One of the foundational books of the Kabalah. This is the most in-depth translation and analysis of the text.

———. *Meditation and Kabbalah.* Jason Aronson, 1994. A brilliant and scholarly discussion of Kosher Kabalah meditation. Complex, difficult, and important.

———. *Sefer Yetzirah.* Weiser, 1997. Many translations and commentaries on this small book are available. This is simply the best one ever published. In my opinion, the *Sefer Yetzirah* is a crossover text between earlier mysticism and Kabalah. Some consider it the first book of the Kabalah.

There are smaller and less expensive editions of this book that are in print, but as a magician, this is the one you should get and study.

Kelder, Peter. *The Eye of Revelation.* Booklocker.com, 2008. This is the source of the physico-spiritual exercises given in Lesson Five. When *Modern Magick* was first published, *Eye* was a rare book. Now there is an entire cottage industry that has developed around the "Five Tibetans." I have a rare book from the same year this was first published without the silly story at the beginning and indicating that the source is not Tibet, but India. Whatever the source, I have found the exercises to be very powerful and useful.

King, Francis. *The Rites of Modern Occult Magic.* MacMillan Co., 1971. A famous and sturdy history of how magick regained popularity.

———. *Sexuality, Magic and Perversion.* Feral House, 2002. An acerbic survey of groups and individuals practicing sex magick. Pretty much the standard concept of the subject. My book, *Modern Sex Magick*, covers an entirely different and more esoteric tradition.

King, Francis, and Stephen Skinner. *Techniques of High Magic.* Destiny Books, 2000. I always recommend that people look at multiple books on any subject when they are available. This one purports to be complete, but it is sadly superficial. Embarrassingly, this is still one of the better books available . . . other than *Modern Magick*.

Knight, Gareth. *A Practical Guide to Qabalistic Symbolism.* Red Wheel/Weiser, 2008. A voluminous book that was originally a two-volume set, the first part really expands on Fortune's *The Mystical Qabalah*. The second part goes into amazing detail on the paths of the Tree of Life, something Fortune didn't cover. Another must for any ceremonial magician.

Konstantinos. *Summoning Spirits.* Llewellyn, 2002. A great book with lots of practical advice on the magickal evocation of spirits.

Kraig, Donald Michael. *Modern Sex Magick.* Llewellyn, 2002. Perhaps the most complete and practical book on Kabalistic sex magick. It explores the secret history of sex magick and where the information was hidden, how it was rediscovered, and is filled with practical techniques and rituals. Explicit by not obscene.

———. *The Resurrection Murders.* Galde Press, 2009. A thrilling novel that shows such things as how a magickal order functions, astral projection and astral travel, magickal battles, evocation, and sex magick in a contemporary fictional setting. A great way to learn about magick from something other than a cold, dry textbook.

———. *Tarot & Magic.* Llewellyn, 2002. This book shows a wide variety of ways that the Tarot can be used for magick, meditation, etc.

———. *The Truth About the Evocation of Spirits.* Llewellyn, 1994. A small booklet with correct information on how spirits are evoked.

Kuhn, Alvin Boyd. *Lost Light.* Filiquarian Publishing, 2007. This is a fascinating and amazing interpretation of ancient scriptures. I once asked Regardie if he had read this, and he said that he had read many of Kuhn's books, and this was the only one worthwhile. That was good enough for me. Although I was fascinated by this book, I never looked at his other works.

Laycock, Donald. *The Complete Enochian Dictionary.* Weiser Books, 2001. The most complete dictionary on Dr. Dee's techniques. An Enochian *777*.

Leadbeater, Charles. *The Chakras.* Quest Books, 1973. When Western Theosophists found out that one of the chakras was associated with the sexual organs, they almost went into apoplexy. So they switched it to the spleen(!). Read this to see how the Theosophists were altering traditional Indian concepts to fit their philosophy. Then read Judith's book for the real deal.

Leitch, Aaron. *Secrets of the Magickal Grimoires.* Llewellyn, 2005. I'm always disappointed and surprised that more people don't know about this book. Leitch has done an incredible job, giving out precise and accurate information on the major grimoires. This book is a must for real magicians.

Lipp, Deborah. *The Elements of Ritual.* Llewellyn Publications, 2003. Although primarily focused toward Paganism, this book's focus on the elements and their use in ritual can add to what you've learned in these lessons.

Lloyd, William J. *The Karezza Method.* BiblioBazaar, 2008. A book that describes a simple technique that can help men to last longer when making love.

Louis, Anthony. *Tarot Plain and Simple.* Llewellyn, 2002. The title says it all. A great introduction to using the Tarot.

Massey, Gerald. *Gerald Massey's Lectures.* Book Tree, 2008. Sorry, fundamentalists, this book shows that much of the Christian myth has its source in ancient Egyptian myth.

Mathers, Samuel. *The Greater Key of Solomon.* Digireads.com, 2007. One of the classic grimoires used in the evocation of spirits.

———. *The Grimoire of Armadel.* Weiser, 2001. Until recently a little-known grimoire used by members of the Golden Dawn. Great for talisman workers.

———. *The Kabbalah Unveiled.* Kessinger Publishing, 2007. A translation of a few small sections of the *Zohar,* the classic Kabalistic text. Personally, I found the highly literate introduction written by Mathers' wife to be the most interesting part of the book.

McCoy, Edain. *Past Life & Karmic Tarot.* Llewellyn, 2004. As the title indicates, this book shows you how to look at and work with your past lives and karma using the Tarot. Great for personal exploration.

Michaels, Mark A., and Patricia Johnson. *The Essence of Tantric Sexuality.* Llewellyn Publications, 2006. These students of Dr. Mumford now run his course in Tantra. Here they present some of his previous lectures on Tantra and sex magick that

had been unavailable for three decades. Still provocative, accurate, and informative.

Mumford, Jonn. *A Chakra & Kundalini Workbook.* Llewellyn Publications, 2002. Currently the finest practical book on working with the chakras and kundalini energy. Dr. Mumford has a distance course (via e-mail) now run by two of his students that uses this as a textbook. Highly recommended.

———. *Ecstasy Through Tantra.* Llewellyn, 2002. Previously published as *Sexual Occultism,* this was one of the first books to compare Western sex magick with Eastern Tantric sexuality. Now, it is expanded to be one of the finest books available on Tantra. The author of the lessons you are reading wrote a chapter that is included in this book.

Omega, Kane. *Cosmic Sex.* Lyle Stuart, Inc., 1973. Although long out of print, this humorous autobiographical introduction to Tantra will teach you more about the spirituality of Tantric sexuality than just about any other book. Find it if you can.

Ophiel (pseud. of Edward Peach). *The Art & Practice of Astral Projection.* Red Wheel/Samuel Weiser, 1976. One of the most direct, most basic, and best introductions to astral projection around. I always got the feeling that Ophiel was not very smart, so he wrote the way he wished things would be written: clear enough so that even he could understand them. As a result, anyone can use them. If you're having trouble with astral projection, try the techniques in this book. His out-of-print book, *The Art & Practice of Getting Material Things Through Creative Visualization,* has a horribly unwieldy title and isn't as famous as some of the other books on that topic, but it, too, is one of the best around. Be careful if you become interested in his books. These two are his best efforts. His others range from average to embarrassingly bad. I have no idea how an editor let them get published. Perhaps an early example of the curse of self-publishing.

Patai, Raphael. *The Hebrew Goddess.* Wayne State University Press, 1990. This is a much-beloved book by Pagans. It clearly shows that the ancient Hebrews worshipped a goddess as well as a god until the destruction of the second temple in 70 C.E. A vital part of any occultist's library.

Penczak, Christopher. *Instant Magick*. Llewellyn Publications, 2006. Although the title implies that you can do things instantly, the real meaning is that through preparation and practice you can become able to do magick quickly and whenever you need to do it. I strongly agree with this concept.

Peterson, Joseph. *Arbatel*. Ibis, 2009.

———. *The Lesser Key of Solomon*. Weiser Books, 2001.

These two books by Peterson are absolute classics, some of the best researched and presented versions of these two grimoires.

Pike, Albert. *Morals and Dogma*. Forgotten Books, 2008. The most famous text of mystical Masonry. Filled with mystical wisdom intended for Freemasons, but applicable to anyone on a spiritual path. The old style of writing may be difficult, but it's worth it.

Pollack, Rachel. *Rachel Pollack's Tarot Wisdom*. Llewellyn, 2008. This is an all-around great book on the Tarot, with history, spreads, interpretation keys, and wisdom gained from her years of study and teaching. There are lots of good introductory books on Tarot. This is one you should study after you've read those introductions.

Prasad, Rama. *Nature's Finer Forces*. Kessinger Publishing, 1997. The little-known book is a classic book of Tantric Indian occultism. Although the Hermetic Order of the Golden Dawn was a Western magickal order, they used a small amount of Eastern concepts. Practically everything they used was taken from this book.

Raphael. *Raphael's Ancient Manuscript of Talismanic Magic*. Kessinger Publishing, 1942(?). A source book for making talismans. Handwritten in the form of a grimoire.

Ready, Romilla, and Kate Burton. *Neuro-Linguistic Programming for Dummies*. For Dummies, 2004.

This was the textbook used when I trained to become a certified practitioner of NLP in 2008. (I'm currently certified as a master practitioner of NLP by the Association for Integrative Psychology. My main trainer was Dr. Matthew James, son of Tad James.) NLP is a young science, and it's amazing how fast it's evolving. Some of the ideas presented in this book were already obsolete when I took my trainings. Still, this will give you the basic concepts of NLP.

Regardie, Israel. *Ceremonial Magic*. Aeon books, 2004. Although the Watchtower ritual first appeared in this book, it was edited out of its obvious order that was taught to me by one of Regardie's students. Still, its value for learning about magick and the concepts of that ritual shouldn't be overlooked.

———. *Foundations of Practical Magic*. Aeon Books, 2004. A collection of small booklets by Regardie that are unmatched in their clarity in discussing several occult topics.

———. *A Garden of Pomegranates*. Llewellyn Publications, 1995. A good explanation of the Kabalah.

———. *The Golden Dawn*. Llewellyn Publications, 2002. The classic text of Western occultism. Probably copied directly or indirectly by more writers than any other occult book . . . usually without giving credit.

———. *How to Make and Use Talismans*. Thorsons, 1983. Simple but clear little book on this topic from a ceremonial magick point of view. Probably the best individual book on this subject. As of this writing it is regrettably out of print. If you can find a copy, get it.

———. *The Middle Pillar*. Llewellyn Publications, 2002. This book has become the source book for information on the Middle Pillar Ritual. Now used by many "ancient" traditions as well as modern ones.

———. *The One Year Manual*. Red Wheel/Weiser, 2007. A system of spiritual development that can be powerful, especially if you read between the lines.

———. *The Tree of Life*. Llewellyn Publications, 2000. A much ignored book on magickal theory and practice due to its difficulty. Also discusses alchemy and sex magick. Regardie was clearly under the influence of his teacher and mentor (and maybe father figure?), Aleister Crowley, when writing this book.

Reich, Wilhelm. *The Function of the Orgasm*. Farrar, Straus, and Giroux, 1986. A book that blends science and sex magick. When I talked to Regardie about this book he agreed with me that all magicians should study it. Of course, he was a Reichian therapist, so he may have been prejudiced.

Rowe, Benjamin. *Enochian Temples*. Black Moon Publishing, 2008. Although in these lessons I only slightly mentioned Enochian magick, those who are really interested in the subject tend to focus on the original writings of Dee and try to reproduce his work. The late Mr. Rowe wrote several brief (this "book" is only thirty-eight pages) monographs that expand on the Enochian system and imaginatively move it into the future. All of his works are highly recommended for advanced practitioners.

Saraswati, Swami Janakananda. *Yoga, Tantra and Meditation in Daily Life*. Weiser, 1992. I purchased this book when it first came out in the mid-1970s, in part because I was a hormonal young man and there were pictures of a naked woman in it. But very quickly, I was confused. What did nudity have to do with meditation? And how did meditation and yoga relate to Tantra? This is a small book and I learned a great deal from it. The author is out of a Tantric tradition where everyone takes the last name "Saraswati." Most of the writers in this tradition are published by the Bihar School of Yoga, and I recommend their publications highly.

Shaw, Scott. *Chi Kung for Beginners*. Llewellyn Publications, 2004. I first started taking lessons in chi kung via mail order about thirty years ago. I quickly realized that it was a way to work with the same energies used in magick. As such, the practice of chi kung is a great way to learn how to develop and become familiar with this energy. Shaw's book is an excellent introduction to chi kung. It's clear and easy to use, but don't let that fool you. The practice of chi kung can give you great personal power.

Sheba, Lady (pseud. of J. W. Bell). *The Grimoire of Lady Sheba*. Llewellyn, 2001. An excellent, if controversial, introduction to what is primarily Gardnerian Witchcraft.

Sherwin, Ray. *The Book of Results*. LULU, 2005. One of the key books for Chaos magicians. It helped turn the focus of magick to results rather than method. Some people even refer to Chaos Magick as "results magick."

Skinner, Stephen. *The Complete Magician's Tables*. Llewellyn Publications, 2007. This is the most complete book to date for magicians looking for lists of correspondences with which to design rituals, talismans, etc. Just as Godwin's book superseded Crowley's *777*, this book can replace Godwin. Personally, I have all three. They each have their uses. This, however, is currently the ultimate guide for designing magickal rituals, talismans, amulets, etc.

———. *Veritable Key of Solomon*. Llewellyn, 2008. A fantastic and perhaps the most complete version of what is commonly known as the *Greater Key of Solomon*. Another must-read.

Skinner, Stephen, and David Rankine. *The Goetia of Dr. Rudd*. Golden Hoard Press, 2007. This is perhaps the ultimate current edition of the *Goetia*. We should thank Skinner and Rankine for their hard work on these volumes.

Spare, Austin Osman. *The Writings of Austin Osman Spare*. NuVision Publications, 2007. Features his theories and ideas. A key book for those looking for background to the Chaos Magick movement, as well as a means to improve their magickal practices.

Sperling, Harry, Maurice Simon, and Paul Levertoff (translators). *The Zohar* (5 volumes). Soincino Press, 1984. The *Zohar* is one of the key documents of the Kabalah, and this is one of the most complete English translations available. A must for those who wish to puzzle over the mysteries of the Kosher Kabalah.

Starhawk. *The Spiral Dance.* HarperOne, 1999. A feminist and political view of the history and rebirth of Witchcraft in the modern era.

Sterling, Stephen. *Tarot Awareness.* Llewellyn, 2000. Examines the spiritual and practical sides of the Tarot. A great book for people looking for more information on the cards.

Stockham, Alice. *Karezza.* Forgotten Books, 2008. One of the most valuable books for potential male sex magicians, and for their partners. It teaches the value of extending sexual activity.

Tyson, Donald. *Enochian Magic for Beginners.* Llewellyn Publications, 2002. There are very few books that are beginners' guides to the Enochian system, but Tyson's book is the one decent one that I would recommend. I disagree with some of Tyson's philosophy—I don't think working Enochian magick is going to bring on the Christian apocalypse—but on a practical level this book is a great introduction.

Valiente, Doreen. *An ABC of Witchcraft Past and Present.* Phoenix Publishing, 1988. Set up a bit like an encyclopedia with an alphabetical listing of entries, this book is an excellent overview of Witchcraft when it was first published in 1973. Today it is an important historical document for people to learn about Wicca at that time, but Witchcraft has moved on.

———. *Witchcraft for Tomorrow.* Robert Hale, 1993. Originally published in 1978, a great introduction to Wicca as it was practiced thirty years ago by one of the most respected women in all of Pagan-

ism, and the author of the famous "Charge of the Goddess."

Vitimus, Andrieh. *Hands-On Chaos Magic.* Llewellyn Publications, 2009. Not just a good introduction to Chaos Magick, but a practical introduction to its techniques. A good starting book for those interested in Chaos Magick.

Waite, A. E. *The Book of Ceremonial Magic.* Cosimo Classics, 2007. A famous source book of sections from grimoires purposely designed to be unusable. Virtually the same as his *The Book of Black Magic and of Pacts*, so don't get them both.

Wang, Robert. *The Qabalistic Tarot.* Marcus Aurelius Press, 2004. The most brilliant introduction to the Tarot from a Kabalistic viewpoint that I've ever read. Also a good introduction to Kabalah in general.

———. *The Secret Temple.* Marcus Aurelius Press, 1993. Although some of his ideas are flawed, this is a simple and direct book giving instructions on how to build the basic magickal tools and a Golden Dawn–style temple.

Weed, Joseph. *Wisdom of the Mystic Masters.* Prentice Hall Press, 1971. If you've been around occult-oriented magazines for more than a few years, you've seen the ads for the Rosicrucian Order, AMORC. This book features the core of their teachings.

Westcott, W. Wynn. *The Complete Golden Dawn Cipher Manuscript.* Holmes Publishing Group, 1996. A high-quality and meticulously researched (by editor Darcy Kuntz) printing and translation of the documents that are responsible for founding the Hermetic Order of the Golden Dawn. Great for historical reference and for seeing how Mathers took the simple concepts and expanded them into full-blown rituals and informational lectures.

Williams, Brandy. *Ecstatic Ritual.* Megalithica Books, 2008. A unique book on sex magick in that it comes from a woman's point of view and is also based in ceremonial magick.

Winkler, Gershon. *The Soul of the Matter.* Judaica Press, 1982. A simple explanation of Kosher Kabalistic theories of reincarnation.

Within, Inquire (pseud of Christina Stoddard). *Light-Bearers of Darkness.* Christian Book Club of America, 1983. Now rare and difficult to find, this is a history of the Golden Dawn by a one-time member who turned against the order and became a hate-filled, paranoid anti-Semite. It was thought that she was going to be a great adept, and she was rushed through the degrees without having the time to really absorb the mystical energies of each grade. An example of what can happen if you do not spend time and earn your advancement rather than just being given a wide range of information.

INDEX

GET MORE AT LLEWELLYN.COM

Visit us online to browse hundreds of our books and decks, plus sign up to receive our e-newsletters and exclusive online offers.

- **Free tarot readings • Spell-a-Day • Moon phases**
- **Recipes, spells, and tips • Blogs • Encyclopedia**
- **Author interviews, articles, and upcoming events**

GET SOCIAL WITH LLEWELLYN

Find us on     @LlewellynBooks
www.Facebook.com/LlewellynBooks

GET BOOKS AT LLEWELLYN

LLEWELLYN ORDERING INFORMATION

 Order online: Visit our website at www.llewellyn.com to select your books and place an order on our secure server.

 Order by phone:
- Call toll free within the US at 1-877-NEW-WRLD (1-877-639-9753)
- We accept VISA, MasterCard, American Express, and Discover.
- Canadian customers must use credit cards.

 Order by mail:
Send the full price of your order (MN residents add 6.875% sales tax) in US funds plus postage and handling to: Llewellyn Worldwide, 2143 Wooddale Drive, Woodbury, MN 55125-2989

POSTAGE AND HANDLING

STANDARD (US):
(Please allow 12 business days)
$30.00 and under, add $6.00.
$30.01 and over, FREE SHIPPING.

INTERNATIONAL ORDERS, INCLUDING CANADA:
$16.00 for one book, plus $3.00 for each additional book.

Visit us online for more shipping options. Prices subject to change.

FREE CATALOG!

To order, call
1-877-
NEW-WRLD
ext. 8236
or visit our
website